SAP PRESS e-books

Print or e-book, Kindle or iPad, workplace or airplane: Choose where and how to read your SAP PRESS books! You can now get all our titles as e-books, too:

- By download and online access
- For all popular devices
- And, of course, DRM-free

Convinced? Then go to www.sap-press.com and get your e-book today.

Configuring SAP® Business Technology Platform

SAP PRESS is a joint initiative of SAP and Rheinwerk Publishing. The know-how offered by SAP specialists combined with the expertise of Rheinwerk Publishing offers the reader expert books in the field. SAP PRESS features first-hand information and expert advice, and provides useful skills for professional decision-making.

SAP PRESS offers a variety of books on technical and business-related topics for the SAP user. For further information, please visit our website: *www.sap-press.com*.

Glavanovits, Haider, Koch, Krancz
SAP Build: No-Code Development, Centralized Access, and Process Automation
2024, 801 pages, hardcover and e-book
www.sap-press.com/5772

Aron, Gakhar, Vij
SAP Integration Suite
2021, 343 pages, hardcover and e-book
www.sap-press.com/5326

Martin Koch, Siegfried Zeilinger
Cloud Connector for SAP
2023, 352 pages, hardcover and e-book
www.sap-press.com/5683

Martin Koch, Siegfried Zeilinger
Security and Authorizations for SAP Business Technology Platform
2023, 355 pages, hardcover and e-book
www.sap-press.com/5627

Banda, Chandra, Gooi
SAP Business Technology Platform (2nd Edition)
2024, 729 pages, hardcover and e-book
www.sap-press.com/5919

Martin Koch, Siegfried Zeilinger

Configuring SAP® Business Technology Platform

The Practical Guide for Administrators

Editor Meagan White
Acquisitions Editor Hareem Shafi
German Edition Editor Eva Wigger, Nicole Gürgens
Translation Martin Koch, Siegfried Zeilinger
Copyeditors Melinda Rankin
Cover Design Noah Neuhaus, Silke Braun
Photo Credit Shutterstock: 381507790/© pk_roaming
Layout Design Vera Brauner
Production Hannah Lane
Typesetting SatzPro, Germany
Printed and bound in the United States of America, on paper from sustainable sources

ISBN 978-1-4932-2707-5
1st edition 2025
1st German edition published 2024 by Rheinwerk Verlag, Bonn, Germany

© 2025 by:
Rheinwerk Publishing, Inc.
2 Heritage Drive, Suite 305
Quincy, MA 02171
USA
info@rheinwerk-publishing.com
+1.781.228.5070

Represented in the E.U. by:
Rheinwerk Verlag GmbH
Rheinwerkallee 4
53227 Bonn
Germany
service@rheinwerk-verlag.de
+49 (0) 228 42150-0

Library of Congress Cataloging-in-Publication Control Number: 2025030593

All rights reserved. Neither this publication nor any part of it may be copied or reproduced in any form or by any means or translated into another language, without the prior consent of Rheinwerk Publishing.

Rheinwerk Publishing makes no warranties or representations with respect to the content hereof and specifically disclaims any implied warranties of merchantability or fitness for any particular purpose. Rheinwerk Publishing assumes no responsibility for any errors that may appear in this publication.

"Rheinwerk Publishing" and the Rheinwerk Publishing logo are registered trademarks of Rheinwerk Verlag GmbH, Bonn, Germany. SAP PRESS is an imprint of Rheinwerk Verlag GmbH and Rheinwerk Publishing, Inc.

All screenshots and graphics reproduced in this book are subject to copyright © SAP SE, Dietmar-Hopp-Allee 16, 69190 Walldorf, Germany.

SAP, ABAP, ASAP, Concur Hipmunk, Duet, Duet Enterprise, ExpenseIt, SAP ActiveAttention, SAP Adaptive Server Enterprise, SAP Advantage Database Server, SAP ArchiveLink, SAP Ariba, SAP Business ByDesign, SAP Business Explorer (SAP BEx), SAP BusinessObjects, SAP BusinessObjects Explorer, SAP BusinessObjects Web Intelligence, SAP Business One, SAP Business Workflow, SAP BW/4HANA, SAP C/4HANA, SAP Concur, SAP Crystal Reports, SAP EarlyWatch, SAP Fieldglass, SAP Fiori, SAP Global Trade Services (SAP GTS), SAP GoingLive, SAP HANA, SAP Jam, SAP Leonardo, SAP Lumira, SAP MaxDB, SAP NetWeaver, SAP PartnerEdge, SAPPHIRE NOW, SAP PowerBuilder, SAP PowerDesigner, SAP R/2, SAP R/3, SAP Replication Server, SAP Roambi, SAP S/4HANA, SAP S/4HANA Cloud, SAP SQL Anywhere, SAP Strategic Enterprise Management (SAP SEM), SAP SuccessFactors, SAP Vora, TripIt, and Qualtrics are registered or unregistered trademarks of SAP SE, Walldorf, Germany.

All other products mentioned in this book are registered or unregistered trademarks of their respective companies.

No part of this book may be used or reproduced in any manner for the purpose of training artificial intelligence technologies or systems. In accordance with Article 4(3) of the Digital Single Market Directive 2019/790, Rheinwerk Publishing, Inc. expressly reserves this work from text and data mining.

Contents at a Glance

1	Introduction to SAP BTP	17
2	User Administration	57
3	Advanced Identity Authentication Service Topics	111
4	Global Account Administration	155
5	Subaccount Administration	199
6	Cloud Connector	253
7	Activating and Setting Up SAP Business Application Studio	297
8	Activating and Setting Up SAP Integration Suite	323
9	Activating and Setting Up SAP Cloud Transport Management for SAP Integration Suite	349
10	Activating and Setting Up SAP Build	391

Contents

Preface 13

1 Introduction to SAP BTP   17

1.1	History and Positioning	19
1.2	License Models, Service-Level Agreements, and Important Documents	22
1.3	Global Accounts and Subaccounts	26
1.4	SAP Discovery Center	29
1.5	Entitlements and Service Plans	36
1.6	Best Practices	40
	1.6.1 Structure of a Governance Model	41
	1.6.2 Structure of an Account Model	44
	1.6.3 Setting Up a Security and Compliance Model	50
	1.6.4 Reference Architectures	52
1.7	Troubleshooting	53
1.8	Resources	55
1.9	Summary	56

2 User Administration   57

2.1	Security and Authorizations	57
	2.1.1 Basics of Secure Communication	58
	2.1.2 Authentication	62
	2.1.3 Authorization	71
2.2	SAP Cloud Identity Services	72
	2.2.1 Identity Authentication	72
	2.2.2 Identity Provisioning	101
2.3	Summary	109

3 Advanced Identity Authentication Service Topics — 111

3.1	SAML 2.0	112
3.2	OpenID Connect	114
3.3	Practical Example: Identity Authentication as a Proxy to Microsoft Entra ID	118
	3.3.1 Integrate Microsoft Entra ID into Identity Authentication with SAML 2.0	118
	3.3.2 Integrate Microsoft Entra ID into Identity Authentication with OpenID Connect	131
3.4	Practical Example: Two-Factor Authentication/Risk-Based Authentication	144
3.5	Practical Example: Conditional Authentication	150
3.6	Summary	153

4 Global Account Administration — 155

4.1	Access to the Global Account	156
4.2	Authentication and Authorization Management	157
	4.2.1 User Management	157
	4.2.2 Roles and Role Collections	166
	4.2.3 Practical Example: Setting Up Authentication via SAP Cloud Identity Service	169
4.3	Directories	175
4.4	Boosters	182
4.5	System Landscape	188
4.6	Resource Provider	190
4.7	Entitlements	192
4.8	Usage Monitoring	193
4.9	Summary	196

5 Subaccount Administration — 199

5.1	Creating a Subaccount	199
5.2	Authentication and Authorization	204
	5.2.1 User Administration	206
	5.2.2 Trust Configuration and Other Identity Providers	208
	5.2.3 Roles and Role Collections	215
	5.2.4 Practical Example: Authentication on a Subaccount with Identity Authentication	227
	5.2.5 Practical Example: Subaccount with Microsoft Entra ID as the Identity Provider	233
5.3	Organizations, Spaces, and Quotas	241
5.4	Subscriptions and Services	247
5.5	SAP Audit Log Viewer Service for SAP BTP	249
5.6	Summary	250

6 Cloud Connector — 253

6.1	Installation and Configuration	253
	6.1.1 Prerequisites	254
	6.1.2 Installing the Cloud Connector	255
	6.1.3 Initial Steps	261
	6.1.4 Configuring the User Interface	264
	6.1.5 Cloud Configuration	267
	6.1.6 On-Premise Configuration	270
	6.1.7 Reporting Configuration	274
	6.1.8 Advanced Configuration	275
6.2	Ensuring High Availability	276
6.3	SAP Connectivity Service	286
6.4	Summary	295

7 Activating and Setting Up SAP Business Application Studio 297

7.1	Setting Up SAP Business Application Studio	297
7.2	Granting Authorizations	303
7.3	Working with Dev Spaces	304
7.4	Using External Systems	305
7.5	Versioning with Git Repositories	311
7.6	Summary	321

8 Activating and Setting Up SAP Integration Suite 323

8.1	Functions and History of SAP Integration Suite	323
8.2	Creating a Subaccount and Assigning Entitlements	326
8.3	Creating a Subscription	329
8.4	Activating Capabilities	334
8.5	Instantiating the SAP Process Integration Runtime	341
8.6	Create Service Key	344
8.7	Summary	347

9 Activating and Setting Up SAP Cloud Transport Management for SAP Integration Suite 349

9.1	Activating SAP Cloud Transport Management	350
9.2	Deploying SAP Cloud Transport Management	352
9.3	Creating a System Landscape in SAP Cloud Transport Management	361
9.4	Adding the SAP Content Agent Service to a Subaccount	365
9.5	Configuring SAP Cloud Transport Management in SAP Integration Suite	380
9.6	Summary	389

10 Activating and Setting Up SAP Build — 391

10.1	**SAP Build Apps**	391
	10.1.1 Installation	393
	10.1.2 Configuration	399
10.2	**SAP Build Process Automation**	404
10.3	**SAP Build Work Zone**	412
	10.3.1 Initial Steps	412
	10.3.2 Run the Booster	418
	10.3.3 Configuring SAP Build Work Zone, Advanced Edition	422
10.4	**SAP Build Code**	438
10.5	**Summary**	444

The Authors 445
Index 447

Preface

The cloud isn't just a promise for the future: It's a defining part of our present. SAP Business Technology Platform (SAP BTP) is *the* cloud application for your SAP ecosystem. It combines the power of the cloud with the solid foundation of traditional IT systems. This book is your guide through the complex terrain of cloud administration. It brings clarity to the often-complex structures and hybrid configurations that characterize today's business world.

This book is your guide to discovering the ins and outs of SAP BTP. It starts by taking you back to its humble beginnings and development, then moves on to its many possibilities and services. We're going to highlight the technical aspects and the philosophy behind SAP BTP. The goal of SAP BTP is to simplify processes and enable companies to increase their efficiency and innovation.

Our goal is to give you the tools you need to understand SAP BTP and administer it at its best. Our wish is that you will walk away feeling confident in your use of this platform. SAP BTP is critical to the business growth and technological advancement of many companies. We build on this foundation chapter by chapter. By the time you reach the end of the book, you will have mastered all aspects of SAP BTP administration and be able to help shape the future of the cloud.

Target Audience

We're talking to system admins, developers, system architects, security experts, and anyone else who's into integrating the cloud and on-premise worlds. The book's structured approach and clear layout provide step-by-step insight into every facet of SAP BTP. It covers everything from basic installation to advanced configurations and administration. If you're interested in connecting the cloud and on-premise worlds within the SAP ecosystem, then this book is a must-read.

Notes on Reading this Book

Each chapter builds on the knowledge gained in the previous chapter while also providing enough flexibility to read and understand individual sections independently. This book will equip you with the knowledge you need to master the challenges and opportunities of SAP BTP administration and successfully implement your cloud strategy. Screenshots illustrate the instructions.

Structure of the Book

This book is the only comprehensive guide to administering SAP BTP. It is divided into the following chapters:

- **Chapter 1** gives you the full picture of SAP BTP: its history, licensing models, and platform structure. It also covers SAP Discovery Center, highlights entitlements and service plans, and concludes with best practices and troubleshooting resources.
- **Chapter 2** focuses squarely on security and permissions. You will learn about SAP Cloud Identity Services and gain deep insights into Identity Authentication and Identity Provisioning.
- **Chapter 3** is the place to go for in-depth knowledge of authentication with protocols such as SAML and OpenID Connect. You will learn how to implement advanced authentication mechanisms through practical examples.
- **Chapter 4** provides a comprehensive overview of global account administration, including user management, roles, collective roles, and practical examples of authentication and monitoring.
- **Chapter 5** provides clear guidance on managing subaccounts and offers practical instructions for authentication with Identity Authentication and for connecting to Azure Active Directory.
- **Chapter 6** will teach you how to install and configure the cloud connector, which acts as a bridge between on-premise systems and SAP BTP. It also explains the connectivity options and monitoring of the cloud connector.
- **Chapter 7** will show you how to set up and configure the development environment for cloud applications. We also discuss spaces and organizations, and we provide tips for setting up SAP Business Application Studio.
- **Chapter 8** will show you how to set up SAP Integration Suite to integrate data via the cloud.
- **Chapter 9** explains how to manage the lifecycle of SAP Integration Suite and how to set it up.
- **Chapter 10** explains how to set up and administer SAP Build, which allows you to create and run cloud applications without writing code.

This book contains info boxes that provide tips, hints, and examples to help you. You'll see the following box types:

[Ex] *For example:* Examples marked this way refer to real-world scenarios and illustrate the functions described.

[+] *Tip:* This title indicates tips and hints from professional practice that provide practical recommendations to make your work easier.

[»] *Note:* Boxes marked this way contain definitions, related topics, or important content that you should remember.

[!] *Caution:* This title indicates special features that you should be aware of. It also warns you of common mistakes and problems.

Summary

This book is not a mere technical guide; it's a resource that will empower you to operate your systems efficiently and securely. You will learn how to manage subscriptions and quotas, implement best practices, and master monitoring your subaccounts to ensure high availability and security for your connections.

Each chapter is meticulously designed to teach you both theory and practical application. This book is your comprehensive guide to effective SAP BTP administration. It includes detailed instructions, best practices, and warnings about common pitfalls.

You are invited to join us on an exciting journey into the world of cloud administration. After reading this book, you will be able to realize your cloud implementation projects and operate them securely.

—**Martin Koch** and **Siegfried Zeilinger**

Chapter 1
Introduction to SAP BTP

SAP BTP is the central component in hybrid and cloud SAP system landscapes. It is the most important element for developing and extending applications, integrating SAP and non-SAP solutions, and analyzing data.

SAP Business Technology Platform (SAP BTP) provides a wide range of functions for low-code application development, artificial intelligence (AI), integration, and data analysis. These functions can be seamlessly integrated into SAP applications. They also enable connections to other applications and data sources. SAP BTP is the foundation for developing innovative solutions that provide a unified user experience for business processes. This sentence may sound a bit pretentious and provocative, but it essentially reflects the functionality of SAP BTP.

SAP's path is clearly defined. It is (almost) entirely in the *cloud-first* direction. The statement that on-premise systems will be excluded from innovations in the future has shocked SAP's customers like an earthquake and caused some resistance. In the medium term, there will be no way for businesses to avoid cloud offerings—whether public or private—and other providers, such as Microsoft with its Office 365, have been pursuing this path for some time.

Cloud software, or *software as a service* (SaaS), offers many advantages. For example, businesses receive all new features immediately. In a world where business models are constantly changing or being reinvented, this is an incredible advantage that can make the difference between a company's economic survival and its failure. Many SAP users can tell you a thing or two about consultants, who are up-to-date with the latest technology, answering every second question with "the latest release can do that"—and then having to confess that their release is three or maybe even five years old.

As SAP drives SaaS solutions, hybrid system landscapes that include both cloud and on-premise solutions will shape their customers' architectures. For these system landscapes, SAP BTP provides extensive functionality to integrate them and provide end users with a single point of access.

SAP BTP plays a key role in driving digitalization forward and helping companies adapt their business models and secure competitive advantages. The platform is a central component, particularly in hybrid environments, for consolidating data and processes from a wide variety of sources, processing them intelligently, and providing innovative services. Offerings such as SAP Business Application Studio, SAP Integration Suite, and SAP Build are just a few examples of tools that enable developers to work faster and more efficiently.

Another advantage of SAP BTP is its ability to seamlessly integrate new technologies such as artificial intelligence and machine learning. This allows companies to not only optimize existing processes but also develop completely new business models that would not be possible without these technologies.

Companies that adopt SAP BTP early on also benefit from a high degree of futureproofing, as the platform is continuously developed and new innovations are made available in a timely manner. Although the move to the cloud may present challenges, the long-term benefits—such as increased agility, lower operating costs, and faster innovation cycles—are clear competitive advantages in an increasingly digital world.

> **Note: What Is an On-Premise System?**
>
> An on-premise system is a system that is physically located on the premises of a company, typically in its data center. In contrast to cloud systems, which are hosted externally, the data and IT infrastructure of an on-premise system are the sole responsibility of the company. This also includes systems that are operated by a hosting provider but are set up and managed specifically for the customer. On-premise systems enable complete control over data and security, which is particularly important in industries with strict data protection or compliance requirements. However, operating such systems requires continuous investment in hardware, software licenses, maintenance and IT personnel, which is often more costly than cloud solutions.

In Section 1.1, we look at the eventful history of SAP BTP, which has been characterized by numerous name changes and rebranding measures. We will discuss this history in detail and shed light on its background. In Section 1.2, we will look at the various licensing options available for SAP BTP and explain them in detail. In addition, we will present the platform's service-level agreements (SLAs) and show you where to find important documents such as audit reports.

In Section 1.3, you will get a comprehensive overview of the basic concepts and architecture of SAP BTP, based on global accounts and subaccounts. SAP Discovery Center, a central resource of the platform, is presented in Section 1.4. There you will find detailed descriptions of the services offered, pricing information, and details on the geographical availability of each service.

We then turn to the topics of entitlements and service plans in Section 1.5. These two mechanisms enable you to flexibly control the provision and scope of services in your subaccounts and to adapt them to your requirements. This allows you to retain control over which services are available in your subaccounts and to what extent.

In Section 1.6, we discuss the best practices that have been established for working with SAP BTP. These practices provide valuable guidelines and recommendations to help you use the platform efficiently and successfully.

Troubleshooting is essential when operating services or application on SAP BTP. We will cover this in Section 1.7.

Finally, in Section 1.8, we introduce some essential resources for working with SAP BTP and provide instructions on how to perform troubleshooting if needed. With this section, we want to ensure that you have all the necessary tools and information at your disposal to effectively overcome any challenges that may arise.

1.1 History and Positioning

SAP BTP is a platform service from SAP that was first introduced in 2012 under the name *SAP NetWeaver Cloud*. Just one year later, in 2013, the platform was renamed to *SAP HANA Cloud Platform*, emphasizing its close connection to the SAP HANA database. With the continuous expansion of the platform to include additional services and functions, a further adjustment was made in 2017: the term *HANA* in the name was removed, making its name *SAP Cloud Platform*. In January 2021, the platform was given its current name, *SAP Business Technology Platform*, which underscores its positioning as a comprehensive technology platform.

Over the years, SAP BTP has been developed and positioned for a variety of use cases. It offers a comprehensive collection of services that help companies develop innovative solutions and make their business processes more efficient. The areas of application for SAP BTP can be divided into three central categories:

- **Innovate**
  SAP BTP enables customers to develop and deliver new and innovative applications. With tools such as SAP Business Application Studio and with low-code/no-code approaches, companies can create applications tailored to their specific needs, enabling them to respond more quickly to changing business requirements.

- **Extend**
  Existing SaaS products from SAP can be seamlessly extended using SAP BTP. These so-called side-by-side extension scenarios provide a flexible way to add functionality without modifying the core systems. This is particularly important for making adjustments that are preserved during system upgrades.

- **Integrate**
  SAP BTP facilitates integration between different systems—whether cloud to cloud, or cloud to on premise. With SAP Integration Suite, companies can seamlessly connect heterogeneous system landscapes, synchronize data, and create end-to-end processes. This ensures that all areas of the company work smoothly together.

In addition to these core areas, SAP BTP also helps companies integrate advanced technologies such as artificial intelligence and machine learning into their solutions. With these functions, the platform enables not only the optimization of existing processes but also the creation of completely new business models. Continuous development and close integration with SAP core systems make SAP BTP an indispensable tool for companies that want to succeed in the digital age.

In 2019, SAP introduced SAP Extension Suite and SAP Integration Suite to more clearly structure and unify the core use cases of SAP BTP. These suites include not only the core services needed for extensions and integrations, but also all the supporting services required to develop, operate, and optimize modern applications.

SAP BTP provides solutions in several key areas to help companies digitize and optimize their processes. These include, but are not limited to, the following:

- **Artificial intelligence**
  SAP BTP offers advanced AI capabilities and tools that enable organizations to develop intelligent applications and implement automation processes. AI services such as machine learning, image recognition, and natural language processing help to make data-driven decisions and make business processes more efficient.

- **Application development and automation**
  Developers can use SAP BTP resources to create, customize, and automate applications to meet the specific needs of their organization. Tools such as SAP Business Application Studio and low-code/no-code platforms facilitate development and enable rapid customization in dynamic business environments.

- **Data and analytics**
  The platform provides powerful data management and analysis tools. With services such as SAP HANA Cloud, SAP Analytics Cloud, and SAP Datasphere, companies can use their data effectively, gain in-depth insights, and make informed decisions. These features support both operational and strategic business decisions.

- **Advanced planning and analysis**
  This area enables the optimization of planning, budgeting and forecasting processes. Organizations can use performance-management tools to improve their business results and promote collaboration across teams.

- **Foundation and cross services**
  The basic services of SAP BTP form the basis for all other areas of the platform. These include essential functions such as security, identity management, API management, and other cross-cutting services that ensure a stable and secure operating environment.

- **Integration**
  SAP Integration Suite on SAP BTP enables seamless connection of applications and systems. Whether you need cloud-to-cloud or cloud-to-on-premise integration, the platform provides tools to ensure end-to-end data communication. This enables

companies to harmonize heterogeneous system landscapes and create end-to-end processes.

With these comprehensive functions, SAP BTP supports companies in developing innovative solutions, expanding existing systems, using their data intelligently, and building future-proof business models. The introduction of SAP Extension Suite and SAP Integration Suite has helped to make the complexity of the platform easier to understand and to maximize the benefits for companies.

Initially, SAP BTP was operated exclusively in SAP's own data centers and in the proprietary Neo environment. In parallel with SAP, other cloud providers have established themselves on the market with their own offerings, such as Amazon with Amazon Web Services (AWS), Microsoft with Azure, Google with Google Cloud, and Alibaba with Alibaba Cloud. To standardize the operation and provision of services in the cloud across providers, well-known cloud providers have joined forces under the umbrella of the Cloud Foundry Foundation to define a uniform standard (see *https://www.cloudfoundry.org/*).

SAP is relying on this Cloud Foundry architecture not only for SAP BTP but also for other products. These include, for example, SAP HANA extended application services, advanced model (SAP HANA XSA) and SAP HANA extended application services, classic model (SAP HANA XS)—that is, the SAP HANA integrated runtime and development environment.

SAP BTP provides a set of capabilities that comprise various technical components such as services, tools, APIs, and applications. Within SAP BTP, SAP allows customers to consume these services in either the Neo or Cloud Foundry environment. The services enable, facilitate, or accelerate the development of business applications and other platform services on SAP BTP. SAP categorizes these services into two different types: *Business services* are those that enable, facilitate, or accelerate the development of business process components or provide industry-specific functionality or content within a business application. *Technical services*, meanwhile, enable, facilitate, or accelerate the development of generic or domain-independent content within a business application, independently of the business process or task of the application.

From a commercial perspective, it makes no difference whether you use a service in the Neo environment, the Cloud Foundry environment, or both. In all cases, you enter a contract with SAP, not with the infrastructure-as-a-service (IaaS) provider. Billing therefore always happens through SAP. In this book, we only cover the Cloud Foundry environment as SAP has announced that SAP BTP, Neo environment will be discontinued on December 31, 2028. Information on the sunsetting of this environment can be found in SAP Note 3365019. New services are now provided exclusively in the Cloud Foundry environment, which is part of the multicloud environment. In the multicloud environment, services are provided by the following SAP IaaS partners:

1 Introduction to SAP BTP

- Amazon
- Microsoft
- Google
- Alibaba

These IaaS partners operate the infrastructure layers for the respective regions, while SAP operates the platform layer and runtime environments. Companies running SAP only have access to the platform layer and not to the infrastructure layer. In the multicloud environment, runtimes are offered for Cloud Foundry, Kyma, and ABAP.

The Cloud Foundry Foundation is a nonprofit, open-source project. The foundation's vision is to make Cloud Foundry the world's leading application platform for cloud computing. It aims to promote awareness and acceptance of the project and create a vibrant community of companies contributing to it. It has set itself the following goals:

- Establish and maintain Cloud Foundry as a global, industry-standard platform-as-a-service (PaaS) open-source technology with a thriving ecosystem.
- Maintain and ensure quality, value, and innovation for user organizations, operators, and providers of Cloud Foundry technology.
- Ensuring a vibrant, agile experience for community contributors who are rapidly delivering top-quality, native cloud applications worldwide.

SAP BTP is a certified Cloud Foundry distribution. The Cloud Foundry environment of SAP BTP enables the development and operation of cloud applications in various programming languages. Cloud Foundry applications can be deployed on SAP BTP in various regions. Each region forms the location of a separate data center. SAP is constantly developing SAP BTP, and planned features can be found on the roadmap. You can access this information at *https://roadmaps.sap.com/*. For example, you can find information there about which new data centers are planned.

1.2 License Models, Service-Level Agreements, and Important Documents

SAP provides enterprise customers with two different licensing models for SAP BTP: the consumption-based model and the subscription-based model. These versatile options enable companies to select the most suitable licensing model for their individual requirements.

The *consumption-based model* gives companies access to all current and future services available for this model. They enjoy unlimited flexibility to activate or deactivate services as required and to switch between different services during the term of the contract. This commercial model offers three different options to choose from: the Cloud

Platform Enterprise Agreement (CPEA), the SAP BTP Enterprise Agreement (SAP BTPEA), and the pay-as-you-go (PAYG) model for SAP BTP. Each option is suitable for different business situations and financial commitments.

The CPEA is characterized by the following features:

- Your company invests in cloud credits in advance for the term of the contract and agrees to use SAP BTP services annually.
- This model is suitable for customers who have well-established and planned use cases and who want the flexibility to switch services on and off and to switch between services without being tied to a single service for the entire contract period.
- You will receive a monthly invoice that includes information on the use of each service and the corresponding costs. The total monthly costs are deducted from your cloud credit.
- This model requires a minimum investment and allows for volume-based discounts. Billing occurs annually in advance. Overages are billed in arrears at list price.
- You can top up your cloud credit at any time to avoid overages.

SAP BTPEA is characterized by the following features:

- Your organization makes an up-front payment for cloud credits for the term of the contract with an annual commitment to consume SAP BTP services.
- This model is suitable for customers with well-defined and planned use cases who want the flexibility to activate and deactivate services and switch between services without being tied to a single service for the entire term of the contract.
- You will receive a monthly bill that includes information on the usage of each service and the corresponding costs. The total monthly costs are deducted from your cloud credit.
- This model has a minimum investment, and volume-based discounts are available.
- You will be billed annually in advance. Any additional usage will be charged retrospectively at the list price.
- You can top up your cloud credit at any time to avoid overuse.
- You will have access to new SAP BTP services that are added to the consumption-based service catalog.

The pay-as-you-go model is characterized by the following features:

- You have equal access to all services available in CPEA, but with a highly flexible, no-commitment model.
- You pay nothing up front, and there are no minimum usage requirements or annual commitments. You only pay for the SAP BTP services as you consume them.
- You will be invoiced monthly in arrears.
- The service fees are not excluded from rebates.

- This low-risk model is suitable for customers whose use cases are not yet well defined and who want to create a proof of concept in a production environment.
- This model offers the flexibility to switch services on and off and to switch between services as needed during the contract period.
- A seamless transition to the CPEA model is possible, provided you do not have other CPEA-based global accounts.

Cloud Foundry Runtime

In global accounts with the consumption-based commercial model, the SAP BTP, Cloud Foundry runtime does not appear on the **Entitlements** page within the SAP BTP cockpit. By default, each subaccount is allocated a technical limit of 200 GB of Cloud Foundry runtime memory. This limit specifies the maximum runtime memory available for use in the subaccount.

In the subscription-based model, your company selects only the services that you want to use. These services can then be subscribed to at a fixed price, regardless of actual use. This model is characterized by the following properties:

- You are only entitled to use the subscribed services.
- You can change your contract through your sales or customer care representatives to access additional services that incur additional costs.
- You pay a fixed amount regardless of your use of the subscribed services. You pay in advance when the contract period begins.
- Your company can renew the subscription at the end of the contract period.

It is important to note that you can subscribe to some services based on user metrics or resource metrics. For example, a portal service can be based on the number of site visits or the number of users. Resource-based metrics are common when many users, such as suppliers, access a portal to interact with your organization. Because it is often difficult to predict exactly how many resources will be needed over a three-year period, you have the option to increase your initial order if resource usage exceeds your subscribed quota. The SAP BTP cockpit enables you to monitor resource consumption within your global account monthly. You also get access to bundles or packages that include multiple related services and applications. In most cases, this is more cost-effective than subscribing to individual SAP BTP services separately. This enables your organization to make optimal use of resources and keep costs under control.

Of course, SAP offers corresponding SLAs for the services provided in SAP BTP. These can be found at *https://www.sap.com/about/trust-center/agreements.html* (see Figure 1.1).

1.2 License Models, Service-Level Agreements, and Important Documents

Figure 1.1 SAP Cloud Agreements

It is important to note that the SLA for SAP BTP services has some unique features. We want to make a fair assessment here, without criticizing unnecessarily. Nevertheless, we must mention that the system availabilities specified in the SLAs are calculated fundamentally differently compared to other cloud providers. This is because certain downtimes are excluded from the calculation. This means that it is possible that a service you want to use may not be available for two hours a week, for example, but still has 100% system availability according to the SLA. It is advisable to take these subtleties into account to have realistic expectations regarding service availability.

The downtimes, calculated based on maintenance windows and major upgrade windows, can be viewed for each service at *https://support.sap.com/en/my-support/systems-installations/cac/maintenance-windows.html*. Figure 1.2 shows an example of the maintenance windows for SAP Integration Suite. Although there are no planned maintenance windows, there are downtimes of up to four hours for major upgrades up to four times a year.

As emphasized, it is not our intention to present SAP in a negative light. Nevertheless, we recommend that you keep this method of calculating system availability in mind, especially if you need to guarantee a certain system availability to your customers in your SLAs. This enables you to make transparent and realistic commitments that consider the actual operating status of the SAP BTP services.

SAP follows a *shared responsibility model* for SAP BTP, which means that SAP manages the platform while you develop and manage applications. SAP is responsible for operating the entire SAP BTP infrastructure, including monitoring, patching, software

1 Introduction to SAP BTP

updates, and maintenance of the infrastructure and underlying operating systems. SAP is also responsible for technical operations, such as monitoring the SAP BTP services, providing health check services, capacity management, error recovery, and housekeeping, implementing regular updates, and incident management. SAP creates your global account and provides you with the resources and services you have purchased.

Systems & Installations / Cloud Availability in SAP for Me
Maintenance Windows and Major Upgrade Windows for SAP Clou... SAP Cloud Services | Vendor-Branded Cloud Services | SAP NS2 Cloud Services

Cloud Service	MAINTENANCE WINDOWS				MAJOR UPGRADE WINDOWS			
	MENA	APJ	Europe	Americas	Frequency	MENA	APJ	Europe
SAP Cloud Integration	FRI 7 pm (2 hrs)	SAT 3 pm (2 hrs)	SAT 10 pm (2 hrs)	SUN 4 am (2 hrs)	Up to 4 times per year	FRI 5 pm (12 hrs)	SAT 1 pm (12 hrs)	SAT 8 pm (12 hr)
SAP Continuous Integration and Delivery	Zero downtime	Zero downtime	Zero downtime	Zero downtime	Up to 4 times per year	FRI 5 pm (4 hrs)	SAT 1 pm (4 hrs)	SAT 8 pm (4 hrs)
SAP Data Privacy Integration	Zero down-time	Zero down-time	Zero down-time	Zero down-time	Up to 4 times per year	SAT 3 pm (3 hrs)	SAT 3 pm (3 hrs)	SAT 3 pm (3 hrs)
SAP Integrated Business Planning	FRI 7 pm (4 hrs)	SAT 3 pm (4 hrs)	SAT 10 pm (4 hrs)	SUN 4 am (4 hrs)	Up to 4 times per year	FRI 1 am (24 hrs)	FRI 9 pm (24 hrs)	SAT 4 am (24 hr)
SAP Integration Suite	Zero down-time	Zero down-time	Zero down-time	Zero down-time	Up to 4 times per year	FRI 5 pm (4hrs)	SAT 1 pm (4 hrs)	SAT 8 pm (4 hrs)

< 1 2 >

(1) These Major Upgrade Windows are separate from and in addition to Major Upgrade Windows of underlying SAP Business Technology Platform.
(2) These Maintenance Windows are separate from and in addition to Maintenance Windows of underlying SAP HANA Cloud.
(3) These Maintenance Windows are separate from and in addition to Maintenance Windows of underlying SAP Data Intelligence.

Figure 1.2 Maintenance Windows

As an SAP BTP customer, you are responsible for managing your global account and any subaccounts. This includes creating an account concept, creating and configuring your subaccounts based on the requirements of your development projects, and distributing resources and services accordingly. You are also responsible for developing and operating applications. You are also responsible for building and deploying applications, managing application-specific role assignments, integrating with existing systems and applications, monitoring and implementing health checks, and performing housekeeping, troubleshooting, and regular updates for your applications running on SAP BTP.

1.3 Global Accounts and Subaccounts

A *global account* is the implementation of a contract that you or your company has made with SAP. This type of account is used to manage subaccounts, members, authorizations, and quotas (known as *entitlements*). You will find a detailed introduction to global accounts and subaccounts in Chapter 4 and Chapter 5.

As an SAP BTP customer, you receive authorizations and quotas for the use of platform resources per global account, and you then distribute these authorizations and quotas to subaccounts for actual use. As already mentioned, there are two types of commercial models for global accounts: the consumption-oriented model and the subscription-based model.

Global accounts are region- and environment-independent. Within a global account, you manage all your subaccounts, which in turn are specific to a region or environment. This structure enables you to effectively organize your resources and services while maintaining a global view of your SAP BTP portfolio. You can set up and control subaccounts for different geographical locations (see Figure 1.3) or business purposes, giving you the flexibility to use your platform resources exactly where they are needed. This makes it easier to scale and adapt your solutions to the requirements of your company in different contexts.

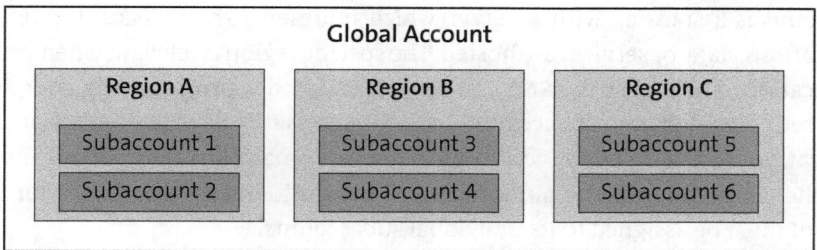

Figure 1.3 One Global Account with Several Subaccounts in Different Regions

Subaccounts enable you to structure a global account according to the requirements of your organization and your projects in terms of members, services, and permissions. A global account can contain one or more subaccounts in which you provide applications, use services, and manage subscriptions (see Figure 1.4). Different subaccounts in a global account are independent of each other. This must be considered when planning your system landscape and overall architecture in terms of security, user administration, data management, integration, and so on.

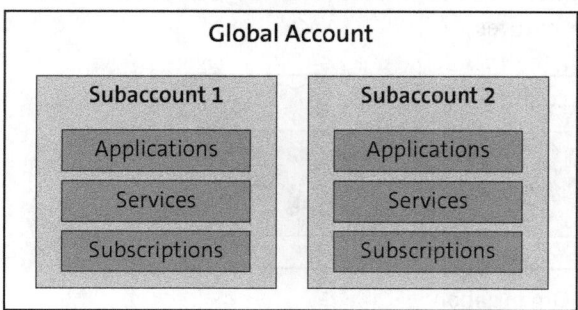

Figure 1.4 Mutually Independent Subaccounts

> **EU Access**
>
> Some customer contracts include the EU access option, which restricts the processing of personal data to the European Economic Area (EEA) and Switzerland. If a global account is marked with EU access, then the actual EU access compliance status of its subaccounts will be displayed during subaccount creation.
>
> If you need a subaccount with EU access, make sure you select a provider and a region where EU access is available. Regions that enable EU access are marked accordingly in the map view of SAP Discovery Center. Note that for some services there is generally no EU access option, even if the provider and region generally support EU access. It is therefore advisable to check the availability of EU access in your specific region and for the desired service to ensure that the data processing requirements can be met according to the contractual agreements.

Each subaccount is associated with a *region*, which represents the physical location where applications, data, or services are hosted. The specific region is relevant when you deploy applications and access the SAP BTP cockpit using the corresponding cockpit URL. The current region of your subaccount does not necessarily have to be associated with your location. For example, you could be located in Germany but operate your subaccount in the United States. The authorizations and entitlements purchased for a global account must be assigned to its individual subaccounts.

When you activate the Cloud Foundry environment in one of your subaccounts, the system automatically creates a Cloud Foundry organization (org) for you. The subaccount and the org have a 1:1 relationship and are on the same navigation level in the cockpit, even though they may have different names. Within this Cloud Foundry org, you can create *spaces* (see Figure 1.5). These spaces allow you to further structure your account model and use services and functions in the Cloud Foundry environment. Spaces in a Cloud Foundry organization make it possible to organize resources and development projects. They serve to refine and specialize your development and deployment processes by providing logical separation for different tasks or teams within the Cloud Foundry environment. This promotes flexibility and efficiency in the use of Cloud Foundry services and features.

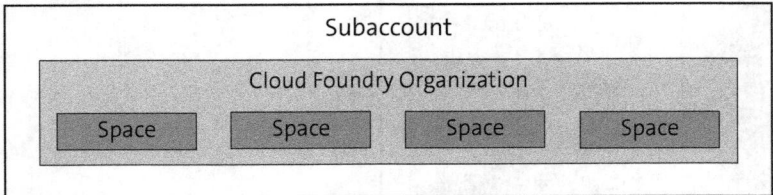

Figure 1.5 Spaces in a Cloud Foundry Organization

1.4 SAP Discovery Center

SAP Discovery Center is your central point of contact if you need information about the services provided on SAP BTP. It can be accessed at *https://discovery-center.cloud.sap/*. Here you will find both service descriptions, in the **SAP BTP Services** area, and **Missions**, which help you explore the SAP BTP services (see Figure 1.6). In addition, a new **Reference Architectures** area was introduced at SAP TechEd 2023. We will discuss this in more detail in Section 1.6.4. The **SAP Business AI Features** section was added toward the end of 2024.

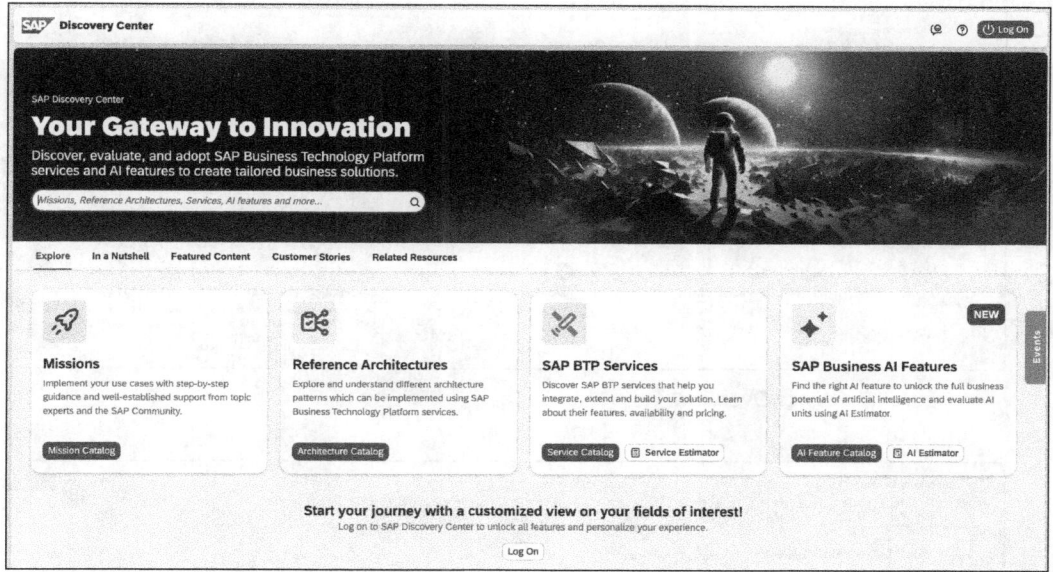

Figure 1.6 SAP Discovery Center

All the services offered on SAP BTP are listed in the **Services** area (see Figure 1.7). In the side menu, you can filter either by solutions, such as **AI** or **Application Development and Automation**, or by capabilities, such as **DevOps** or **Process Automation**. In addition, newly available services are marked with the label **New**. Services that are currently still in the beta stage are marked with a **Beta** label, and services that will be discontinued soon are marked with the label **Deprecated** (or **Retiring Soon**). As you can see from this description, some services are also being discontinued or not further developed by SAP. This affected, for example, the workflow service on SAP BTP, which became obsolete with the introduction of SAP Build Process Automation and was replaced by it.

Clicking a service will take you to the description of the respective service. There you will find a wide range of helpful information. For an example, we have selected the SAP Integration Suite service (see Figure 1.8).

1　Introduction to SAP BTP

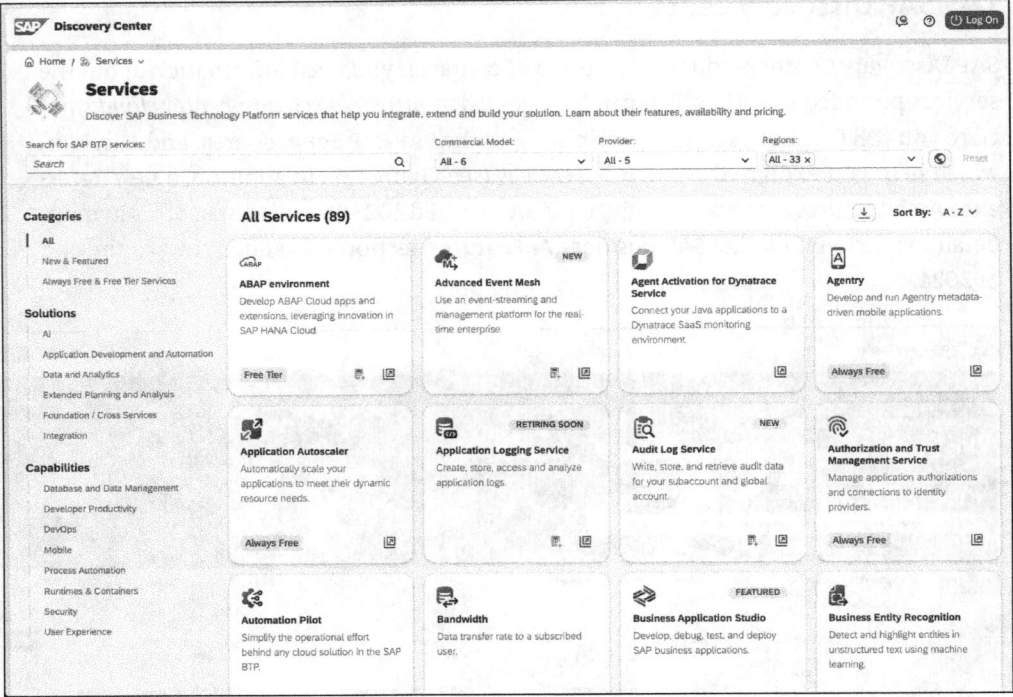

Figure 1.7 Service Overview

Figure 1.8 Overview Tab for SAP Integration Suite

On the first tab page, **Overview**, the features of the respective service are displayed in the main area. This information is usually offered at an abstract level. If you want to learn more details about a service, we recommend that you look at the documentation for that service. The menu on the right-hand side is particularly useful. There you will find links to the service and its tools, as well as links to resources that further explain the service. In most cases, you will also see a **Tutorials & Learning** section. There you will find links to tutorials, openSAP training courses, and SAP learning paths for the selected service.

The **Pricing** tab is particularly interesting. Here you will find information about the license models under which SAP offers the service (see Figure 1.9). This section also tells you whether a free service plan is available for the service. This entitles you to use the service free of charge, usually for a certain period and to a certain extent. This allows you to familiarize yourself with the service, evaluate it, and thus determine whether the service meets your requirements.

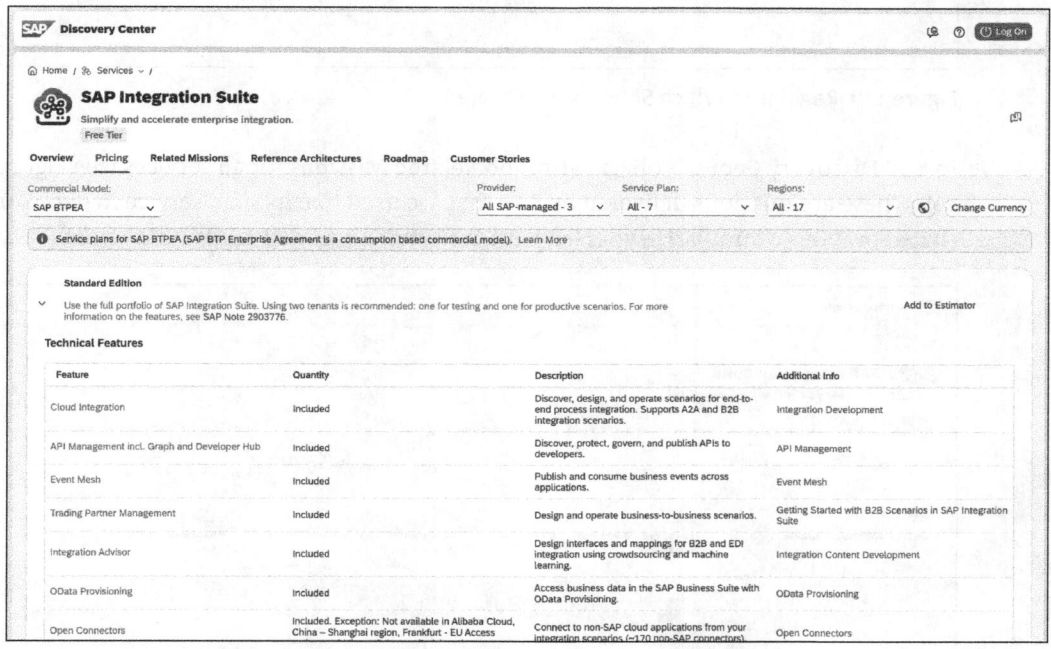

Figure 1.9 Pricing Tab for SAP Integration Suite

By clicking the globe icon (to filter services using a map), you can see a graphical display showing in which geographical regions the desired service is offered. Figure 1.10 shows this for SAP Integration Suite. The legend shows you which color corresponds to which hyperscaler. You can decide for yourself via which hyperscaler the subaccount containing the desired service should run.

1 Introduction to SAP BTP

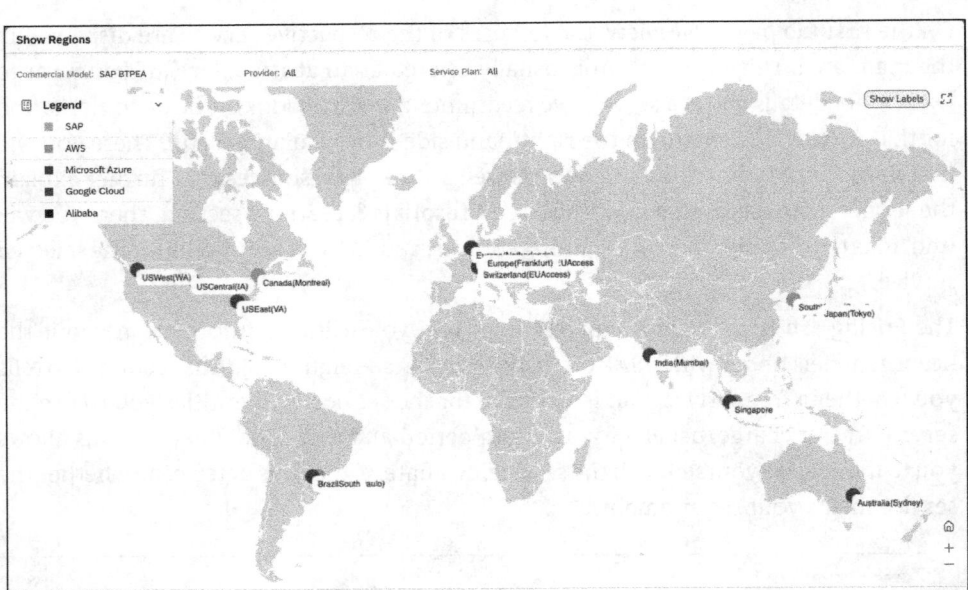

Figure 1.10 Regions in Which Services Are Offered

In SAP Discovery Center, you can also find **Related Missions** for all services (see Figure 1.11). These are missions delivered by SAP that are used to explain a service in detail or that allow you to familiarize yourself with the service via a self-study guide from SAP.

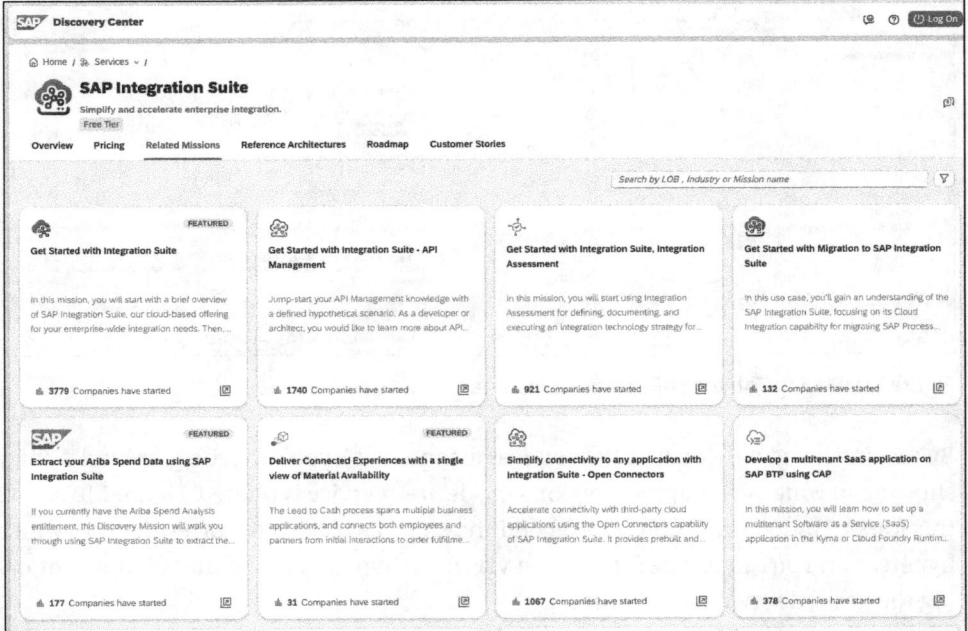

Figure 1.11 Related Missions Tab for SAP Integration Suite

In the **Reference Architectures** tab, you will find typical use cases for this service (see Figure 1.12).

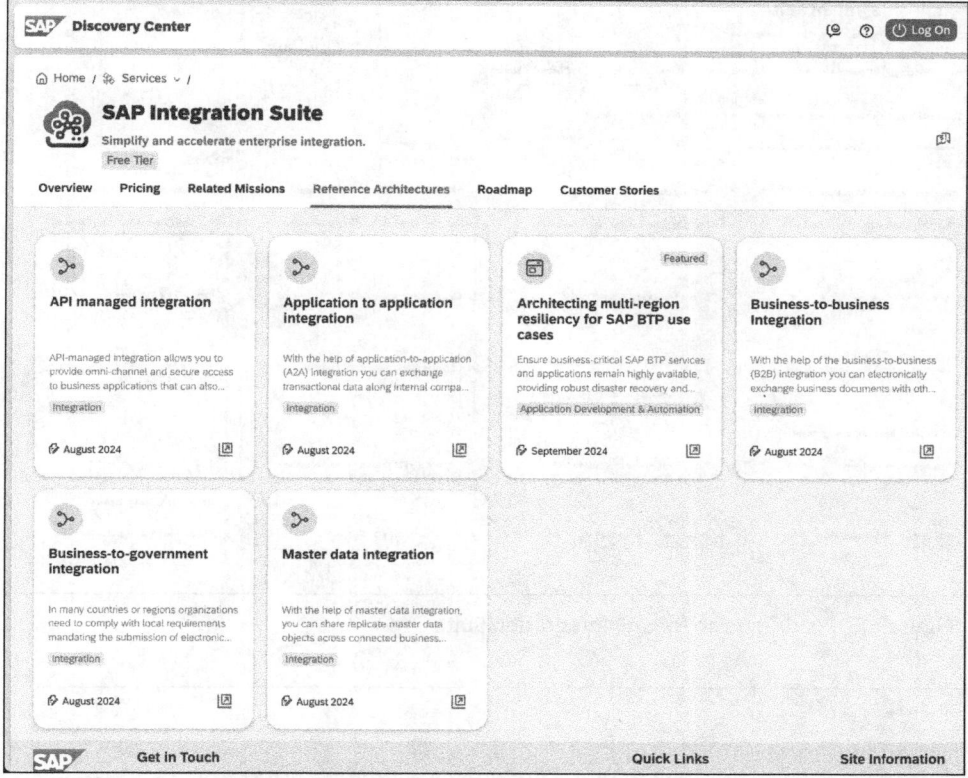

Figure 1.12 Reference Architectures for SAP Integration Suite

In SAP Discovery Center, you can also find the roadmaps for the respective services on the **Roadmap** tab. The current planning statuses of new features are presented here (see Figure 1.13). The roadmap time frame usually covers the next four to five quarters. However, it is important to emphasize that this is planning only on the part of SAP and can change at any time. Note that you have no legal right to expect the implementation of any announced features.

With missions, you can solve your use cases on SAP BTP with step-by-step instructions and in-depth support from subject matter experts from SAP and the SAP community. The use case of a mission is always divided into three parts (see Figure 1.14):

- The **Current Position** explains what challenge the mission is intended to solve.
- The **Destination** describes the expected result.
- The **Route** states what is required to get from the current position to the desired destination.

1 Introduction to SAP BTP

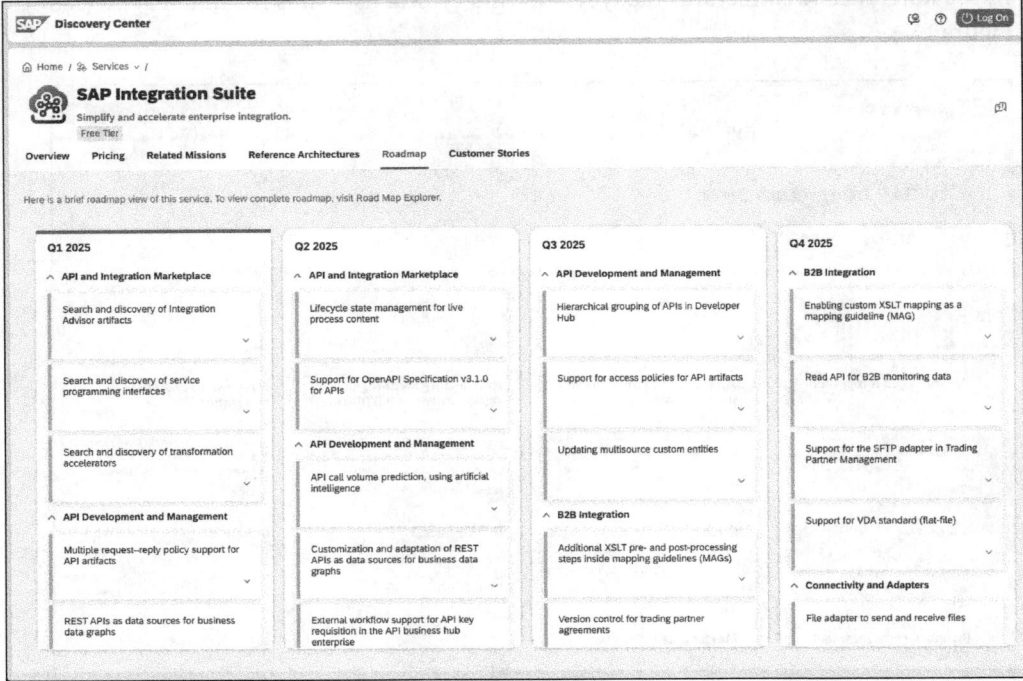

Figure 1.13 Roadmap Tab for SAP Integration Suite

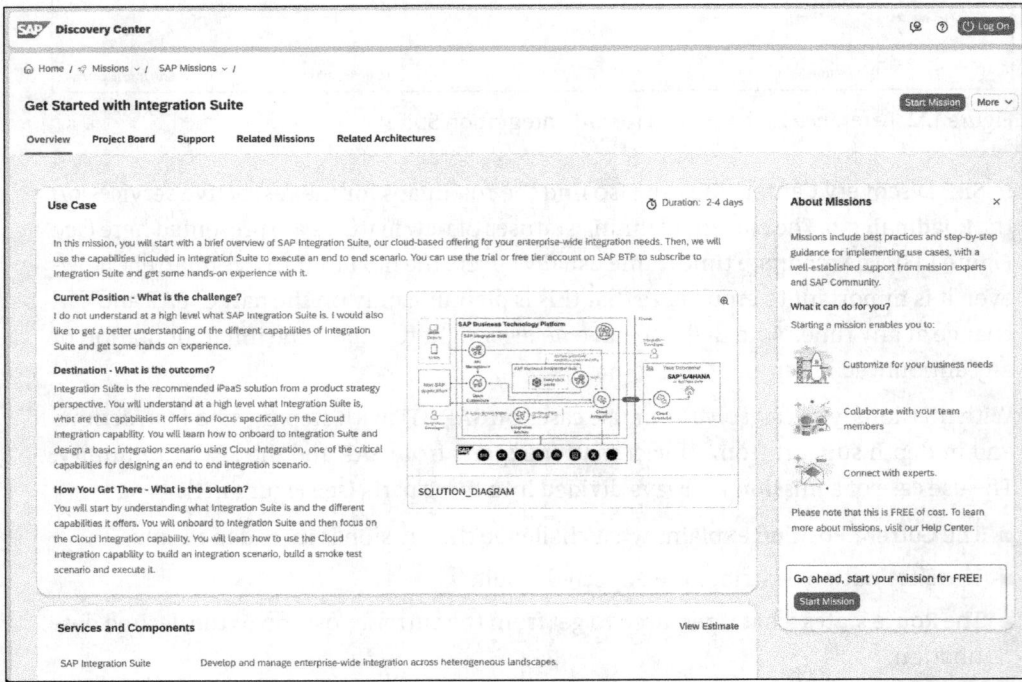

Figure 1.14 Overview of Mission

You can start the mission by clicking the **Start Mission** button. To do this, you must be logged in with an SAP Universal ID (as an S-user). For more information about SAP Universal ID, see the text box in Chapter 2, Section 2.1.2. Starting a mission does not incur any costs.

After you have started a mission, you can jump to the **Project Board** tab. There you will find a Kanban board that guides you through the desired goal in several phases (see Figure 1.15). You start from the left column and work your way to the right. In each column, you work your way from top to bottom. The individual tasks are texts, videos, links to tutorials, or openSAP training courses.

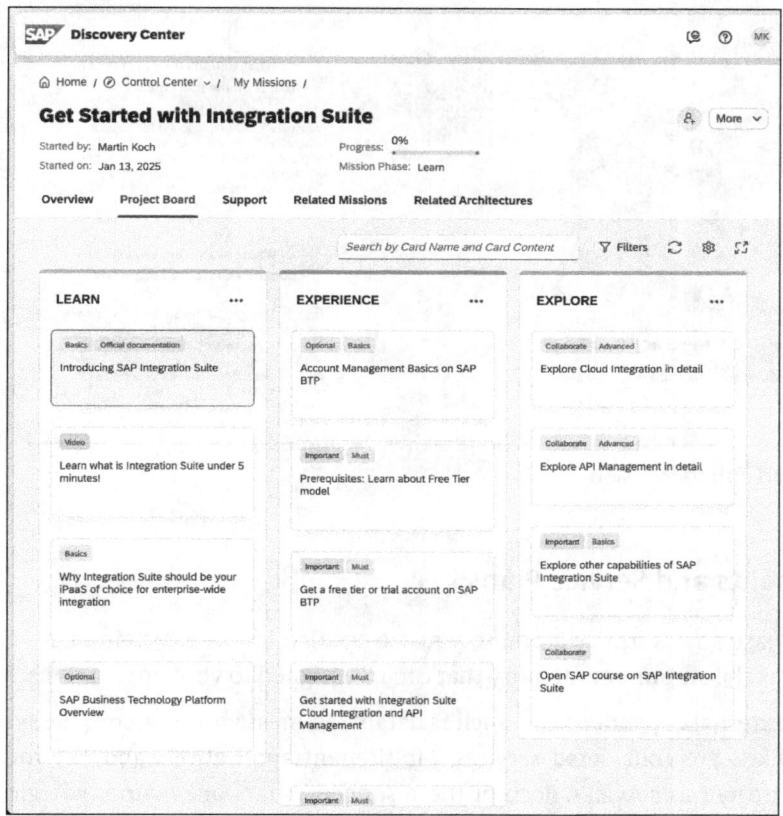

Figure 1.15 Project Board Tab for Mission

If you encounter a problem while working through the mission, you can use the **Support** tab to ask an SAP expert for help (see Figure 1.16).

These missions can help you learn about individual SAP BTP services via self-study. However, we would also like to mention at this point that missions are not available for all services. Furthermore, although the services are generally explained very well in the missions, they do not go into full details. For this, you need to consult the relevant product documentation at *https://help.sap.com*.

1 Introduction to SAP BTP

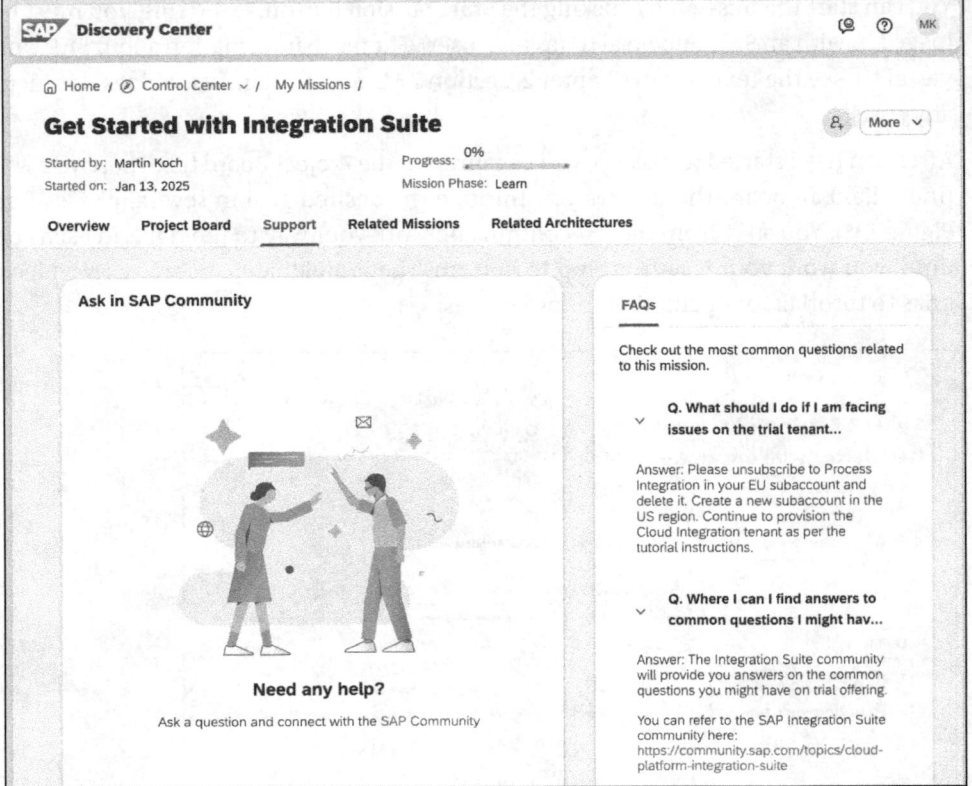

Figure 1.16 Support Tab for Mission

1.5 Entitlements and Service Plans

When you purchase an enterprise account, you are entitled to use a certain quota of resources, such as the amount of memory that can be assigned to your applications.

On SAP BTP, all external dependencies—such as databases, messaging systems, file systems, and the like—are considered *services*. Multitenant applications and environments are also treated as services. Each of these services offers one or more service plans to choose from. A *service plan* represents the costs and services for a specific variant of a particular service. For example, a database may be available in different configurations, each represented by a different service plan, comparable to different T-shirt sizes.

An *entitlement* is your right to use a resource. In other words, entitlements correspond to the service plans that you are authorized to use. A *quota* is a numerical value that indicates the maximum permissible consumption of a resource. Some service plans use a numeric quota, which means that you can increase or decrease the number of available units in a subaccount. Depending on the service, these units represent different things and can affect the number of service instances, applications, or routes you can have in a subaccount (see Figure 1.17).

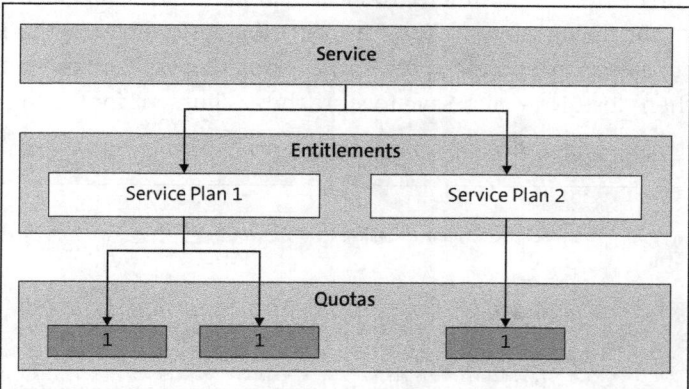

Figure 1.17 Entitlements

Entitlements are assigned at the global account level to the respective subaccounts. To do this, you must navigate in the SAP BTP cockpit in the side menu to **Entitlements • Entity Assignments**. There you must select the desired subaccount in the **Subaccounts/ Directories** input field. After that, you will see the currently assigned service. Click **Edit** to change the assignments (see Figure 1.18).

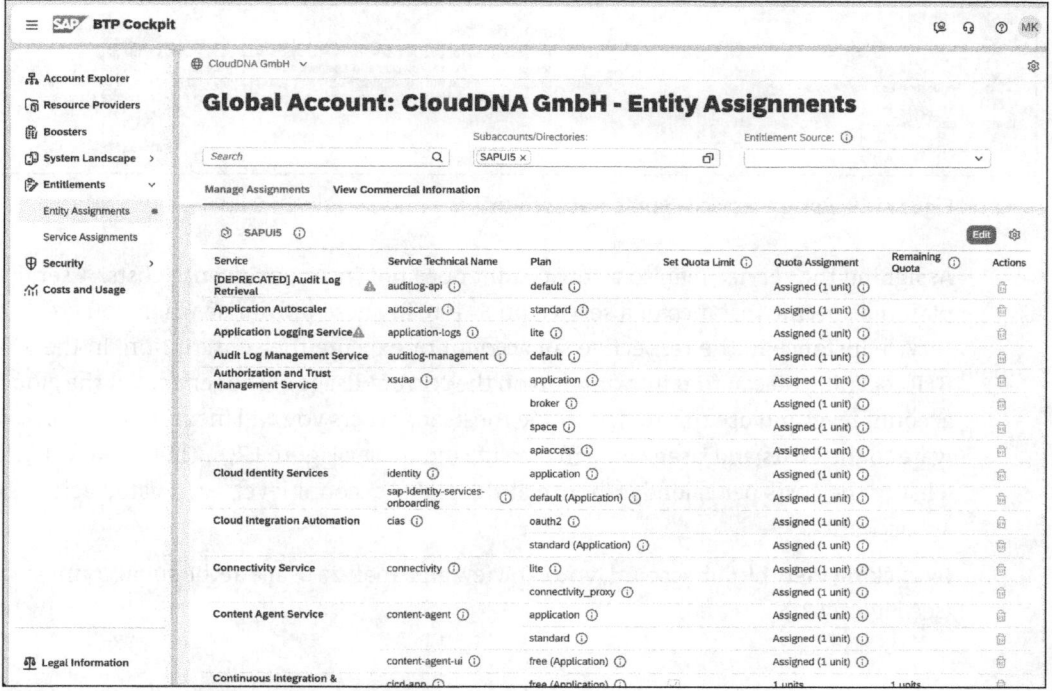

Figure 1.18 Assign Entitlement to Subaccount

You must then click the **Add Service Plans** button to open the dialog for assigning service plans. You can select the desired entitlement in this dialog window. Figure 1.19 shows this using the SAP BTP ABAP environment. You will then see the available service plans on the right side of the dialog window. You can select the desired plan(s) there. Once you have made your selection, you can apply it by clicking the **Add Service Plans** button. The dialog will then close. Now click **Save** to store the assignment for this subaccount.

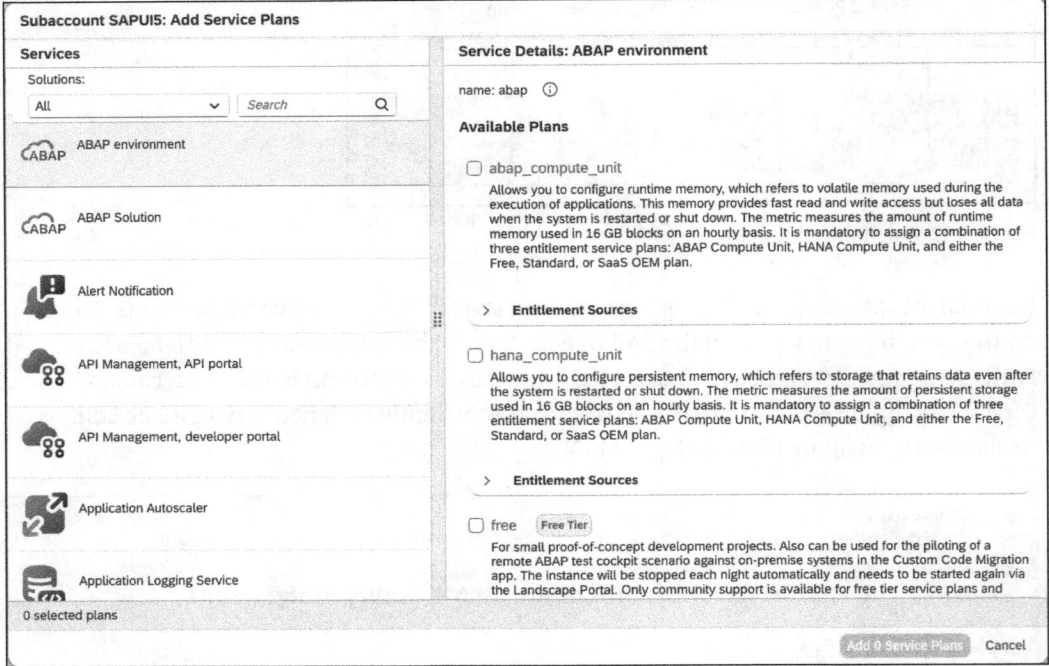

Figure 1.19 Assign Service Plan to Subaccount

Assigning the service plan to a subaccount does not incur any license costs. A service plan is a specific instance of a service on SAP BTP. These only arise when you create a service instance in the respective subaccount or execute the subscription. In the SAP BTP cockpit, you can find information on the current usage of the services at the global account level and use this to determine the license costs you will incur. To do this, navigate to the **Costs and Usage** area in the side menu (see Figure 1.20). There you will find a list of the costs per calendar month at the global account level, aggregated across all subaccounts.

By clicking **View by Subaccount**, you can view and analyze usage at the subaccount level (see Figure 1.21).

1.5 Entitlements and Service Plans

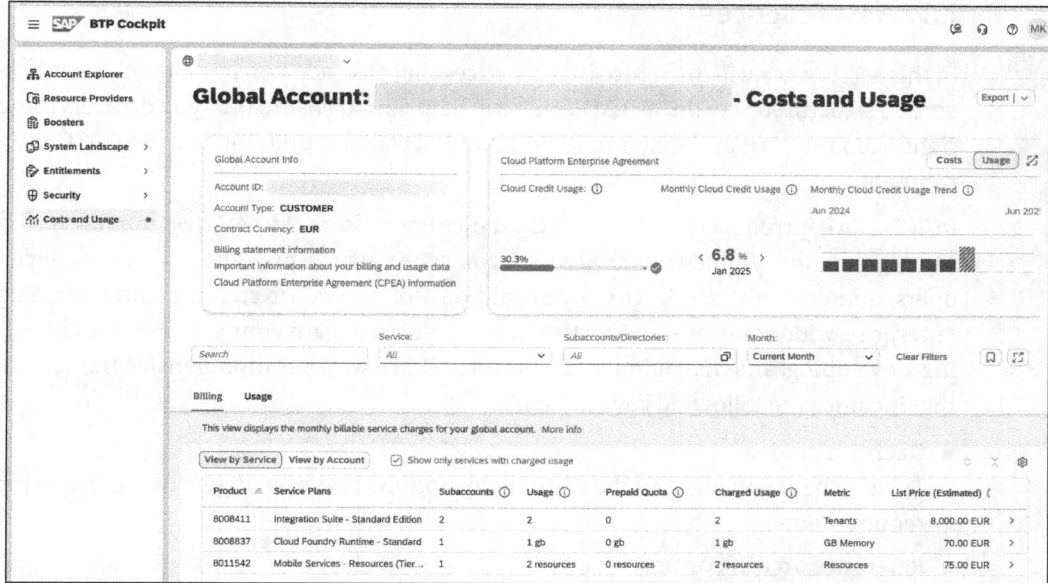

Figure 1.20 Costs and Usage

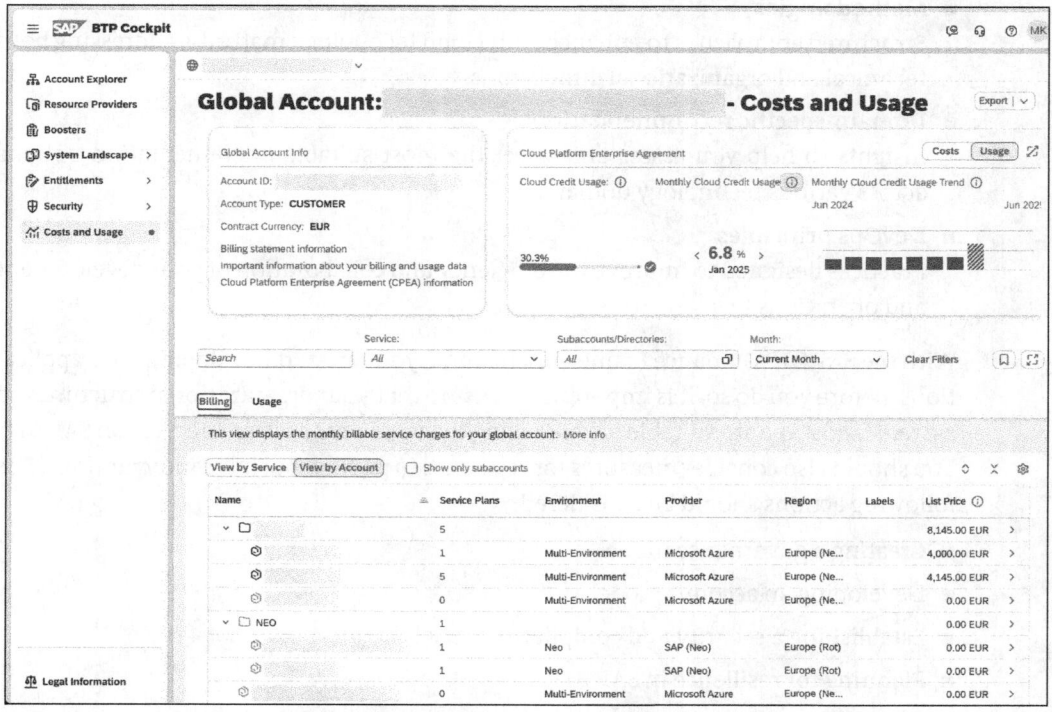

Figure 1.21 Cost and Usage per Subaccount/Directory

1.6 Best Practices

In this section, we will introduce best practices that will help you implement your project in a structured way on SAP BTP. This will help you to ensure that you do everything right from the start and that a solid foundation is laid for building your SAP BTP environment.

In 2024, SAP introduced the SAP BTP Guidance Framework (*https://help.sap.com/docs/sap-btp-guidance-framework/guidance-framework*), which provides architects, developers, and administrators with a central point of access for creating and executing enterprise-wide solutions on SAP BTP. It helps you navigate your journey to architecting, developing, and managing solutions on SAP BTP with a comprehensive framework that includes the following key elements:

- **Decision guides**
  Tools to help you identify the technology options that best align with your specific requirements.
- **Reference architectures**
  Curated solution templates that illustrate how to design and implement solutions on SAP BTP effectively.
- **Methodologies**
  Structured approaches to enhance your cloud technology maturity, addressing both technical and organizational dimensions.
- **Domain-specific recommendations**
  Insights to help you assess and select the most suitable implementation options across various technology domains.
- **DevOps principles**
  Practices designed to improve the efficiency and collaboration of your development and operations teams.

With the SAP BTP Guidance Framework in mind, you can start developing your applications. Before you do so, it is important to ensure that your organizational structure and system landscape are suitable for managing the whole application lifecycle on SAP BTP. You should also consider measures for resilience to prevent business interruptions. The following actions should be considered:

- Creating a governance model
- Developing an account model
- Establishing a security and compliance model
- Planning for resilience in SAP BTP

1.6.1 Structure of a Governance Model

One of the first and most important steps on your journey to the cloud is to establish a suitable organizational structure and governance model. A clear and well-thought-out organizational structure makes it easier for your employees to adopt agile processes.

SAP recommends setting up two types of teams: one or more *cloud development teams* to develop and operate the applications, and a central *platform engineering team* or *center of excellence* (CoE) that is responsible for all operational activities of the global accounts and subaccounts. This latter type of team also defines central governance and compliance guidelines and drives cloud adoption in your organization. Cloud development teams are responsible for developing and operating the applications that run on SAP BTP. In many cases, organizations separate development from operations. The development team builds the application and then hands it off to the operations team, which keeps it running and maintains it. However, this split is not optimal in a cloud application development environment. We recommend that cloud development teams adopt a *DevOps* approach, which means that the team both develops and operates applications. The team should regularly monitor applications after deployment and troubleshoot any issues. For example, if the team members are developing an SAPUI5 user interface, they should check at least every three to six months to see if the UI elements they are using are still supported by the latest SAPUI5 version. Performing this check doesn't require a lot of effort, but it should happen to ensure that the application continues to run properly.

The platform engineering team defines, sets up, and maintains the cloud environment. This team's job is to operate a stable and secure cloud environment. Its members should provide the infrastructure so that developers can start developing cloud applications without delay. The members of this team are experts with experience in developing and building as well as operating an infrastructure for continuous delivery and continuous integration. This team can support your development teams by providing knowledge and defining guidelines that meet your company's quality and security requirements. Normally, the platform engineering team should not be responsible for the lifecycle management of specific applications; this task should be assumed by the cloud development team. The platform engineering team can also serve as a CoE that drives the adoption, migration, and operation of cloud solutions in your organization. The CoE is also responsible for identifying, evaluating, and implementing use cases for SAP BTP.

SAP recommends that the platform engineering team/CoE create the following documents and make them available to developers:

- Onboarding document
- Security document
- Service catalog

Onboarding Document

An *onboarding document* ensures that a new application is fully and correctly integrated into the organization and documented. Onboarding can take place through various channels—for example, via email, a ticketing system, or another tool that is suitable for your organization. The following is an extended list of information that can be captured in an onboarding document and a brief description of each item:

- **Organization or department**
  The unit in which the application is developed.
- **Application name**
  Both the technical and business names.
- **Business case and application description**
  The purpose and benefits of the application.
- **Planned go-live date**
  Time frame for the launch.
- **Application owner**
  Person responsible for the application.
- **Access requests**
  List of colleagues who need access to the subaccount for development (especially in the case of a staged development environment).
- **Target group**
  Clarification of whether the application should be accessible to external users.
- **End-to-end data flow**
  Description of data flows and connectivity to backend systems.
- **Technologies and programming languages**
  Information on the planned technical basis.
- **Git repository URL**
  If available, a link to the repository.
- **Test strategy**
  Plan for quality assurance.

After the document has been reviewed and approved, the owners and developers will be given access to the development subaccount. It is important to point out to the development team that applications and data in the development subaccount can be deleted at any time without warning.

Security Document

SAP recommends creating a standardized *security document* that is completed and approved by the security team before the development of new applications begins. The template should cover the following information:

- **Application owner**
  Person responsible.
- **Scenario description**
  Business need and use case.
- **User groups**
  Target groups, data classification, and security requirements (confidentiality, integrity).
- **Security guidelines**
  Compliance with relevant company guidelines.
- **End-to-end data flow**
  Detailed description of the data paths.
- **Data storage**
  Location and type of stored data.
- **System overview**
  Overview of all connected cloud and on-premise systems, protocols, and ports used.
- **Authentication concept**
  High-level approach to authentication and authorization.
- **Auditing and logging**
  Traceability and security monitoring.

Service Catalog

For companies with multiple development projects, SAP recommends setting up a *central service catalog*. This catalog combines all services offered by the platform engineering team, especially with restricted access to test and production subaccounts. This facilitates collaboration between teams and accelerates processes.

The following are examples of services you might see in such a catalog:

- Adding or managing destinations
- Creating and managing build plans
- Restarting applications
- Read access to a test or production subaccount
- Creating database schemas and assigning access

All services should be provided as templates in a ticketing system or similar tool. To make using the services as easy as possible, SAP recommends automating processes. To do this, you can use SAP BTP APIs, the SAP BTP command line interface (CLI) or the SAP BTP setup automator. The latter can be used for the automation of database schema creation and access management through scripts. The SAP BTP setup automator can be found at *https://github.com/SAP-samples/btp-setup-automator*.

You can also facilitate the Lifecycle Management API so that the cloud development team can restart applications in productive subaccounts without requiring direct access to the subaccount. A service catalog and automation of this kind promotes efficiency and reduces the potential for errors in the collaboration between teams.

1.6.2 Structure of an Account Model

The hierarchical structure between global accounts, directories, and subaccounts allows you to define an *account model* that precisely matches your business and development requirements. Once you have signed your contract with SAP, you will receive the access data for your global account. This global account is the implementation of your commercial contract with SAP; you will use it to manage the resources and authorizations for your development projects. You will also receive one invoice for all consumed resources per global account.

To develop and deploy applications, consume services, and subscribe to applications provided by SAP, you need to create subaccounts. You can create any number of subaccounts in any environment and region. For example, if you are based in Germany, you can create subaccounts in different regions, such as Europe, the United States, or Japan, to support the customers who use your applications. Subaccounts are independent of each other, which means that each subaccount enables its own entitlement and user management. You can configure a separate identity provider for end users for each subaccount. If you have many subaccounts, you can use *directories*, which group subaccounts and/or further subdirectories, to keep track of them and make administration easier. You can use directories to manage permissions or users for entire groups of subaccounts. You can also use directories to distribute the resources assigned to the global account to its subordinate subaccounts.

> **Scalable Account Structure**
>
> SAP recommends building an account structure that can be easily scaled as your organization grows or additional projects are added. That is, you should start with only subaccounts and add directories to group these subaccounts as needed.

How many subaccounts and directories you create and for what purpose depends on your organizational structure and your use case. In general, SAP recommends using subaccounts for a multilevel development process in which you distinguish among a subaccount for development, one for testing, and one for production.

The development subaccount is intended for development purposes and for testing individual increments in the cloud. The test subaccount can be used to carry out integration tests and tests in a production-like environment before they are made publicly available, to ensure quality. In companies where DevOps is highly developed, this subaccount is also used for production applications as the tests take place in the development subaccount. You create the production subaccount for production applications.

Other typical reasons for creating subaccounts include the following:

- Separating development scenarios and projects for easier configuration—for example, with regard to access restrictions
- Separating the work of different development teams
- Restricting access to applications and their administration—for example, by setting up highly secure subaccounts with restricted access or by creating separate subaccounts for connectivity with your various backend systems
- Sharing an SAP HANA cloud database in a subaccount with similar projects that are managed in other subaccounts

When creating different subaccounts, keep the following considerations in mind:

- Connectivity to on-premise systems must be set up separately for each subaccount, which means more work for your platform engineering team. However, it may be easier for you to switch off all integration paths for a project if you have maintained them all in a subaccount. This also allows you to control which application uses which on-premise connections.
- When selecting a region for your subaccount, you should ensure that the region is close to the geographical location of your customers to reduce network latency. In enhancement scenarios, you should choose a region that is close to the systems involved. When selecting a region, also consider all legal requirements and load distribution.
- If your SAP S/4HANA clients need to be separated for legal or regulatory reasons (e.g., to separate the subsidiaries of a company), use different subaccounts for their extensions.
- If the DevOps or application operating teams within a subaccount are completely separate, you should set up separate subaccounts for them for better maintainability.

Although creating a multistage development environment is a good idea in any case, there are some Cloud Foundry–specific considerations that you should keep in mind.

You can use both subaccounts and spaces to develop applications and use services. You therefore need to decide whether you will create different subaccounts or spaces within a subaccount, for example, to set up a multistage development environment.

> **Data Access Separation at the Subaccount Level**
> Think of a subaccount as a tenant: Data access and data visibility are separated at the subaccount level, not at the application or Cloud Foundry space level. Remember that

> services used by every application within a subaccount collect messages from all those services. If you do not want these to be visible across applications, then you need to create different subaccounts.

In general, we recommend creating different subaccounts for a multitier development environment. This allows for dedicated user management between the different tiers, as well as dedicated data management. You can then create a separate scope for each application, extension, solution, or any other project within these subaccounts if you don't need separate user management for these applications and projects. You can only monitor the consumption of resources in your global account for each subaccount, directory, or Cloud Foundry space, not per application. To monitor the resources consumed by a specific project, department, or application, create a dedicated subaccount, directory, or space for it. Exact billing is only possible for global accounts. For the usage-based model, you can calculate the costs after use, but bear in mind that this is only an approximation.

As mentioned earlier, SAP presents the account model with subaccounts and the account model with directories and subaccounts as best practice in the SAP BTP documentation.

Account Model with Subaccounts

With a separate account landscape for each functional area, you can use multiple instances of the same SaaS subscription (e.g., in case you need to keep data or user access separate). You can see these account landscapes in Figure 1.22 for the HR and sales areas.

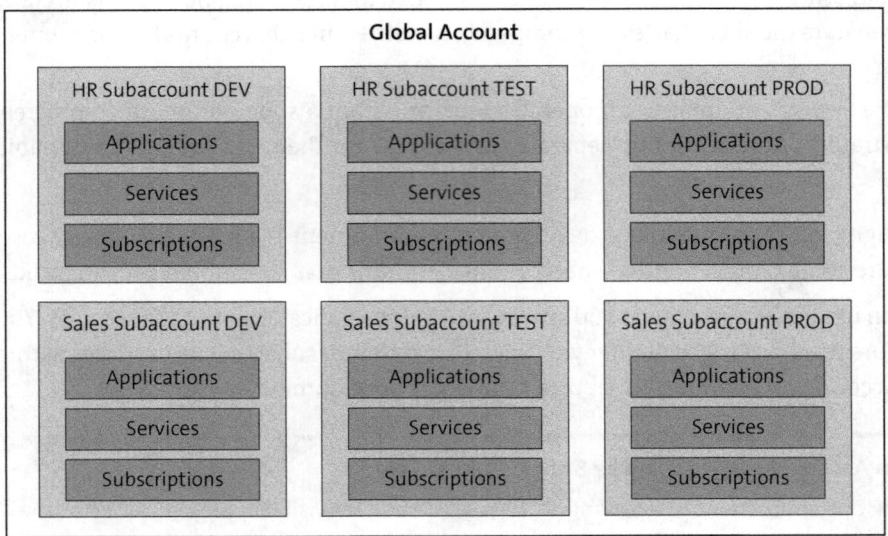

Figure 1.22 Separated Account Landscape for Sales and HR

For example, an internal identity provider would be used for HR subaccounts, while an external identity provider could be used for public or external scenarios. This account model allows you to distribute the administration of the subaccounts across several teams, which makes it easy to scale as the number of cloud projects grows, while keeping maintenance and governance manageable. If possible, you should assign a colleague to be responsible for each group of three subaccounts—that is, each account landscape. An SaaS application can only be used once within a subaccount. So if each functional area has its own subaccount (for development, test, and production), you will not encounter any restrictions when using the same SaaS offering in different projects. In the Cloud Foundry environment, however, you can divide different projects into different areas within a subaccount. This model can easily be expanded later to use directories as additional structuring elements.

Account Model with Directories and Subaccounts

Not only can you structure your global account into multiple subaccounts, you can also combine individual subaccounts into directories in order to manage, operate, and analyze these groups of subaccounts together. A global account can contain up to five levels of directories, each of which can contain a subaccount. The following are some possible reasons for creating directories to make managing your subaccounts easier:

- **Administrative reasons**
  Structure your global account according to responsibilities within your organization. For example, give each branch office, department, or LOB its own directory.

- **Billing purposes**
  Structure your global account into directories for billing purposes.

- **Geographic separation**
  Group subaccounts based on geographic location to manage different local regulations or to improve network performance for groups located in common sites.

- **Business scenario**
  Group subaccounts by business scenario or other business requirement. This enables you to control each business solution separately.

- **Resource constraints**
  Use the directory structure to control access to resources and limit usage by creating separate usage and cost reports, or to define usage restrictions, give critical directories more resources, or enable different monitoring per directory. You can also structure the subaccounts according to usage restrictions in different landscapes.

- **Technical reasons**
  Structure directories and subaccounts according to technical restrictions and then add labels for virtual grouping or vice versa.

These approaches can be categorized into three distinct models based on functional areas, geographic regions, and subsidiaries, as outlined ahead.

Directories per Functional Area

In this account model, each functional area uses its own directory. Within each of these directories, three subaccounts (for development, test, and production) are created (see Figure 1.23). For each directory, the functional area can use its own identity provider and manage its permissions. In addition, you can use labels—for example, to denote the person responsible, the cost center, or other aspects that you need for later reports.

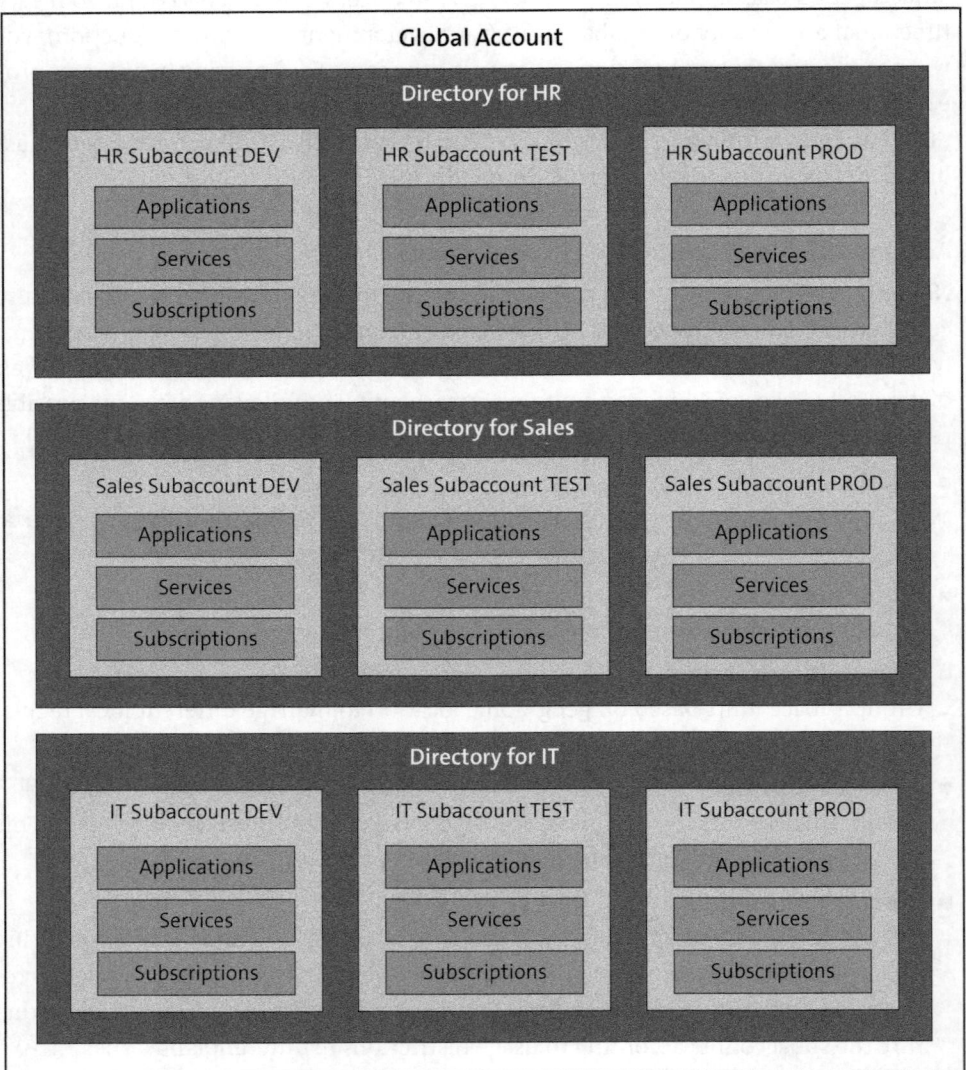

Figure 1.23 Separate Directories for Each Functional Area

Directories per Geographic Area

In this account model, you create a directory for each geographic area. In Figure 1.24, we show this using the example of the Europe, Middle East, and Africa (EMEA) region, and the Americas (AMER) region. There could possibly be a further distinction between North and South America. In addition, there is the Asia Pacific and Japan (APJ) region. You can also use labels at this point to describe the subaccounts in more detail.

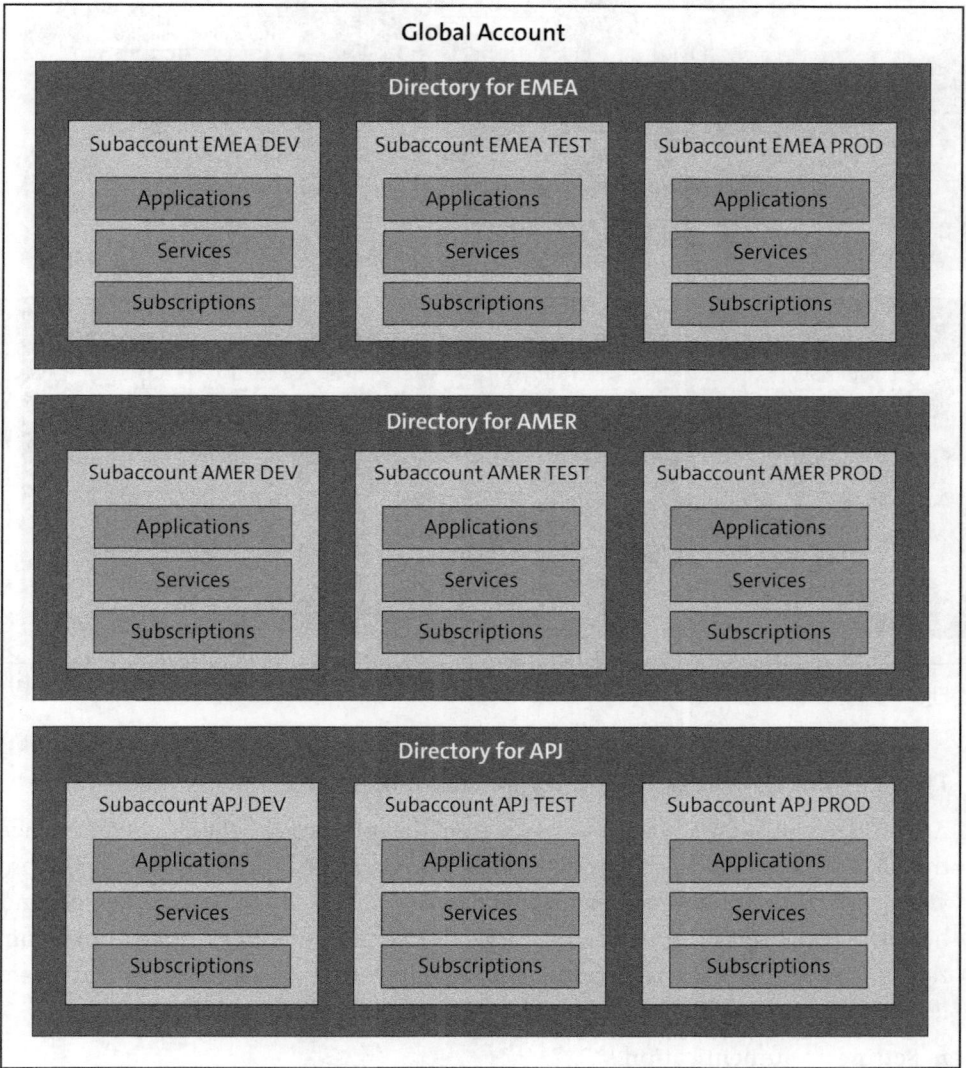

Figure 1.24 Separate Directories for Each Geographic Area

Directories per Subsidiary

In this account model, you create a directory for each subsidiary of your company (see Figure 1.25). Again, you can use labels to add information about cost centers or responsible persons, for example.

1   Introduction to SAP BTP

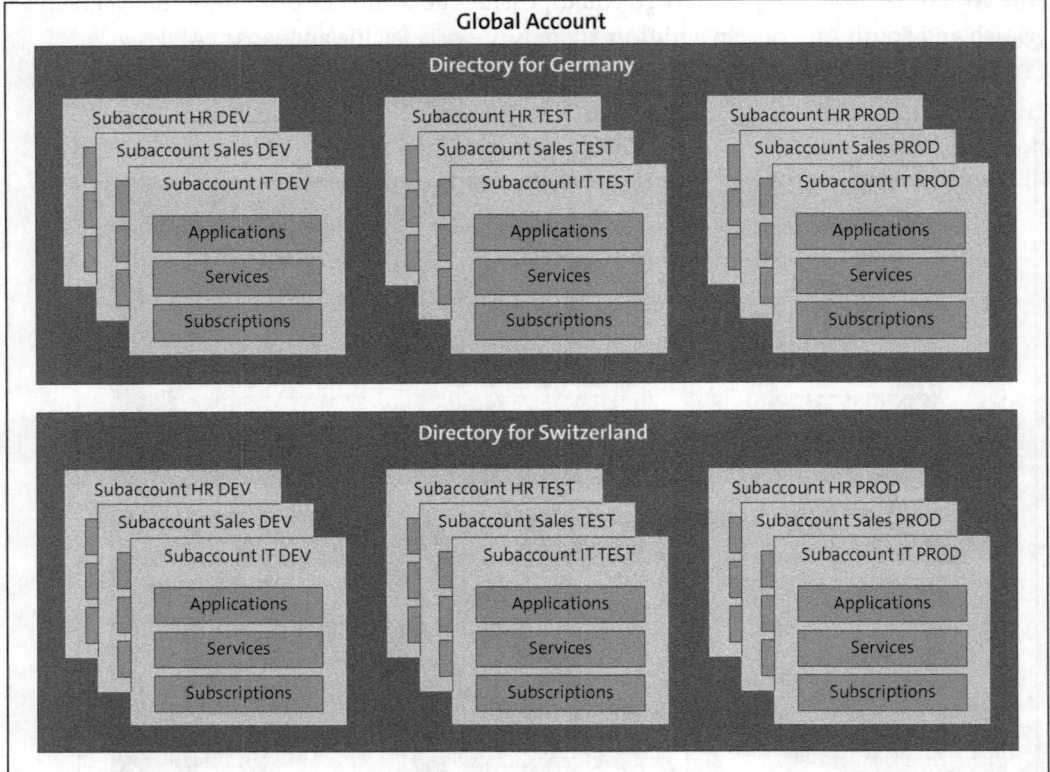

Figure 1.25 Separate Directories for Each Subsidiary

1.6.3   Setting Up a Security and Compliance Model

Applications on SAP BTP can be accessed from the internet and should therefore meet the highest possible security requirements to prevent unauthorized access. SAP provides various recommendations for this. The level of security implemented depends heavily on your specific use case and the general security requirements of your organization. However, SAP recommends several best practices that should be applied regardless of your implementation to ensure a high level of security, as follows:

- **Setting up authentication**
  Initial access to the SAP BTP platform is granted through the default identity provider. After the first scenarios have been tested, your company's own identity and access management solution should be integrated. This gives you full control over your security policies, including authentication methods and password policies. Multifactor authentication (MFA) and single sign-on (SSO) can be implemented for added security.

- **Set up the identity lifecycle**
  Effective identity management encompasses the onboarding, management and offboarding of employees. Small businesses may be able to handle this manually, but larger organizations should rely on automated processes to minimize errors and increase efficiency. Tools such as identity provisioning services and workflow automation can help here.

- **Manage and assign authorizations**
  Permissions are usually assigned in SAP BTP using three methods:
  - Manual assignment: Suitable for smaller environments or infrequent changes.
  - Federation: Enables the synchronization of identities and authorizations between different systems.
  - Provisioning: Automated assignment based on roles and attributes.

  In practice, companies combine these approaches to be able to react flexibly to different scenarios. Make sure that authorizations are regularly checked and that access rights that are no longer required are removed (per the principle of minimal rights).

- **Setting up access to remote systems**
  To access external systems and services, use the SAP Connectivity service:
  - Internet services: Use APIs and destinations to establish a secure connection.
  - Cloud-to-on-premise scenarios: Use the cloud connector, which enables a secure connection to your on-premise systems. The cloud connector ensures encrypted communication and controls access based on defined rules.

- **Comply with data protection and privacy**
  The protection of personal data and compliance with data protection guidelines such as the General Data Protection Regulation (GDPR) are crucial. Consider data protection requirements as early as the planning phase of your application to avoid later adjustments. The following measures should be integrated:
  - Data minimization: Collect and store only the data that is necessary.
  - Encryption: Secure data both during transmission and at rest.
  - Transparency: Ensure that users can view and manage their data.
  - Auditing: Implement mechanisms to track all data access and changes.

- **Security monitoring and incident management**
  Set up a continuous monitoring and alert system to detect security incidents early. Use tools such as the SAP Alert Notification service for SAP BTP and SAP Cloud ALM to identify anomalies and potential threats.

- **Regular security assessments and testing**
  Conduct regular security assessments, including penetration testing, vulnerability assessments, and configuration reviews. Keep all systems and dependencies up to date with timely updates to address known vulnerabilities.

1 Introduction to SAP BTP

1.6.4 Reference Architectures

In SAP Discovery Center, as shown in Figure 1.26, SAP provides reference architectures for various use cases. These are each assigned to a category, such as integration.

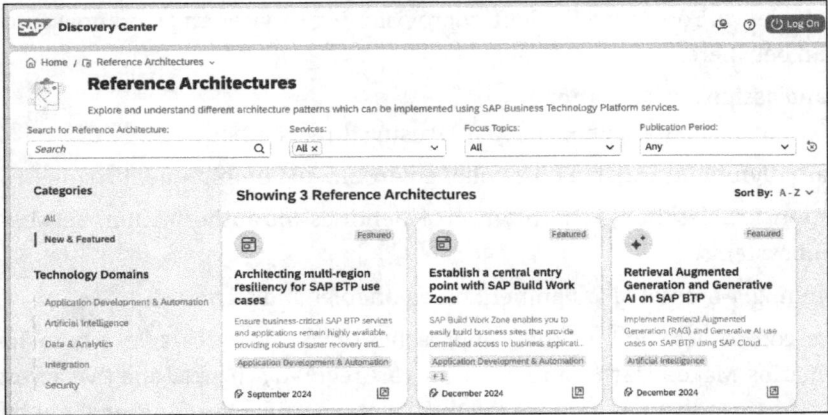

Figure 1.26 SAP BTP Reference Architectures

Figure 1.27 shows the reference architecture for application-to-application integration. In principle, you will find an architecture diagram in each reference architecture. This shows the components involved and, where applicable, various options.

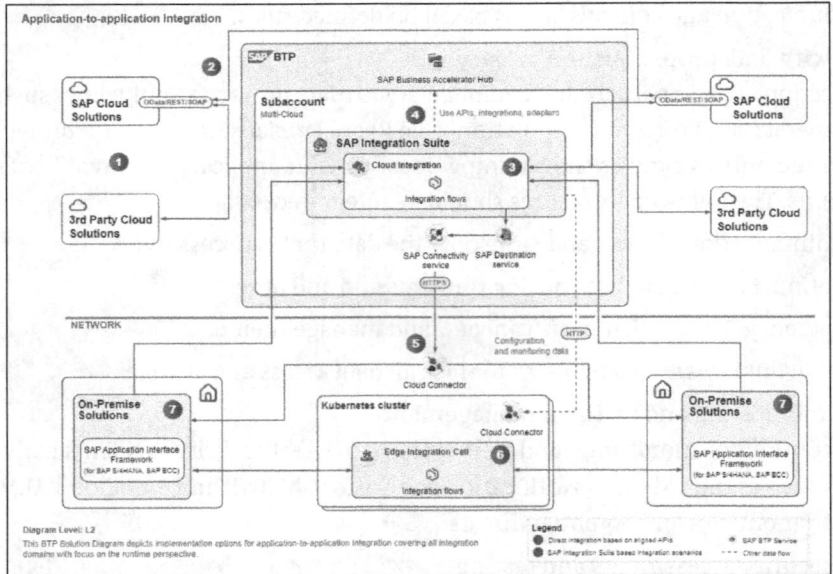

Figure 1.27 Reference Architecture for Application-to-Application Integration

A textual description of the architecture and its various forms can be found below each diagram.

1.7 Troubleshooting

In this section, we will explore the art of troubleshooting to effectively manage the challenges and issues that may arise when managing SAP BTP. We will provide practical insights, proven methods, and strategies for identifying and overcoming potential stumbling blocks to keep your SAP BTP environment running smoothly and efficiently.

For troubleshooting SAP BTP problems, there are several resources and/or websites provided by SAP that can be useful for identifying the cause of the error. First, you should check whether SAP is aware of any current problems or service interruptions. The **Cloud Service Status** page, available at *https://www.sap.com/about/trust-center/cloud-service-status.html*, allows you to do so. This page provides an overview of all services provided by SAP in the cloud. You can use the search function on this page to find the service you are looking for.

We also recommend that you regularly check the **What's New** area in the SAP BTP documentation at *http://s-prs.co/v608000* for news. In addition to current changes, you will also find announcements for future changes including dates.

Another central point of contact for the services you have licensed is SAP for Me. In the **Finance & Legal** area, on the **Cloud** tab page (see *https://me.sap.com/financelegal/cloud*), you will find a list of all packages that you have licensed (see Figure 1.28). You will also find information about the contract terms there.

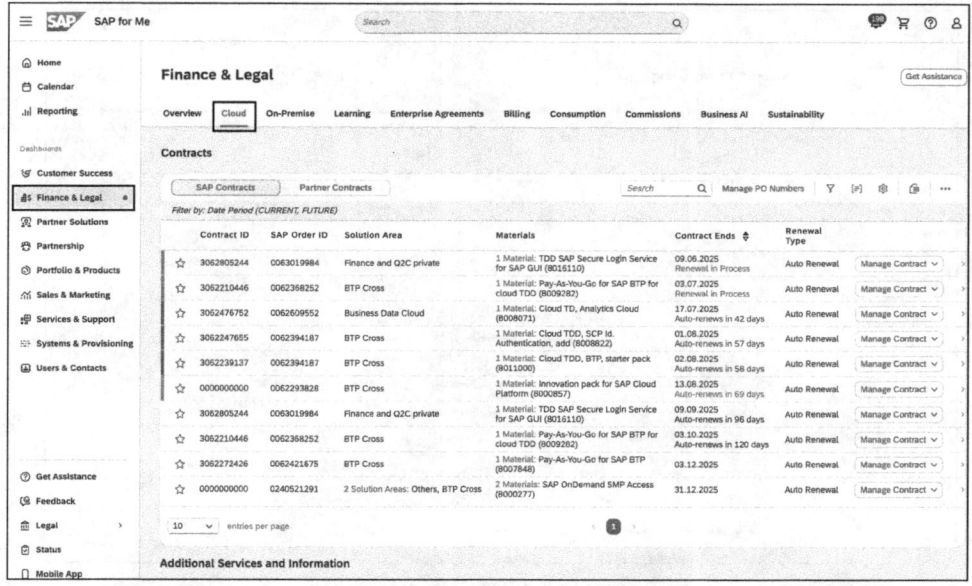

Figure 1.28 SAP for Me: Finance & Legal: Overview of Licensed Packages

On the **Enterprise Agreements** tab, you can find an overview of the costs incurred during the past months (see Figure 1.29).

1   Introduction to SAP BTP

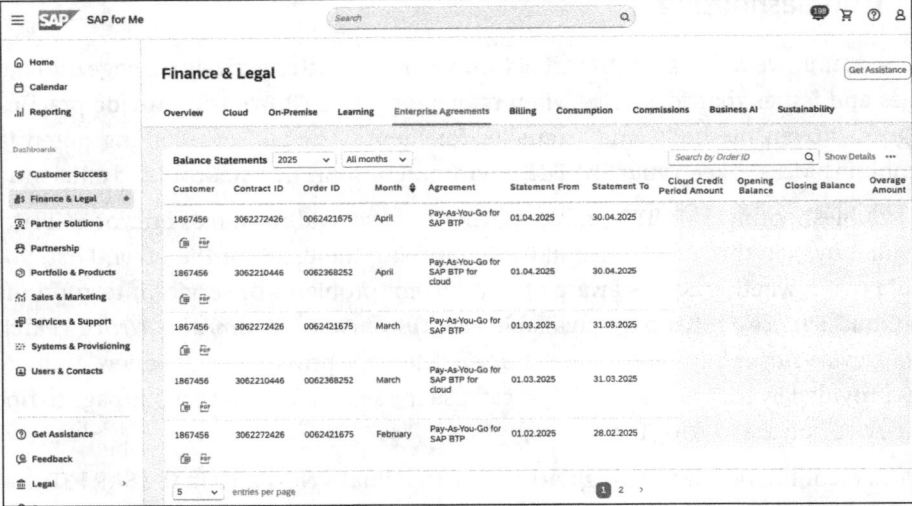

Figure 1.29 SAP for Me: Enterprise Agreements: Overview of Costs Incurred in Previous Months

Another useful resource in SAP for Me is the **Systems & Provisioning** area. As shown in Figure 1.30, the **Availability** tab in this area contains information on upcoming maintenance work and the associated service downtimes.

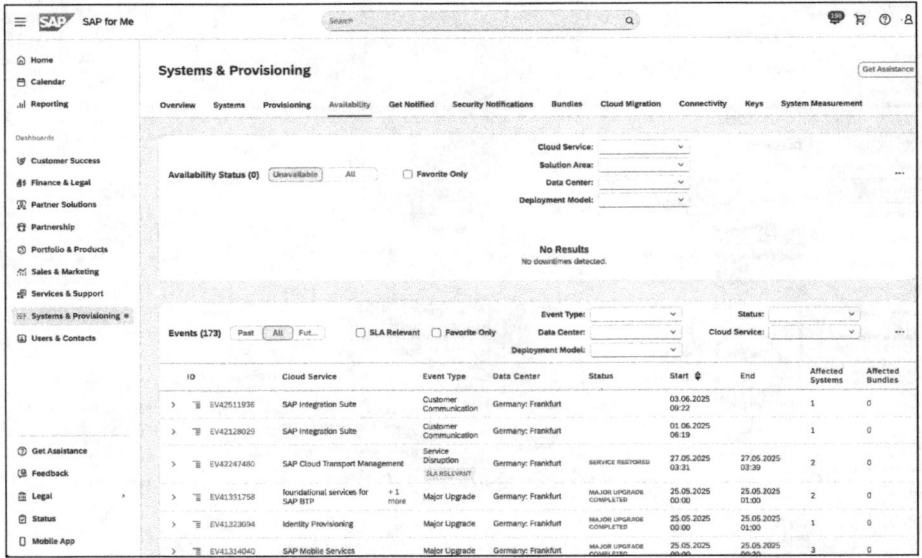

Figure 1.30 SAP for Me: Systems & Provisioning: Availability: Overview of Upcoming Maintenance

Another resource that can help you with error analysis is the Guided Answers wizard, which guides you step by step through the process of correctly classifying the cause of an error. It starts by determining what you are having a problem with—for example, the login process (see Figure 1.31).

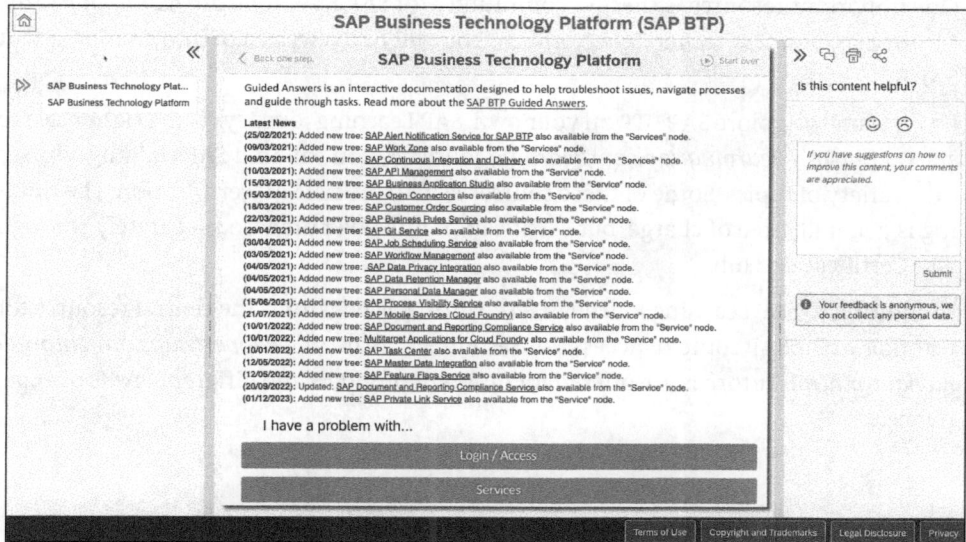

Figure 1.31 Guided Answers: Start Screen

After that, you will be asked questions that will lead you ever closer to the cause of the problem. After a few questions, you will be offered a few suggested solutions—for example, in the form of SAP Notes (see Figure 1.32). If the suggested solutions do not solve your problem, then you can create an incident. In our experience, Guided Answers can be used to solve most problems.

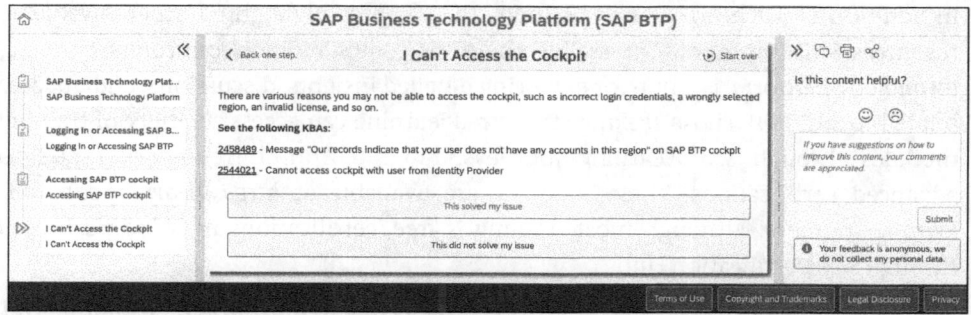

Figure 1.32 Guided Answers: Proposed Solution

1.8 Resources

In this section, we will discuss other important resources available to you as an administrator. We will show you where you can find valuable information, tools, and support

1 Introduction to SAP BTP

to optimize your administrative tasks and get the most out of your SAP BTP implementation.

One important resource is the SAP community for SAP BTP, at *https://community.sap.com/topics/business-technology-platform*. You will find a wealth of information about SAP BTP there.

If you want to explore SAP BTP on your own, SAP Learning Journeys is the right place to start. At *https://learning.sap.com/learning-journeys*, you will find SAP training courses on a variety of topics. Some of these courses lead to official SAP certification. The training is generally free of charge, but certification must be purchased separately through SAP Certification Hub.

In addition to SAP Learning Journeys, SAP Tutorial Navigator is the central resource for tutorials in the SAP context. Access this resource at *https://developers.sap.com/tutorial-navigator.html*. Tutorials are offered for different products and different levels of experience.

1.9 Summary

This book provides a comprehensive overview of the tools and resources designed to help administrators with their SAP BTP implementations. One key tool is Guided Answers, a wizard that helps diagnose and resolve errors systematically. Starting with a simple query about the issue at hand, Guided Answers navigates through a series of targeted questions to narrow down the possible causes of a problem. By the end of the process, it provides suggested solutions, such as implementing particular SAP Notes. You also have the option to create an incident if none of the proposed solutions are effective.

In addition to such error analysis tools, this chapter highlighted other invaluable resources. SAP Community, accessible via *https://community.sap.com/topics/business-technology-platform*, is a hub for exploring detailed insights, discussions, and updates related to SAP BTP. Those seeking structured learning can access a variety of training modules through SAP Learning Journeys, ranging from introductory topics to advanced certifications. These modules are available at *https://learning.sap.com/learning-journeys*. Although most training is free, certifications must be purchased through SAP Certification Hub.

SAP Tutorial Navigator, located at *https://developers.sap.com/tutorial-navigator.html*, is also recommended. It offers a centralized platform that presents tutorials covering a wide range of products and skill levels. Together, these resources provide administrators with the knowledge and practical tools necessary to optimize their tasks and unlock the full potential of their SAP BTP systems. This holistic approach ensures a strong foundation and continued learning opportunities for professional growth.

Chapter 2
User Administration

With digital transformation, user management in the cloud is critical for organizations running on SAP BTP.

This chapter provides a comprehensive guide to effectively organizing user identities and permissions on SAP BTP. Learn how to use authentication, authorization, and encryption to ensure the security of your data and how to use SAP Cloud Identity Services to ensure smooth and automated user administration. Effectively managing user identities and access in the cloud is becoming increasingly important due to the growing complexity of business applications and increasing data security and compliance requirements. In this chapter, you will learn what is involved in user management and the critical role that user management plays in ensuring a secure and efficient operation.

In Section 2.1, you will learn the central principles of security and authorizations in SAP BTP. We explain key concepts such as authentication, authorization, and encryption to ensure a comprehensive understanding of the protection mechanisms implemented in this state-of-the-art cloud environment.

In Section 2.2, we look at SAP Cloud Identity Services. The two central elements, Identity Authentication and Identity Provisioning, are explained in detail here. Identity Authentication provides advanced methods for securely verifying user identities, while Identity Provisioning ensures seamless access to resources by automating the management of user accounts and privileges. These two services play a key role in the overall context of user management on SAP BTP and form the backbone of a robust and flexible security infrastructure.

With a deep understanding of the principles of user management and a clear overview of SAP Cloud Identity Services, organizations can optimize their operations while meeting the highest security and compliance standards.

2.1 Security and Authorizations

Security and permissions are fundamental to the protection of data and range from the selection of secure transmission technologies to the identification of users and the assignment of permissions. Seamless integration with the existing infrastructure is critical: A new user must be able to log in to the cloud and receive the appropriate rights, and invalid users must be immediately registered by cloud applications and services. This integration begins at the technical level and enables seamless connection with business applications.

This section provides insight into the security mechanisms of SAP BTP. In Section 2.1.1, we introduce secure communication paths. In Section 2.1.2, we explain various methods of authentication, and in Section 2.1.3 we discuss methods of authorization. We will also show how to manage users as identities and how to ensure correct permissions.

2.1.1 Basics of Secure Communication

To illustrate the importance of secure communication, we will use a trivial example that is often used in technical literature. Imagine the following scenario: You want to send a message by mail to a certain recipient. In this scenario, insecure communication would be equivalent to sending your message by postcard. This can be read by anyone along the way, such as the postman or postwoman. If, on the other hand, you send the message to the recipient in a sealed envelope, this is secure communication. Only the recipient can read the message, provided that the envelope is not opened en route.

In the digital world, the unencrypted exchange of messages (in the example, those sent by postcard) corresponds to Hypertext Transfer Protocol (HTTP) transmission. Any network node can read an HTTP message in clear text. The encrypted exchange of messages (in the example, those sent in envelopes) corresponds to Hypertext Transfer Protocol Secure (HTTPS) transmissions. Although every node in the network can read the message, it is encrypted and can only be cracked with immense computing power if the private key is not available.

The HTTP protocol is found in layer 5 of the Open Systems Interconnection (OSI) model from the International Organization for Standardization (ISO). This is the basis for internet communication. Encrypted communication, according to the OSI model, uses either symmetric or asymmetric encryption.

Symmetric encryption uses a single key that must be known to both the sender and receiver of a message. The sender encrypts the message with the key, and the recipient decrypts the message with the same key. The oldest and probably best-known cipher, the Caesar cipher, dates back to the year 100 BC. It was named after Gaius Julius Caesar, who used this type of encryption for military correspondence. The Caesar cipher uses simple substitution.

Of course, the requirements for encryption have changed. Today, Data Encryption Standard (DES), Triple DES, Advanced Encryption Standard (AES), Blowfish, and International Data Encryption Algorithm (IDEA) are among the best-known symmetric encryption algorithms. The key length is of crucial importance for the quality of the encryption. However, longer key lengths require more computing power for encryption and decryption. The biggest challenge of symmetric encryption is the exchange of keys between sender and receiver. Any network node located between the sender and receiver could decrypt the message if the key is known.

With *asymmetric encryption*, both the sender and the recipient have a pair of keys, consisting of a private key and a public key. The sender can encrypt the contents of the message using the recipient's public key. Only the owner of the private key—in this case, the recipient—can decrypt the message with the private key. Asymmetric encryption provides security but has the disadvantage of being significantly slower than symmetric encryption. Modern network communication relies on a combination of symmetric and asymmetric encryption.

Secure Socket Layer (SSL) was released as version 1.0 by Netscape in November 1994 and is located in the OSI model between the application layer and the transport layer. Only nine months after version 1.0, SSL version 2.0 was introduced. Over time, several security vulnerabilities became known. Version 3.0 of the protocol was released in 1996 to address these vulnerabilities and provide new, more secure cipher suites with longer key lengths and new algorithms.

Meanwhile, SSL has evolved to Transport Layer Security (TLS), which is essentially a symmetric method for secure data transfer. The use of SSL/TLS is a prerequisite for SAP cloud applications and can be used by default without further activation in the configuration.

SAP BTP offers the SAP Destination service, which enables services to be addressed via standard protocols, including the following:

- **HTTP**
  An HTTP destination enables data communication via the HTTP protocol for both internet and on-premise connections.
- **RFC**
  A Remote Function Call (RFC) destination enables connections to ABAP on-premise systems via the RFC protocol using the Java connector and the cloud connector.
- **LDAP**
  A Lightweight Directory Access Protocol (LDAP) destination enables the activation of LDAP-based user management if an LDAP server is operated in the on-premise network.
- **Mail**
  A destination of this type allows you to connect to an email provider for sending and receiving emails using Simple Mail Transfer Protocol (SMTP), Internet Message Access Protocol (IMAP), or Post Office Protocol (POP3).

The addressed services can either be directly accessible via a public network or located in the customer's on-premise environment and addressed via the cloud connector.

The functionality of the SAP Destination service can be compared to the functionality of RFC destinations in ABAP systems, which are maintained via Transaction SM59.

Destinations ensure that the configuration of the connections does not have to be hard-coded in the application. Instead, the configuration can be read from the application using the name of the destination and performed dynamically.

Destinations can be defined at the subaccount level by specifying the communication protocol and other properties, as shown in Figure 2.1.

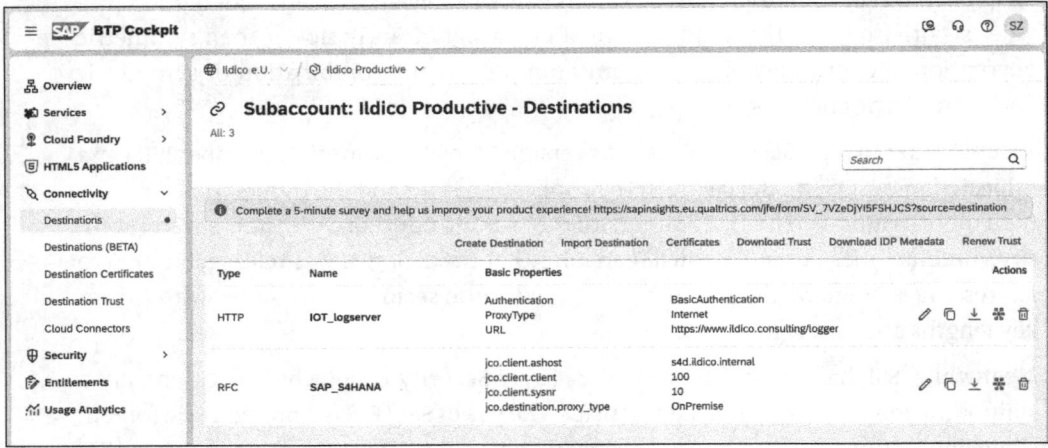

Figure 2.1 Destinations on Subaccount Level Within SAP BTP Cockpit

In addition to creating destinations via the SAP BTP cockpit, it is also possible to create destinations using the command line. Furthermore, destinations can be created using an OData API.

SAP BTP comes with preinstalled root certificates from renowned certification authorities in the standard trust store. This procedure corresponds to the approach of renowned browser manufacturers, which also provide a fixed set of certificates that are trusted by default.

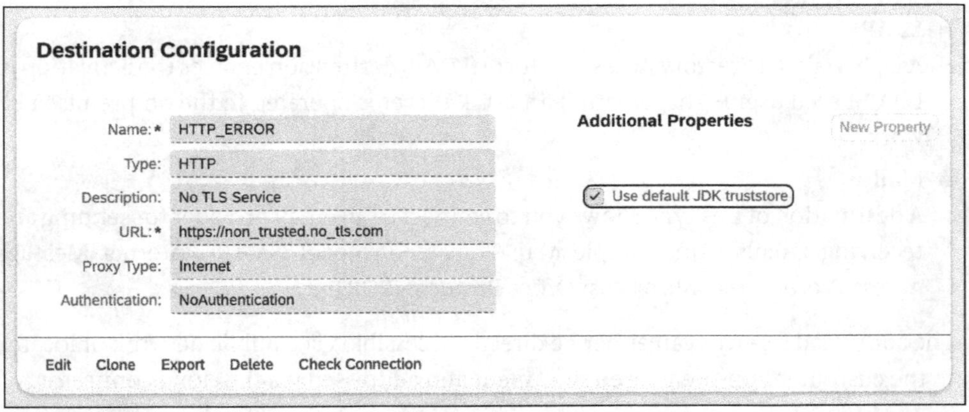

Figure 2.2 Destination with Untrusted Endpoint

If, as in the example shown in Figure 2.2, you use a destination set to an HTTPS endpoint whose certificates are not in the default trust store, then this can lead to potential errors that may not be immediately apparent when you set up the destination.

If this is the case, click the **Check Connection** button to perform a connection test. You will receive an **SSLHandshake** error message (see Figure 2.3), indicating that the negotiation of key information has failed due to lack of trust.

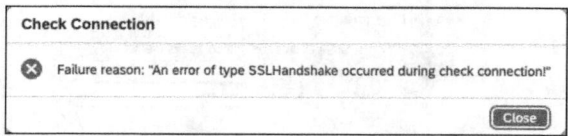

Figure 2.3 SSL Handshake Error

You can solve this problem by using your own trust store. To do this, uncheck the **Use Default JDK Truststore** option in the **Destination Configuration**. This will allow you to select your own trust store location and enter the appropriate password (see Figure 2.4).

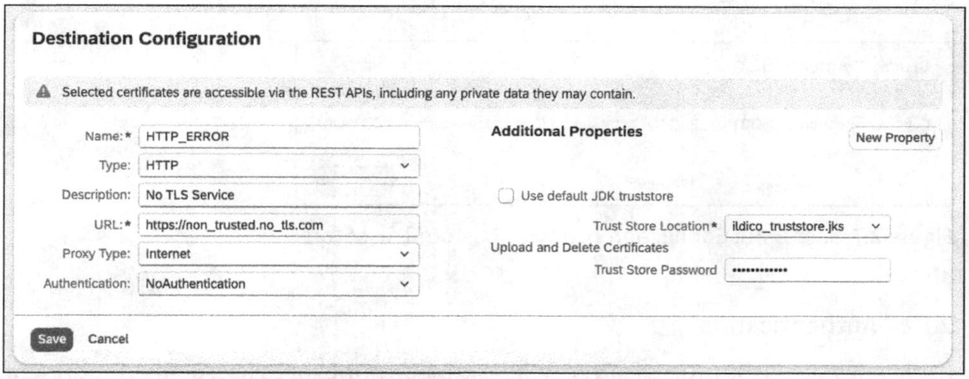

Figure 2.4 Using Custom Trust Store

You can create a trust store using standard Java commands, but you can also use tools with a graphical user interface, such as KeyStore Explorer (available at *https://keystore-explorer.org/*). After you have created a trust store, you can click the **Upload and Delete Certificates** link to upload your new trust store (see Figure 2.5).

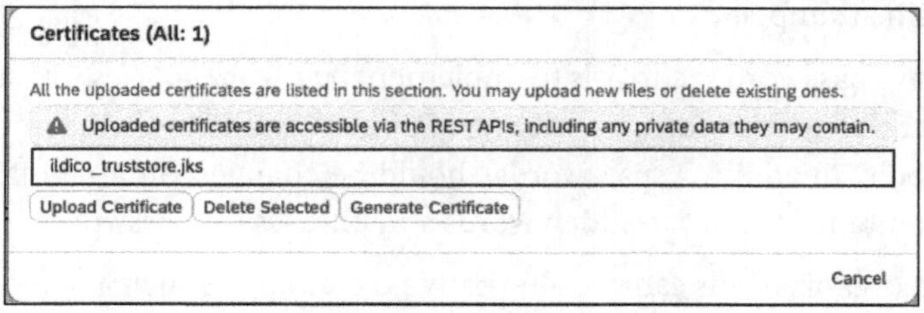

Figure 2.5 Uploading Custom Trust Store

61

2 User Administration

Figure 2.6 shows how the custom trust store can be configured in a destination.

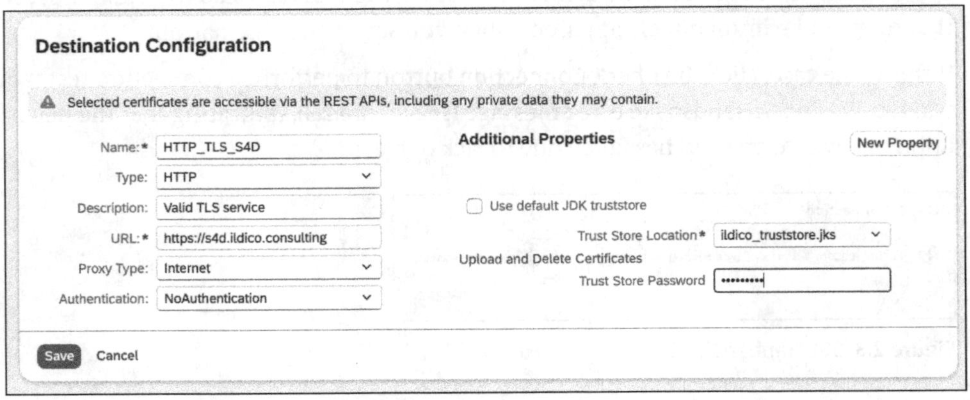

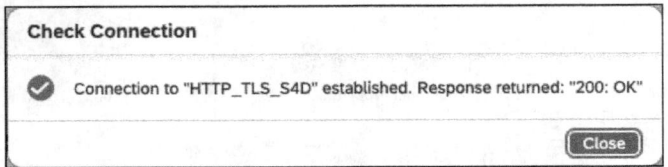

Figure 2.6 Configuration with Custom Trust Store

Figure 2.7 shows the result of a successful connection test after using a custom trust store.

Figure 2.7 Successful Connection Test with Custom Trust Store

2.1.2 Authentication

Authentication is the process of verifying and confirming that a user actually represents the identity he or she claims to have. Typically, this verification is performed by the user by entering an appropriate password. Upon successful entry, the system grants access to the user account.

However, this simple authentication method is susceptible to *brute force attacks*, in which an attacker tries to gain access to an account by repeatedly logging in with different passwords. To make such attacks more difficult, accounts can be locked after a certain number of failed login attempts.

An effective way to improve password security is to implement *password policies*. These policies enforce the use of strong passwords consisting of uppercase and lowercase letters, numbers, and symbols. In addition, passwords should be changed on a regular basis. It is also wise to maintain a list of forbidden words and phrases for passwords.

In addition to passwords, organizations can use alternative technologies such as client certificates, biometrics, one-time tokens, or custom authentication applications. SAP BTP offers high flexibility in the selection of these authentication methods.

When using client certificates, an identity is verified through the exchange of a digital certificate issued by a trusted authority and uniquely associated with a user account. For example, SAP Passport allows you to create digital client certificates for S-users and use them to log on to different SAP platforms.

SAP Universal ID and SAP ID Terminology

Understanding the SAP Universal ID, S-user ID, P-user ID, and SAP ID is essential for accessing and administering SAP BTP. Figure 2.8 illustrates the relations between these ID types.

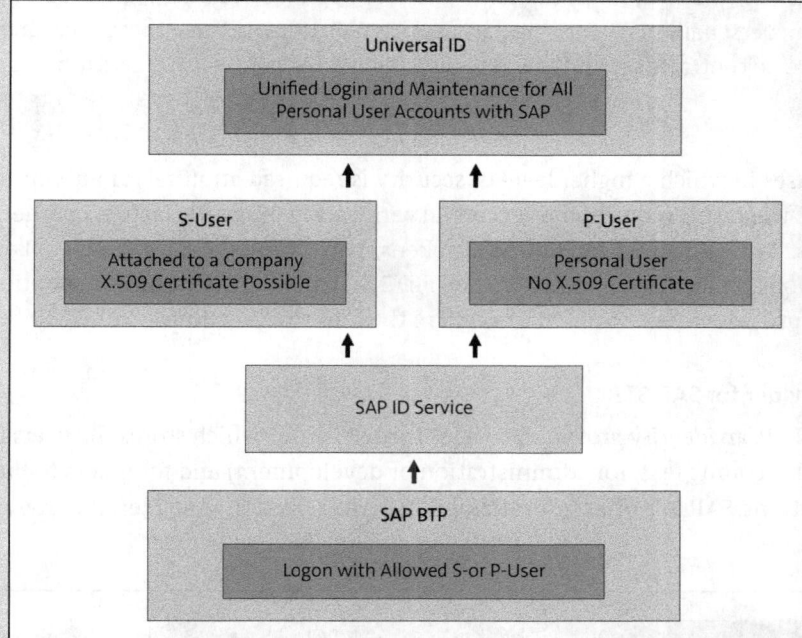

Figure 2.8 SAP Terminology for User ID Types

Here's a breakdown of the terminology and how these concepts relate to each other:

- **SAP ID**
  SAP ID is the central identity provider authentication system used across SAP BTP, SAP Support Portal, SAP for Me, and others. You could also call SAP ID SAP's login engine. It supports various user types (S-user IDs, P-user IDs, and SAP Universal IDs) and enables single sign-on (SSO) using these accounts.

- **SAP Universal ID**
  SAP Universal ID is a unified login system introduced by SAP to streamline identity management. It can link multiple SAP accounts (S-user and P-user, and SAP-internal I-user and D-user) under one personal identity. With this ID, you no longer need to remember multiple S-user or P-user credentials. This can be essential for users who work with SAP in multiple roles (e.g., consultant, partner, customer, or test user).

2 User Administration

- **S-user ID**
  S-user IDs are corporate accounts issued by SAP to their customers or partners. Your organization must have an SAP support agreement to be able to request S-user IDs. S-users are used for administering SAP BTP global accounts and subaccounts (unless deactivated and replaced by other identity providers). Because SAP knows these users, you can request an X.509 certificate for a S-user, which can then be used to sign onto different SAP services and platforms.
- **P-user ID**
  P-user IDs are personal accounts, typically used by individuals who register directly with SAP (e.g., via *community.sap.com*). They are not linked to a company. You can use them personally or for training purposes. As SAP does not know these users and there are no contracts set up, there is no possibility to obtain an X.509 certificate for a P-user.

In certain cases in which a higher level of security is required, multifactor authentication (MFA) is used. This requires the successful verification of several factors in order to grant access. Typical factors include SMS tokens, hardware tokens, software tokens, authentication applications, phone calls, and FIDO2 security keys. The different options for identity providers are explained in detail in the following sections.

Identity Provider for SAP BTP

Within SAP BTP, an *identity provider* provides the user store, which stores the users for access to subaccounts (e.g., for administration or development) and for access to business applications. SAP BTP offers great flexibility in the selection of an identity provider (see Figure 2.9).

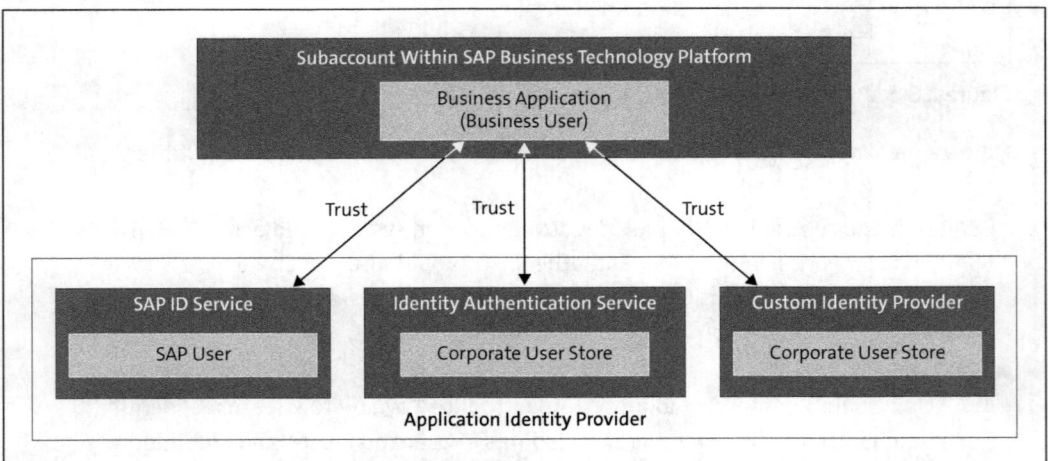

Figure 2.9 Identity Provider for SAP BTP

A distinction is made between the *platform identity provider* and *application identity provider*. The platform identity provider in SAP BTP uses the SAP ID service by default, but it can also use Identity Authentication (see Figure 2.10). No separate facilities are required for user authentication via the organization's own corporate user store. Using your own identity provider is not allowed in this case.

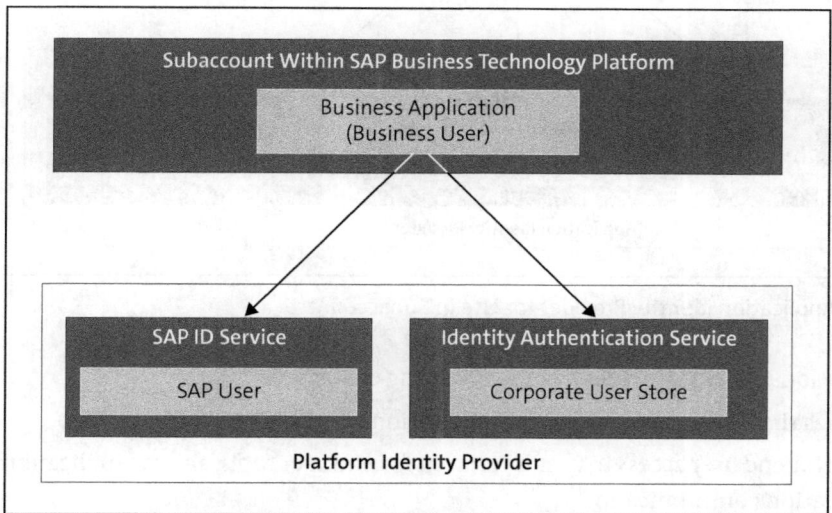

Figure 2.10 Platform Identity Provider for Subaccount Users

The platform identity provider is characterized by the following features:

- It provides the user base for accessing the subaccount.
- It is used in the SAP BTP cockpit, in various development tools, and in the command line.
- By default, the SAP ID service is used in the global account and all subaccounts.
- Optionally, the Identity Authentication tenant can be used.
- Users managed in the platform identity provider are typically administration and development users.

The application identity provider authenticates end users for applications on SAP BTP. In addition to the SAP ID service and Identity Authentication, a custom identity provider can be used as an application identity provider. The custom identity provider must be a SAML-based identity provider, such as Microsoft Entra ID, formerly known as Microsoft Azure Active Directory (see Figure 2.11).

2   User Administration

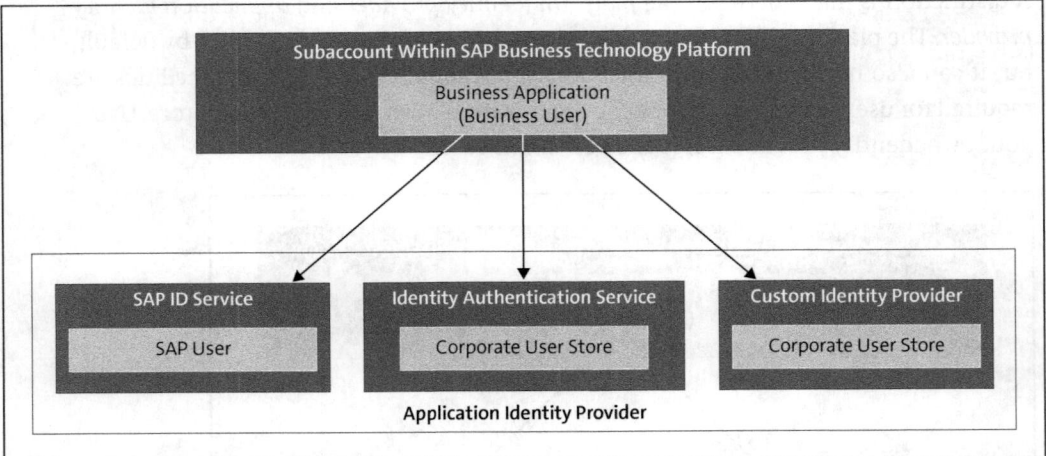

Figure 2.11 Application Identity Provider for Use in Subaccount

The application identity provider has the following characteristics:

- It provides the user base for accessing applications in an SAP BTP subaccount.
- It is used for end user access to user interfaces, for end user tools, and for application-to-application communication.
- By default, the SAP ID service is used.
- Optionally, the Identity Authentication tenant or a third-party corporate identity provider can be used.
- Users managed with the application identity provider are typically end users.

SAP BTP is preconfigured with a trust relationship to SAP ID by default. SAP ID is used as both the platform identity provider and the application identity provider. No further configuration is required except for the assignment of the user to the subaccount. There are no additional costs for using SAP ID.

SAP ID manages the users of the official SAP sites, including the SAP developer and partner community. Users can be created via self-service or via the SAP Support Portal by authorized users within their own organization. SAP ID includes the following elements:

- A central user store for all identities that require access to the application's protected resources.
- A standards-based SSO service that allows users to log on once and gain seamless access to all applications on SAP BTP.

Optionally, a customer-specific identity provider can be used. In this case, there are no additional costs associated with SAP BTP services, except for the license costs for this identity provider.

Another option is to use Identity Authentication as a platform identity provider. This service can act as a proxy for corporate user stores or third-party identity providers such as Microsoft Entra ID. For a detailed discussion of Identity Authentication, see Section 2.2.1. The use of this service requires the purchase of a license, for which the number of registrations is used as a billing metric.

In summary, SAP BTP supports the following scenarios for user authentication via the identity provider:

- **Standard identity federation via SAP ID**
  The SAP ID trust relationship is preconfigured by default in SAP BTP, which means that you can use this service without any further adjustments. Optionally, additional trust settings can be configured in SAP BTP, such as the registration of the service provider, role assignments to users and groups, and much more.
- **Identity federation through the Identity Authentication tenant**
  Here, user authentication is performed via a special tenant that acts as the Identity Authentication service. This allows for centralized authentication and identity management, especially when corporate user stores such as LDAP directories or third-party identity providers are used.
- **Identity federation through a corporate identity provider**
  In this scenario, companies can use their own identity provider based on SAML—for example, Microsoft Entra ID. Using a corporate identity provider provides flexibility and the ability to continue to use established authentication infrastructures.

Figure 2.12 illustrates using the SAP ID service for standard identity federation. If a user wants to access SAP BTP, SAP ID is used for the authentication. Using SAP BTP's trust, the user is classified as trustworthy. Therefore, access is possible if SAP ID has confirmed a positive authentication.

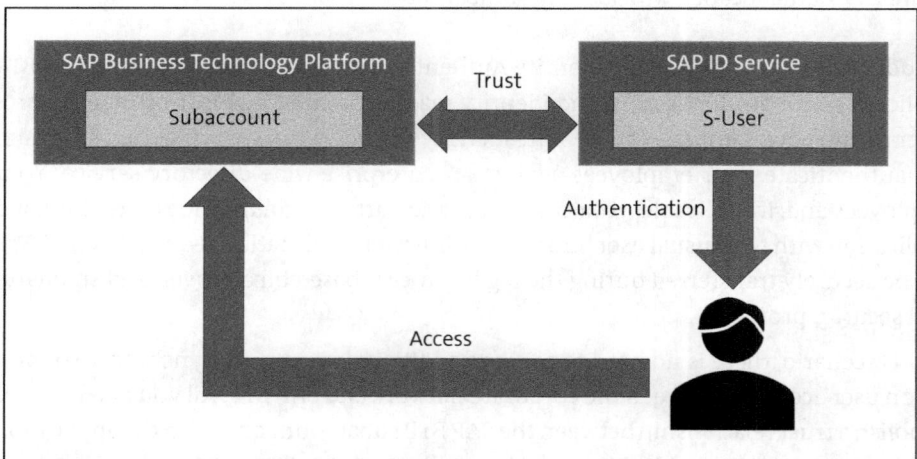

Figure 2.12 Authentication Using SAP ID Service as Identity Provider

If you want to use subaccount users (members) from your company's user base instead of creating S-users for these users, you can use the Identity Authentication tenant as the identity provider for your applications. Identity Authentication is a cloud service that manages the lifecycle of the identities you manage. You have the option to integrate your own user base on SAP BTP. In addition, you can use corporate branding (e.g., integrating the company logo on the authentication page) and identity providers from social media such as Facebook, X (formerly known as Twitter), Google, or LinkedIn. This provides the foundation for provisioning users in various cloud and on-premise applications.

The Identity Authentication tenant (i.e., your Identity Authentication instance) is available to all subaccounts within your global account (see Figure 2.13).

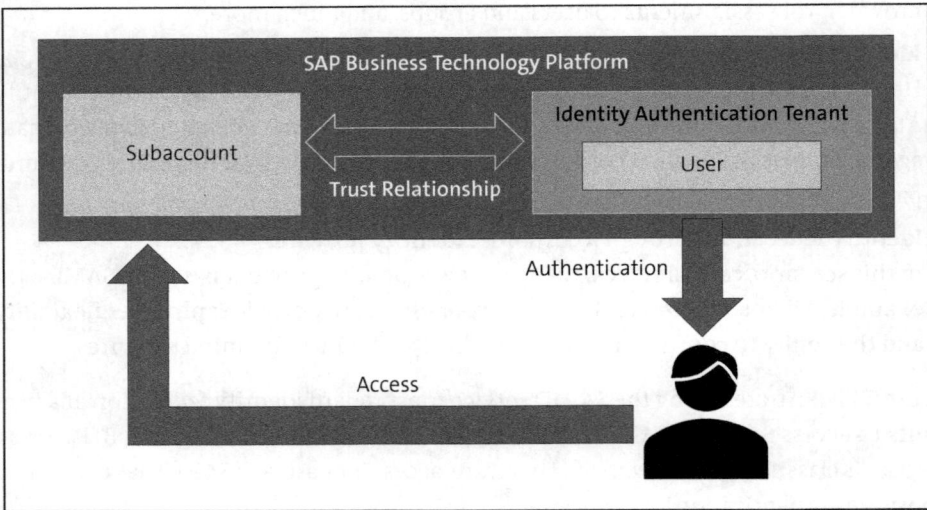

Figure 2.13 Authentication with Identity Authentication Tenant as Identity Provider

In addition to using SAP ID and Identity Authentication, you can also delegate SAP BTP applications for authentication and identity management to an existing identity provider within your company (a corporate identity provider). This provider can, for example, authenticate your employees against an enterprise-wide directory service. Your employees and, if applicable, your customers and partners can then log on to the cloud application with their usual user information. All user information required by SAP BTP can be securely transferred during the logon process based on a proven and standardized security protocol.

In this scenario, there is no need to manage additional systems to synchronize or provision user accounts between the corporate network and SAP BTP. All you need to do is establish a trust relationship between the SAP BTP subaccount on which the application runs and your corporate identity provider, as illustrated in Figure 2.14.

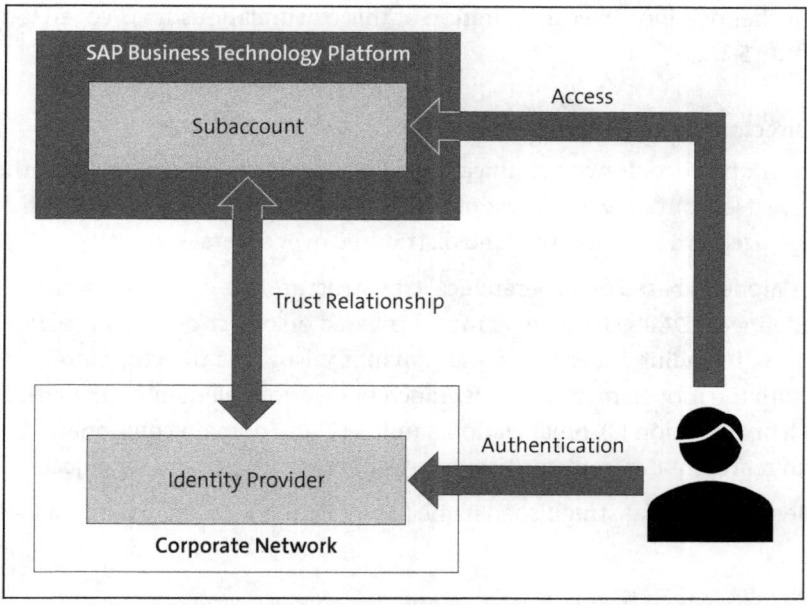

Figure 2.14 Authentication with Corporate Identity Provider as Identity Provider

Configuring the Identity Provider on SAP BTP

In SAP BTP, Cloud Foundry environment, both the platform identity provider and the application identity provider are configured at the subaccount level using the **Security • Trust Configuration** path.

SAP ID is also preconfigured here as the default identity provider (see Figure 2.15).

Figure 2.15 Default Identity Provider

If you want to use Identity Authentication as the platform identity provider instead, you must first establish a trust relationship between the Cloud Foundry subaccount and Identity Authentication. The configuration of this trust relationship is covered in Chapter 5, Section 5.2.2.

Lightweight Directory Access Protocol

LDAP is a network protocol for communicating with a directory service; it is not the directory service itself, but only the access protocol. LDAP enables the simple search of a directory organized in a tree structure and distributed over several servers.

The LDAP data model is based on a hierarchical tree structure, the essential features of which are predefined. LDAP's simple data model is based on object-oriented programming approaches, including inheritance and polymorphism. The directory structure always starts with the root element and can branch into various elements—in particular, country (C), organization (O), organizational unit (OU), and domain component (DC). Individuals can represent different entities, such as documents, persons, or objects.

An object is identified by its distinguished name (DN). A distinguished name might look like this:

CN=Martin Koch, OU=Consulting, DC=Clouddna, DC=at

This means that the individual named Martin Koch is assigned to the consulting organization unit within the CloudDNA domain in Austria. Figure 2.16 shows an example of the position of a distinguished name within an LDAP hierarchy tree.

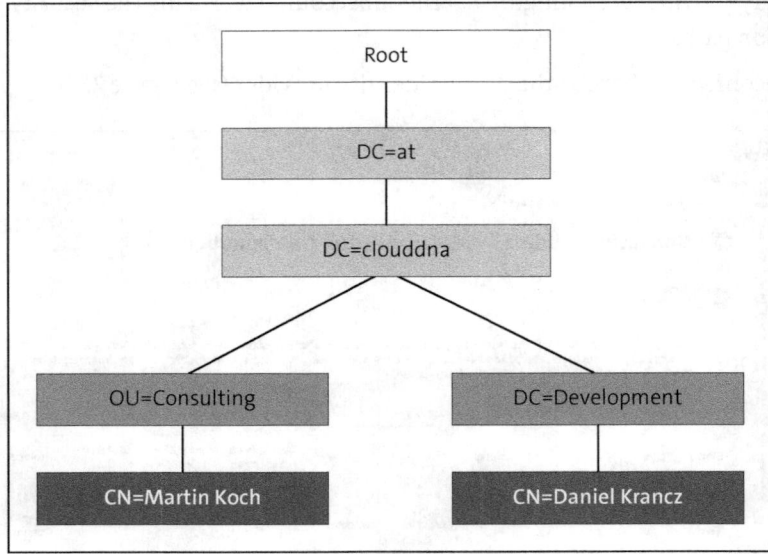

Figure 2.16 Example of LDAP Structure

SAP BTP enables the configuration of an existing LDAP directory from an on-premise system as a user store. This requires the use of the cloud connector. Applications in SAP

BTP can then use the on-premise user store for various purposes, including credential checking, user search, reading user details, and group membership.

Another use of LDAP in SAP BTP is in identity federation through the Identity Authentication tenant. In this scenario, Identity Authentication acts as a proxy to the local LDAP directory. Enabling this scenario requires the use of Identity Authentication.

The Identity Authentication tenant authenticates using the open OAuth protocol to the subaccount where the add-on is deployed. The Identity Authentication add-on then uses the cloud connector to connect to the LDAP server (see Figure 2.17).

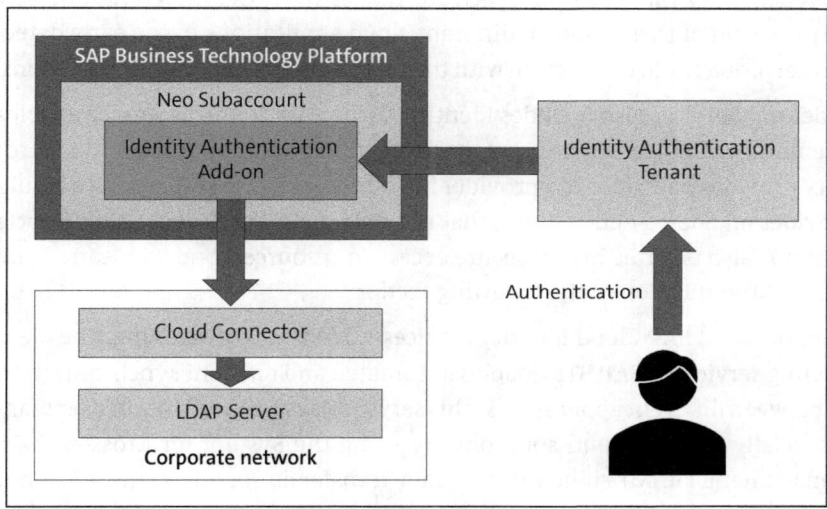

Figure 2.17 User Authentication Against On-Premise LDAP Server

2.1.3 Authorization

Authorization refers to the process of granting a user permission to access a particular resource or functionality. In secure environments, authorization is always performed after authentication; users must prove their identity before being granted access to the requested resources.

SAP BTP uses two different standards for authorization, as follows:

- *SAML* is an open standard that enables the exchange of authentication and authorization identities between security domains. In the Neo environment, authentication is based on SAML tokens.
- *OAuth 2.0* is an authorization framework that allows third-party applications to obtain restricted access to an HTTP service. It is described in more detail in Chapter 3.

OpenID Connect, an identity layer based on OAuth 2.0, allows clients to verify the identity of end users based on authentication by an authorization server. In SAP BTP, Cloud Foundry environment, authentication is based on the OAuth protocol. The application router, which serves as a central entry point, creates access tokens in the form of JSON Web Tokens (JWTs), which represent the access rights for applications for the current user.

2.2 SAP Cloud Identity Services

SAP Cloud Identity Services is available on SAP BTP, and its elements cover a wide range of tasks. Within this collection of services, the entire lifecycle of user and identity security is comprehensively mapped. The spectrum ranges from the integration of new users to the provision of these users in different cloud applications to the early detection of potential problems in connection with the assignment of critical authorizations.

SAP Cloud Identity Services also includes Identity Authentication. This service enables the implementation of SSO scenarios and the delegation of authentication to a third-party identity provider or an identity provider in your on-premise systems. As a result, SAP BTP provides an end-to-end solution that not only enables efficient user lifecycle management but also ensures highly secure access to resources. You will learn more about Identity Authentication in the following section.

Another component of SAP Cloud Identity Services is Identity Provisioning. The Identity Provisioning service on SAP BTP enables automated and efficient synchronization of user data between different applications. This service plays a central role in user management, especially for SAP cloud solutions. By using the System for Cross-domain Identity Management (SCIM) standard, the data transfer is seamless and does not require specific connectors for each application. Identity Provisioning automates the user data maintenance process, especially in scenarios in which different applications have their own user management. This automation ensures that changes to user accounts in one application are reflected in other applications in a timely manner. As a result, Identity Provisioning provides an effective solution for synchronizing user information and helps minimize the administrative burden of user management. For more information, see Section 2.2.2.

Depending on your SAP BTP license and version, SAP Cloud Identity Services is available for subscription in your subaccount under **Services • Instances and Subscriptions** (for Identity Authentication and Identity Provisioning together), or you may have received links to SAP Cloud Identity Services from SAP. We will describe the setup of Identity Provisioning at the beginning of Section 2.2.2.

2.2.1 Identity Authentication

Identity Authentication is a platform as a service (PaaS) service provided by SAP that acts as a SAML identity provider. Its main task is the authentication of users in SAP BTP applications as well as in all SAP SaaS products. Optionally, the service can also be used for on-premise applications. Identity Authentication offers several central functions (see Figure 2.18), as follows:

- **Authentication**
  The service verifies the credentials provided by the user and issues a SAML assertion upon successful authentication.

- **Identity federation and single sign-on**
  The service allows the delegation of authentication to a third-party identity provider, enabling SSO across applications.

- **Risk-based authentication**
  If required, identity authentication enables multifactor authentication for access to highly protected business applications.

- **User management**
  Identity Authentication enables efficient user management.

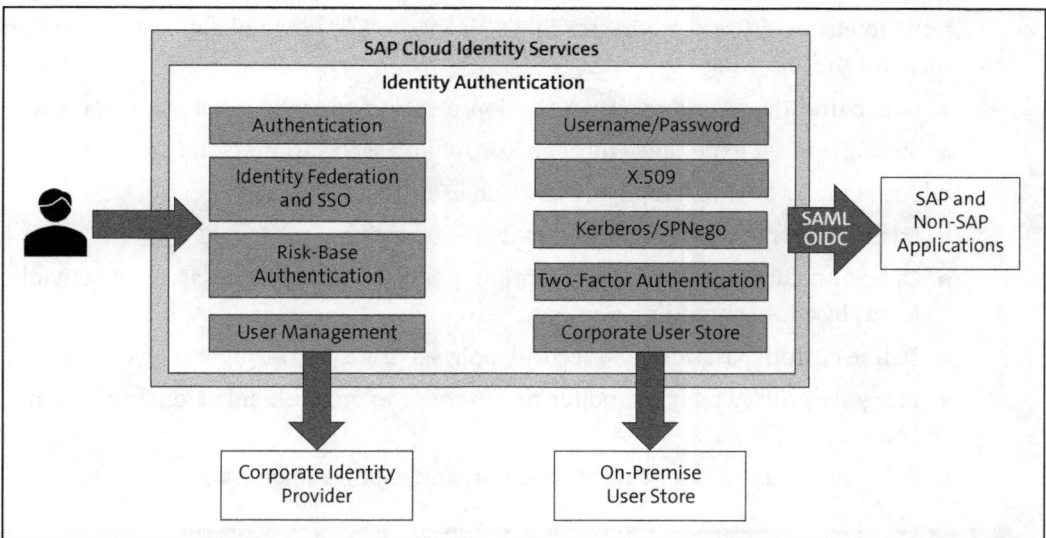

Figure 2.18 Functions of Identity Authentication

SAP offers an Identity Authentication tenant regardless of the number of user contracts signed. The tenant is purchased in a bundle with other SAP products and allows full use of the Identity Authentication functionality. The production tenant license also allows you to request a second tenant for test purposes free of charge. Additional tenants must be purchased separately.

After purchasing the license, you will receive an email invitation to register the initial Identity Authentication administrator. The administration console for the Identity Authentication tenant is activated via a provided link.

2 User Administration

> **Number of Administrators**
> It is recommended to add another administrator immediately after the first administrator is activated.

Identity Authentication supports several scenarios, including business-to-consumer (B2C), business-to-business (B2B), and business-to-employee (B2E). B2C scenarios cover all the security aspects related to end users using applications, including registration, authentication, and authorization. The following sections will also cover tenant login and tenant settings to provide a complete overview of the supported Identity Authentication scenarios.

Business-to-Consumer

Identity Authentication on SAP BTP enables the seamless integration of various functions to ensure a smooth and secure B2C scenario. The range of supported functions includes the following:

- User name and password authentication, also known as the *classic login* approach
- Simplified user experience through SSO for access to various cloud applications
- Social media sign-on for an efficient and user-friendly login process
- Enables users to self-register for flexible onboarding
- Option to customize login, registration, password change, and account activation forms by adding branding elements
- Define custom password and security policies to ensure the highest level of security
- Integrate privacy policies and terms of service to ensure transparency and compliance
- Efficiently manage user data with import and export capabilities

> **A Web Shop as an Example of a B2C Scenario**
> As an illustrative example, let's consider a web shop or a mobile shopping app, the kind often found for online bookstores—perhaps even the kind you used when you bought this book! Here are the details:
>
> - **Initiated by the customer**
>   In this case, you are the customer. The process begins when you decide to create an account with the store to personalize your shopping experience.
>
> - **Registration steps**
>   Registration involves multiple steps:
>   – Forwarding to the registration page: After you have decided to shop, you will be directed to a user-friendly registration page.

> - Create a user account: Create a new user account using your email address. Acceptance of the terms of use is required.
> - Optional social media login: For added convenience, you can log in using your social media credentials, such as Facebook, Twitter, LinkedIn, or Google.
> - Respect password policies: If you choose to create your own password, you must follow certain password guidelines.
>
> - **Account activation**
>   After your account is created, there are a couple of steps to activate it:
>   - Email confirmation: After successful registration, you will receive an email with an activation link.
>   - Activate your account: Clicking on the link will activate your account and make it available for further interactions.
>
> - **Purchasing options**
>   With an activated account, you can purchase both physical and electronic items from the web store.
>
> - **Self-service options**
>   If you forget your password, a convenient self-service option is available to reset your password.
>
> This example illustrates how seamless and user-friendly registration can be in a B2C scenario to ensure an optimal shopping experience.

Business-to-Business

In the B2B scenario, the same proven security mechanisms are applied, but with specific adaptations for corporate customers, as follows:

- **Invite-based registration**
  In contrast to the B2C scenario, registration is not automatic. Business customers are invited by the service provider or an authorized person in their own company.

- **B2B shops**
  For this scenario, there are B2B shops developed specifically for corporate customers. Here companies can purchase specific products such as spare parts.

- **Activation and acceptance of terms of use**
  Similar to the B2C scenario, the activation of a corporate account requires the acceptance of the terms and conditions of the provider.

- **Waiving social media sign-on**
  Due to business-specific requirements, social media sign-on usually is not required in the B2B scenario.

This customized B2B scenario enables targeted interaction with corporate customers and ensures that the security and sign-on processes meet the specific requirements of this audience.

SAP Support Portal as an Example of a B2B Scenario

In a B2B scenario, especially in the context of support portals, the benefits of Identity Authentication on SAP BTP manifest. We will illustrate this using the SAP Support Portal as an example.

Let's assume that you are already familiar with the SAP Support Portal, which allows you to create tickets and access SAP notifications. To perform these actions, you require an authorized user, usually in the form of an S-user, which SAP provides to your company. This S-user has administrator rights, can create additional users, and can assign the appropriate authorizations.

Identity Authentication supports you in this scenario with a variety of functions:

- User name and password authentication to ensure secure logon
- SSO for cloud applications to simplify the user experience
- Partner invitation to enable access to specific B2B applications
- Administered partner enrollment to simplify the onboarding process
- Creating branding elements to customize enrollment, registration, password update, and account activation forms
- Defining password and security policies to ensure the highest security standards
- Creating privacy policies and terms of service to ensure transparency and legal compliance
- Importing and exporting users to ensure efficient management of user data

These comprehensive identity authentication capabilities not only simplify access to and use of SAP Support Portal but also enhance the security and flexibility of your B2B applications.

Business-to-Employee

The SAP Fiori launchpad plays a central role in the B2E scenario, which covers all the actions performed by an organization's employees when using enterprise applications.

You might already be familiar with SAP Fiori launchpad, the central entry point for modern SAP applications. The majority of applications in SAP S/4HANA are delivered as SAP Fiori apps. This launchpad can be deployed both on-premise and via SAP BTP. When delivered via SAP BTP, identity authentication can be used to integrate your existing user store and ensure a consistent user experience. Employees can log on to the system with their existing credentials and authentication mechanisms.

Hybrid system landscapes, consisting of a combination of on-premise and SaaS solutions, are widespread in the SAP world. Examples include the use of SaaS solutions such as SAP SuccessFactors and SAP Concur in conjunction with an on-premise SAP Business Suite or SAP S/4HANA system. In this context, the SAP Fiori launchpad on SAP BTP serves as the central entry point, while Identity Authentication provides user authentication and SSO.

In B2E scenarios, Identity Authentication provides a variety of functions to make it easier for employees to use applications:

- User name and password authentication to ensure a secure login
- Cloud application SSO for seamless access to multiple cloud applications
- Creating branding elements to customize enrollment, registration, password change, and account activation forms
- Defining password and security policies to ensure the highest level of security
- Creating privacy policies and terms of service for transparency and legal compliance
- Importing and exporting users for efficient management of user data

These comprehensive features not only enable a seamless experience with the SAP Fiori launchpad but also provide security and flexibility for all B2E scenarios.

Identity Authentication Tenant Login

To enroll in the Identity Authentication tenant, go to *https://<IdentityAuthentication-TenantID>.accounts.ondemand.com*, replacing *<IdentityAuthenticationTenantID>* placeholder with the ID of your Identity Authentication tenant.

The tenant ID is generated automatically by SAP. The first administration user created for the tenant receives an activation email with a URL. This URL contains the tenant ID. You also have the possibility to jump directly from the SAP BTP cockpit to the Identity Authentication tenant.

The prerequisite for the jump is that a trust relationship has been established between the subaccount and the Identity Authentication tenant. Navigate to the **Security • Trust Configuration** path and click the link in the **Name** column; in the example in Figure 2.19, this is **IAS Ildico**.

In the resulting overview of user-defined Identity Authentication tenants, click the link corresponding to the host name of your identity authentication tenant (in the **Single Sign-On URL (Redirect Binding)** field; see Figure 2.20).

2   User Administration

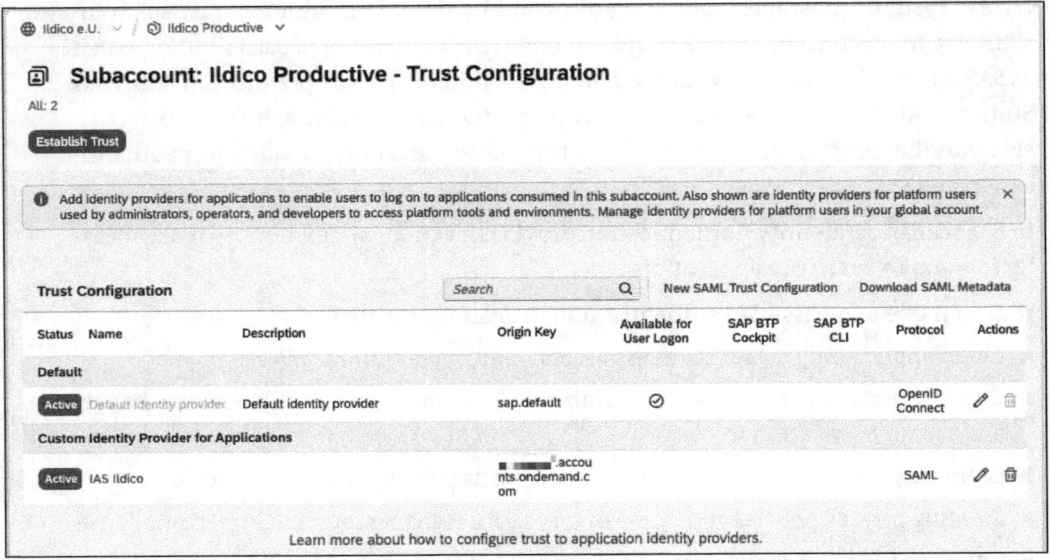

Figure 2.19 Trust Configuration on SAP BTP

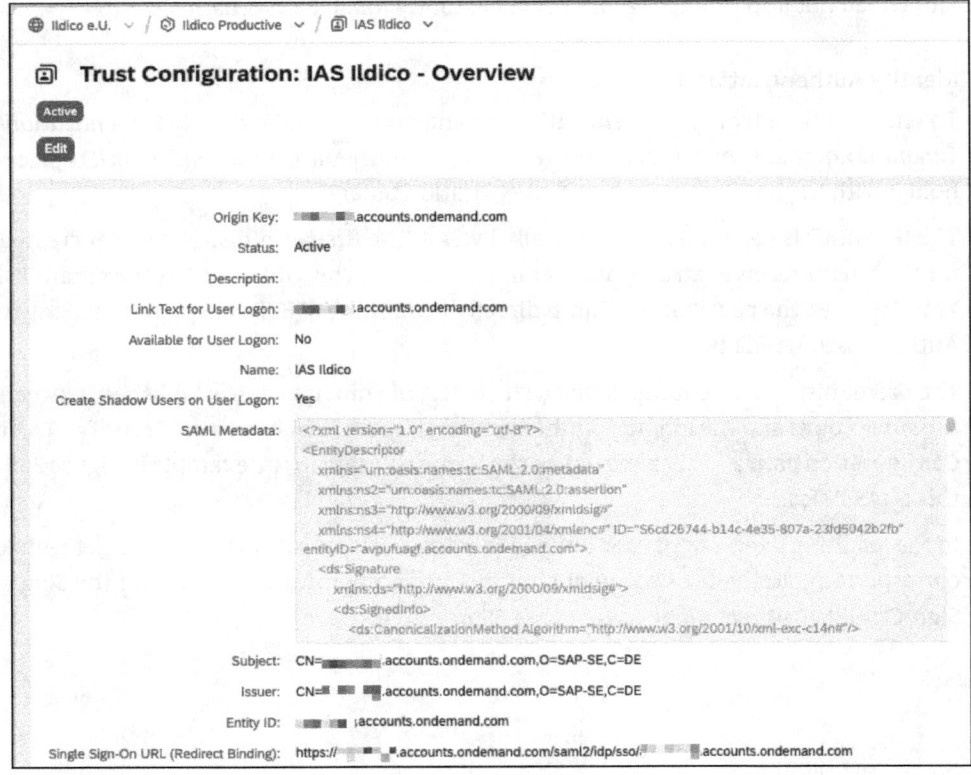

Figure 2.20 Jumping to Identity Authentication Tenant from Within SAP BTP

Figure 2.21 shows the login screen of your Identity Authentication tenant's administration console. You must first log on with the user name that you received in the invitation email. If you have already created an additional administration user, you can use that one as well.

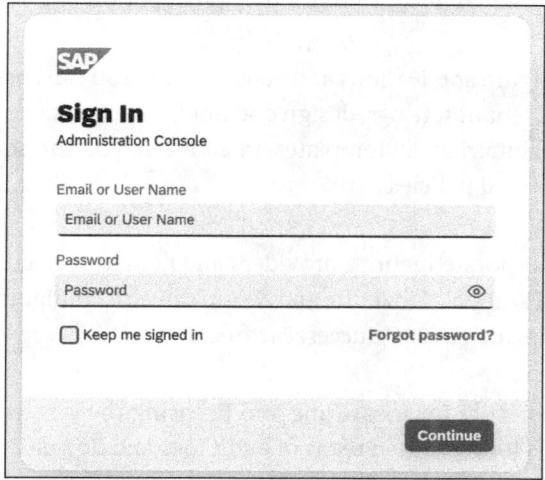

Figure 2.21 Login Dialog for Identity Authentication Client

After successful login, you will be taken to the Identity Authentication overview (see Figure 2.22). The home page is built dynamically based on the permissions assigned to you.

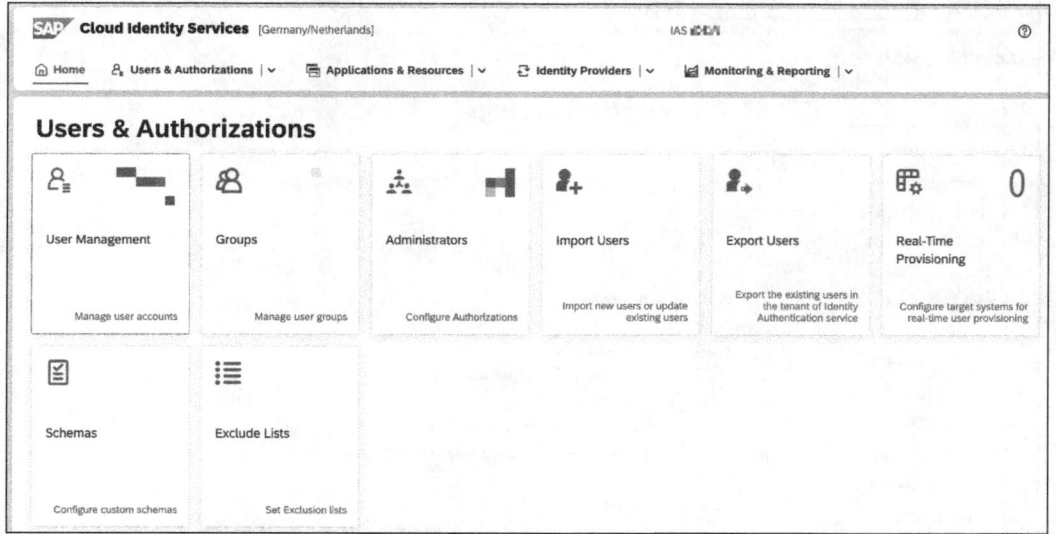

Figure 2.22 Identity Authentication Overview

2 User Administration

The menu of Identity Authentication is divided into different areas that allow you to manage and administer the system:

- **Users & Authorizations**
  In this area, you can manage users, user groups, and administration users. Here you can import/export users and configure target systems for user provisioning.

- **Applications & Resources**
  This is where you register and configure applications and subaccounts. You can customize the Identity Authentication tenant settings, design documents such as terms of use and privacy policies, and maintain email templates. In addition, you can set up custom CSS and customize password policies here.

- **Identity Providers**
  In this section you can integrate corporate identity providers and configure social identity providers such as Google, Facebook, LinkedIn, and X. You can also configure external user data retrieval systems, such as SAP SuccessFactors.

- **Monitoring & Reporting**
  Here you have access to relevant metrics for measuring and licensing the system. You can generate access credentials for API-based reads of audit logs and download change and troubleshooting logs as CSV files.

To maintain administration users, navigate to the **Users & Authorizations • Administrators** menu path (see Figure 2.23).

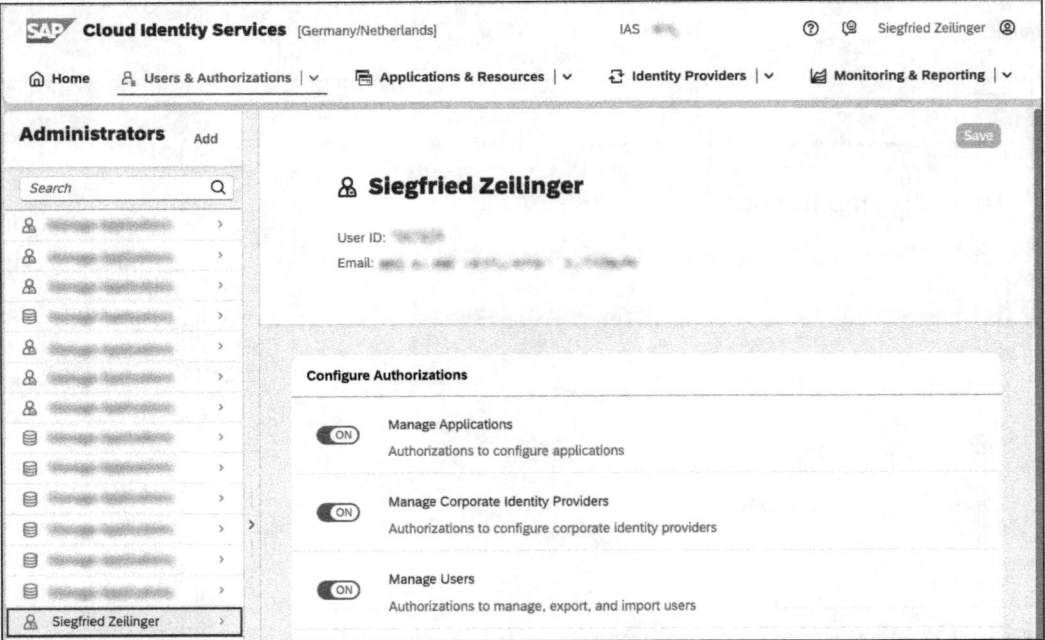

Figure 2.23 Overview of Identity Authentication Administration Users

2.2 SAP Cloud Identity Services

In the overview, personal administrators are represented by the personal icon 🔓 and system administrators by the administrator icon 🗄. Both can perform the same roles and actions.

To add a new administration user, click **Add**. Enter an email address and a first and last name. Several administration roles are available to toggle on or off, including the following:

- **Manage Applications** (configure applications)
- **Manage Corporate Identity Providers** (configure identity providers)
- **Manage Users** (manage, import, and export users)
- **Read Users** (retrieve user data, import via the SCIM REST API)
- **Manage Groups** (create, edit, and delete user groups)
- **Manage Tenant Configuration** (manage tenant configuration and assign permissions to users)

> **SICM Protocol**
>
> System for Cross-Domain Identity Management (SCIM) is an HTTP-based protocol that enables the administration of identities in multidomain scenarios (e.g., between the customer's own domain and the standard domain of SAP BTP, *ondemand.com*). The SCIM standard is managed by the Internet Engineering Task Force (IETF). The following specifications cover the SCIM standard:
>
> - RFC7642 (SCIM: Definitions, Overview, Concepts, and Requirements)
> - RFC7643 (SCIM: Core Schema)
> - RFC7644 (SCIM: Protocol)
>
> SCIM-enabled systems can be used as source or target systems in Identity Authentication. In addition, Identity Authentication provides a SCIM API, which can be used to create and manage users and user groups.
>
> SCIM 2.0 is based on an object model, as shown in Figure 2.24. A *resource* is the core element from which all other SCIM objects are derived.

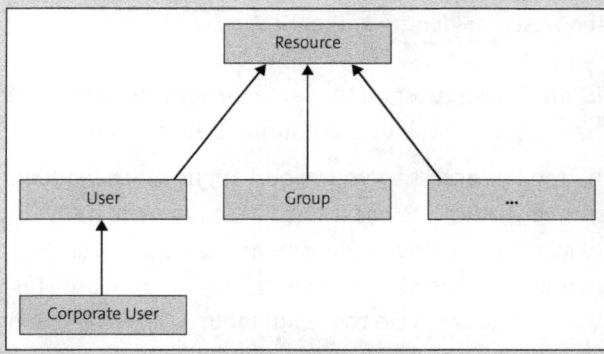

Figure 2.24 SCIM Object Model

Assign the desired roles to the new administration user and save the user using the **Save** button (see Figure 2.25).

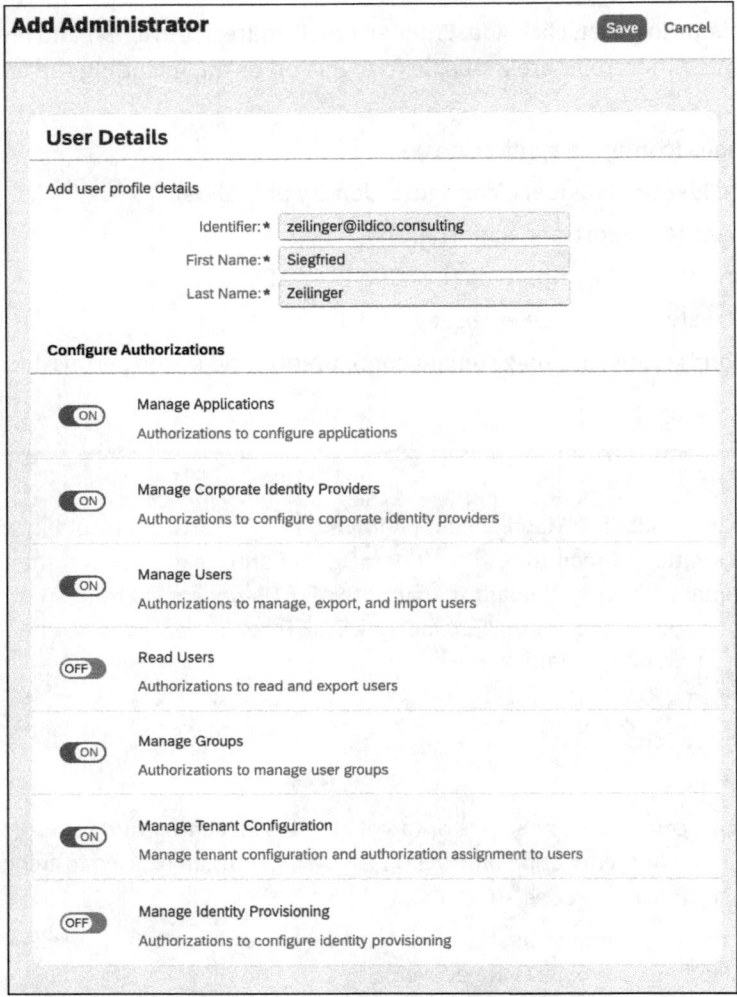

Figure 2.25 Creating Administration User for Identity Authentication

The system now issues a user ID for the new user. At the same time, the user receives an email. This email contains a link with which the user account can be activated.

To manage the other users who require access to your cloud applications via Identity Authentication, select the **Users & Authorizations** • **User Management** path in the menu. You will now see a list of all users created in Identity Authentication (see Figure 2.26). Because this list usually contains a large number of entries, you can search for different attributes, such as the user ID. Click a row in the result table to view the details of a user.

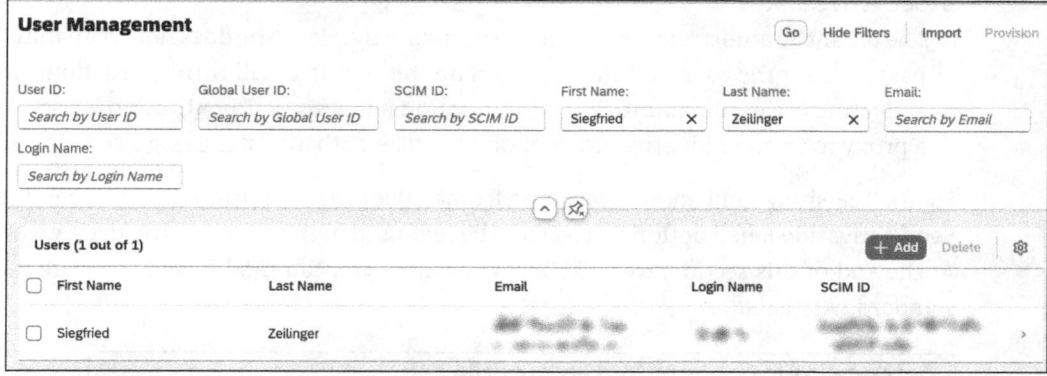

Figure 2.26 User Overview for Identity Authentication

Click the **+Add** button to create a new user. In the creation dialog, you must specify the last name, the email address, the user type, and the account activation method (see Figure 2.27). In the **User Type** field, the **Employee** option is selected by default. You can choose the **Customer**, **Employee**, **Partner**, or **Public** option.

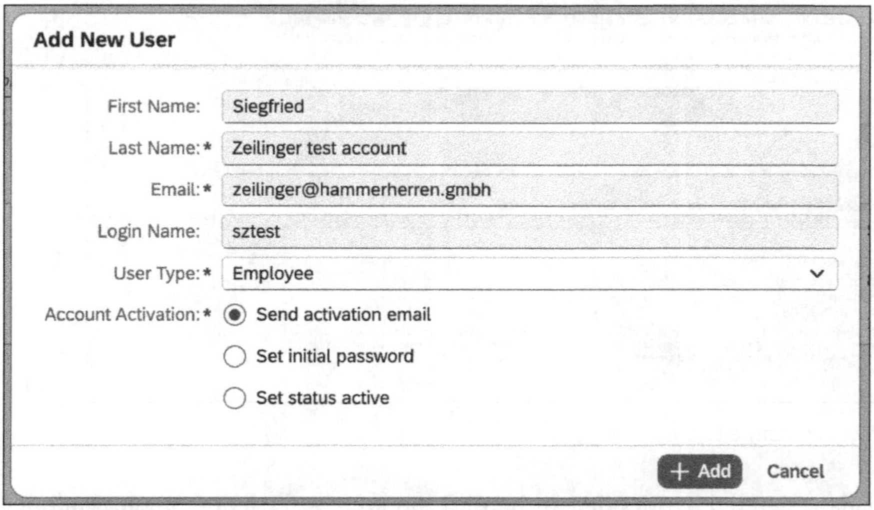

Figure 2.27 Creating User

The following options are available for activating the user account:

- **Send Activation Email**
  The user receives an email with instructions for activating the user account.
- **Set Initial Password**
  The tenant administrator sets the password for the user. The user will be prompted to change the password upon first authentication.

- **Set Active Status**
  The tenant administrator sets an active user directly. He or she does not set an initial password for the user, and the user does not receive an email with instructions for activating the user account. Choose this option if Identity Authentication is used as a proxy to another identity provider or if the user authenticates using a certificate.

Figure 2.28 shows an example of the welcome email that the user receives when the **Send Activation Email** option is selected. The text used in the email is provided by SAP. At the end of this section, we will show you where you can modify and translate the standard SAP texts.

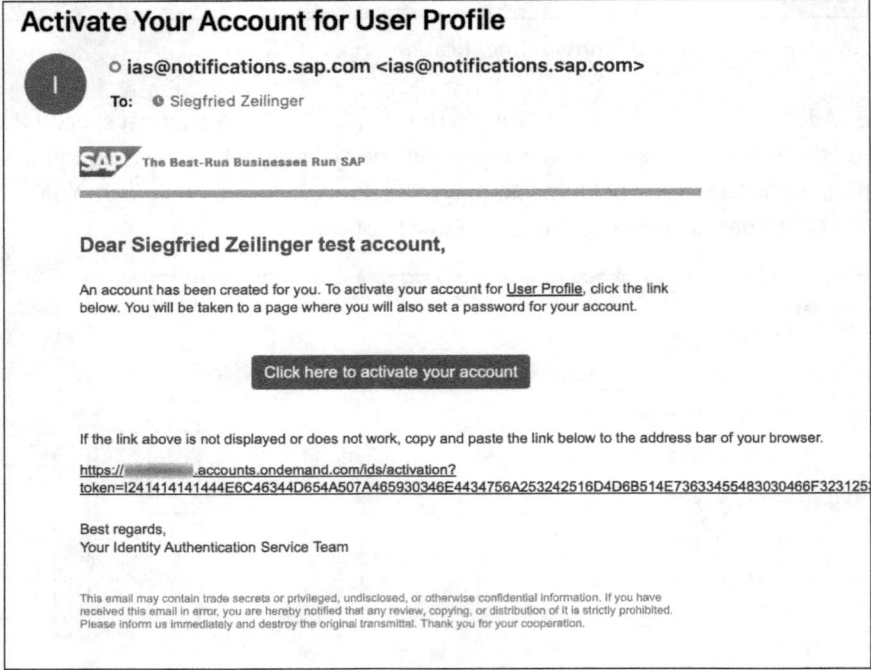

Figure 2.28 Welcome Email

The emails generated by Identity Authentication are always sent from *ias@notifications.sap.com*. However, it is also possible to use your own email server for this purpose. You will find the necessary configuration at the end of this section.

When creating a new user, you only need to maintain the most important attributes from an Identity Authentication point of view. In many cases, however, you may want to maintain additional information about the user. To do so, you can access the **User Details** tab (see Figure 2.29) by clicking the user or the > icon. Here you can maintain personal information, employee information, company information, and custom attributes.

Figure 2.29 User Details

The personal information is interesting for many scenarios. For example, you can configure the validity period of a user account. Say that an employee leaves your company. With the validity period settings, you don't have to delete the corresponding user account; instead, you can set the date in the **Valid To** field to the date the employee will be leaving and thus limit the validity period (see Figure 2.30). In this section, you can also partially control the behavior of identity authentication when sending notifications by setting the language of the user. Email notifications are always sent in the appropriate language if possible.

On the **Legal** tab, which you can select in the upper part of the user display, you can find important information such as when a user last successfully logged in, whether the password is locked, when the password was set, and from which system the password was taken (see Figure 2.31). This information can only be read; it is not possible to manipulate this data.

2 User Administration

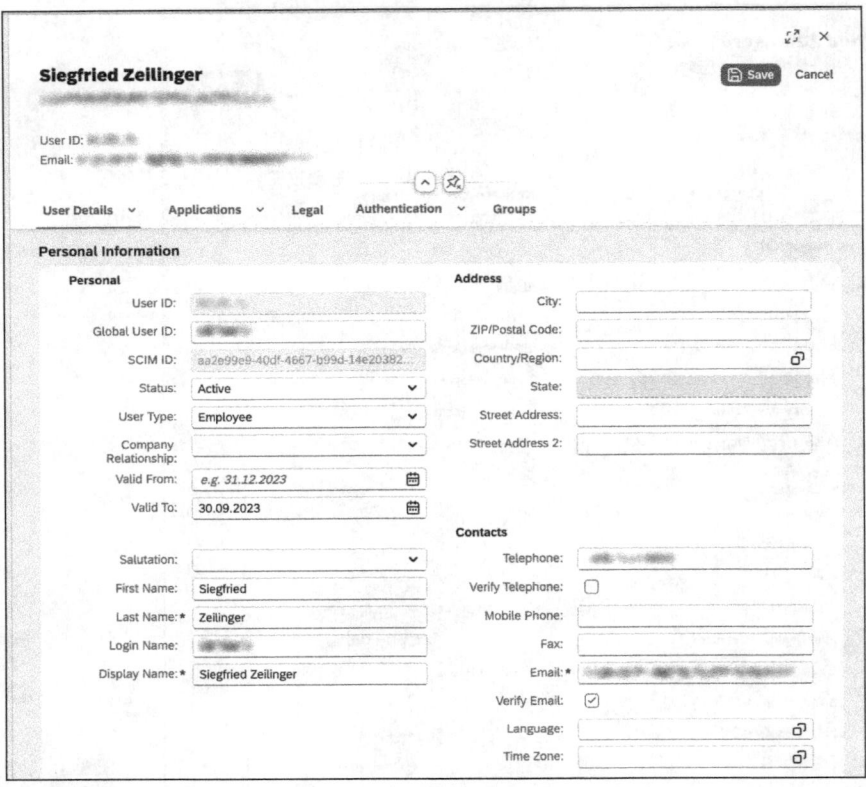

Figure 2.30 Personal Details in User Account

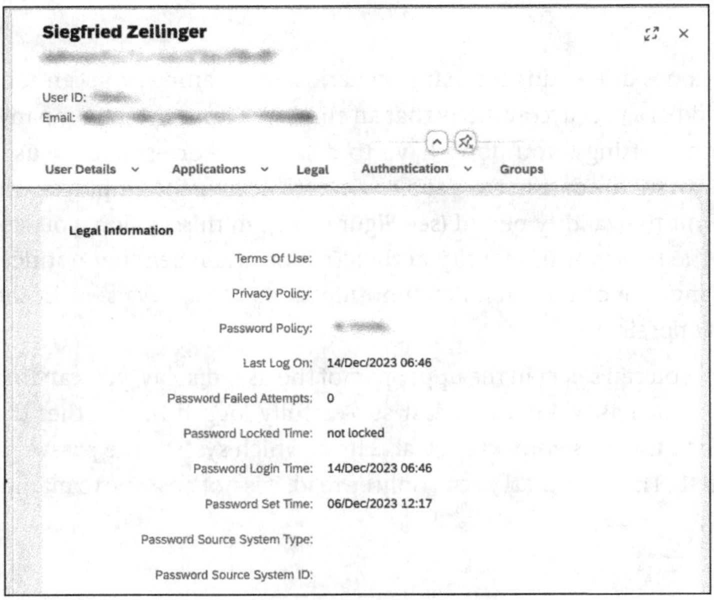

Figure 2.31 Legal Tab in Details of User Account

2.2 SAP Cloud Identity Services

Support staff often need to unlock user accounts or reset passwords. You can perform these actions in the user details. To do so, navigate to the **Authentication** tab and click **Password Details** (see Figure 2.32).

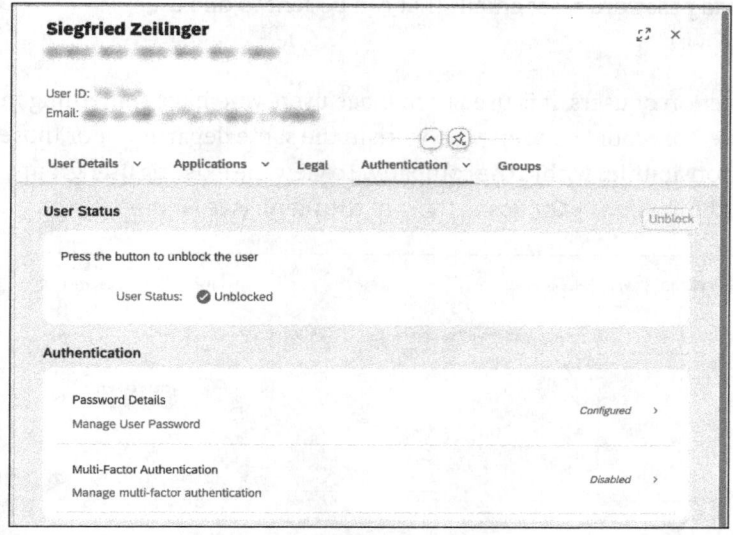

Figure 2.32 Password Details for User Account

In the password details, you can perform the following actions (see Figure 2.33):

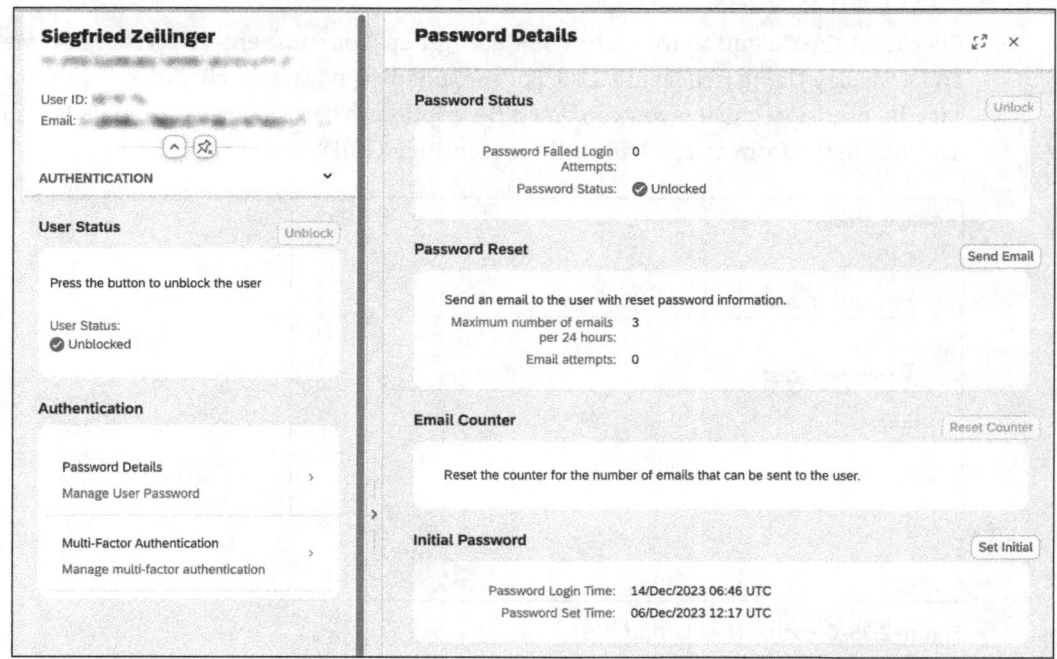

Figure 2.33 Available Actions in Password Details of User Account

2   User Administration

- Unlock a locked user account
- Send an email with information about resetting the password
- Reset the email sending counter per user in order not to exceed the maximum number of activation and password reset emails that can be sent to one user
- Set an initial password

A *user group* is a collection of users. It is used to manage users who have something in common. For example, this could be users who work in the same department or those who have similar responsibilities within the company. To view the existing user groups, select the **Users & Authorizations • Groups** path from the menu (see Figure 2.34).

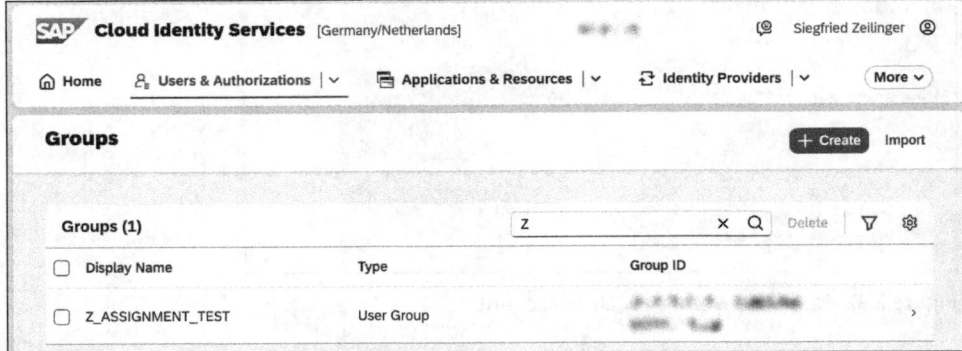

Figure 2.34 Maintaining User Groups

Click the **+ Create** button to create a new user group. You must enter a technical **Name** and a **Display Name** (see Figure 2.35). For these names, no special characters or spaces may be used. Optionally, you can add a **Description**. When saving, a group ID is also assigned in the form of a globally unique identifier (GUID).

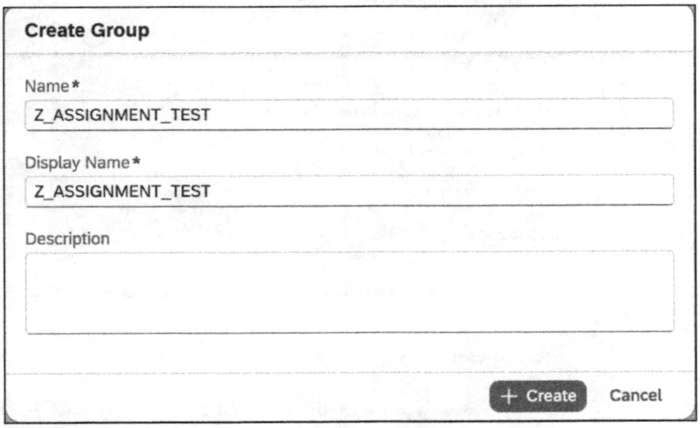

Figure 2.35 Creating User Group

2.2 SAP Cloud Identity Services

The assignment of users to a group is done via user administration. Navigate to the details of the user account as described previously, then click the **Assign** button on the **Groups** tab (see Figure 2.36).

Figure 2.36 Assigning User to User Group

In the popup window that opens, select the desired user group and click the **Assign** button again (see Figure 2.37).

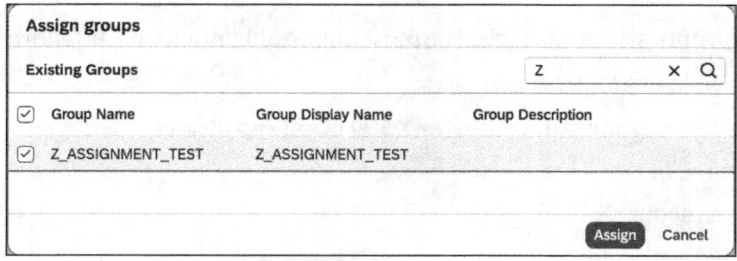

Figure 2.37 Selecting User Group for Assignment

Identity Authentication Tenant Settings

SAP provides the Identity Authentication tenant with preconfigured default settings, which you can customize to meet your requirements. To do so, follow the **Application & Resources • Tenant Settings** path in the menu (see Figure 2.38).

2   User Administration

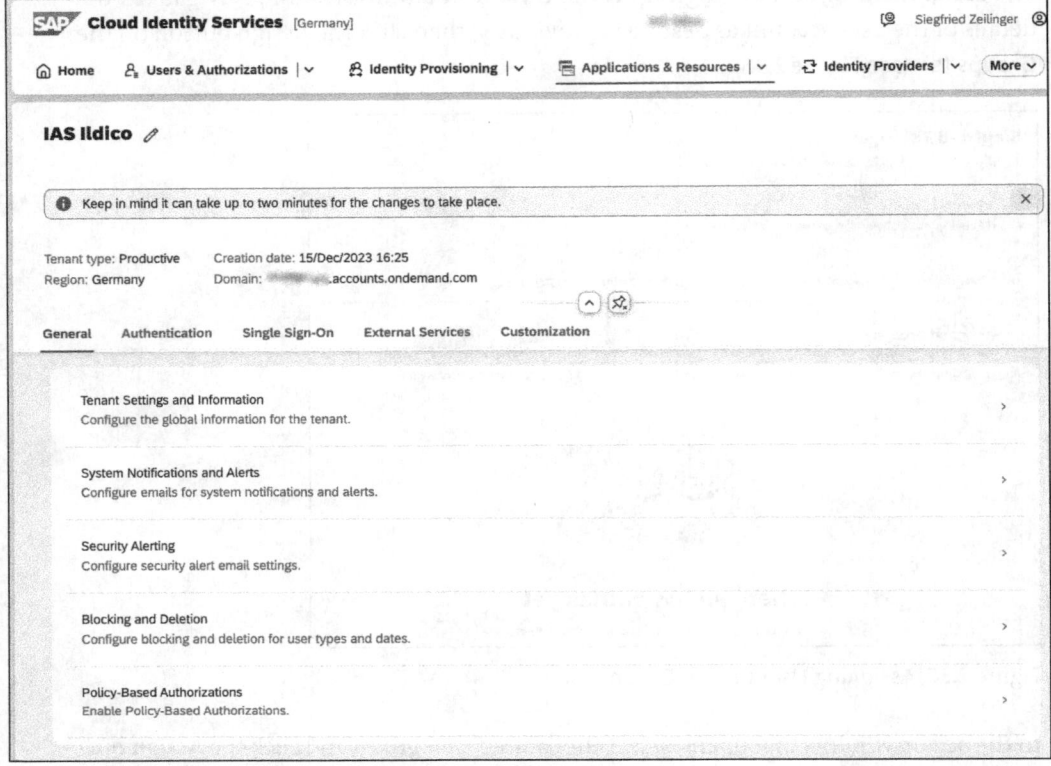

Figure 2.38 Tenant Settings

Several customization options are available. The most important options are as follows:

- Customize and download SAML 2.0 metadata
- Configure trusted certification authorities for X.509 client certificates
- Configure the lifetime of email links
- Configure session timeout
- Configure risk-based authentication
- Configure the corporate user store
- Email server setup and configuration
- Enable security alerts
- Configure a custom domain

Let's take a closer look at the practical settings for email link expiration and session timeout.

You can customize the email link expiration time, setting it somewhere between one hour and 30 days. For password-based actions, it is recommended to limit the validity to a few hours. You can find this setting within the **Tenant Settings** via the **Authentication • Initial Password and Email Link Validity** path (see Figure 2.39).

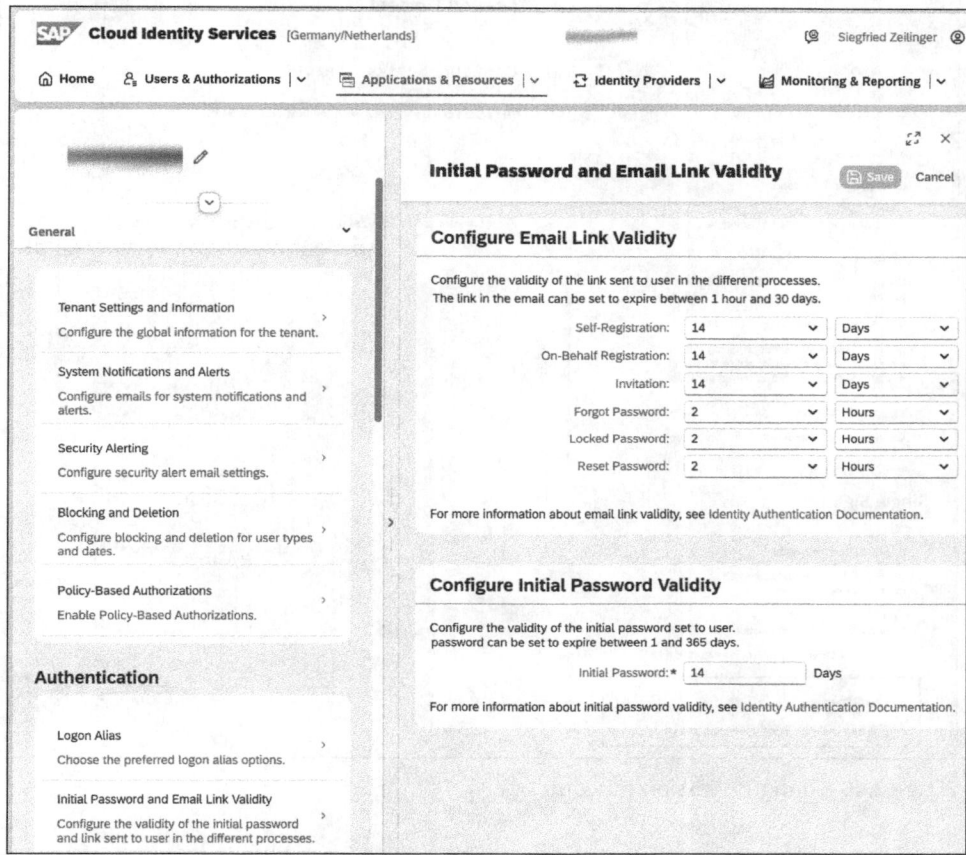

Figure 2.39 Configuring Email Link Expiration

Identity Authentication also allows you to configure the session timeout window after which a new authentication is required. Navigate to **Tenant Settings • Single Sign-On** and click **Session Timeout** (see Figure 2.40).

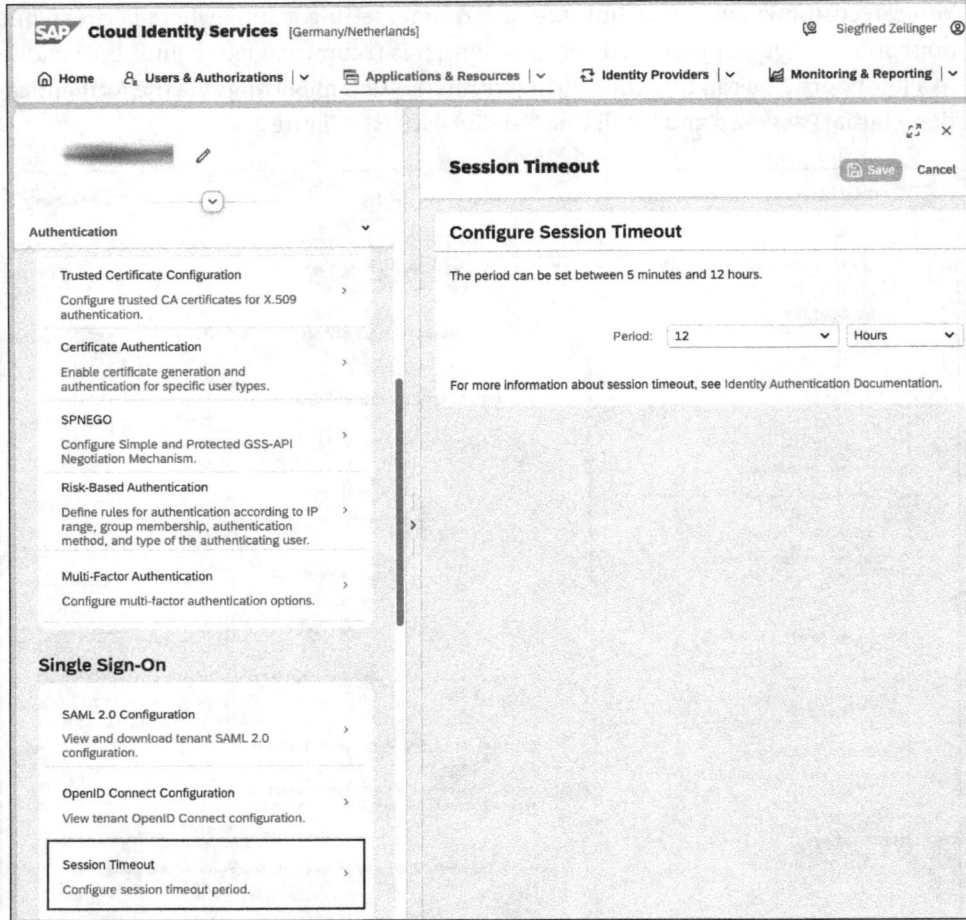

Figure 2.40 Configure Session Timeout

As mentioned earlier, Identity Authentication offers the ability to send notification emails through your own email server. To configure this, in **Tenant Settings** under **External Services**, select **Mail Server Configuration** (see Figure 2.41).

Identity Authentication also allows you to send alerts when a user's email address, login name, or password is changed. By default, these alerts are disabled. To enable the sending of alerts, go to **Tenant Settings** • **General** • **Security Alerting** and set the toggles for the desired alerts to **On** (see Figure 2.42). Subscribers will then be notified of changes to their credentials via the email address they have provided.

2.2 SAP Cloud Identity Services

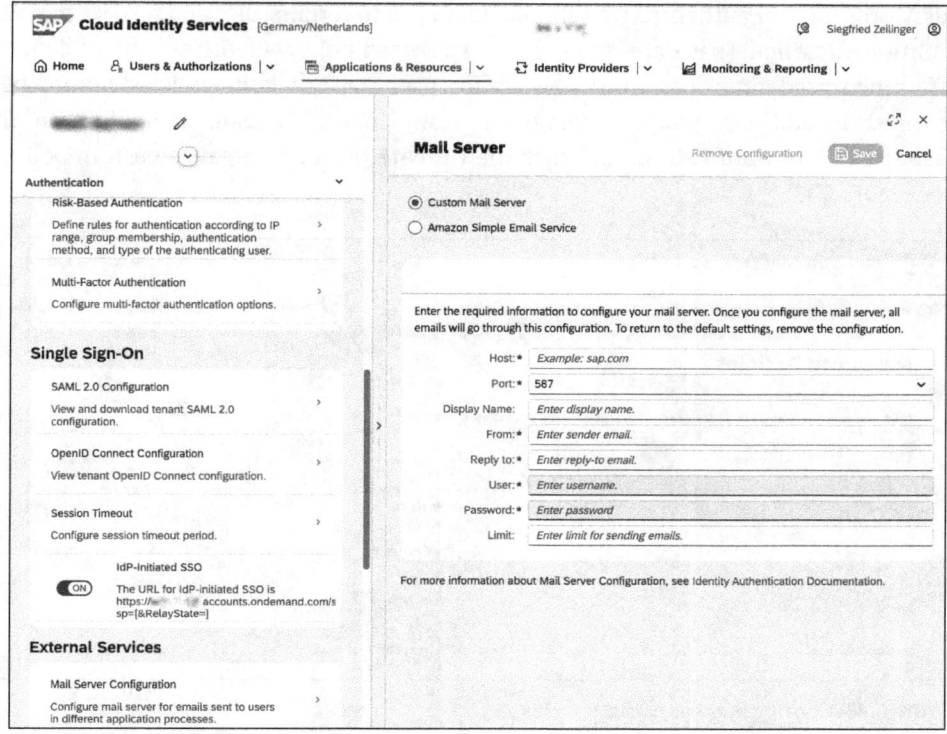

Figure 2.41 Configure Your Own Mail Server

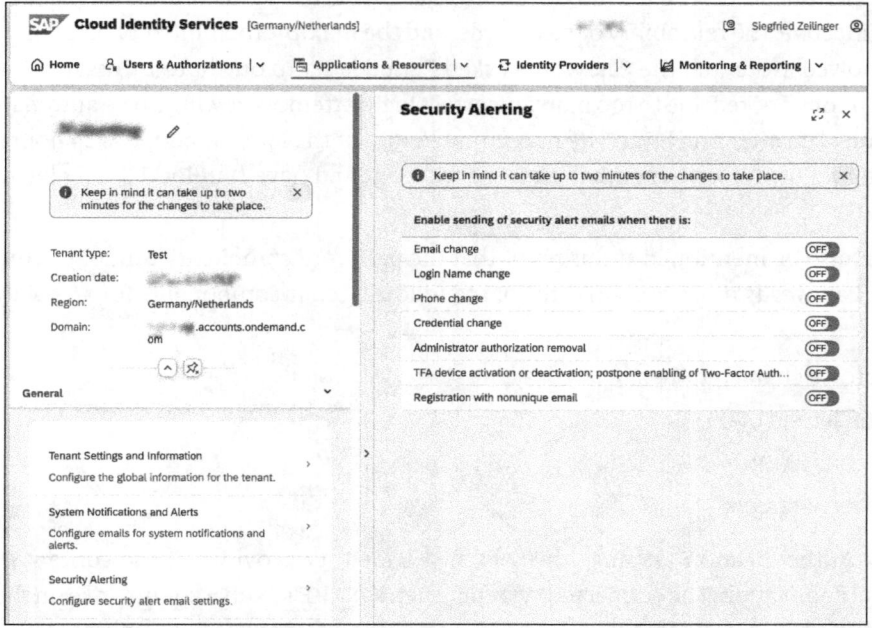

Figure 2.42 Configuring Security Alerting

Passwords for user authentication should be subject to certain rules and restrictions, as mentioned earlier. These are defined in a password policy. Identity Authentication offers two predefined password policies for use. These default policies cannot be changed. In addition, you can create a custom policy. Navigate to **Application & Resources • Password Policies** and click the **+ Create** button to create a custom policy (see Figure 2.43).

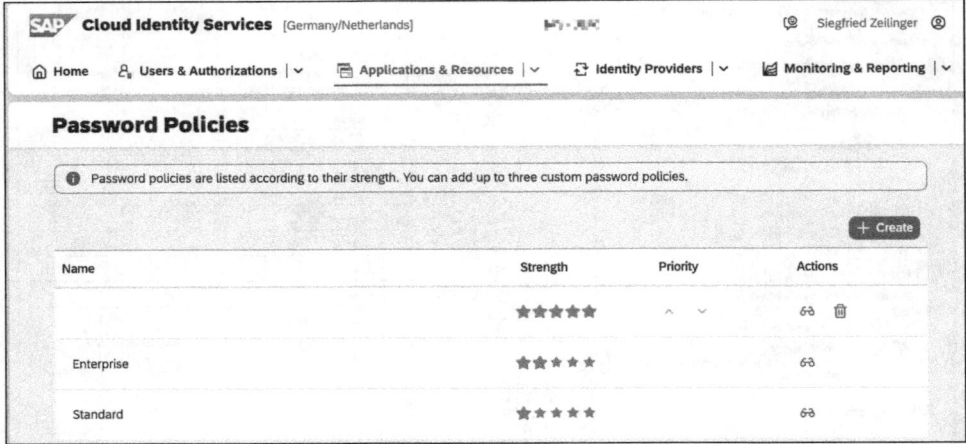

Figure 2.43 Configuring Password Policies

Figure 2.44 shows which restrictions you can define for passwords, such as the password length, the time after which a password must be changed, the maximum time a user may be inactive, the reusability of passwords, and the maximum number of error messages allowed. Note that the **Password Locked Period** is set to one hour by default. If a user account is locked due to too many incorrect login attempts, it will also be automatically unlocked after one hour. The maximum length of the lockout period is 24 hours. It is not possible to permanently lock a user account and have it unlocked only by an administrator.

It should also be mentioned at this point that the password complexity cannot be configured. Passwords must contain three of the following four components for all policy types:

- Lowercase characters (a–z)
- Capital letters (A–Z)
- Numerals (0–9)
- Special characters

Identity Authentication assumes the role of the identity provider in the context of SAML authentication. The connected systems, such as SAP BTP subaccounts, take on the role of the service providers. These service providers are managed as applications in Identity Authentication and can be configured independently.

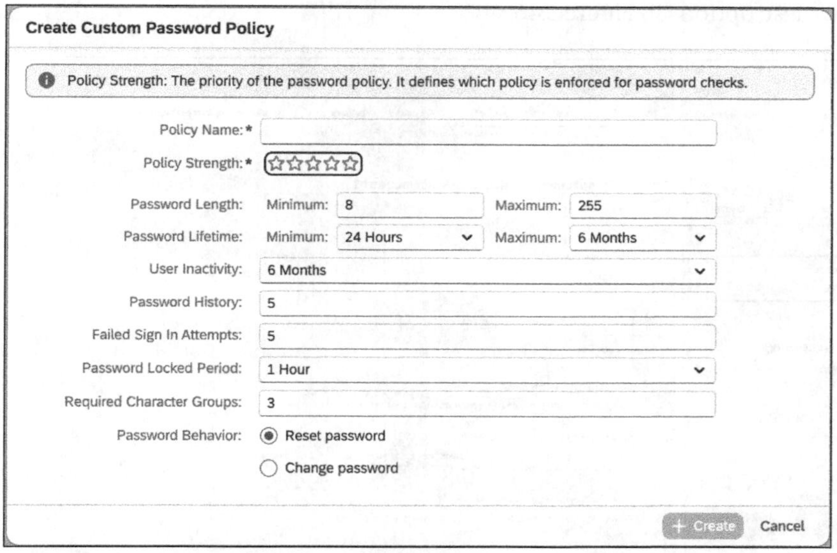

Figure 2.44 Password Policy Details

Navigate to **Applications & Resources • Applications** to see the connected subaccounts (see Figure 2.45). From the list of applications, select the subaccount you wish to configure. If your desired subaccount is not visible in the list, the SAP Platform Identity Provider service for SAP BTP has not been enabled for it.

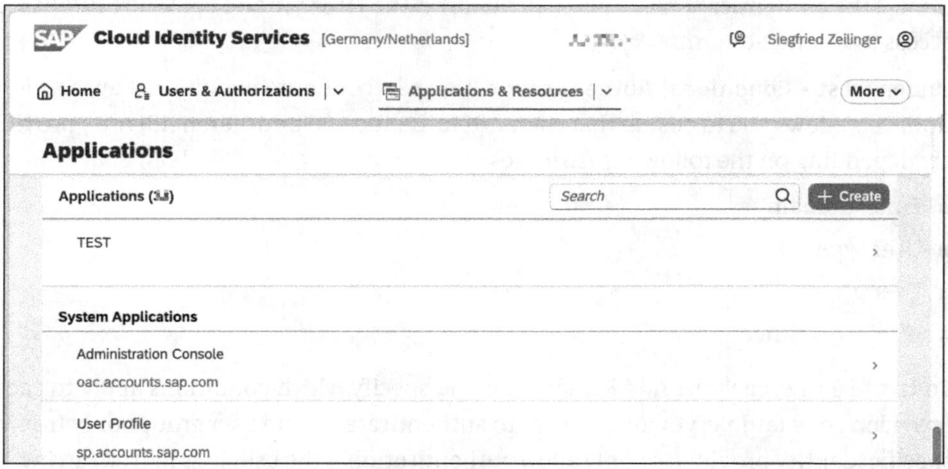

Figure 2.45 Configuring Applications for Identity Authentication

In the application settings, you can make settings in the following areas:

- Trust settings
- Authentication and access control settings
- Setting the branding and layout of forms

You can see these options in Figure 2.46.

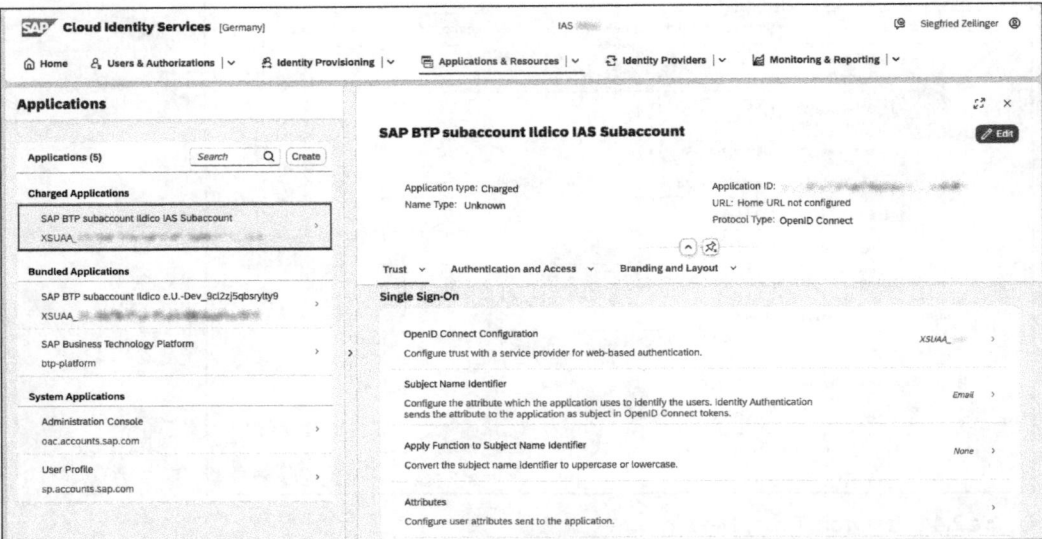

Figure 2.46 Detailed View of Application in Identity Authentication Subaccount

On the **Trust** tab, the most important setting is the authentication type. This can be either SAML 2.0 or OIDC. Subaccounts in SAP BTP, Neo environment use SAML 2.0, and subaccounts in the Cloud Foundry environment use OIDC by default. You also can customize the authentication assertion attribute on the **Trust** tab and configure API-based access to the subaccount.

Under **Trust • Conditional Authentication**, you can configure conditional authentication. This allows you to ensure that users are authenticated by different identity providers depending on the following attributes:

- Email domain
- User type
- User group
- IP address range

To create a rule, click the **Add Rule** button and specify which conditions apply to each provider. For example, you might want to authenticate certain user groups only from a specific identity provider, or only allow authentication if the user logs in from an internal IP address (see Figure 2.47).

The **Authentication and Access** tab is used to configure how users log onto the system and which policies are used and must be accepted by the users (see Figure 2.48).

2.2 SAP Cloud Identity Services

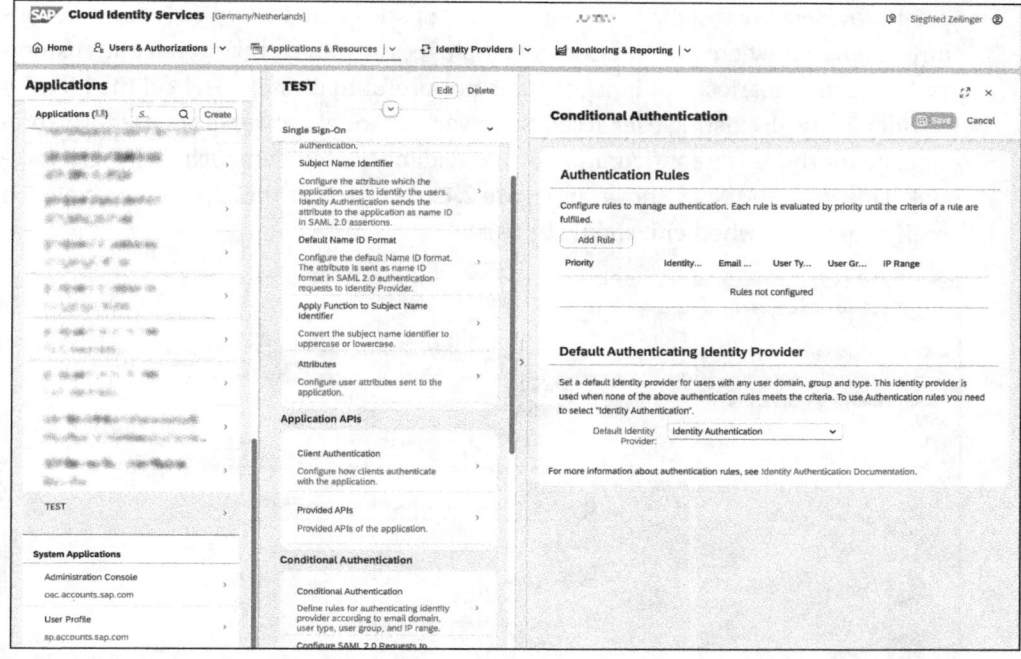

Figure 2.47 Defining Authentication Rule

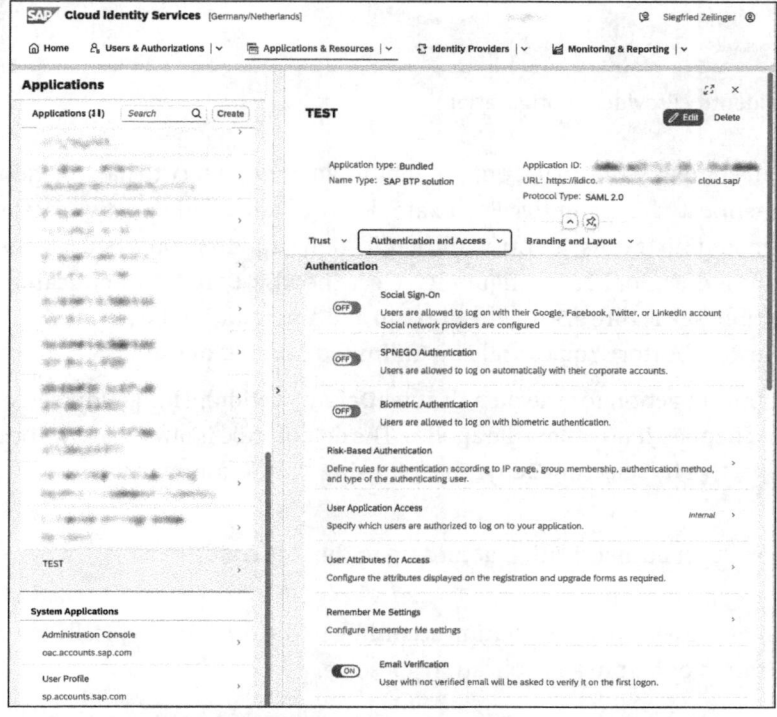

Figure 2.48 Configuring Authentication and Access Control

97

Social providers are disabled by default. This logon method is typically used in consumer scenarios where the users are not employees of your company, but end customers. For such scenarios, it is in most cases not useful to create a user on the Identity Provider. Instead, existing user accounts in various social networks are used. The prerequisite for this is the configuration of social identity providers such as Google, Facebook, LinkedIn, and X, as shown in Figure 2.49. For each of these providers, you can specify separately whether it should be used.

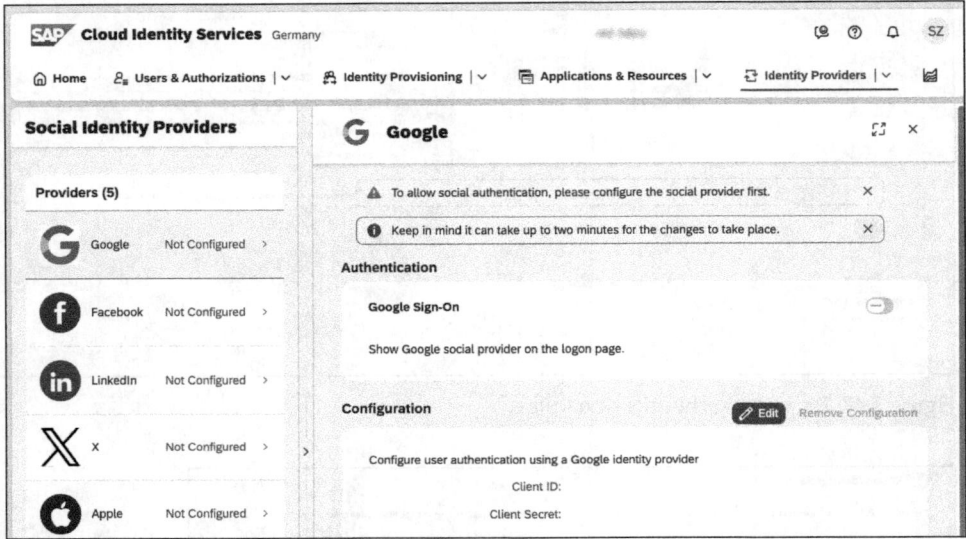

Figure 2.49 Social Identity Provider Configuration

Depending on your company-internal requirements, it can be necessary to have certain user groups authenticated differently. For example, you can configure two-factor authentication for administrators. Identity Authentication supports you in such cases with risk-based authentication. To configure it, select the **Risk-Based Authentication** configuration section (see Figure 2.50). Here you can add a new authentication rule by clicking the **Create Rule** button. You can add an unlimited number of rules.

You must also define an action for the default rule (**Default Action**). This action determines what should happen if no other rule applies. The default rule is always active, but you can make it inactive by selecting **Deny**. The following actions are available:

- **Allow**
  This action allows user authentication according to the rule conditions.
- **Deny**
  This action denies the user's authentication according to the rules. It is typically used for a test application or before an application goes live.

2.2 SAP Cloud Identity Services

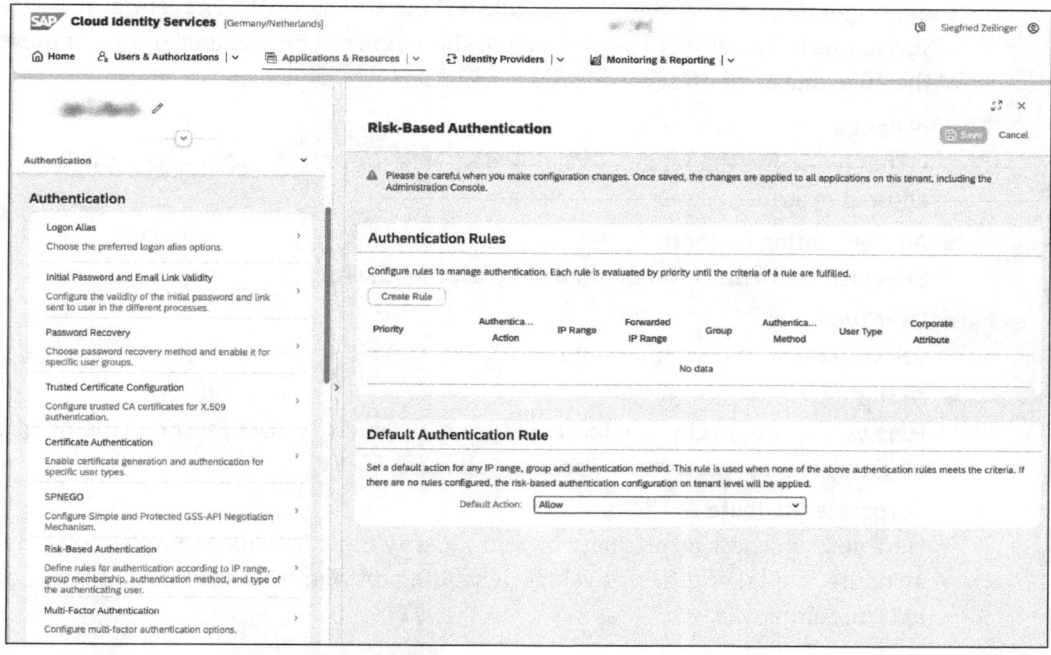

Figure 2.50 Configuring Risk-Based Authentication

- **TOTP Two-Factor Authentication**
  This action uses two factors to authenticate users. In addition to their primary credentials, users must provide a time-based one-time password (TOTP)—that is, a passcode. To do this, they must install an authenticator application, such as SAP Authenticator, on their mobile devices to generate the TOTP passcodes.

- **SMS Two-Factor Authentication**
  With this type of two-factor authentication, users must provide an SMS code that is sent to their mobile device in addition to their primary credentials. To use two-factor SMS authentication, you must have licensed SAP Authentication 365 and configured it in the Identity Authentication administration console.

- **Web Two-Factor Authentication**
  Users must authenticate with a device such as a built-in biometric scanner, USB, Bluetooth, or near-field communication (NFC) device in addition to their primary credentials.

- **RADIUS Server Two-Factor Authentication**
  Users must provide a RADIUS passcode in addition to their primary login credentials. To do this, they must have a RADIUS token configured through a RADIUS dial-in server so that they can generate passcodes. RADIUS is a standard for dialing into other networks and is often used for two-factor authentication.

The configuration of an authentication rule is shown in Figure 2.51. The central attribute of such a rule is the action to be performed. The action can be triggered by one or more of the following attributes:

- **IP Range**
  Here you define the range of valid IP addresses or proxies from which the user is allowed to authenticate.
- **Authentication Method**
  Select the authentication method to be used by the user.
- **User Type**
  Select the type of user you want to authenticate.
- **Group**
  Here you indicate a cloud or local user group of which the user must be a member. If no group is selected, the rule applies to all users.
- **Corporate Attribute**
  Here you can check an attribute in your identity provider—for example, a separate attribute that takes different values depending on whether a user is an internal or external employee.

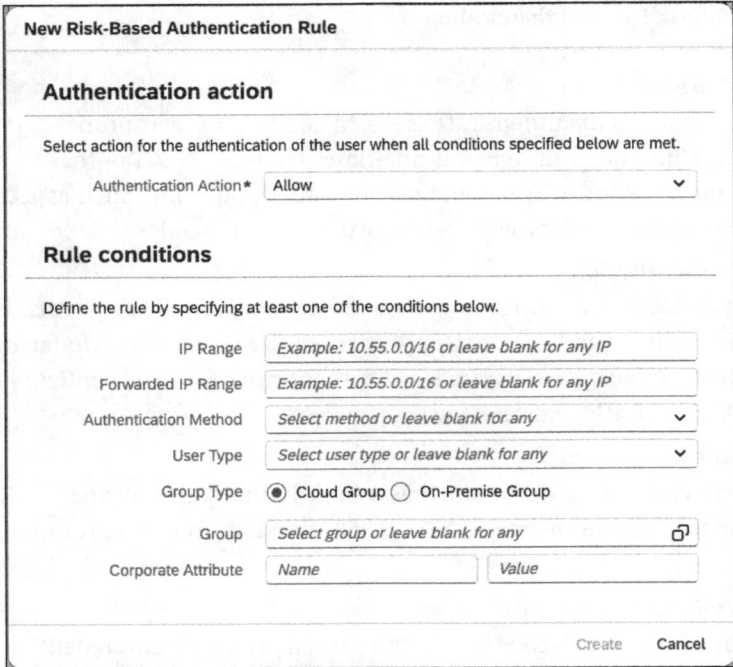

Figure 2.51 Define Risk-Based Authentication

On the **Branding and Layout** tab, Identity Authentication allows you to customize the appearance and behavior of the generated pages and emails (e.g., login or password reset). This includes the logo, the branding style in the form of CSS code, and the email templates to be used (see Figure 2.52).

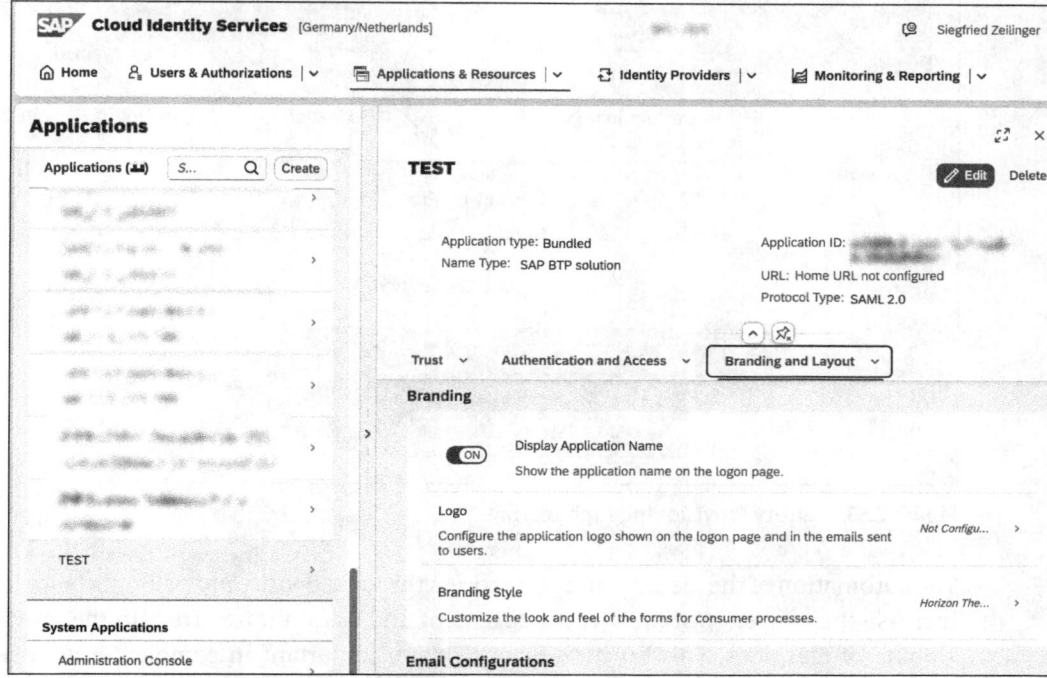

Figure 2.52 Configuring Branding, Layout, and Email Templates

2.2.2 Identity Provisioning

A key component of SAP Cloud Identity Services is the Identity Provisioning service. This service provides support for automating the identity lifecycle process and facilitates the provisioning of identities and their privileges to business applications running in the cloud as well as on premise.

The service extracts user information from one or more query systems, performs transformations, and customizes the information. A *transformation* can, for example, be the adjustment of attribute-specific information from a query system to match standard attributes in SAP BTP. After these adjustments, the user information is written to one or more target systems.

Figure 2.53 illustrates the data flow and interactions that occur during the identity provisioning process. This process ensures that identities are consistent and correctly synchronized between different systems. The adaptation and transformation of the user information ensures that the data can be correctly interpreted and used in the target system.

2   User Administration

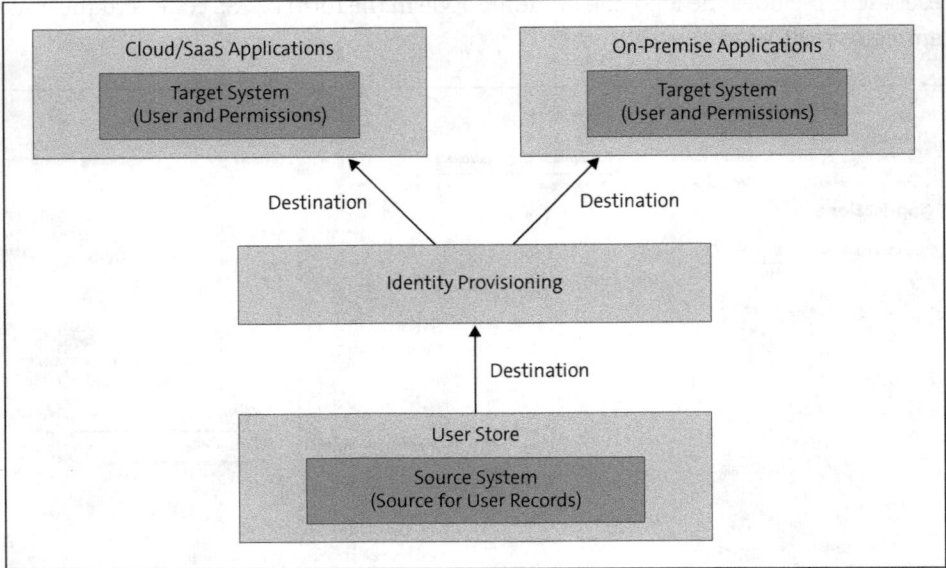

Figure 2.53 Identity Provisioning Architecture

The automation of the identity lifecycle process through identity provisioning helps to increase the efficiency of identity management and to minimize errors in the provisioning of identities. This function is particularly important in complex enterprise environments, in which several applications and systems must be integrated.

The *source system* is typically an organization's existing corporate user store, which can be a cloud or on-premise system. Identity Authentication can also be a source system. You can maintain a maximum of 20 sources. The following source systems are supported by Identity Provisioning:

- Identity Authentication
- Google G Suite
- Local Identity Directory
- SAP Analytics Cloud
- SAP NetWeaver Application Server for ABAP
- SAP BTP ABAP environment
- SAP BTP subaccounts
- Java or HTML5 applications on SAP BTP
- SAP Concur
- SAP CPQ
- SAP Fieldglass
- User account and authentication server of SAP HANA extended application services, advanced model

- SAP Integrated Business Planning for Supply Chain
- SAP Jam
- SAP Marketing Cloud
- SAP S/4HANA Cloud
- SAP S/4HANA (on premise)
- SAP SuccessFactors
- SAP SuccessFactors Learning Marketplace
- SAP SuccessFactors Incentive Management
- SAP Build Work Zone
- Cloud Foundry user accounts and authentication servers
- Google Workspace
- LDAP server
- Microsoft Active Directory
- Microsoft Entra ID
- SCIM system
- Databricks in SAP Business Data Cloud (in beta at time of printing)

Your bundle determines which combinations are allowed. You can find an overview of the bundles at *https://help.sap.com/docs/cloud-identity-services/cloud-identity-services/get-your-tenant*.

The target system is the cloud or on-premise system in which you want to create or customize the identities from your source system. You can maintain a maximum of 50 target systems. The same systems allowed as source systems are allowed as target system. In addition, you can use the following systems as target systems: SAP Sales Cloud and SAP Service Cloud (formerly SAP Cloud for Customer).

A *proxy system* is a special connector that is used in hybrid scenarios in which cloud systems are connected to on-premise systems. This means that you can provision entities from a cloud system to an on-premise system and vice versa, without establishing a direct connection between these systems. Identity Provisioning can be used as a proxy system to perform the provisioning operations requested by the on-premise system, such as creating, updating, and deleting entities.

You can receive Identity Provisioning free of charge bundled with an SAP cloud solution—for example, SAP S/4HANA Cloud, SAP Marketing Cloud, SAP Sales Cloud, or SAP SuccessFactors. For a complete list of available bundles, see the product documentation or contact your SAP representative.

Each customer receives two Identity Provisioning tenants per region. You can use one of these for testing purposes and the other for production configuration and job provisioning. A tenant bundled with an SAP Cloud product receives access to all source,

2 User Administration

target, and proxy systems that are relevant for this product. If a customer has purchased multiple SAP Cloud products, then all relevant systems are activated for both tenants, and in both Identity Provisioning administration consoles. As of October 2020, Identity Provisioning could no longer be purchased as a standalone product.

To use SAP Cloud Identity Services, including Identity Provisioning, a subscription is required via your subaccount. In a newly installed SAP BTP environment, you can find this under **Services** • **Instances and Subscriptions** (see Figure 2.54).

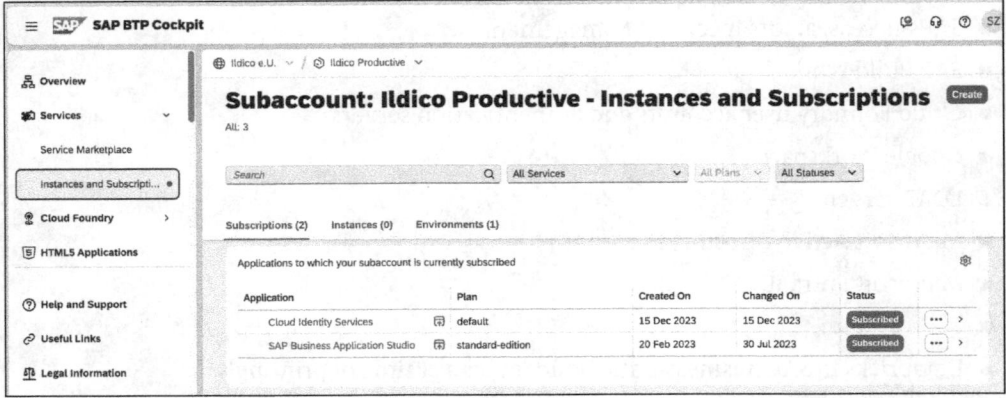

Figure 2.54 Subaccount Subscriptions

> **SAP Cloud Identity Services Cannot Be Found**
> If SAP Cloud Identity Services cannot be found, you can instantiate it via the **Create** button.

By clicking **Cloud Identity Services** in the details, you can use the **Go to Application** button to jump to the SAP Cloud Identity Services (see Figure 2.55).

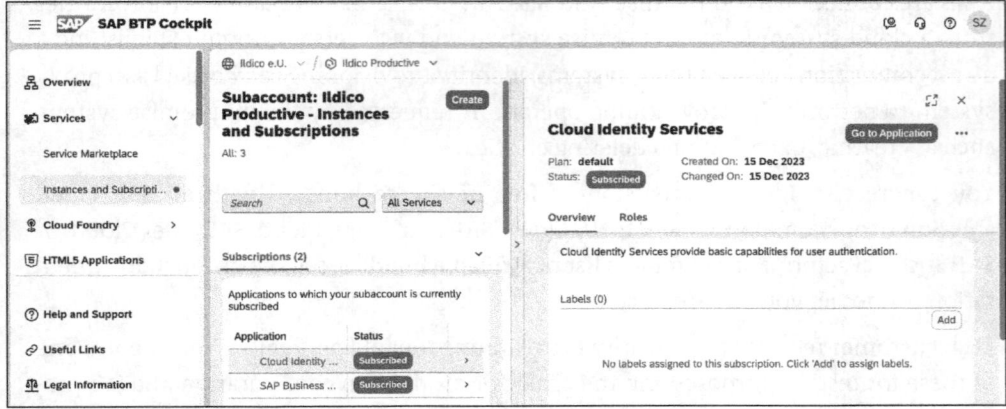

Figure 2.55 Details for SAP Cloud Identity Services

2.2 SAP Cloud Identity Services

Now you can create source and target systems under Identity Provisioning and configure the transformation of the identities (see Figure 2.56).

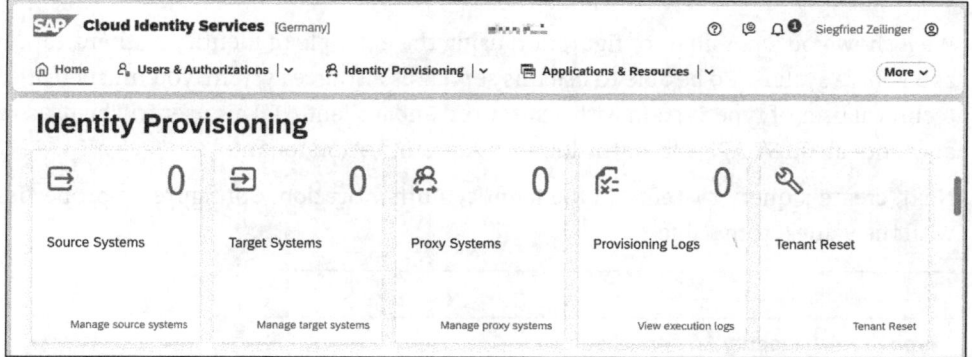

Figure 2.56 Identity Provisioning Section of SAP Cloud Identity Services

To create a new source system for Identity Provisioning, choose the **Source Systems** menu item, then click the **Add** button in the list of source systems. The following dialog for creating the source system is shown in Figure 2.57.

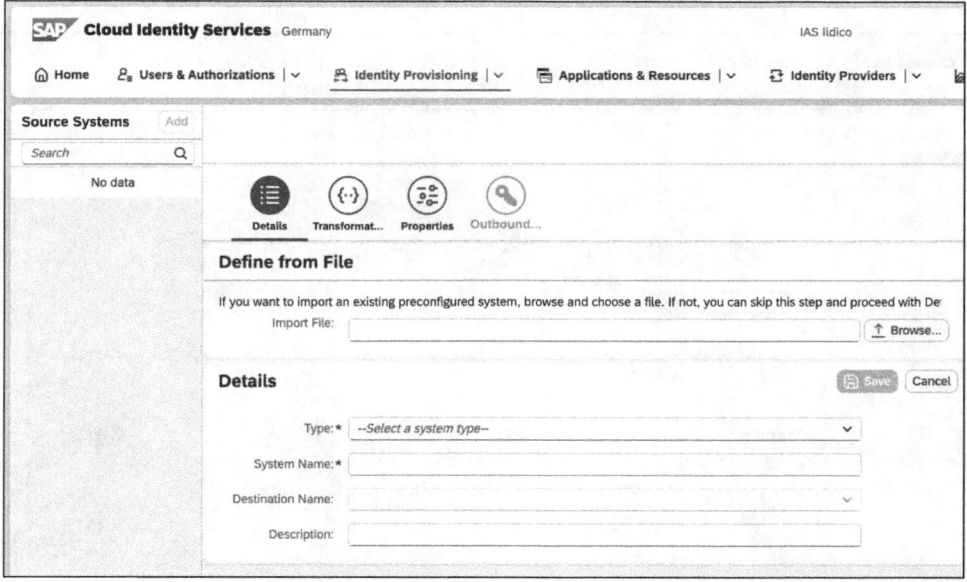

Figure 2.57 Create Source System

Select the type of the call system and enter a name for the system. You also can enter a destination and a description. If you select a destination, it will be used for technical communication with the call system.

2   User Administration

Alternatively, you have the option to maintain the connection parameters on the **Properties** tab. Refer to the respective documentation to find the specific properties of the selected call system type.

We'll show you a possible configuration using the example of Identity Authentication as a source system. To be able to use this service as a source system, you must create a technical user of type **System** with a password and a client ID. This user will be used to authenticate REST API calls to the Identity Authentication tenant.

Next, create a query system of type **Identity Authentication**. Configure its properties with the values from Table 2.1.

Field	Value
Type	Identity Authentication
Name	Default technical name for the queueing system

Table 2.1 Properties of Identity Authentication Client as Call System

Create a new target system under the **Target Systems** menu item. To do so, click the **Add** button below the list of target systems (in Figure 2.58, the list is empty).

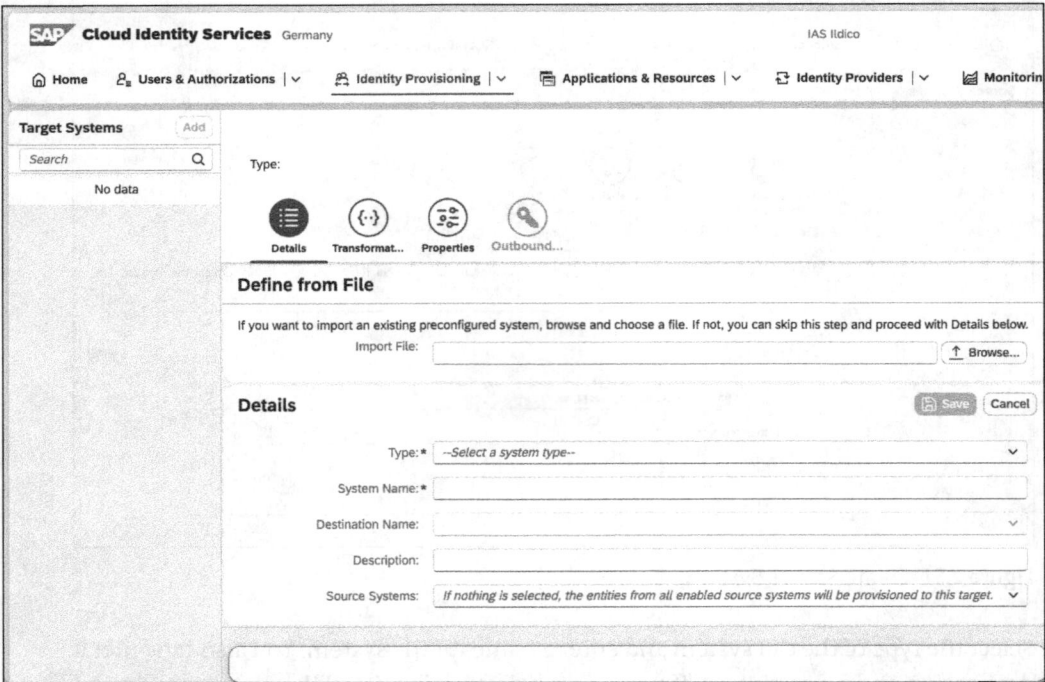

Figure 2.58 Create Target System

For the target system, you must specify the same properties as for the source system (see Figure 2.59). In addition, you can select the source systems from which the identities are to be obtained. You maintain the properties for the system connection in the same way as for the source system. Refer to the documentation for the system-specific properties at *https://help.sap.com/docs/cloud-identity-services/cloud-identity-services/source-systems*.

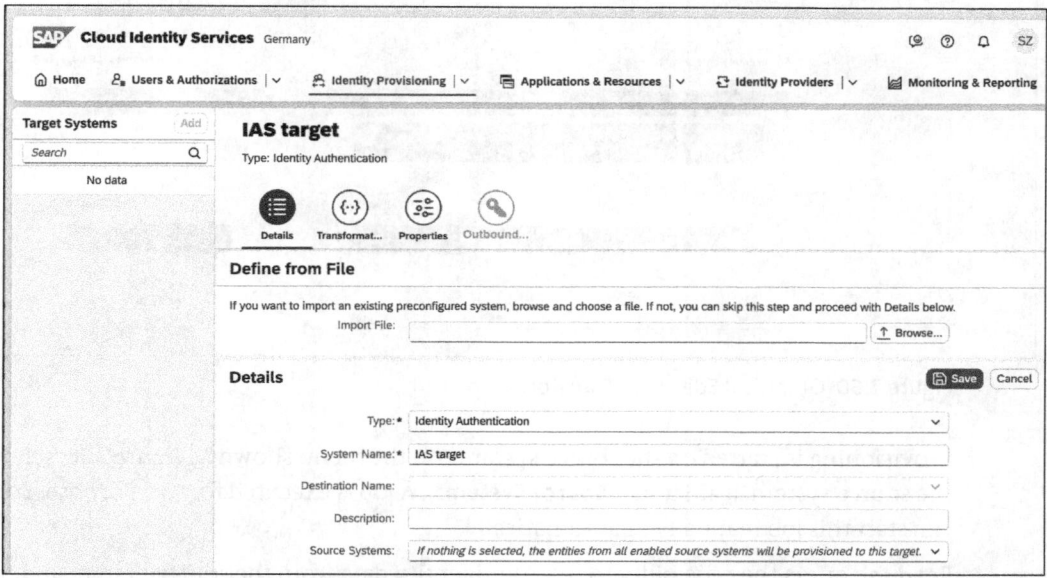

Figure 2.59 Maintaining Target System Details

Source and target systems typically use different data structures. Therefore, it is necessary to map these data structures. In Identity Provisioning, the mapping is performed in the form of transformations. Identity Provisioning processes the data in JavaScript Object Notation (JSON) format. After you have configured and saved a query system, a default transformation is created. This transforms the data from the source system, which is already in JSON format, into generic JSON, which is used by Identity Provisioning.

When the identities are deployed to the provisioning target system, another transformation is run. This transformation converts the generic JSON to a JSON format that can be processed by the target system. The transformations can be customized on both the source and target systems. Since 2023, there is also a practical graphical editor for these transformations, which you can see in Figure 2.60.

2 User Administration

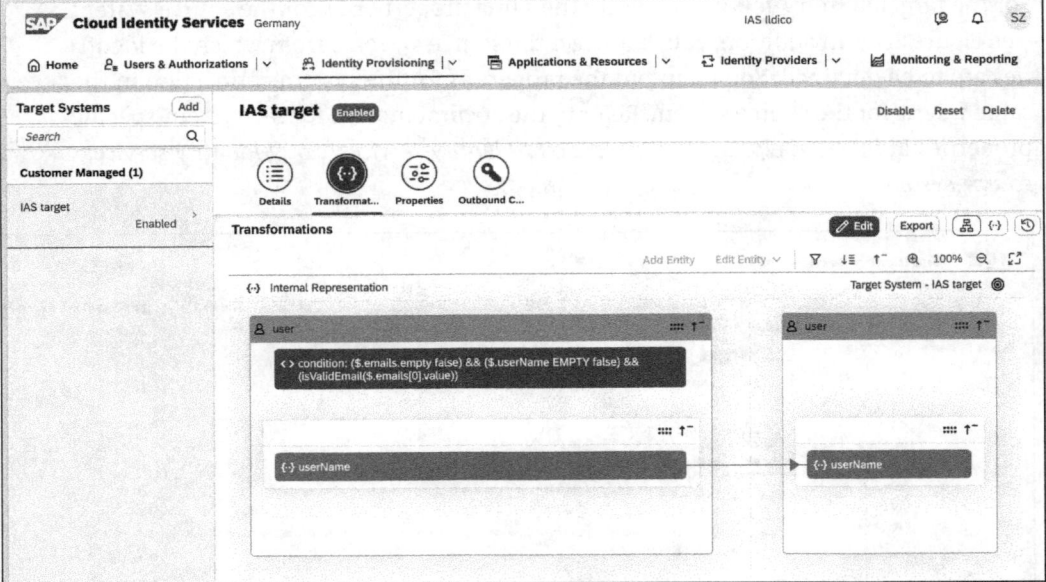

Figure 2.60 Graphical Editor for Transformations

Provisioning is started on the source systems (in the menu shown in Figure 2.56, select the source system again under **Source Systems**). A job is executed for this purpose. You can start this job manually or automatically.

Read Job offers the possibility to read out identity data from the source system and to make that data available in the target system after the execution of transformations. Two different operations are available for this purpose (see Figure 2.61):

- **Run Now**
  This option allows you to run the job immediately. The job reads all identities from the source system and transfers them to the target system. The target system only checks whether changes have been made to the identities in the source system. Note that any manual changes made in the target system will be overwritten by the job.

- **Schedule**
  Here you can plan the regular execution of the job, whereby the smallest interval is 30 minutes. The read job will not be started immediately, but after the specified interval has elapsed.

Resync Job enables the resynchronization of the data in the target system if changes have been made in the source system. The available operation for this job type is **Run Now**. This option starts the resynchronization job immediately. Unlike **Read Job**, **Resync Job** will overwrite any changes you have made manually in the target system in the meantime.

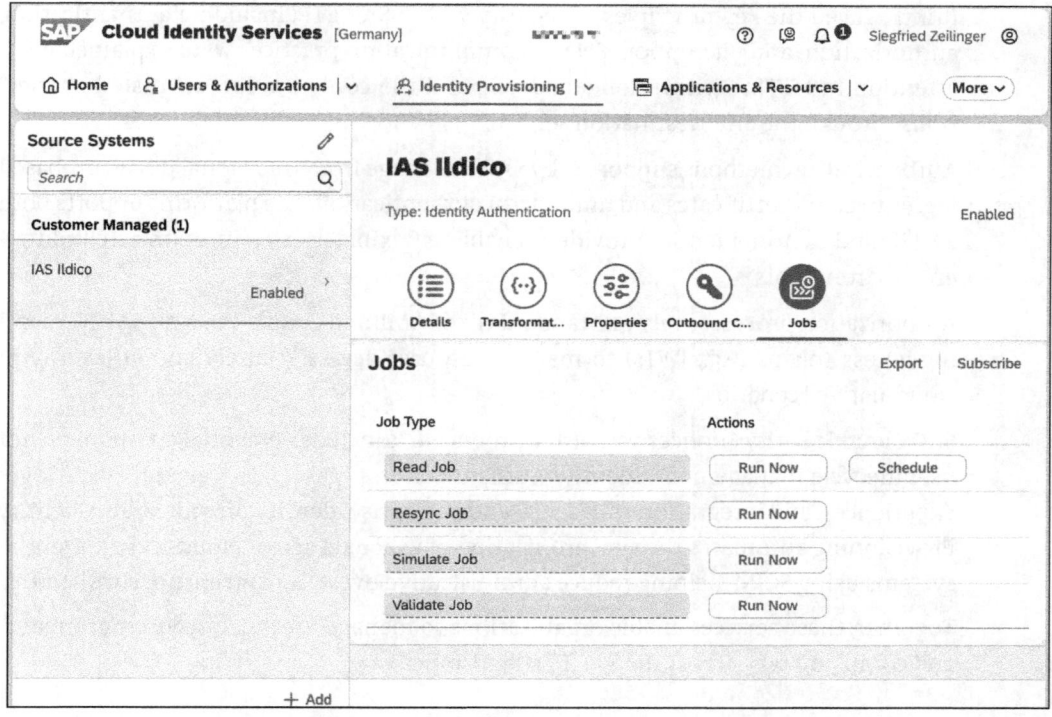

Figure 2.61 Scheduling Identity Provisioning Job

Simulate Job reads identities from the source system, performs transformations, and simulates the transfer of data to the target system. It is useful for understanding the potential impact of changes in the source system on the target system without actually changing the data. The **Run Now** operation allows you to start the simulation immediately.

Validate Job allows you to check the configuration and identity data without actually performing any transfers. The **Run Now** operation can be used to start the validation immediately. **Validate Job** reads identities, performs transformations, and validates the configuration and data. It helps you to identify potential problems in advance, before actual transfers take place.

Taken together, these four job types in Identity Provisioning provide comprehensive control over the identity lifecycle process, from simulation and validation to the actual synchronization of data between source and target systems.

2.3 Summary

This chapter offered a detailed overview of user administration in SAP BTP, highlighting the importance of secure identity and access management in cloud environments.

2 User Administration

It introduced the key principles of security within SAP BTP, including authentication, authorization, and encryption. Secure communication practices were explained, with attention to HTTPS, encryption standards, and the configuration of trusted connections through the SAP Destination service.

Authentication methods supported by SAP BTP range from traditional password-based logins to client certificates and multifactor authentication. The platform supports both SAP ID and custom identity providers, enabling flexible user verification across different environments.

Authorization processes rely on standards like SAML and OAuth 2.0, with SAP BTP issuing access tokens (e.g., JWTs) to manage resource access securely and efficiently in cloud-native scenarios.

SAP Cloud Identity Services was also introduced. It includes essential components for user lifecycle management: Identity Authentication supports SSO, customizable login experiences, and integration with social and enterprise identity providers, and Identity Provisioning automates the synchronization of user data across cloud and on-premise systems using SCIM, helping reduce administrative overhead and ensure consistency.

Together, these services enable organizations to manage users in a secure, automated, and compliant way across the SAP BTP landscape.

Chapter 3
Advanced Identity Authentication Service Topics

In combination with Identity Authentication, SAP BTP offers a wide range of options for a variety of requirements in the standard system. The central feature is that you can configure a customer-specific identity provider for any number of your subaccounts in one place. Options such as attribute-based authentication are also possible.

In this chapter, we dive deeper into the world of advanced concepts and technologies that are cenkntral to the Identity Authentication service domain. Our journey takes us through various key technologies and real-world examples that provide a comprehensive understanding of this complex and dynamic domain.

At this point, we would like to remind you about single sign-on (SSO). SSO is a process that allows users to log in to multiple applications or services with a single set of authentication credentials (such as a user name and password). Instead of having to log into each application separately, SSO provides a platform that allows access to multiple systems or resources after a single authentication. SSO offers many benefits that make it an attractive solution for both users and administrators.

One of the key benefits is ease of use, as only a single user name and password combination is required for authentication. This greatly simplifies the logon process and reduces the likelihood of forgotten passwords. As a result, SSO increases efficiency because employees spend less time on logon processes and more time doing their jobs. For the administration team, SSO simplifies the management of user accounts and access rights by allowing them to monitor and maintain one central platform instead of several separate authentication systems. Because Identity Authentication helps with SSO, we will cover the technical basics of Security Assertion Markup Language (SAML 2.0) and OpenID Connect (OIDC) in this chapter.

SAML 2.0 and OIDC are both standards for web-based authentication and authorization. However, they have different characteristics and application areas. Both standards play an important role in SAP BTP.

In Section 3.1, we provide an overview of SAML, a core component for identity management in corporate environments. SAML enables the secure transmission of authentication information between different parties, and we will examine its functionality, benefits, and challenges in detail. In Section 3.2, we cover OIDC, a modern identity layer built on the OAuth 2.0 protocol. We explore how OIDC simplifies yet secures authentication and authorization on the internet through practical examples. In Section 3.3, we cover the practical application and integration of Identity Authentication as a proxy to Microsoft Entra ID. We show how this configuration efficiently supports the management of user identities and access rights in cloud-based environments. Two-factor authentication is a crucial element of modern security architecture. In Section 3.4, we examine various methods and technologies used in two-factor authentication and demonstrate their implementation in real-life scenarios. Conditional authentication is an advanced technique that helps improve the level of security based on user context and behavior. Finally, in Section 3.5, we explain how this method increases security without compromising the user experience.

3.1 SAML 2.0

SAML 2.0 is the standard for exchanging authentication and authorization information. SAML 2.0 is used in corporate environments to enable SSO. The OASIS open consortium, a nonprofit organization that develops open standards for information technology, manages the SAML standard. IBM, Microsoft, and Novell originally developed SAML. The first version of the standard was published in 2002, and SAML 2.0, the current version, was published in 2005.

SAML is an XML-based authentication protocol that identity providers use to communicate with service providers. Identity providers manage the login data of users, while service providers are the applications that require authentication.

SAML 2.0 supports two ways to start a login process: service provider–initiated SSO, and identity provider–initiated SSO. The main difference between these two is where the login process begins. With *service provider–initiated SSO*, the login process starts with the application that the user wants to open. With *identity provider–initiated SSO*, the login process begins with the identity provider that manages the user's login data.

Figure 3.1 shows the process of service provider–initiated SSO. Here's how it works:

❶ The user visits the website of an application that supports service provider–initiated SSO.

❷ The application (which fulfills the function of the service provider in this context) recognizes that the user is not yet logged in and creates and signs a SAML request.

❸ The application then redirects the user to the identity provider login URL.

❹ The identity provider verifies the signature, parses the SAML request, and prompts the user to authenticate.

❺ The user enters their credentials.

❻ The identity provider authenticates the user and returns a SAML response.

❼ This directs the user to the service provider.
❽ The application verifies the signature of the SAML response, validates it, and performs an authorization check of the user.
❾ The service provider makes the requested resource available.

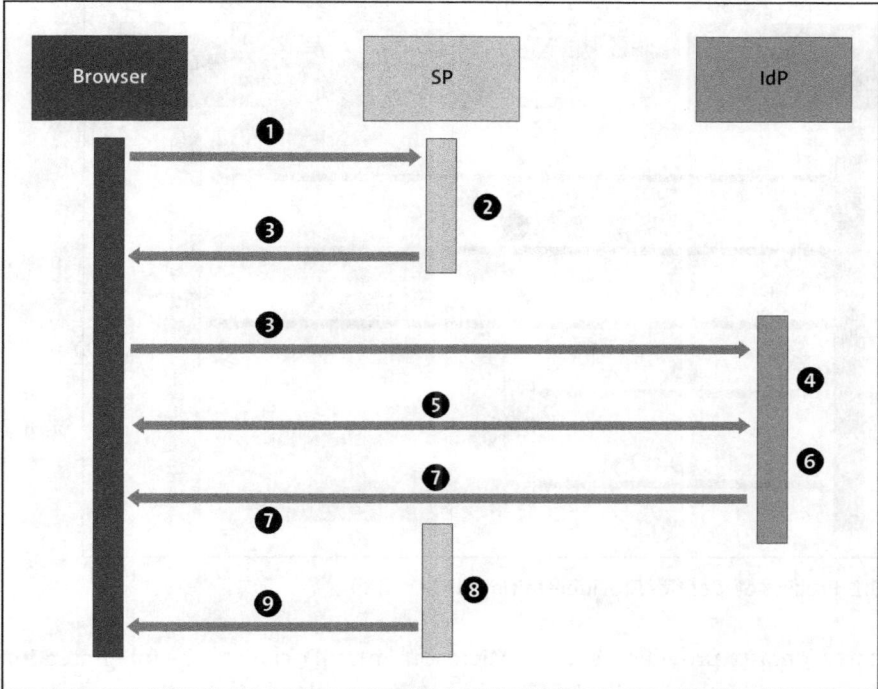

Figure 3.1 Flow of Service Provider–Initiated SSO

The process of identity provider–initiated SSO is shown in Figure 3.2. It works as follows:

❶ The user visits the identity provider's website.
❷ The user enters their login details with the identity provider.
❸ The identity provider authenticates the user and creates a SAML assertion.
❹ The SAML assertion is sent back to the browser.
❺ The browser sends the user information along with the SAML response to the application.
❻ The service provider checks the signature of the SAML response, validates it, and carries out a correction check for the user.
❼ The application provides the desired resource.

SAML is supported on SAP BTP for various scenarios. SAP provides SAP BTP in two technology stacks: the old Neo environment and the new multicloud environment. In the Neo environment, SAML was used exclusively because OIDC had only been published in 2014 and was not available when the Neo environment was introduced. SAML 2.0 was the de facto standard at the time, and SAP relied on it. SAML 2.0 is therefore used in the Neo environment for the integration of Identity Authentication in the role of platform identity provider and as application identity provider.

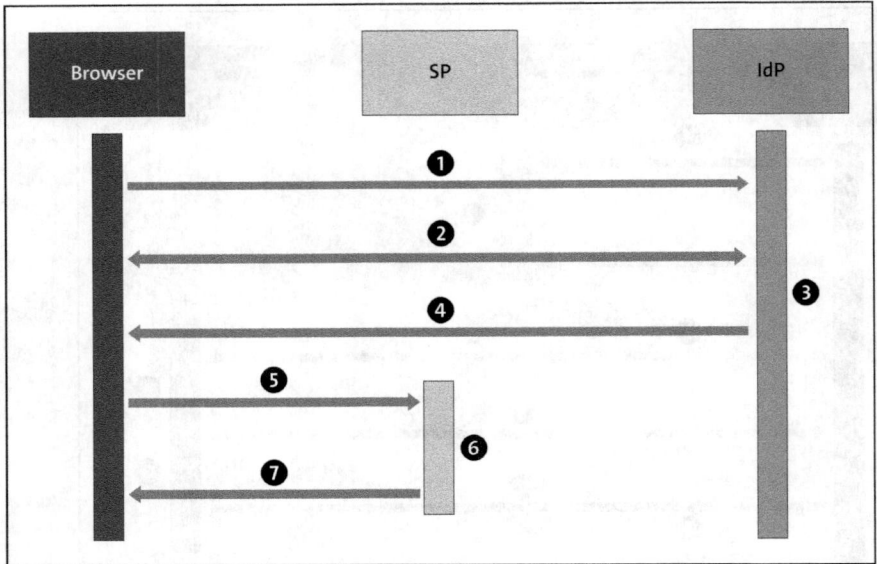

Figure 3.2 Process of Identity Provider–Initiated SSO

Third-party identity providers, such as Microsoft Entra ID, can also be integrated into the Neo environment as application identity providers via SAML 2.0. For more details and practical examples, refer to Chapter 5 of this book.

In the Cloud Foundry environment, you can use SAML 2.0 for the integration of third-party identity providers as application identity providers. The Identity Authentication service is connected in the Cloud Foundry environment both as a platform identity provider and as an application identity provider exclusively via OIDC.

3.2 OpenID Connect

OpenID Connect is an authentication protocol that enables user authentication and authorization via third-party identity providers. It is based on the OAuth 2.0 protocol and offers additional functions for the secure management of user identities and access tokens. Before we look at the details of OIDC, let's first explain OAuth 2.0.

OAuth 2.0 is a protocol for the authorization of web applications and APIs. It allows an application to access the resources of another application without requiring the user's login data. OAuth 2.0 is based on the principle of consent, meaning the user grants permission to an application to access their resources, and the application can then request a token from an authorization server that confirms the user's permission. OAuth 2.0 simplifies the implementation of authorization for client developers while offering specific authorization processes for different application types. The OAuth 2.0 standard and its extensions are defined by the Internet Engineering Task Force (IETF). The framework is specified in Request for Comments (RFC) 6749; RFCs are collections of internet specifications. OAuth 2.0 defines four roles within the authorization process:

- **Resource**
  The resource owner is an entity that can grant access to a protected resource. If the resource owner is a person, they are referred to as a *user*.
- **Resource server**
  The server on which the protected resources are hosted can accept and respond to requests for protected resources using access tokens. That makes it the resource server.
- **Client**
  The client is an application that requests protected resources on behalf of the resource owner and with their permission. The term *client* does not imply any special implementation features (e.g., a form factor or the type of device).
- **Authorization server**
  The server that issues access tokens to the client after the resource owner has been successfully authenticated and authorized is called the *authorization server*.

To request an access token, the client receives authorization from the resource owner. The authorization is expressed in the form of an authorization grant. The client then uses this authorization to request the access token (see Figure 3.3).

OAuth 2.0 defines four types of authorization (*grant types*):

- Via an authorization code
- Via an implicit authorization
- Via the login data (password) of the resource owner
- Via the login data of the client (the client credentials)

OAuth 2.0 also provides an extension mechanism for defining additional types of authorization. OAuth 2.0 offers a variety of use cases, including the following:

- **Social login**
  Users can log into applications with their social media accounts.
- **SSO**
  Users can log into multiple applications with a single set of credentials.
- **API authentication**
  Applications can access protected resources and services without users having to enter their credentials.

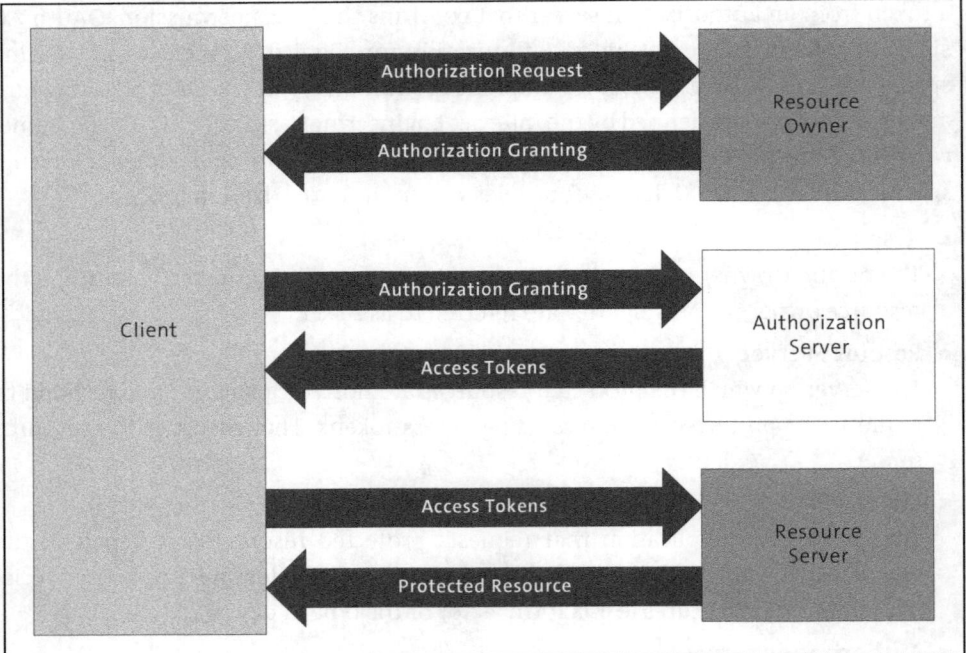

Figure 3.3 Authorization Process Flow with OAuth 2.0

Now that you have a clearer idea of OAuth 2.0, let's go back to OIDC and look at how the two protocols interact. Both OAuth 2.0 and OIDC are open-standard protocols used for authentication and authorization of users. OAuth 2.0 is an authorization protocol that allows an application to access another application's resources without the application needing to know the user's credentials. OIDC is an authentication protocol that enables users to authenticate themselves to an application by authenticating themselves to an identity provider. OIDC is based on OAuth 2.0 and adds additional features to simplify and improve authentication, including the following:

- **JSON Web Token–based authentication**
  OIDC uses JSON Web Tokens (JWTs) to transmit the identity and authorization of the user. JWTs are compact, signed tokens that can be transmitted securely over the network.

- **Centralized authentication**
  OIDC allows users to authenticate to an application by authenticating to an identity provider. This simplifies the authentication process for users and makes it easier to comply with security guidelines.

- **Decentralized identity management**
  OIDC enables identity providers to manage the identity data of users, simplifying the management of user data and improving security.

Now, let's explain JWTs in more detail as they are the central element in connection with OIDC. A JWT consists of three parts, separated by dots:

- **Header**
  The header contains information about the token, such as the signature method used.
- **Payload**
  The payload contains the actual data of the token, such as the identity and authorization of the user.
- **Signature**
  The signature is a digital signature that guarantees the integrity of the token.

Figure 3.4 shows an example of a JWT and its decoded representation.

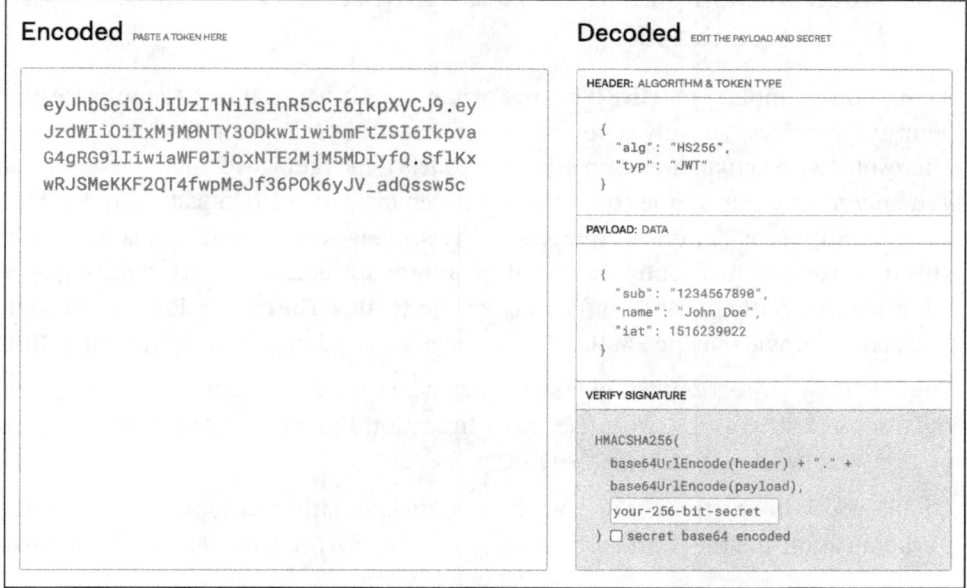

Figure 3.4 Example of JWT

OAuth 2.0 and OIDC work together to allow users to log in to an application safely and easily. Here's how it's done:

1. The user wants to log in to an application.
2. The application asks the user to prove who they are to an identity provider.
3. The user enters their login details with the identity provider.
4. The identity provider checks the user's identity and authorizes them.
5. The application receives the JWT from the identity provider.
6. The application uses the JWT to check whether the user is allowed to access the resources they're trying to access.

OAuth 2.0 is responsible for authorizing the application that the resource owner wants to access. OIDC is responsible for authenticating the user, transmitting the user's identity, and authorizing the user to the application.

OIDC is used at various points in the multicloud environment of SAP BTP. At the global account level, Identity Authentication can be connected using OIDC as an identity provider for global account users. In addition, Identity Authentication is integrated into the multicloud environment at the subaccount level, acting as both a platform identity provider and an application identity provider, again with the help of OIDC. If Identity Authentication is used as a proxy to a third-party identity provider, OIDC can be used for the connection.

3.3 Practical Example: Identity Authentication as a Proxy to Microsoft Entra ID

A common example in practice is the use of Identity Authentication as a proxy to other identity providers. This gives you the option of using Microsoft Entra ID (formerly Microsoft Azure Active Directory) in proxy mode. The advantage of this approach is that you only must establish the connection between Identity Authentication and a third-party identity provider once, regardless of how many subaccounts it is later used in. This reduces the initial configuration effort and the administration effort during operation. Identity Authentication offers two options for this: The first option is to integrate the identity provider using SAML 2.0, and the second option is to integrate using OIDC.

The following two sections will give step-by-step instructions for how to configure Identity Authentication and Microsoft Entra ID. In Section 3.3.1, we use SAML 2.0 for the integration, and in Section 3.3.2, we use OIDC.

To follow our instructions, you must have sufficient authorizations in both Identity Authentication and the third-party identity provider (in this case, Microsoft Entra ID).

3.3.1 Integrate Microsoft Entra ID into Identity Authentication with SAML 2.0

In the context of SAML, the Identity Authentication Service now takes the role of the service provider and Microsoft Entra ID takes the role of the identity provider. As usual in SAML configuration, metadata must be exchanged between the service provider and the identity provider. Therefore, you must first locate the metadata for your Identity Authentication instance and download it to your computer.

First, log onto Identity Authentication. You will see the initial screen (see Figure 3.5). In the **Applications & Resources** area, click the **Tenant Settings** tile.

Go to the **Applications & Resources** tab and select the desired application from the list (**clouddna** in our example). In the view that opens, click the **SAML 2.0 Configuration** entry in the **Single Sign-On** area (see Figure 3.6).

3.3 Practical Example: Identity Authentication as a Proxy to Microsoft Entra ID

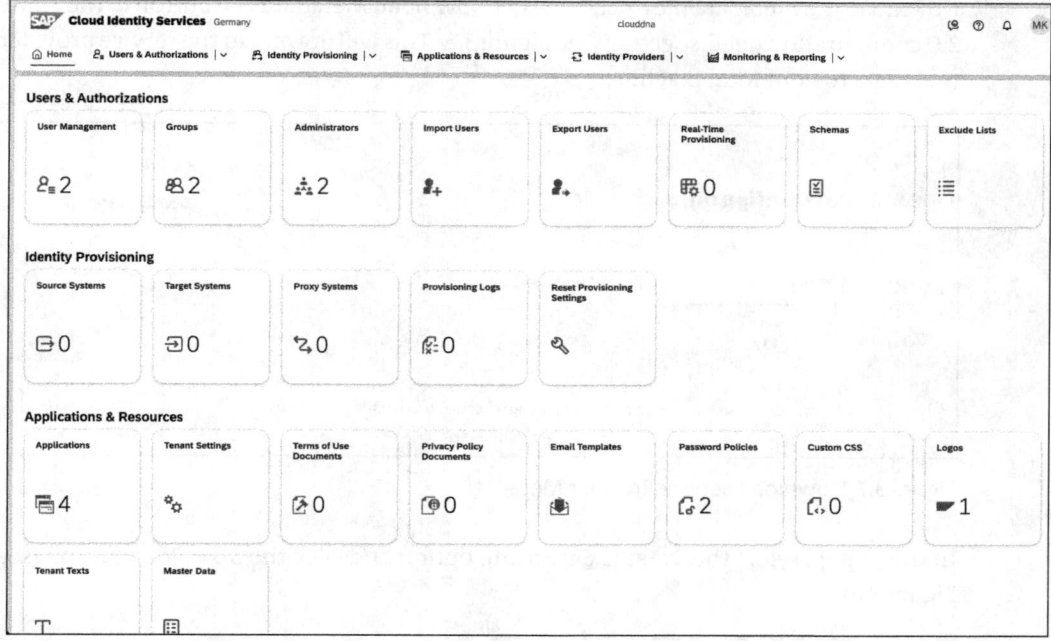

Figure 3.5 Start Screen of Identity Authentication

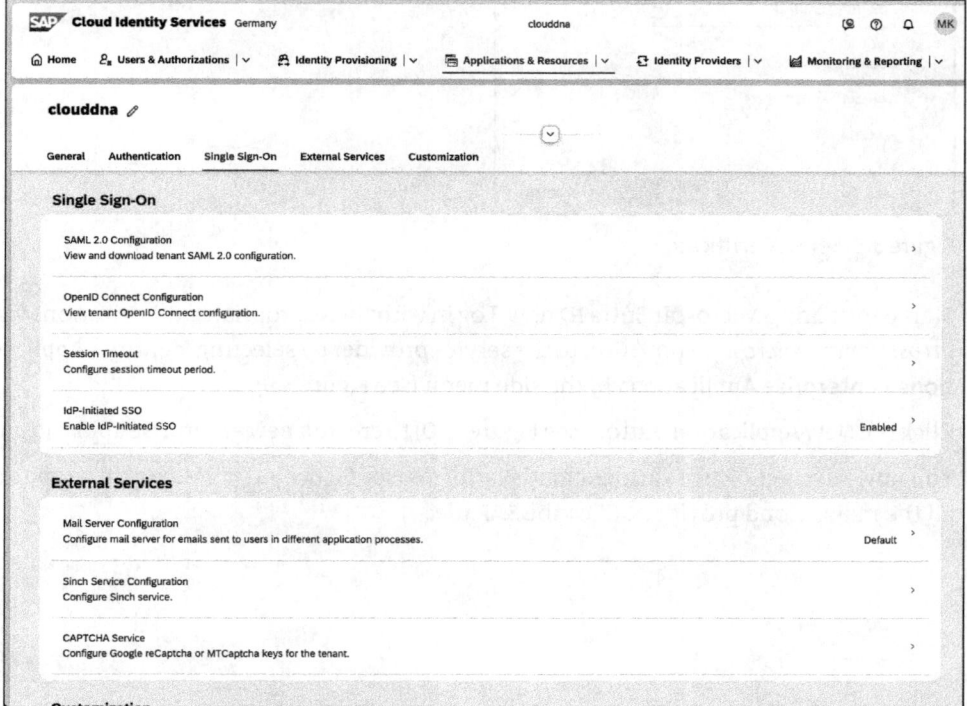

Figure 3.6 Open SAML 2.0 Configuration

Download the metadata file by clicking the **Download Metadata File** button in the SAML 2.0 configuration details section (see Figure 3.7). This will download the service provider metadata to your local machine.

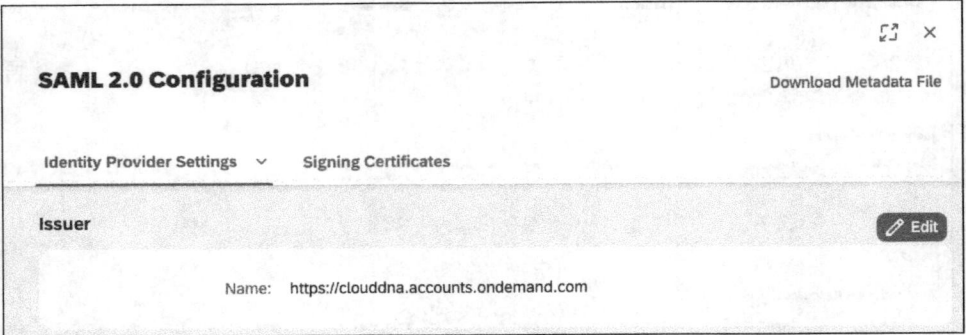

Figure 3.7 Download Service Provider Metadata

In the popup, select the **Default Certificate** option and click the **Download** button (see Figure 3.8).

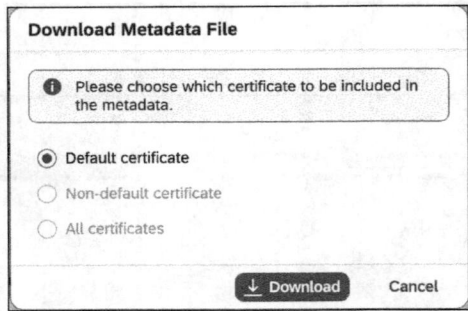

Figure 3.8 Select Certificate

Start configuring Microsoft Entra ID now. Log in with the appropriate authorizations via *https://entra.microsoft.com/*. Create the service provider by selecting **Identity • Applications • Enterprise Applications** in the side menu (see Figure 3.9).

Click the **New Application** button (see Figure 3.10) to create a new enterprise application.

You now have a choice of various cloud platforms (see Figure 3.11) as Microsoft supports all the major cloud providers. Click the **SAP** tile.

3.3 Practical Example: Identity Authentication as a Proxy to Microsoft Entra ID

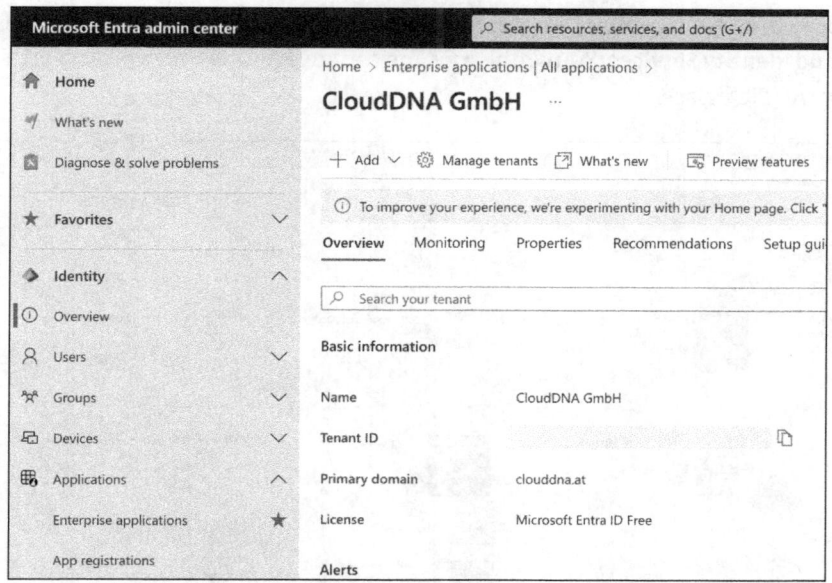

Figure 3.9 Launch Enterprise Applications

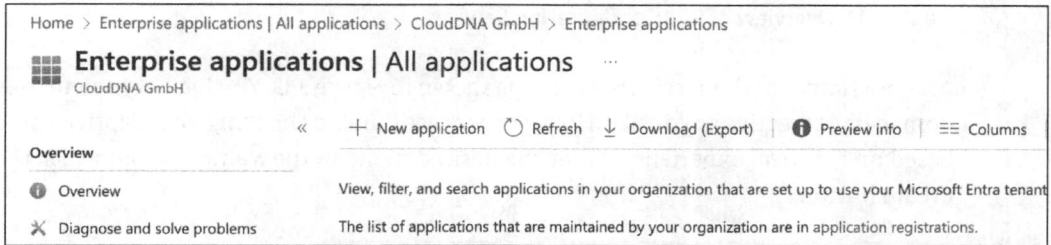

Figure 3.10 Create New Enterprise Application

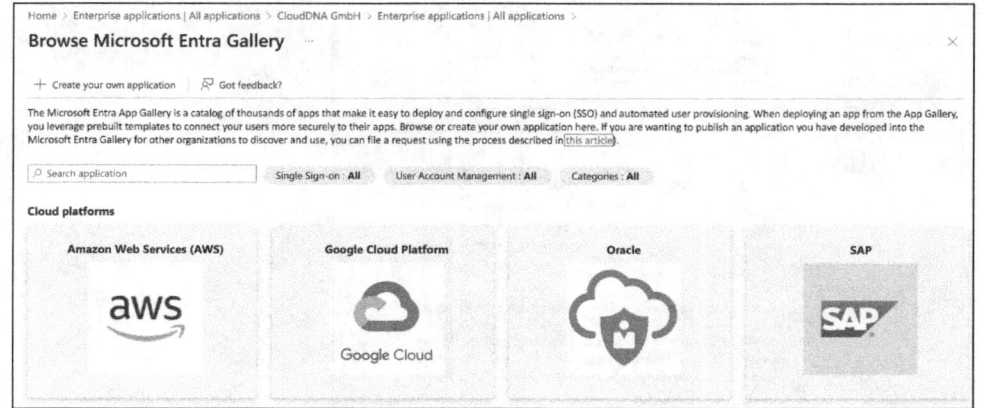

Figure 3.11 Select Cloud Platform

You can choose from a range of SAP applications here (see Figure 3.12). For this example, click **SAP Cloud Identity Services**. You can also perform a configuration for SAP Analytics Cloud or for SAP Fieldglass.

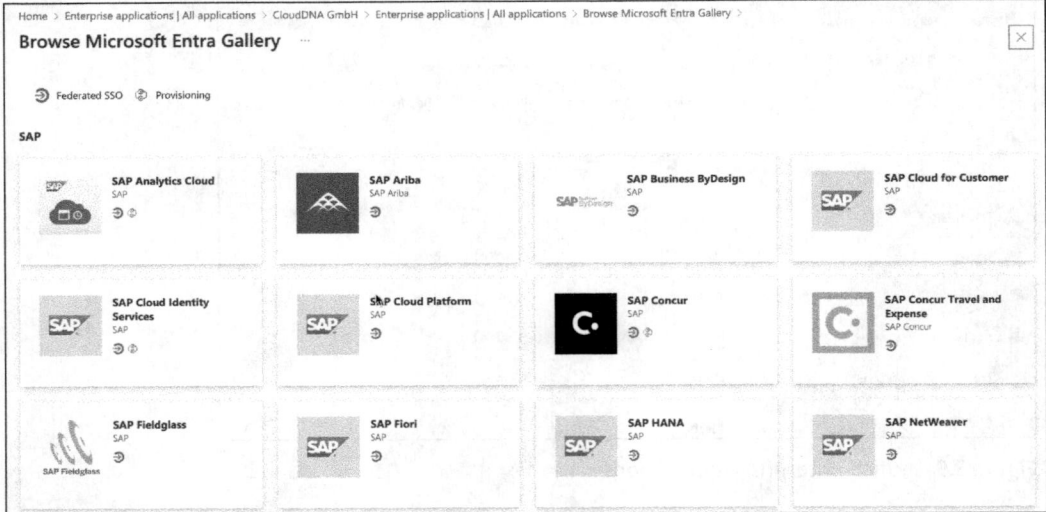

Figure 3.12 Overview of SAP Configuration Services

Assign a **Name** for the service provider, as shown in Figure 3.13. You have complete freedom to be as creative as you like. However, we recommend choosing a descriptive name based on practical experience. Enter the desired name in the **Name** field and click the **Create** button.

Figure 3.13 Assign Service Provider Names

3.3 Practical Example: Identity Authentication as a Proxy to Microsoft Entra ID

It takes a few seconds to create the enterprise application. You will then be redirected to the enterprise application details page, as shown in Figure 3.14. Click the **Set Up Single Sign-On** tile.

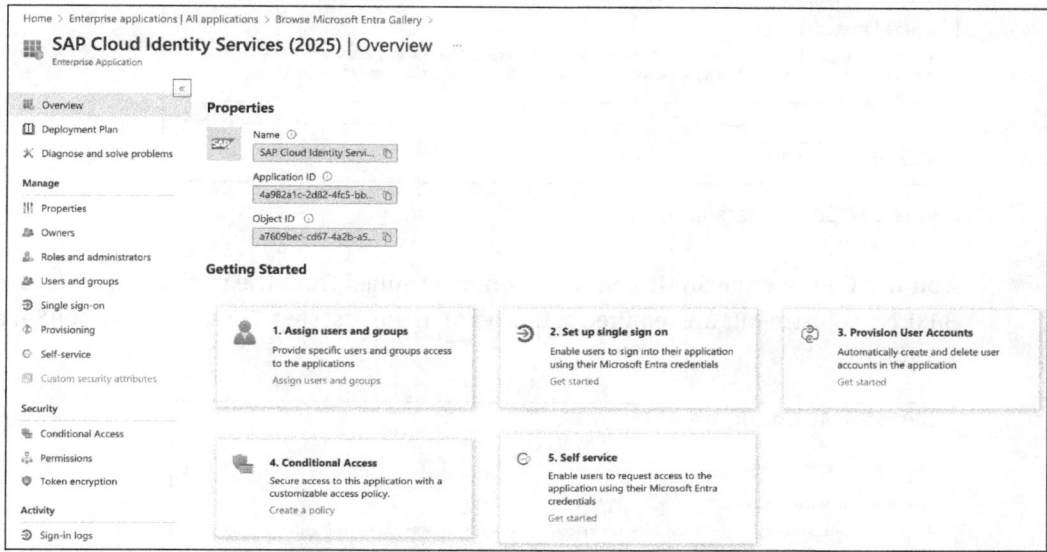

Figure 3.14 Enterprise Application Overview

Now select SAML as the single sign-on method (see Figure 3.15) by clicking the **SAML** tile.

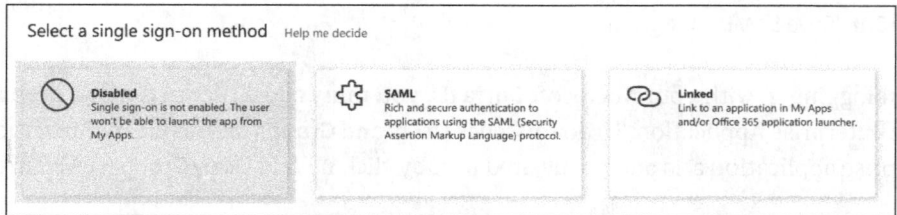

Figure 3.15 Select Single Sign-on Method

Now you need to upload the metadata. To do this, click the **Upload Metadata File** button (see Figure 3.16).

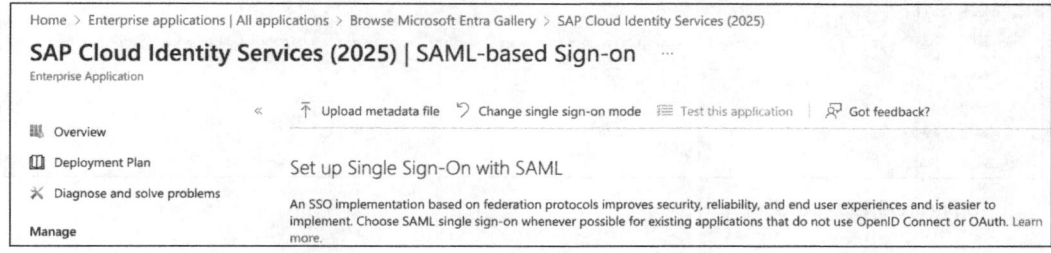

Figure 3.16 Upload Metadata

123

3 Advanced Identity Authentication Service Topics

Now select the service provider (Identity Authentication) metadata file that you previously downloaded to your computer. Then click the **Add** button to upload the metadata (see Figure 3.17).

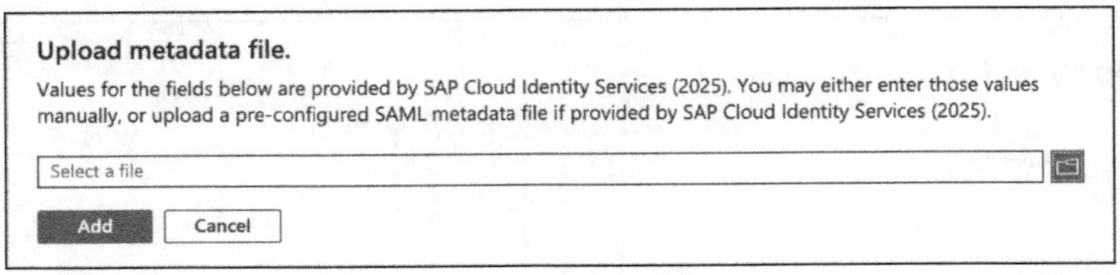

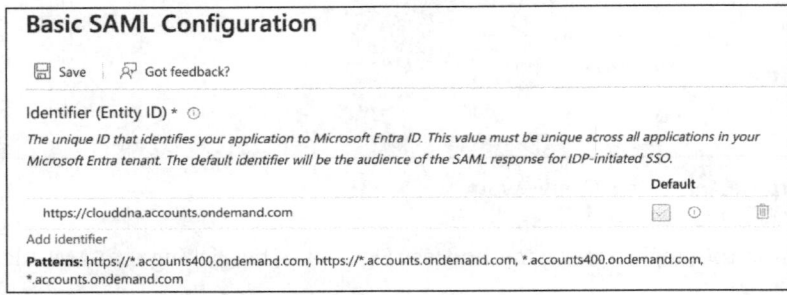

Figure 3.17 Select Metadata

You will then see the SAML configuration determined from the metadata (see Figure 3.18). No adjustments are required at this point in the first step. Therefore, click the **Save** button.

Figure 3.18 Save SAML Configuration

To test logging in with your Microsoft Entra ID, you must add either a user or a group to the Enterprise Application. To do this, click **Users and Groups** in the side menu of the enterprise application and add the desired user by clicking **Add User/Group** (see Figure 3.19).

Figure 3.19 Add User

3.3 Practical Example: Identity Authentication as a Proxy to Microsoft Entra ID

You are now ready to download the identity provider metadata. To do this, navigate to the **Single Sign-On** section in the **Enterprise Application** side menu. In the **SAML Certificates** section, click the **Download** link next to the **Federation Metadata XML** entry. This will save the metadata to your local computer (see Figure 3.20).

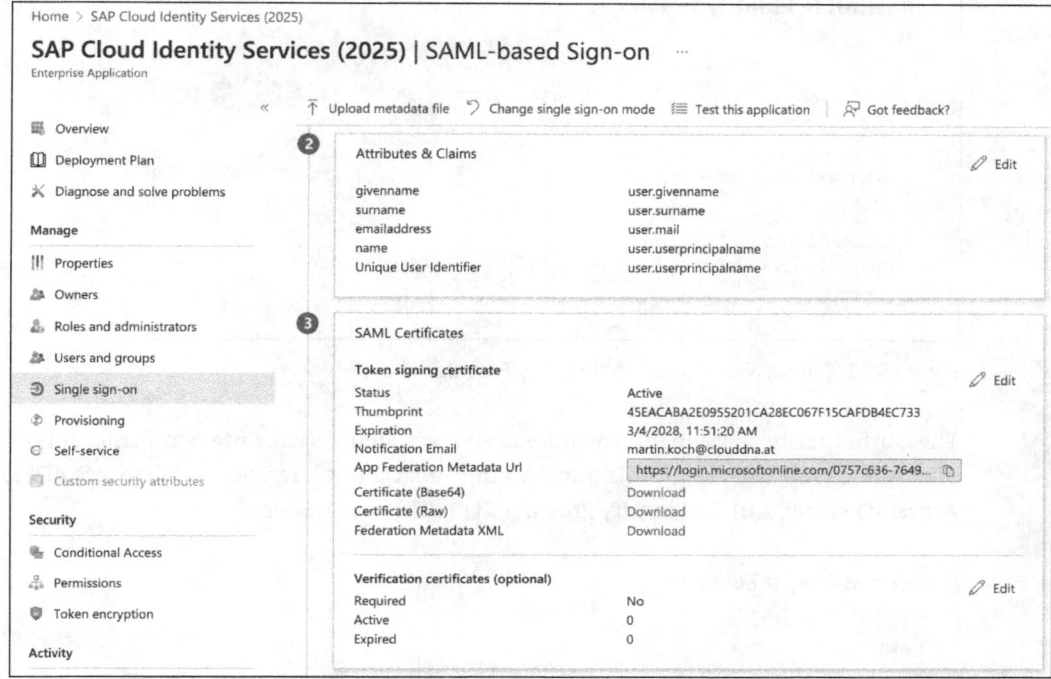

Figure 3.20 Download Metadata from Identity Provider

Now you need to import the metadata you just downloaded from the identity provider into Identity Authentication. To do this, you need to create something called a *corporate identity provider*. Therefore, expand the **Identity Providers** menu and click **Corporate Identity Providers** (see Figure 3.21).

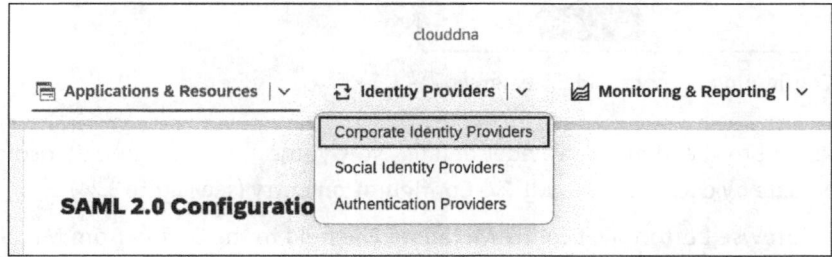

Figure 3.21 Go to Corporate Identity Providers

Now click the **Create** button to create a new identity provider (see Figure 3.22).

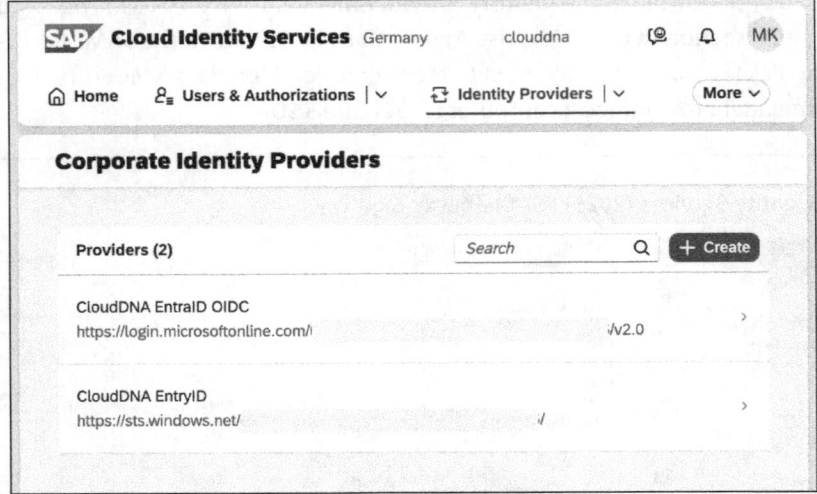

Figure 3.22 Create New Corporate Identity Provider

The configuration is done in a separate dialog (see Figure 3.23). Enter a meaningful **Display Name**. You will assign this name to the subaccount later. Select **Microsoft ADFS/ Azure AD (SAML 2.0)** for **Identity Provider Type**. Then click **Save**.

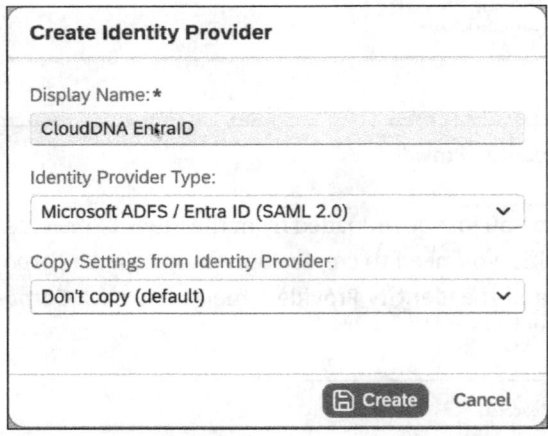

Figure 3.23 Configuring Corporate Identity Provider

This will take you to the identity provider details. Now you can upload the Microsoft Entra ID metadata by clicking the **SAML 2.0 Configuration** entry (see Figure 3.24).

Now click the **Browse** button next to the **Metadata File** field in the **Define from Metadata** area (see Figure 3.25).

3.3 Practical Example: Identity Authentication as a Proxy to Microsoft Entra ID

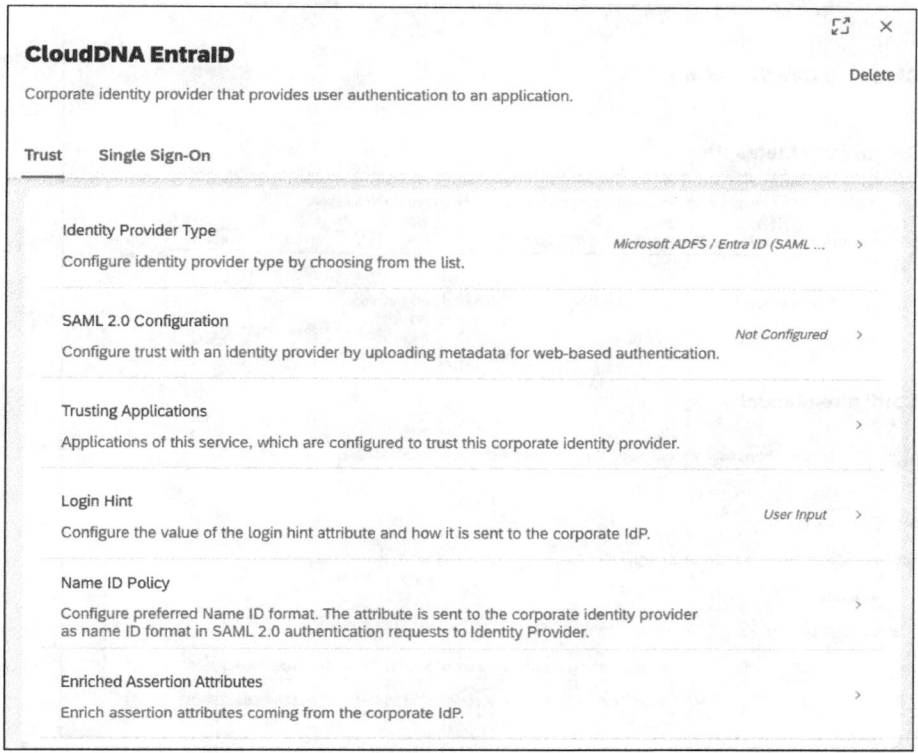

Figure 3.24 Configure SAML 2.0

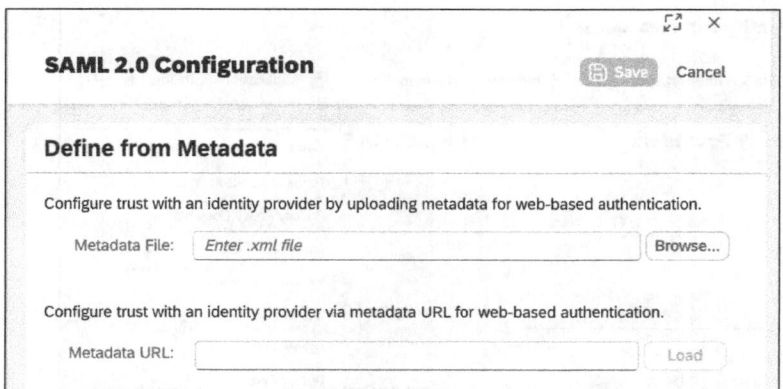

Figure 3.25 Begin Uploading Metadata from Microsoft Entra ID

Select the previously downloaded metadata, then click **Save** (see Figure 3.26).

The easiest way to test the configuration is to store it in the conditional authentication of a subaccount. To do this, navigate to the **Applications & Resources · Applications** path (see Figure 3.27).

3   Advanced Identity Authentication Service Topics

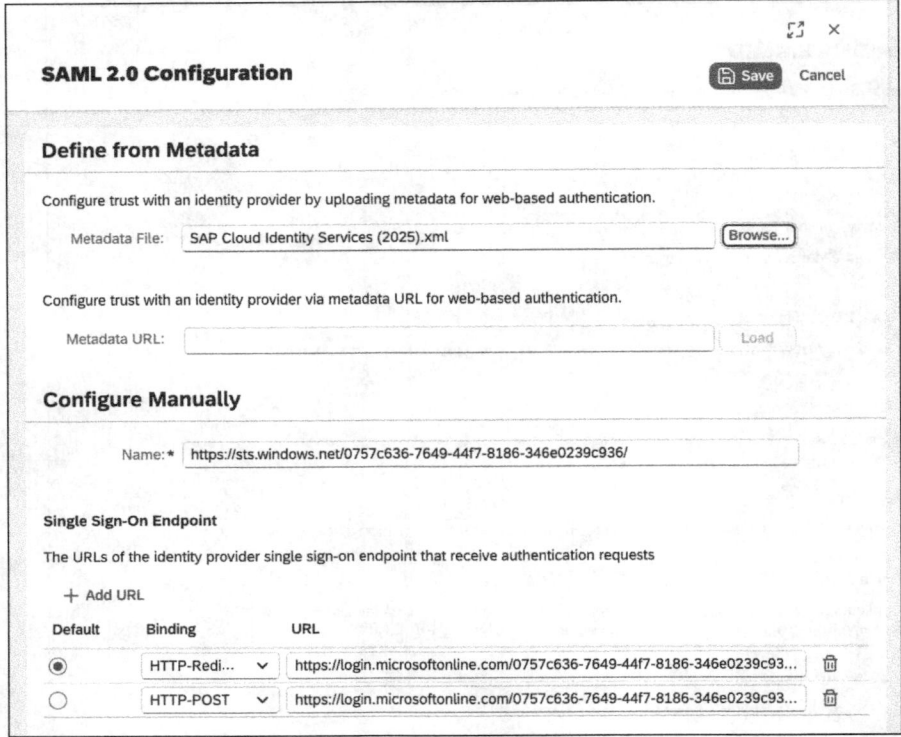

Figure 3.26 Save SAML 2.0 Configuration

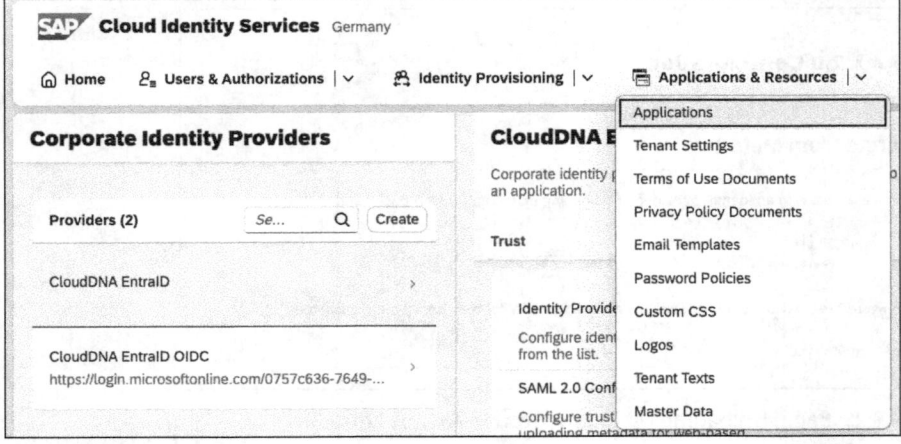

Figure 3.27 Open Applications

From the side menu, select a subaccount that is registered with Identity Authentication. In this example, we have already created a subaccount called IAS Proxy Demo and set up a trust with Identity Authentication. Click the **Conditional Authentication** entry in the details in the **Conditional Authentication** section (see Figure 3.28).

3.3 Practical Example: Identity Authentication as a Proxy to Microsoft Entra ID

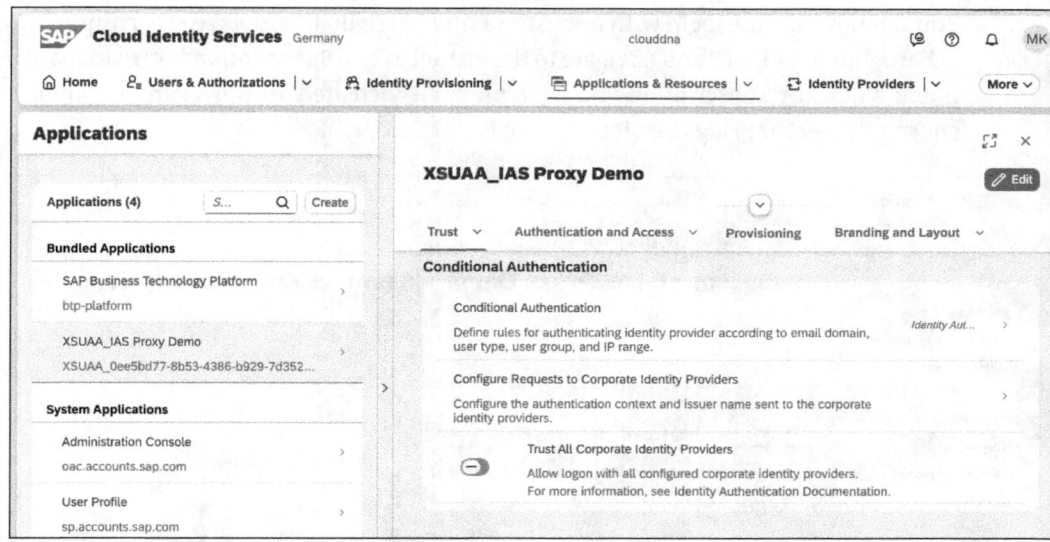

Figure 3.28 Jump to Conditional Authentication of Subaccount

In the **Default Authenticating Identity Provider** section, select the corporate identity provider you just created in the **Default Identity Provider** field, then click **Save** (see Figure 3.29).

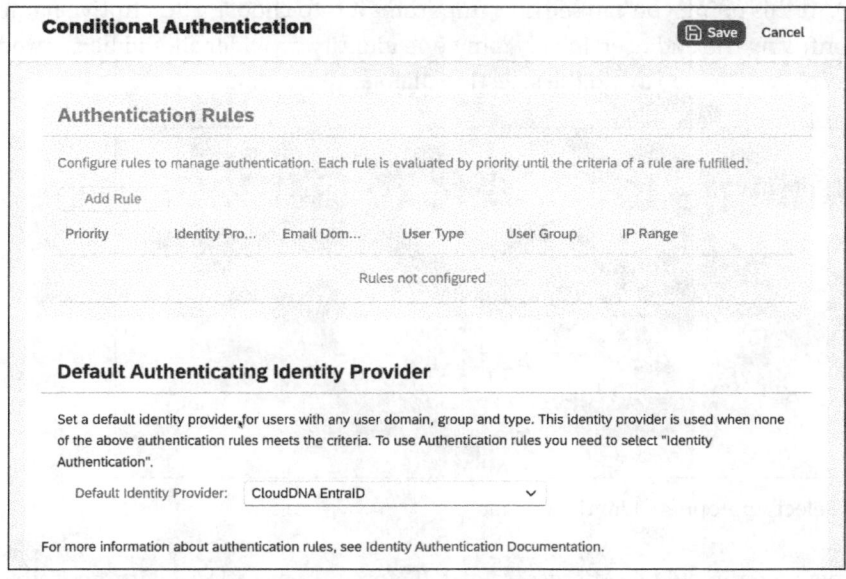

Figure 3.29 Select Default Identity Provider

This tells Identity Authentication that user authentication for this subaccount should always be performed against the Microsoft Entra ID and not against the user store in Identity Authentication.

3   Advanced Identity Authentication Service Topics

You can now test the login with Microsoft Entra ID. To do this, open the corresponding subaccount in SAP BTP and navigate to the **Instances and Subscriptions** entry in the side menu. Click any subscription you have previously created. In this example, we have chosen the **Feature Flags Service** app (see Figure 3.30).

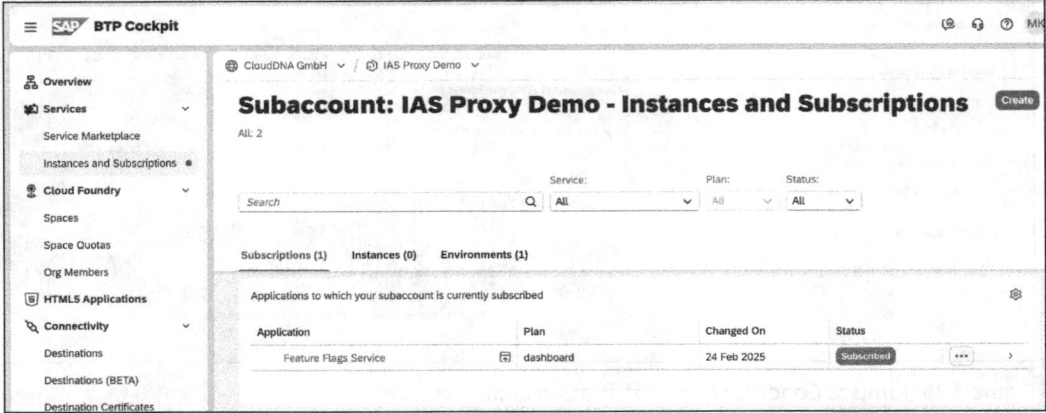

Figure 3.30 Open Subscription

If more than one identity provider has been configured and these identity providers are enabled for enrollment, you must now select the identity provider you want to use (see Figure 3.31). At this point, you can see how important it is to choose a descriptive name to avoid confusing the end user. Ideally, only one identity provider should be allowed to register. This will let you avoid the selection dialog.

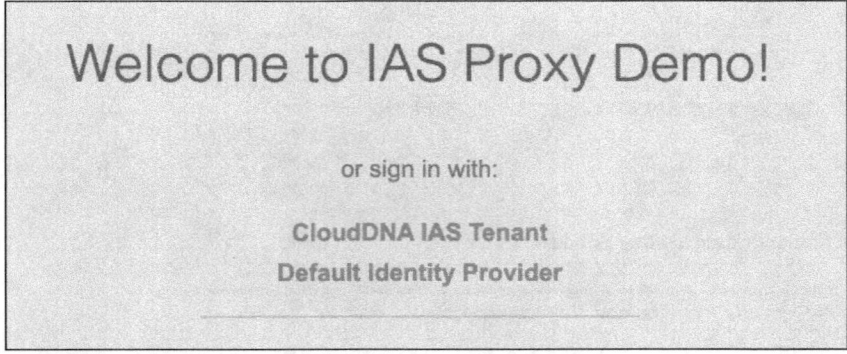

Figure 3.31 Select Appropriate Identity Provider

You will now be redirected to Microsoft Entra ID for authentication—with no visible contact to Identity Authentication. Once there, you can log in with your username and password.

3.3 Practical Example: Identity Authentication as a Proxy to Microsoft Entra ID

After successful login, you are redirected to the Feature Flags Service application (see Figure 3.32). There you will see an authorization error. This means that you have completed the authentication, but the authorization checks have not yet been completed. Therefore, it is necessary to assign the appropriate role collections to the user. This can be done either directly or via security groups derived from Microsoft Entra ID.

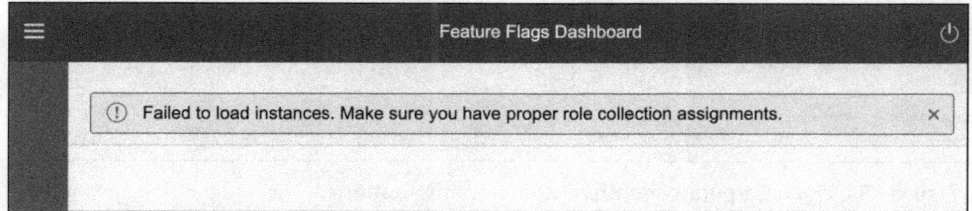

Figure 3.32 Error Message in Feature Flags Service App

3.3.2 Integrate Microsoft Entra ID into Identity Authentication with OpenID Connect

Integration using OIDC differs from SAML-based configuration because OIDC is based on OAuth 2.0. The first step is to determine the tenant ID in Microsoft Entra ID (see Figure 3.33).

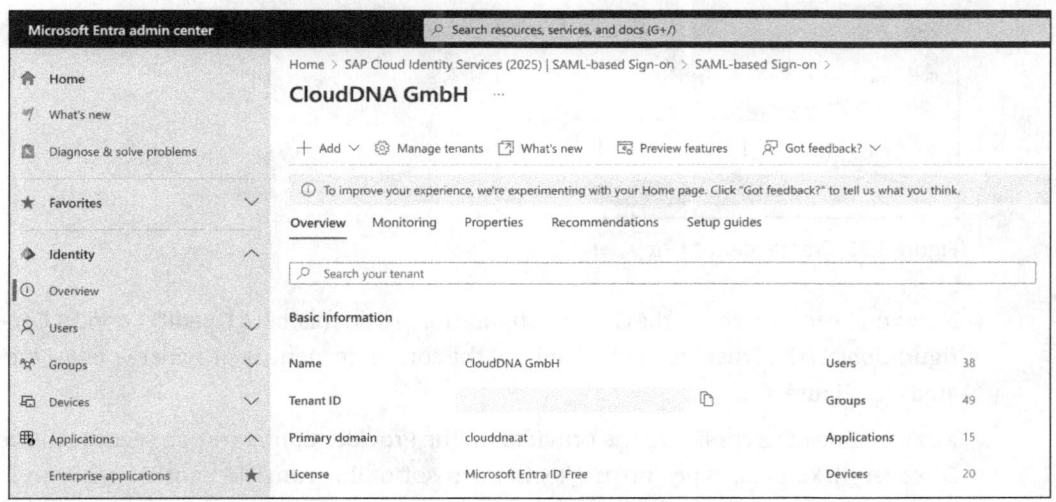

Figure 3.33 Determine Tenant ID from Microsoft Entra ID

Next, you need to set up a corporate identity provider in Identity Authentication. To do this, navigate to **Identity Providers • Corporate Identity Providers** in the menu, as shown in Figure 3.34.

3 Advanced Identity Authentication Service Topics

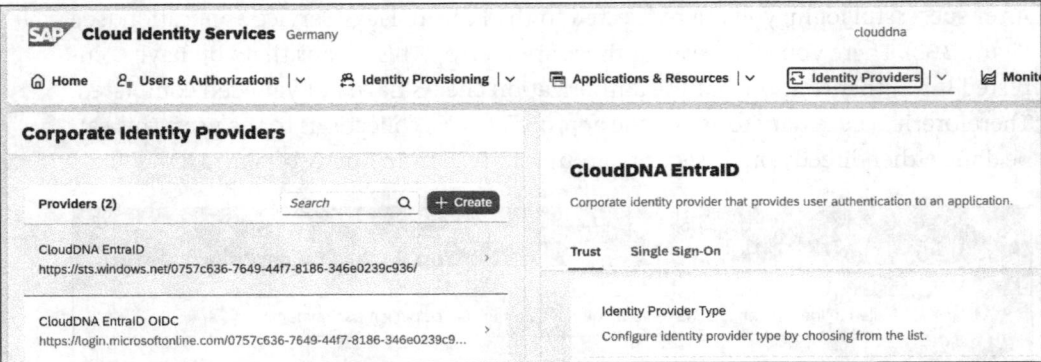

Figure 3.34 Open Corporate Identity Provider Configuration

Create a new enterprise identity provider. Enter a descriptive name in the **Display Name** field and select **OpenID Connect Compliant** in the **Identity Provider Type** field. Then click **Save** (see Figure 3.35).

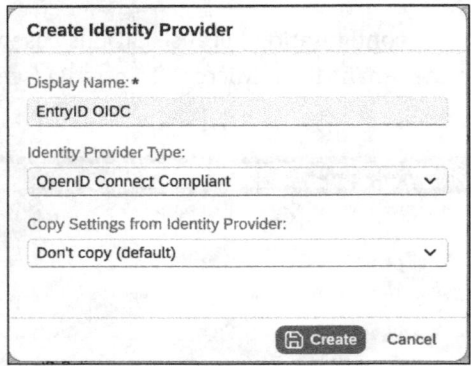

Figure 3.35 Create Identity Provider

Now you need to perform the OIDC configuration. To do this, click **OpenID Connect Configuration** on the **Trust** tab in the details of the corporate identity provider you just created (see Figure 3.36).

Next, you need to configure the provider. In the **Provider Configuration** section, in the **Discovery URL** field, type "https://login.microsoftonline.com/<TenantID>/v2.0/.well-known/openid-configuration" (see Figure 3.37), but replace "<TenantID>" with the Microsoft Entra ID tenant ID you determined earlier. Then click the **Load** button. The remaining configuration fields will be filled in automatically. Save these settings.

3.3 Practical Example: Identity Authentication as a Proxy to Microsoft Entra ID

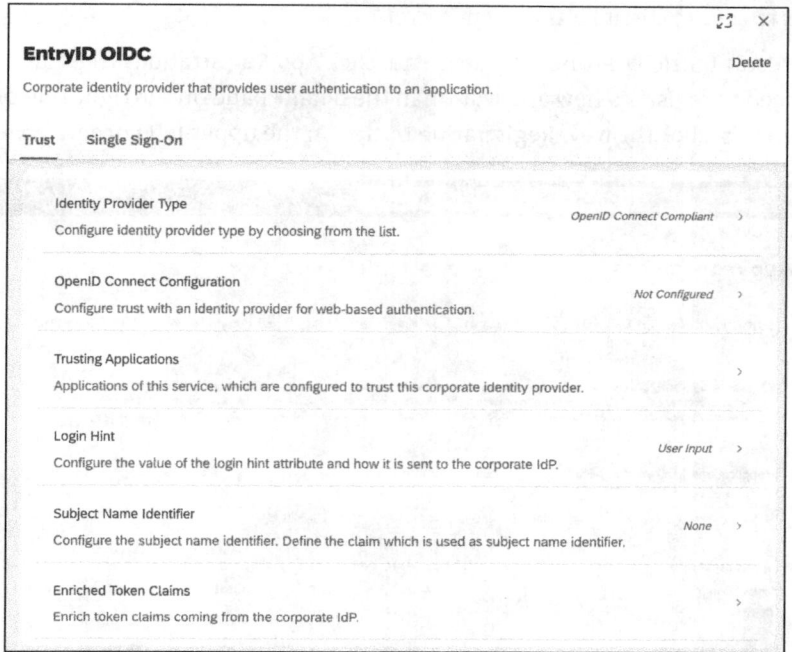

Figure 3.36 Open OIDC Configuration

Figure 3.37 Enter Discovery URL

3   Advanced Identity Authentication Service Topics

The next step is to set the client ID and client secret.

Go back to Microsoft Entra ID. From the side menu, click **App Registrations** (see Figure 3.38). You will need to register a new application in the details pane on the right side of the screen. To do this, click the **New Registration** button in the upper-left corner.

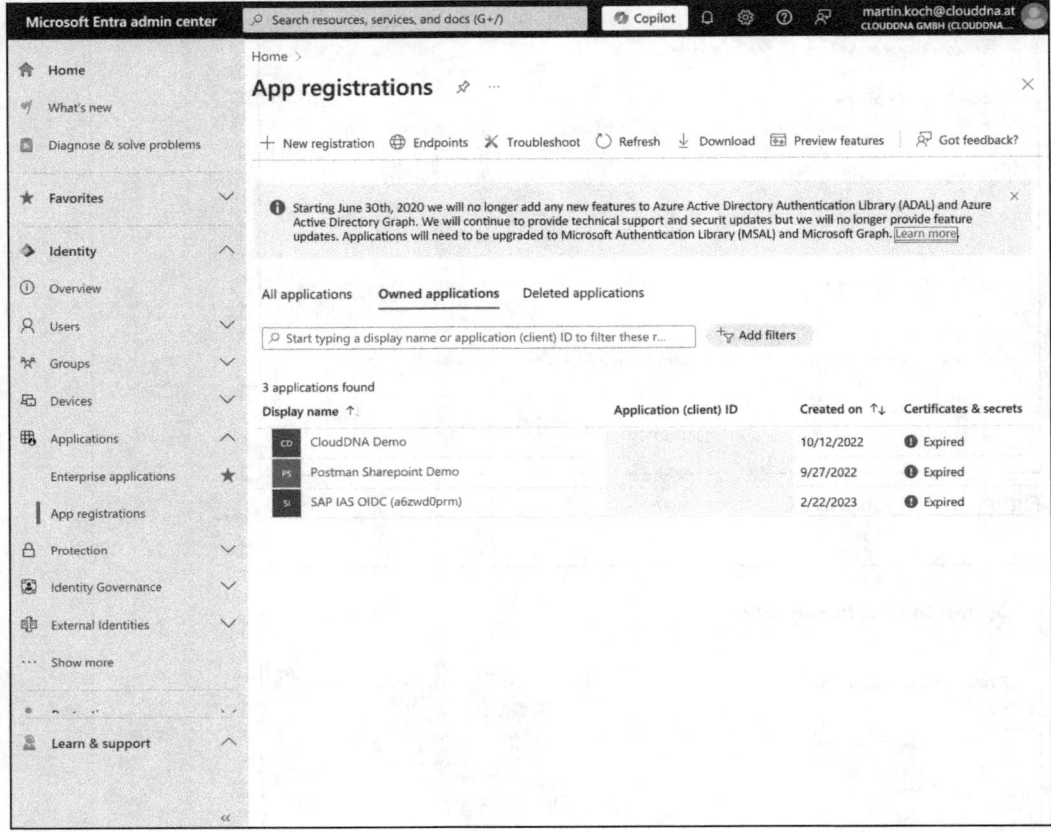

Figure 3.38 App Registration Overview

Again, type a meaningful name in the **Name** field. Select the **Accounts Only in This Organizational Directory** option (see Figure 3.39). Create a **Redirect URI** of type **Web**. Enter the host name of your Identity Authentication tenant and add the path "/oauth2/callback". The URL should look like this: *https://<iastenant>.accounts.ondemand.com/oauth2/*. Then click the **Register** button.

After registering the application, the registration details pane opens (see Figure 3.40). In the **Essentials** section, you will find an attribute called **Application (Client) ID**. Copy this ID. It is the same as the client ID that must be entered in Identity Authentication. In addition to the client ID, you also need the client secret.

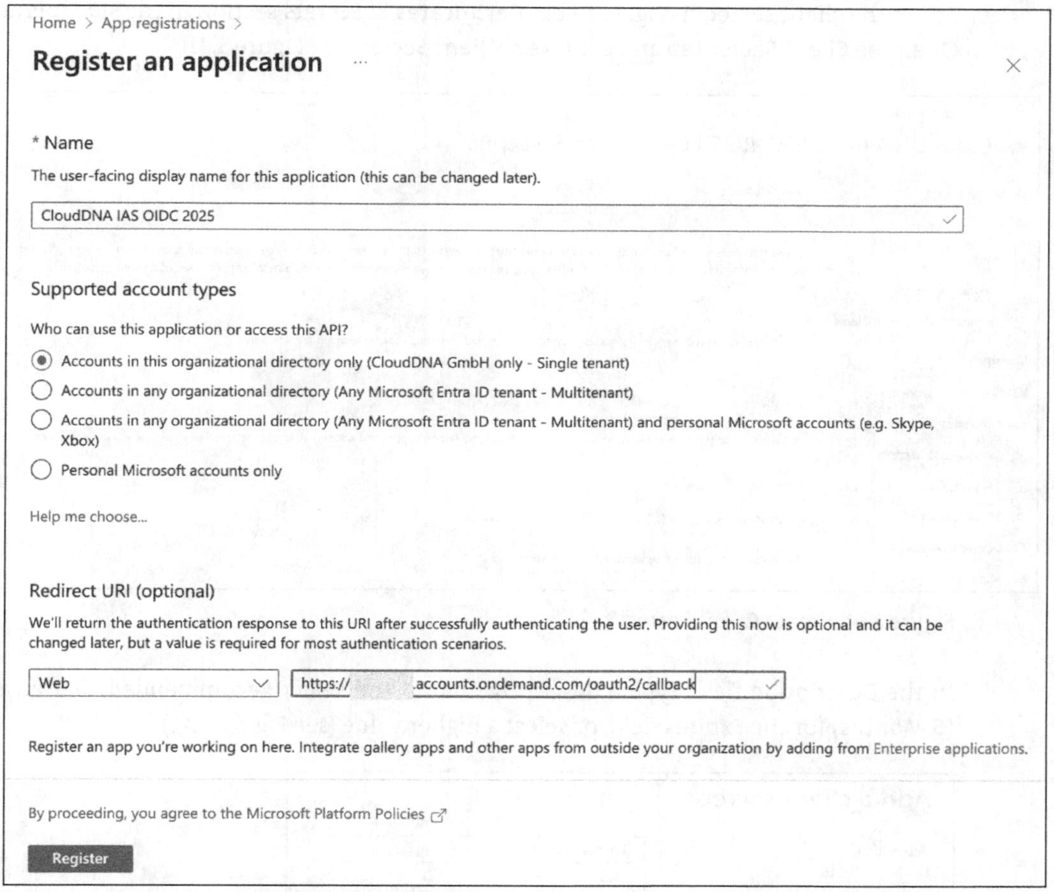

3.3 Practical Example: Identity Authentication as a Proxy to Microsoft Entra ID

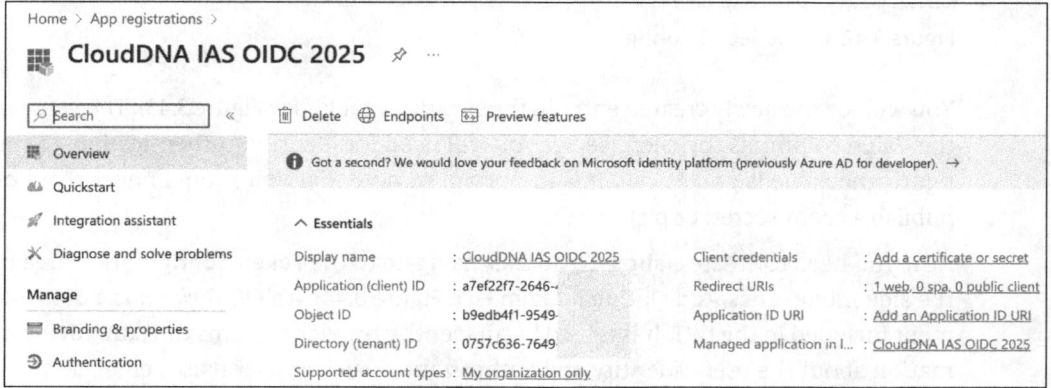

Figure 3.39 Details of App Registration

Figure 3.40 Determine Application ID

To set the client secret, navigate to the **Certificates & Secrets** section in the side menu. Open the **Client Secret** tab and click **New Client Secret** (see Figure 3.41).

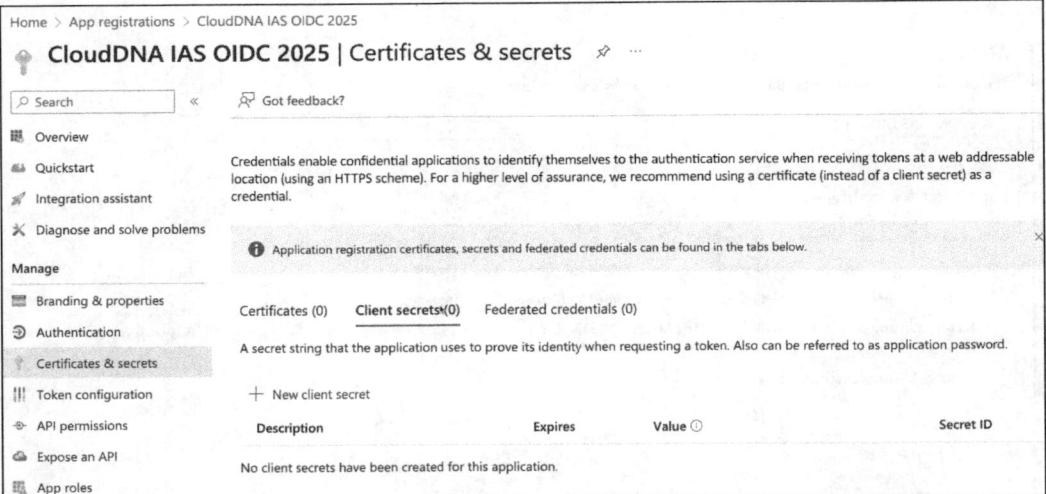

Figure 3.41 Create Client Secret

In the **Description** field, type a descriptive name and select **Recommended: 180 days (6 Months)** for the **Expires** field, or select a higher value (see Figure 3.42).

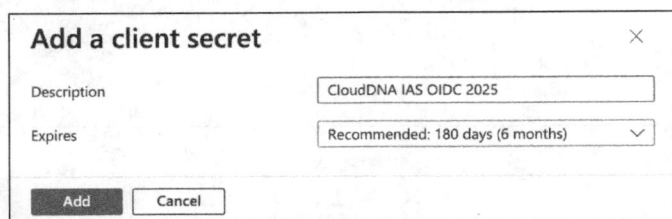

Figure 3.42 Client Secret Configuration

You will see the newly created entry in the summary table (see Figure 3.43). The value in the **Value** column is the client secret you will need for Identity Authentication. In the figure, the value is grayed out. It is important to note that you should never share or publish a client secret! Copy the value.

Now you need to create claims. To do this, navigate to the **Token Configuration** area in the side menu. Click **Add Optional Claim** (see Figure 3.44). An *OIDC claim* is a data element included in the JWT. It is issued by an identity provider. Claims can contain information about the user's identity and authorization, such as user name, email address, roles, or permissions.

Select **ID** for **Token Type** and select the **email** claim type from the table below. Then click **Add** (see Figure 3.45).

3.3 Practical Example: Identity Authentication as a Proxy to Microsoft Entra ID

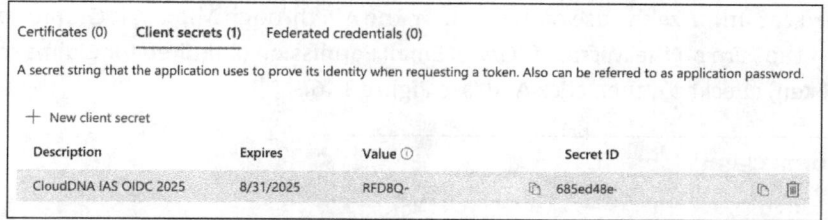

Figure 3.43 Copy Client Secret

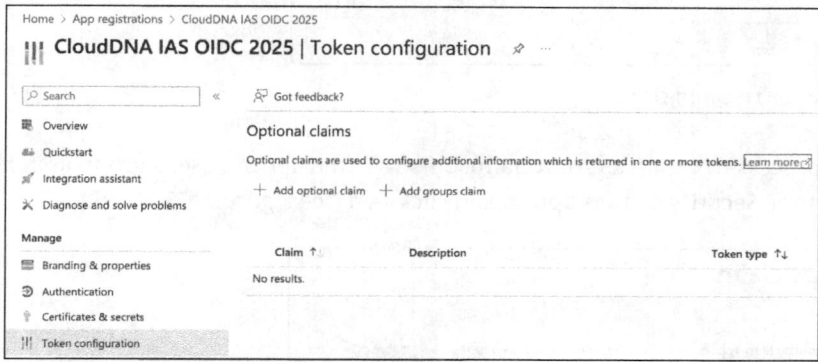

Figure 3.44 Create OIDC Claim

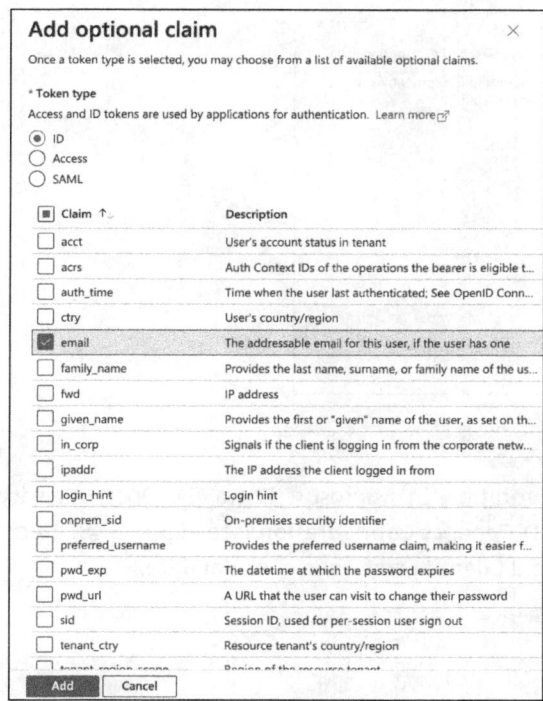

Figure 3.45 Configure OIDC Claim

3 Advanced Identity Authentication Service Topics

You now need to authorize the use of the claim in the API through Microsoft Graph. To do this, select the **Turn on the Microsoft Graph Email Permission (Required for Claims to Appear in Token)** checkbox, then click **Add** (see Figure 3.46).

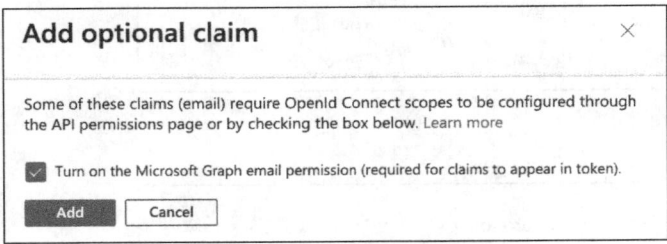

Figure 3.46 Agree to Claim Usage

Repeat this process to create a group claim. This will transfer the users' group assignments. Select the **Security Groups** option and click **Add** (see Figure 3.47).

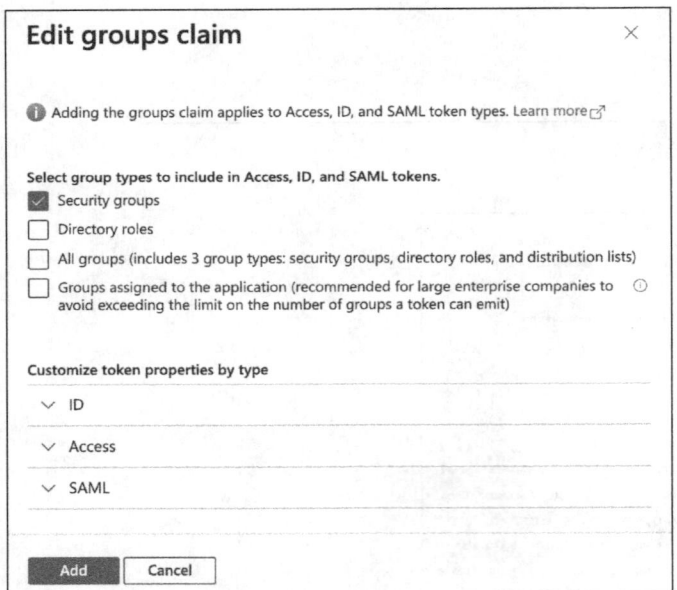

Figure 3.47 Create Groups Claim

You have now completed the configuration in Microsoft Entra ID. Open Identity Authentication and go back to **OpenID Connect Configuration** (see Figure 3.48). Enter the previously determined **Client ID** and **Client Secret**, then click **Validate**.

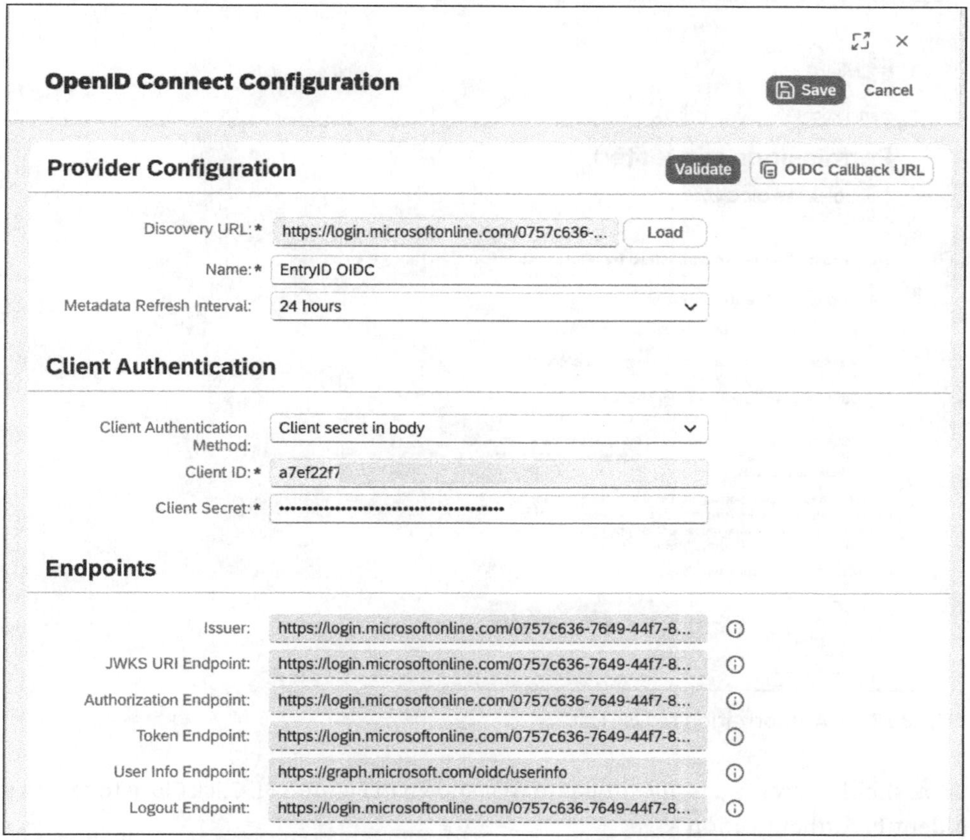

3.3 Practical Example: Identity Authentication as a Proxy to Microsoft Entra ID

Figure 3.48 Maintain Client ID and Client Secret During Identity Authentication

A message appears informing you that the validation will be performed in a separate browser tab (see Figure 3.49). Click **OK**.

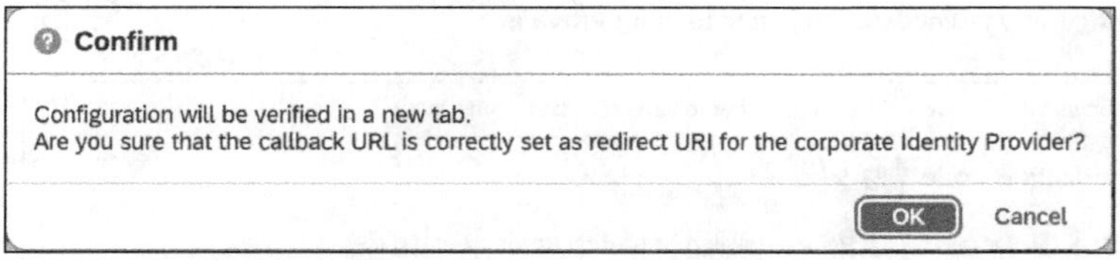

Figure 3.49 Confirm Validation in New Browser Tab

In the next step, a popup window asks you to confirm that you accept the authorization to use the data in the application on behalf of your organization. To do this, click **Accept** (see Figure 3.50).

3   Advanced Identity Authentication Service Topics

Figure 3.50 Authorization to Use Data

You should now see a result similar to that shown in Figure 3.51. Click **Close** to return to Identity Authentication.

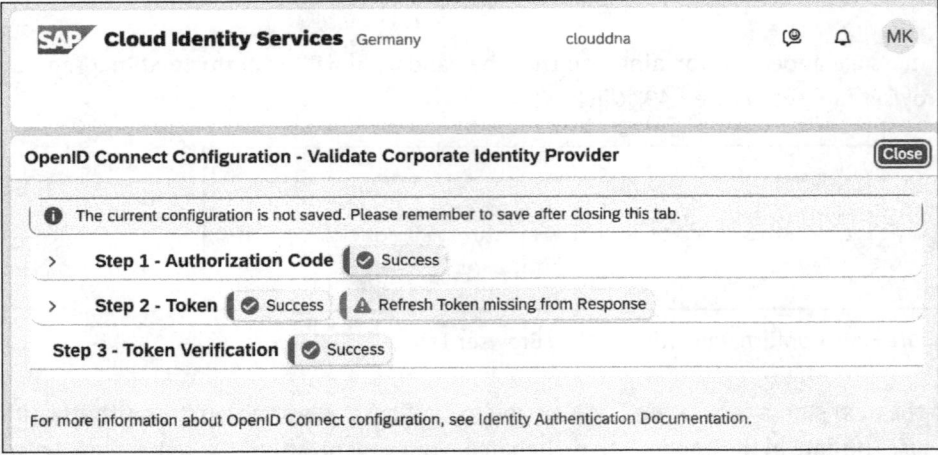

Figure 3.51 Validation Result

3.3 Practical Example: Identity Authentication as a Proxy to Microsoft Entra ID

The next step is to configure the SSO settings. To do so, open the **Single Sign-On** tab in **OpenID Connect Configuration** under Identity Authentication, then click the **Identity Federation** entry (see Figure 3.52).

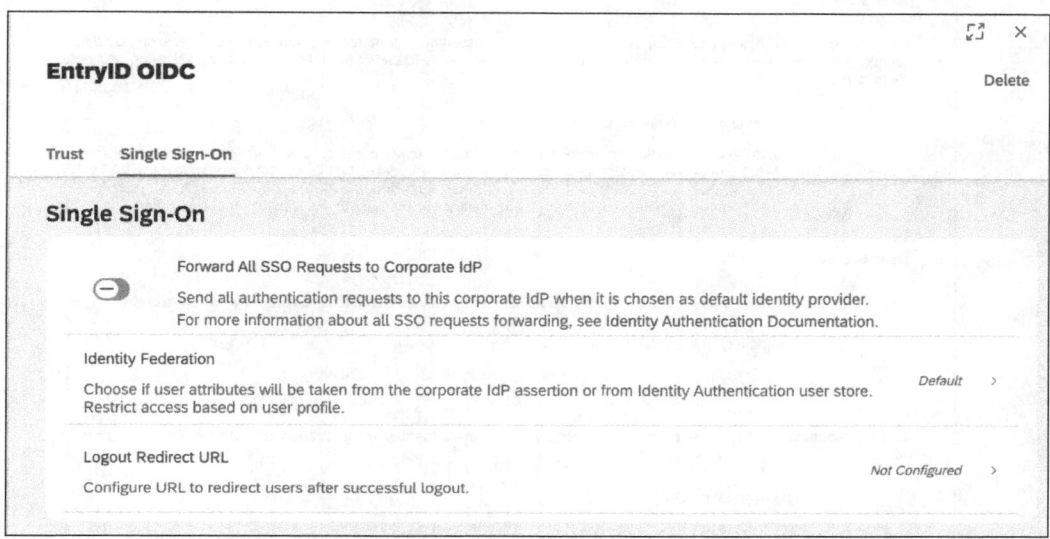

Figure 3.52 Configure Single Sign-on

Select the **Use Identity Authentication** user store option. Then enable the **Allow Identity Authentication Users Only** and **Apply Application Configurations** options (see Figure 3.53).

The **Use Identity Authentication User Store** option allows you to use the data from the Identity Authentication user store and send the subject name identifier (*name ID* for SAML 2.0 or *subject* for OpenID Connect), assertion, and default attributes according to the application configuration. For users without a profile in Identity Authentication, the application receives the subject name identifier from the enterprise identity provider assertion and attributes, according to the application configuration.

The **Allow Identity Authentication Users Only** option restricts access to only those users who have a profile in Identity Authentication.

The **Apply Application Configurations** option applies custom application configurations to authentication and access policies. This includes risk-based authentication, terms of service, privacy policies, upgrade forms, and registration forms.

3 Advanced Identity Authentication Service Topics

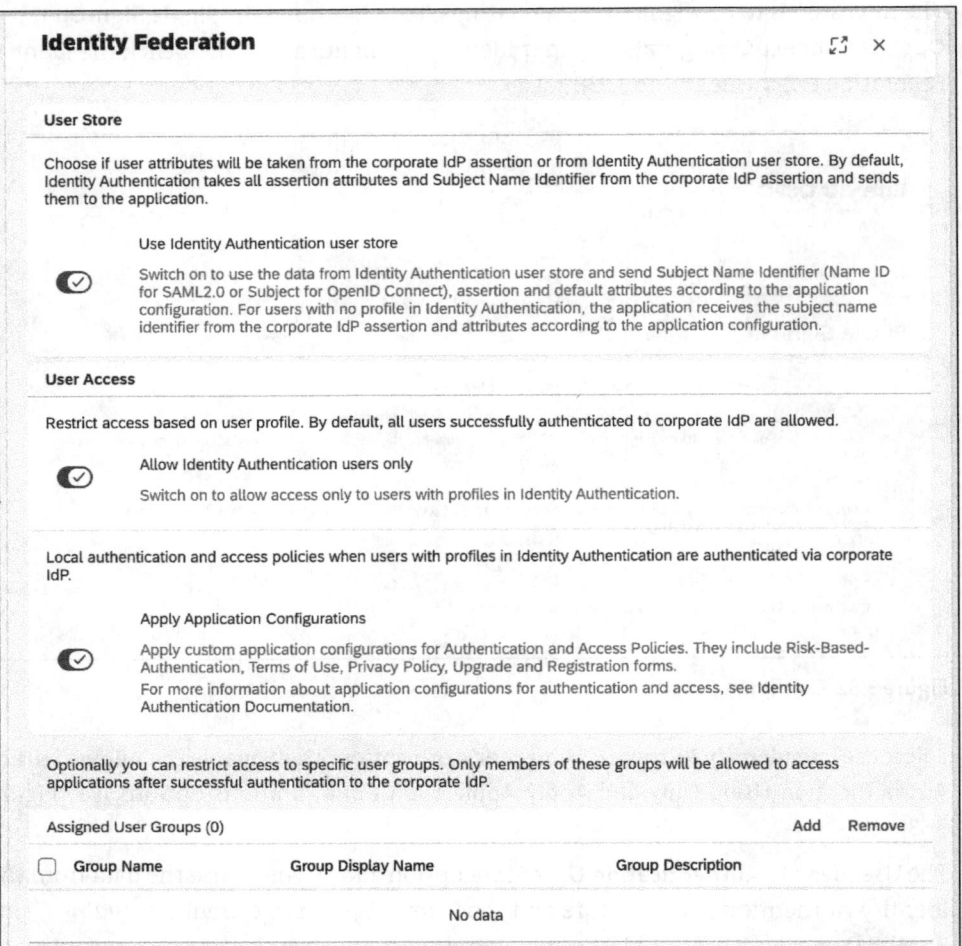

Figure 3.53 Activate User Store and User Access

Finally, you need to configure the subject name identifier. To do this, go back to the **Trust** tab and click **Subject Name Identifier** (see Figure 3.54).

Select the **Email** option and click **Save** (see Figure 3.55).

3.3 Practical Example: Identity Authentication as a Proxy to Microsoft Entra ID

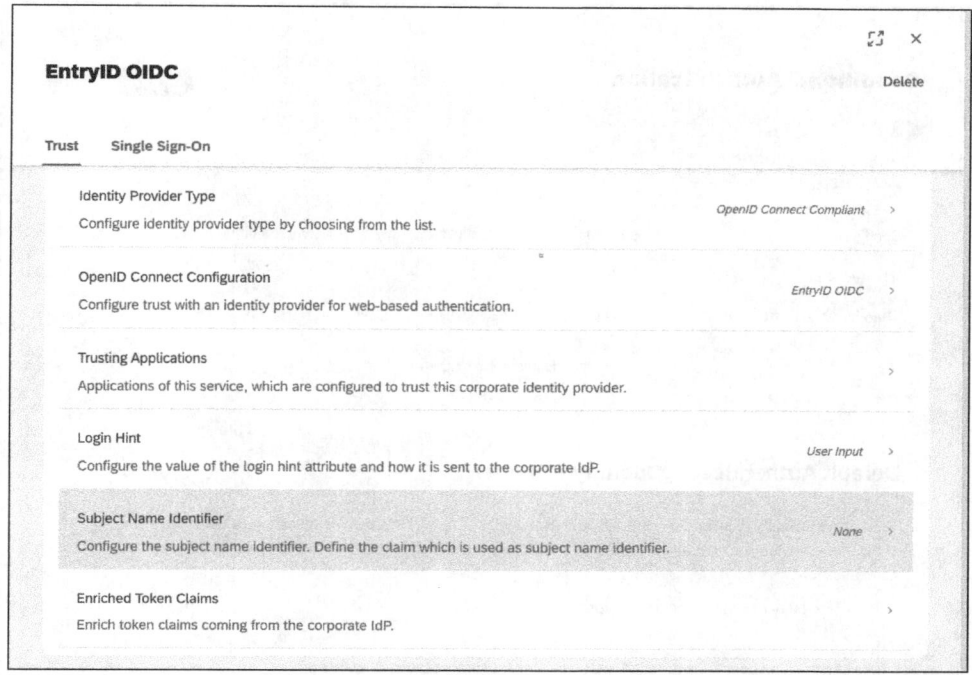

Figure 3.54 Configure Subject Name Identifier

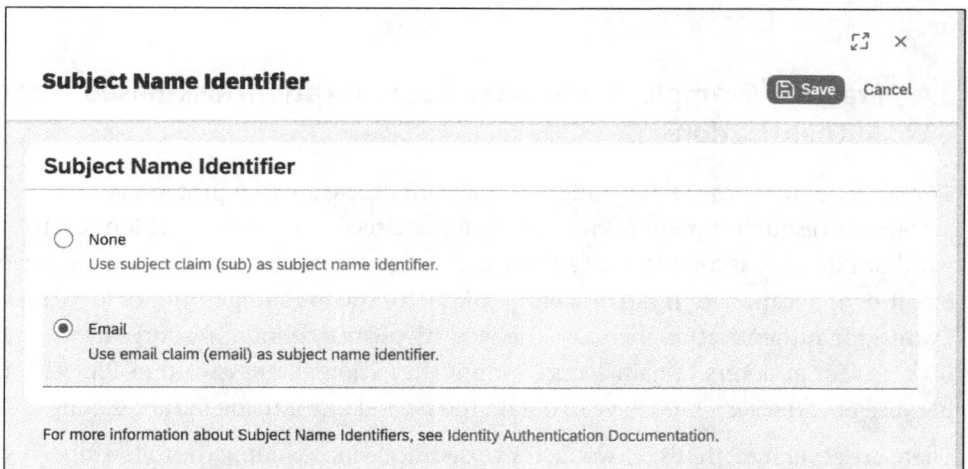

Figure 3.55 Select Email for Subject Name Identifier

Now you can test the configuration. The easiest way to do this is to set the conditional authentication to the OIDC identity provider you just created, as shown with SAML (see Figure 3.56). You can then open the application in the SAP BTP subaccount and authenticate against Microsoft Entra ID using OIDC.

143

3   Advanced Identity Authentication Service Topics

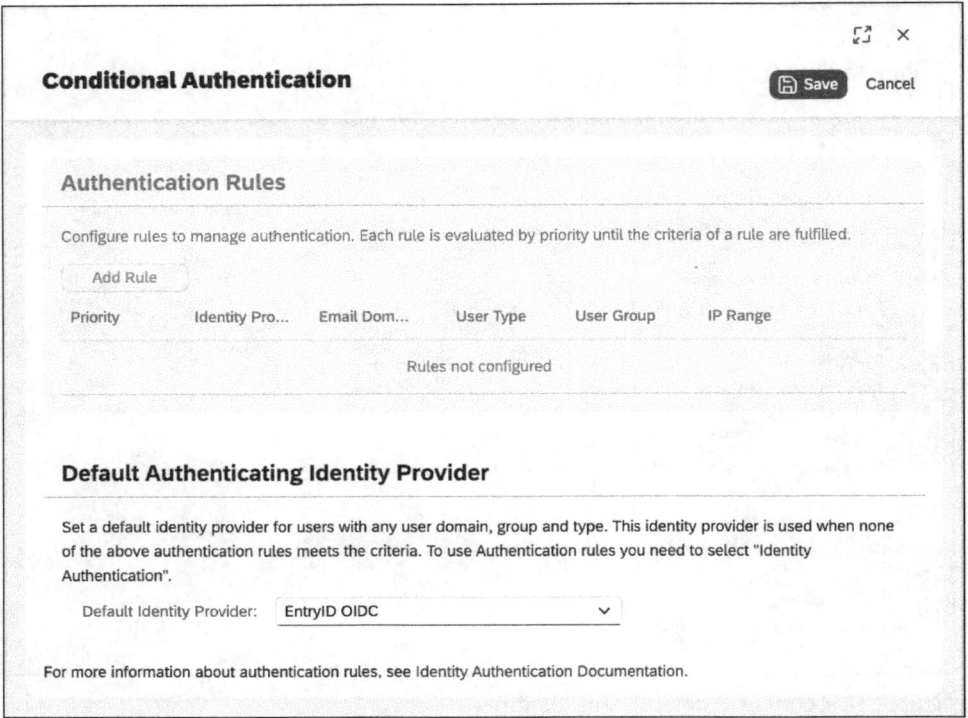

Figure 3.56 Test Configuration

3.4   Practical Example: Two-Factor Authentication/Risk-Based Authentication

Two-factor authentication is an additional security measure that protects access to an account or resource. It requires the user to enter a second factor in addition to a password or PIN. This second factor can be a one-time code generated by a text message, email, or application; or it can be a biometric factor such as a fingerprint or facial scan. Two-factor authentication increases the security of an account or resource by making it harder for attackers to gain access, even if they know the password or PIN. This is because the attacker would have to obtain the second factor to log in successfully.

There are several methods of two-factor authentication, including the following:

- **SMS or email transaction authentication number (TAN)**
  The user receives a one-time code via SMS or email that must be entered to log in.
- **App TAN**
  The user uses an authentication app to generate a one-time code that must be entered to log in.
- **Biometric**
  The user uses a biometric factor, such as a fingerprint or face scan, to log in.

3.4 Practical Example: Two-Factor Authentication/Risk-Based Authentication

Two-factor authentication can help stop attackers in the following scenarios:

- **Phishing attacks**
  Phishing attacks attempt to trick users into revealing their login credentials. If a user has two-factor authentication, it is much more difficult for the attacker to gain access to the account, even if they know the credentials.

- **Password brute force attacks**
  In password brute force attacks, attackers try to gain access to an account by repeatedly trying passwords. Two-factor authentication makes it much harder for attackers to gain access to an account, even if they guess a password.

- **Device recovery**
  If a user loses their device or the device is stolen, an attacker can use the device to log in to the user's account if the user doesn't use two-factor authentication. Two-factor authentication makes it much harder for attackers to gain access to an account even if they can get their hands on a user's device.

Identity Authentication can also implement two-factor authentication. It is in the risk-based configuration area. Configuration always takes place at the level of a subaccount or application that has registered with Identity Authentication as a service provider. The following example shows how to set up risk-based authentication for a subaccount. In Identity Authentication, on the **Applications and Resources** tab, click **Applications** to see a list of all registered applications. Click the application that represents the subaccount. In the application details, open the **Authentication and Access** tab (see Figure 3.57). Click the **Risk-Based Authentication** entry to open the configuration.

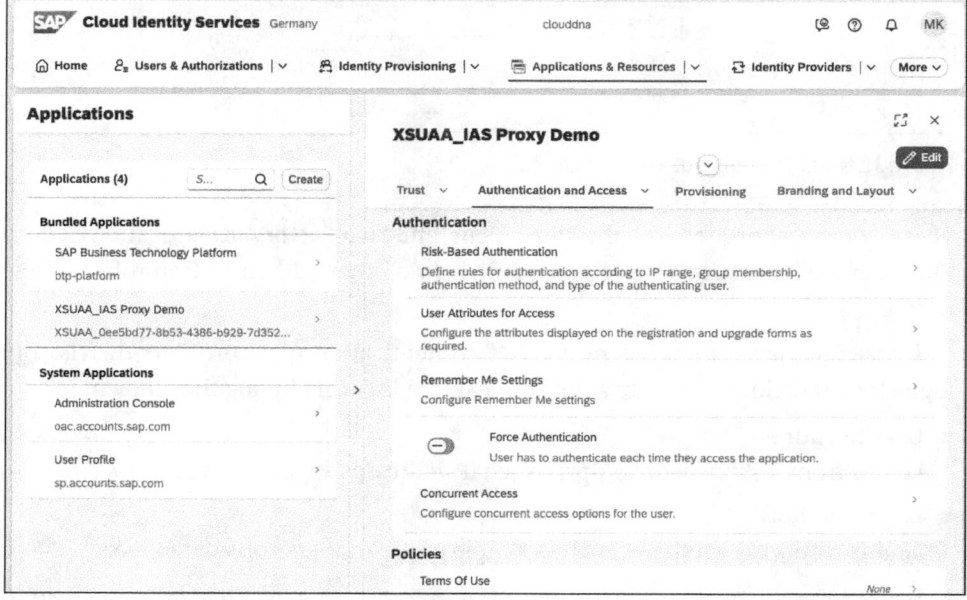

Figure 3.57 Configure Risk-Based Authentication

145

3   Advanced Identity Authentication Service Topics

You now have the option of defining a default authentication role. This is done within the **Default Authentication Rule** area, in the **Default Action** field (see Figure 3.58).

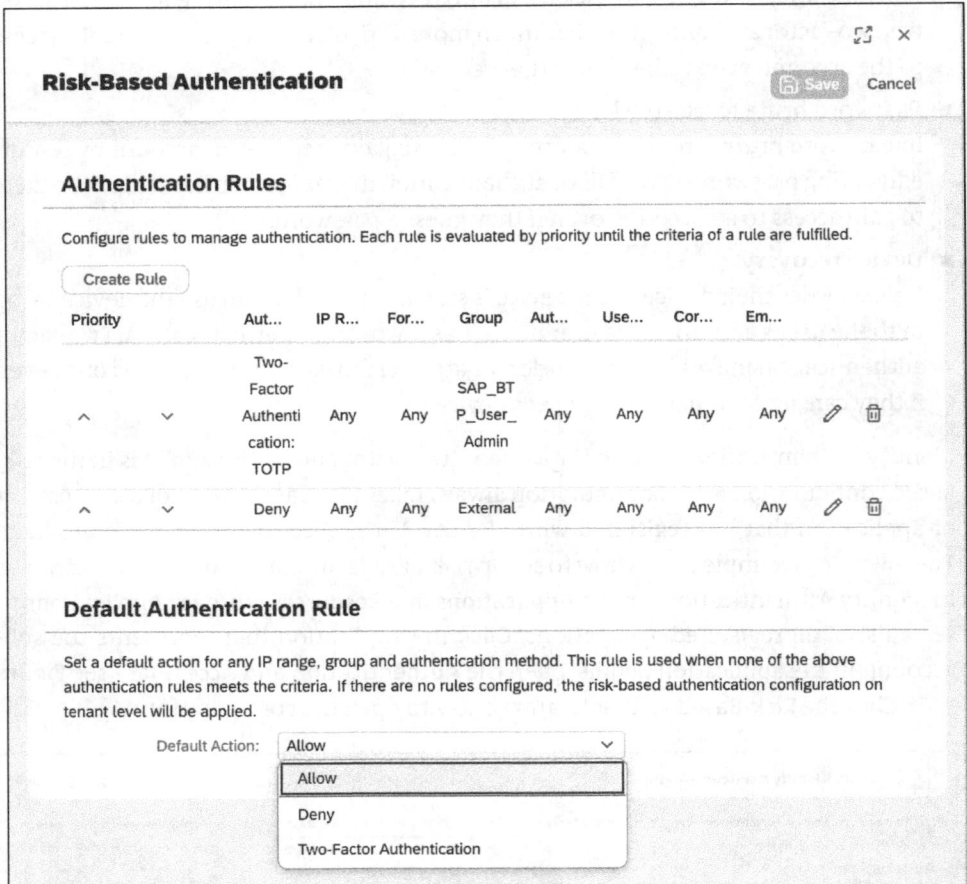

Figure 3.58 Set Default Authentication Rule

There, you can choose among the **Allow**, **Deny**, and **Two-Factor Authentication** options. The default authentication rule only applies if no other authentication rule has been found.

Risk-based authentication is a method of authentication that considers the risk of a login. It uses various factors to assess the risk of a login, including the following:

- **User IP address**
  Logins from unknown or compromised IP addresses are considered risky.
- **Login method**
  Logins with weak methods, such as simple passwords, are considered risky.
- **User type**
  Logins from external users are considered risky.

3.4 Practical Example: Two-Factor Authentication/Risk-Based Authentication

- **Group membership**

  Logins from users assigned to a specific group, such as administrators, are considered risky.

Click **Create Rule** to create rules for user authentication. As shown in Figure 3.59, select **Two-Factor Authentication** for **Authentication Action**.

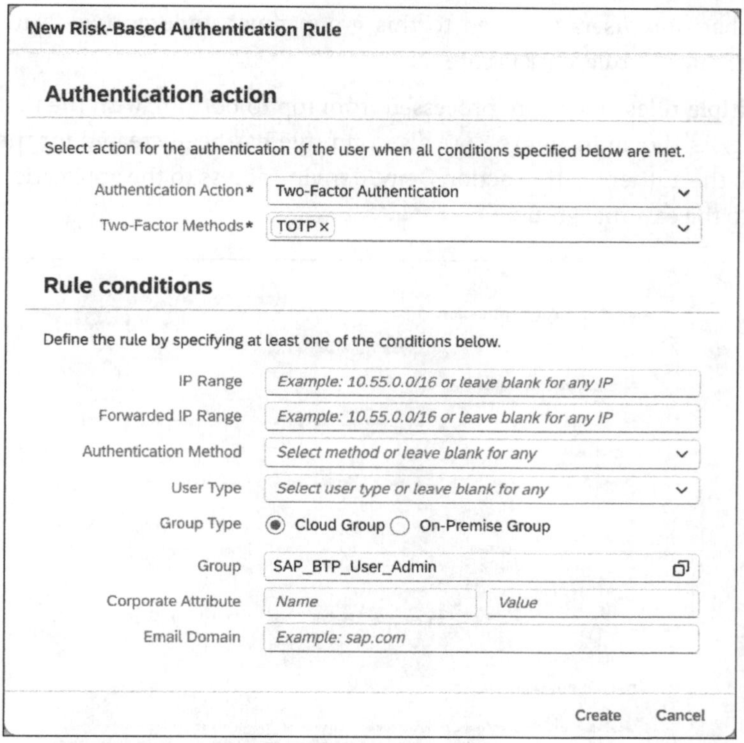

Figure 3.59 Create Authentication Rule

In the **Two-Factor Methods** field, choose **TOTP**, or you can select **Web Authentication** or **Email OTP Code**. Let's look at these options:

- **Time-based one-time password (TOTP)**

  In the case of identity authentication, two factors are used to verify the user. If you set up TOTP two-factor authentication, users must enter a TOTP, also known as a *passcode*, in addition to their primary credentials. Users also need to install an authentication application on their mobile devices to generate TOTPs.

- **Web authentication**

  Users must authenticate with a device such as an integrated biometric scanner or a USB, Bluetooth, or near-field communication (NFC) device in addition to their primary credentials.

3   Advanced Identity Authentication Service Topics

- **Email OTP code**
  When setting the email OTP code, users must provide the code sent to their email in addition to their primary credentials. Note that an email OTP code is not a method of two-factor authentication that SAP recommends. Use one of the other methods instead.

In our example, the rule for the SAP_BTP_User_Admin group was created in the **Group** field. This means that only users assigned to this group must undergo two-factor authentication. To create the rule, click **Create**.

You can create multiple rules, which are processed from top to bottom, with the first rule found applying. As shown in Figure 3.60, a second rule has been created for the external group with the authentication action **Deny**, denying access to the application for users assigned to the external group.

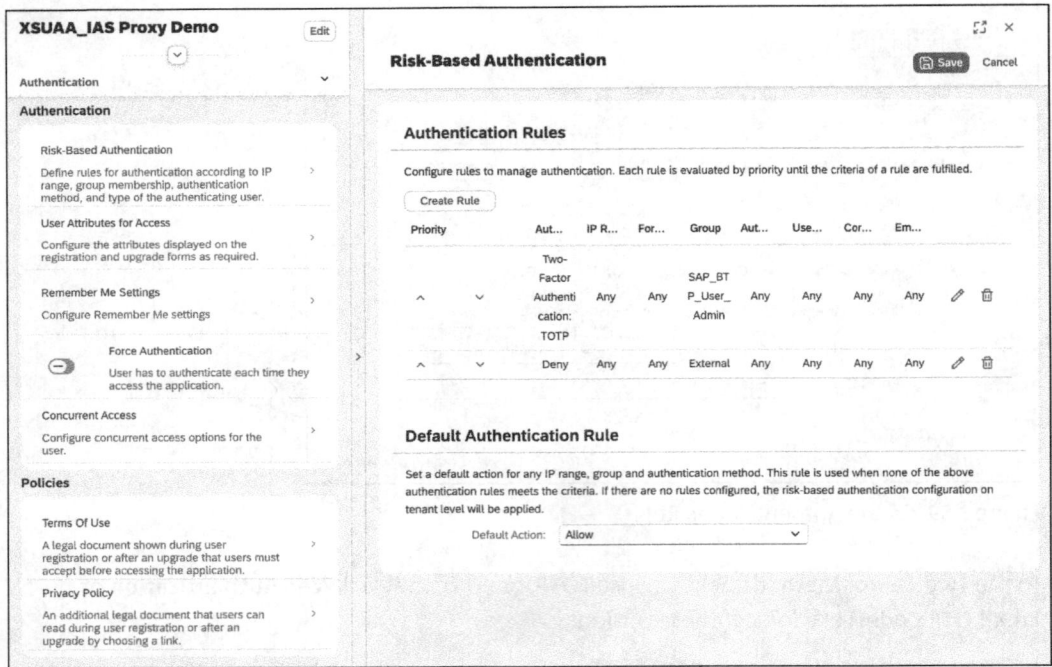

Figure 3.60 Authentication Rules

After creating the authentication rules, test access to the application. Two-factor authentication is activated after successful identification (see Figure 3.61). In this example, we are testing with a user in the SAP_BTP_User_Admin group. The first time the user accesses the application, they must scan the QR code with a TOTP app, such as Google Authenticator. The TOTP code will then be displayed in the app and must be entered in the **Passcode** field.

Figure 3.61 TOTP Authentication

In the user profile, you can check whether multifactor authentication is active for your user account (see Figure 3.62).

If you use Identity Authentication as a proxy to a third-party identity provider, then multifactor authentication can also be carried out on the respective identity provider—for example, Microsoft Entra ID.

3   Advanced Identity Authentication Service Topics

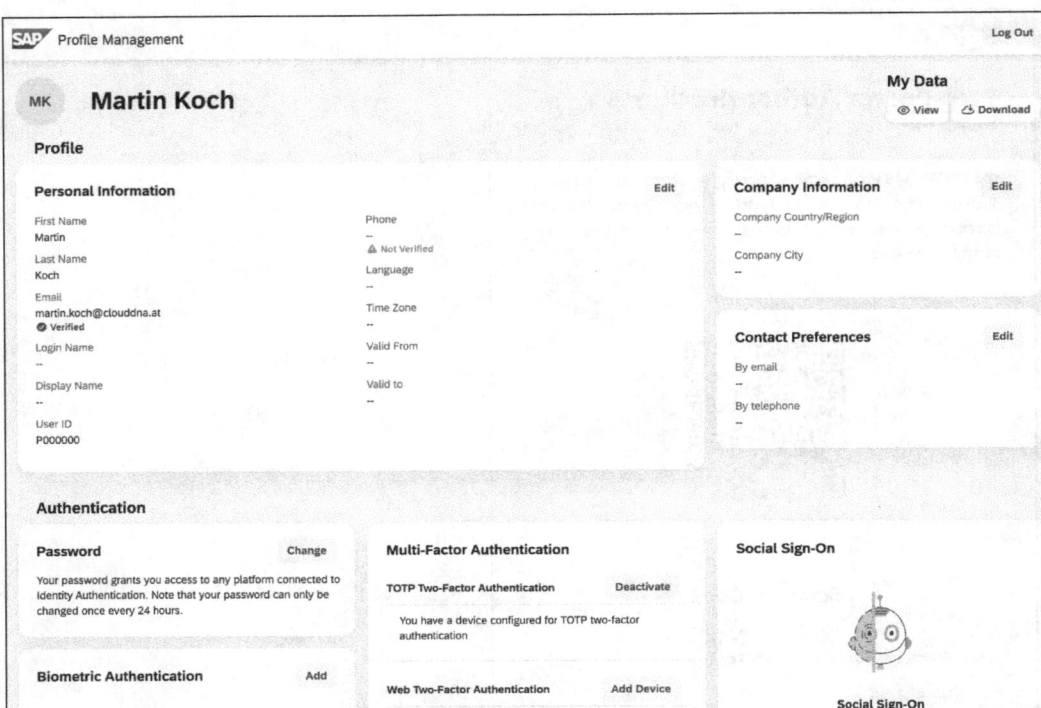

Figure 3.62 Multifactor Authentication in User Account

3.5 Practical Example: Conditional Authentication

Some users should be identified using the company's internal identity provider, such as Microsoft Entra ID, while you authenticate all other users against Identity Authentication. Map this scenario in Identity Authentication using *conditional authentication*. Define rules for authentication by the email domain, user type, user group, and IP range of the users. Set conditional authentication for each subaccount. To enable conditional authentication, navigate to the **Applications & Resources** tab in Identity Authentication and select **Applications**. Then, click the **Trust** tab page and select the **Conditional Authentication** area (see Figure 3.63).

Define a default identity provider in the **Default Authenticating Identity Provider** area. In the standard system, this is always set to **Identity Authentication** (see Figure 3.64), meaning that users are authenticated against Identity Authentication. You can change the default identity provider to any corporate identity provider that has previously been created in Identity Authentication. In this case, Identity Authentication acts as a proxy. You're likely already familiar with this configuration from Section 3.3. To create additional rules that are checked before the default identity provider is called, click **Add Rule**.

3.5 Practical Example: Conditional Authentication

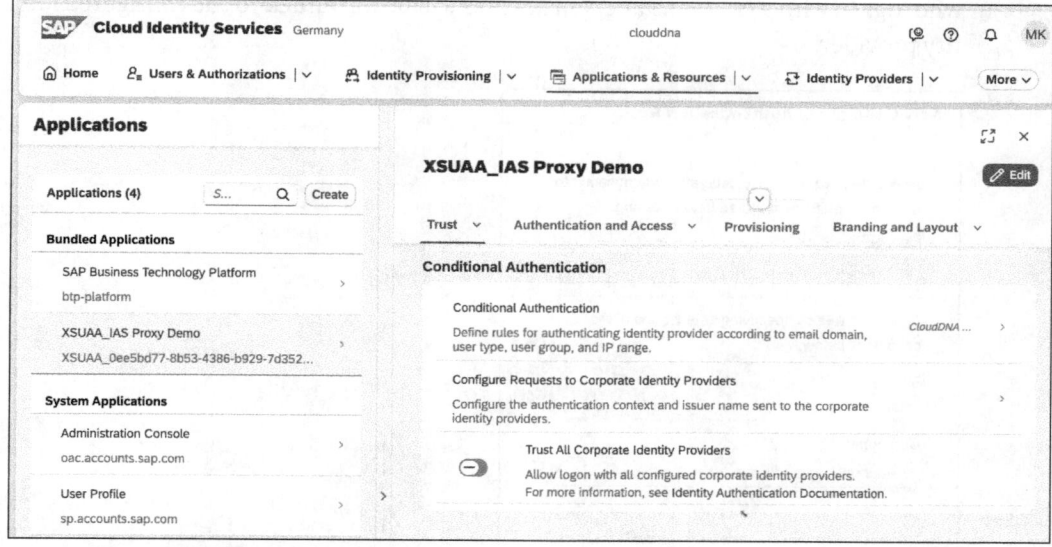

Figure 3.63 Configure Service Provider

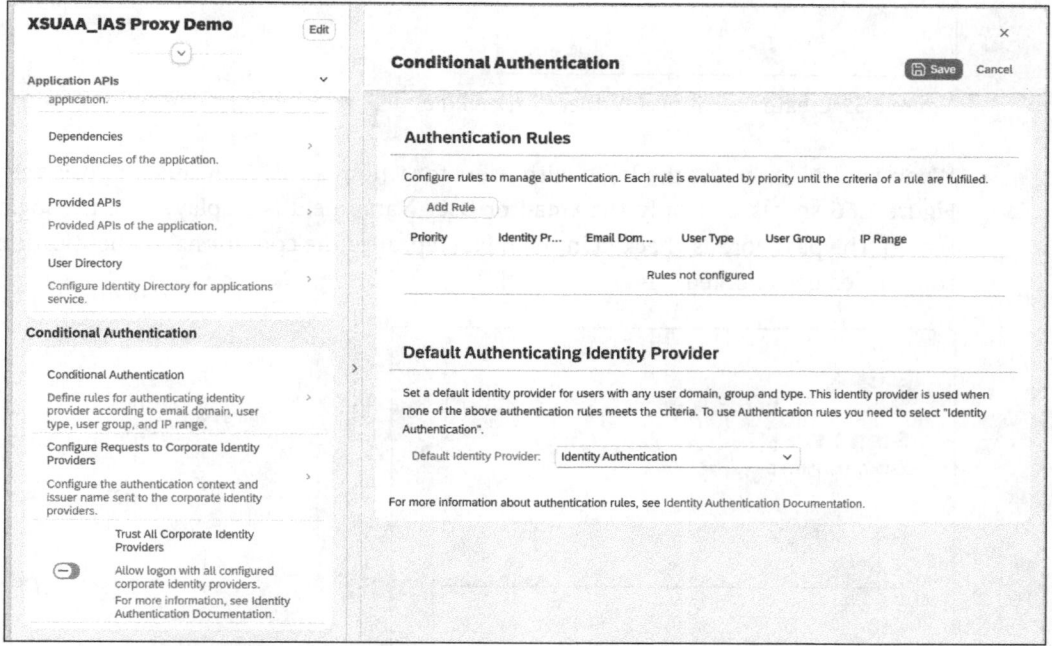

Figure 3.64 Set Up Conditional Authentication

As shown in Figure 3.65, you can configure a conditional authentication rule. First, select the identity provider that will be called if the rule is evaluated positively. Then, maintain the conditions that will be checked for this rule. In this example, you can see that the **Email Domain** field has been filled with "clouddna.at". This means that a user who logs in with a clouddna.at email address will be forwarded to the configured identity provider.

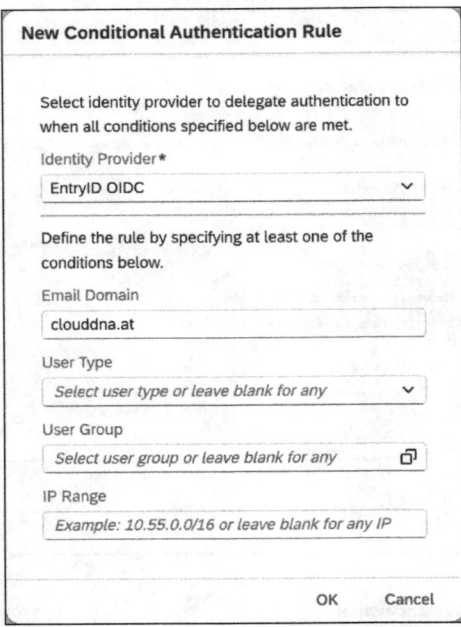

Figure 3.65 Create Conditional Authentication Rule

When you're done, test the login with users for whom a rule is evaluated positively. Figure 3.66 shows that only the **Email or User Name** field is displayed on the login screen. The password is checked in the next step, after the conditional authentication rules have been checked.

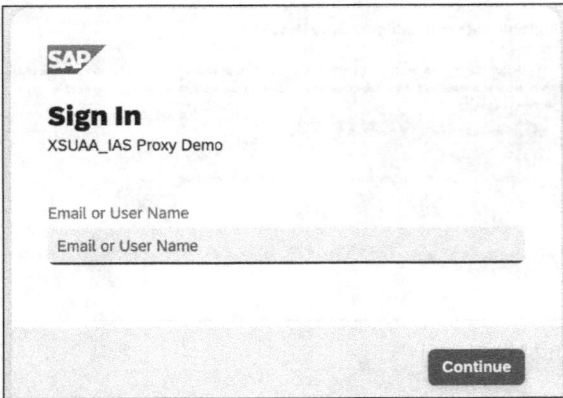

Figure 3.66 Test Login

3.6 Summary

This chapter provided a comprehensive overview of advanced topics related to Identity Authentication. It began with an introduction to the two central authentication protocols: SAML 2.0 (Section 3.1) and OpenID Connect (Section 3.2). The chapter then moved on to a practical example, demonstrating the Identity Authentication service's role as a proxy for Microsoft Entra ID (Section 3.3). Two integration approaches were considered: integrating Microsoft Entra ID in Identity Authentication using SAML 2.0 (Section 3.3.1) and integrating with OpenID Connect (Section 3.3.2).

We also examined advanced security mechanisms such as two-factor authentication and risk-based authentication (Section 3.4), used to improve the protection of user accounts. Finally, we discussed conditional authentication (Section 3.5), which makes it possible to control access based on defined criteria.

Chapter 4
Global Account Administration

When you dive into the world of SAP BTP, your journey begins with the assignment of a global account. This central element is far more than just a user account; it is the control center for cloud resources, licenses, and user management. A comprehensive understanding of global account management is essential to fully unlock the potential of SAP BTP.

As soon as you license SAP BTP services, you receive a global account. Originally, the idea was that each organization would have exactly one global account. However, in practice, organizations may have multiple global accounts. This can happen, for example, when organizations use the integration services of SAP BTP in addition to an SaaS product like SAP SuccessFactors. You may also receive two global accounts if you acquire some services through a subscription model and others via a Cloud Platform Enterprise Agreement (CPEA). Global accounts are provided only by SAP and cannot be created independently by organizations. In general, the global account is where you consolidate your subaccounts and define overall (global) settings.

Global accounts are geographically independent, unlike the next level down—the subaccount level—where you can choose the region in which each subaccount is hosted. At the global account level, you manage the licenses available in your organization and allocate them to different environments where development takes place or where your cloud solutions are productively operated. It is the entry point for managing and grouping subaccounts and for assigning resources and licenses.

In Section 4.1, you will learn how to access your global account and switch between multiple global accounts. Section 4.2 covers user management in the global account, including roles and role collections. This topic is less complex than it is for the subaccount level, but it is important to note that admin permissions in the global account are very powerful and therefore critical. In Section 4.3, you will learn how to use directories to organize and authorize subaccounts in a structured way. Section 4.4 introduces boosters, which are used in the SAP BTP environment to speed up new subscriptions and administrative tasks. Further information about the system landscape and the resource providers as administrative units spanning subaccounts can be found in Section 4.5 and Section 4.6. How to assign resources or services using entitlements is explained in Section 4.7. Section 4.8 finally addresses the topic of usage monitoring. In

4 Global Account Administration

this last section, you will learn how to monitor key performance indicators and use your resources efficiently to make the most of SAP BTP.

4.1 Access to the Global Account

You can access your SAP BTP cockpit via *https://<region>.cockpit.btp.cloud.sap/cockpit/#/globalaccount/*, changing *<region>* to, for example, *us10*. Until recently, registration was handled at *https://hana.ondemand.com/*. This URL still works, but it will redirect the request. After successful authentication, you will be redirected to the global account you last viewed (see Figure 4.1).

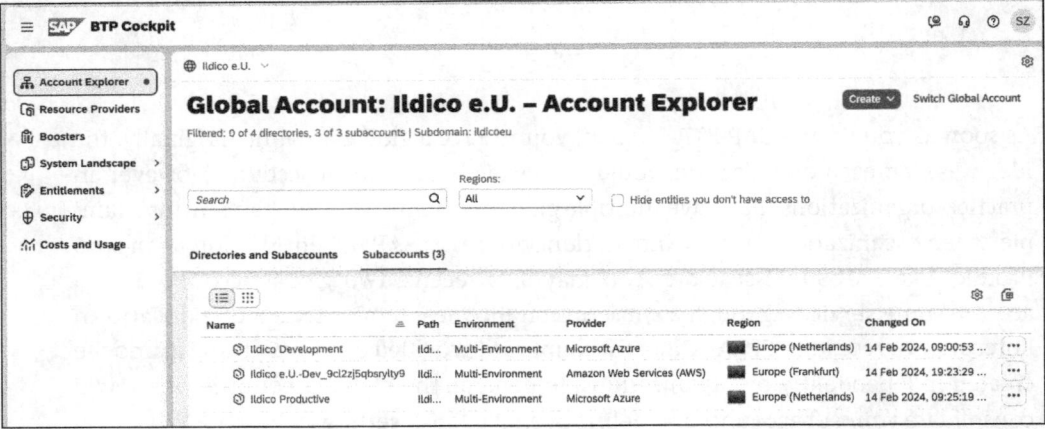

Figure 4.1 Overview of Subaccounts After Logging into Global Account

If you have more than one global account, you can switch between them by clicking the **Switch Global Account** link (see Figure 4.2).

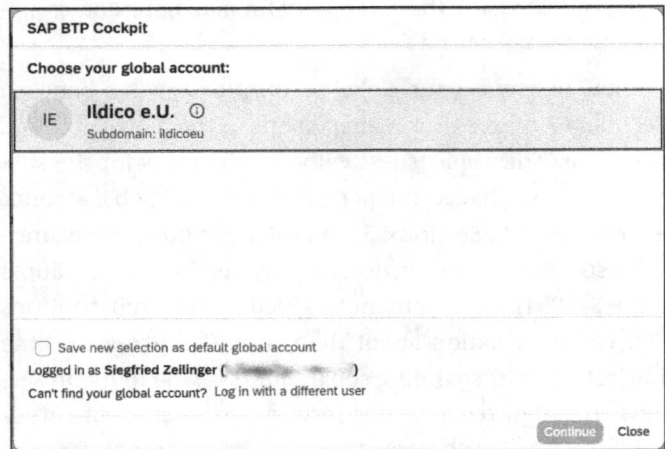

Figure 4.2 Switching Between Global Accounts

4.2 Authentication and Authorization Management

A global account can have as many subaccounts as you like, which you can create and manage yourself. The creation and management of subaccounts is described in more detail in Chapter 5.

> **Lost Subaccount Privileges**
>
> From the global account, you can use the **Add Me as Admin** function in the context menu of each subaccount to get authorization for that subaccount. This is especially helpful if there has been a change in administration or if someone is suddenly unavailable. These actions are of course documented in the audit log.

4.2 Authentication and Authorization Management

User authentication at the global account level is first performed by the SAP ID service. You typically log on with your S-user that is defined for the global account. This S-user will be sent a welcome email and is responsible for the administration of the global account. They are the only one with initial access to Identity Authentication and is assigned the administrator role by default.

Recently, it has also become possible to use your own Identity Authentication service tenant for authentication in the SAP BTP cockpit. We will introduce this in Section 4.2.1 and will demonstrate a practical example in Section 4.2.3 by setting up a platform identity provider. Section 4.2.2 will cover roles and collective roles for granting permissions within the global account.

4.2.1 User Management

You can find the users of your global account under **Security** • **Users** in your SAP BTP cockpit (see Figure 4.3).

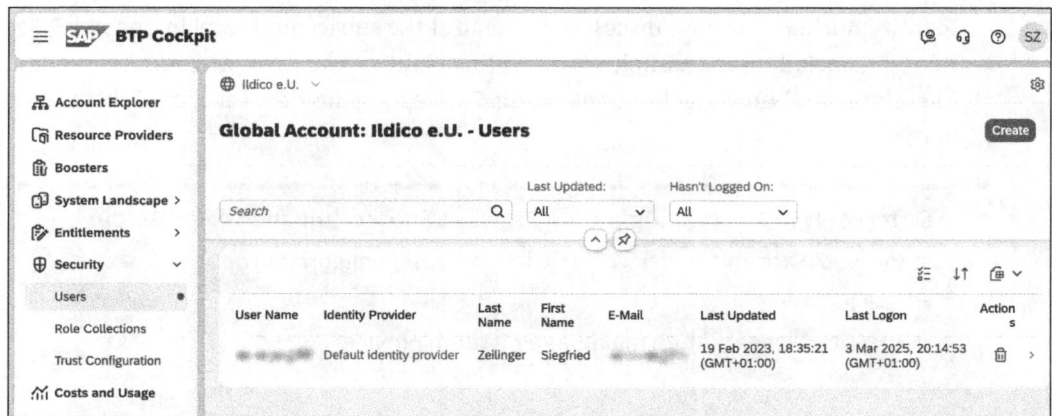

Figure 4.3 Users in Global Account

We recommend that you use at least two administrators as it's possible to be locked out of SAP BTP for an hour if you enter the wrong password. It is also useful to have a substitute in case of illness or vacation.

> **Who Needs Access to the Global Account?**
>
> From our point of view, only users who are involved in creating new subaccounts or monitoring and configuring existing ones, similar to the SAP Basis department, need access to the global account.
>
> Users who develop or use an application in a subaccount do not need access to the global account as these users can be authorized in the subaccount and access to the global account does not provide any added value.
>
> Persons from the auditing department, the internal audit department, and the works council may be granted read-only access to the global account (see Section 4.2.2).

The **Default Identity Provider** setting, as shown in Figure 4.3, means that the SAP ID service is configured. Authentication using this identity provider is sufficient. However, you can also use *SAP Cloud Identity Services*. This includes, among other elements, *Identity Authentication*, which can store data individually. This means that users who are authenticated using Identity Authentication do not necessarily need an account with SAP but can be created directly in Identity Authentication. Identity Authentication can also be used to pass the authentication to your local directory server (e.g., Microsoft Entra ID or Microsoft Active Directory on-premise). The decisive advantage of such a configuration is that the users exist in the lifecycle of your organization; that is, the validity data is transferred from your company servers and changes are therefore reflected in the global account administration.

Another aspect of setting up SAP Cloud Identity Services is that the included Identity Authentication service becomes a platform identity provider. It can be used in all subaccounts.

Identity Authentication is discussed in detail at the subaccount level in Chapter 5, Section 5.2.2, including an example of connecting Identity Authentication to a subaccount. Therefore, we abbreviate the content here. Connecting the global account is a side issue at this point.

> **Differences in Trust Configuration Between Subaccount and Global Account**
>
> In the global account, you have the following trust configuration options:
> - SAP ID
> - Identity Authentication tenant as a platform provider

4.2 Authentication and Authorization Management

In the subaccount, you can choose from among the following options:

- SAP ID
- Identity Authentication tenant
- SAML configuration

In the global account, you *cannot configure SAML directly*. However, doing so is possible via Identity Authentication. An important advantage of this is that all authentication methods involved in the global account are under SAP's control, and therefore you can get better help from SAP in case of a SAML error or a hack in your trusted system.

To add users, you can create a new user with **Create** (see Figure 4.4).

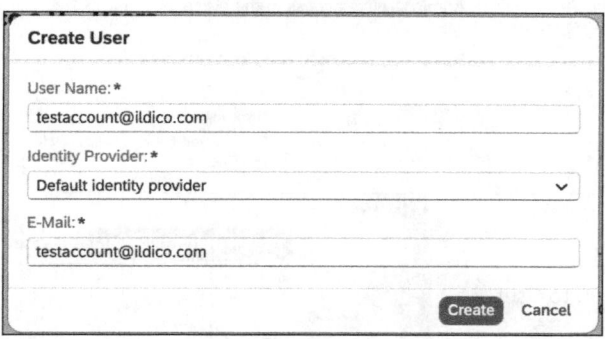

Figure 4.4 Creating New User

As shown in Figure 4.5, enter the mail address of the new user. The underlying S-user or P-user must be associated with the email address entered.

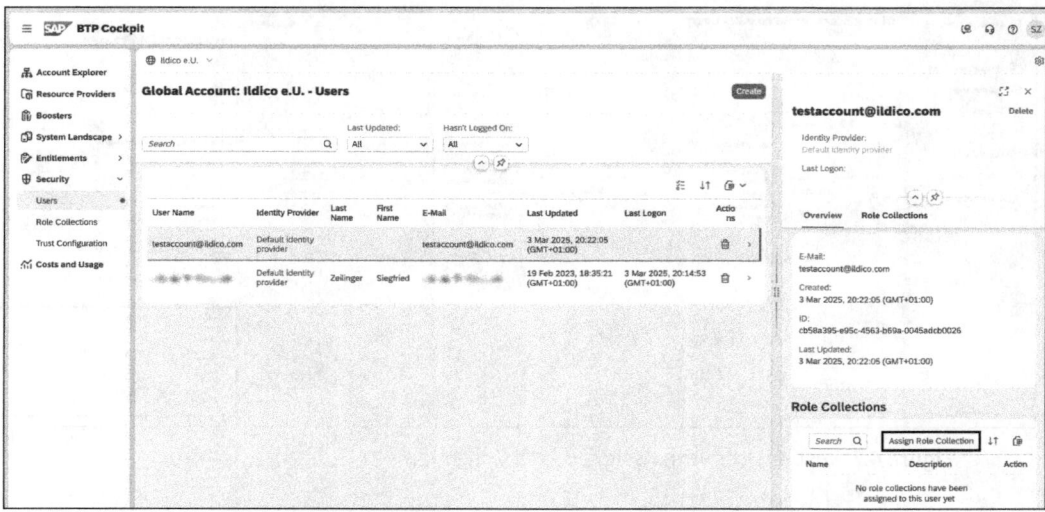

Figure 4.5 Created User with User Details Opened

4 Global Account Administration

After creating the user, you can select a **Role Collection** in the lower-right area. For more information about role collections, see Section 4.2.2.

For test purposes, click **Assign Role Collection** and assign the **Global Account Viewer** role to the new user (see Figure 4.6).

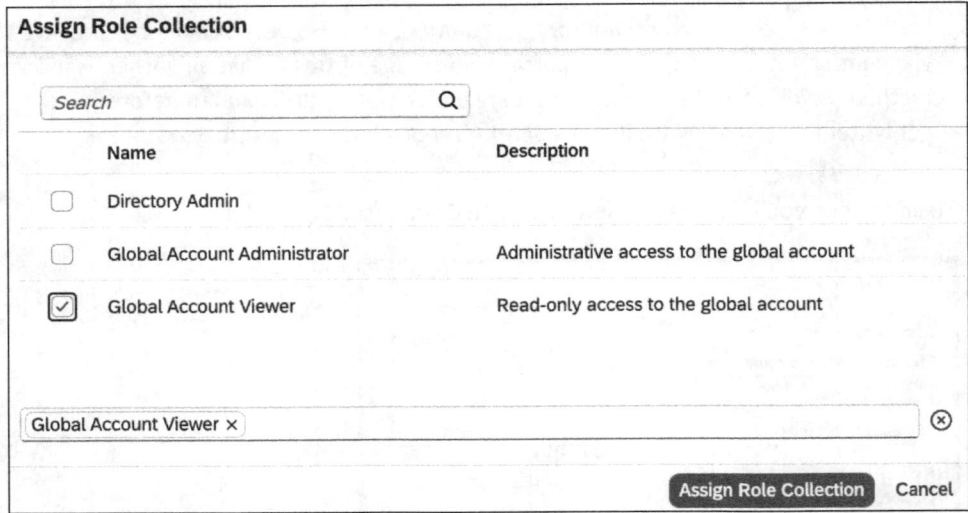

Figure 4.6 Assigning Role Collection to User

Click **Assign Role Collection** again to assign the collection role. Figure 4.7 shows the assigned composite role in the user overview under **Role Collections**.

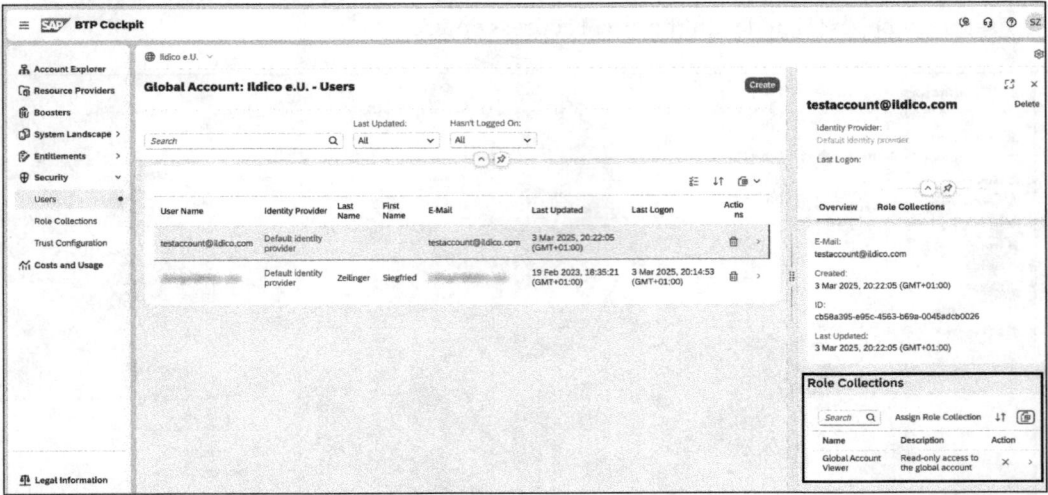

Figure 4.7 Result: User with Assigned Role Collection

4.2 Authentication and Authorization Management

> **Users in SAP ID**
>
> Users that you assign with an SAP ID authentication type must also be known in your company with the same email address. To ensure this, you can register an SAP Universal ID (a P-user) or—and this is what we recommend—register an S-user via your company. This way, you have the account validity under control.

If you have not yet created the selected user in your company, go to *https://me.sap.com/userscontacts/usermanagement* and log onto SAP for Me as a user administrator. Once there, click **Users & Contacts** (see Figure 4.8).

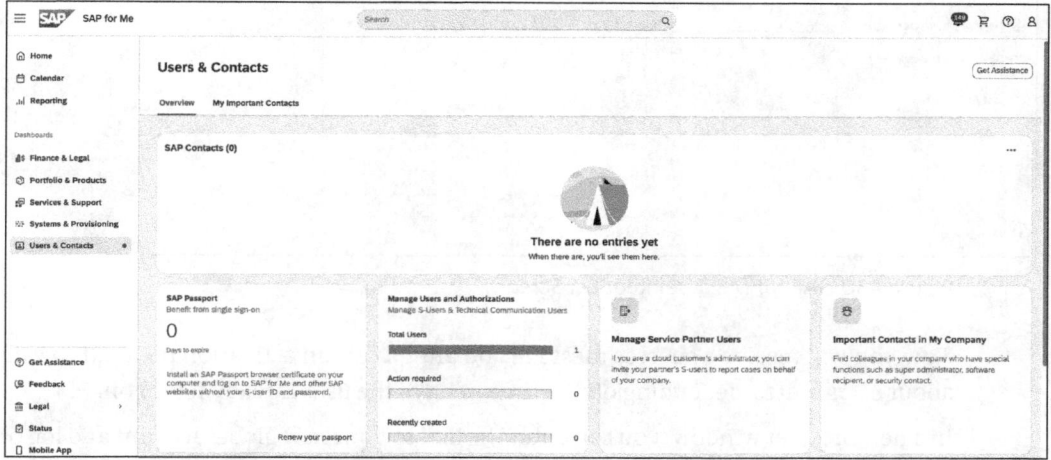

Figure 4.8 Logging onto SAP Support User Management

On the next screen (see Figure 4.9), create a new user for your company by choosing **Request User**.

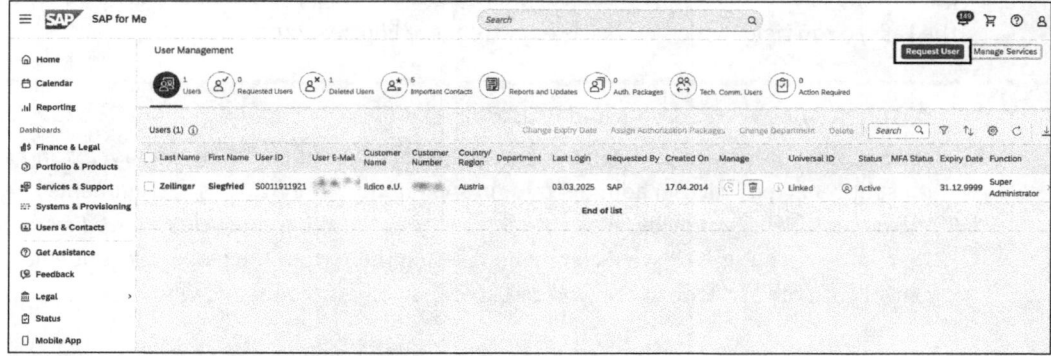

Figure 4.9 User Overview in SAP for Me

161

On the **Request User** screen, enter your **First Name**, **Last Name**, and **Email** address, then click **Submit** (see Figure 4.10).

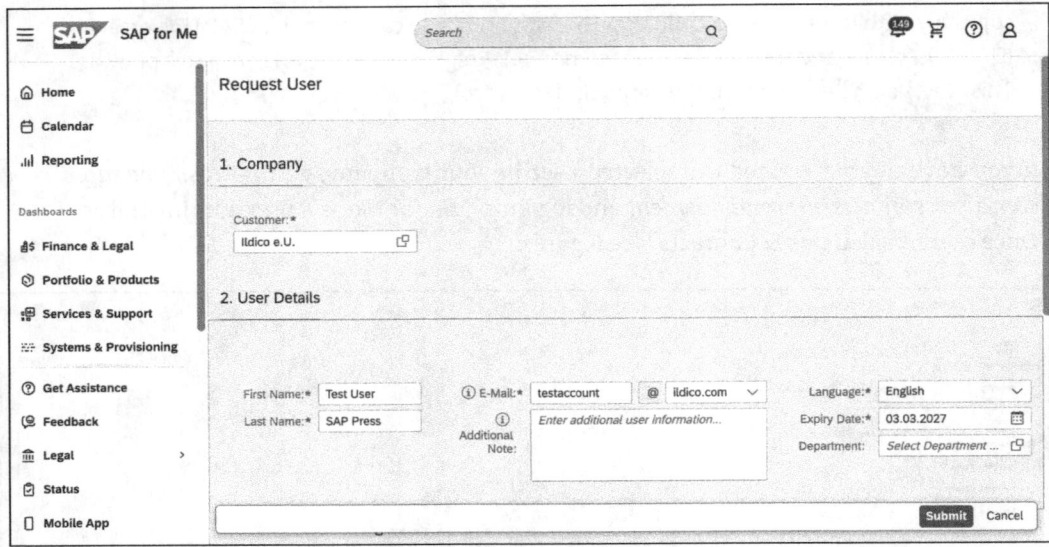

Figure 4.10 SAP for Me: User Request Screen

Now you will receive a success message and after a certain activation period (typically about 60 minutes, depending on the time of day), the user is ready for logon.

In a new browser window, you can enter the link to your new global account and log on with the email address of the newly created user.

After logging in (see Figure 4.11), you can immediately see from the lock icon beside the **Subaccount** label that you have read-only access to the global account (because you have only assigned the Global Account Viewer role).

Back in the user overview, you can see that the newly created user now shows a date in the **Last Logon** field, which works as expected (see Figure 4.12).

> **Difference Between S-Users and P-Users**
>
> Note another difference between S-users and P-users: S-users expire after two years and must be renewed by a user administrator in SAP for Me. P-users and the assignments in the default identity provider never expire; the role collection must be removed from them at least, but in fact we recommend deleting them from the global account. You can still use the audit log to see who accessed the global account and when.

4.2 Authentication and Authorization Management

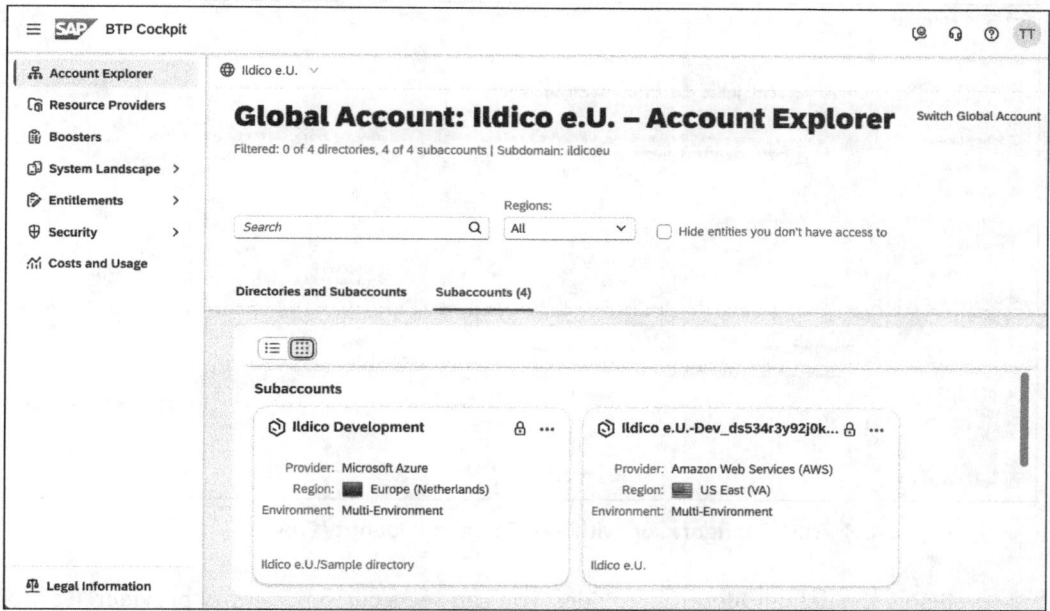

Figure 4.11 Read-Only Access with Test User Just Created

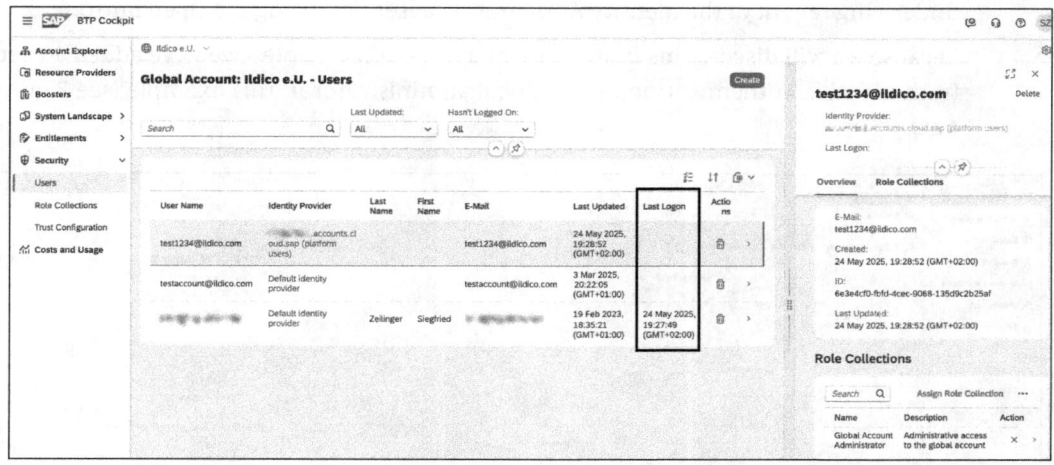

Figure 4.12 Last Login Date in User Overview

We have already written several times about the default identity provider. In the SAP BTP cockpit of your global account, click **Security • Trust Configuration**. There you will see the linked identity providers, as shown in Figure 4.13.

163

4   Global Account Administration

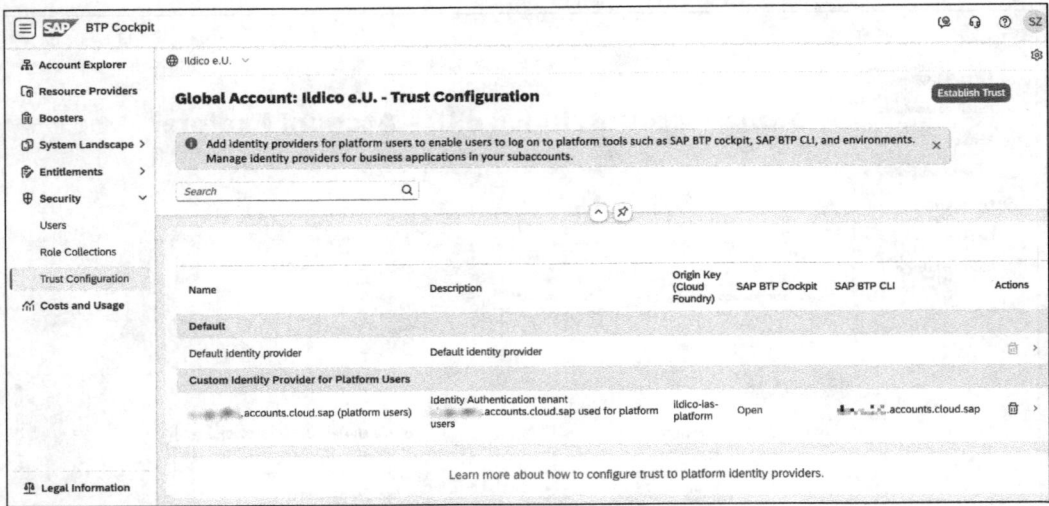

Figure 4.13 Trust Configuration with SAP ID: Default Identity Provider

Below the default identity provider, you can see a custom identity provider. (Section 4.2.3 describes how to create this identity provider.) You can also authorize users of this identity provider in your SAP BTP cockpit. You also can also jump to the provider (the underlying tenant of the Identity Authentication service) using the **Open** button.

Because we will discuss this in more detail later in this chapter, we have added a user from Identity Authentication as the global administrator in this example (see Figure 4.14).

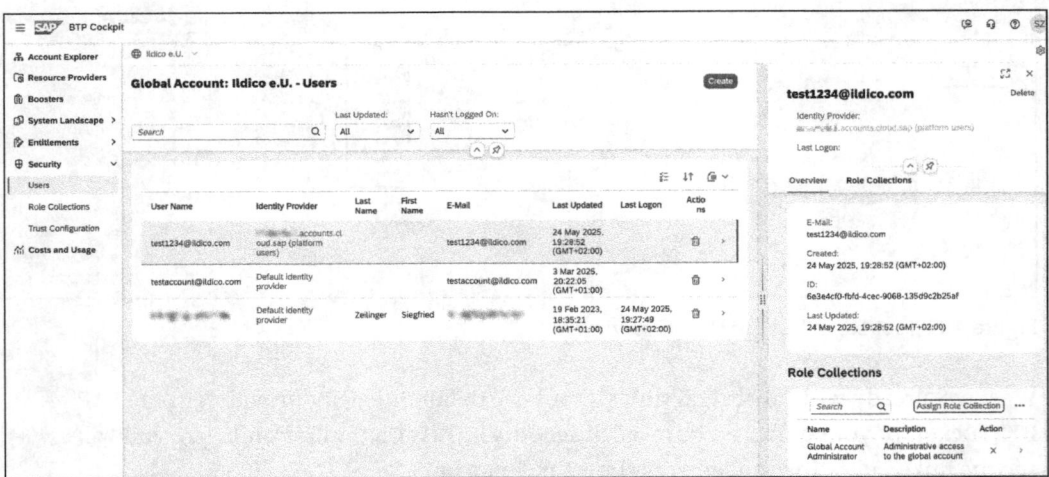

Figure 4.14 Example of Identity Authentication User in User List of Global Account

4.2 Authentication and Authorization Management

As you can see in Figure 4.15, you can now configure multifactor authentication (via the **Multi-Factor Authentication** menu item) in Identity Authentication and also define a user lifecycle with start and end dates (**Valid From** and **Valid To**, shown in Figure 4.16).

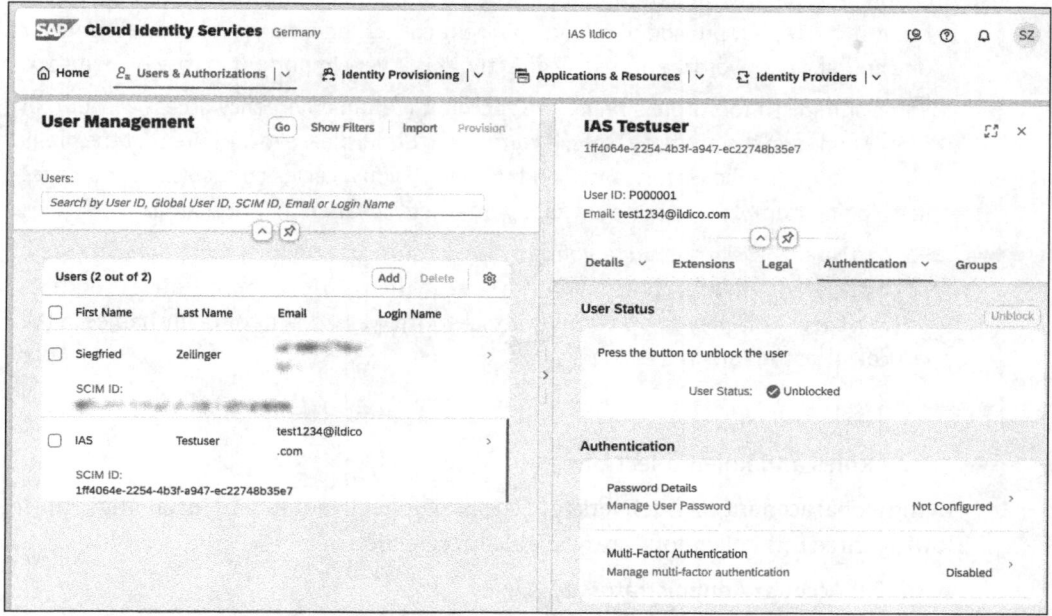

Figure 4.15 Test User in Identity Authentication Tenant

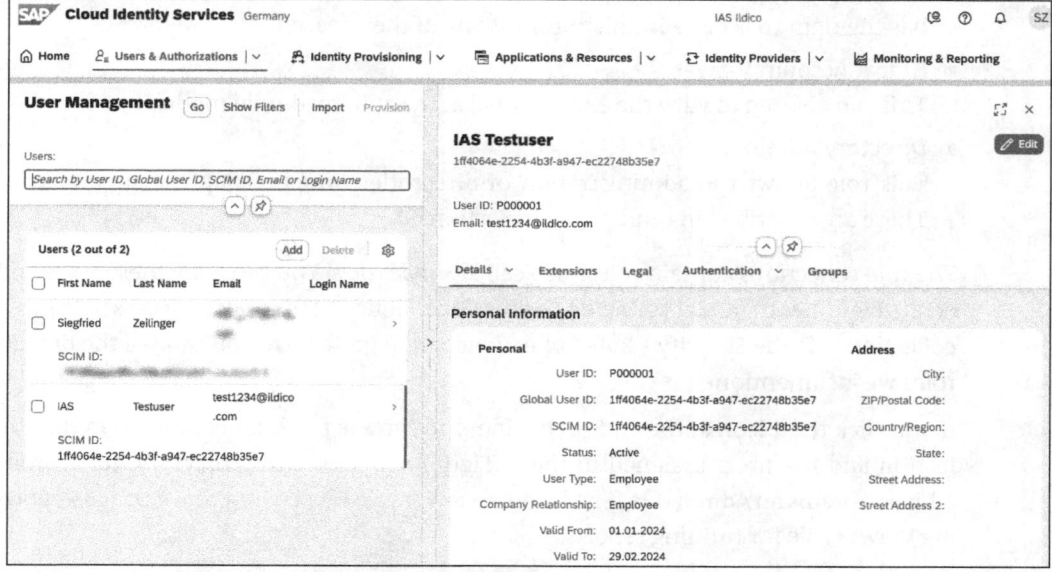

Figure 4.16 User Details with Test User Start and End Dates

4 Global Account Administration

> [+] **Practical Considerations for Using Identity Authentication and Global Accounts**
>
> We recommend connecting global account administration users via Identity Authentication and using two-factor authentication. We also recommend deactivating SAP ID because it does not provide two-factor authentication and because it locks accounts for one hour if a password is entered incorrectly. This is very important in case of an attack.
>
> Some administrators store a *break glass* account (i.e., an emergency access account) in SAP ID and keep the password safe. If you wish to do so, please make sure that the break glass account mailbox is forwarded and checked. If you receive any suspicious messages (e.g., login attempts or attempted password resets), change the username.
>
> For particularly tricky scenarios, you can also consider having a separate domain that is not associated with your company, which you can then use for administrative users (e.g., *domain1.dev*). This prevents dictionary attacks with well-known company names in the critical infrastructure in the cloud.

4.2.2 Roles and Role Collections

In the global account, SAP delivers collections of roles. In a standard installation, the following three role collections are available for selection:

- **Global Account Administrator**
  This role collection provides full access to the global account. You can manage users; create, modify, and delete subaccounts; and manage technical settings such as quotas and permissions (more on technical topics in Section 4.7). This kind of user also has the right to act as administrator for any of the subaccounts.

- **Global Account Viewer**
  This can be used to view the entire global account in read-only mode.

- **Directory Admin**
  This role allows the administration of directories, which group the subaccounts. These are described in more detail in Section 4.3.

The role collections contain roles, also called *single roles*. You can copy these roles and create new ones to model your own permissions. Figure 4.17 shows the access to the role collections via the **Security • Role Collections** menu path. Here you can see the default roles we just mentioned.

If you click the > icon at the end of the line, you can see the roles contained in the collection and the users assigned to them. Figure 4.18 shows the **Directory Admin** role, which contains an **Admin** role for editing, a **Viewer** role for viewing, and a **Usage Reporting Viewer** role for running reports.

Figure 4.19 shows the contents of the **Global Account Administrator** collection role, which contains all the individual roles for the global account, the system landscape administrator, and the user administration.

4.2 Authentication and Authorization Management

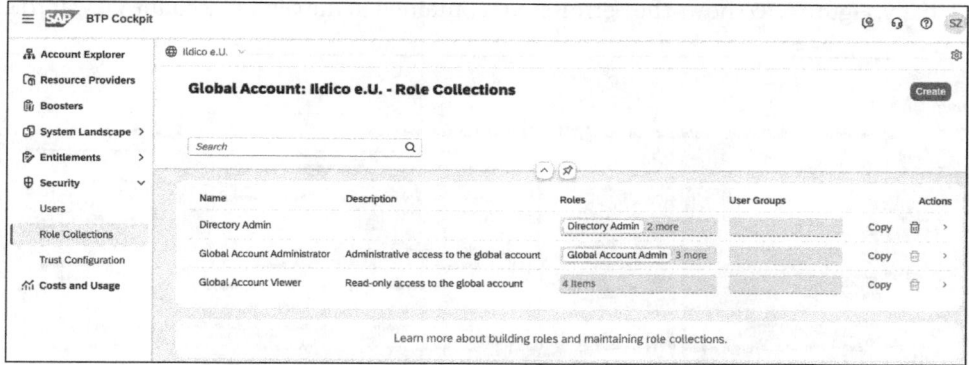

Figure 4.17 Overview of Role Collections in Global Account

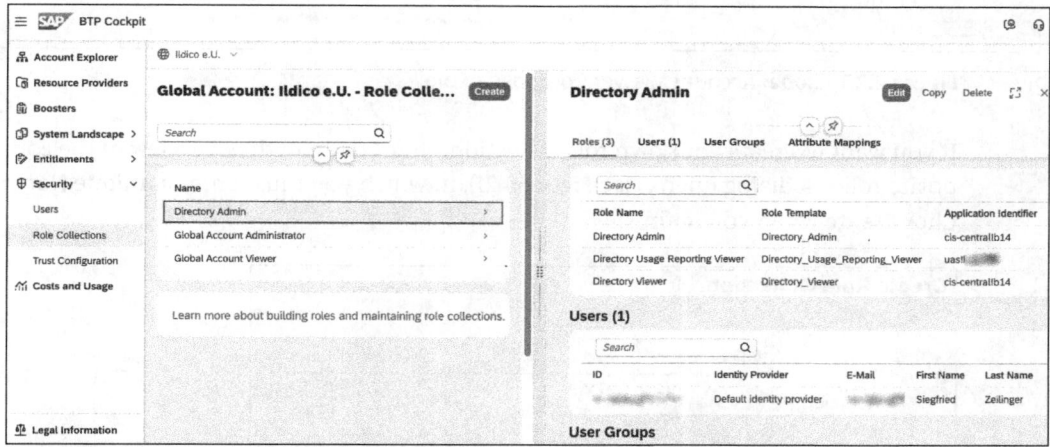

Figure 4.18 Individual Roles Assigned to Composite Role and Overview of Assigned Users

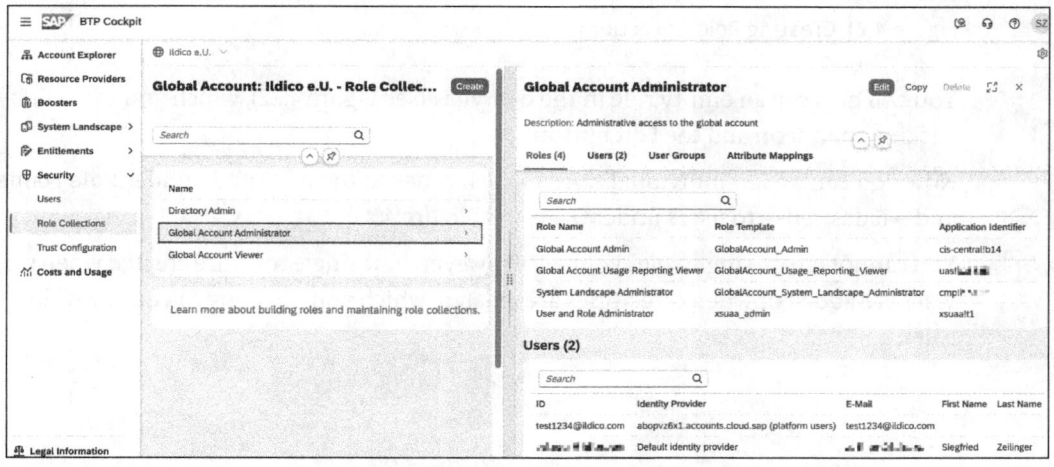

Figure 4.19 Contents of Global Account Administrator Role

167

4 Global Account Administration

Finally, Figure 4.20 shows the permissions contained in the **Global Account Viewer** role.

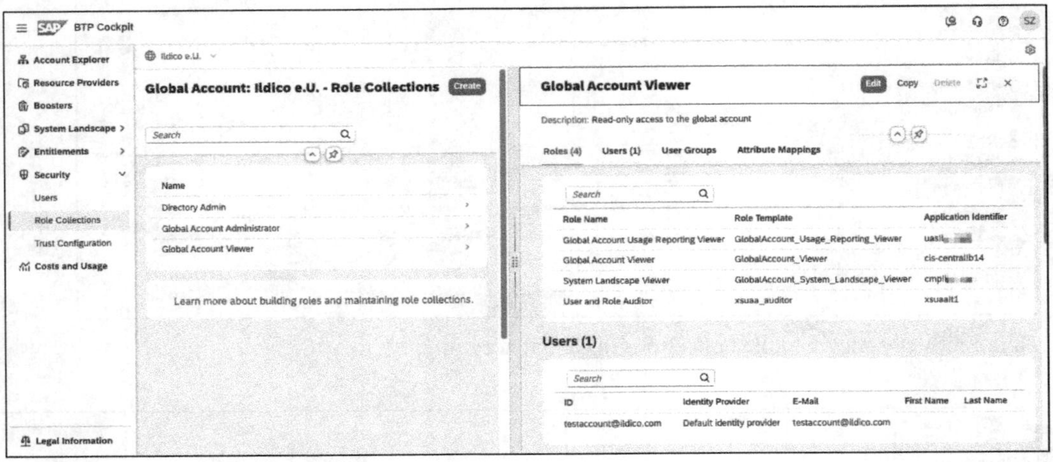

![Figure 4.20 screenshot of SAP BTP Cockpit showing Global Account Viewer composite role]

Figure 4.20 Global Account Viewer Composite Role

If you want to create your own role collection, click **Create** in the overview of the composite roles. A dialog opens (see Figure 4.21), in which you must enter a unique **Name**. Click **Create** when you're finished.

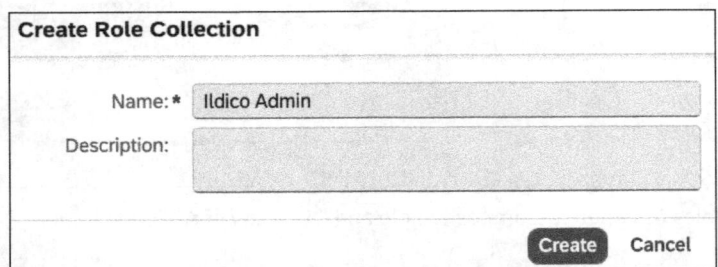

Figure 4.21 Creating Role Collection

You will now see an empty role in the overview (see Figure 4.22), which you can edit by clicking the > icon and the **Edit** button.

Now you can assign individual roles to each other in the edit mode under **Role Name** and—if desired— to users under **Users** (see Figure 4.23).

You cannot create single roles yourself. However, new single roles are created when services are added or when directories are created, which you can copy to your own single roles.

4.2 Authentication and Authorization Management

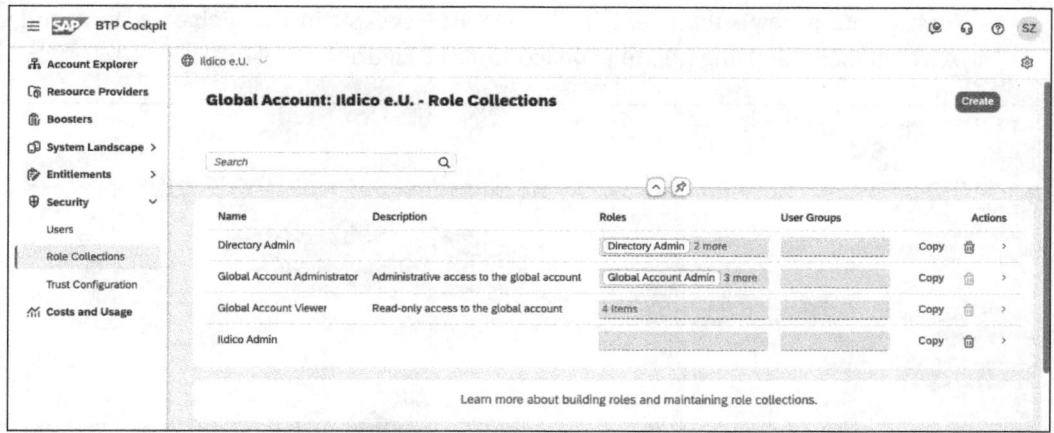

Figure 4.22 Display of Roles, Including Newly Created Composite Role

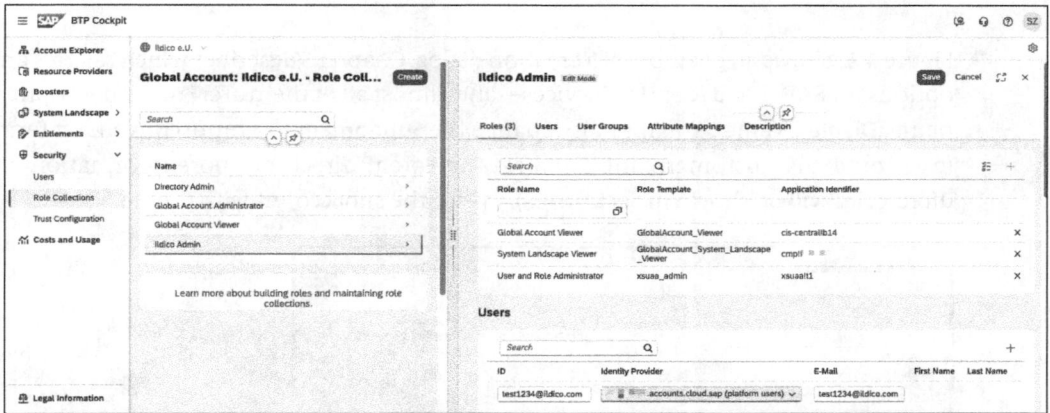

Figure 4.23 Edit Mode for Composite Role

When naming new roles, note that they should not start with the same name as the SAP default roles (e.g., do not use Global Account Editor for your own role). This is for protection in case SAP wants to extend its collection of roles. Including a company name is recommended, rather than having the roles start with Y or Z as in old ABAP times.

4.2.3 Practical Example: Setting Up Authentication via SAP Cloud Identity Service

In this practical example, we will show you how to set up authentication via SAP Cloud Identity Services, which Identity Authentication is a part of, in the global account. A more detailed explanation of SAP Cloud Identity Services can be found in Chapter 5, Section 5.2.4, where this topic is described in more detail for subaccounts, and the initial setup is also described in more detail.

4 Global Account Administration

First create a new subaccount in the SAP BTP cockpit in the global account under **Account Explorer** using **Create · Subaccount** (see Figure 4.24).

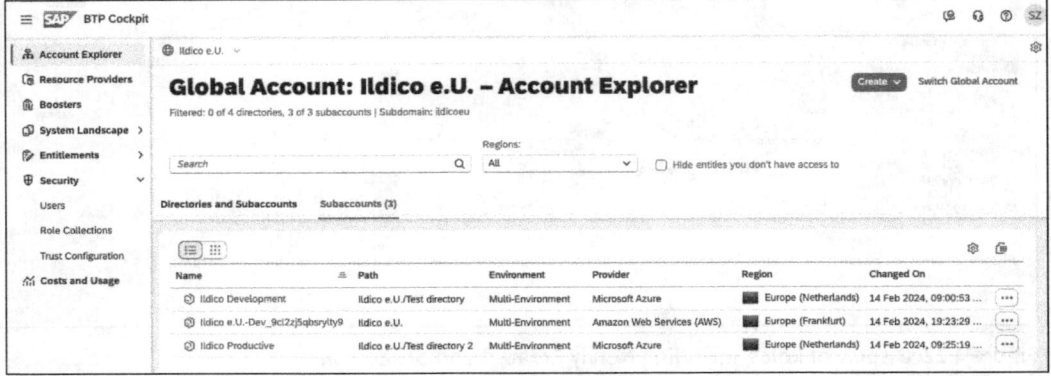

Figure 4.24 Account Explorer in SAP BTP Cockpit

Figure 4.25 shows an example of a creation dialog. Chapter 5 describes which regions are options for SAP Cloud Identity Services—and almost all of them are. Enter a descriptive name (**Display Name**). You may also change the **Subdomain** to a more convenient term (e.g., "prod_ids_customername") and set the **Parent** directory (more information on directories will be shown in Section 4.3). Create the subaccount with **Create**.

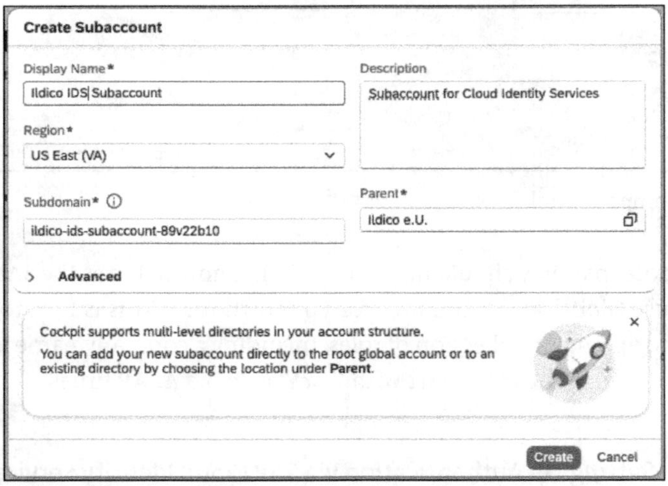

Figure 4.25 Subaccount Creation Dialog

During the creation of the subaccount, you will see a waiting icon, then the name will turn blue and you can log into the subaccount (see Figure 4.26). You will be taken to the **Overview** page (see Figure 4.27).

4.2 Authentication and Authorization Management

Figure 4.26 Subaccount Setup Progress Indication

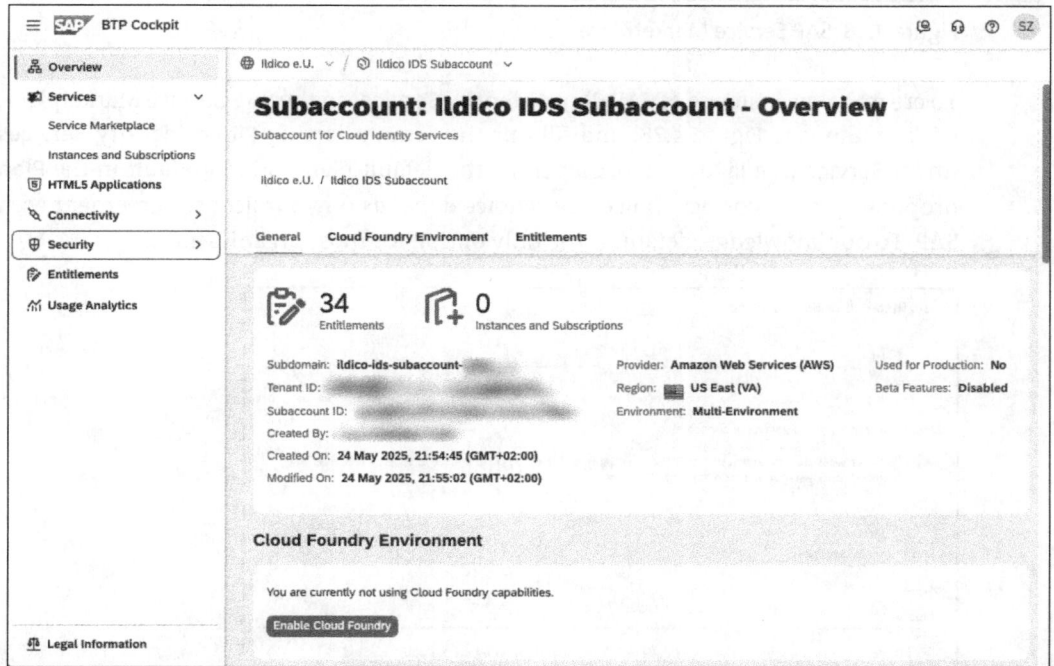

Figure 4.27 New Subaccount Overview Page

The first time you log into the subaccount, you can access the **Service Marketplace** directly from the home page of the subaccount via **Services • Service Marketplace**, as shown in Figure 4.28.

4 Global Account Administration

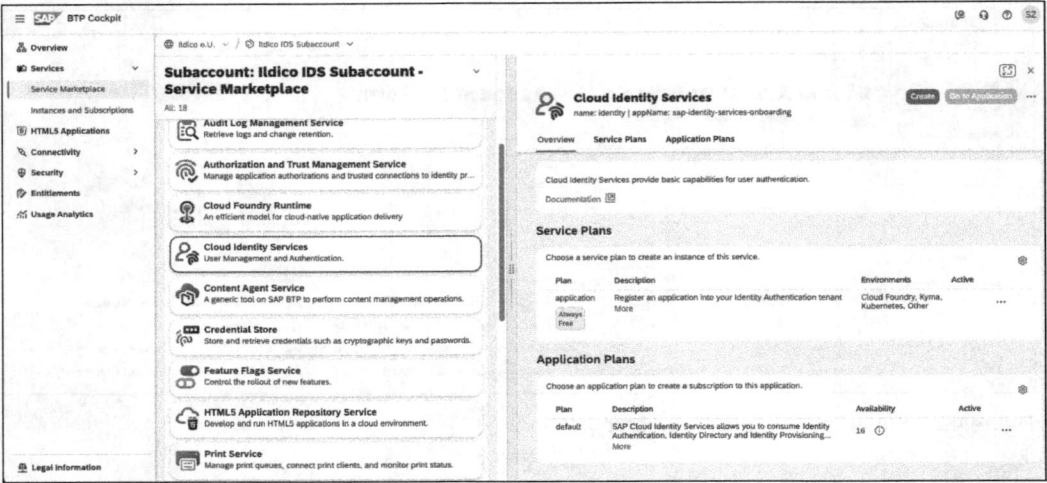

Figure 4.28 SAP Service Marketplace

To create a new instance of SAP Cloud Identity Services in the SAP Service Marketplace, click **Create** (see Figure 4.28) and fill out the form, selecting **Cloud Identity Services** under **Service** (see Figure 4.29). Currently, the default plan option (**default** in the **Plan** dropdown) is the correct choice. This choice depends on your license agreement with SAP. To our knowledge, default is the only option for most organizations.

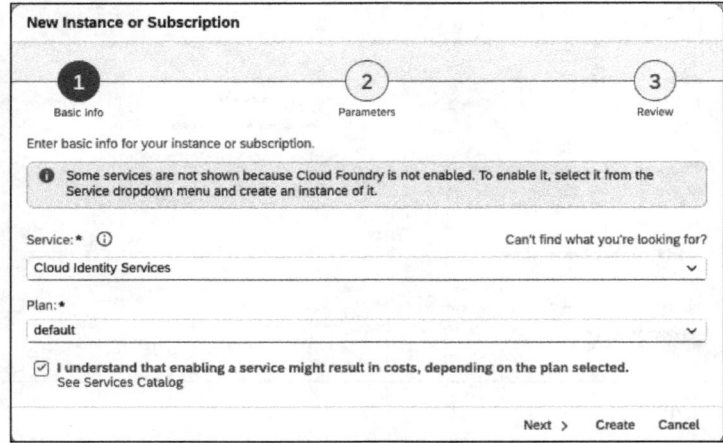

Figure 4.29 Creating Identity Authentication Tenant

Click **Create** to create the SAP Cloud Identity Services instance.

4.2 Authentication and Authorization Management

> **SAP Cloud Identity Services Instance**
>
> The creation screen differs if you have already activated Cloud Foundry in your tenant. Compare Figure 4.29 with Figure 9.11 in Chapter 9: The difference is in the choice of space and runtime environment.
>
> Also note that using SAP Cloud Identity Services means that a corresponding tenant for each global account is created once as a shared instance. This sharing means that creation happens only once and is then only shared. Our screenshots may not be 100% accurate at this point as an SAP Cloud Identity Services instance was already created on the training tenant beforehand.

You can view this instance in the SAP BTP cockpit under **Services • Instances and Subscriptions**, as shown in Figure 4.30.

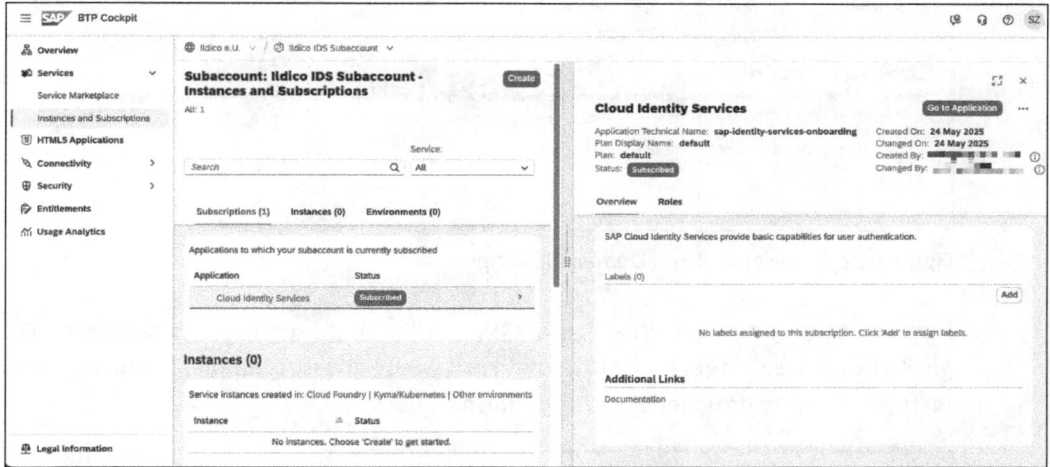

Figure 4.30 Overview of Instances and Subscriptions with Open SAP Cloud Identity Services Instance

This setup is sufficient for use with the global account. Additional options on the subaccount level are explored in Chapter 5.

Now navigate back to the SAP BTP cockpit of your global account under **Security • Trust Configuration**. Use **Establish Trust** to select the SAP Cloud Identity Service tenant to be used in the global account (see Figure 4.31).

Select your Identity Authentication tenant and click **Next**. On the next screen, select the internet domain under **Domain**. As shown in Figure 4.32, this should match the link in the browser and should end in *cloud.sap*. Click **Next**.

4   Global Account Administration

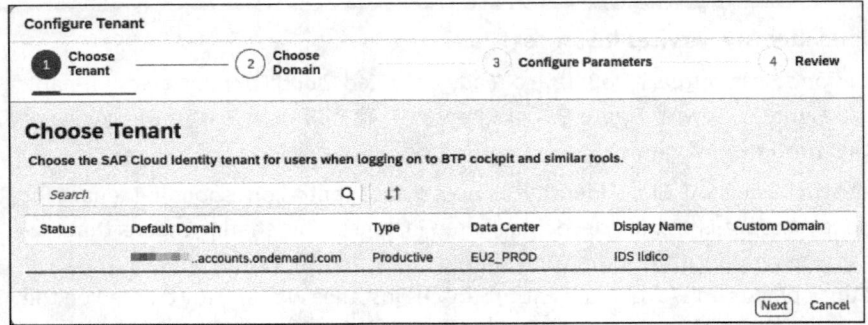

Figure 4.31 Selecting Identity Authentication Tenant

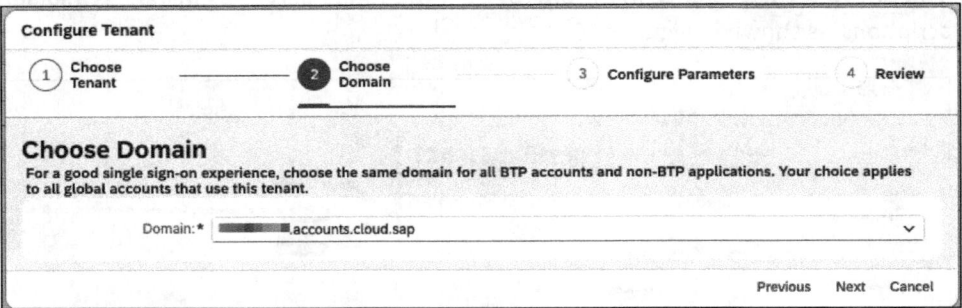

Figure 4.32 Browser Link and Domain Selection

Now enter the parameters (see Figure 4.33), ideally using a self-explanatory key for **Origin Key**. Click **Next** to get to the final overview, where you can complete the setup of the platform identity provider by clicking **Finish**.

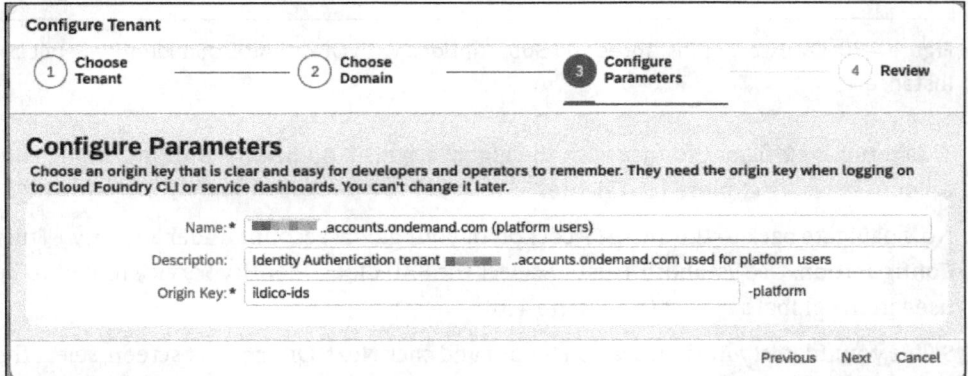

Figure 4.33 Identity Authentication Connection Parameters

Pay attention to the final message shown in Figure 4.34: The configuration setup now is not only valid for the global account but is also available for *all* subaccounts (but does not have to be used).

4.3 Directories

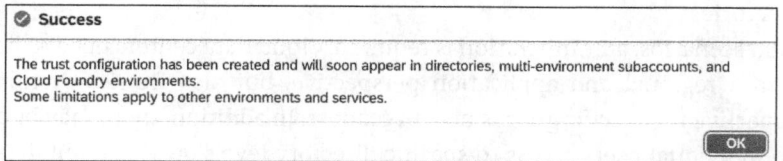

Figure 4.34 Final Message: Platform Identity Provider Has Been Set Up

The target screen is shown in Figure 4.35.

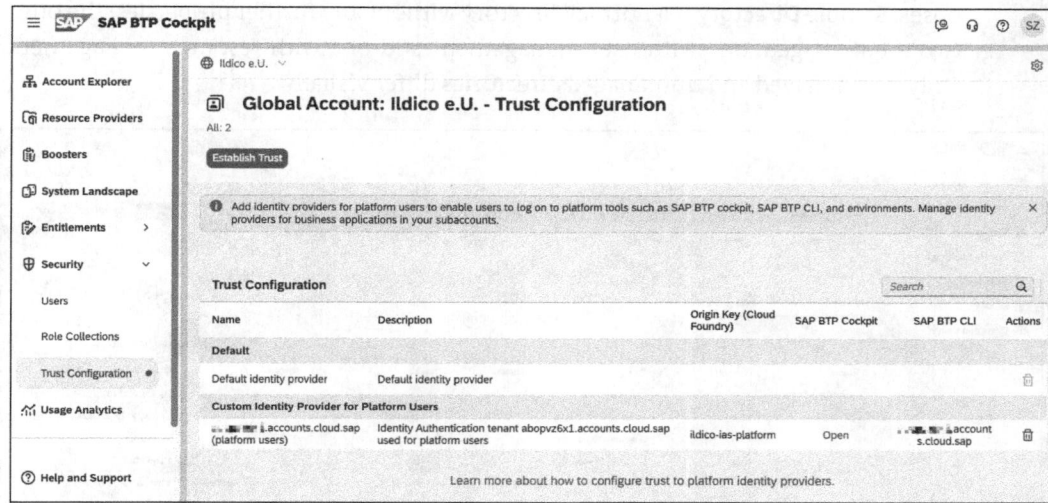

Figure 4.35 Trust Configuration with Platform Identity Provider Setup

In this practical example, we configured the platform identity provider based on identity authentication. You can now use and authorize users in your global account based on this configuration.

4.3 Directories

Directories help you to better structure your accounts in your account explorer. You are completely free to determine the division of the directories. For example, whether you separate development and quality assurance from production tenants in one directory or whether you group them by projects, is your individual decision.

SAP distinguishes between two different types of directories, as follows:

- **Simple directories**
  Simple directories are used for structuring purposes only. You can create simple tree structures with them. This is also explained in Chapter 5, Section 5.1. Simple directories are recommended, for example, if you want to subdivide similar subaccounts and need to centrally manage a set of up to 20 subaccounts.

4 Global Account Administration

- **Managed directories**

  For larger cloud scenarios, administration is required. Cloud data centers need to be managed from a regional and application perspective, but also from a system resource perspective for specific groups of subaccounts. In addition, there may be a need to grant individual users access to specific directory levels. At this point, it is time to look into managed directories.

You can find the directories in the SAP BTP cockpit of your global account, in the account explorer. In Figure 4.36, we have created three test directories for testing purposes. **Sample Directory** is a normal directory without any further properties; the other two are managed, one with user management and one with resource management. Only the managed and unmanaged directories differ visually.

Figure 4.36 Example Directories in Account Explorer

> **[+] Splitting Directories**
>
> Note that there can only be one managed directory in a directory hierarchy. Things like inherited permissions that overlap and the like currently are not possible.

To create a directory, select **Create** • **Directory** to reach the creation screen shown in Figure 4.37.

Click **Advanced** to display the additional options at the bottom of the screen. You can enter a name under **Display Name** and a root node under **Parent**. If you click the icon beside the directory name, a selection dialog for the object's root node opens.

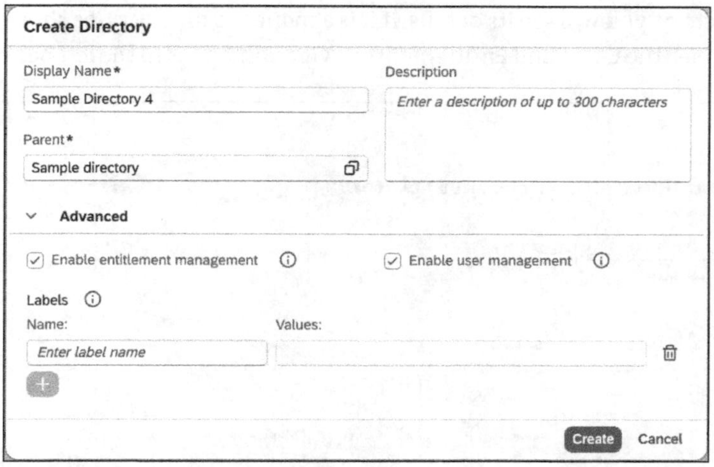

4.3 Directories

Figure 4.37 Directory Creation Screen

If you do not specify anything else, you will create a default directory node. With the **Enable Entitlement Management** and/or **Enable User Management** checkbox, you can make the new directory a managed directory. Click **Create** to create the directory. Figure 4.38 shows the created directory.

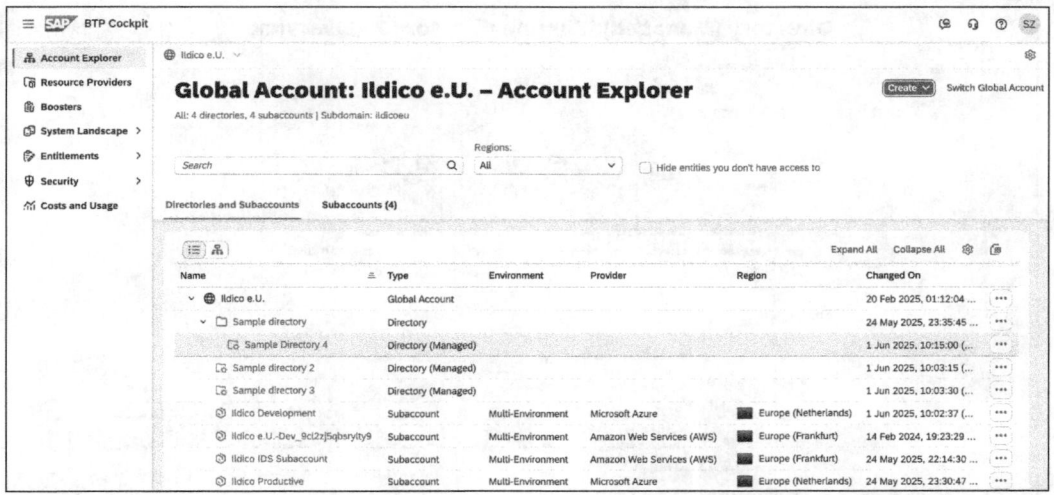

Figure 4.38 Subaccounts in Account Explorer with Updated Directory Structure

Now you can move the subaccounts into the directories by simply clicking and dragging the subaccount row, then releasing the mouse button. You can see an example result in Figure 4.39.

4   Global Account Administration

If you now click a directory, you will see its details. If it is a managed directory, as shown in Figure 4.40, you will see the **Users** and **Entitlements** navigation nodes in the left pane.

Figure 4.39 Subaccounts in Directories

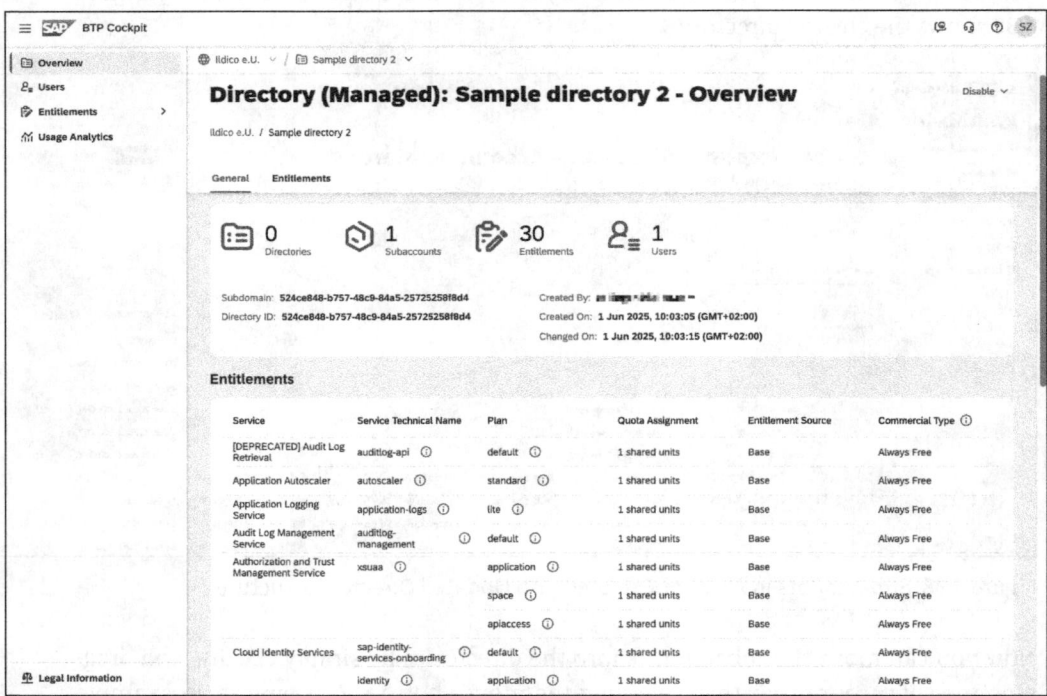

Figure 4.40 Detailed View of Directory

The example Sample Directory 2 was configured for entitlement management only. Figure 4.41 shows what happens when you navigate to an inactive item such as this. By clicking **Enable User Management**, you can easily configure user management for the directory.

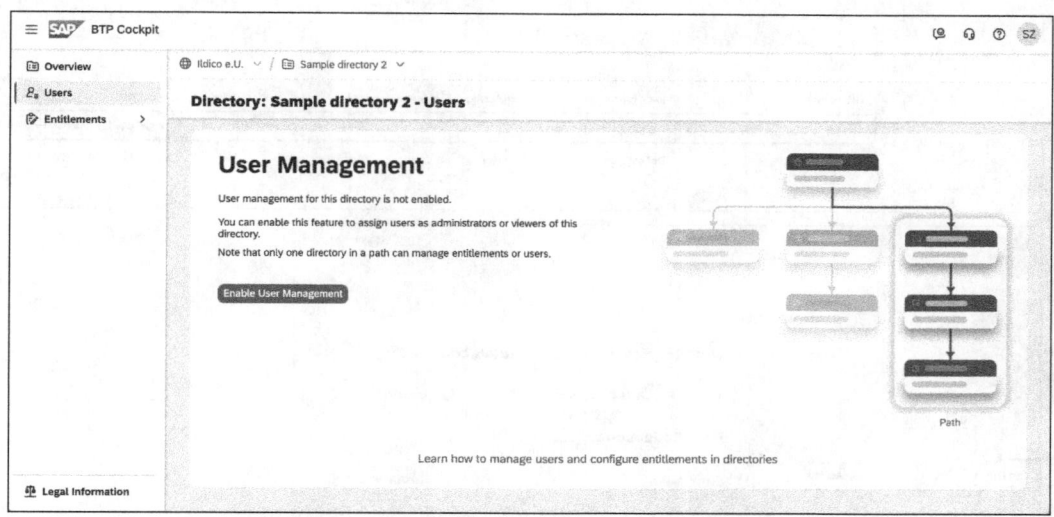

Figure 4.41 Access to User Management in Directory

In user management, users can be created with **Create User** in the same way as in the global account. These users are then specifically authorized for a directory. Figure 4.42 shows an example of a user creation screen.

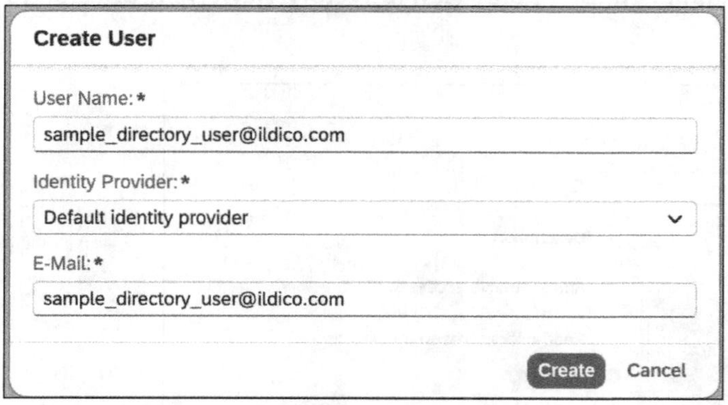

Figure 4.42 Creating Directory User

For the user to receive permissions, a few steps are necessary. First, navigate from the user overview via the ▷ icon to the user details (Figure 4.43). At the bottom right, you will find the assigned **Role Collections**.

4 Global Account Administration

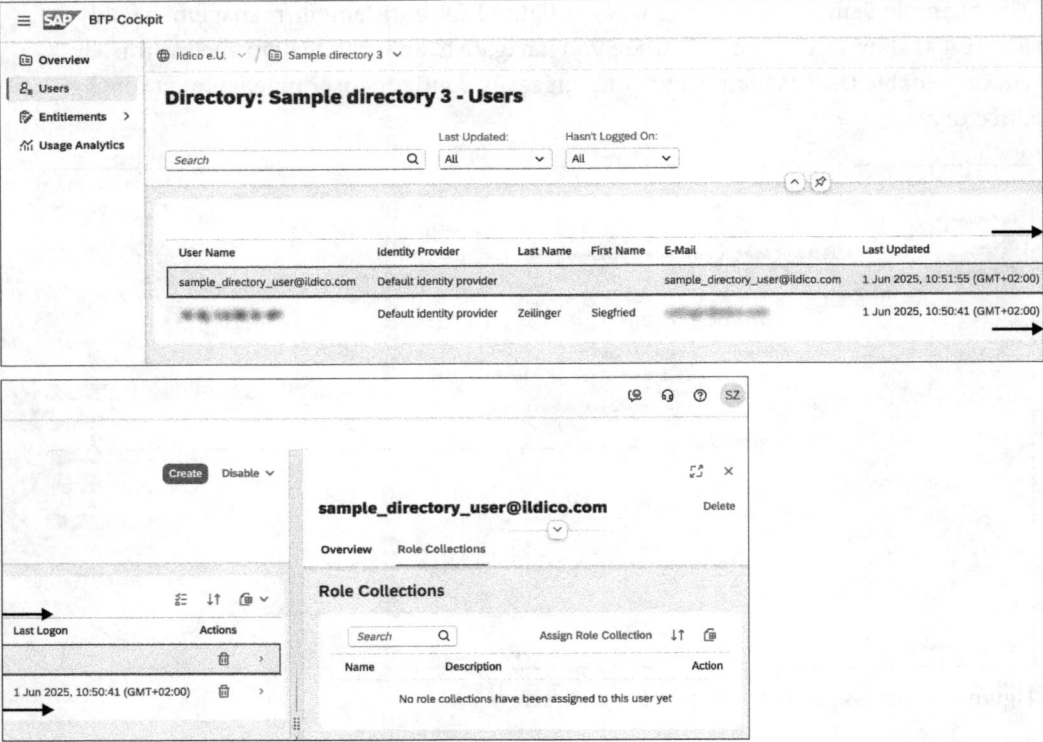

Figure 4.43 User Detail View At Directory

Click the **Assign Role Collection** link and choose whether the selected person may administrate (**Directory Administrator**) or only view (**Directory Viewer**) the directory, as shown in Figure 4.44.

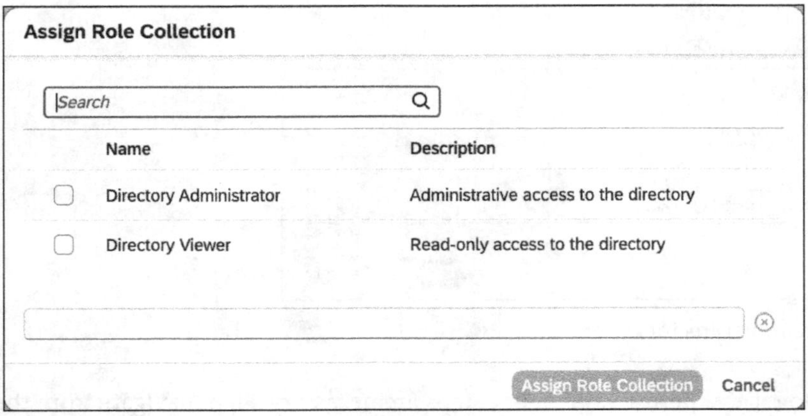

Figure 4.44 Directory Role Assignments

4.3 Directories

The entitlements, which we will discuss in the Section 4.7, can also be analyzed at the directory level in the corresponding menu item. This can be used to determine which assignments exist at the directory level. You will also find these mappings in the global account, but they are not broken down. Figure 4.45 shows the filtered selection of subaccounts in the directory.

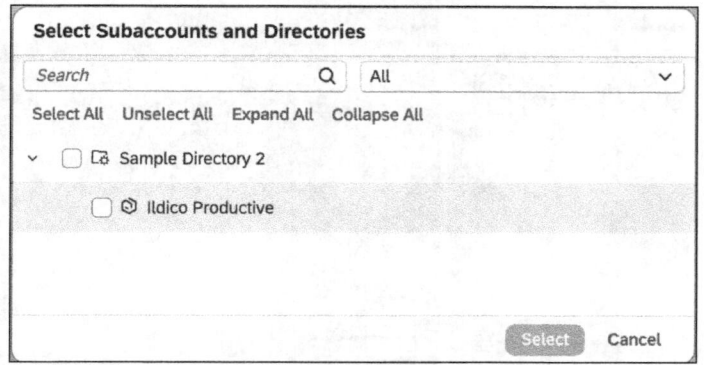

Figure 4.45 Selection in Subaccount Field

The **Service Assignments** in the directories are also filtered and prepared according to the assigned subaccounts (see Figure 4.46).

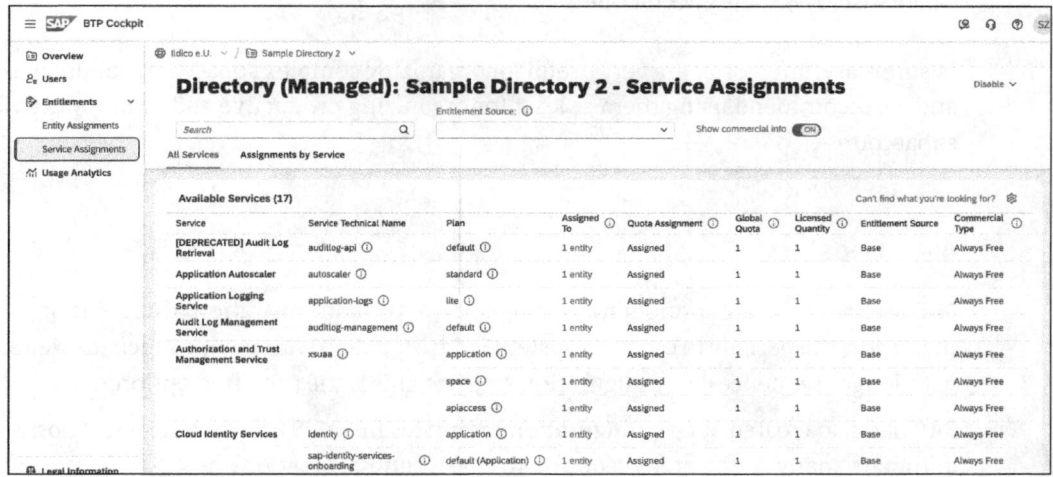

Figure 4.46 Service Assignments in Directory

Another tool to help with the administration of directories is **Usage Analytics**, which we will discuss in Section 4.8 and which you can see a preview of in Figure 4.47.

181

4 Global Account Administration

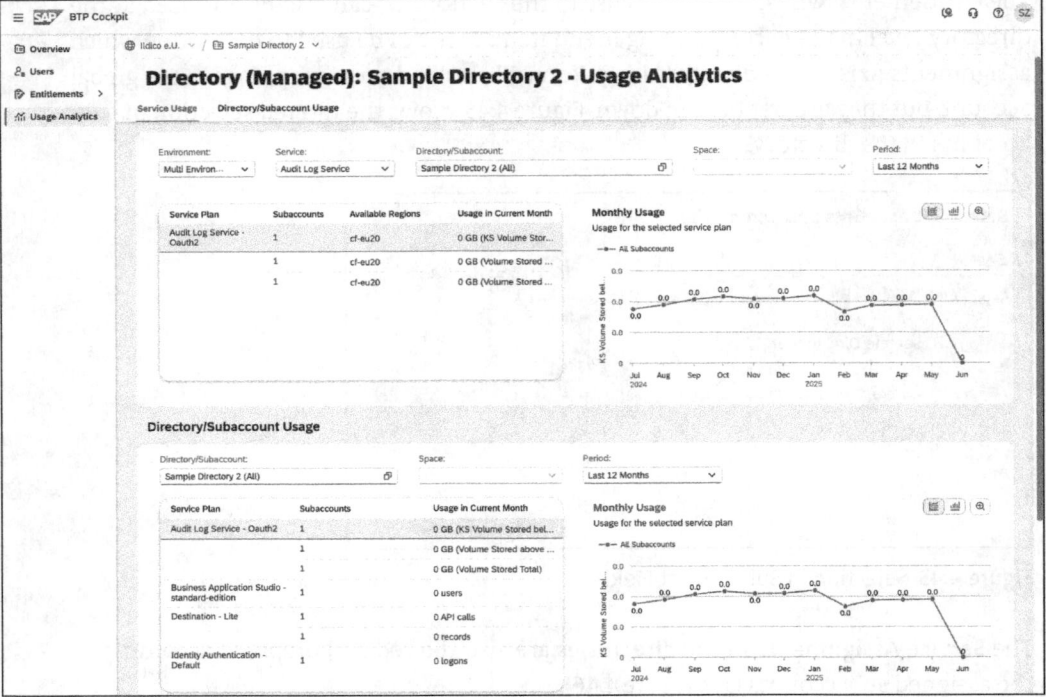

Figure 4.47 Usage Analytics for Directory

In summary, directories are very useful for organizing complex subaccount landscapes, and we recommend using them at least for organizing productive and nonproductive subaccounts.

4.4 Boosters

SAP uses ready-made configuration templates for the administration of its solutions in many areas. Especially in complex system landscapes and with new products, as well as with longer sequences of configuration settings, this is the preferred option.

SAP has also created such configuration templates in SAP BTP with boosters. *Boosters* automate many of the steps required to make certain functions or solutions quickly available, such as integrating data, setting up authentication mechanisms, or configuring connectivity services.

Boosters are offered in SAP BTP in your global account in the navigation under **Boosters**. They are subdivided into a filterable overview of tiles (see Figure 4.48), and detailed representations (see Figure 4.49). All configurations can be performed using a wizard-based interface, which reduces the complexity of administration.

4.4 Boosters

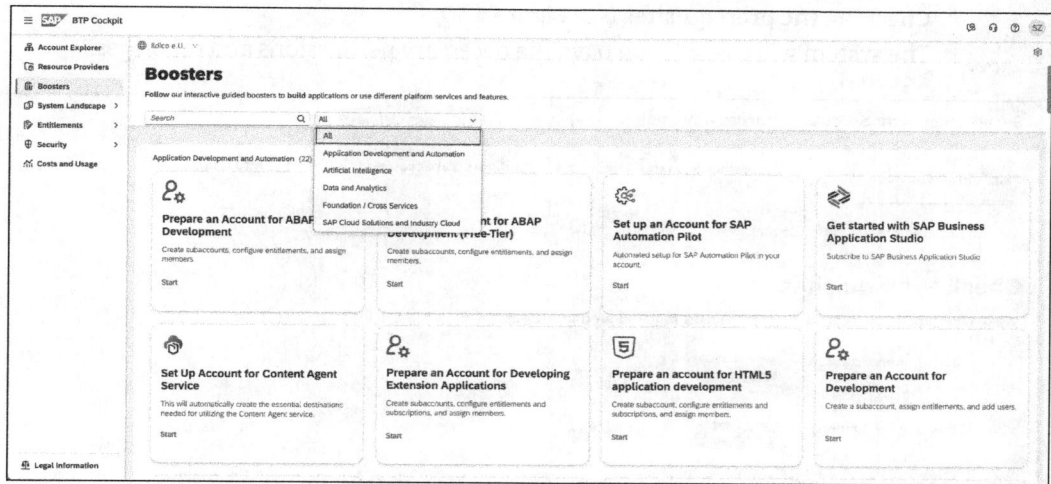

Figure 4.48 Filterable Entry to Boosters

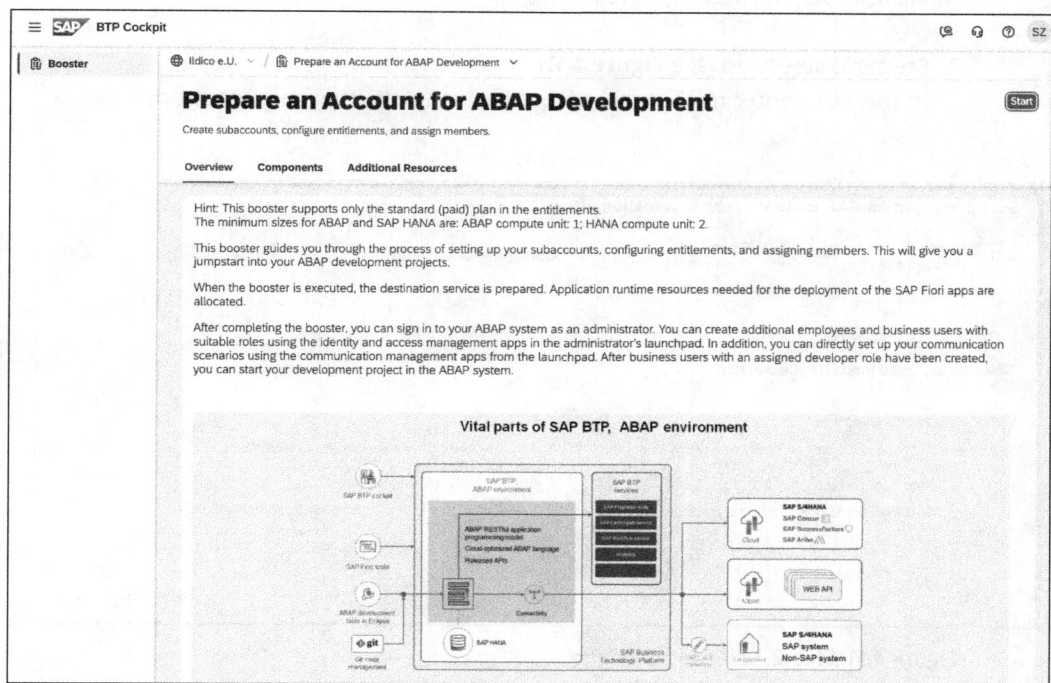

Figure 4.49 Details of Sample Booster

The following example walks through the steps to set up a (free) booster in SAP BTP. Start the booster via the **Start** button (as shown in Figure 4.49). The remaining steps, each completed by clicking **Next**, are as follows:

1. **Checking the prerequisites (see Figure 4.50)**
   The system will check if you have the necessary permissions and privileges.

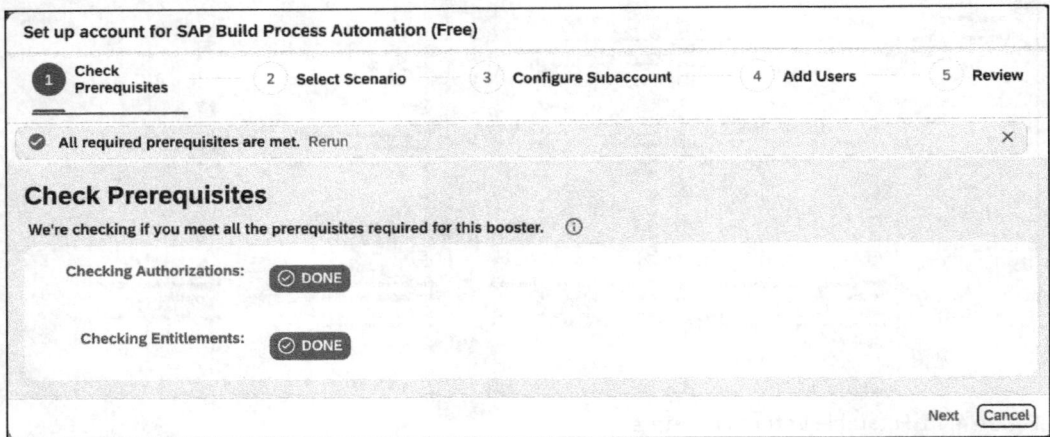

Figure 4.50 Step 1: Checking Prerequisites

2. **Scenario selection (see Figure 4.51)**
   In this step, you can choose whether to use an existing subaccount or create a new one.

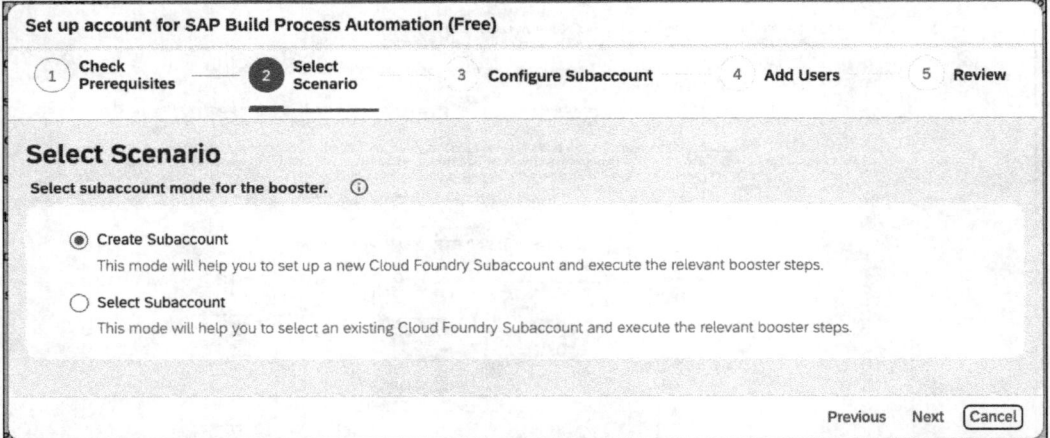

Figure 4.51 Step 2: Selecting Scenario

3. **Subaccount settings (see Figure 4.52)**
   This is where you specify how the subaccount will be included in your global account.

Figure 4.52 Step 3: Subaccount Settings

4. **Identity provider and user (see Figure 4.53)**
   In the last step, you specify the identity provider and can also specify authorized users.

5. **Summary (see Figure 4.54)**
   On the last screen, the summary, you can check all your settings and start the booster by clicking **Finish**.

4 Global Account Administration

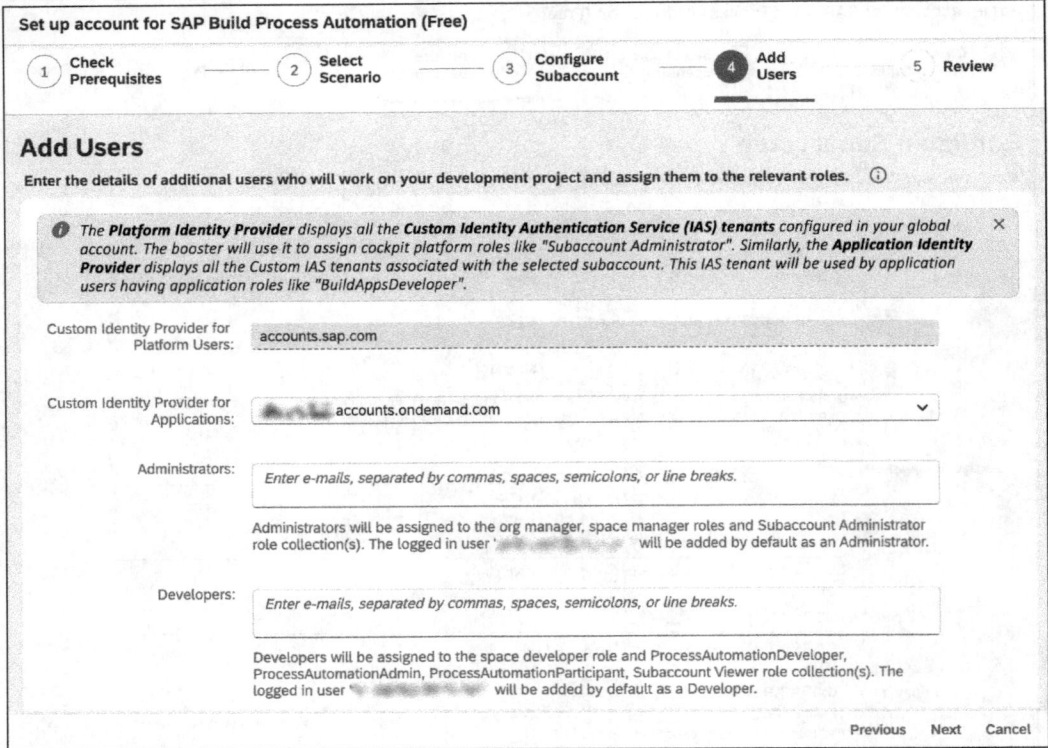

Figure 4.53 Step 4: Identity Provider and User

Figure 4.54 Step 5: Summary

Now you will see a progress screen, and when it completes, everything will be prepared for you (see Figure 4.55).

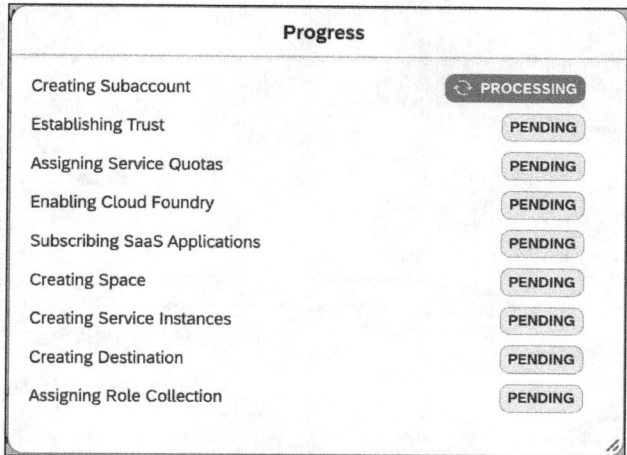

Figure 4.55 Wizard Execution: Progress Bar

The final **Success** screen (see Figure 4.56) allows you to navigate directly to the new subaccount using the **Navigate to Subaccount** link.

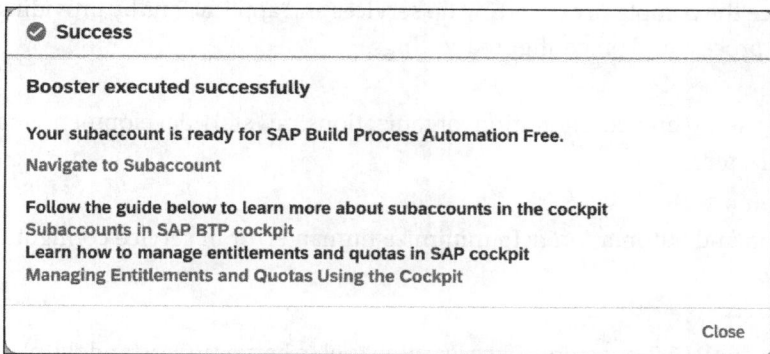

Figure 4.56 Success Message After Booster Execution

If you go to the subaccount and then navigate to **Services • Instances and Subscriptions**, you will see that the Cloud Foundry runtime, the corresponding service instance, and the corresponding application have been added and set up in this process (see Figure 4.57).

4 Global Account Administration

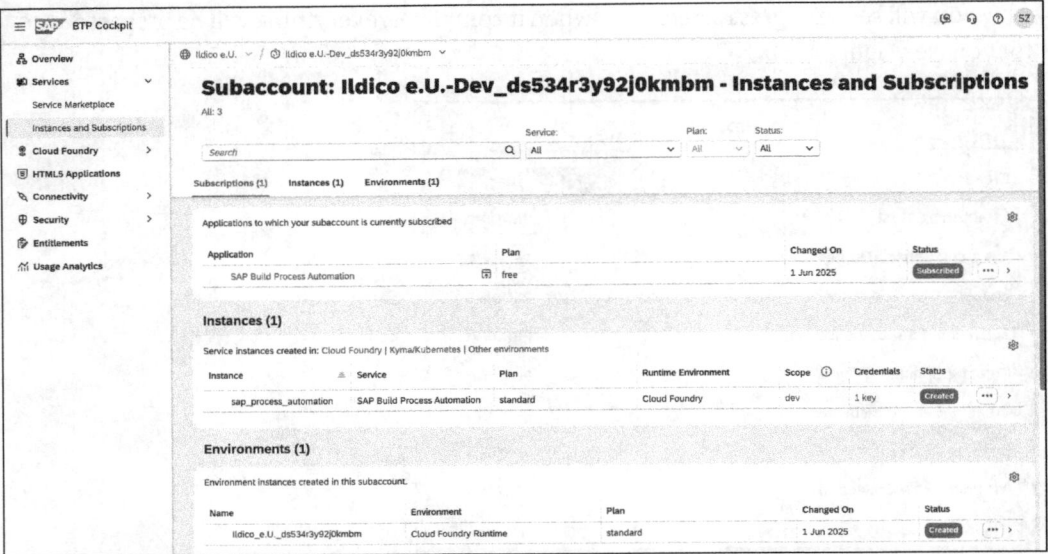

Figure 4.57 SAP BTP Cockpit of Created Subaccount

The benefits of an SAP BTP booster are, in a nutshell, as follows:

- **Simplification**
  Boosters reduce the complexity of setting up services and applications by providing a step-by-step process and preconfigured settings.

- **Time savings**
  By automating setup and configuration, organizations can start development and get to market faster.

- **Error reduction**
  Standardization and automation help minimize human error in service configuration.

- **Learning support**
  For new users of SAP BTP, boosters offer a learning tool to better understand the platform and its capabilities.

Boosters cover a wide range of use cases, including the integration of SAP and non-SAP applications, the development of new applications, the implementation of security and authentication mechanisms, and much more.

4.5 System Landscape

If you want to connect an SAP cloud solution such as SAP SuccessFactors or SAP Marketing Cloud to your global account, you can do so using an integration token. The integration takes place in the SAP BTP cockpit of your global account under the **System Landscape** menu item. The following SAP solutions can be connected:

- SAP S/4HANA Cloud
- SAP Marketing Cloud
- SAP SuccessFactors
- SAP Commerce Cloud
- SAP Cloud for Customer
- SAP Field Service Management

The basic procedure is as follows: First, under **System Landscape • Systems**, click **Add System** (see Figure 4.58).

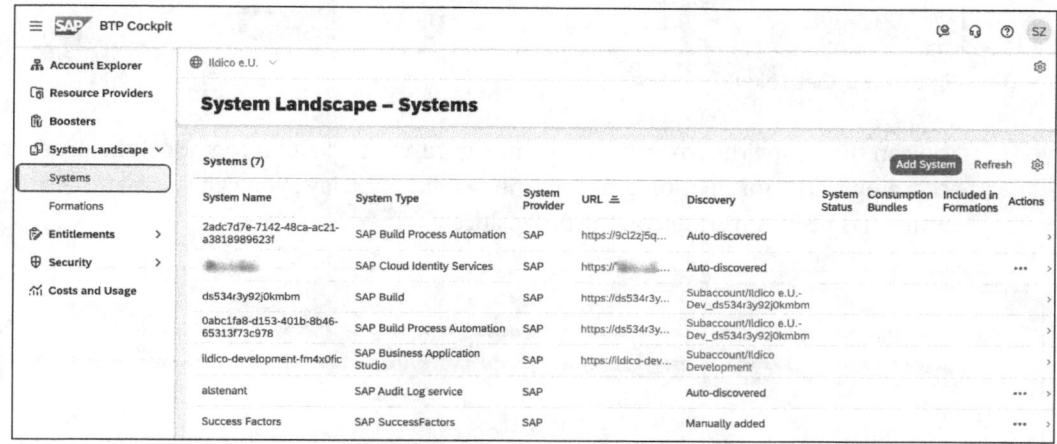

Figure 4.58 Accessing System Landscape

In the next step, select the **System Type** and enter a **System Name** (see Figure 4.59). In this example, we have chosen **SAP SuccessFactors**.

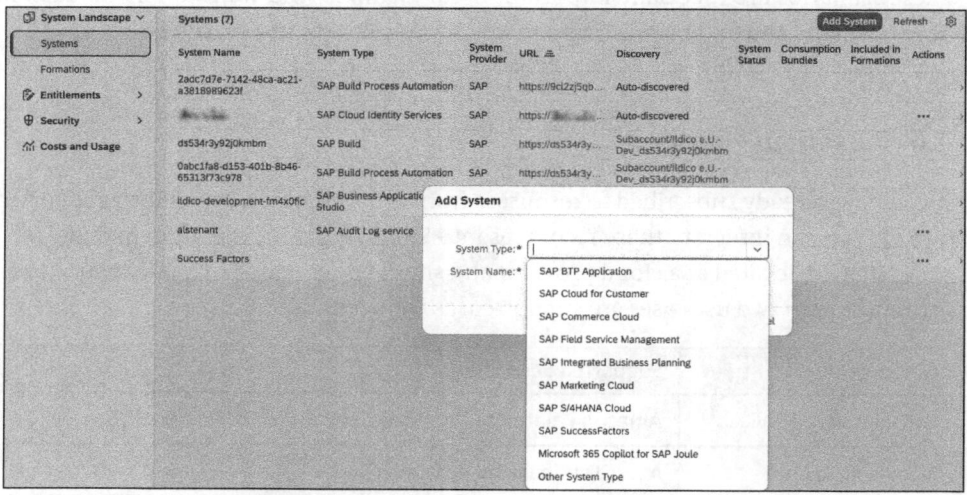

Figure 4.59 Selecting System Type

4 Global Account Administration

Now you can directly create the token for the authentication in the target system (see Figure 4.60) by clicking **Get Token**.

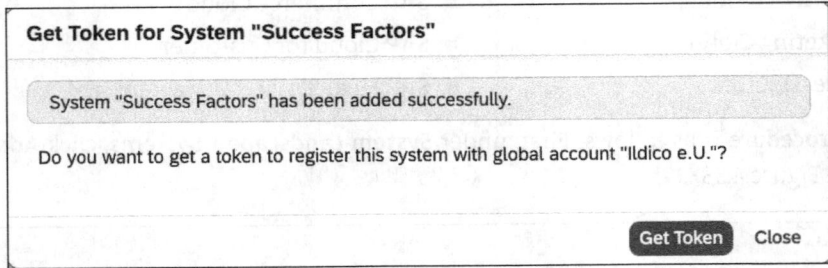

Figure 4.60 Get Token

You can then copy the token as shown in Figure 4.61 and add it to your cloud product according to the installation guide. In the system overview, you can see that the trust setting has been confirmed on the other side.

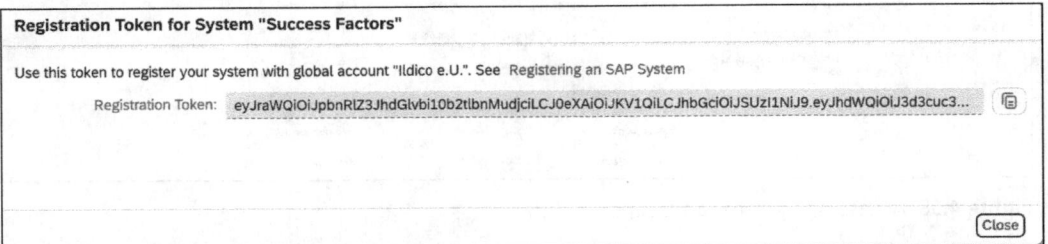

Figure 4.61 Receiving SAP BTP Token for Target System

These scenarios are especially important if, for example, you want to rely on custom developments and extensions for your SAP SuccessFactors installation.

4.6 Resource Provider

If you have already subscribed to resources from one of the cloud providers supported by SAP, you can integrate these resources into SAP BTP. Examples might include databases that are located at a cloud provider and should be accessed by your applications. Currently, only two use cases are supported, as shown in Table 4.1.

Cloud Vendor	Supported Services
Amazon Web Services	Amazon Relational Database Service (RDS)—PostgreSQL
Microsoft Azure	Azure Database for PostgreSQL

Table 4.1 Services Supported by Cloud Providers

4.6 Resource Provider

To create a resource provider, navigate to **Resource Providers** in your global account in the SAP BTP cockpit (see Figure 4.62). Now use the **New Provider** button to access the creation dialog.

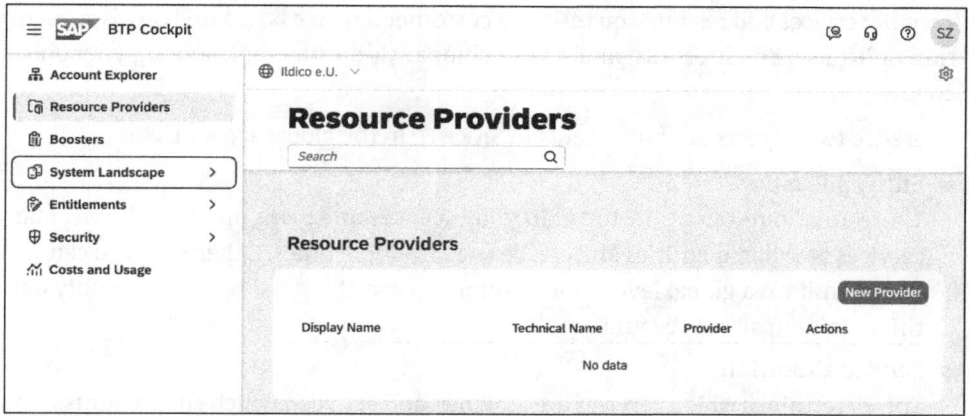

Figure 4.62 Overview of Resource Providers in Global Account

The resources received from the providers are now entered in the configuration dialog (see Figure 4.63).

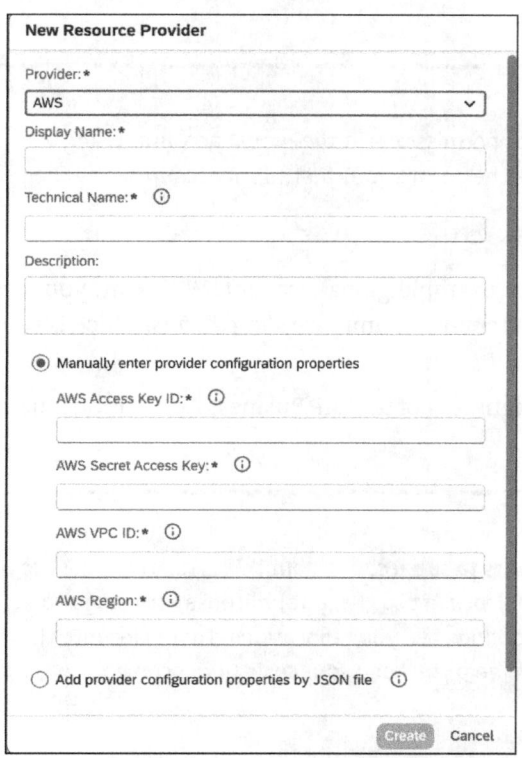

Figure 4.63 Resource Provider Registration Dialog

4.7 Entitlements

Entitlements can be thought of as *rights*; they determine the allocation of resources and services made available to an organization or user. These entitlements define which specific services and resource quantities a customer has access to based on his subscription or license. You must distribute your company's entitlements among your subaccounts.

There are two aspects of entitlements in SAP BTP in the global account:

- **Entity allocations**
  These are the resources included in your licenses and plans and their limits. Many services are shared entities and can be used multiple times. Otherwise, you can set a quota limit on a global level—for example, to specify that a service may only exist three times in all subaccounts.

- **Service allocation**
  This determines which services are assigned and active in which subaccounts.

The management of entitlements is an essential part of administration as it allows you to use and control cloud resources efficiently and can save you a lot of money. You can manage your entitlements via the SAP BTP cockpit under the **Entitlements** menu option. There, you can view your current allocations, make adjustments, and monitor the usage of your subscribed services.

> **Configuring Entitlements in Practice**
>
> In practice, you start the distribution of permissions in the global account. Using the optional directories, you then distribute the permissions first to subaccounts, and then to spaces.

Figure 4.64 shows the allocations of an example global account. With **Edit**, you can change the quotas. Note that in our test tenant, all units are *shared units*, which is why they are difficult to see in the example.

Figure 4.65 shows an example of the assignment of the SAP Business Application Studio service in our example tenant.

> **Common Issues Related to Entitlements**
>
> People often forget to assign entitlements to subaccounts, but this is relatively easy to fix. If you are using a usage-based model, be sure to check your license terms and conditions; you will quickly incur costs if you increase your allocations. That leads into the next topic, usage monitoring, which will help you keep your costs under control.

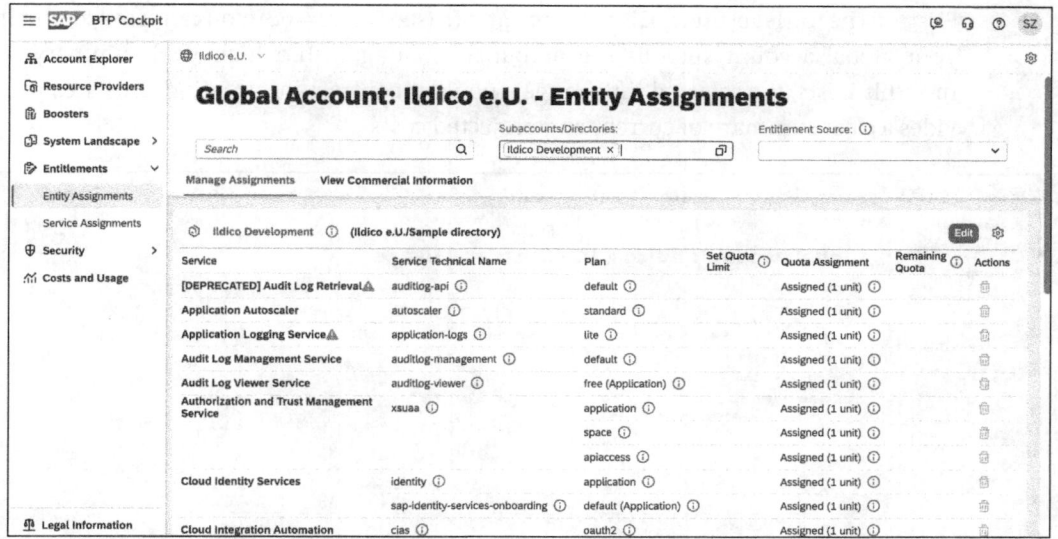

Figure 4.64 Entity Assignments

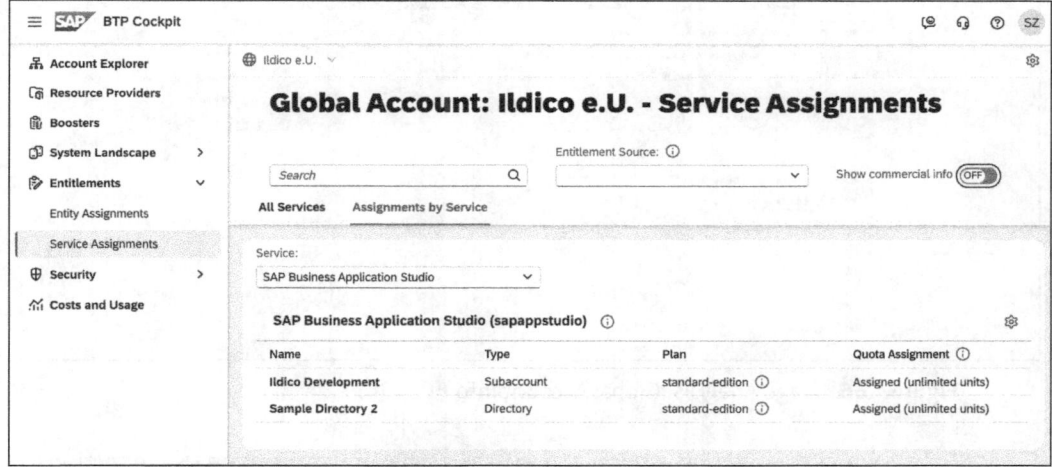

Figure 4.65 Service Assignments

4.8 Usage Monitoring

With the **Costs and Usage** menu of the SAP BTP cockpit, you can monitor cloud resources and services and also get an overview of the (forecasted) running costs. If you navigate to the **Costs and Usage** menu in the SAP BTP cockpit, you will find different sources of information.

First, on the top level under **Global Account Info** (see Figure 4.66), you can see facts about your global account such as the **Account ID**, along with a high-level summary of monthly costs, the selected time range, and your contract information. This area provides a clear summary of current and projected costs.

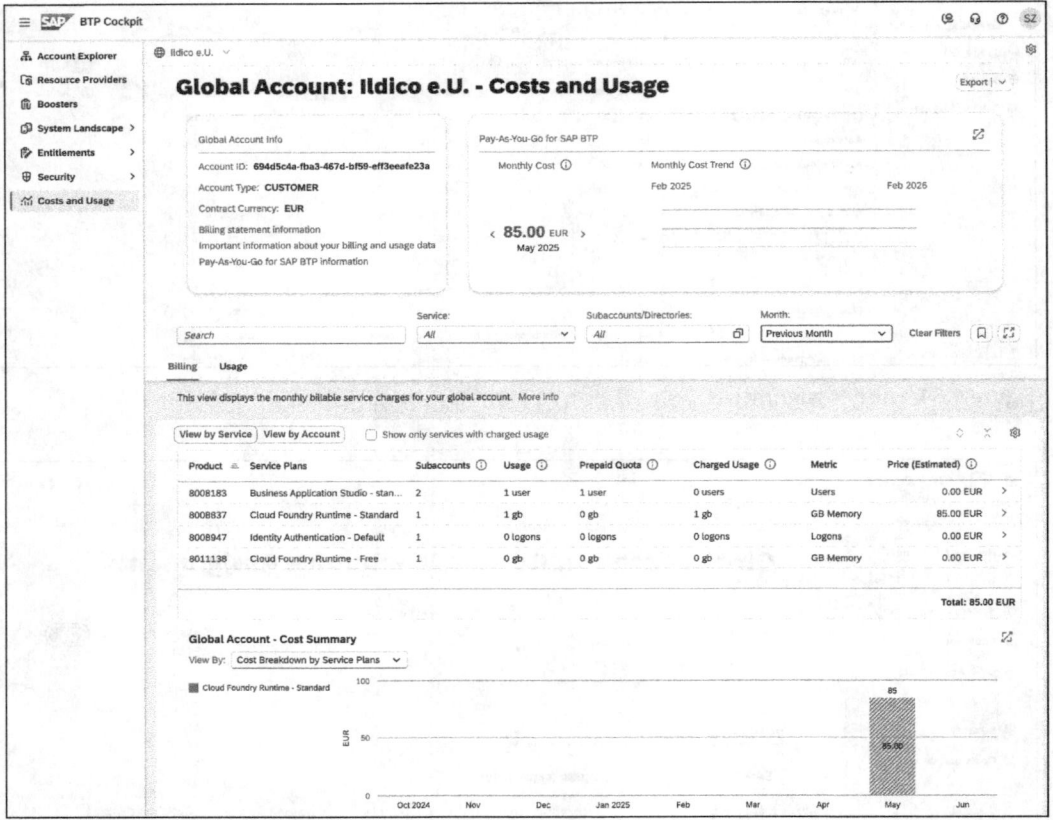

Figure 4.66 Usage Analysis: Global Account Info

Below, when you filter by **Service**, you will see a table under the main **Usage** section that shows resource usage grouped by service plan. This table includes information like **Service Plan**, **Usage**, and **Metric**. This helps identify which services and plans are consuming the most resources (see Figure 4.67).

If you drill down into a particular service plan from the usage table, you'll see detailed consumption data by subaccount or directory for that service. This provides insights into how the service is being used across different parts of your organization (see Figure 4.68).

4.8 Usage Monitoring

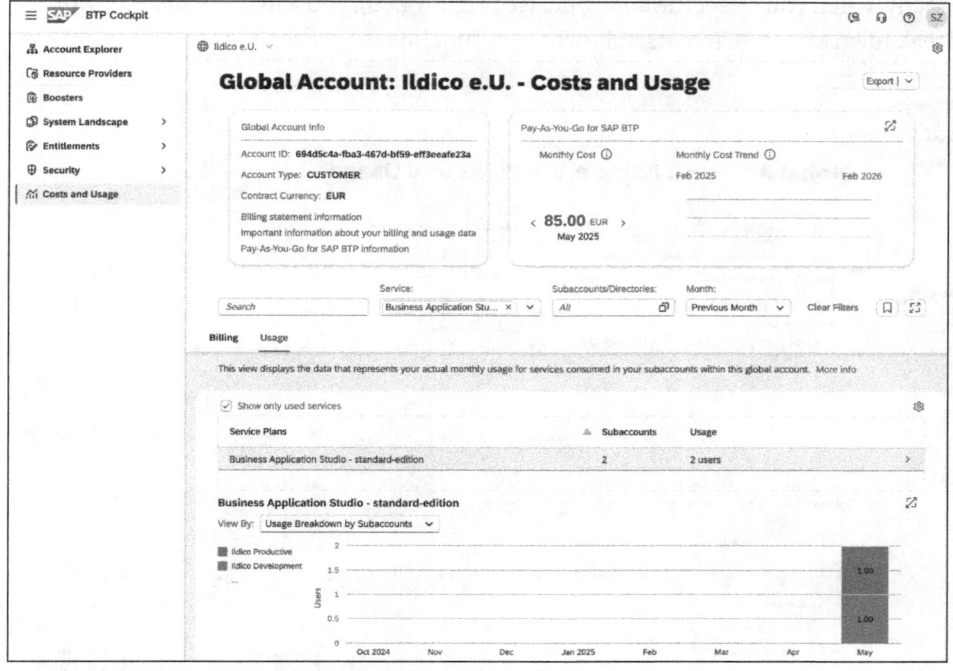

Figure 4.67 Usage Analysis: Service Plans

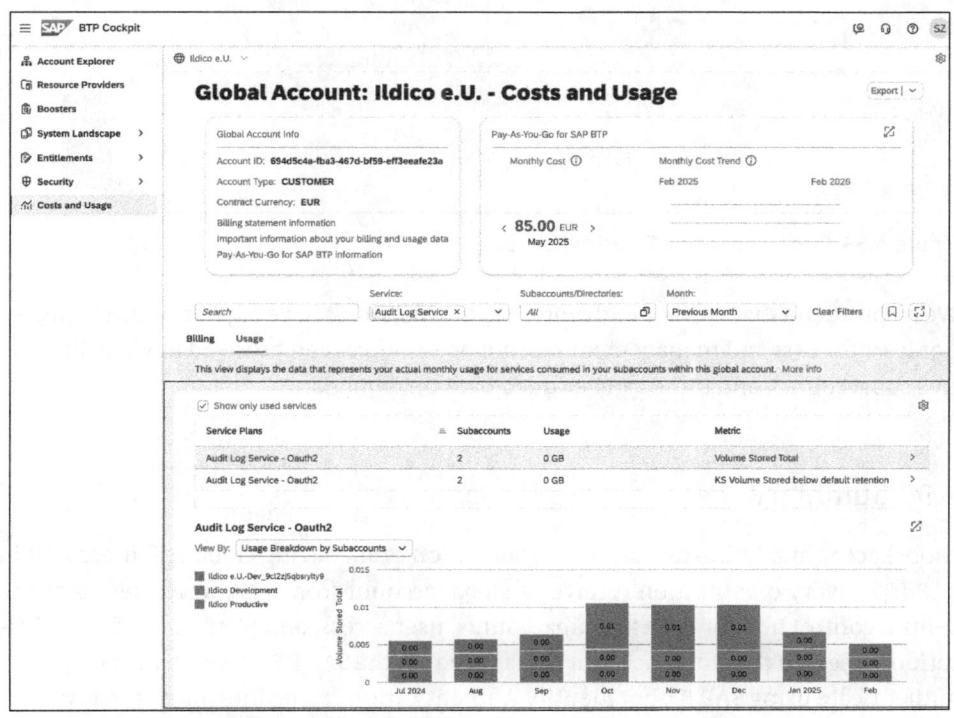

Figure 4.68 Usage Analysis: Service Usage

Finally, when you select the **Billing** tab (see Figure 4.69), you will see a subaccount-based breakdown of SAP BTP costs, followed by a timeline diagram.

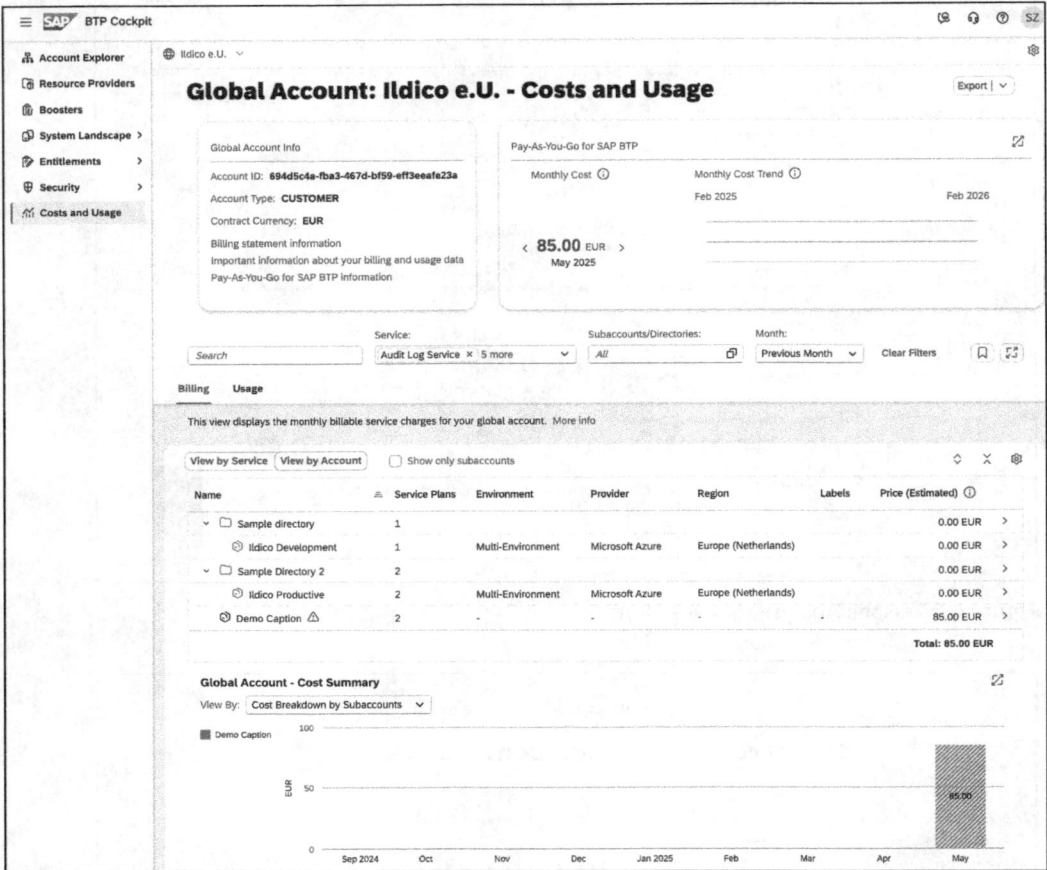

Figure 4.69 Subaccount and Directory Usage

We recommend that you regularly monitor the costs and usage of your cloud services—not least for cost and management reasons as resources can be saved in virtually inactive subaccounts, and these can be added back on demand.

4.9 Summary

Global account administration is the foundation of managing cloud resources within SAP BTP. Every organization receives a global account from SAP, which serves as the central control hub for licenses, subaccounts, user access, and platform-wide configuration. Access to the global account is managed via the SAP BTP cockpit. Users typically authenticate using SAP ID, but Identity Authentication can be integrated for advanced scenarios, such as connecting to corporate identity stores and enabling multifactor authentication. Managing users, assigning role collections, and controlling access is crucial for maintaining secure administration.

Role collections in the global account—such as administrator, viewer, or directory admin—determine user capabilities. These can be customized to suit organizational needs. Directories help in structuring and organizing subaccounts logically, either for purely visual grouping or for managed control of entitlements and user permissions across large landscapes.

Boosters are SAP's wizard-based tools to quickly configure and deploy common SAP BTP scenarios, automating many setup tasks and reducing errors.

The system landscape feature allows integration of other SAP cloud solutions (e.g., SAP SuccessFactors or SAP Marketing Cloud) by using authentication tokens, thus simplifying centralized administration. SAP BTP also supports integrating cloud infrastructure resources via resource providers, expanding flexibility in hybrid deployments.

Entitlements determine which services and resources are allocated to which subaccounts. Managing entitlements effectively is key to optimizing usage, avoiding unnecessary costs, and staying within license limits. Finally, usage monitoring tools offer visibility into service consumption and cost trends, enabling better governance and cost control across the cloud environment.

Chapter 5
Subaccount Administration

Well-designed subaccount user management is the key to running your cloud environment securely. In this chapter, we will show you how to lay the groundwork for this task via roles and role collections.

This chapter provides a holistic approach to efficient subaccount management and dives deep into the nature of authentication and authorization management. In Section 5.1, you will learn how to create a subaccount. Section 5.2 next emphasizes the importance of roles and role collections for user management by explaining the underlying principles and the versatility of their practical application. This includes the design of security policies and access protection, which are central to the management of subaccounts. Practical instructions follow, showing you how to configure authentication by using Identity Authentication for subaccounts. We go into detail about how these configuration steps enable seamless integration with Microsoft Entra ID (formerly Azure Active Directory) as the identity provider, ensuring secure and efficient user management within the cloud infrastructure. In addition, we examine the organizational structure of a directory in detail.

In Section 5.3, you will learn how to efficiently manage the use of cloud resources with organizations, spaces, and quotas. Section 5.4 then shows you how to use subscriptions and services strategically to customize your subaccounts to meet your unique needs. You will also see how a well-organized Cloud Foundry structure can help increase efficiency. Another focus is on the SAP Audit Log Viewer service for SAP BTP, a powerful tool that is essential for monitoring management. In Section 5.5, we present methods for analyzing audit logs to identify and investigate security-related events. This is critical to ensuring security and compliance within the subaccount environment.

In summary, this chapter is a comprehensive resource that covers not only the technical implementation but also the strategic planning and security management of subaccounts in the SAP BTP environment. These contents will enable you to manage subaccounts with a higher degree of professionalism.

5.1 Creating a Subaccount

With the help of subaccounts, you can structure your global account according to your needs and the organization of your projects. You can structure the management of members and permissions as well as entitlements.

5 Subaccount Administration

Each subaccount must be created within a region and a data center. The region reflects the physical location of the data center in which applications, data, and services are hosted. The region does not have to be the same as your company's location.

The subaccounts structured under a global account are independent of each other. You must take this into account when planning the overall architecture regarding security, member administration, data management, data migration, and integration. In the SAP BTP cockpit, under the **Account Explorer** menu, all subaccounts assigned to your global account are displayed (see Figure 5.1).

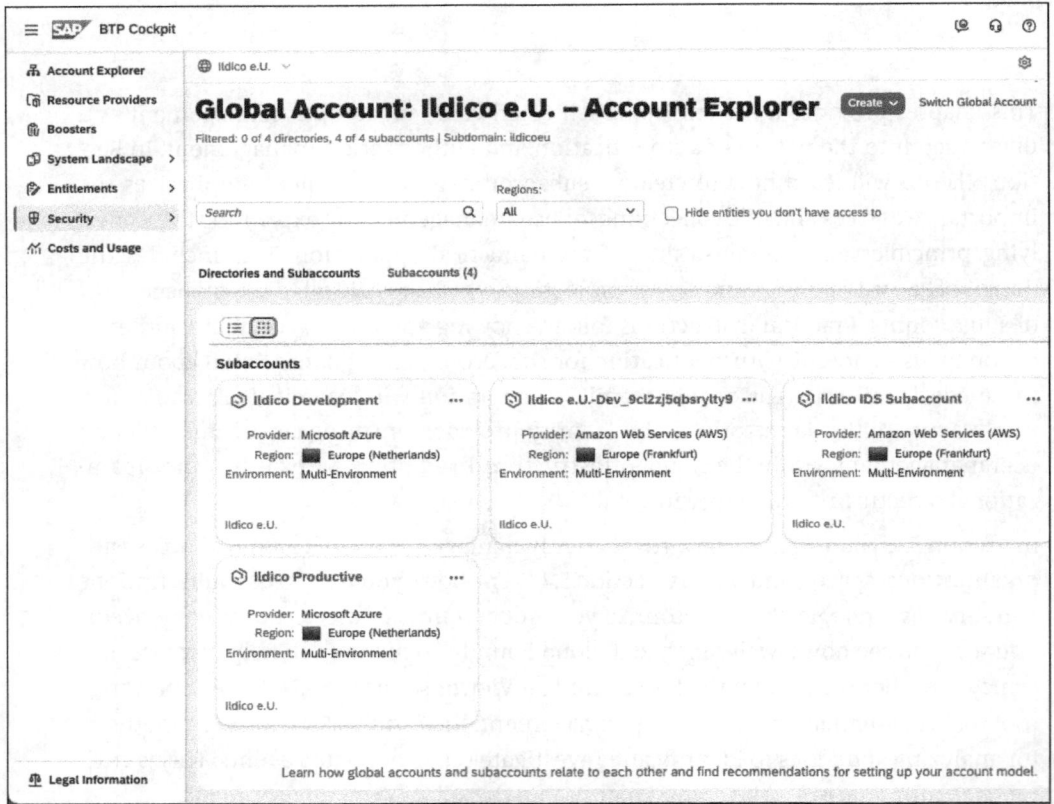

Figure 5.1 Overview of Subaccounts in SAP BTP Cockpit

> **[+] Select a Reasonable Subaccount Structure**
>
> At the subaccount level, you can configure system connections, among other things. Separate subaccounts for production systems and development are recommended, just to separate resources and system connections. Furthermore, you can create additional security by separating the backends used (SAP ERP HCM, SAP ERP, etc.) or the responsible teams.

200

5.1 Creating a Subaccount

In contrast to global accounts, you can create subaccounts yourself, as follows:

1. In the account explorer, navigate to **Create • Subaccount**.
2. In the dialog to create the subaccount, select a name under **Display Name**.
3. In the dropdown menu for **Region**, select an option. The options are sorted by the service host, then by region. You can choose **Amazon Web Services (AWS)**, **Google Cloud Platform**, or **Microsoft Azure**, each of which offers multiple regions. Your data will be hosted by the provider in a data center in that region (see Figure 5.2).

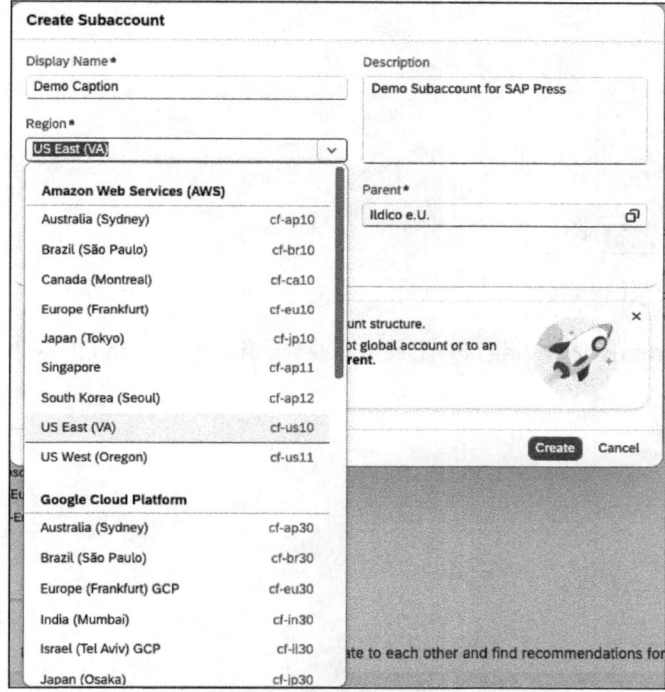

Figure 5.2 Selecting Subaccount Region

4. Next, you can select a **Subdomain** (see Figure 5.3). This step is optional. The subdomain is automatically generated as a suggestion and can be overwritten by a customer name, which must be unique within SAP BTP. We'll discuss the subdomain in more detail ahead.
5. In the **Advanced** section, you can check the **Used for Production** box if this is a production account (see Figure 5.3). This has no direct effect on your subaccount, but it helps the SAP system to prioritize your support tickets when it is a productive subaccount.
6. Finally, click **Create** to create the subaccount.

5   Subaccount Administration

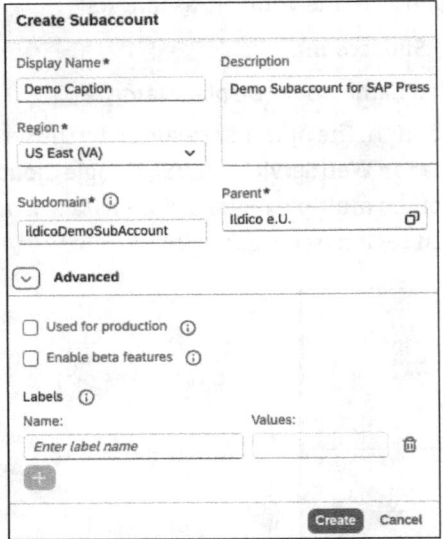

Figure 5.3 Advanced Settings for Subaccount Creation

7. After a short while, the **Creation Pending** label (see Figure 5.4) disappears, and the subaccount is ready for use.

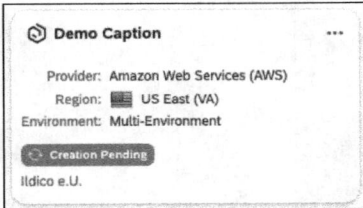

Figure 5.4 Subaccount Being Created

When choosing the subdomain, you should pay attention to the following points:

- The subdomain name may only contain letters, numbers, and underscores.
- The subdomain name must not contain any hyphens at the beginning or end.
- The subdomain must be unique across all subaccounts in the selected region. If another customer already uses the subdomain you want, you must choose a different subdomain.
- Upper- and lowercase letters are allowed, but the case will not affect name matching.

[»] **Neo Environment**

In the lower part of the region selection of the subaccount creation dialog, you will see several entries with the prefix *neo*. Note that the Neo platform will be retired by SAP at the end of 2028 and is therefore no longer covered in this book.

When creating subaccounts, you may have noticed that there is also an option to create directories. If you have a lot of accounts to manage, it is a good idea to divide them into directories. As you can see in Figure 5.5, you can customize the view in the account explorer. In addition, you can access a graphical view by clicking the **Distribution** button 🔲, as shown in Figure 5.6.

Figure 5.5 Example of Using Directories

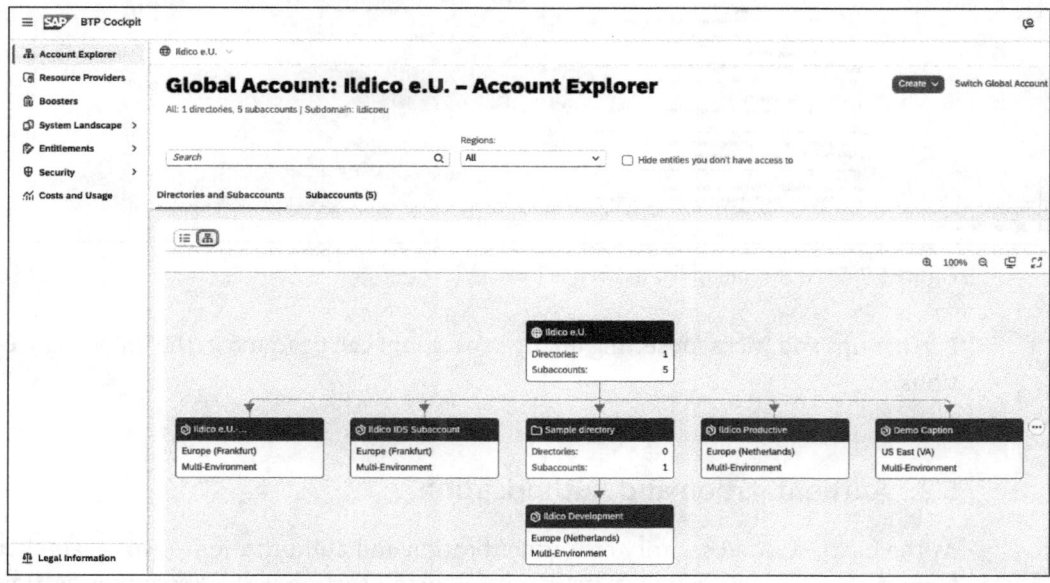

Figure 5.6 Graphical View of Directories

5   Subaccount Administration

> **[+] Selecting Alibaba Cloud as the Provider**
>
> Alibaba Cloud cannot be selected as a provider at this point. If you want to use Alibaba Cloud, you must contact your SAP sales manager.

Because not all services are available in all environments and regions, we recommend that you check in advance in the SAP BTP documentation whether the desired services are available from the preferred provider in the desired region. SAP Discovery Center (available at *https://discovery-center.cloud.sap/index.html*) lists all cloud services and their geographical availability. When you activate a service via the **Services • Service Marketplace** path, you can also see in which data centers the service is offered (see Figure 5.7).

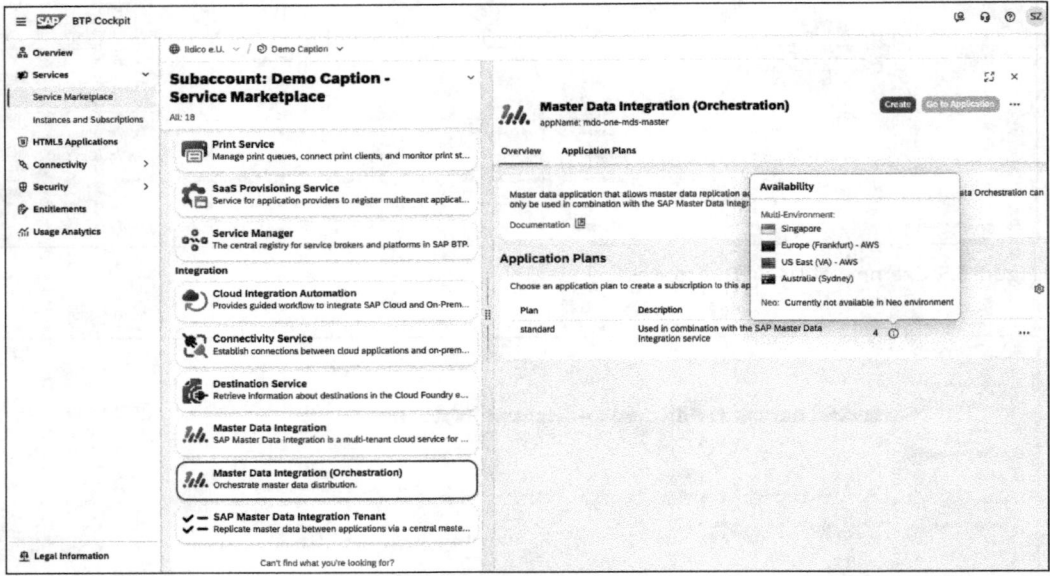

Figure 5.7 Service Availability in Service Detail View

Further tips and tricks for setting up the subaccount can be found in the following sections.

5.2   Authentication and Authorization

At the heart of cloud security are authentication and authorization—two pillars that form the basis for protecting digital resources. In this section, we look at authentication and authorization within an SAP BTP subaccount and how these two processes work together seamlessly to ensure a secure environment.

Within this section, you will find some general information about authentication and authorization. In Section 5.2.1, we'll examine user management, and Section 5.2.2 will cover trust configuration within the subaccount.

Authentication is the process of validating and confirming that a user is who they say they are. Passwords are the most commonly used authentication method. If a user enters the correct password for his or her user account or user name, then the system assumes that the identity is valid and grants access.

However, this simple authentication method is susceptible to *brute force attacks*, in which an attacker tries to log in with different passwords until the right password is found. Often, the passwords used in such attacks are not chosen at random but are read from a list of frequently used passwords. Brute force attacks can be made more difficult by ensuring that user accounts are locked after a certain number of incorrect login attempts.

Another measure against such attacks is to enforce strong passwords with password policies. Passwords for access to SAP applications should always consist of upper- and lowercase letters, numbers, and special characters. Passwords should also be changed at regular intervals. In addition to password policies, you should also maintain a list of words and terms that should not be used in passwords.

Other technologies such as client certificates, biometrics, one-time tokens, or custom authentication applications can also be used for authentication. SAP BTP offers you a lot of flexibility at this point. When using client certificates, the user's identity is verified by exchanging a digital certificate. The certificate is issued by a trusted authority and uniquely assigned to a user account. With SAP Passport, for example, SAP offers the possibility to create a digital client certificate for your S-user or P-user. You can then log onto various SAP websites, SAP Support Portal, and SAP BTP. You can find detailed information about this in SAP Support Portal at *https://support.sap.com/en/my-support/single-sign-on-passports.html*.

In certain cases, systems require the successful verification of more than one factor or characteristic before access is granted. This is referred to as *multifactor authentication* (MFA) and is often used to increase security compared to traditional password authentication. An additional proof of identity is required when logging in. The following factors are typically used:

- SMS token
- Hardware token
- Software token
- Authentication apps
- Phone call
- FIDO2 security key

These additional authentications and verifications are usually performed by the identity provider, which has to enable the corresponding components. The different options for identity providers are explained in Section 5.2.3. Successful authentication is followed by authorization, which determines which resources and actions an authenticated user can

5   Subaccount Administration

access. Section 5.2.3 also shows how to implement permissions and how to use roles and role sets to control access control.

Authorization is the process of granting a user permission to access a particular resource or functionality. This term is often used synonymously with *access control*. If you allow someone to download a certain file from your server, this is an example of authorization. Granting administrative access to an application to a single user is also an example. In secure environments, authorization always occurs after authentication. Users must first prove that their identity is genuine before they are granted access to the requested resources. SAP BTP uses three different standards for authorization: SAML, OAuth, and OpenID Connect (OIDC—which is based on OAuth).

In Section 5.2.4 and Section 5.2.5, we show practical examples for setting up identity authentication and for setting up Microsoft Entra ID as an identity provider.

5.2.1   User Administration

You can add users as members to an organization within your SAP BTP subaccount. You assign roles to these members to enable them to perform actions. The prerequisite for adding members and assigning roles is that you yourself are assigned the Organization Manager role. The user who created the subaccount is automatically added as a member and assigned this role. See Section 5.2.2 for more information on organizations and roles.

User management is accessed from the **Security** · **Users** path in the SAP BTP cockpit of the subaccount. Figure 5.8 shows the standard view of user administration for an administration user that has been assigned as the default identity provider via the SAP ID service. The user's email address is specified in the **User Name** column (blurred in the figure).

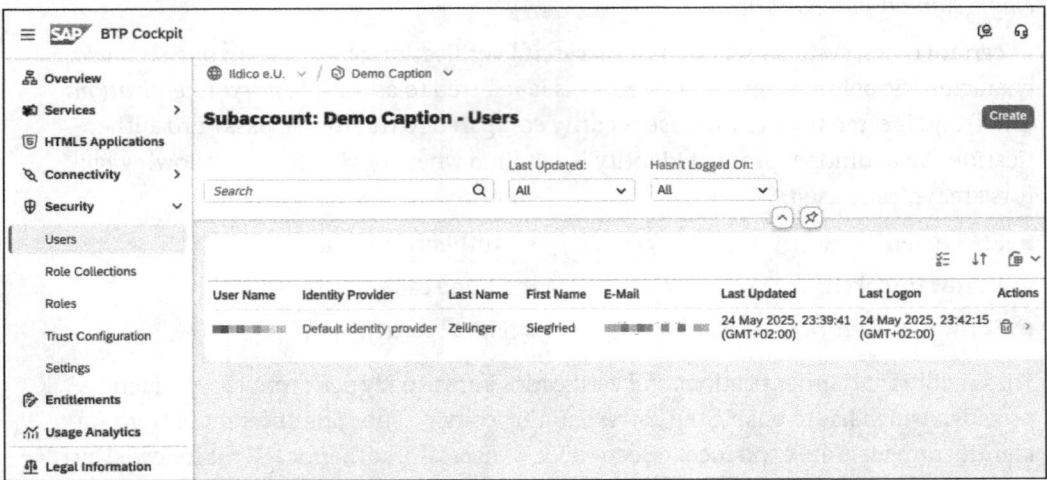

Figure 5.8 Overview of Subaccount Users

You can use the **Create** button to create new users. For users that come from the SAP ID service (labeled **Default Identity Provider** in the **Identity Provider** column on this screen), this should be done explicitly. For other identity providers, you do not need to add the users explicitly.

In the dialog for creating a new user, enter the user's email address as a unique identifier in the **User Name** and **E-Mail** fields (see Figure 5.9). In addition, enter the identity provider that provides this user. Confirm your entries with the **Create** button.

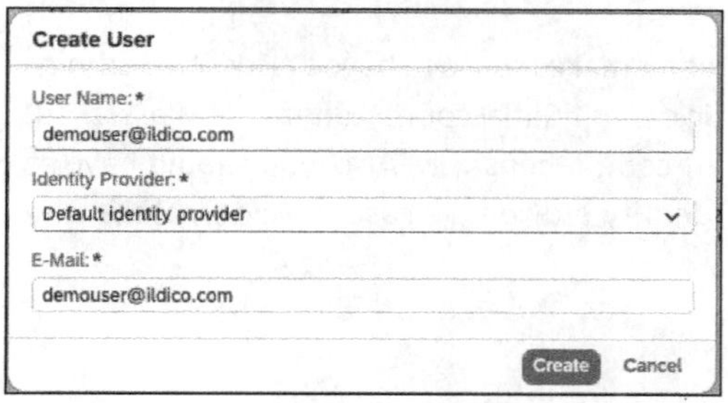

Figure 5.9 New User Creation

After creating the user, you can check the user data again by clicking the arrow button on the right side of the line to display the user details (see Figure 5.10). At this point, you can also assign roles directly to the user, as explained in Section 5.2.3. It is also possible to delete a user by clicking first the three-dot button and then **Delete**.

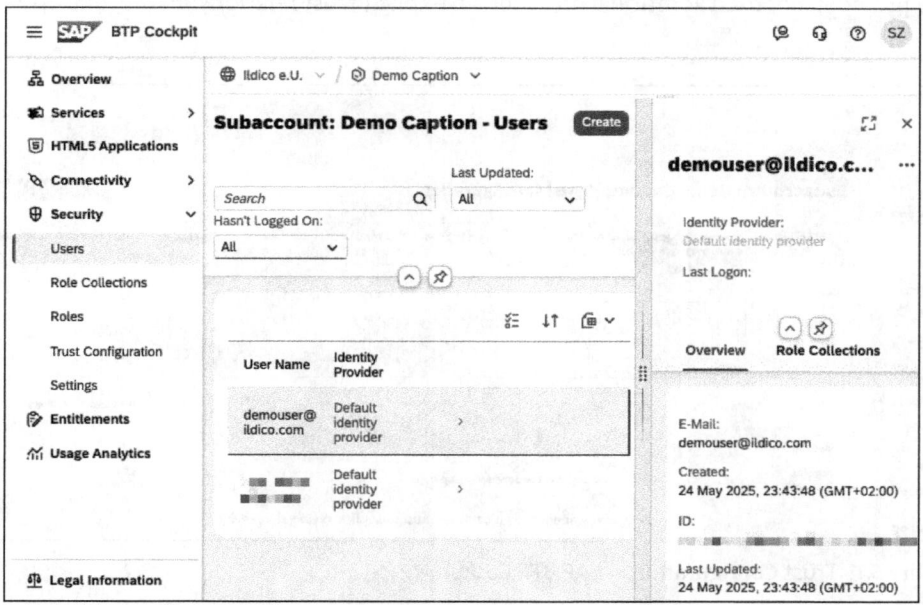

Figure 5.10 Display User Details

5 Subaccount Administration

For administrators, this is the default way to create new users at the subaccount level. However, if end users need access to a cloud application that is run in an SAP BTP subaccount, it is common to automatically create the users from the company's own identity provider.

To do this, you must set a checkmark in the identity provider configuration (see Section 5.2.5). In practice, this saves steps for creating users for end users.

> **Administration Users**
>
> At this point, it is also worth mentioning that it makes sense to have at least two administrators, to whom the subaccount-specific default Subaccount Admin role is assigned. This allows you to manage the subaccount comprehensively. Also, you should have at least two users managed by the default identity provider, in case the external identity provider is not available.

5.2.2 Trust Configuration and Other Identity Providers

You can find the trusted identity provider administration in the SAP BTP cockpit via the **Security • Trust Configuration** path (see Figure 5.11).

In the overview, you can see all currently configured providers. By default, the default identity provider provided by SAP is activated. Alternatively, you can set up a platform identity provider. If you want to use your own provider, this is set up as a custom identity provider. For each additional provider, an explicit trust relationship must be established.

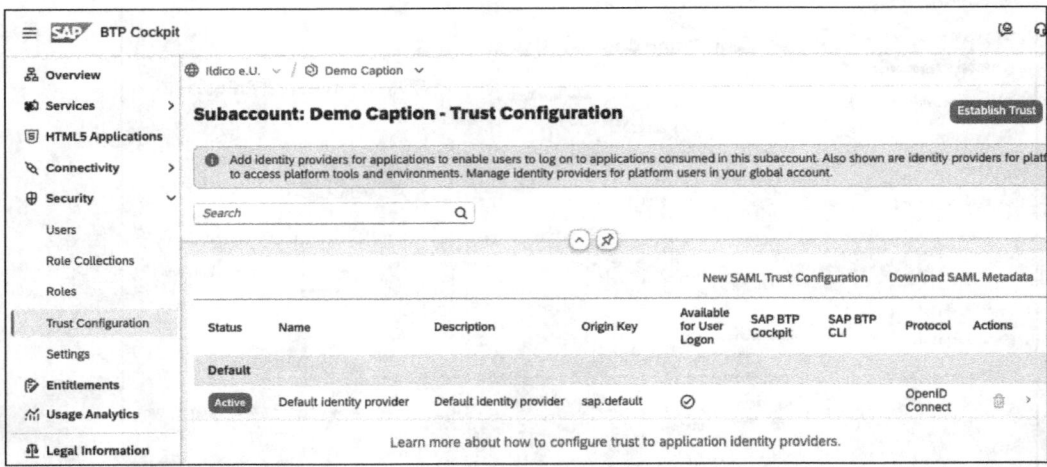

Figure 5.11 Trust Configuration in SAP BTP Cockpit

The following section will cover the SAP ID service as the default identity and authentication provider, followed by a section on platform identity providers. After that, we'll

208

5.2 Authentication and Authorization

examine the role of the Identity Authentication service, part of SAP Cloud Identity Services. Finally, we shed some light on other, third-party identity providers you might want to use.

SAP ID Service

The SAP ID service is the default identity provider. On the screen, it is labeled as the **Default Identity Provider** or with the `sap.default` origin key. This identity provider cannot be deleted, but it can be configured. To configure it, use the arrow icon [>] in the **Actions** column to view the details (see Figure 5.11). If you are sure that your platform identity provider and/or your third-party identity provider on the subaccount level correctly authenticates all required users, then you can deactivate the SAP ID service as an identity provider by clicking **Edit** and removing the checkmark from the **Available for User Logon** checkbox (see Figure 5.12).

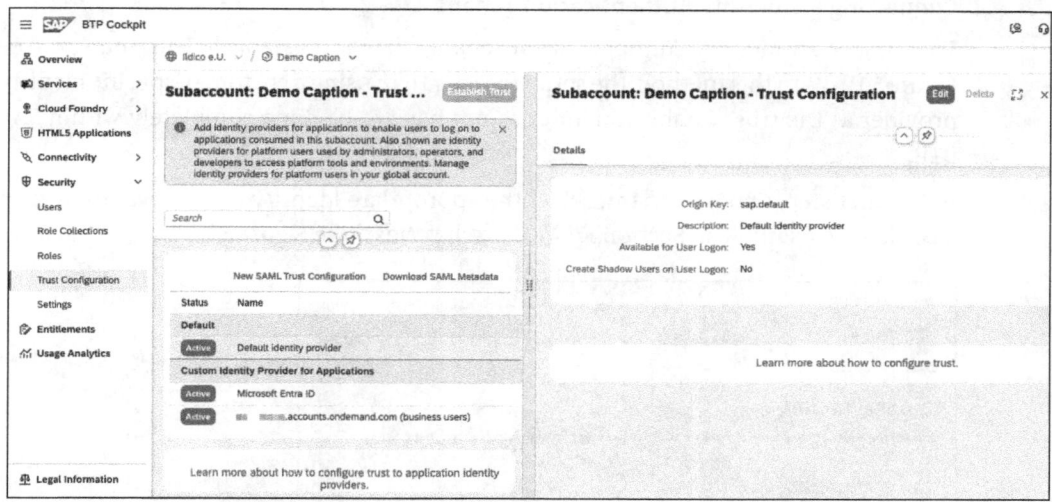

Figure 5.12 Configuring SAP ID Service Identity Provider

By activating the **Create Shadow Users During Logon** checkbox, you can control whether users listed in the default identity provider are automatically created in your SAP BTP tenant. This is useful when you have your own identity providers. In the context of SAP ID, however, this means that all users who have an account with SAP ID can log on as users of your cloud applications. They only need to know the link to launch the application. Therefore, this setting is inactive by default for SAP ID, and we do not recommend enabling it for this identity provider.

Setting Up a Platform Identity Provider

Using a platform identity provider is another method of authentication. The name of the provider comes from the fact that the authentication service runs on SAP BTP. For this purpose, Identity Authentication is used, which is part of the SAP Cloud Identity

5 Subaccount Administration

Services subscription. The use of this service is bundled with most SAP BTP instances and serves as a cross-account identity provider (Identity Authentication can, but does not have to, be used by all subaccounts).

> **[!] Identity Provider and Bundle Licenses for Identity Provisioning**
>
> The bundle licenses for Identity Authentication and Identity Provisioning are often limited to certain features. For example, in a bundle with SAP SuccessFactors, only that solution can be used as the query system. Before deploying, check SAP Help Portal (at *https://help.sap.com/docs/identity-provisioning/identity-provisioning/obtain-bundle-tenant*) to make sure the bundle licenses cover your needs. Details on the licensing models can be found in SAP Note 2717906.

Connecting an Identity Authentication Tenant

To connect an Identity Authentication tenant, click the **Establish Trust** button (see Figure 5.11). With this method, the setup is easier than using a customer-specific identity provider as the trust establishment does not have to be done completely within SAP BTP.

In the first step, **Choose Tenant**, select the appropriate identity authentication tenant (see also the example in Section 5.2.4), then click **Next** (see Figure 5.13).

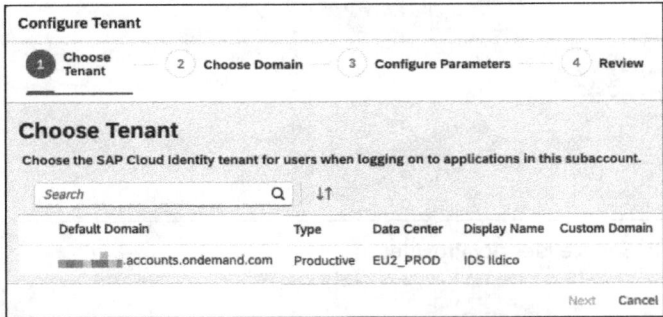

Figure 5.13 Selecting Identity Authentication Client

In the next step, choose the domain. SAP used to use the *ondemand.com* domain; now SAP BTP uses the *cloud.sap* domain. All applications should be accessed from the same domain endpoint, so select the appropriate domain for your applications or end user accesses. Then click **Next** (see Figure 5.14).

In the next step, the **Description**, **Name**, and **Origin Key** displayed in the subaccount are assigned, as well as text that is displayed to the end users on the login screen. Click **Next** to accept the default values (see Figure 5.15).

If you skip the summary, the connection will be created and displayed in the overview (see Figure 5.16).

5.2 Authentication and Authorization

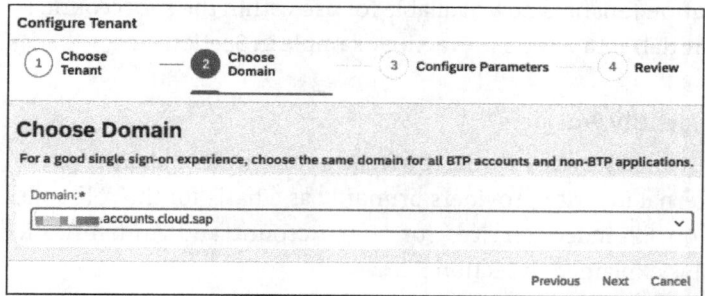

Figure 5.14 Choosing Domain

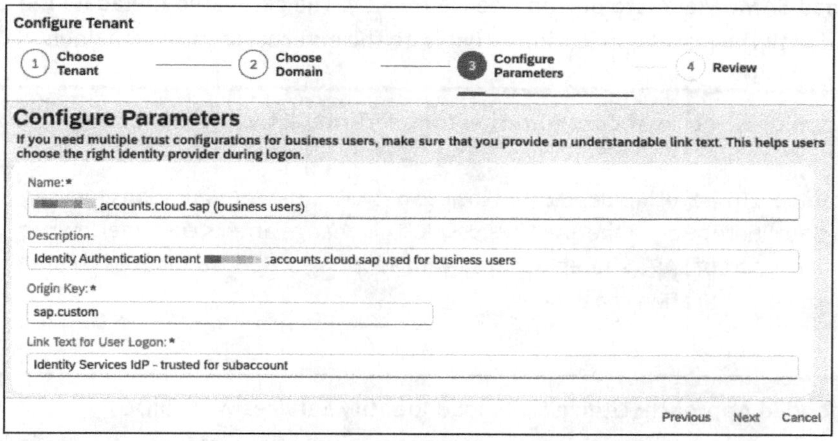

Figure 5.15 Selecting Identity Authentication Connection Parameters

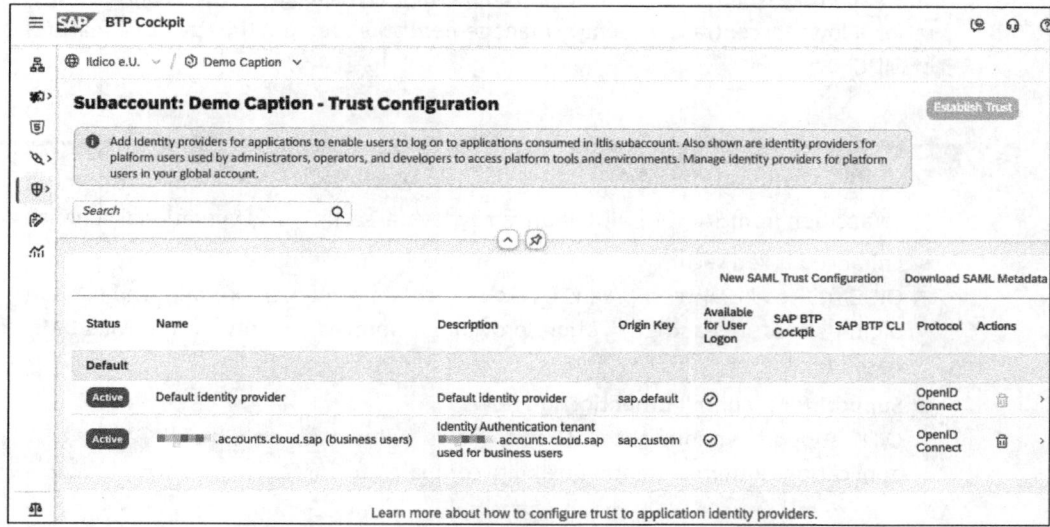

Figure 5.16 Trust Configuration for Default Identity Provider and Identity Authentication Tenant

5   Subaccount Administration

The Identity Authentication tenant is now available for use within the subaccount. For the exact steps of the (initial) setup, see the practice example in Section 5.2.4.

Setting Up Third-Party Identity Providers

Centralized SAML 2.0–enabled services are the most common external identity providers. You need these external identity providers primarily as a basis for the role collection mappings based on Extended Services for User Account and Authentication (XSUAA), a concept that is explained in Section 5.2.3.

To establish a SAML-based trust relationship, start by downloading the service provider's metadata. To do this, navigate to the **Security · Trust Configuration** path and click the **Download SAML Metadata** button (see Figure 5.17). The generated metadata file is then uploaded to the target application—that is, to the external identity provider.

> **Deprecation of SAML Trust Configuration for User-Interactive Authentication in SAP BTP**
>
> As of December 2024, SAP has deprecated the use of SAML trust configurations for user-interactive authentication in the SAP BTP cockpit. This change affects customer-owned accounts and is part of SAP's strategic shift toward adopting OIDC for enhanced security and modern authentication capabilities.

> **Recommended Approach: Utilize SAP Cloud Identity Services with OIDC**
>
> SAP recommends configuring trust between SAP BTP and Identity Authentication in SAP Cloud Identity Services using the OIDC protocol. In this setup, Identity Authentication acts as a proxy to corporate identity providers such as Microsoft Entra ID. This configuration allows for centralized identity management and leverages the advanced features of OIDC.

Security Considerations: Advantages of OIDC over SAML

The transition from SAML to OIDC is driven by several security and operational benefits:

- **Enhanced token security**
  OIDC utilizes JSON Web Tokens (JWTs), which are compact, URL-safe, and support digital signatures and encryption, providing improved security over SAML's XML-based tokens.

- **Support for modern authentication flows**
  OIDC supports various authentication flows suitable for web, mobile, and native applications, offering greater flexibility compared to SAML.

- **Improved performance**
  The lightweight nature of JWTs in OIDC leads to reduced overhead and faster authentication processes compared to the more verbose SAML assertions.
- **Better integration with modern identity providers**
  OIDC aligns well with contemporary identity solutions, facilitating seamless integration and improved user experiences.

After importing the metadata into your identity provider, you can upload the provider's SAML response in the SAP BTP cockpit's trust configuration using the **New SAML Trust Configuration** button (see Figure 5.17). The popup shown in Figure 5.18 will open.

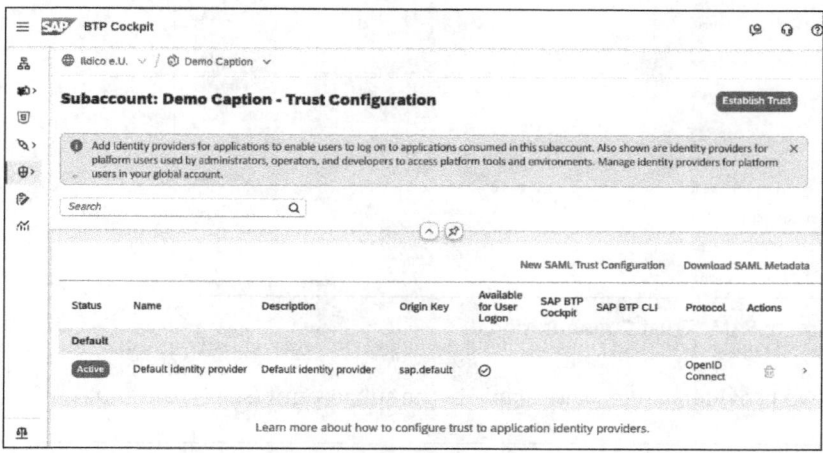

Figure 5.17 Downloading SAML Metadata from SAP BTP

Make the following settings:

1. In the **Metadata** field, use the **Upload** button to upload the XML file containing the identity provider's response. Usually, the **Origin Key** field is prefilled. This key uniquely identifies the identity provider.
2. In the **Name** field, enter an internal name for the identity provider, which you can choose freely.
3. Select the **Available for User Logon** option to allow externally managed users to log on.
4. If you select the **Create Shadow Users During Logon** option, a user is automatically created in the user management of the SAP BTP subaccount when an externally managed user logs on for the first time. This means that you no longer need to explicitly create the user in the subaccount. Both checkboxes are enabled by default.
5. In the **Link Text for User Logon** field, you can optionally enter a display text for the link that will be displayed to users on the login page of the subaccount. Clicking this link takes the user to the linked identity provider.
6. Save your settings by clicking the **Save** button.

5   Subaccount Administration

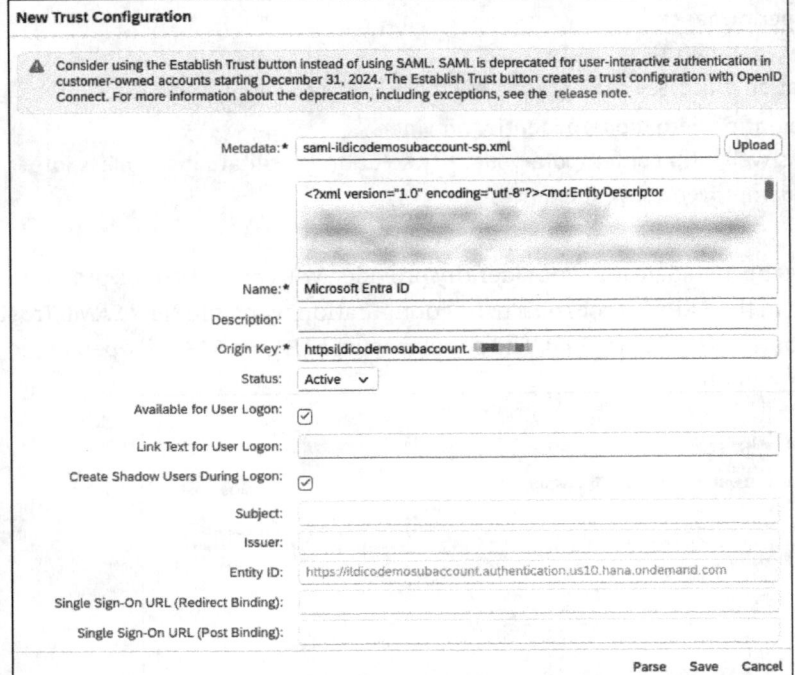

Figure 5.18 Create SAML Trust Configuration

As a result, two providers are now available in the subaccount (see Figure 5.19).

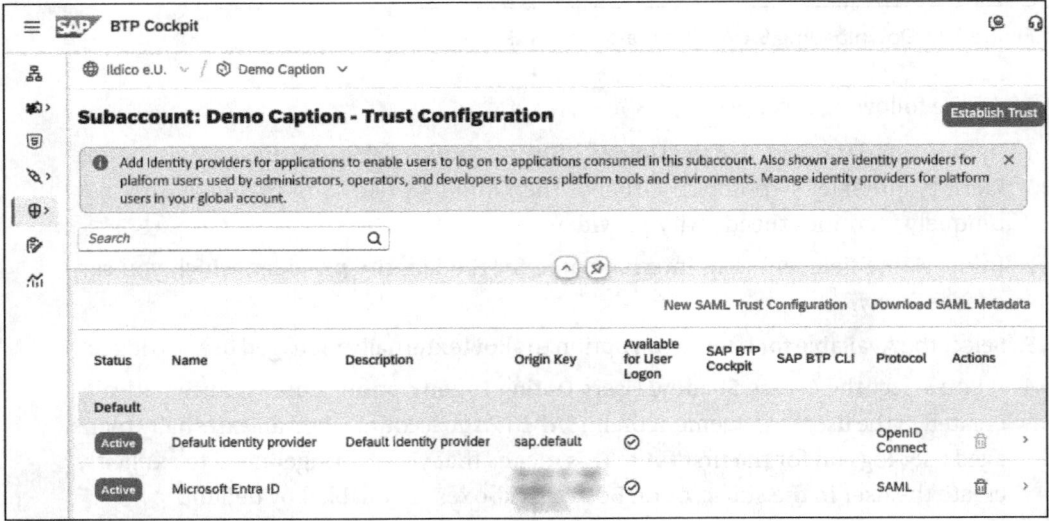

Figure 5.19 Trust Configuration with Two Providers

In Section 5.2.5, we will go through the entire external identity provider setup process using Microsoft Entra ID as an example.

5.2 Authentication and Authorization

5.2.3 Roles and Role Collections

SAP BTP also has comprehensive authorization management at the subaccount level. Roles can be grouped into role collections and assigned to users or user groups. It is also possible to assign roles to users with similar attribute values. In this section, we will show you how to work with roles and role collections.

Roles

The available standard roles are listed in the SAP BTP cockpit via the **Security • Roles** path (see Figure 5.20).

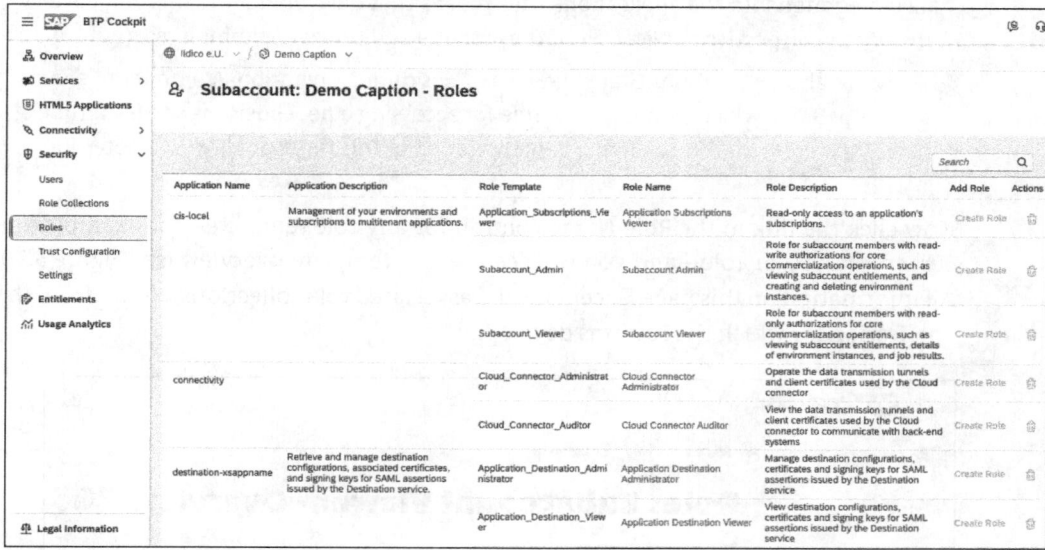

Figure 5.20 Roles in SAP BTP Subaccount

The overview contains the following columns:

- **Application Name**
  This column contains the technical name of the application that contains the role template.
- **Application Description**
  This column contains the description of the application, if a description has been provided by the development teams.
- **Role Template**
  In this section, you can see the role identifier assigned by the development team.
- **Role Name**
  Here you will find the nontechnical name of the role template in the form of a link. By clicking this name, you can jump to the role template assignments and edit them.

5   Subaccount Administration

- **Role Description**
  In this column, you will find explanations about the roles, which have been entered by the development teams.

Using the control fields in the last two columns (**Add Role** and **Actions**), you can create customer-specific roles based on the standard role as a template (**Create Role**) or delete roles.

> **Development of Role Templates**
>
> The role templates are created by SAP BTP application development teams and are usually integrated into the applications. This means that development teams will have to modify the respective applications if they require additional role templates.
>
> There are also applications that create new roles during operation. A prominent example is SAP Build, which creates a new role for accessing a new business site each time a new site is created. You can find a demonstration of this functionality in Chapter 10.

Now click the link in the **Role Name** column for any role template—for example, the Subaccount_Viewer role—and you will see the role template overview (see Figure 5.21). All information on this page, except for the associated role collections, comes from the application for which the role was developed.

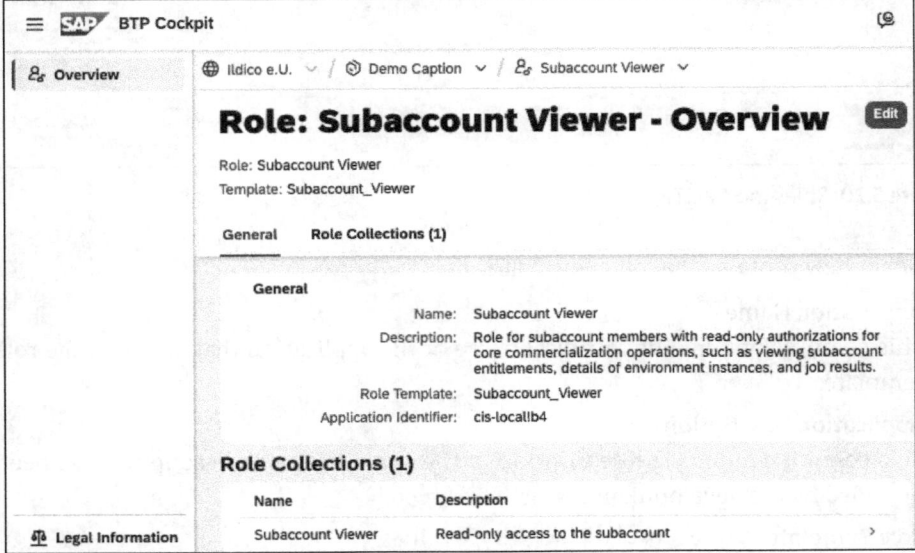

Figure 5.21 Overview of Role Template

You can use the **Edit** button in the upper-right area to edit the role collections assigned to the role template. In edit mode, you can add the role to other role collections by clicking the **Add** button. You can remove the role from these role collections by clicking the **X** button ☒ (see Figure 5.22).

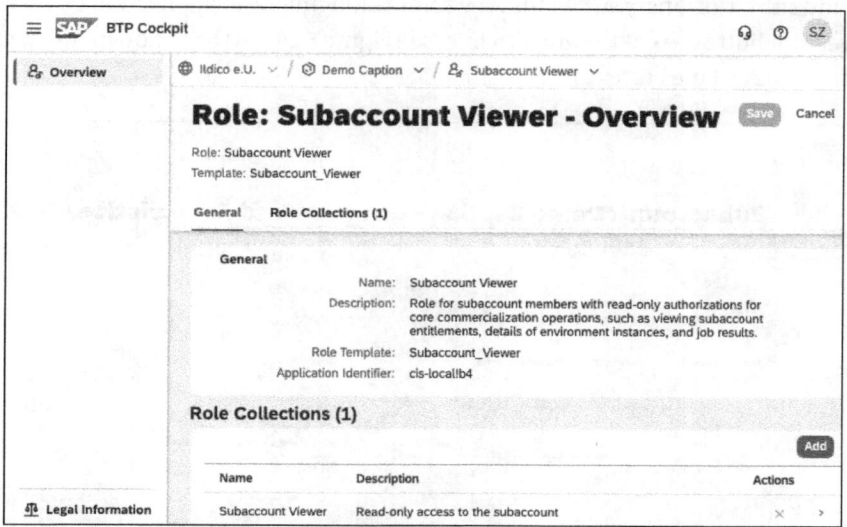

Figure 5.22 Adding and Deleting Role Collection Assignments

It is particularly convenient to use the arrow button at the end of a line to jump directly to the area to edit the role collection (see Figure 5.23). There, you can also check which other roles have already been assigned to the selected role collection.

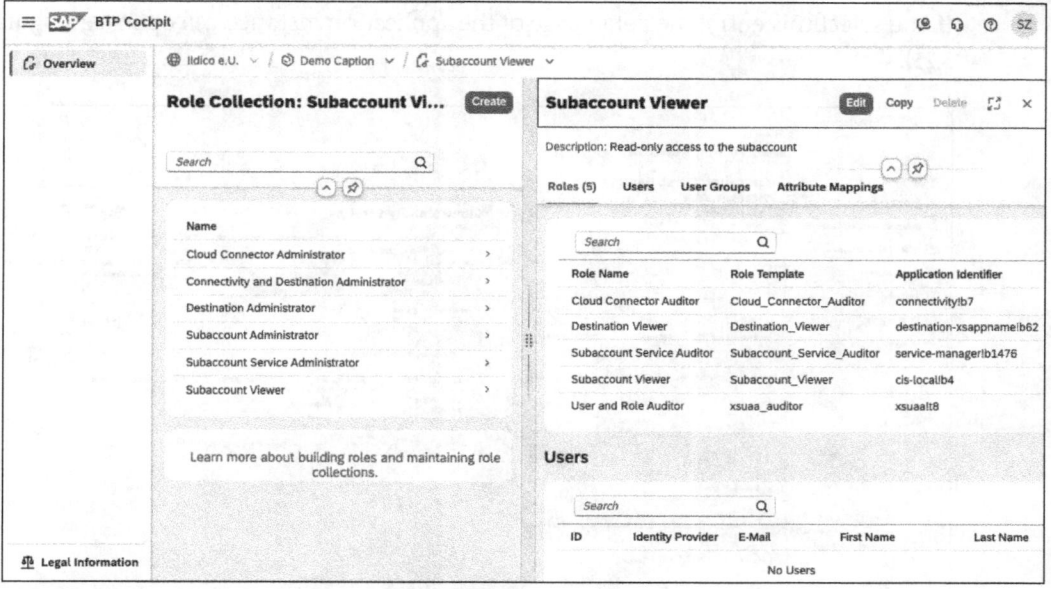

Figure 5.23 Accessing Role Collection via Role in Subaccount

Another way to find role templates for applications is to navigate via the **Instances and Subscriptions** entry under the **Services** menu of the SAP BTP cockpit. In the overview of instances and subscriptions, you can find the roles belonging to an application by clicking the three-dot button ••• at the end of a line (see Figure 5.24). In the action menu, you will find the **Manage Roles** function.

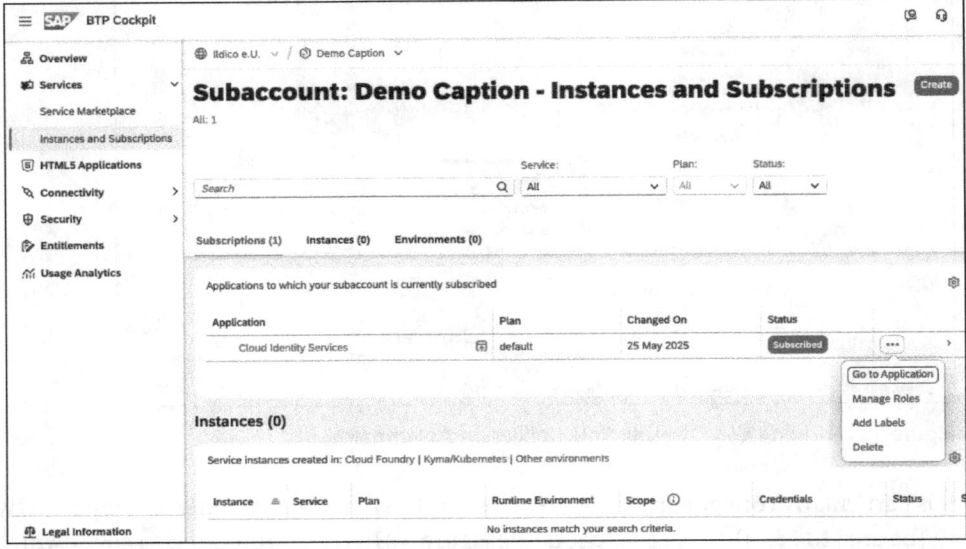

Figure 5.24 Manage Roles Function in Instantiated Applications Menu

If you select this entry, the detail page of the application instance will open (see Figure 5.25).

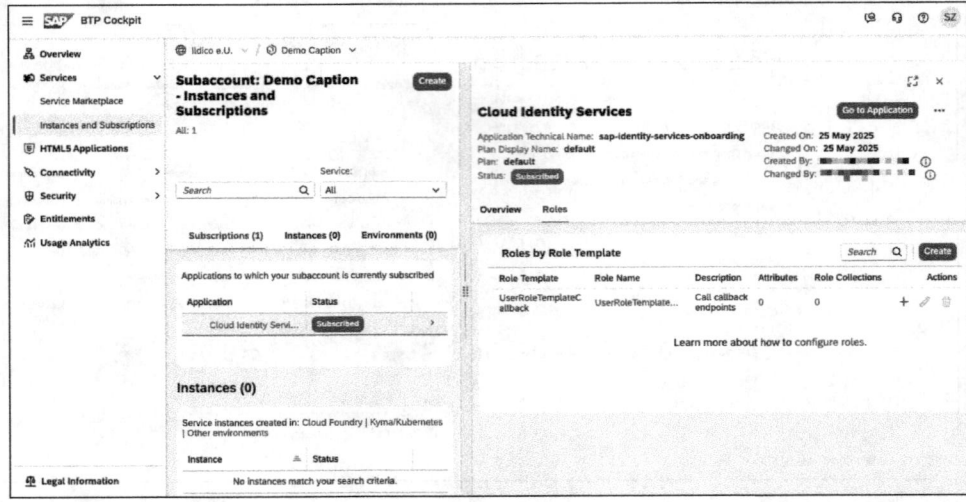

Figure 5.25 Finding and Editing Roles via Application Overview

In the right pane, you can see all the role templates contained here. Starting from this overview, you can add new role collections by clicking **Add** (the plus button ⊞) or edit the existing roles by clicking **Edit** (the pencil button 🖉).

It is especially useful to use this view if you want to find out who has access to a certain application. For example, if the **Role Collections** and **Attributes** columns at this point display the value "0", then you can assume that no one can use the application in question (assuming it has been programmed correctly).

Role Collections

As mentioned earlier, role collections are formed from individual roles and assigned to users or user groups. You can access role collection maintenance via the **Security** • **Role Collections** menu path (see Figure 5.26).

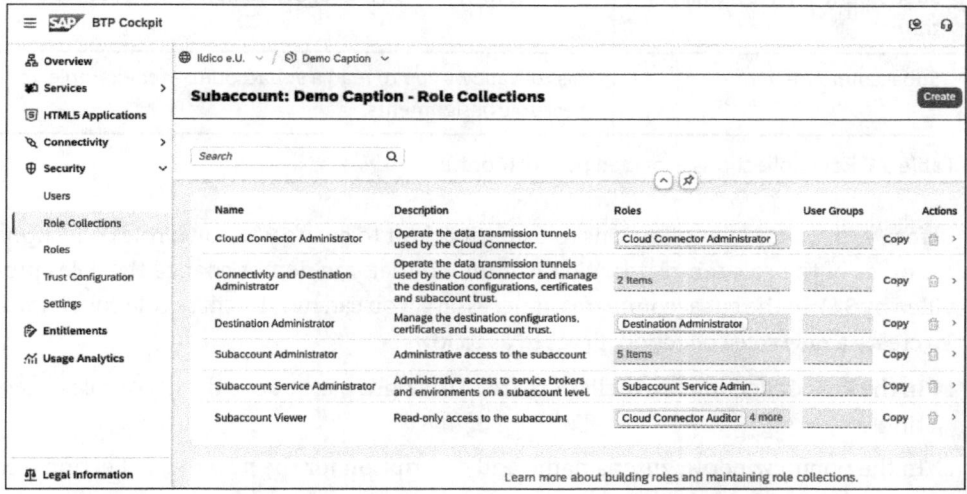

Figure 5.26 Maintaining Role Collections

SAP delivers the standard role collections listed in Table 5.1 with SAP BTP.

Role Collection	Description
Business Application Studio Administrator	This role is intended for the administration of SAP Business Application Studio. You can also export and delete user data with this role.
Business Application Studio Developer	This role is for developers who work in SAP Business Application Studio.
Business Application Studio Extension Deployer	This role allows you to deploy applications from SAP Business Application Studio.

Table 5.1 Role Collections Provided by SAP

5 Subaccount Administration

Role Collection	Description
Cloud Connector Administrator	This role allows you to manage the cloud connector.
Connectivity and Destination Administrator	This role allows you to maintain cloud connector connections and the corresponding destinations in the SAP BTP cockpit.
Destination Administrator	This role allows only the maintenance of destinations, but not the administration of the cloud connector.
Subaccount Administrator	This role is the most important role collection delivered by SAP as it allows you to manage your subaccount comprehensively. Ideally, this role is always assigned to at least two people.
Subaccount Service Administrator	With this role, you can manage the services of a subaccount.
Subaccount Viewer	This role allows you to read a subaccount—for example, to check role assignments.

Table 5.1 Role Collections Provided by SAP (Cont.)

Before you assign role collections to users, it is best to create your own role collections as copies of the role templates. We recommend that you do not change the roles provided by SAP in the subaccount area. If necessary, you can modify these role collections. To create a new role collection, proceed as follows:

1. In the **Role Collections** area, click **Create** in the right pane above the list of role collections.
2. In the popup window, enter a name and description for the new role collection (see Figure 5.27) and save your entries.

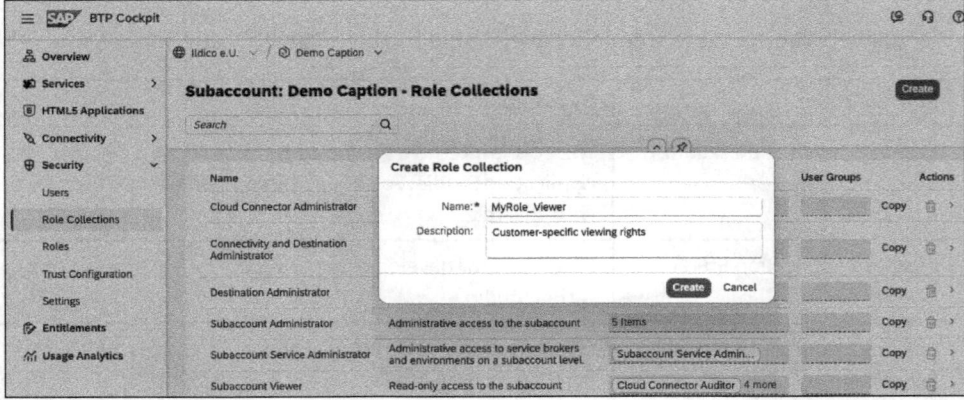

Figure 5.27 Role Collection Creation

220

3. The created role collection is now displayed in the list of role collections. To edit it, click the small arrow button ▷ at the right of the row (see Figure 5.28).

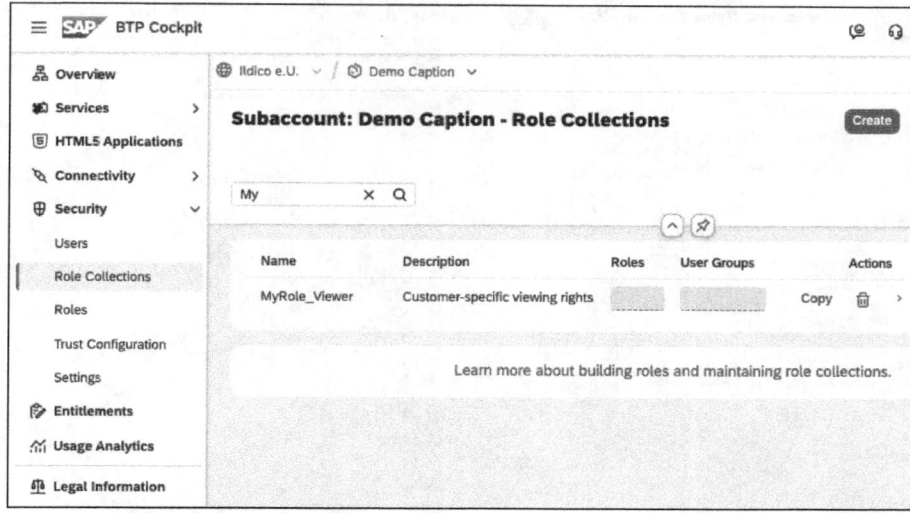

Figure 5.28 Edit Role Collection

> **Naming Conventions for Role Collections**
> SAP usually assembles the names of role collections from the name of the application or application area and the possible actions, such as Viewer for display authorization. In technical names, these elements are separated from each other by underscores. You can use these rules as an orientation for your own role collections, but they are not binding.

4. In the following view, you can add roles to the role collection and add groups or attributes to the role. Use the **Edit** button in the upper-right corner to switch to edit mode (see Figure 5.29).
5. In the **Roles** section, you can add roles to the role collection.
6. The value help is shown in Figure 5.30. Using the dropdown lists provided, you can combine roles from the various applications of your subaccount as well as the subaccount itself.
7. In the **Users** section, you can assign role collections to users by clicking the **+** button or unassign them by clicking the **X** button.
8. The **User Groups** and **Attribute Mappings** sections are important when using role collection mappings; we will explain this in the next section.
9. In the **Description** section (you can find it by scrolling down; it is not shown in the image), you can edit the description of the role collections.
10. Finally, save your changes by clicking the **Save** button.

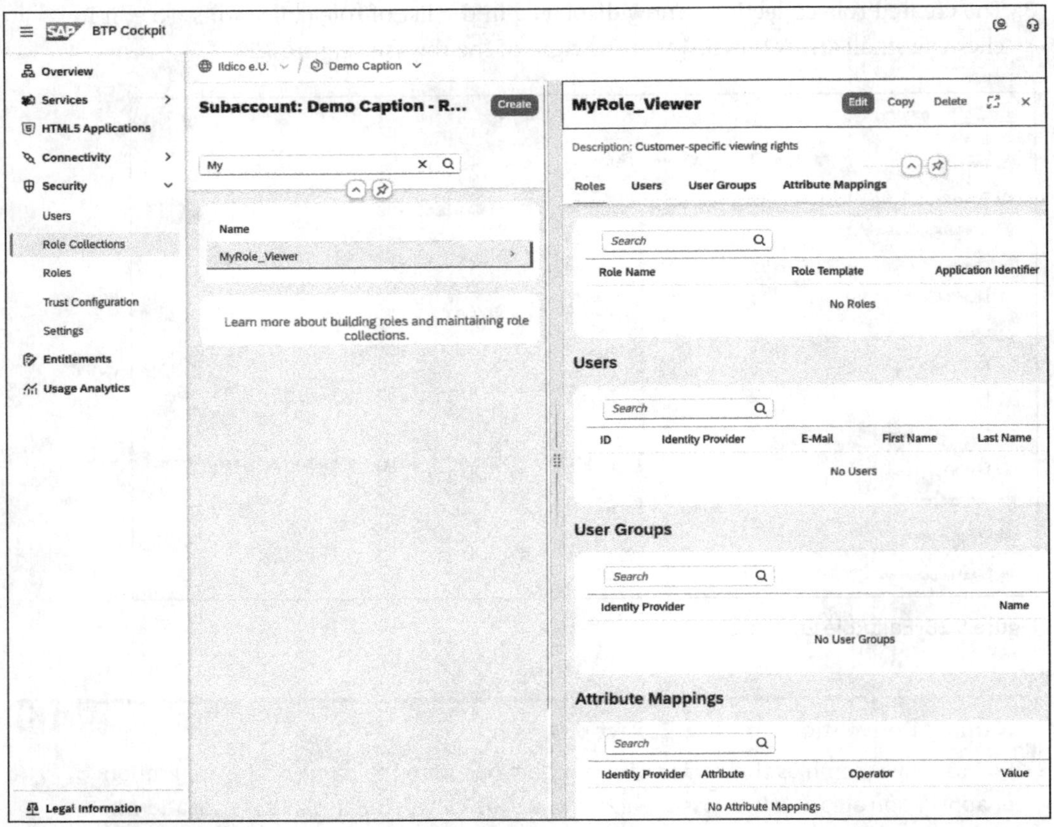

5 Subaccount Administration

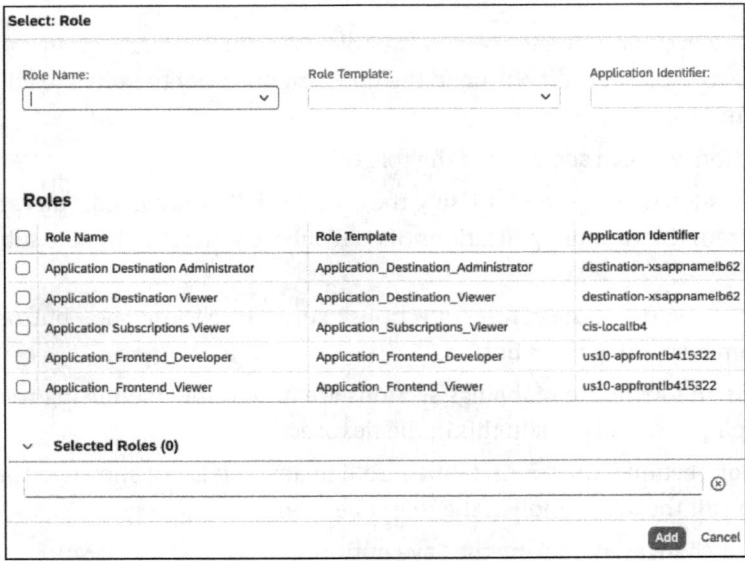

Figure 5.29 Role Collection in Edit Mode

Figure 5.30 Value Help for Role Assignment

222

5.2 Authentication and Authorization

If you have created your own role collection and want to configure further role collections based on it, you can easily copy the role collection via the **Copy** link at the end of the line (see Figure 5.31). You can then specify a new name for the copied role, as shown in the **Create Role Collection** dialog in Figure 5.27.

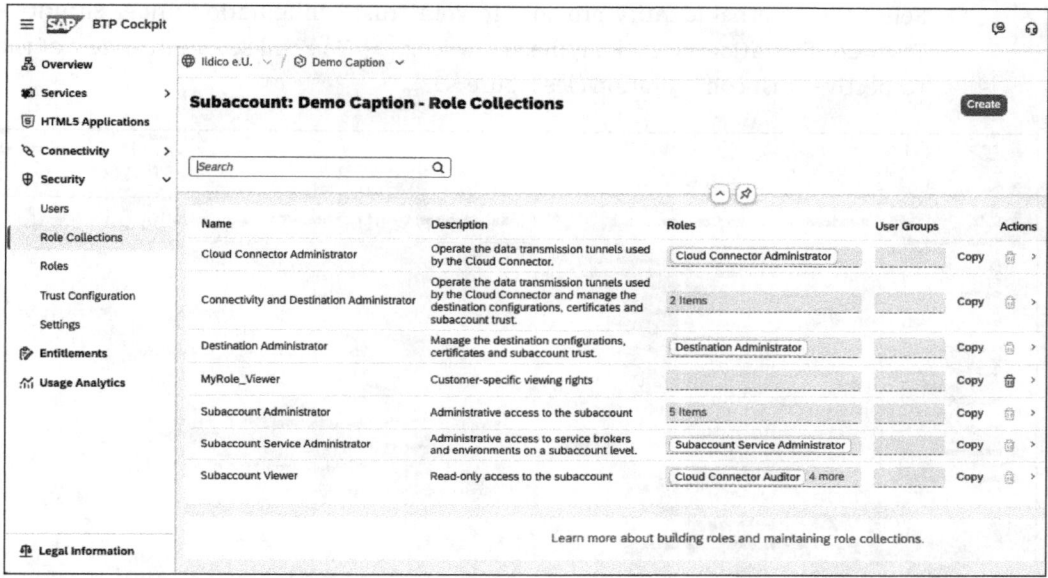

Figure 5.31 Copying Role Collection

> **When Should Role Collections Be Used?**
>
> Similar to roles in ABAP systems, it is a general recommendation to organize role collections according to the positions of the end users in the company's organizational chart or according to business processes and to fill them with different granular roles. Many companies use their own logic here. One possibility would be to name the role collections on SAP BTP the same way as the role collections in the SAP ERP or SAP S/4HANA system, if they are assigned to the same user groups.

Role Collection Mapping

Role collections can be automatically associated with the properties of users provided by external identity providers or by assignments to certain user groups within the external identity provider. This procedure is called *role collection mapping*. The mapping is based on the XSUAA concept. Not only are users, authorizations, and authentications obtained from the external identity provider, but decisions for the assignment of authorizations also can be generated from this source. For example, permissions can be calculated from the user attributes. To do this, it is necessary to transfer these

223

attributes from the identity provider to the Cloud Foundry environment. In Section 5.2.5, we show you this process using Microsoft Entra ID as an example.

If you have the appropriate information from the identity provider, perform the mapping as follows:

1. Select the external identity provider in your trust configuration under **Security** • **Trust Configuration** by clicking the arrow icon ▷. You will see an overview of the respective trust configuration (see Figure 5.32).

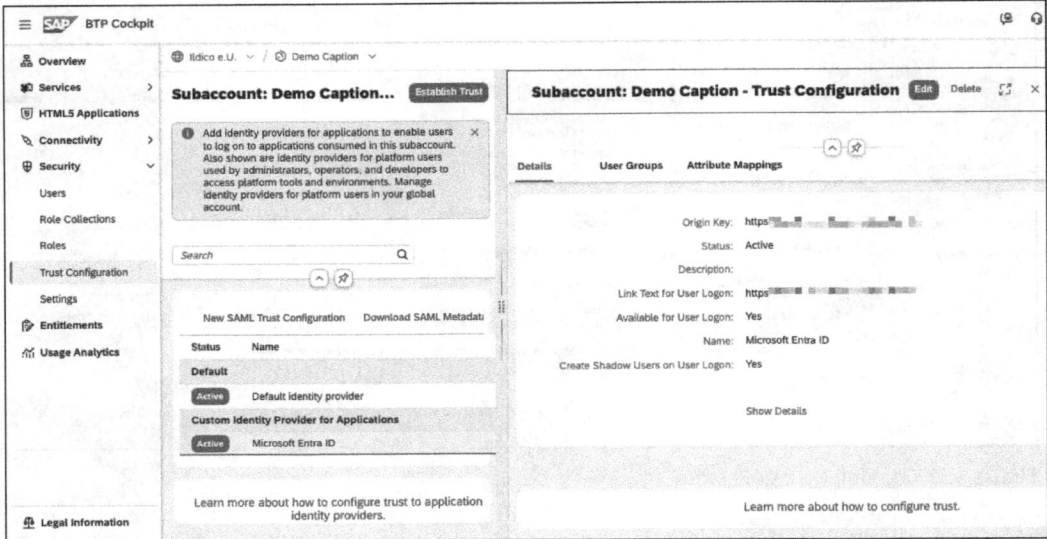

Figure 5.32 Select External Identity Provider

2. Click **Edit** and scroll down to the **User Groups** and **Attribute Mappings** sections.
3. Here you can perform the mapping between the role collections and the provided user groups or attributes. Available role collections can be selected using the **Role Collection** dropdown box. If you need more lines, you can press the + icon (see Figure 5.33).
4. Use **Attribute** and **Value** or **Name** (for the group name) to specify when to assign the role collection.
5. Save the values with **Save**.

 Role Collection Mapping Terminology in the UI

Up to 2024, there was a menu entry called **Role Collection Mapping**, and it was possible to add a role collection mapping with a + icon that has disappeared. This term has disappeared from the UI and has been replaced by user groups and attribute mappings. Note that the old term is still quite present in many corners of the internet.

5.2 Authentication and Authorization

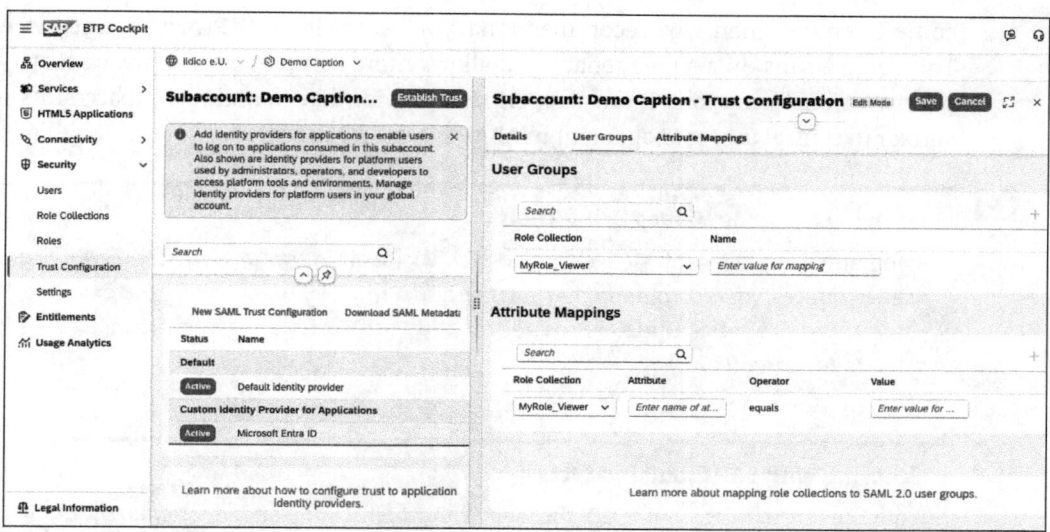

Figure 5.33 Create Role Collection Mapping

For the key/value pairs in **Attribute Mappings**, you can use all the values from the identity provider. The way these values are written does not have to match the way they are written in the identity provider. The result of the automatic assignment of the MyRole_Viewer role to a location in the root record with the Tiefgraben value is shown in Figure 5.34.

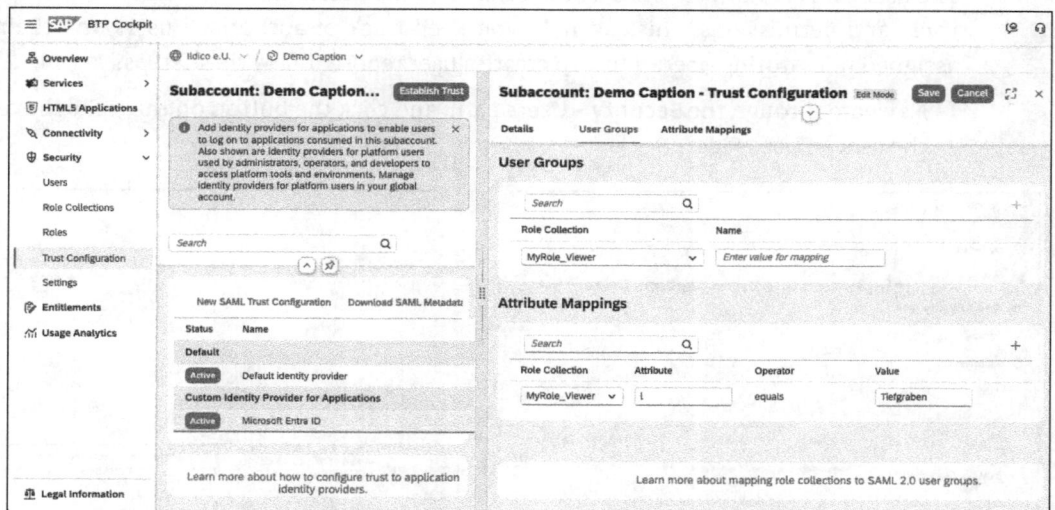

Figure 5.34 Overview of Role Collection Mappings

Role collection mappings are useful if you manage a small number of subaccounts and provide the user data for these subaccounts through a single identity provider. In more complex environments, we recommend that you use the Identity Provisioning service. This service runs on a single tenant and allows more complex operations with attributes via transformations. It can also centrally provide data to multiple subaccounts—similar to central user management in ABAP-based SAP solutions.

> **Verifying Mapping Values Using Tools**
>
> If you are using Microsoft Active Directory or Microsoft Entra ID as the source for the user attributes, we recommend that you use a tool to verify these values. For example, you can use the Active Directory snap-in for the Microsoft Management Console (see *http://s-prs.co/v608001*).

> **Licensing with SAP Cloud Products**
>
> From the fourth quarter of 2020, the Identity Authentication and Identity Provisioning services (together in SAP Cloud Identity Services) will be bundled with many SAP cloud solutions. This makes the use of both services even more attractive from a cost perspective. Currently, we can say that almost every global account can subscribe to SAP Cloud Identity Services.

Reporting

The user overview of your subaccount offers you the possibility to generate reports on users and permissions. This can help you keep track of authorized users and their assigned roles during operations. To create a user report, follow these steps:

1. Navigate through the **Security** • **Users** path, and click the button on the right above the user list (see Figure 5.35).

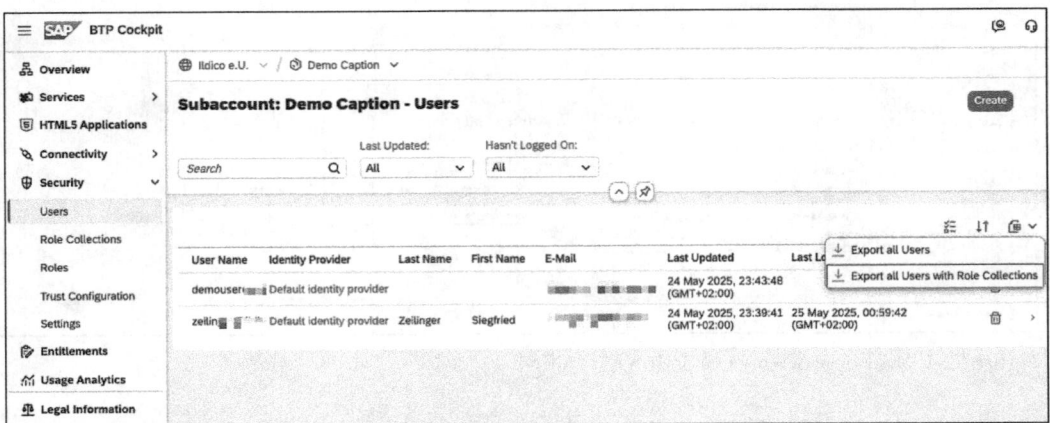

Figure 5.35 Accessing User Reports

2. In the menu that opens, you can choose between a pure user report (**Export All Users**) and a report including role assignments (**Export All Users with Role Collections**).

3. The report is generated as a CSV file and can be opened in a spreadsheet program such as Microsoft Excel.

Figure 5.36 shows the structure of a report including the assigned roles. The structure consists of the user name, the information about the identity provider from which the user comes, the last name, the first name, the email address, the time of the last change, the time of the last login, and the assigned role collections, which are separated by a semicolon.

	A	B	C	D	E	F	G	H
1	User Name	Identity Provider	Last Name	First Name	E-Mail	Last Updated	Last Logon	Assigned Role Collections
2	demou	sap.default			demou	2024-02-04T17:12:09.528Z		
3	zeiling	sap.default	Zeilinger	Siegfried	zeilinge	2024-02-04T14:06:02.730Z	2024-02-07T15:30:35.373Z	Subaccount Administrator;MyRole_Viewer

Figure 5.36 User Report with Assigned Role Collections

5.2.4 Practical Example: Authentication on a Subaccount with Identity Authentication

To perform authentication using an Identity Authentication tenant as part of SAP Cloud Identity Services, you must subscribe to the services. A tenant in a supported data center is sufficient. To view the list of data centers, navigate to the global account in the SAP BTP cockpit, then follow menu path **Entitlements** • **Service Assignments** to see the list of **All Services**. Scroll down or filter for **Cloud Identity Services**, and click the **Information** button next to SAP Cloud Identity Services (see Figure 5.37).

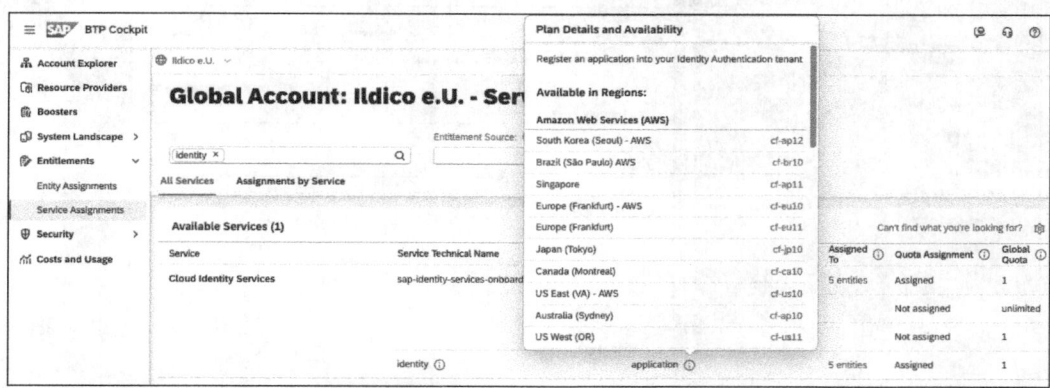

Figure 5.37 Availability of SAP Cloud Identity Services

When creating the subaccount, select one of the data centers for identity authentication or create a new subaccount for it. SAP Cloud Identity Services are offered as a shared unit, or as a shared service if supported by the datacenter. Navigate to the selected subaccount

5 Subaccount Administration

in the SAP BTP cockpit via **Services** • **Service Marketplace** and search for "Identity Services" (see Figure 5.38).

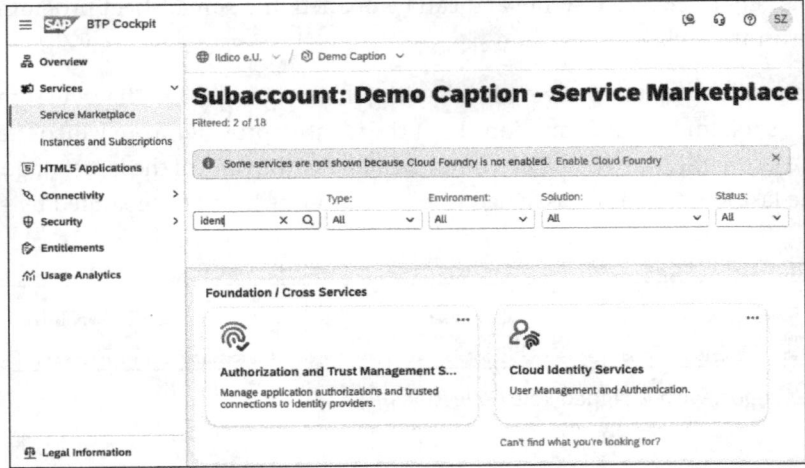

Figure 5.38 Search for SAP Cloud Identity Services in SAP Service Marketplace

Now select SAP Cloud Identity Services and click **Create**. The only thing you have to do is to select a **Plan** and eventually confirm that you are aware of the costs, depending on your SAP BTP licensing contracts, by clicking the checkbox below **Plan** (see Figure 5.39).

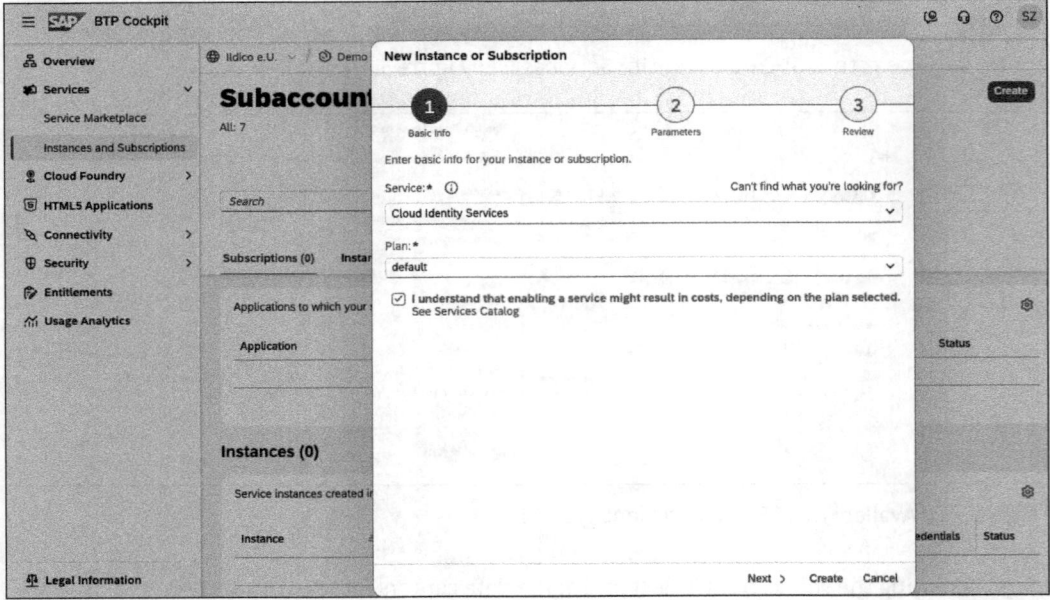

Figure 5.39 Creating SAP Cloud Identity Services Subscription

After setting up SAP Cloud Identity Services, you can, for example, go from the **Subscriptions** page directly to the application (see Figure 5.40), such as by this link: *https://<tenant>.accounts.ondemand.com/admin*.

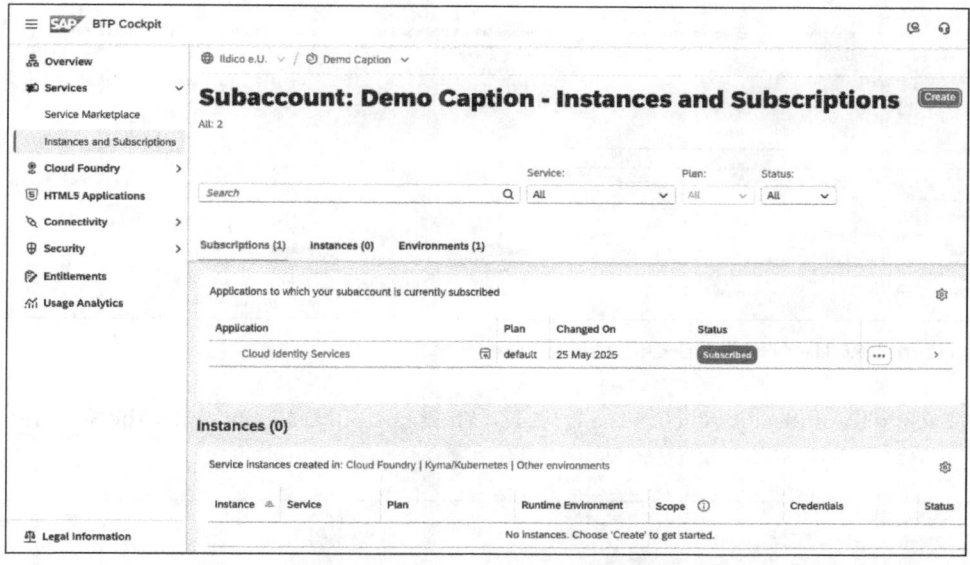

Figure 5.40 SAP Cloud Identity Services in Subscriptions Overview

If you follow the link, you can start the **Add New User** dialog in SAP Cloud Identity Services under **Users & Authorizations** by clicking the **+ Add** button (see Figure 5.41). Enter a **First Name**, **Last Name**, and **Email** address in the corresponding fields, and set the **User Type** to **Employee** for test purposes. For **Account Activation**, you can decide how you want to activate and confirm the user. Leave the default settings for this example. Use the **+ Add** button to add the user to SAP Cloud Identity Services.

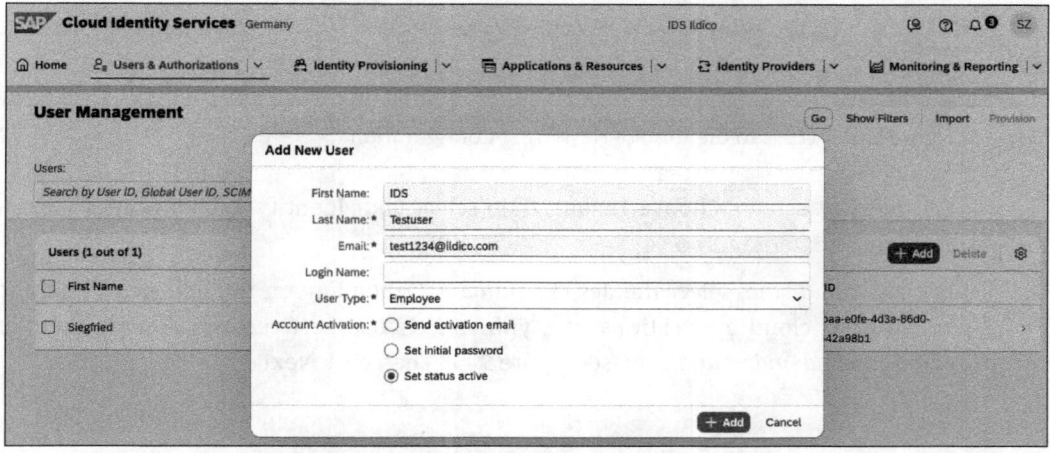

Figure 5.41 Adding New User to SAP Cloud Identity Services

The user is now available in the Identity Authentication service of SAP Cloud Identity Services (see Figure 5.42).

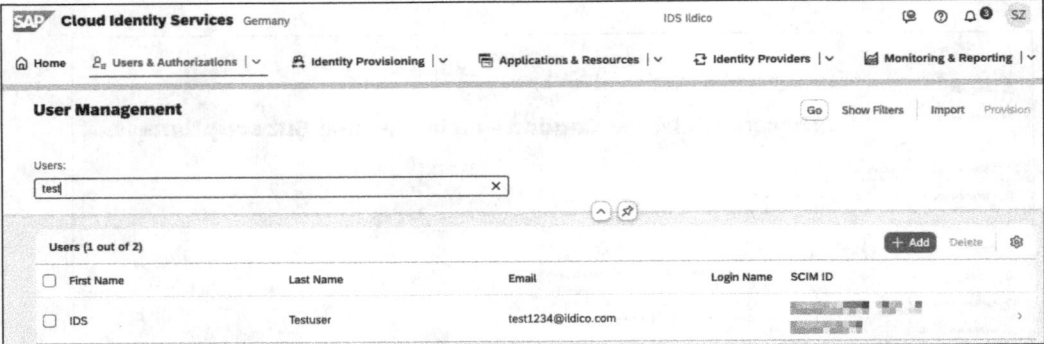

Figure 5.42 User List in SAP Cloud Identity Services

Back in the subaccount, click the **Establish Trust** button, available under the **Security • Trust Configuration** path (see Figure 5.43).

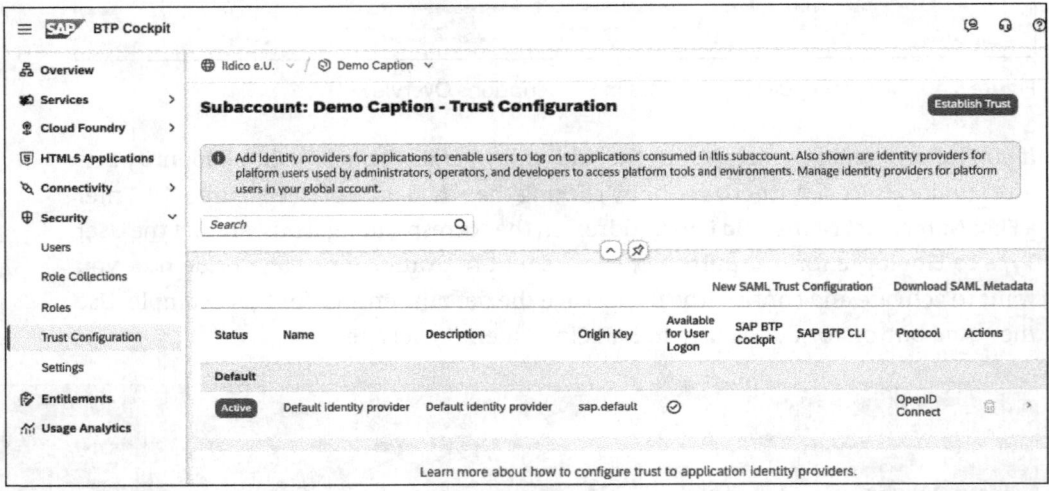

Figure 5.43 Access to Creation of New Trust Configuration

On the next screen, **Choose Tenant**, then select your Identity Authentication tenant from the list (see Figure 5.44).

In the second step, select the desired **Domain**. Depending on the internet domain in which your cloud applications run, you can choose between the domain endings *cloud.sap* and *ondemand.com* (see Figure 5.45). Then click **Next**.

5.2 Authentication and Authorization

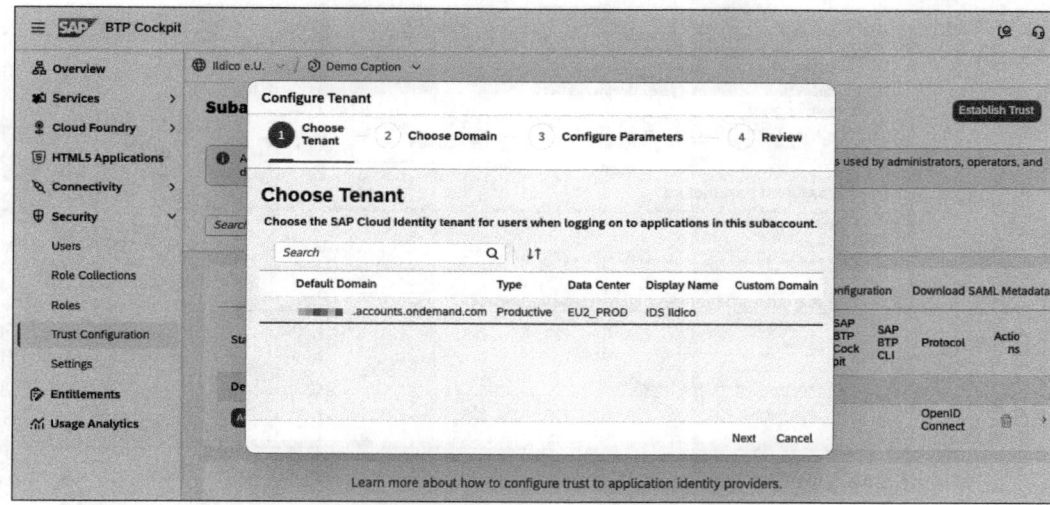

Figure 5.44 Selecting Identity Authentication Tenant

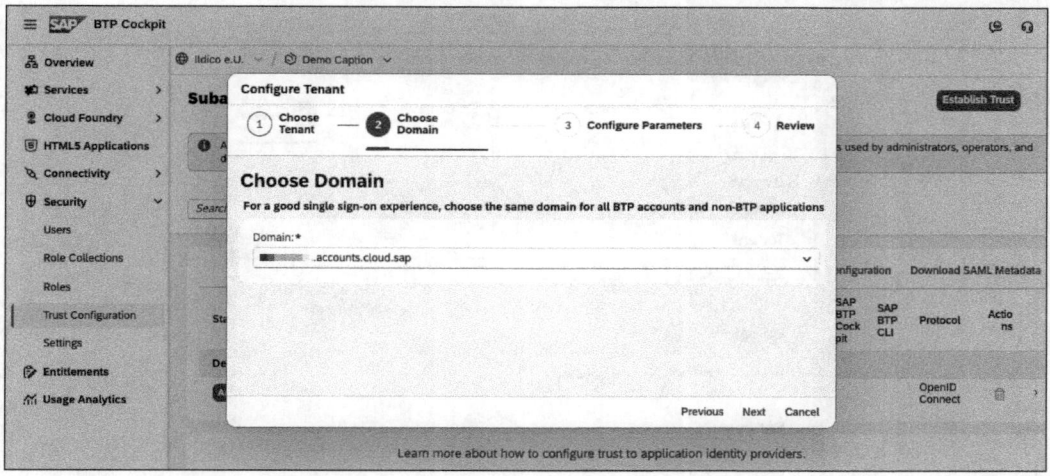

Figure 5.45 Selecting Domain

In the third step, you can perform optional parameter settings. Of particular interest is the text that will be displayed to users when they log in (**Link Text for User Logon**; see Figure 5.46). For testing purposes, you do not need to change anything here and can proceed to the summary by clicking **Next**.

Review the parameters once again and finish the process with **Finish** (see Figure 5.47).

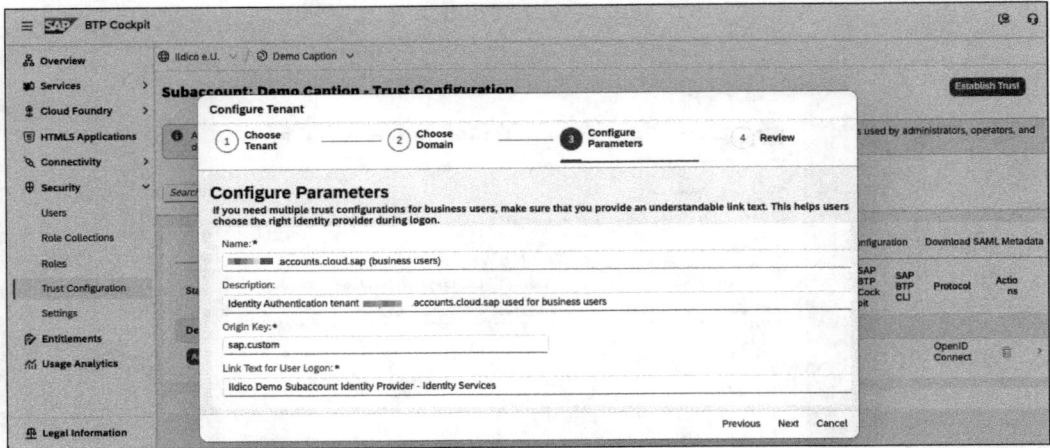

Figure 5.46 Optional Parameter Settings

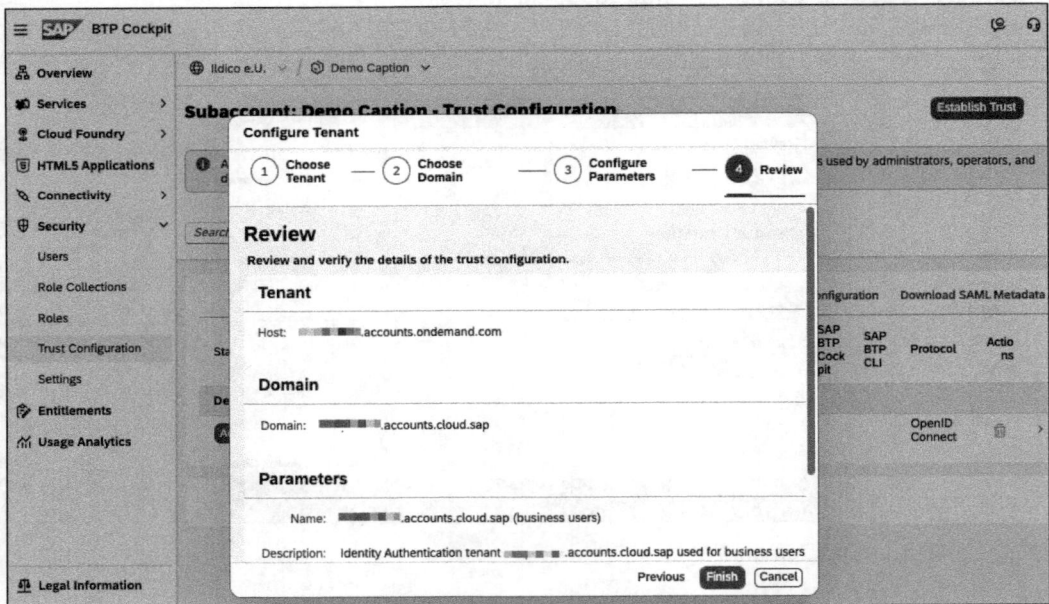

Figure 5.47 Tenant Parameter Review

As a result, you will see the new **Custom Identity Provider for Applications** in the **Trust Configuration** overview in your SAP BTP cockpit (see Figure 5.48).

Now you can, for example, assign a role collection to the selected user. In Figure 5.49, you can see an example in which we have assigned the development rights in SAP Business Application Studio to the newly created user.

5.2 Authentication and Authorization

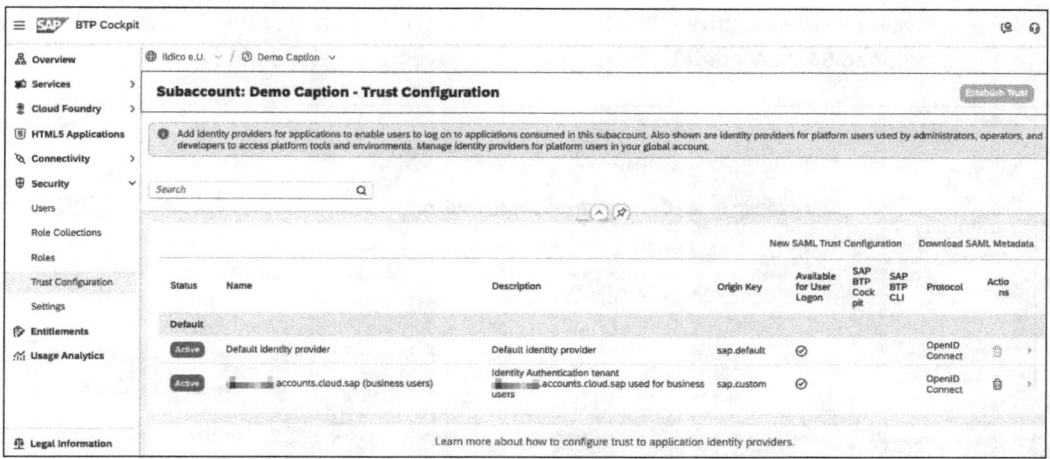

Figure 5.48 Identity Authentication Tenant in Trust Configuration Overview

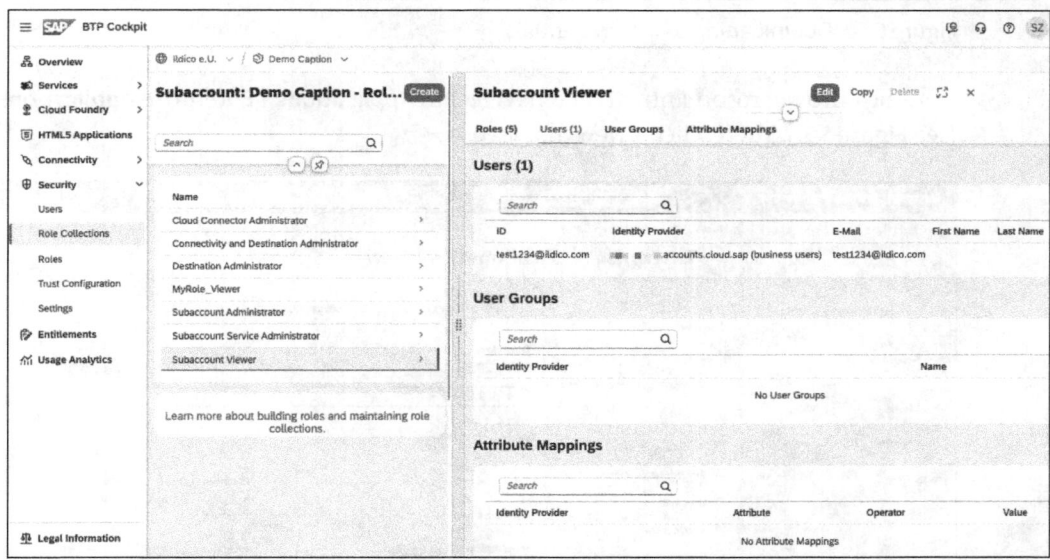

Figure 5.49 Assigning Role Collection to Identity Authentication User

5.2.5 Practical Example: Subaccount with Microsoft Entra ID as the Identity Provider

If you want to use Microsoft Entra ID as your identity provider, you need administrator rights in Microsoft Entra ID. Typically, you register with Microsoft at *https://entra.microsoft.com/*.

Start by downloading the SAML metadata from your subaccount and uploading it to Microsoft Entra ID for trust. The response from Microsoft Entra ID will then be used to complete the trust configuration in your subaccount. To download the metadata, navigate to the **Security • Trust Configuration** path in your SAP BTP cockpit and click **Download SAML Metadata** (see Figure 5.50). Save the received file.

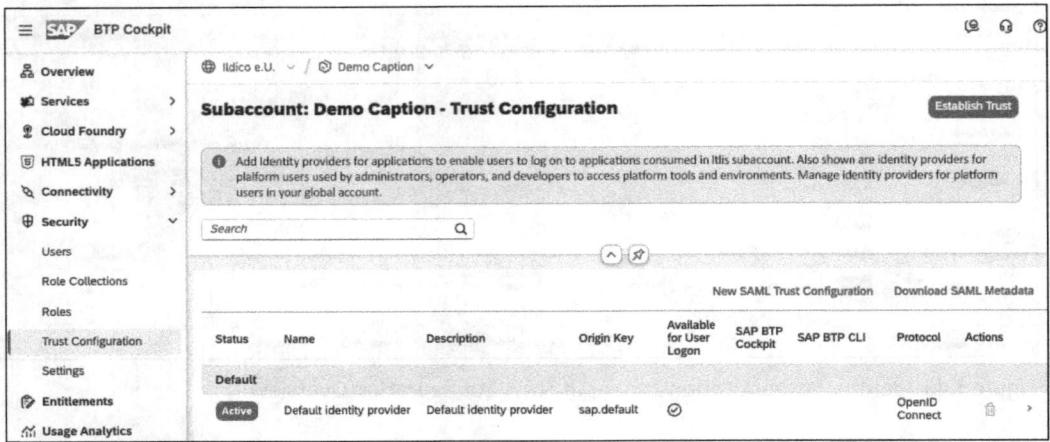

Figure 5.50 Downloading SAML Credentials

Now log onto Microsoft Entra ID and navigate to **Applications • Enterprise Applications** (see Figure 5.51). There, click **+ New application**.

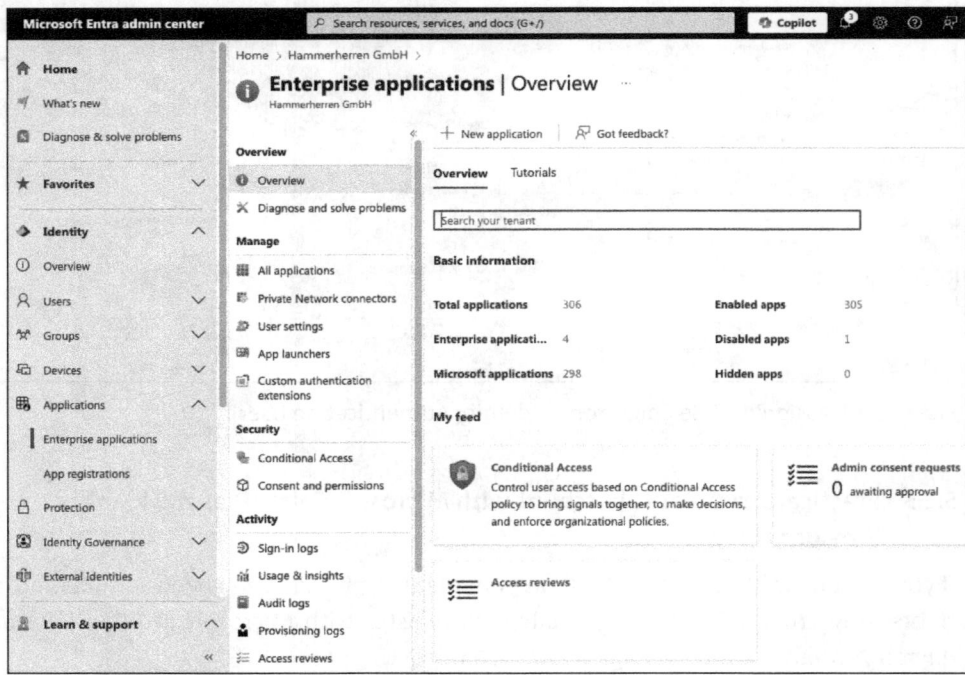

Figure 5.51 Creating Enterprise Application in Microsoft Entra ID

Now click the **SAP** vendor (see Figure 5.52).

5.2 Authentication and Authorization

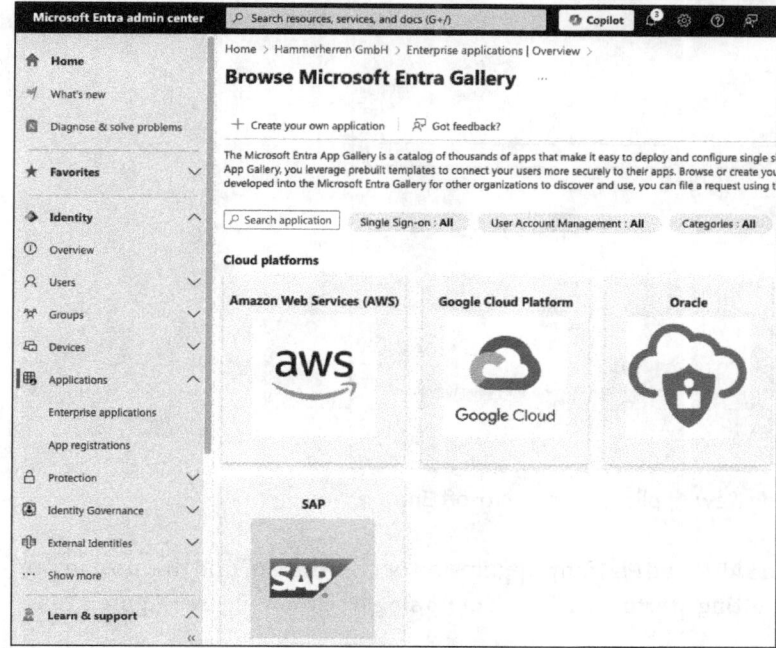

Figure 5.52 Vendor Selection in Microsoft Entra ID

In the SAP application list that appears, select the **SAP Cloud Platform** tile (see Figure 5.53). Click the panel and then click **Create** to create a new application. Optionally, you may assign a **Name** (see Figure 5.54).

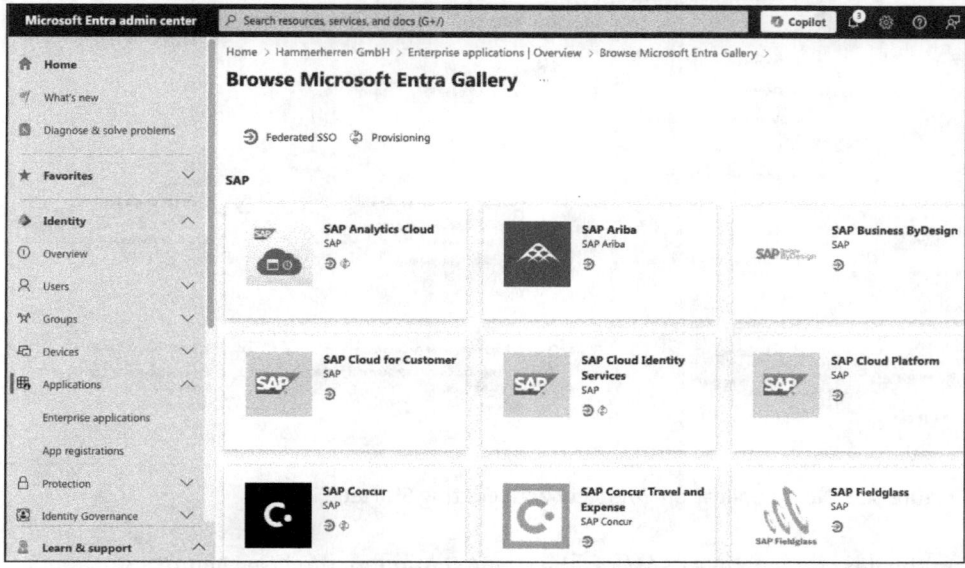

Figure 5.53 SAP Applications in Microsoft Entra ID

235

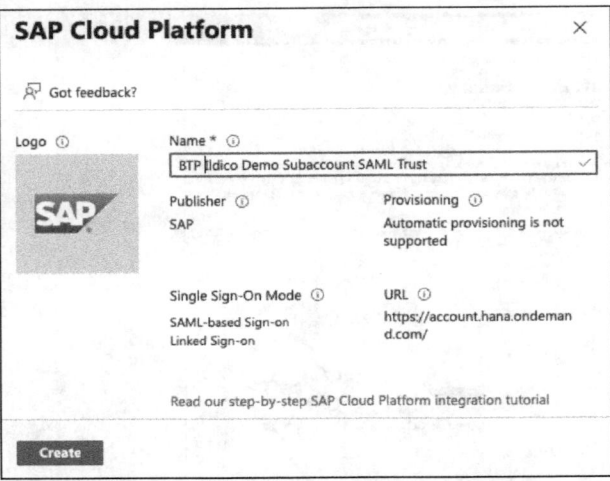

Figure 5.54 Creating New Application in Microsoft Entra ID

The newly created **SAP Cloud Platform** application opens. You can find the most important steps under **Getting Started**. Click the **Set up single sign-on** tile (see Figure 5.55).

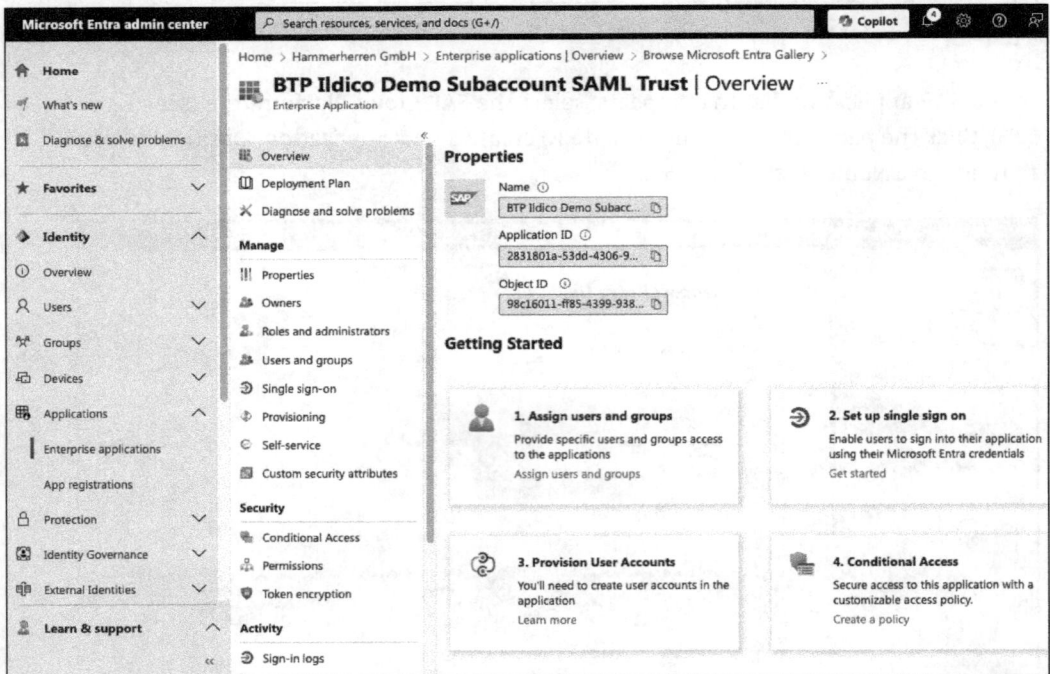

Figure 5.55 New Application Overview with Getting Started Tiles

In the next screen, select **SAML** as the single sign-on method (see Figure 5.56).

5.2 Authentication and Authorization

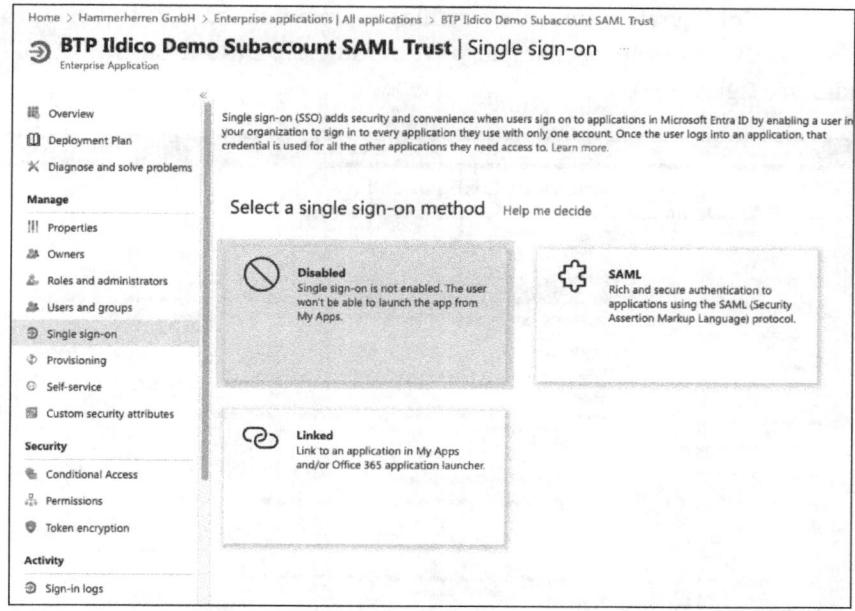

Figure 5.56 Select SAML as SSO Method

In the next screen, you can upload the XML file received from SAP BTP by clicking **Upload Metadata File** (see Figure 5.57).

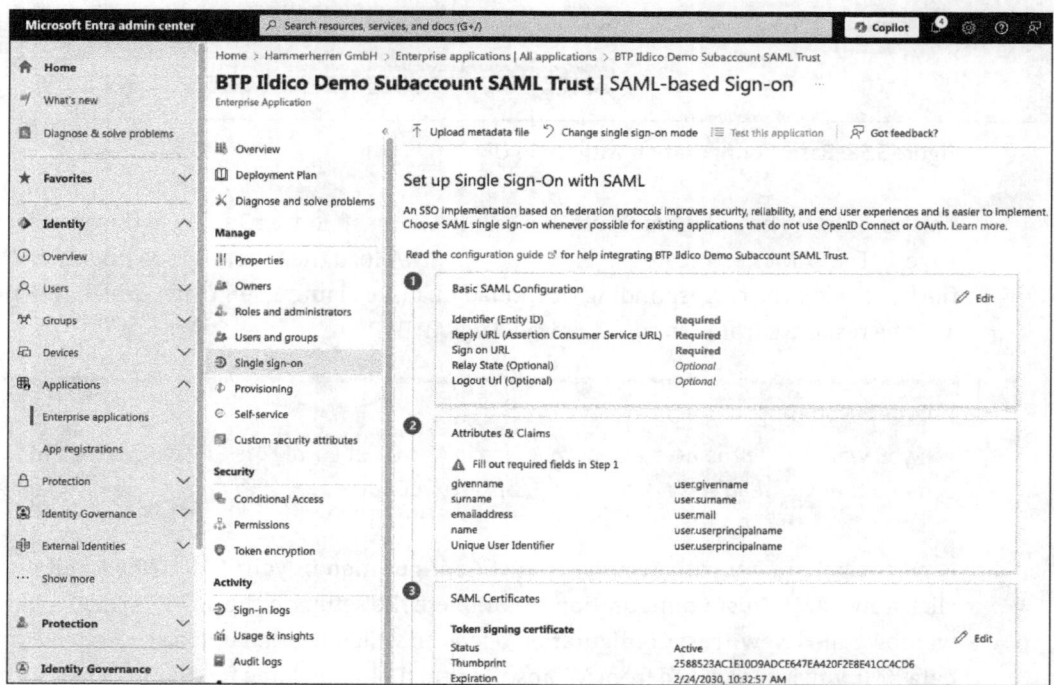

Figure 5.57 Upload Metadata

In the **Basic SAML Configuration** screen, everything is prepopulated. You only have to define the **Sign on URL** yourself; for example, you can add the link to SAP Business Application Studio (see Figure 5.58).

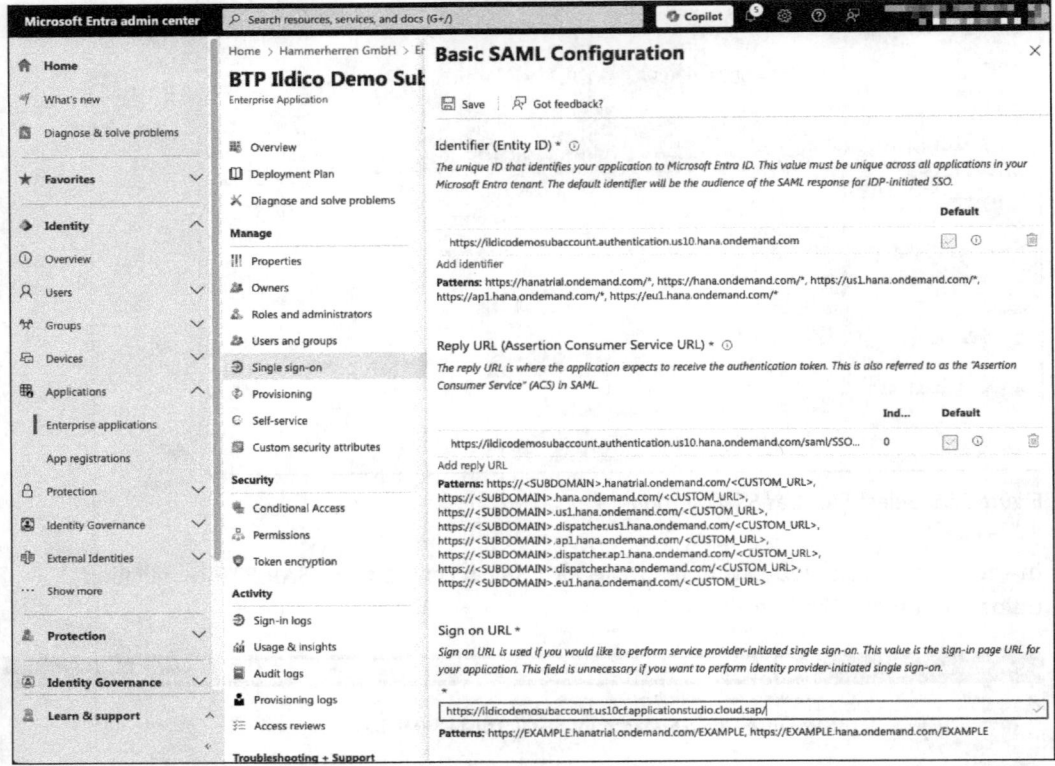

Figure 5.58 Basic Configuration with Login URL

This completes the SAML configuration on the Microsoft Entra ID side. On the overview page, in the **SAML Certificates** section, you can download the **Federation Metadata XML** file by clicking the corresponding **Download** link (see Figure 5.59). You need this file to add the response from Microsoft Entra ID in SAP BTP.

> **Group Mapping**
>
> If you want to use the user groups modeled in Microsoft Entra ID in SAP BTP, we recommend that you read this article: *http://s-prs.co/v608002*.

Now navigate menu path **Security • Trust Configuration** in your SAP BTP cockpit and click **New SAML Trust Configuration** to complete the setup on the SAP BTP side. A new window called **New Trust Configuration** opens, in which you can upload the federation data XML you just received from Microsoft Entra ID. In the **Name** field, enter a name for this trust. The **Origin Key** field should already be filled in. You can also specify a login text for the SAP BTP login screen using **Link Text for User Logon**. Click **Save** to complete the configuration (see Figure 5.60).

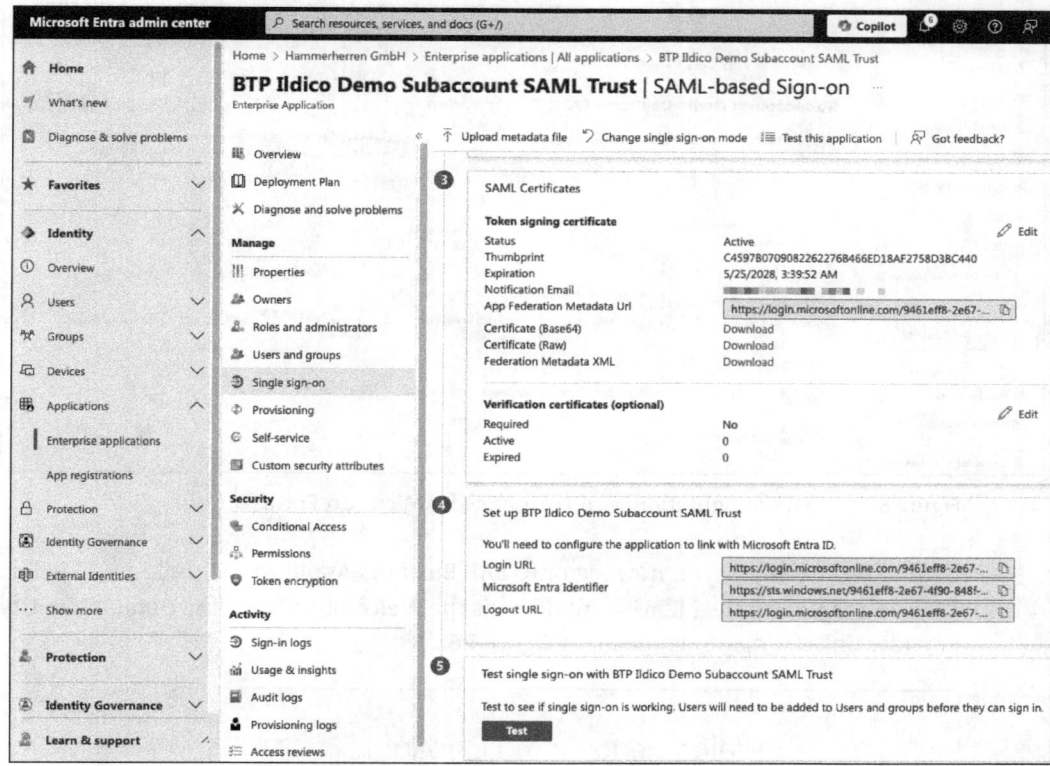

Figure 5.59 Downloading the Federation Data XML

Figure 5.60 Creating Trust Configuration and Uploading Response from Microsoft Entra ID

After the creation process, you will see the new trust provider in the overview (see Figure 5.61).

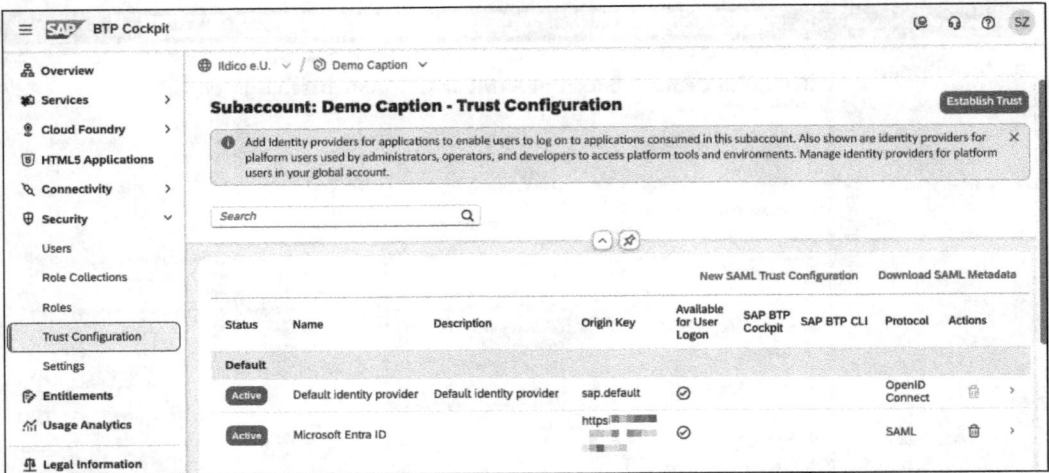

Figure 5.61 Trust Configuration with Trust Provider Microsoft Entra ID

If, as in our example, you now log onto SAP Business Application Studio on SAP BTP, then you can select the identity provider via the **Welcome to the...** and **Default Identity Provider** links to log on, as shown in Figure 5.62.

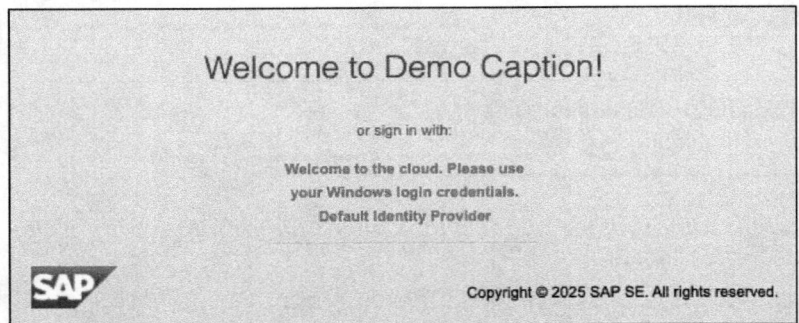

Figure 5.62 Logon to SAP Business Application Studio

If you have several accounts at Microsoft, you will now receive a prompt from Microsoft to select one of these accounts. Use the account that matches the trust you created or log on via your standard Microsoft login procedure (see Figure 5.63).

If the previous configuration works, you will be logged on to SAP BTP directly after logging in to your Microsoft account (see Figure 5.64).

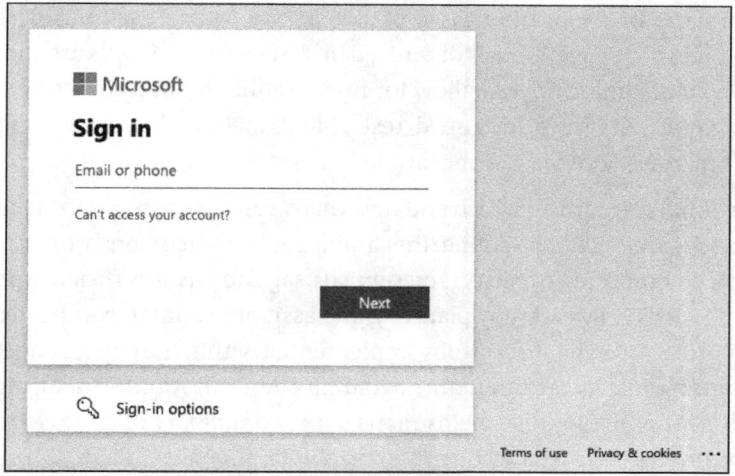

Figure 5.63 Completing Microsoft Login

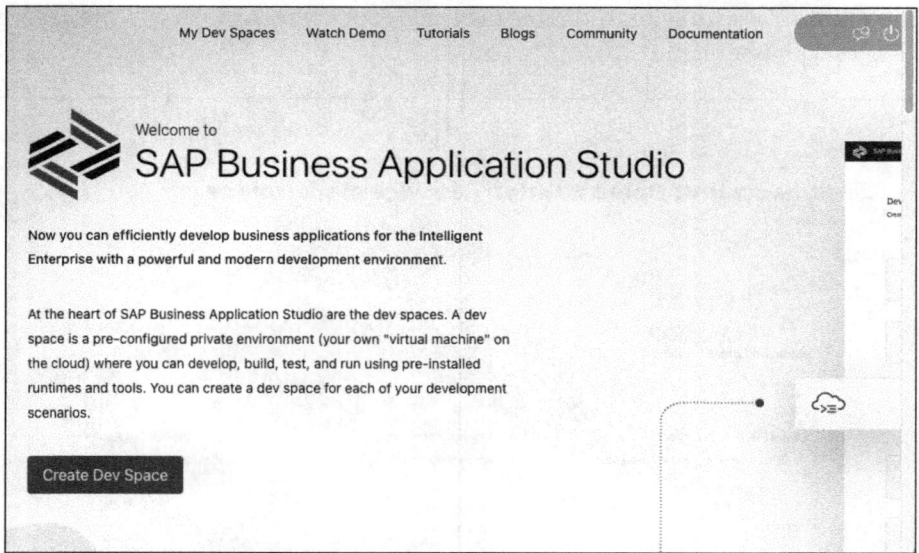

Figure 5.64 Successful Login Using Microsoft Entra ID Account

See Section 5.2.2 for our notes on the depreciation of SAML and our recommendations.

5.3 Organizations, Spaces, and Quotas

Organizations, spaces, and quotas play a central role in SAP BTP to manage resources efficiently and to structure the development and operation of applications. An *organization* (*org*) is the highest structuring point within a subaccount and serves as a framework for collaboration and resource allocation. It can be seen as a virtual shell that

5 Subaccount Administration

contains different projects or application cases of a company, where each business case—that is, each project or application—is organized in its own space. *Spaces* are subordinate areas within an organization that allow for finer granularity in resource allocation and isolation. Applications are developed, tested, and operated in a space, with each space having its own set of services, applications, and resources.

Quotas at the subaccount level control which and how many resources are available to each organization and space. Quotas define the limits for resource consumption, including storage space, computing capacity, and service usage, to ensure efficient and cost-conscious use of SAP BTP. By carefully planning and assigning quotas, companies can ensure that their projects can be successfully implemented within the given budget and resource framework, while at the same time avoiding overutilization. Structuring into orgs and spaces and defining quotas helps manage the complexity of large cloud environments and promotes clear separation of responsibilities, security, and cost control.

To see spaces and orgs, you must have the Cloud Foundry runtime instantiated in SAP Service Marketplace. After instantiation, the **Cloud Foundry** menu item appears in your SAP BTP cockpit (see Figure 5.65).

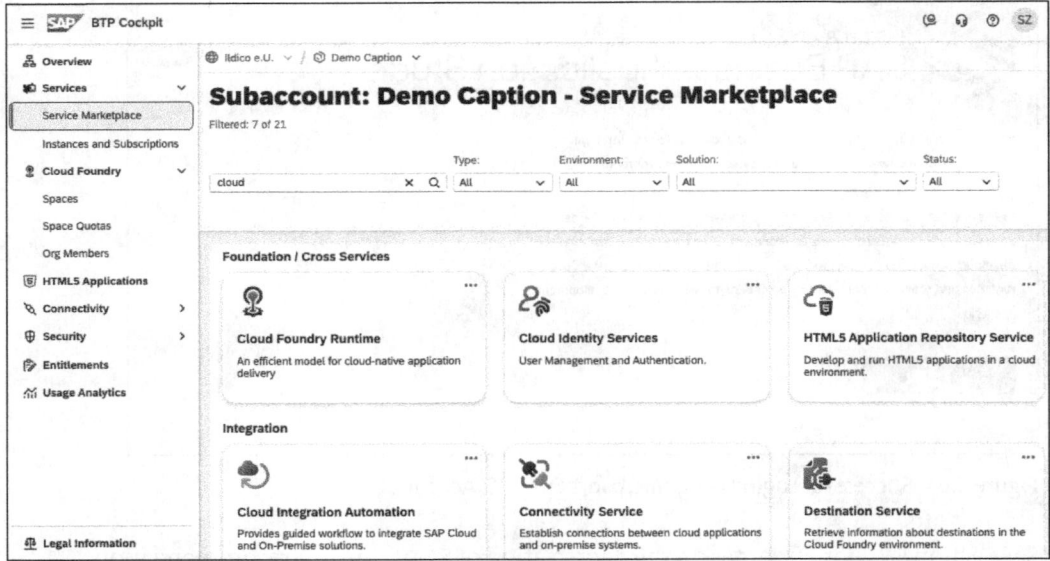

Figure 5.65 Cloud Foundry Menu Item in SAP BTP Cockpit

Before you create a space, you can create a space quota, which is highly recommended. This controls the available resources. You can find the space quotas via menu path **Cloud Foundry** • **Space Quotas** in the SAP BTP cockpit (see Figure 5.66). Note that previously this was a binding requirement, but now the use of space quotas is optional.

5.3 Organizations, Spaces, and Quotas

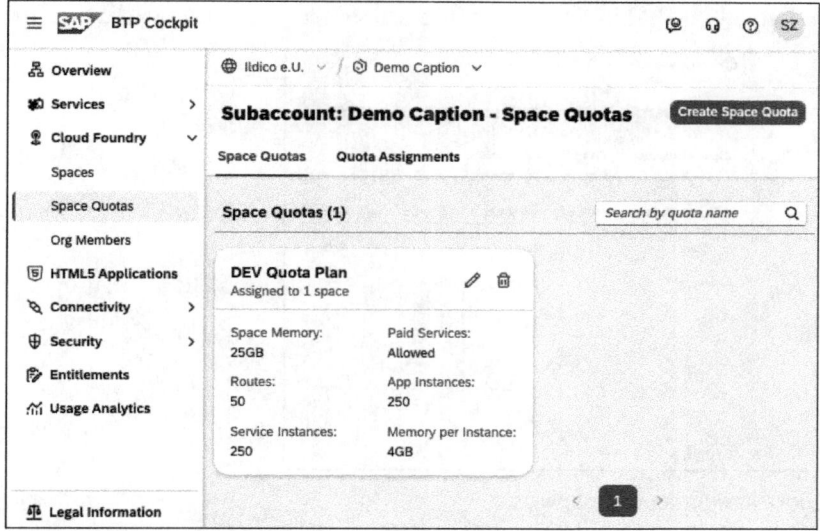

Figure 5.66 Overview of Space Quotas

Figure 5.67 shows which properties are queried when creating a new space quota. If you enable the **Allow Paid Services** switch, the resource limits are calculated based on the additional contracts you have with your hosting provider.

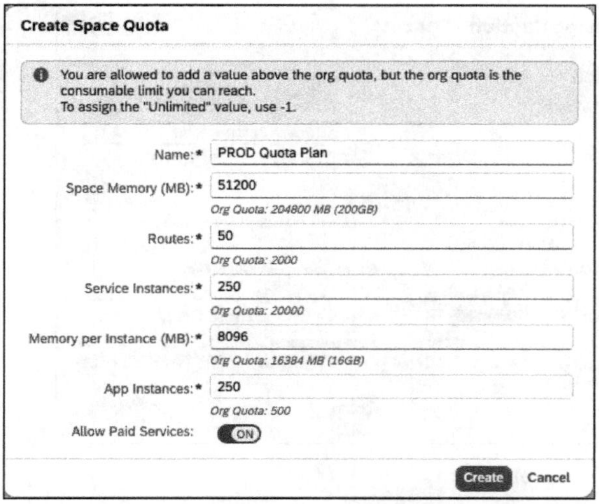

Figure 5.67 Dialog for Creating Space Quotas

On the **Quota Assignments** tab, you can see which spaces have been added to which space quotas (see Figure 5.68).

243

5 Subaccount Administration

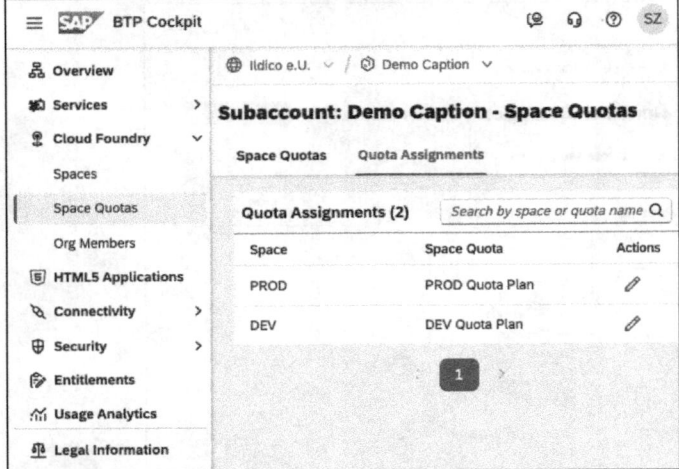

Figure 5.68 Quota Assignments for Spaces

Finally, you can see all available spaces in your subaccount in the SAP BTP cockpit via the **Cloud Foundry** • **Spaces** path (see Figure 5.69).

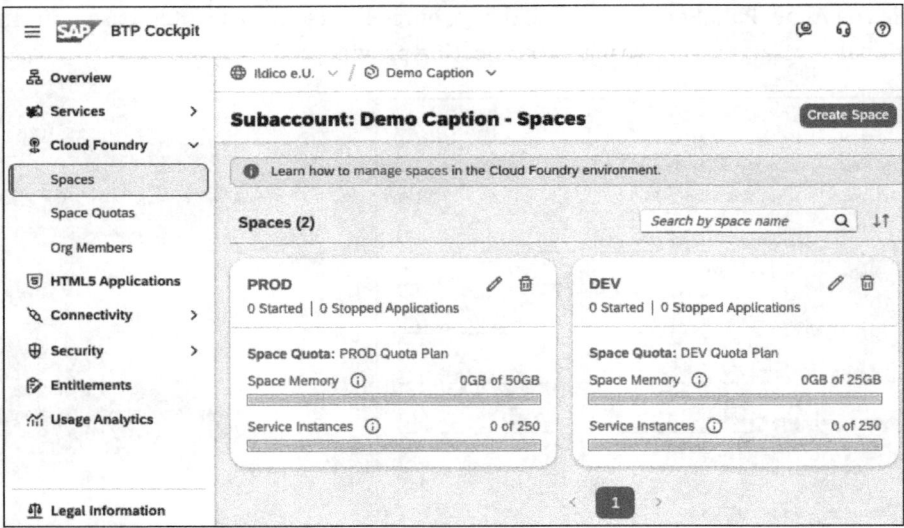

Figure 5.69 Overview of Spaces in Subaccount

For the organizations mentioned here, you can find the representations in the SAP BTP cockpit under **Cloud Foundry** • **Org Members**. You can use the **Add Members** button to add more members to your organizations (see Figure 5.70).

5.3 Organizations, Spaces, and Quotas

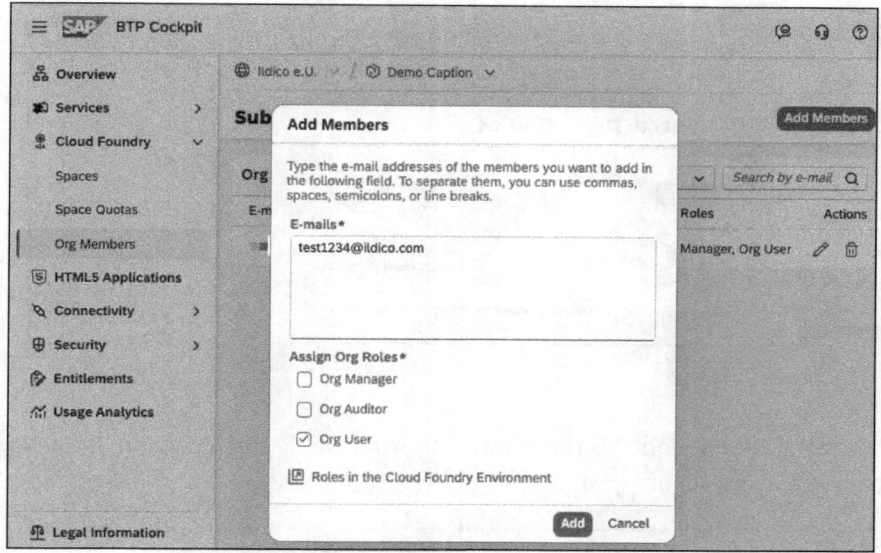

Figure 5.70 Adding Users as Organization Members

Note that when you click a space in the **Spaces** overview shown in Figure 5.69, a new space-specific menu opens. The first entry in this submenu is **Applications** (see Figure 5.71). Here you can see which applications are available in your space or have already been deployed by the developer.

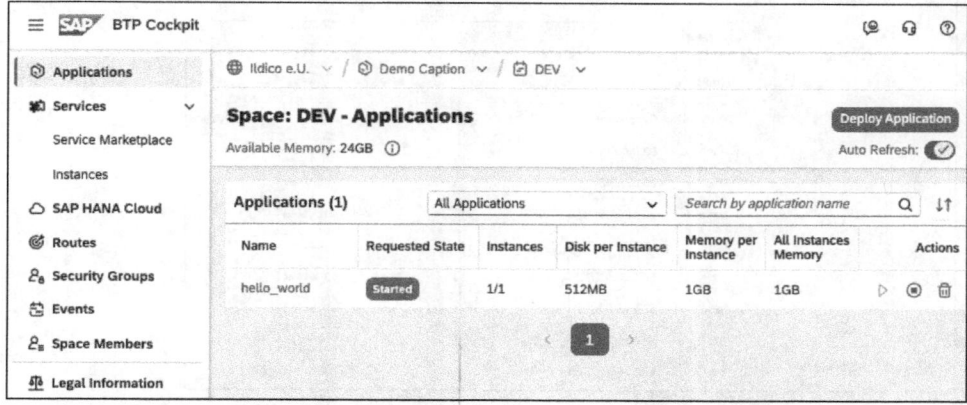

Figure 5.71 Applications of Selected Space

In the **Routes** section, you can see which paths can be used to access your applications from outside the space (see Figure 5.72).

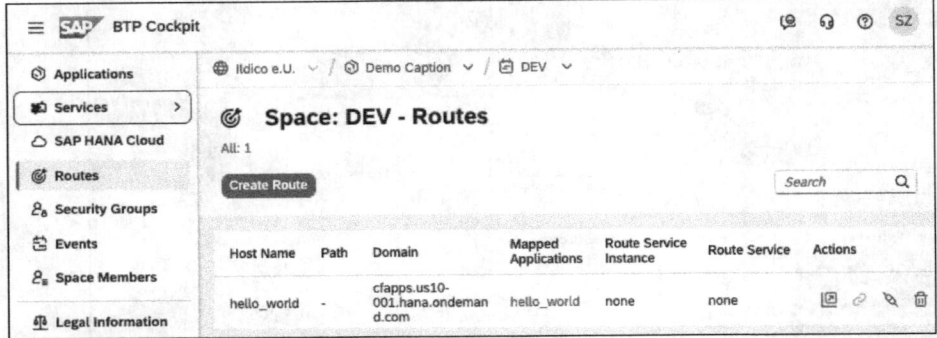

Figure 5.72 Routes to Space

Finally, **Security Groups** controls the allowed network traffic between your space and the outside world (see Figure 5.73).

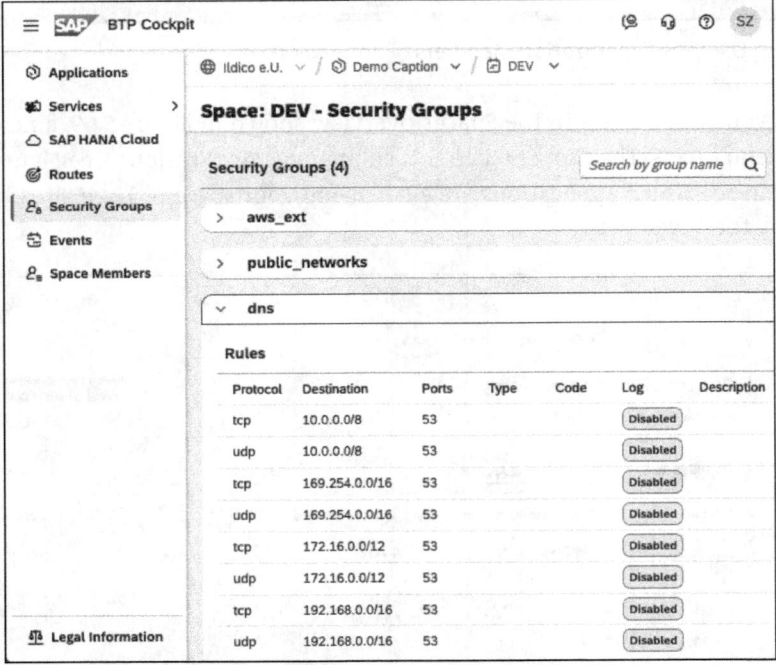

Figure 5.73 Security Groups of Space

The **Events** section aids administration by allowing you to see exactly who made a configuration change to the space at what time (see Figure 5.74).

You can also add members to a space and assign roles to these members. The prerequisite for this is that you have been assigned the Space Manager or Organization Manager role. If you only have the Space Manager role, the users that you want to add as members of the space must have been assigned to the organization as members beforehand.

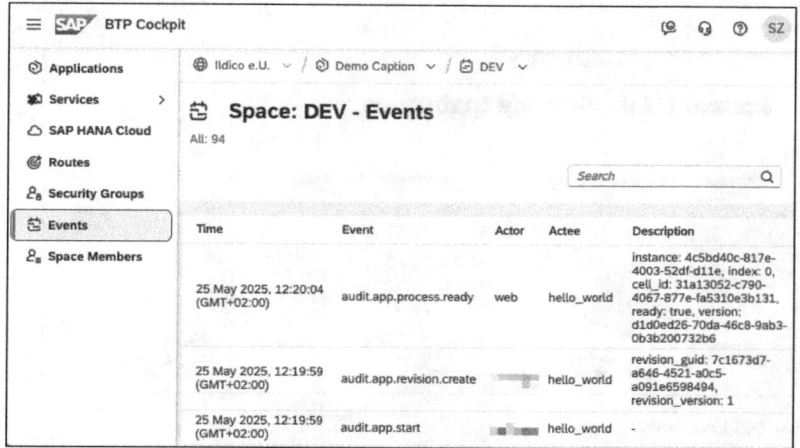

Figure 5.74 Space Event Log

If you have the Organization Manager role, the new member will be added not only to the space but also to the parent organization automatically. In SAP BTP, members are identified on the level of subaccounts and spaces only by their email addresses (partially blurred in the figure; see Figure 5.75).

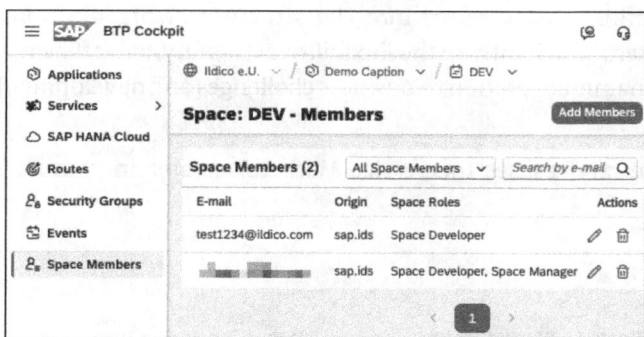

Figure 5.75 Members of Selected Space

5.4 Subscriptions and Services

Subscriptions allow you to select the services or applications you need for your business or development needs and activate them for your subaccounts or within specific spaces. This selective access control allows the platform to be flexibly adapted to individual requirements, so that resources can be used in a targeted and demand-oriented manner. An example of such a subscription model is SAP Cloud Identity Services, which you can integrate into your subaccounts.

You can find an overview of the selected subscriptions in the SAP BTP cockpit and below your space under **Services • Instances** (see Figure 5.76).

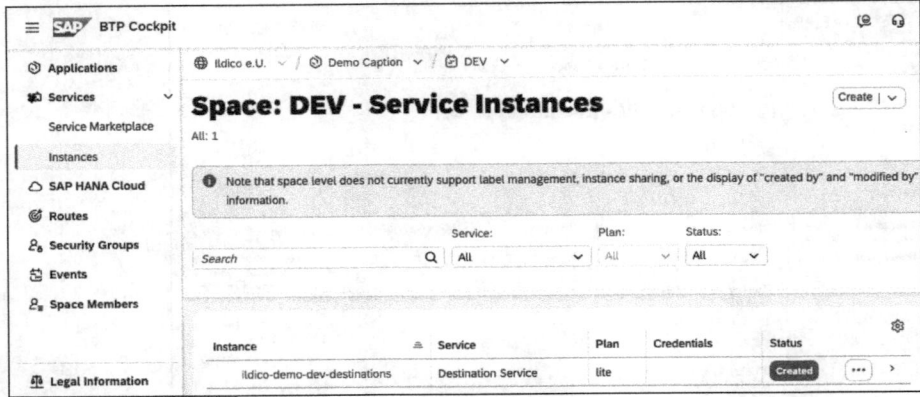

Figure 5.76 Instances Overview

Services are the core offering of SAP BTP and provide a variety of solutions—from data management and analysis to application development and integration. The availability and usage of these services is determined by subscriptions and defined quotas within a subaccount or space, which enables effective control over resource consumption and costs. This architecture helps organizations keep their IT infrastructure agile and cost-conscious by precisely controlling access to technology resources and tools. The seamless integration of subscriptions and services into the structure of organizations, spaces, and quotas contributes significantly to the flexibility, scalability, and efficiency of SAP BTP and promotes dynamic adaptation to business challenges and development requirements.

For an overview of available services, see the **Service Marketplace** area in your subaccount (see Figure 5.77).

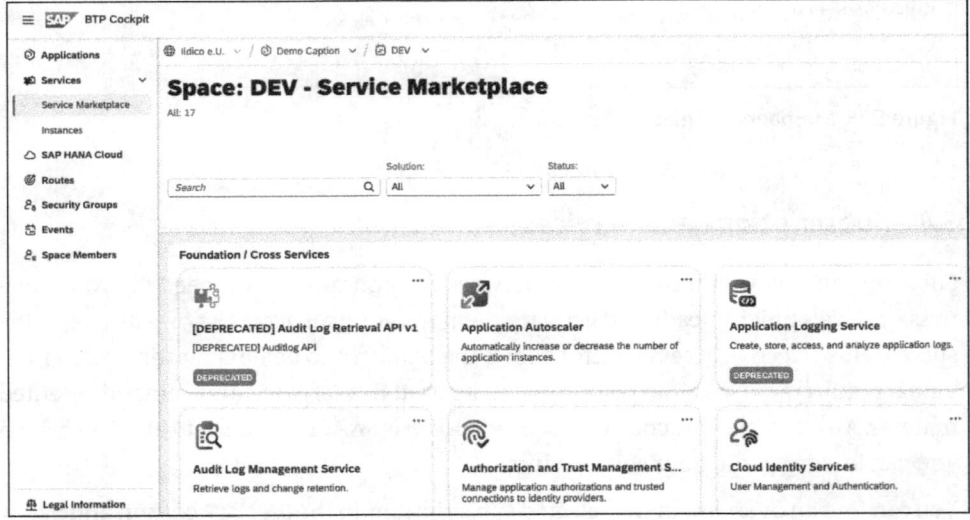

Figure 5.77 SAP Service Marketplace

5.5 SAP Audit Log Viewer Service for SAP BTP

To audit the system, SAP BTP provides the *SAP Audit Log Viewer service*. If you want to use this service, you have to subscribe to the SAP Audit Log service. Be aware of the permissions assignment in the global account, as described in Chapter 4.

In your SAP BTP cockpit, you can create a subscription for the service by going to **Services • Service Marketplace**, clicking the service panel, then clicking the **Create** button (see Figure 5.78).

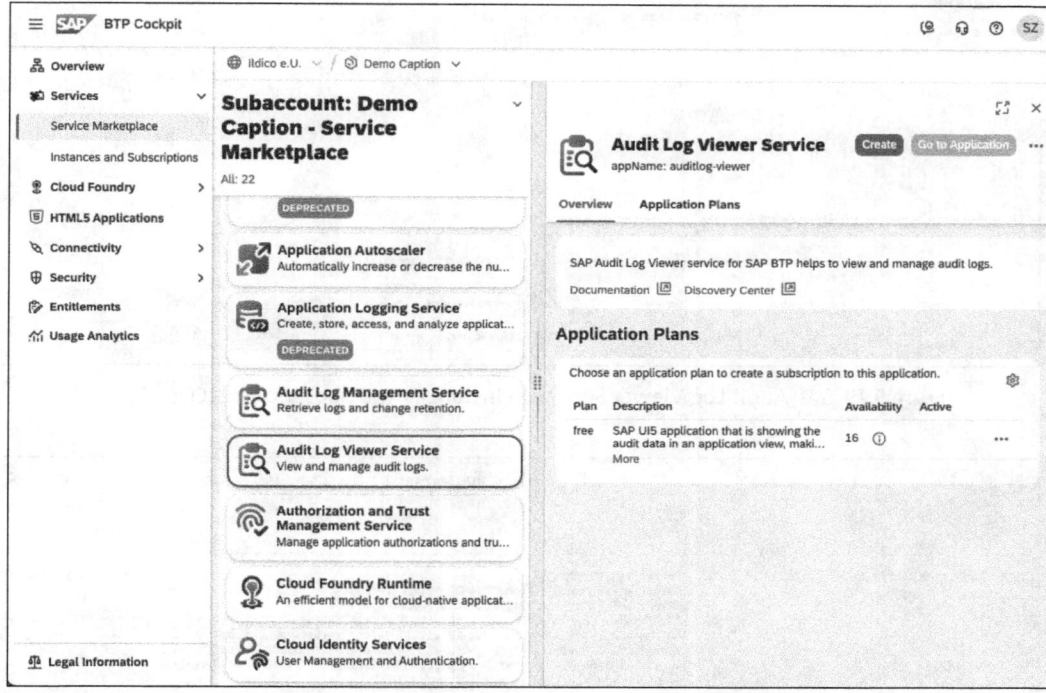

Figure 5.78 SAP Audit Log Viewer Service in SAP Service Marketplace

Now you can access the URL of the SAP Audit Log Viewer service in the overview under **Services • Instances and Subscriptions** by clicking the link highlighted in blue or by right-clicking and selecting **Copy Link** from the context menu (see Figure 5.79).

An example for a filtered audit log is shown in Figure 5.80.

> **Note Audit Log Permissions**
>
> To perform an audit, you need audit permission for the organization and the space you want to audit. A more detailed description can be found at *http://s-prs.co/v608003*.

5   Subaccount Administration

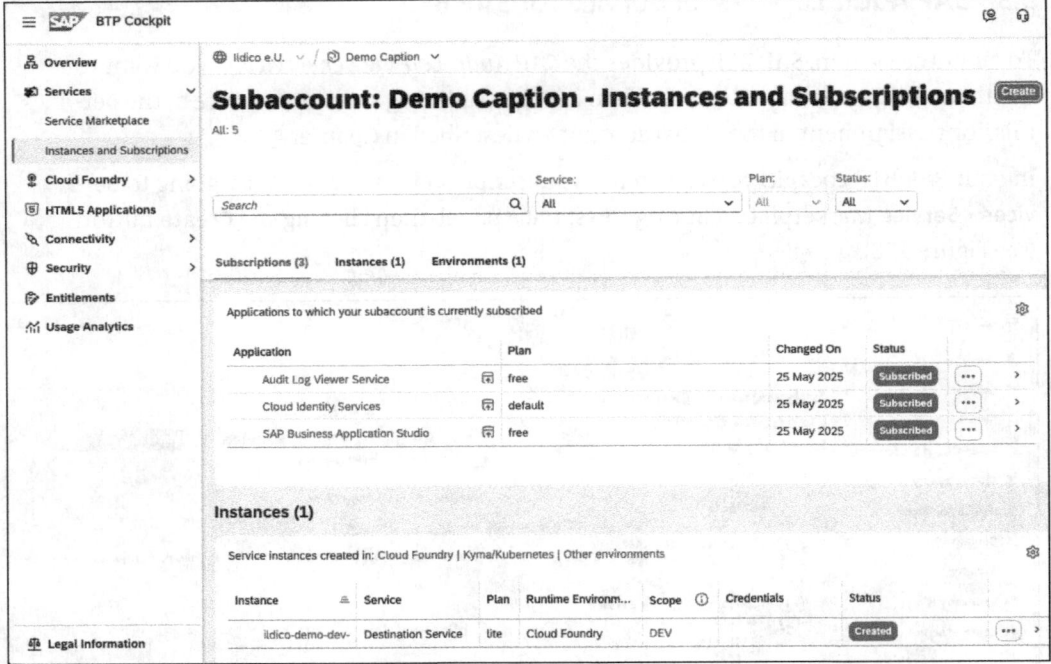

Figure 5.79 SAP Audit Log Viewer Service in Instances and Subscriptions Overview

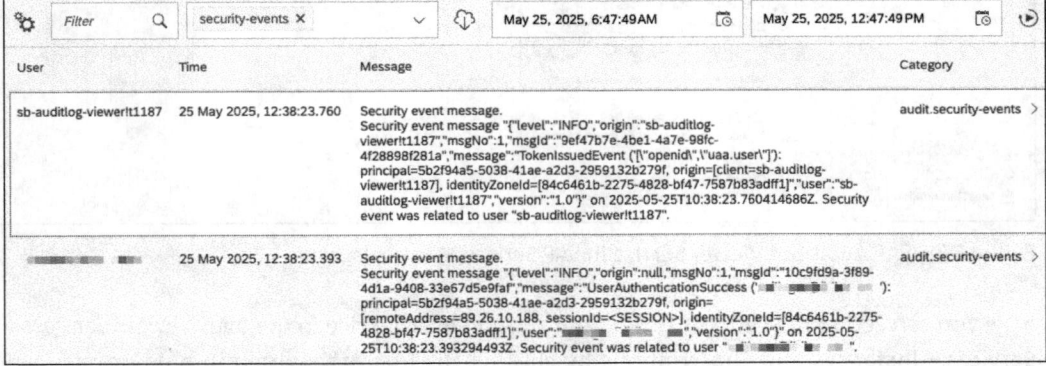

Figure 5.80 Sample Result of Audit Log

5.6   Summary

Effective subaccount administration in SAP BTP forms the backbone of secure and scalable cloud operations. This chapter guided you through creating and managing subaccounts, assigning roles, integrating identity providers, and organizing environments with precision.

It began with subaccount creation, emphasizing thoughtful regional selection and optional directory structures for better manageability. We then covered user authentication and authorization in depth, including best practices for password policies, MFA, and certificate-based login. You also learned how to integrate Identity Authentication, moving toward modern OIDC-based setups and away from legacy SAML.

The chapter also explored role and role collection management. Role collections bundle access rights for easy assignment and can be dynamically mapped to user attributes from external identity providers via role collection mapping.

We also explained how to structure development and operations using organizations, spaces, and quotas within Cloud Foundry. You learned too that subscriptions and services provide flexibility, enabling activation of capabilities such as SAP Cloud Identity Services and the SAP Audit Log Viewer service. In essence, this chapter provided know-how for securely and efficiently managing SAP BTP subaccounts.

Chapter 6
Cloud Connector

The cloud connector is the heart of the modern IT landscape, bridging the gap between local systems and SAP Business Technology Platform.

This chapter provides a detailed roadmap for the cloud connector: from basic requirements to initial installation to advanced monitoring options. Whether you want to prepare the installation, explore the connectivity options, or use the monitoring capabilities of the cloud connector, here you will find the know-how you need for an optimized and secure connection between your on-premise infrastructure and SAP BTP.

Section 6.1 provides installation and configuration instructions to ensure a seamless integration between your on-premise system and SAP BTP. In Section 6.2, we discuss the different options for connectivity with the cloud connector. The chapter concludes with Section 6.3, in which you learn about the monitoring options of the cloud connector.

> **Further Reading**
>
> If you want to learn more about the cloud connector, we recommend our book *Cloud Connector for SAP*, also published by SAP PRESS, which can be found at *https://www.sap-press.com/cloud-connector-for-sap_5683/*.

6.1 Installation and Configuration

To ensure smooth installation and configuration of the cloud connector, it is crucial to understand the requirements and steps involved. This section provides a comprehensive guide.

In Section 6.1.1, you will learn which prerequisites your system and system landscape must meet in order to be able to install the cloud connector. In Section 6.1.2, you will find a step-by-step guide to installing the cloud connector. Next, in Section 6.1.3, we describe the first steps you need to take when setting up the cloud connector for the first time. Then, in Section 6.1.4, we will show you how to customize the cloud connector's login screen, how to change the cloud connector user's user name and password, and how to replace the UI certificate so that administration can use an encrypted connection with a trusted certificate when accessing the cloud connector. In Section 6.1.5, we show some options that are available when connecting with SAP BTP. You will learn how to set up a proxy server and how to set up the cloud user store so that cloud users can authenticate themselves using Lightweight Directory Access Protocol (LDAP). You will also learn how to set up custom regions if your data center is not supported by the cloud connector. Section 6.1.6 explains how to configure the connection to your on-premise systems. Section 6.1.7 tells you where to configure the connection to SAP Solution Manager. Finally, Section 6.1.8 explains the advanced configuration options available.

6.1.1 Prerequisites

The installation of the cloud connector is very simple. However, there are some prerequisites that you should check beforehand. One prerequisite is the use of an operating system supported by SAP. The following operating systems are supported:

- Red Hat Enterprise Linux (x86/64 and PowerPC)
- SUSE Linux Enterprise Server (x86/64 and PowerPC)
- Windows Server
- Windows 11
- macOS (note that you should not use macOS for production scenarios)

The cloud connector is a Java application that requires a Java Virtual Machine (JVM) to run. The JVM loads the Java byte code, validates it, and executes it. This JVM is called an *interpreter* and is the core of the Java programming language because it executes the Java programs. The JVM is platform-specific and performs many functions, including memory management and security.

The cloud connector is implemented as a web application and uses Apache Tomcat as its runtime environment. It requires at least JVM 8 in all currently supported versions. Starting with version 2.14.0 of the cloud connector, SAP JVM version 11 is required; cloud connector version 2.15.0 requires version 17 of the JVM.

The cloud connector must be able to establish an internet connection to the SAP Connectivity service hosts. The *SAP Connectivity service* is the counterpart to the cloud connector on the SAP BTP. The cloud connector will actively connect to the SAP Connectivity service. All connections to cloud hosts are TLS-based and are established on port 443. This means that your firewall must allow outbound connections on port 443 to SAP BTP. In addition, you have the option of restricting outgoing connections to the IP addresses of the data centers used. The IP addresses are not listed here because they change frequently. You can find the current list in the cloud connector documentation.

If you install the cloud connector in a network segment that is isolated from backend systems—for example, in a demilitarized zone (DMZ)—then you must make sure that the exposed hosts with the corresponding ports are network-enabled. This means that you must open the ports in the firewall for incoming traffic.

6.1.2 Installing the Cloud Connector

After you have fulfilled all requirements in your system landscape, the cloud connector can be installed. To do this, the cloud connector must be downloaded from *https://tools.hana.ondemand.com/#cloud*. Unlike most other SAP products, the cloud connector is not obtained through SAP Service Marketplace, and you do not need an SAP Service Marketplace user to download it. On the same page where the cloud connector can be obtained, SAP also offers SapMachine and SAP JVM for download; you will need these to have a supported runtime environment in place (see Figure 6.1).

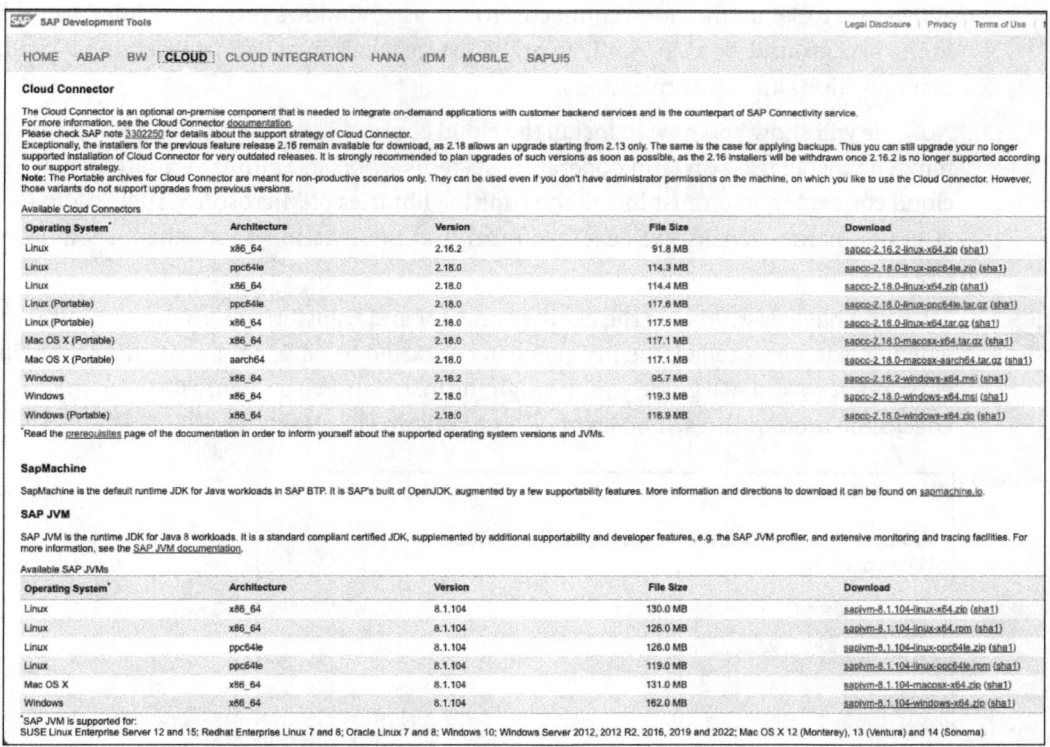

Figure 6.1 Downloading Cloud Connector and SAP JVM

As you can see in Figure 6.1, the cloud connector is also available for download in a portable version. This is a version that only needs to be unpacked and can then be started directly from the command line. Note that no administrator or root rights are required for the installation. You can also run multiple instances on the same host on different ports.

The portable version has the following limitations:

- It is intended for nonproduction scenarios only.
- It does not support an automatic upgrade procedure. To upgrade a portable installation, you must delete the current installation, extract the new version, and then reconfigure it.
- The JAVA_HOME environment variable is relevant when the instance is started, so it must be set correctly.
- You cannot run it in the background as a Windows service or Linux daemon.

The other, nonportable versions, also called *installer versions*, are delivered with an installation program that also sets up the cloud connector as a service in the underlying operating system. This requires administrator or root rights for the installation and allows you to set up the cloud connector to run as a Windows service or Linux daemon in the background. You can easily upgrade the installation version, preserving all your configurations and customizations.

Now, we will show you how to install the cloud connector on a Windows operating system. The installation on Linux operating systems works in a similar way. To install the cloud connector, you must install the runtime libraries of Microsoft Visual Studio C++ 2013 (file name: *vcredist_x64.exe*). You can find information about this in SAP Note 2493763.

After you have downloaded the cloud connector and transferred it to the computer on which it is to be installed, the installer can be started by clicking the MSI file in the file explorer. A wizard will guide you through the installation (see Figure 6.2). The first step checks the prerequisites. If no error occurs, you can click **Next**.

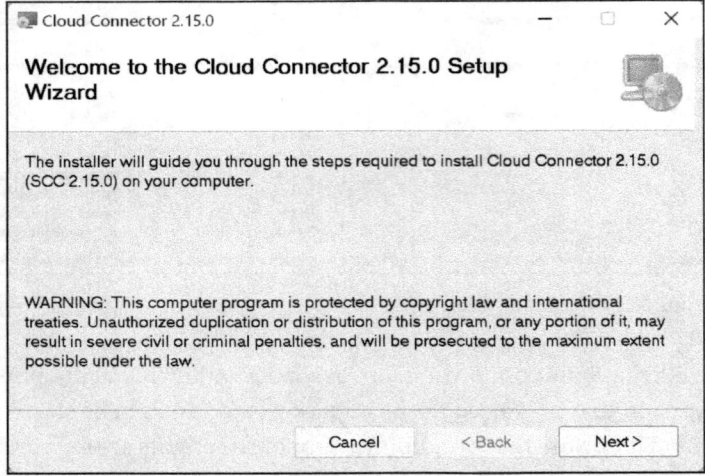

Figure 6.2 Cloud Connector Installation Wizard

In the next step you must select the installation **Folder** (see Figure 6.3), then click **Next**.

6.1 Installation and Configuration

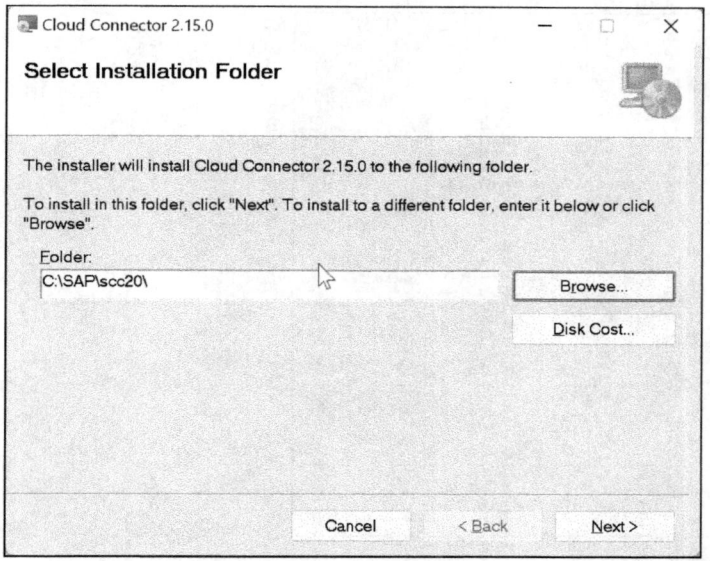

Figure 6.3 Select Installation Directory

After this, you have the option to adjust the **Port** used by the cloud connector. By default, the cloud connector is installed on port 8443 (see Figure 6.4). Click **Next** again.

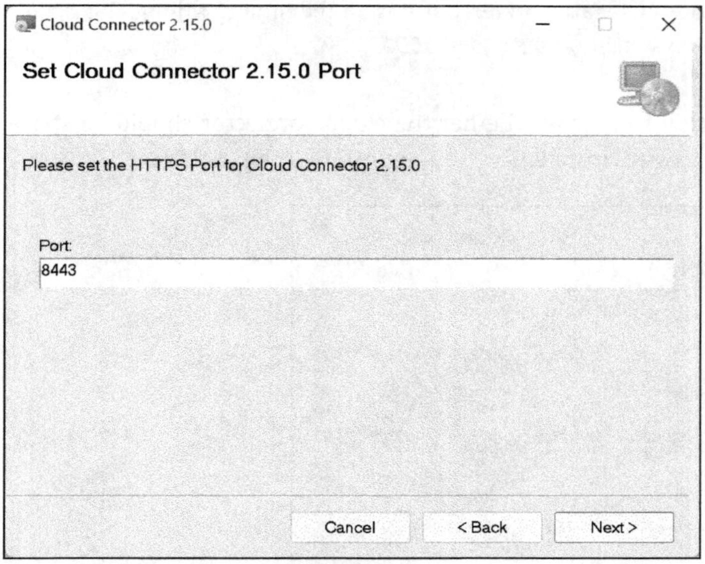

Figure 6.4 Select Port Number

You must now select the Java Development Kit (JDK) installation directory (see Figure 6.5). Make sure that you are using a version supported by SAP. When you are finished, click **Next** again.

6   Cloud Connector

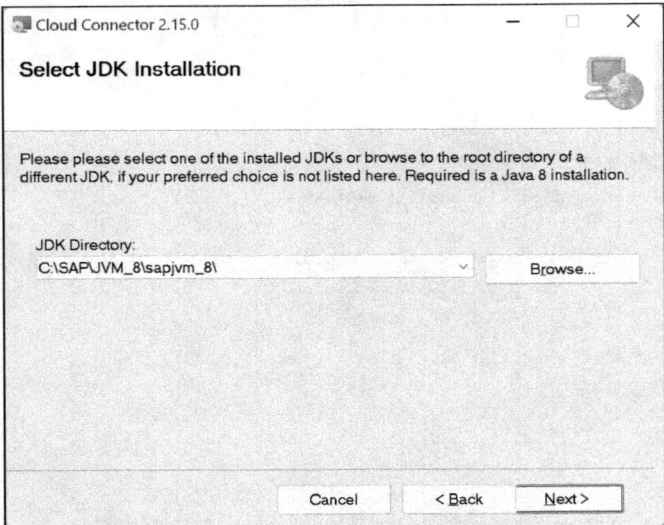

Figure 6.5 Selecting JDK Directory

> **Supported Versions**
>
> You can find the supported versions in the SAP Connectivity service documentation under **Cloud Connector** • **Installation** • **Prerequisites**. At the time of writing, this documentation was available at *http://s-prs.co/v608004*.

You now have the option to specify whether the cloud connector should be started immediately after a successful installation (see Figure 6.6). Then click **Next**.

Figure 6.6 Start Cloud Connector After Successful Installation

Finally, you must confirm that you want to start the installation (see Figure 6.7). Click the **Next** button once again.

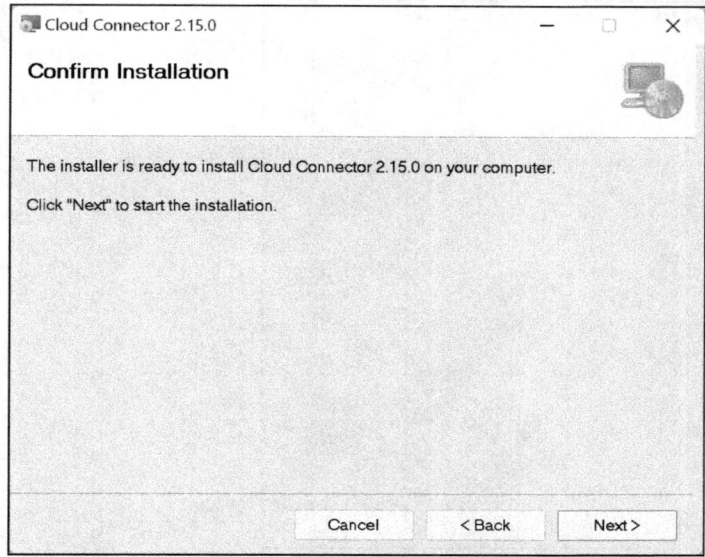

Figure 6.7 Starting Installation

After the successful start of the installation, you will see the status of the installation (see Figure 6.8). Normally, no errors should occur at this point.

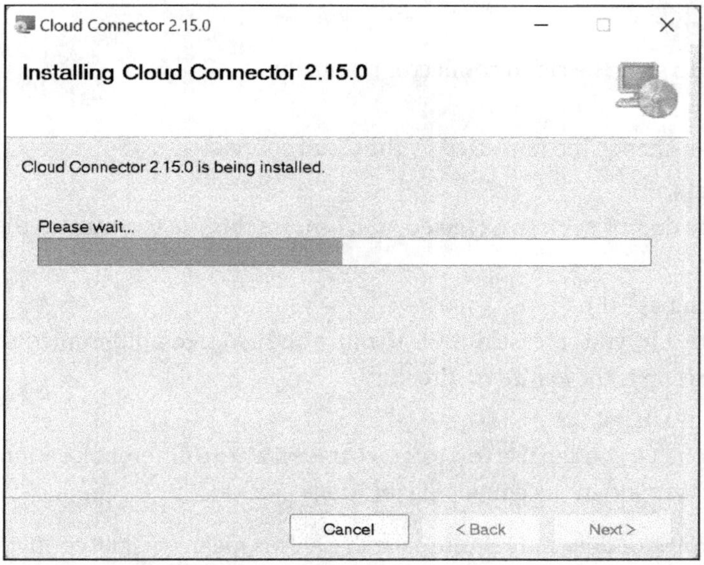

Figure 6.8 Installation Progress

After successful installation, you will be informed about the completion of the installation (see Figure 6.9). Close the dialog by clicking **Close**.

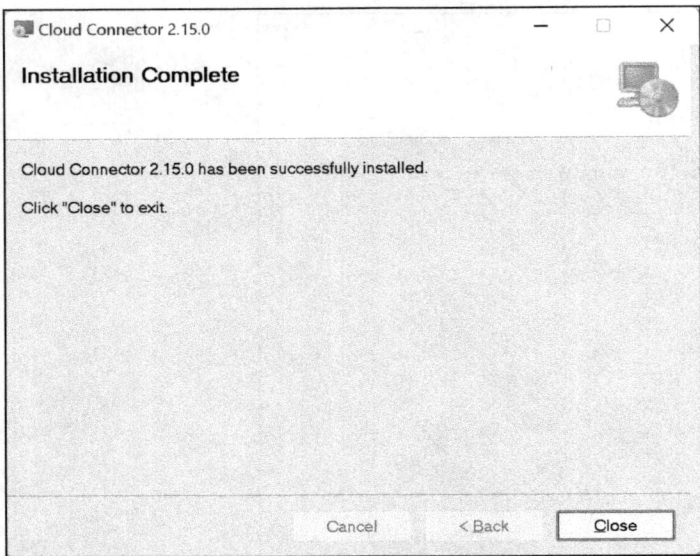

Figure 6.9 Completing Installation

After the installation is finished, you will see the directory structure shown in Figure 6.10. The most important files in the cloud connector installation directory are as follows:

- **go.bat (.sh)**
  You can use this file to start the cloud connector manually.
- **changeport.bat (.sh)**
  With this file, you can change the port used by the cloud connector.
- **useFileUserStore.bat (.sh)**
  If your LDAP settings do not work as expected, you can use this file to revert to the file-based user store.
- **changeAuditLogPath.bat (.sh)**
  As of cloud connector 2.14, you can use this file to move audit logs to a different location. The default location is the *log/audit* directory.
- **changeLogAndTracePath.bat (.sh)**
  As of cloud connector 2.14, you can use this to move trace files to a different location. The JVM-related files remain in the default log location.

Note that the cloud connector does not require a database. This means that all configuration, log, and trace files are stored locally on the cloud connector's file system. Therefore, you should make sure that the installation directory is included in your backup.

6.1 Installation and Configuration

However, you should also restrict access to the directory according to your requirements. You should pay special attention to the log and trace files.

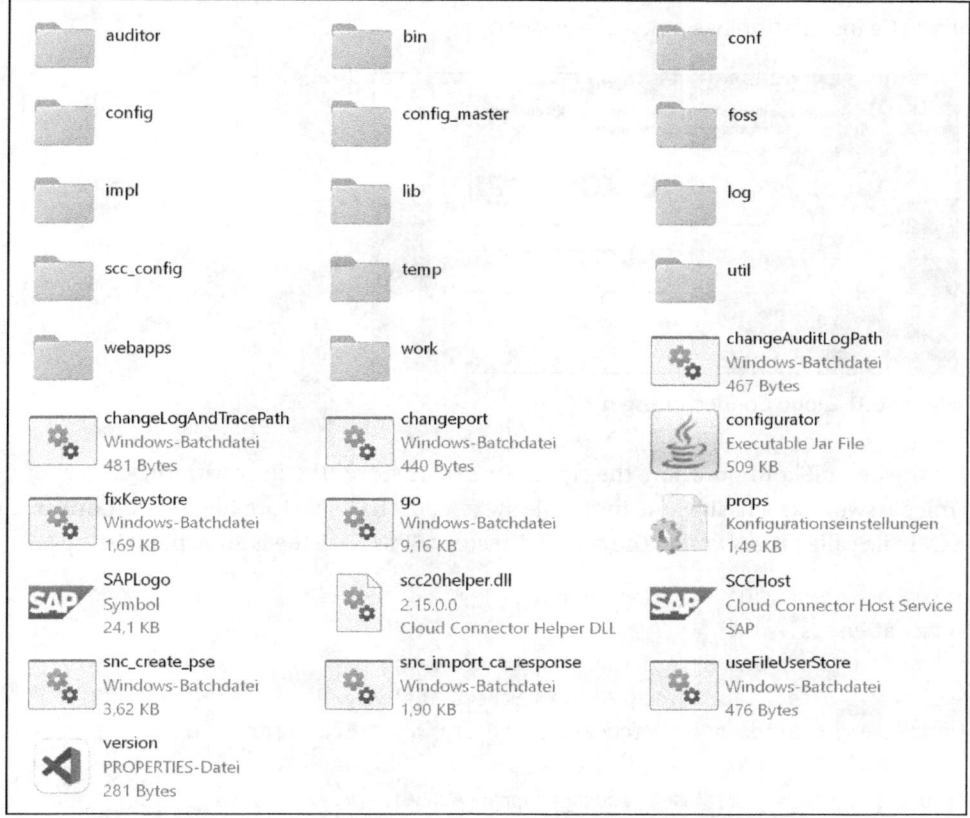

Figure 6.10 Installation Directory Structure

After the cloud connector has been installed, the cloud connector administration interface can be opened in a browser of your choice. Use the host name of the server on which the cloud connector has been installed as the host name. By default, port 8443 is used, but you can change the port during the installation as described in the previous section.

> **Hint**
> The port will be displayed in command line during startup.

6.1.3 Initial Steps

When you log in for the first time, you will receive a security warning. This is because the cloud connector's HTTPS connection is encrypted with a self-signed certificate. This certificate is created when the cloud connector is started for the first time. Section 6.1.4 tells you how to replace this UI certificate. You will also be informed that the cloud connector instance has not assumed the master or shadow role (see Figure 6.11). This means that the installation has not yet been set up.

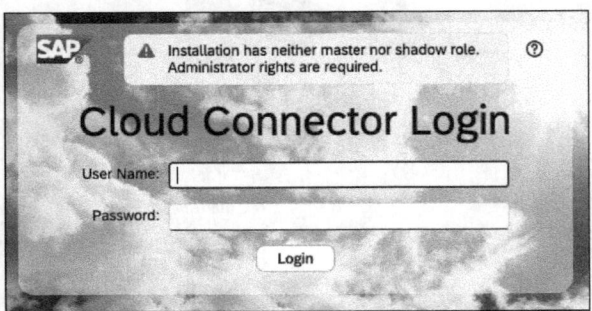

Figure 6.11 Cloud Connector Login

In the default configuration, the cloud connector stores the user with the corresponding password as a hash value in the file system, in the user store file. This is done in an XML file called *users.xml* in the *config* directory. This XML file is shown in Listing 6.1.

```
<?xml version='1.0' encoding='utf-8'?>
<tomcat-users.xml
<tomcat-users xmlns=http://tomcat.apache.org/xml
xmlns:xsi=http://www.w3.org/2001/XMLSchema-instance
xsi:schemaLocation=http://tomcat.apache.org/xml tomcat-users.xsd
version="1.0">
<role rolename="admin"/> <group groupname="admin"/>.
<group groupname="initial" roles=""/> <user name
<user username="Administrator" password=
"280D44AB1E9F79B5CCE2DD4F58F5FE91F0FBACDAC9F7447DFFC318CEB79F2D02" groups=""
roles="admin"/></tomcat-users>
```

Listing 6.1 users.xml

The cloud connector cannot be used by multiple users without integrating an LDAP server. For the first login to the cloud connector, enter "Administrator" for **User Name** and "manage" for **Password**. Note that the user name is case-sensitive. After a successful initial login, you will be prompted to change the user's password (see Figure 6.12). After that, you will have to decide whether this will be the master or shadow instance. There is no set password policy for the user store file, but you should still use a complex password.

6.1 Installation and Configuration

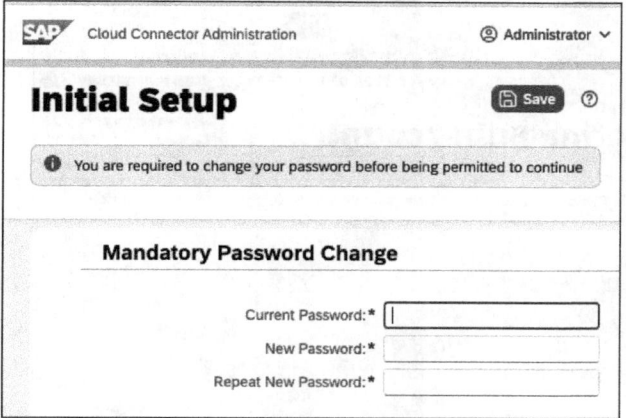

Figure 6.12 Change Credentials After Initial Login

> **Troubleshooting Forgotten Password**
>
> There is no direct way to change a password using scripts in the command line. However, if you have forgotten the password for a user name, there is a solution:
>
> 1. Stop the cloud connector.
> 2. Download a portable version of the cloud connector to your local computer and unzip it.
> 3. Copy the *users.xml* file from the config directory of the portable version to the config directory of your cloud connector installation and overwrite the existing file.
> 4. Start the cloud connector.
> 5. Log in with the default credentials (user name *Administrator* and password *manage*).
>
> You can find more detailed instructions in SAP Note 2388242.

Once you have changed the password, you will be taken to the **Define Subaccount** area (see Figure 6.13). Here you can connect to an SAP BTP subaccount and define an HTTPS proxy. Although the cloud connector only makes sense in connection with a subaccount, you do not need to connect to a subaccount at this point and can also perform the configuration beforehand.

You can access the configuration of the cloud connector via menu path **Connector · Configuration**. The configuration is divided into the areas **User Interface**, **Cloud**, **On-Premises**, **Reporting**, and **Advanced** (see Figure 6.14).

263

6   Cloud Connector

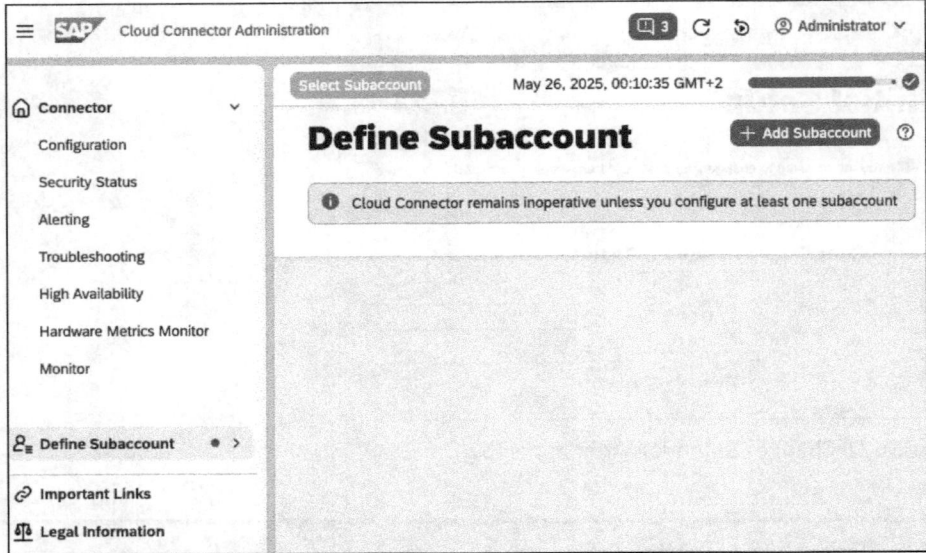

Figure 6.13 Connecting Cloud Connector to SAP BTP Subaccount

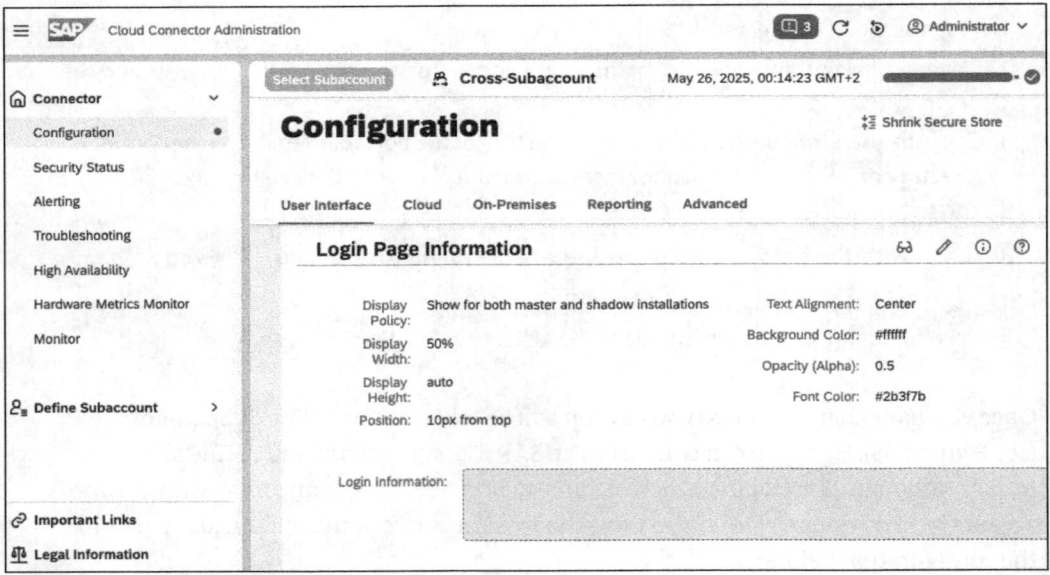

Figure 6.14 Basic Cloud Connector Configuration Options

6.1.4   Configuring the User Interface

On the **User Interface** tab, you have the option to customize the information displayed on the login screen. Click **Edit** (the pencil button ✏️) to do this. You can now make adjustments (see Figure 6.15). The **Login Information** will be displayed in a box with

264

rounded corners. You can use the **Display Policy** section to control whether the information is displayed in the master instance, in the shadow instance, in both instances, or not at all. You can use this option to inform the user whether he is in a development system, a test system, or a production system. At this point, you have the option to use HTML to display the information in an appealing way. However, there are some limitations to using HTML, which you can read about in the cloud connector documentation. These restrictions mainly pertain to the use of headings and list elements.

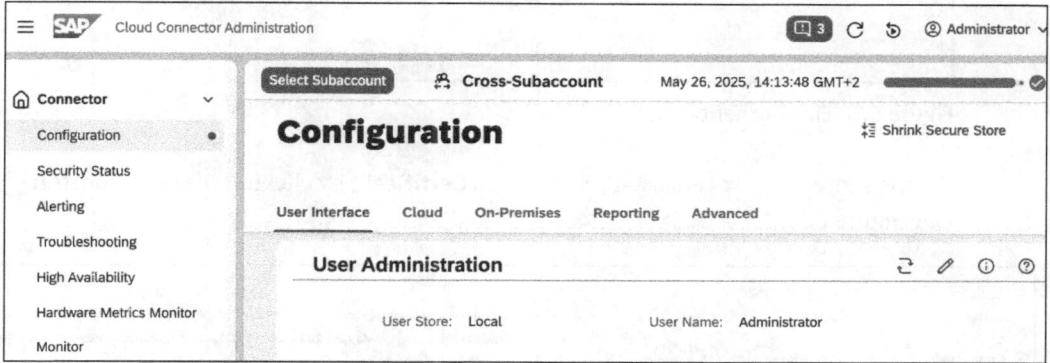

Figure 6.15 Customize Credentials

In the **Authentication** section of the **User Interface** tab, you can perform the LDAP configuration. This configuration is described in Section 6.1.5. However, you can also change the credentials (see Figure 6.15 and Figure 6.16). Click **Edit** to do so.

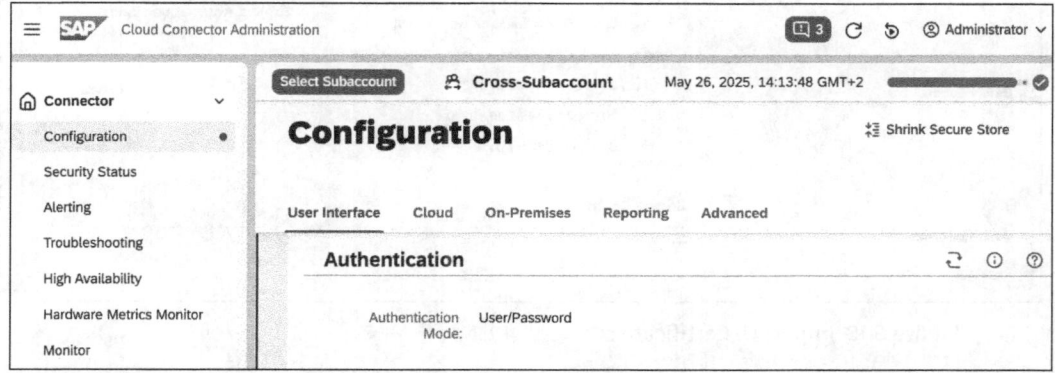

Figure 6.16 Configuring Authentication

At this point, you can also change the user name in the **User Name** field. To change the password, you must enter the user's current password in the **Current Password** field, then enter a new password in the **New Password** field and repeat it in the **Repeat New Password** field (see Figure 6.17).

6   Cloud Connector

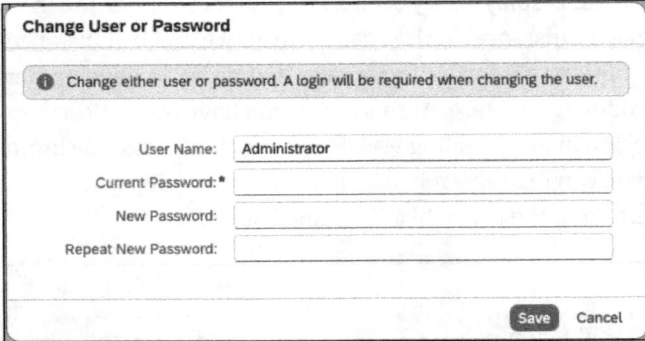

Figure 6.17 Edit Authentication

On the same tab, you can also import the **UI Certificate** by clicking the arrow button ⬆ (see Figure 6.18).

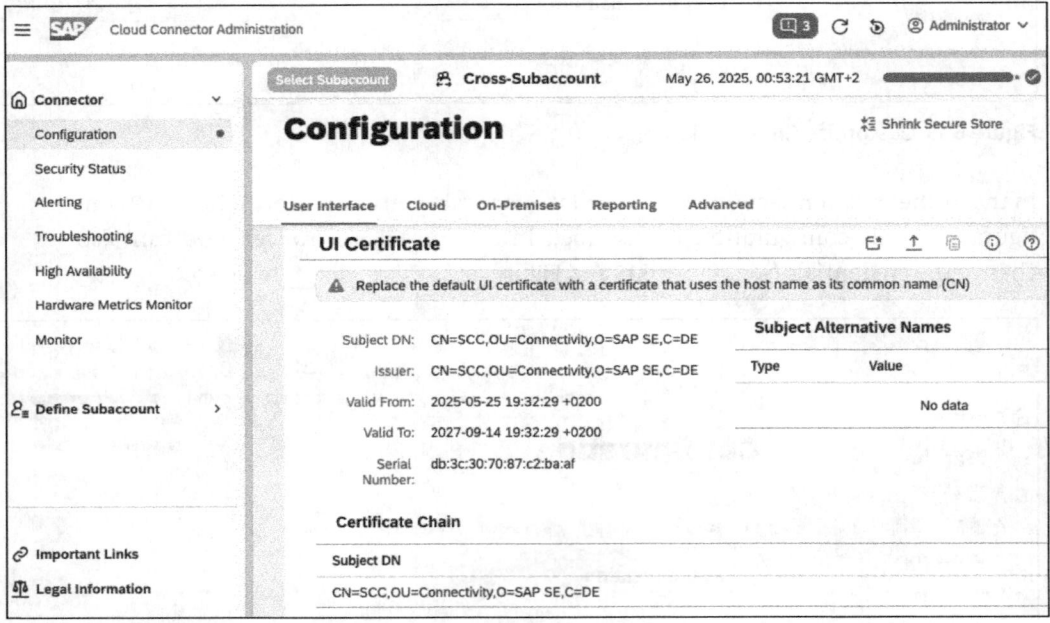

Figure 6.18 Import UI Certificate

The cloud connector ships with several cipher suites, listed in this tab under **Cipher Suites** (see Figure 6.19). A *cipher suite* represents the type and complexity of information encryption. A long key is recommended.

6.1 Installation and Configuration

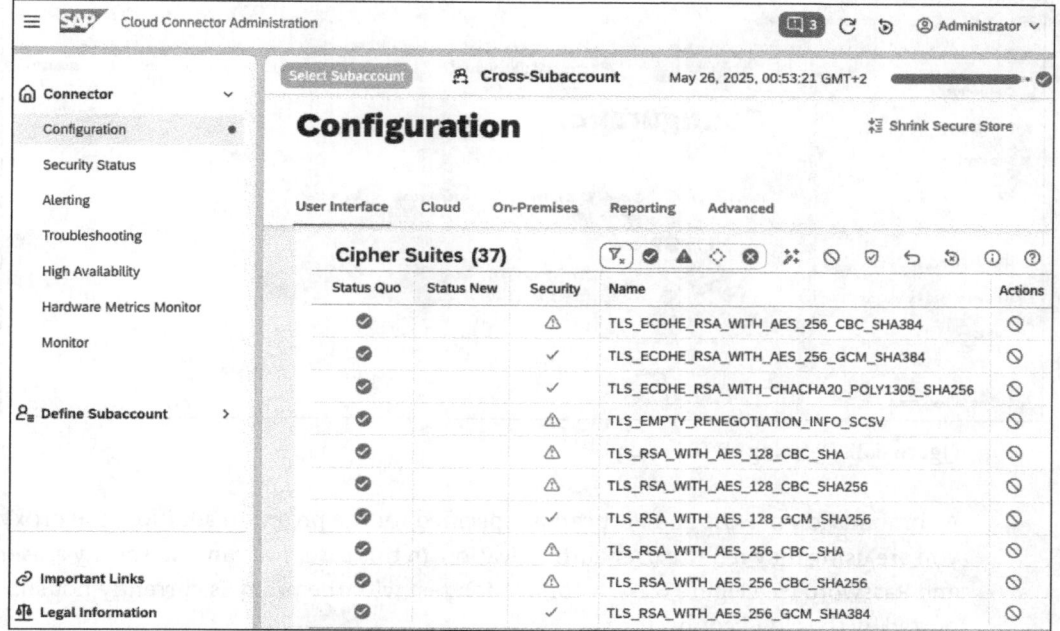

Figure 6.19 Overview of Cipher Suites

6.1.5 Cloud Configuration

In the **Connector Info** section of the **Cloud** tab, you can click **Edit** (the pencil button ✏️) to change the description of the cloud connector that was assigned to it when it was first registered (see Figure 6.20).

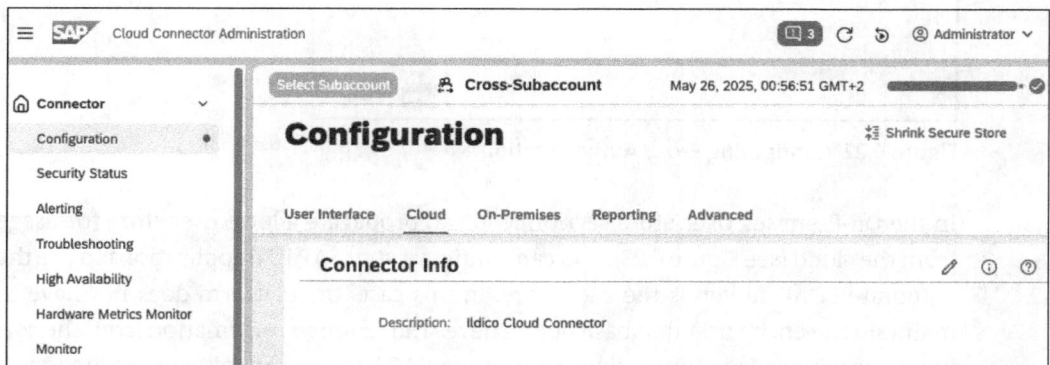

Figure 6.20 Change Cloud Connector Description

In the **HTTPS Proxy** section on the same tab, you can optionally define an HTTPS proxy by clicking the pencil icon. This proxy is used by the cloud connector to establish the TLS tunnel to the SAP BTP subaccounts (see Figure 6.21).

267

6 Cloud Connector

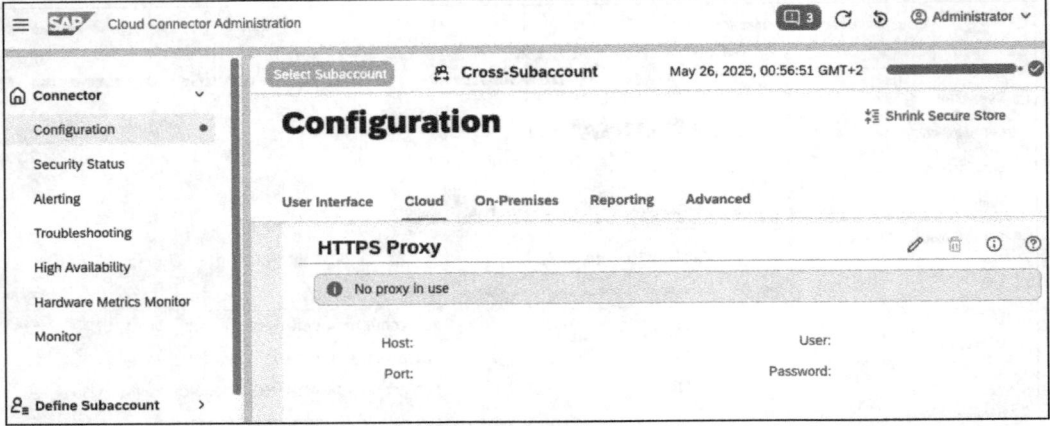

Figure 6.21 Defining HTTPS Proxy

A combination of **Host** and **Port** can be specified for the proxy. In addition, the proxy you are using may require user authentication. In this case, you can also specify a **User** and **Password** (see Figure 6.22). A connection test with the proxy is currently not supported by the cloud connector.

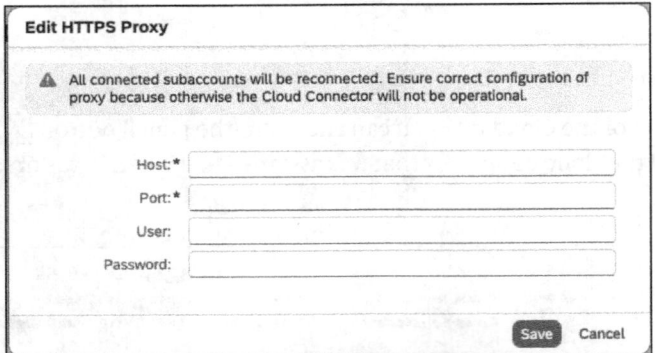

Figure 6.22 Configuring Proxy Authentication

In the **On-Premises User Store** section, you can propagate a local user store for usage from the cloud (see Figure 6.23). You can configure your SAP BTP applications to use the corporate LDAP server as the user store. In this case, the platform does not have to maintain the entire user database but retrieves the required information from the corporate user store. Java applications running on SAP BTP can use this connection to validate credentials, search for users, and retrieve details. In addition to user information, the cloud application can also retrieve information about the groups a user belongs to in LDAP, which can be used to derive SAP BTP permissions.

6.1 Installation and Configuration

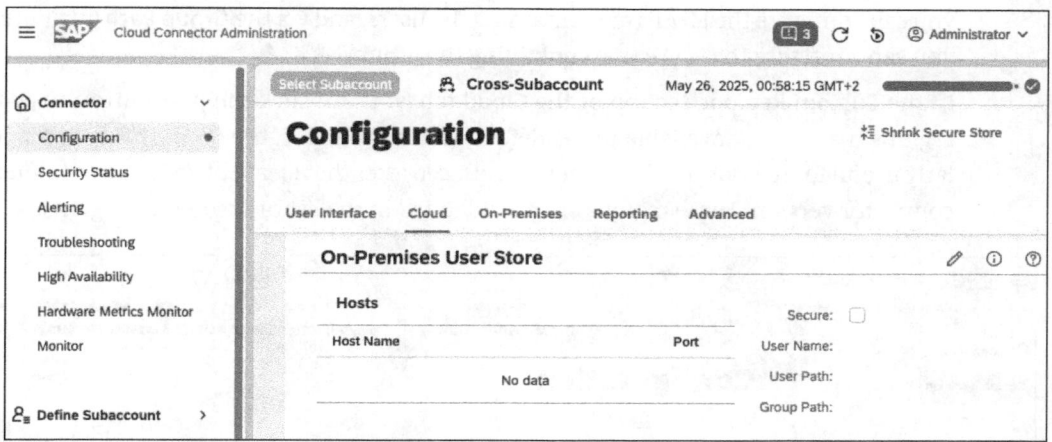

Figure 6.23 Cloud User Store Configuration

For configuring, you need to specify the **Host Name**(s) and **Port**(s), as shown in Figure 6.24. You can enter multiple hosts to achieve a failover data stream.

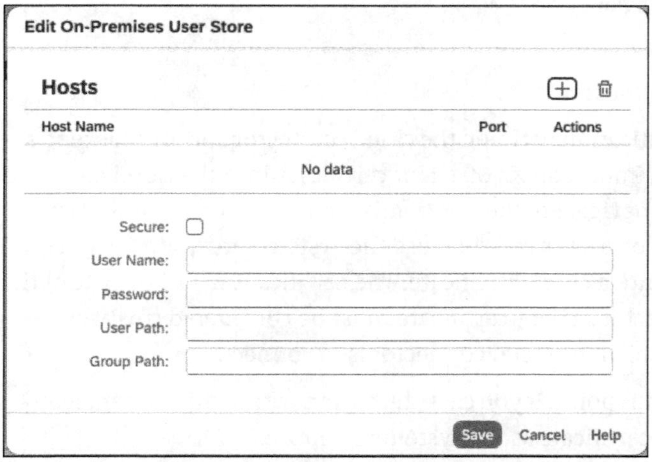

Figure 6.24 Specifying Host Name and Port for Cloud User Store

With the **Secure** checkbox, you can specify whether to use LDAP over SSL/TLS (LDAPS) as the communication protocol. LDAPS is a secure version of LDAP in which the data transfer between client and server is encrypted using a secure SSL/TLS connection. This ensures that the data transmitted over the network is protected from unauthorized access or manipulation. LDAPS is especially important in sensitive networks in which confidential information is stored. The **User Name** attribute contains the name of the technical user with which the connection to the LDAP server is established, and the **Password** attribute contains the corresponding password. Via the **User Path** attribute,

269

you can configure the LDAP tree containing the users, and via the **Group Path** attribute, you can configure the LDAP tree containing the groups.

In the **Custom Regions** section of the **Cloud** tab, you can click the plus button to add regions that are not available in the default selection (see Figure 6.25). This is particularly useful for regions that have been introduced after the release of your current cloud connector version. These regions are not included in the list of predefined regions.

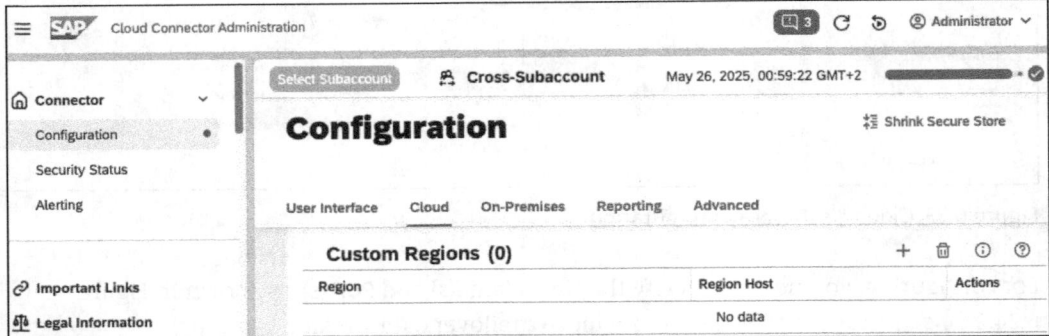

Figure 6.25 Adding Custom Regions

6.1.6 On-Premise Configuration

To establish mutual authentication between the cloud connector and any backend system it connects to, you can import an X.509 client certificate into the cloud connector (see Figure 6.26). To do this, navigate to the **On-Premises** tab and then to the **System Certificate** section. The cloud connector will then use the system certificate for all HTTPS backend requests that require a client certificate. The certification authority (CA) that has signed the cloud connector's client certificate must be considered trustworthy by all backend systems with which the cloud connector is to connect.

There is a useful feature at this point: If you click the button with the document icon, then you can accept the UI certificate as the system certificate.

By default, the cloud connector trusts every local system when it connects to it via TLS. Because this behavior can be undesirable for security reasons, you can configure a trust store that acts as a list of trusted certificate authorities. Any TLS server certificate issued by one of these certification authorities is considered trustworthy.

If the CA that issued a particular server certificate is not in the trust store, the server will be considered untrusted, and the connection will fail. Navigate to the **Backend Trust Store** section and click the plus button to add the desired server certificates to the trust store (see Figure 6.27).

6.1 Installation and Configuration

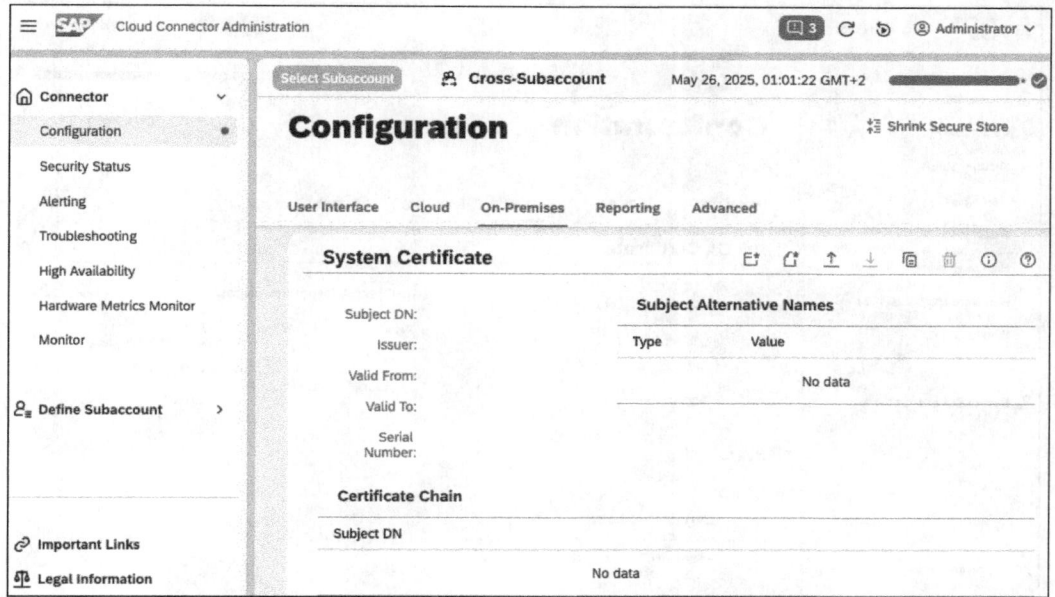

Figure 6.26 Configuring System Certificate

Figure 6.27 Configure Trust Store

The cloud connector uses the configured CA approach to issue short-lived certificates for registration with the same identity in the backend that is registered in the cloud. However, to establish a trust relationship with the backend, the configuration steps are always the same and, as already mentioned, independent of the CA approach you chose (see Figure 6.28).

6 Cloud Connector

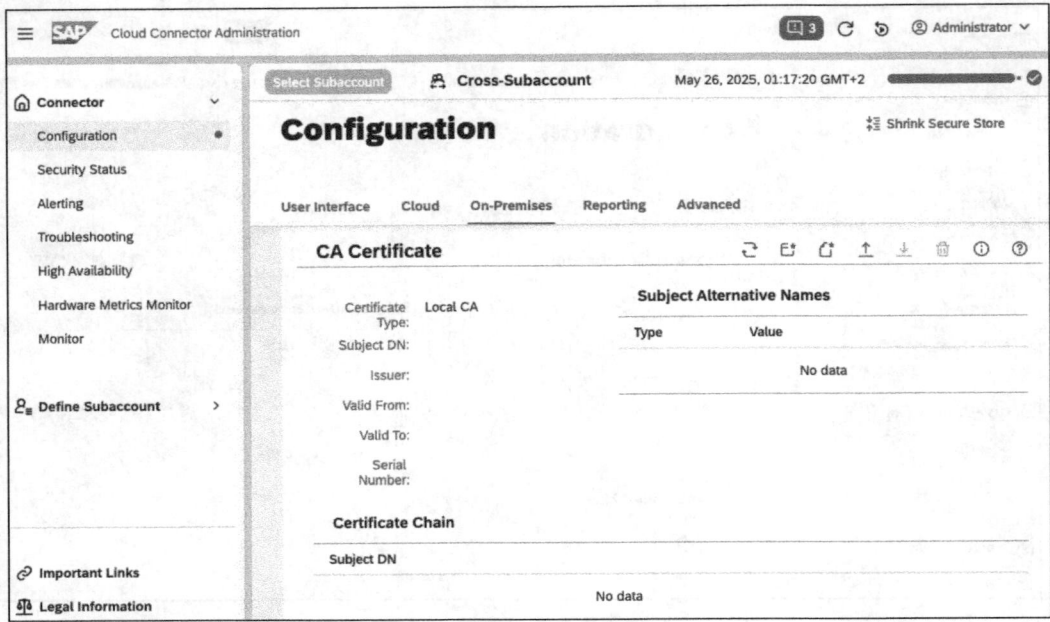

Figure 6.28 Configuring CA Certificate

The cloud connector supports *principal propagation*, which means that the user identity is propagated from the cloud application to the backend system. The required configuration is done in the **Principal Propagation** section (see Figure 6.29). You can find more information about the principal propagation configuration at *https://help.sap.com/docs/connectivity/sap-btp-connectivity-cf/configuring-principal-propagation*.

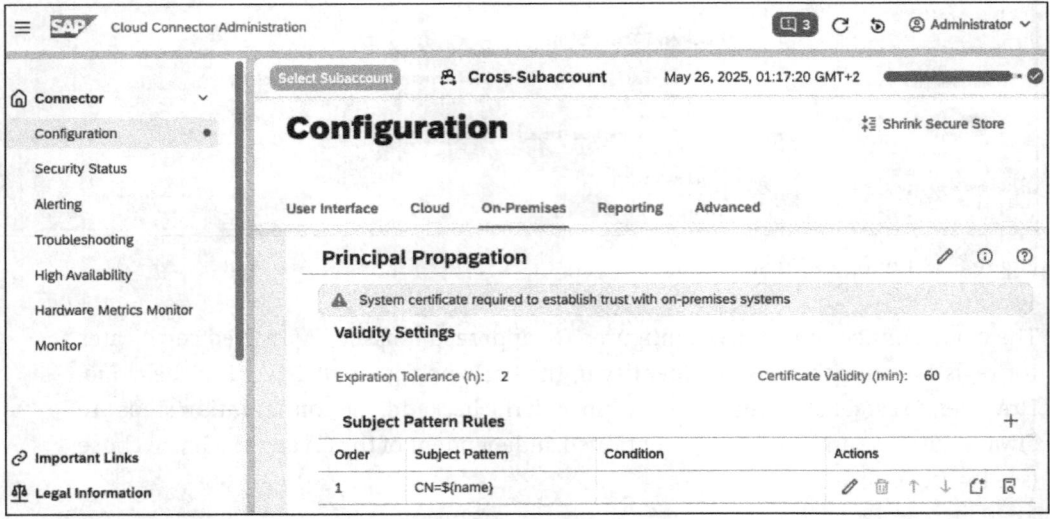

Figure 6.29 Configuring Principal Propagation

The cloud connector allows you to propagate Kerberos-authenticated users from SAP BTP to backend systems. It uses the Kerberos Service for User and Constrained Delegation protocol extensions. This approach uses the Key Distribution Center (KDC) to exchange messages in order to retrieve Kerberos tokens for a specific user and backend system. This feature is not supported for ABAP backend systems. In this case, you can use certificate-based principal propagation. The required configuration can be set in the **Kerberos** area (see Figure 6.30).

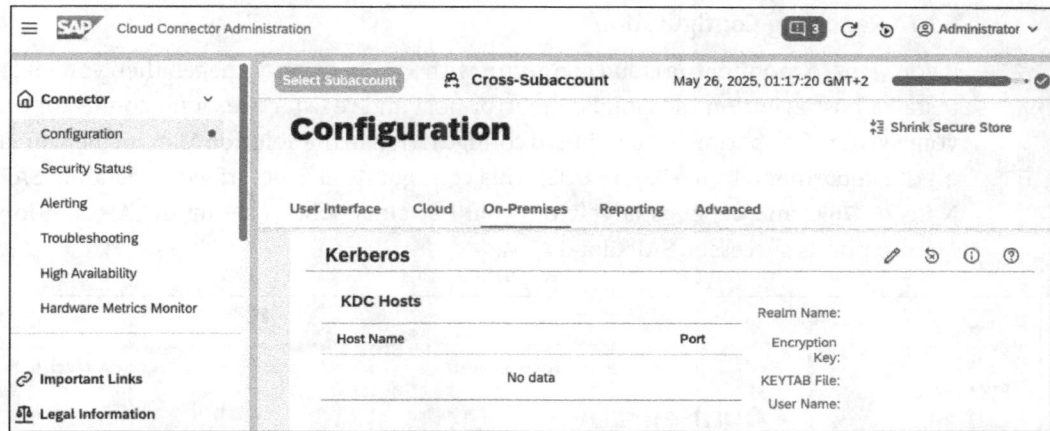

Figure 6.30 Kerberos Configuration

The cloud connector allows access to backend systems via the established RFC protocol. No additional configuration is required for a pure RFC connection. However, if you want to use a secure network connection based on Secure Network Communications (SNC), then you must perform the necessary configuration in the **SNC** area (see Figure 6.31). As a prerequisite, you must install an SNC library. You can find information about configuring SNC at *http://s-prs.co/v608005*.

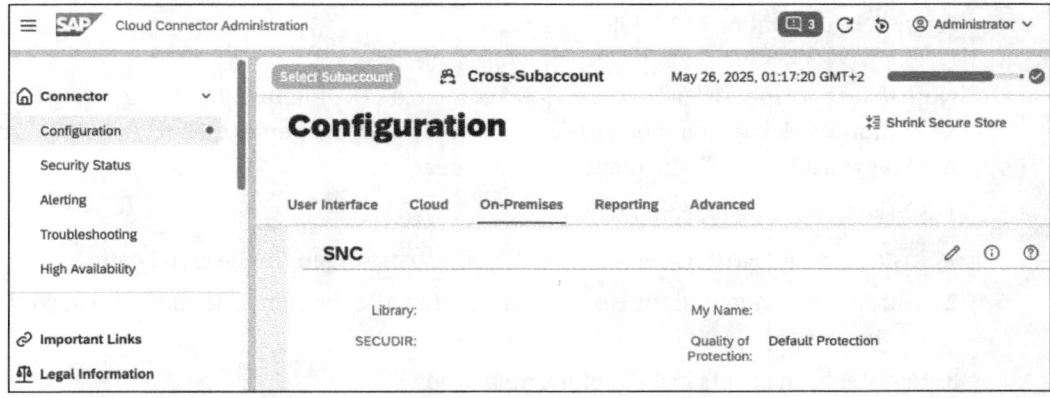

Figure 6.31 Configuring SNC

SNC is a feature in SAP systems that enables the secure transfer of data. With SNC, communication between different SAP systems and components can take place over a secure connection that is protected from manipulation and eavesdropping. SNC is an important component of SAP solutions for security and compliance, especially regarding the transmission of sensitive data. The use of SNC helps ensure that companies can maintain their data security and comply with regulations and laws.

6.1.7 Reporting Configuration

If you want to monitor the cloud connector with SAP Solution Manager, then you must install a host agent on the cloud connector host and register the cloud connector on your system. You perform the required configuration in the **Solution Management** area on the **Reporting** tab (see Figure 6.32). This configuration is described in detail in SAP Note 2607632 and depends largely on what has already been set up in SAP Solution Manager or its successor, SAP Cloud ALM.

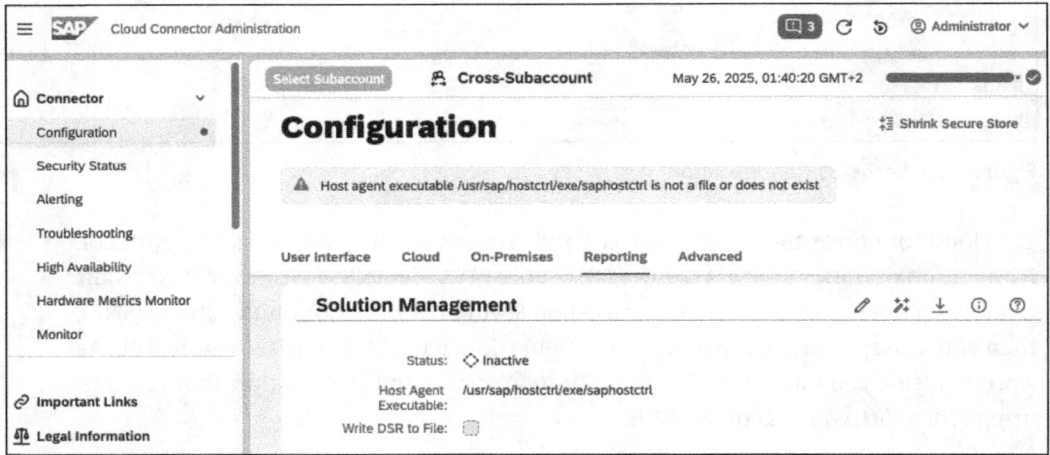

Figure 6.32 Integrating SAP Solution Manager

Note that in former releases of the cloud connector, the menu entry was intended for SAP Solution Manager and had been called **Solution Management**. Now, as SAP Cloud ALM is available as well, the menu entry has been renamed.

The basic procedure is as follows:

1. Install the SAP Host Agent and the SAP Diagnostics Agent in the cloud connector.
2. Add SAP Host Agent to the cloud connector to write the Dynamic Statistical Records (DSR) to a file.
3. Register both agents in SAP Solution Manager.

4. Set the full configuration with the SAP EarlyWatch Alert in the SAP Solution Manager configuration environment, select **SAP Cloud Platform Connector**, and perform an automatic relevance determination. For SAP Cloud ALM, see SAP Note 3391480.
5. Assign a user to connect SAP Solution Manager to the cloud connector.
6. Have your admin apply SAP Note 2556432 with a new SAP Diagnostics Agent setup (see *http://s-prs.co/v608006*).

This configuration may be simplified in the future, so be sure to refer to SAP Note 2556432 for the latest information.

6.1.8 Advanced Configuration

In the **Connectivity** area of the **Advanced** tab, you can adjust the connection settings (see Figure 6.33). This controls the throughput and the HTTP connection to on-premise systems as follows:

- **Application Tunnel Connections**
  This parameter specifies the default value for the maximum number of tunnel connections per application.
- **Tunnel Worker Threads**
  This parameter controls the number of worker threads used for all requests.
- **Protocol Processor Worker Threads**
  This parameter controls the number of worker threads used for protocol processing.
- **Max. Reconnect Attempts**
  This parameter controls the maximum number of reconnect attempts.
- **Max. Chunk Size HTTP Packages (kb)**
  This parameter controls the maximum size of chunks transferred during HTTP streaming. The chunk size affects the throughput of HTTP communication.
- **Max. HTTP Request Header Size (kb)**
  This parameter controls the maximum size of the HTTP request header. A header containing authentication information such as SAML or a JSON Web Token (JWT) may require a larger size. JWT is a standard format for transmitting user authentication information between parties over the internet.
- **Max. HTTP Request-Line Size (kb)**
  This parameter controls the size of the request header of an HTTP request. The HTTP body is not included.
- **Max. HTTP Response Header Size (kb)**
  This parameter controls the maximum size of HTTP response headers.
- **Max. HTTP Response Status-Line Size (kb)**
  This parameter controls the size of the HTTP response body. The HTTP body is not included.

6   Cloud Connector

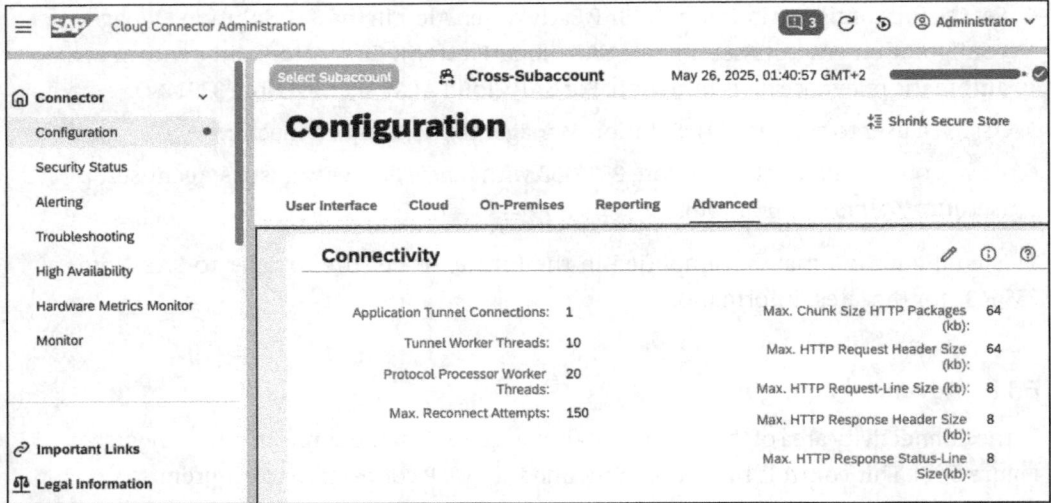

Figure 6.33 Configuring Connection Settings

In the **JVM** section, you can adjust the JVM settings that control memory management (see Figure 6.34). A reboot is required if you change the JVM settings. The **Initial Heap Size**, **Maximal Heap Size**, and **Maximal Direct Memory** parameters can be configured.

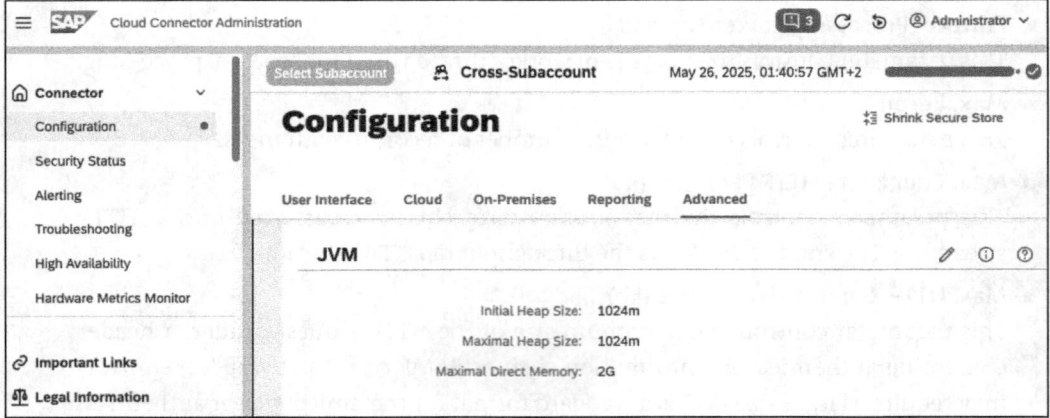

Figure 6.34 Configuring JVM Settings

If you are sizing the cloud connector according to your requirements, then you must adjust the settings at this point.

6.2   Ensuring High Availability

In this section, we go over the basic concepts of high availability and scalability that are essential for IT administrators. We explain why it is important to minimize system downtime, especially in the cloud. Understanding these fundamentals is critical to designing and operating reliable and efficient IT services.

High availability (HA) is about eliminating single points of failure so that applications continue to work even if one of the IT components on which they depend, such as a server, fails.

Scalability refers to the ability to increase or decrease resources as needed to meet changing requirements. There are two types of scalability, as follows:

- *Horizontal scaling* involves adding resources to your system, such as virtual machines, to distribute the workload among them. Horizontal scaling is especially important for organizations that require highly available services with minimal downtime. Horizontal scaling increases high availability because if you distribute your infrastructure across multiple tiers, you can simply use a machine from the other tiers if one fails.
- With *vertical scaling*, you can increase or decrease the capacity of existing services and instances by adding random access memory (RAM), storage, or processing power in the form of CPUs. This usually means that the expansion has an upper limit based on the capacity of the server or computer being expanded.

Horizontal and vertical scaling are often used in combination. Horizontal scaling is usually considered a long-term strategy, while vertical scaling is used more for short-term adjustments. This is because servers can be added to the infrastructure in almost unlimited numbers, while hardware upgrades can run into physical limitations.

With the cloud connector, direct horizontal scaling is not possible. Instead, the load can be distributed by operating multiple cloud connector instances with different site IDs across the participating subaccounts. In this way, identical configurations can be used for different targets, with the exception of the location ID. A distinction is made between the master instance and the shadow instance.

To set up high availability, the primary instance (called the *master instance*) transfers all configurations to the secondary instance (called the *shadow instance*). During operation, the master instance regularly updates the shadow instance with the latest configurations, ensuring synchronization between the two instances. The shadow instance periodically checks the availability of the master instance. If the master instance is unavailable, the shadow instance attempts to reestablish the connection based on the specified takeover delay. If no connection is established within this time, it attempts to assume the role of the primary instance and establish a tunnel to SAP BTP (see Figure 6.35). However, it is possible that the master instance is still active and simply facing a network problem. In this case, the shadow instance tries to connect to the corresponding SAP BTP subaccount. If this attempt is rejected because the master instance is still active, then the shadow instance remains on standby by continuing to try to communicate with the cloud until the master instance is reached.

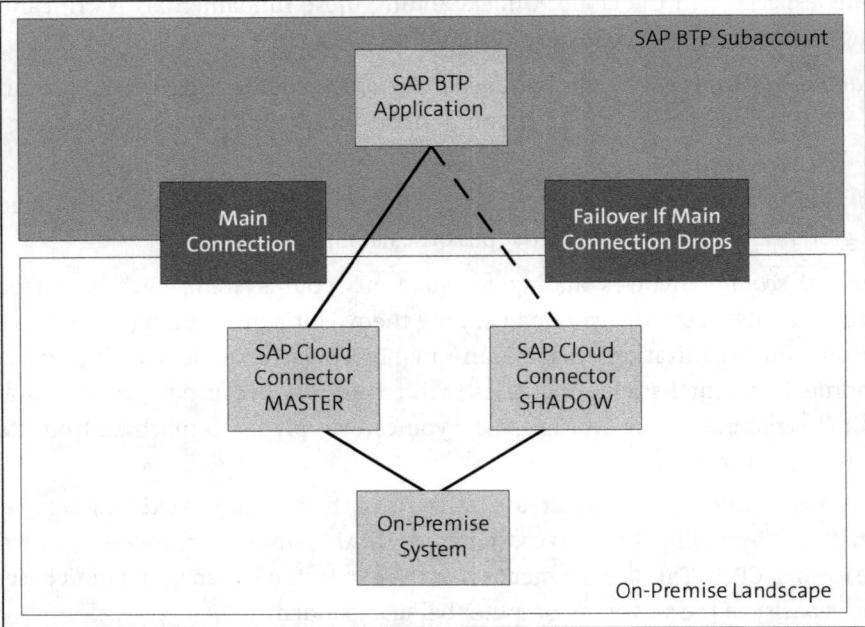

Figure 6.35 Master/Shadow Configuration Scheme

After the takeover delay has elapsed and the shadow instance has successfully established a connection, the cloud side opens a tunnel, and the shadow instance assumes the role of the master instance. From this point on, the shadow instance acts as the master instance and performs all standard operations. If the original master instance reboots and finds that the shadow instance has taken over, it registers with the new master instance as the shadow instance. In this way, the two cloud connector installations swap roles.

The installation processes for the master and shadow instances are identical, using the same installation package for both instances. It is recommended to install the shadow instance on a dedicated server or on a separate virtual machine. By default, the shadow instance listens on port 8443 and uses HTTPS only (note that in our examples, we had set the port to 8444 as both instances, master and shadow, were running on the same host in parallel). The initial login credentials for the shadow instance are preset with *Administrator* as the user name and *managed* as the password. After the first login with these credentials, you will be prompted to change the password (see Figure 6.36). You must also select **Shadow (Backup Installation)** in the **Choose Installation Type** section. Click **Save**.

In the next step, you have to connect the shadow instance to the master instance. Click **Edit** (the pencil button 🖉) in the **Connection to Master** area (see Figure 6.37).

6.2 Ensuring High Availability

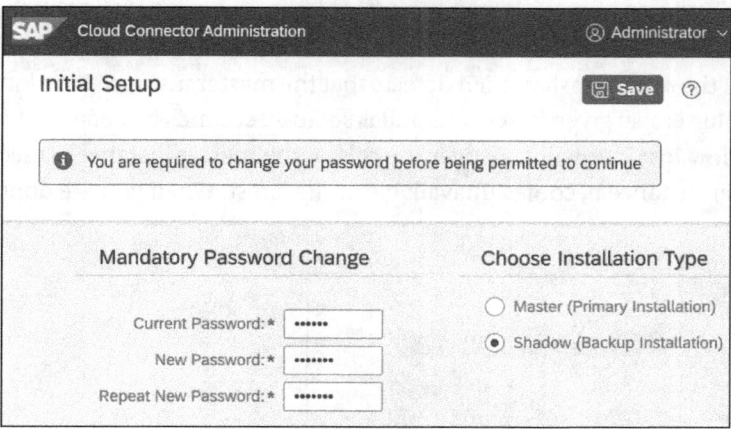

Figure 6.36 Setting Up High Availability Shadow Instance

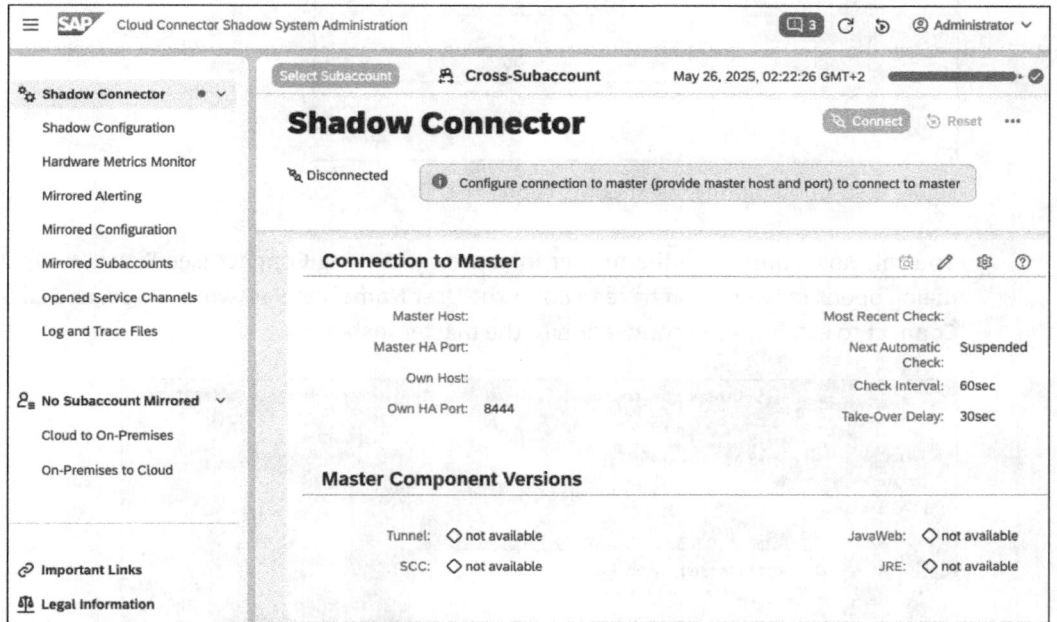

Figure 6.37 Shadow Host High Availability Configuration

In the dialog, maintain the **Master Host** and the **Master HA Port** (see Figure 6.38). These are the host name and the high availability port number of the master machine. In addition, you can select your own host name from the **Own Host** dropdown list. This is especially important if the shadow instance can be addressed with different host names. With the **Check Interval** parameter, you can control at what intervals the shadow instance should check if the master instance is still reachable. This value must be specified in seconds and is set to 60 seconds by default. This means that in the worst case you would recognize after 60 seconds that the master is no longer available. With the **Take-Over Delay** parameter, you can control the time after which the shadow instance takes over the role of the master instance if it detects that the master instance is no longer available. This value is also given in seconds and is set to 30 seconds by default. This means that the shadow instance will take over the role of the master instance 90 seconds after the master instance becomes unavailable at the latest. When you are done, click **Save**.

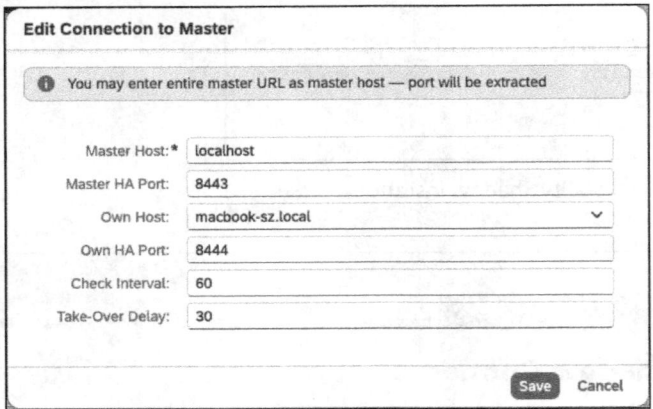

Figure 6.38 Configuring Master Connection

You can now connect to the master instance by clicking **Connect** (see Figure 6.39). A dialog opens in which you have to enter the **User Name** and **Password**. Do so, and click **Connect** to establish the connection to the master instance.

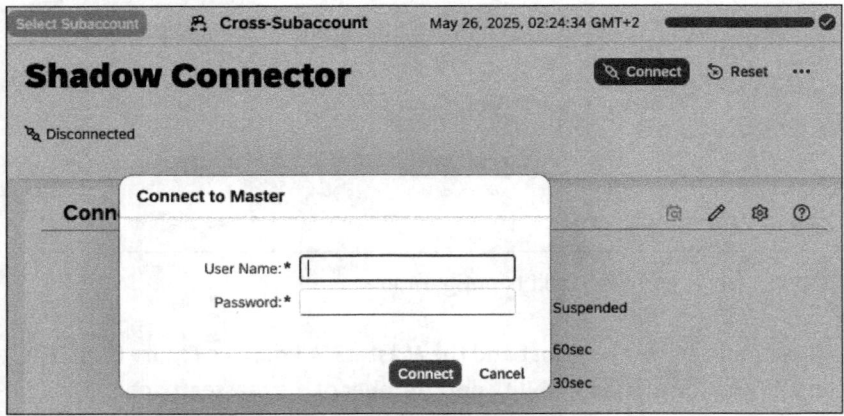

Figure 6.39 Enter Master Host Credentials

You will be surprised to see that despite correct configuration and valid credentials, the connection to the master cannot be established. An error message indicates that the master instance is not configured for high availability yet (see Figure 6.40).

6.2 Ensuring High Availability

Figure 6.40 Connection to Master Failed

Log into the master instance and navigate to the **High Availability** section in the side menu. Once there, click **Enable** (see Figure 6.41).

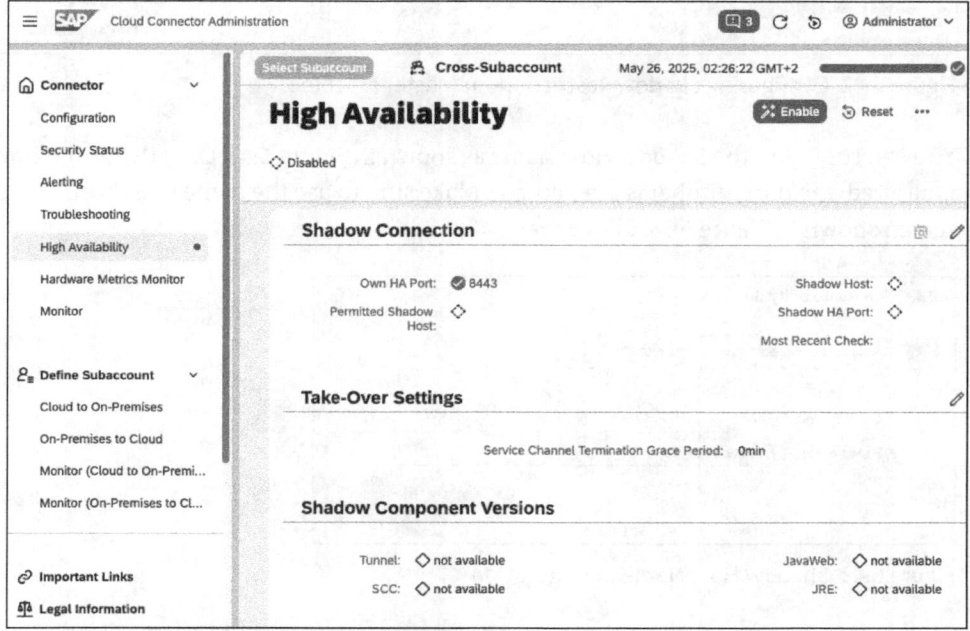

Figure 6.41 Enabling High Availability in Master Instance

6 Cloud Connector

After the configuration, the **No Shadow Host Restrictions** message informs you that no restrictions have been configured for the shadow instance (see Figure 6.42). This means that any shadow instance can connect to this master instance. At this point, you can configure a restriction for a particular host name, and we recommend doing so. Click **Edit**, the pencil icon, to set up your restrictions.

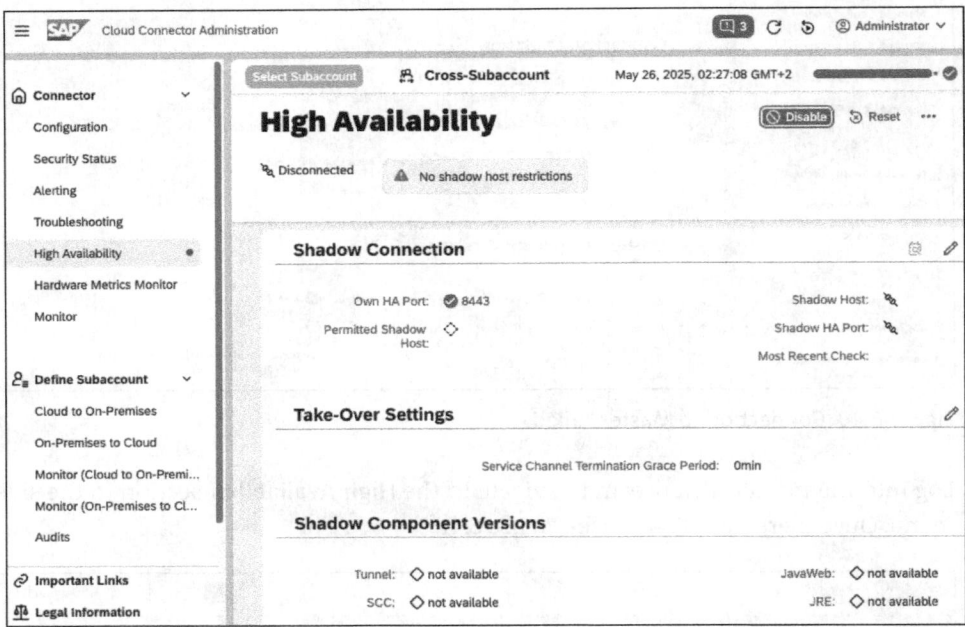

Figure 6.42 Configuring Shadow Restrictions in Master Machine

You can configure the **Shadow Host** name as shown in Figure 6.43. Only the host name is allowed; the port number is not allowed. Make sure to use the name you chose in the screen shown in Figure 6.38. Click **Save**.

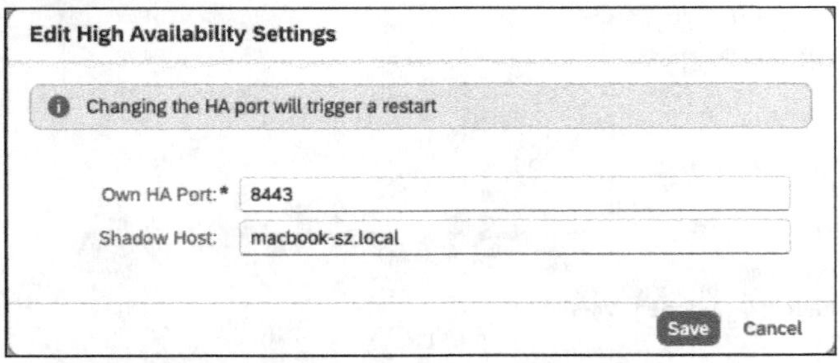

Figure 6.43 Shadow Host Name Configuration

You can now log onto the shadow machine and connect to the master machine. After the connection has been successfully established, you should see the confirmation information of the master instance (see Figure 6.44).

282

6.2 Ensuring High Availability

Figure 6.44 Master Information Screen

The master also shows that a shadow instance is connected to this master instance (see Figure 6.45).

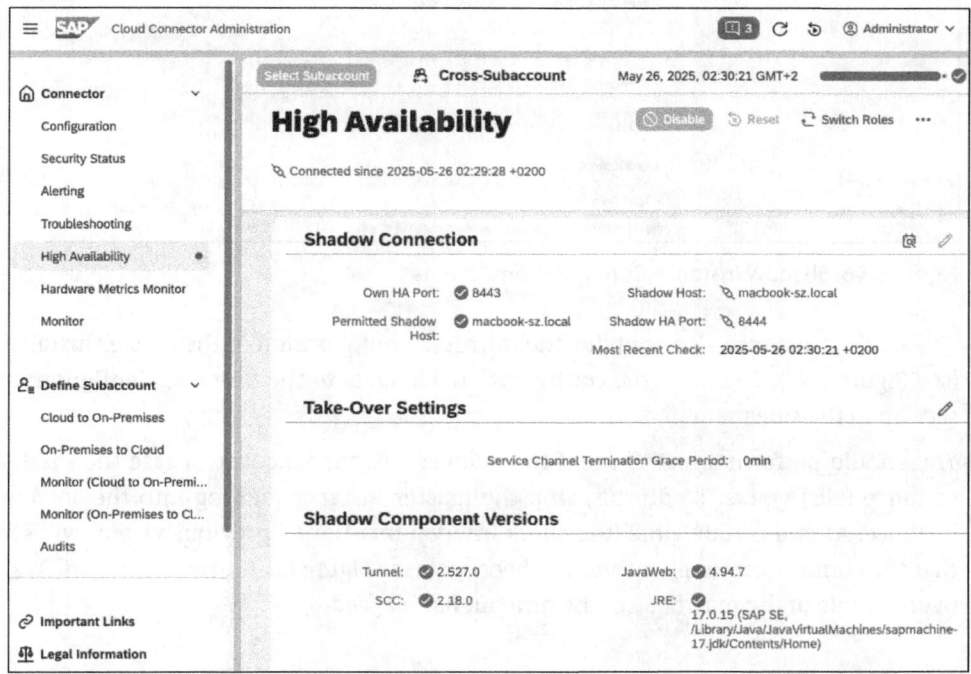

Figure 6.45 High Availability with Connected Shadow Instance in Master Instance

6 Cloud Connector

For the shadow instance, you have similar configuration options as for the master instance (see Figure 6.46). To set these options, navigate to the **Shadow Configuration** section in the side menu. Again, it is important that the shadow instance has a valid SSL certificate, so you need to create a certificate signing request, request an SSL certificate from a certificate authority, and import it into the cloud connector. The configuration is identical to the configuration for the master.

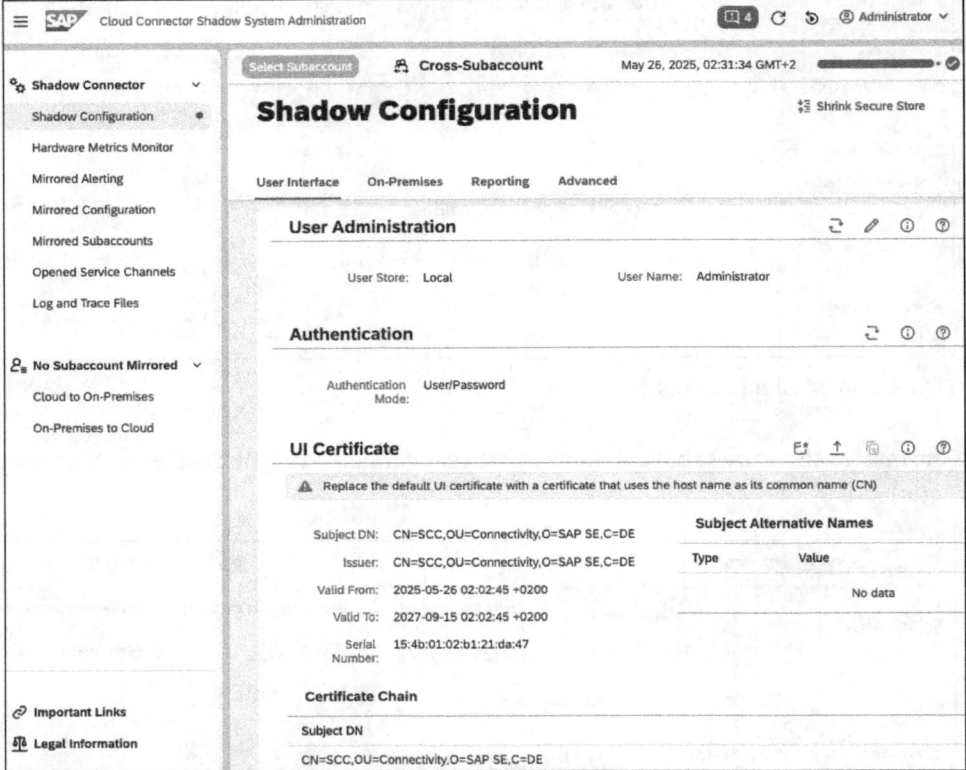

Figure 6.46 Shadow Instance Configuration Options

The shadow instance also contains the mirrored configuration of the master instance (see Figure 6.47). To accept the configuration, navigate to the **Mirrored Configuration** section in the side menu.

You should perform a test to see if the failover (i.e., the takeover in case the master instance fails) works. To do this, stop the master instance and log into the shadow instance. After a certain time (the check interval mentioned previously), you will see that the connection to the master has been lost (see Figure 6.48). The shadow will take over the role of the master after the timeout has elapsed.

6.2 Ensuring High Availability

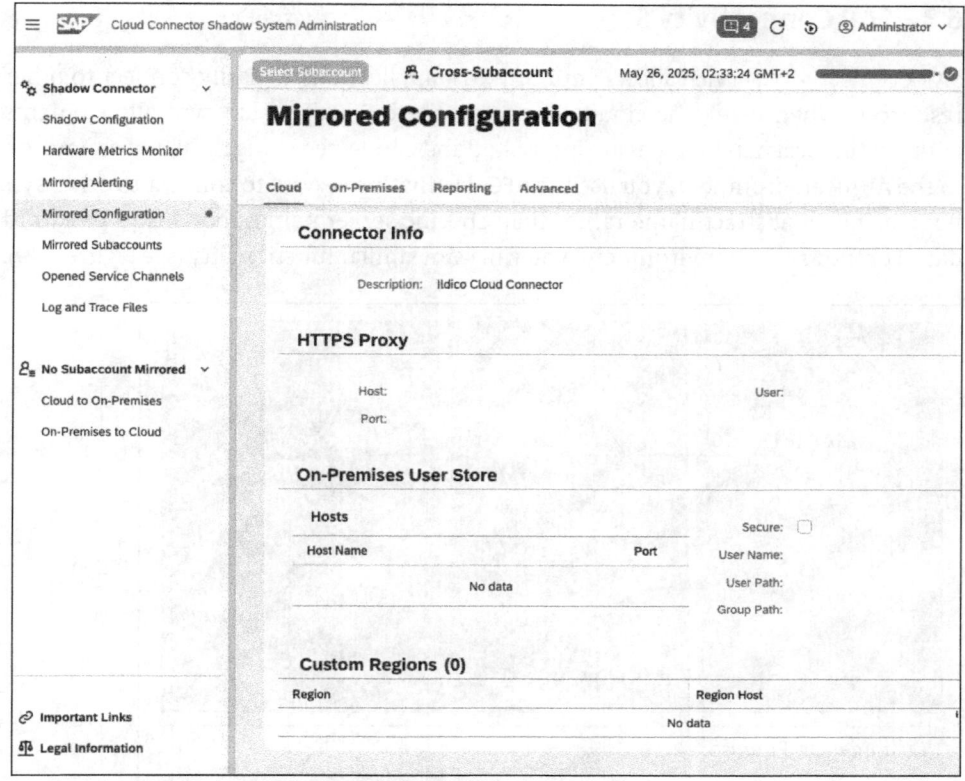

Figure 6.47 Shadow: Mirrored Master Configuration

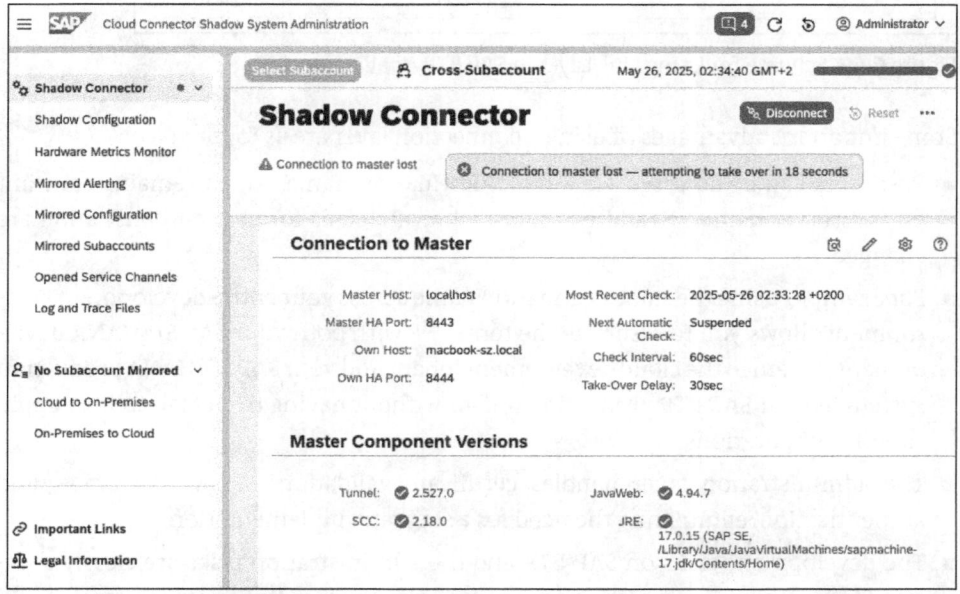

Figure 6.48 Lost Connection to Master Instance

6.3 SAP Connectivity Service

SAP Connectivity service allows your SAP BTP applications to easily connect to other resources. When using the cloud connector, these resources are typically elements within your local network that are integrated and connected using the cloud connector. In the ABAP environment, you use the RFC destination service to connect to other systems using an abstract name rather than specific server names, ports, and password data. For the SAP BTP environment, you will want similar functionality (see Figure 6.49).

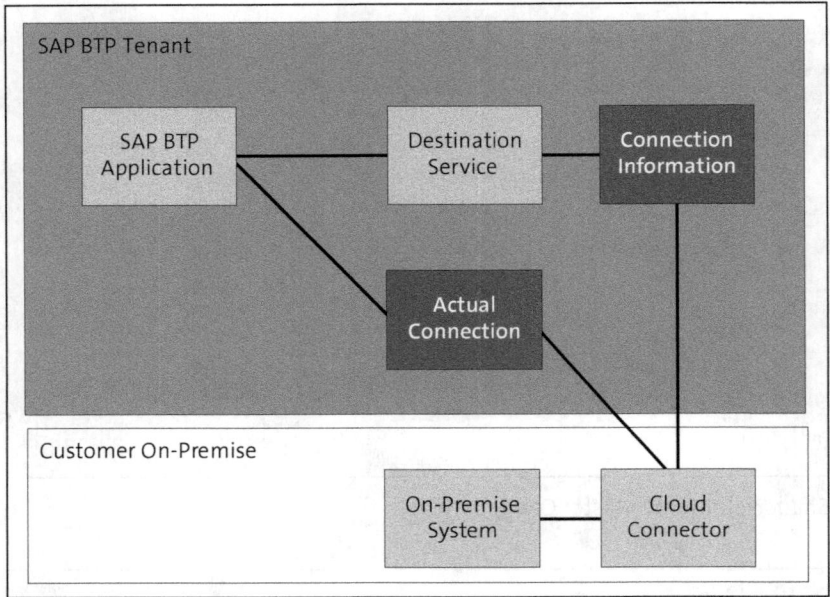

Figure 6.49 Scheme for Using Link Layer in SAP BTP Applications

Some important advantages of using a connection layer are as follows:

- Resources can be accessed via a fixed destination name, which remains constant even if server names, IP addresses, or technical details for user authentication are changed.
- For example, using the same destination name across your entire development environment allows you to associate the term *ERP* with both your SAP S/4HANA development system in the cloud development tenant and your SAP S/4HANA production system in your SAP BTP production tenant without having to change code or application configurations.
- The administration layer handles certificate validation, password storage, and authentication, eliminating the need for a separate implementation.
- The development tasks on SAP BTP and the administration tasks are clearly separated from each other, which corresponds to the usual company structures.

There are two types of connectivity services:

- SAP Destination service, which manages the technical details of a resource
- SAP Connectivity service, which provides the proxy functions for your applications to access and use the resources

> **Unofficial terminology**
> Sometimes the unofficial term *SAP BTP Connectivity* is used to refer to the combination of the SAP Destination service and SAP Connectivity service.

The prerequisite for using destinations is the activation of the SAP Destination service in the SAP BTP cockpit. It is possible to model destinations without activating this service, but if you want to access a destination from a cloud application, the service must be active in your space.

Destinations can be defined at the subaccount level. The destination is created for the entire subaccount. The communication protocol used and other properties, such as authentication method, proxy type, and URL, are specified.

To be able to use the created destinations, you first need an instance of the SAP Destination service. To find the SAP Destination service, navigate to the **Services • Service Marketplace** path in the SAP BTP cockpit and enter "Destination" in the search field (see Figure 6.50).

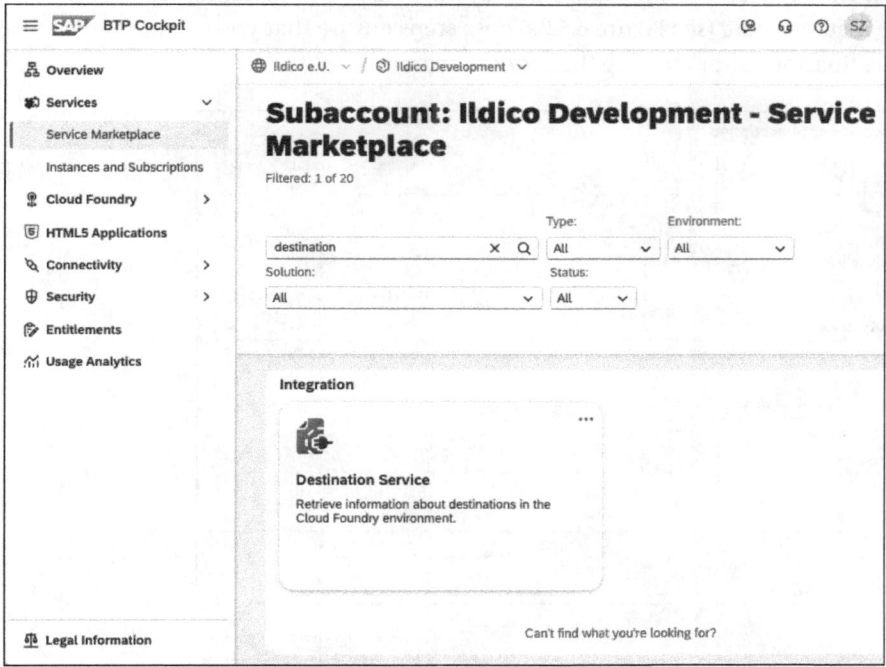

Figure 6.50 Finding Destination Service in SAP Service Marketplace

6 Cloud Connector

Click the **Destination Service** tile. The **Service Marketplace** detail view opens (see Figure 6.51). Click the **Create** button in the upper-right corner.

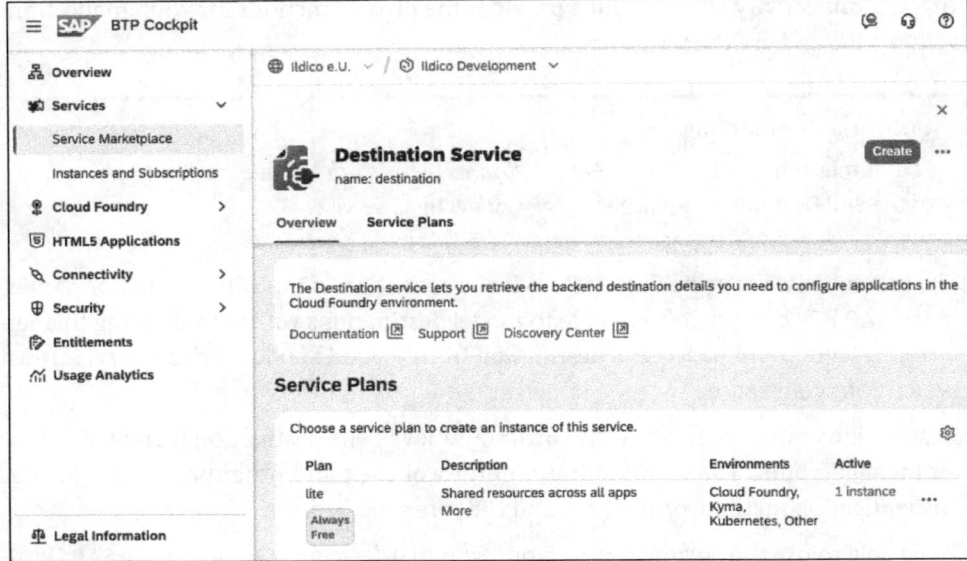

Figure 6.51 Detail View of Target Service in SAP Service Marketplace

The **New Instance or Subscription** window opens. Except for the instance name in the **Instance Name** field, all the fields are already filled in. Enter a meaningful name for your service instance here (see Figure 6.52). These steps ensure that you can properly access your destinations after creating the service instance.

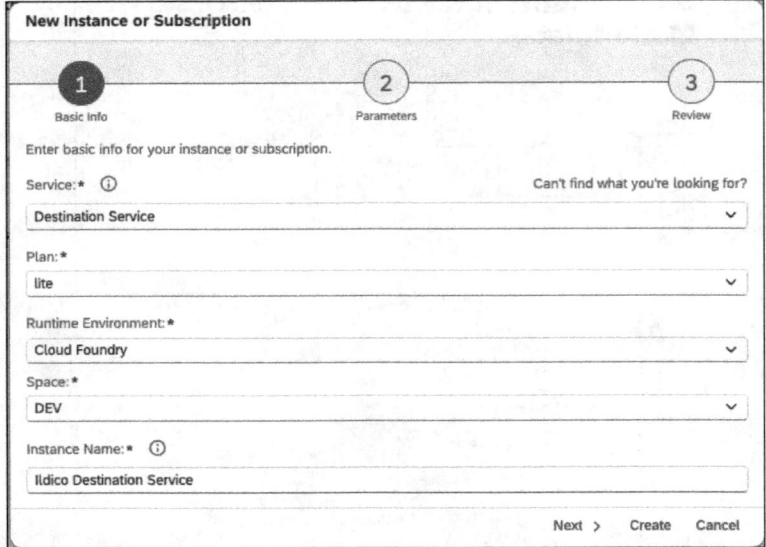

Figure 6.52 Specifying Service Instance Name

6.3 SAP Connectivity Service

You can proceed directly with creating the instance by clicking **Create**. The next **Information** window can be confirmed by clicking **Close** (see Figure 6.53).

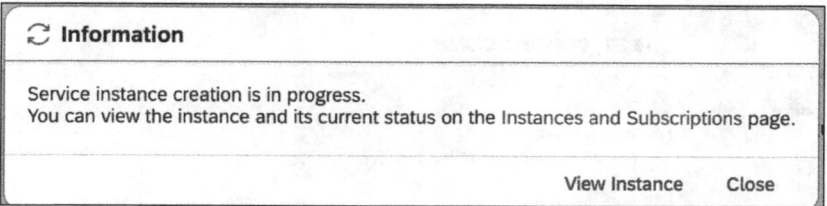

Figure 6.53 Information About Instance Creation

If a destination refers to a specific subaccount, the destination is created in the SAP BTP cockpit via the **Connectivity • Destinations (New)** path (see Figure 6.54). In addition to creating destinations using the SAP BTP cockpit, it is also possible to create destinations using the command line. Destinations can also be created using an OData API.

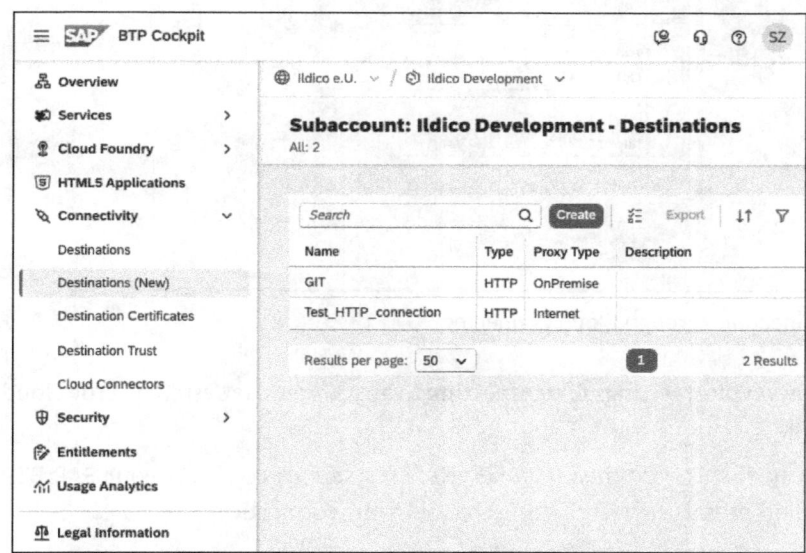

Figure 6.54 Destinations at Subaccount Level in Cloud Foundry Environment

To create a destination on SAP BTP, navigate to the **Connectivity • Destinations (New)** path in your subaccount. Click the **Create** button. Enter the name of the virtual host in the **URL** field to establish a connection via the cloud connector. Selecting **OnPremise** in the **Proxy Type** field indicates that the connection should be routed through a cloud connector (see Figure 6.55).

289

6 Cloud Connector

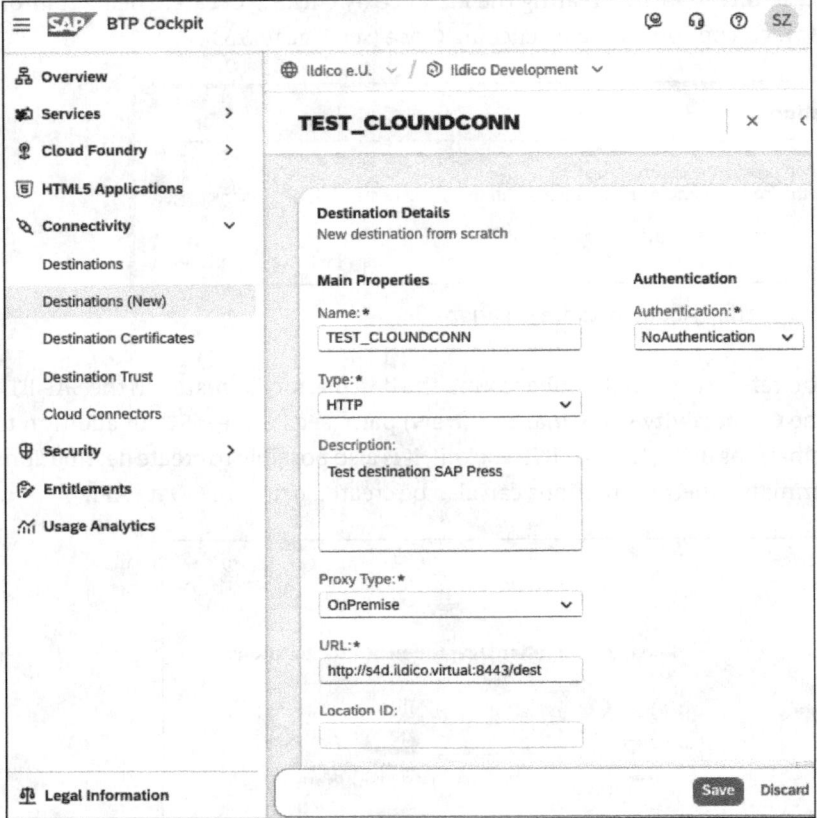

Figure 6.55 Connection Through Cloud Connector

Figure 6.56 shows typical settings for connecting to an on-premise system via the cloud connector.

Now let's turn to the SAP Connectivity service. This service connects your SAP BTP applications to on-premise systems using the following connections:

- HTTP/HTTPS
- RFC
- SAP HANA database via service channels

The SAP Connectivity service can be described as a kind of proxy, where the SAP Destination service only stores the technical details and does not establish a connection to your application.

This service is not needed if you only want to access the technical information stored in the destination service (for accessing URIs in the cloud, on the internet, etc.). The main reason for the introduction of this layer is that cloud applications usually use the OAuth standard for authentication, while in the backend you may use RFC authentication via the SAP Java Connector or other authentication means.

6.3 SAP Connectivity Service

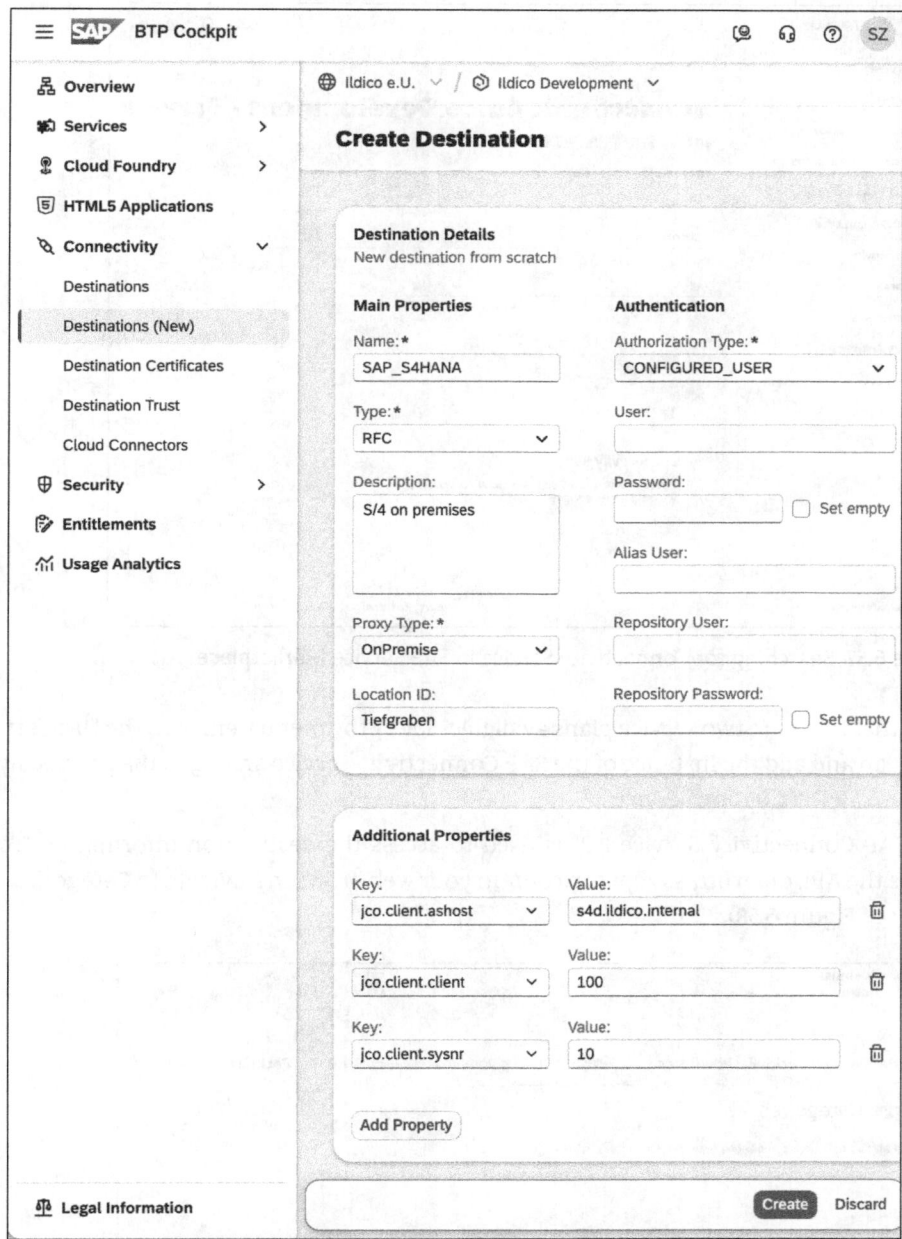

Figure 6.56 Typical Connection Properties for On-Premise RFC Connection

To activate the SAP Connectivity service, click the **Service Marketplace** menu item in your SAP BTP cockpit and enter "Connectivity" in the search field (see Figure 6.57).

6   Cloud Connector

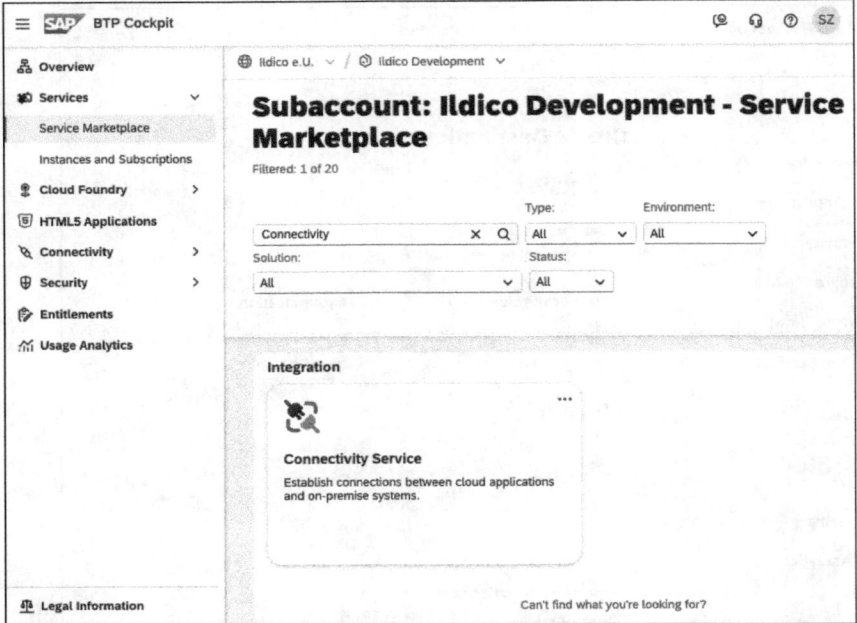

Figure 6.57 Searching for Connectivity Service in SAP Service Marketplace

Note that there are two service plans available. Select the menu item with the "lite" service plan and add the instance of the SAP Connectivity service analog to the previously shown SAP Destination service.

The SAP Connectivity Service API is used to access the destination information. To access the API, open *https://api.sap.com/* in your web browser. Navigate to **Categories · APIs** (see Figure 6.58).

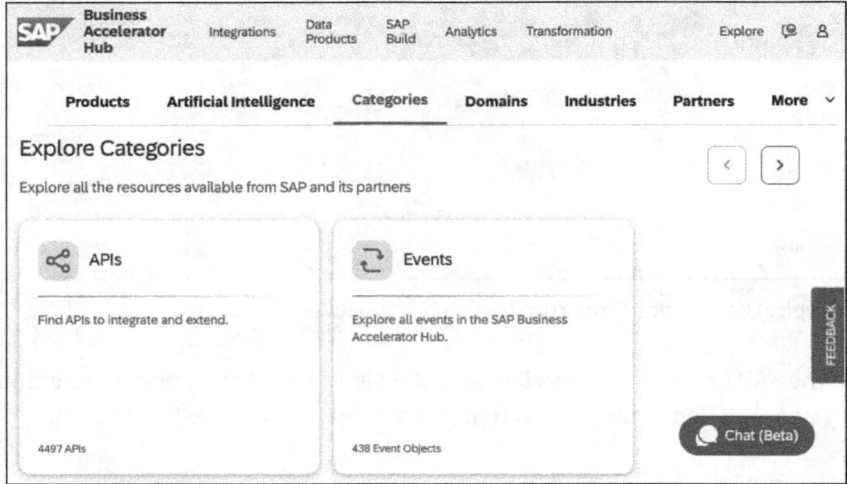

Figure 6.58 Menu Item in SAP Business Accelerator Hub

6.3 SAP Connectivity Service

On the following screen, you can search for the corresponding API services (see Figure 6.59). To do this, enter "Connectivity" in the search field.

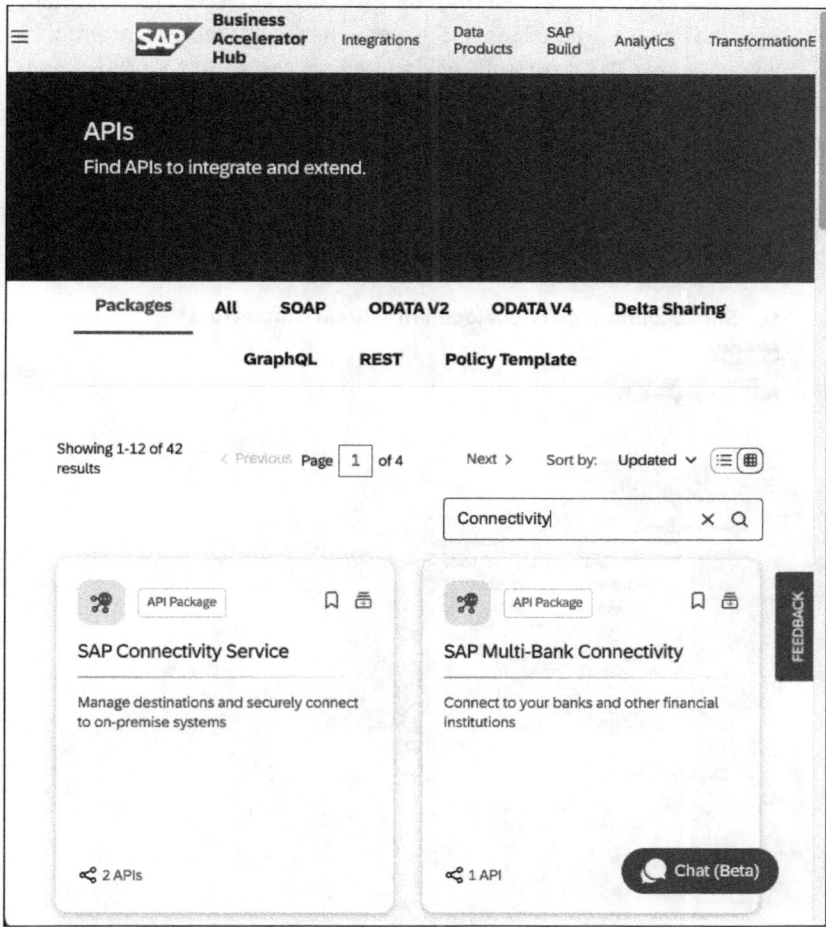

Figure 6.59 Selecting SAP Connectivity Service API

The possible operations include finding destinations by their names (globally or at the subaccount level) and accessing their properties. If available, certificates can also be accessed. This gives your developers the information available in the SAP Destination service. This information can then be used to access on-premise systems through the SAP Connectivity service.

For more information, visit the SAP Help Portal at *https://help.sap.com/docs/connectivity/sap-btp-connectivity-cf/connectivity*.

In the SAP BTP cockpit, you can use the **Connectivity • Cloud Connectors** menu path to view the cloud connector instances associated with your subaccount and their version status (see Figure 6.60). All connected connectors should be known to you.

293

6 Cloud Connector

Outlook

For the future, SAP has announced that it will introduce a REST API that will allow the management of active and passive subaccount certificates, which will enable uninterrupted rotation of signer certificates. This is currently only announced for SAP BTP, Cloud Foundry environment. For more information about this and other announced features, see *https://help.sap.com/docs/connectivity/sap-btp-connectivity-cf/developing-applications*.

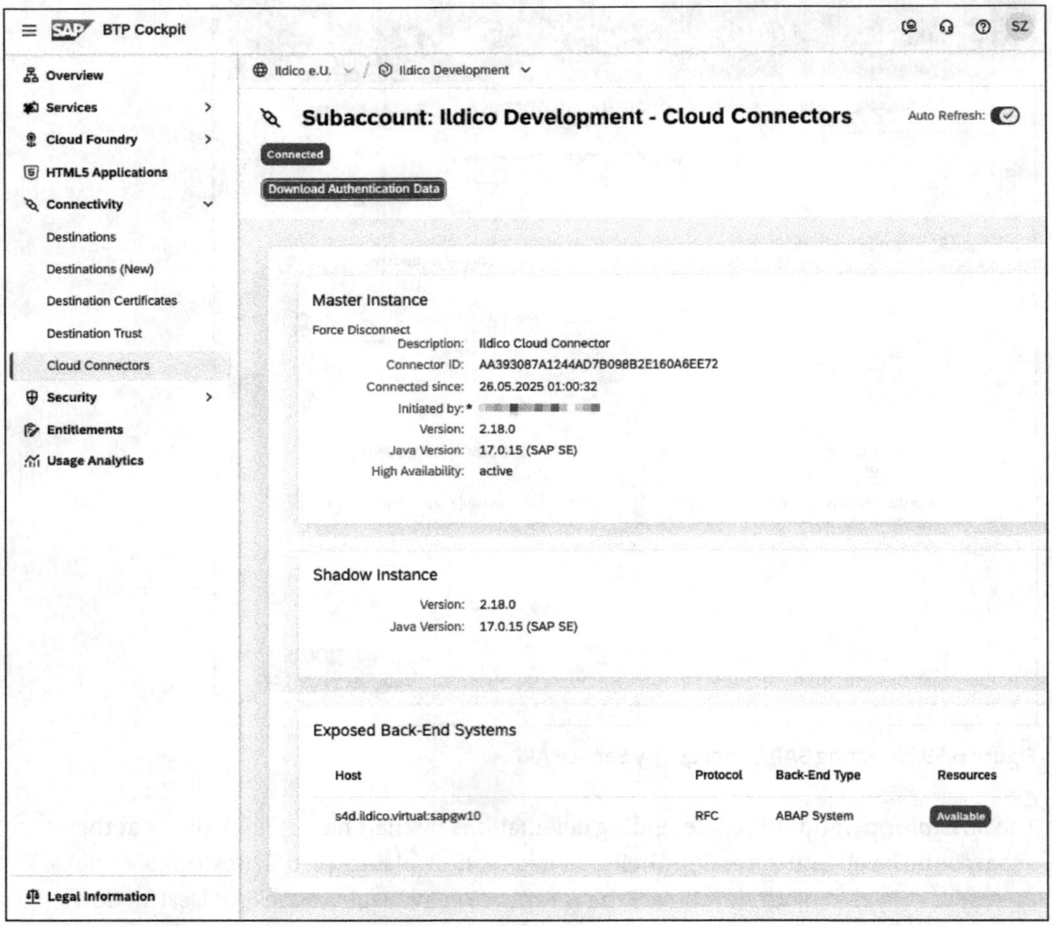

Figure 6.60 Displaying Cloud Connector Instances Associated with Selected Subaccount in SAP BTP Cockpit

On the side of the cloud connector—also on the other side—you can also perform monitoring—for example, of hardware and connection utilization.

6.4 Summary

The cloud connector serves as the secure bridge between on-premise systems and SAP BTP. It ensures seamless, secure, and monitored connectivity for hybrid system landscapes. This chapter outlined how to set up, configure, and manage the cloud connector from installation to high availability and monitoring.

It started with the technical prerequisites and installation methods, including steps for both installer and portable versions, followed by an overview of first-time setup procedures like initial login, password changes, and subaccount connections. We also discussed the customizable user interface authentication.

Cloud-specific settings like proxies, cloud user stores, and custom regions are supported. For backend connectivity, the connector allows importing system certificates, trust configuration, principal propagation (via certificate or Kerberos), and secure network communication through SNC.

Monitoring integration with SAP Solution Manager and SAP Cloud ALM is possible, provided the necessary agents and configuration are in place. Advanced configuration options let you fine-tune memory usage and connection behavior for performance and scalability.

High availability is achieved via a master-shadow setup, enabling automatic failover with mirrored configurations. The shadow instance can take over in case of master instance failure, ensuring continuous operations. Finally, the SAP Destination service and SAP Connectivity service work in tandem with the cloud connector to enable abstract, secure access to backend resources from SAP BTP applications.

Chapter 7
Activating and Setting Up SAP Business Application Studio

Discover SAP Business Application Studio, the heart of cloud development. Learn how to use the powerful development spaces for isolated and secure development and create a solid foundation for your development teams.

SAP Business Application Studio is the integrated development environment (IDE) provided by SAP for SAP cloud applications. You can use it in your company to develop, test, and deploy applications. This chapter guides you through the seamless setup of the IDE, which is designed for efficiency and customization.

Section 7.1 describes the steps involved in setting up SAP Business Application Studio. Section 7.2 deals with the authorizations you can grant to the development team so that they can work easily and develop good software. Section 7.3 shows you how to separate multiple developments and developers by using dev spaces.

The external systems that your development team needs to access are described in detail in Section 7.4. These system accesses should be centrally configured and then made available. Finally, in Section 7.5, we show you how to use the Git version control system in your company to manage, version, and authorize developments. We also discuss the basics of the software lifecycle with Git.

7.1 Setting Up SAP Business Application Studio

SAP Business Application Studio is a web-based cloud service offered as part of SAP BTP. The architecture of the service is shown in Figure 7.1. You can see that you can use software-as-a-service (SaaS) applications as well as on-premise applications.

7   Activating and Setting Up SAP Business Application Studio

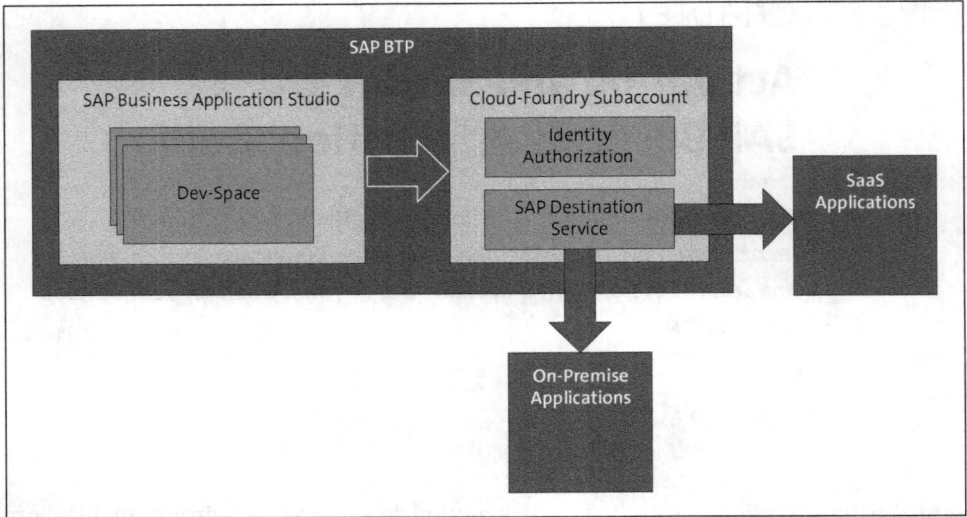

Figure 7.1 Architecture of SAP Business Application Studio

The development itself takes place in SAP Business Application Studio in *dev spaces*. These can be created and personalized and are completely isolated from the dev spaces of other developers. This has the decisive advantage that the developments of one developer cannot interfere with the developments of another developer, so long as they have not yet been released. In addition, it allows convenient management of development quality assurance and production code lines.

Similar to the integration services described in Chapter 6, SAP Business Application Studio is available as a subscription. To start the subscription, navigate to the SAP BTP cockpit, choose **Services** • **Service Marketplace** • **SAP Business Application Studio**, and click the **Create** button (see Figure 7.2).

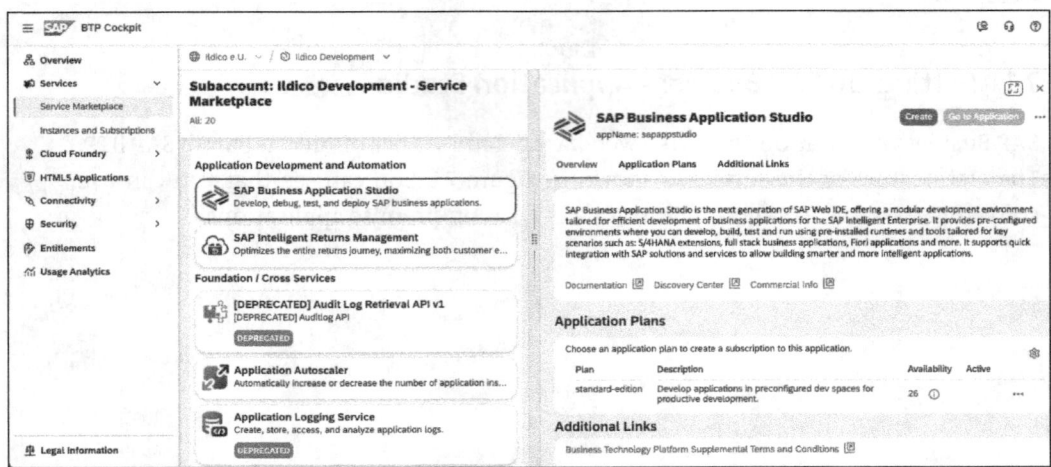

Figure 7.2 SAP Service Marketplace in SAP BTP Cockpit

7.1 Setting Up SAP Business Application Studio

> **If SAP Business Application Studio Is Not Displayed**
> If SAP Business Application Studio is not displayed in the marketplace, make sure that your subaccount for SAP Business Application Studio has an assignment (called an *entitlement*; see Chapter 5).

Now select your desired **Plan** and click **Create** (see Figure 7.3). The **standard-edition** option can be used for development, while the **free** option should only be used for testing or smaller projects (it offers all tools, but you can only use one of a maximum of two dev spaces at the same time).

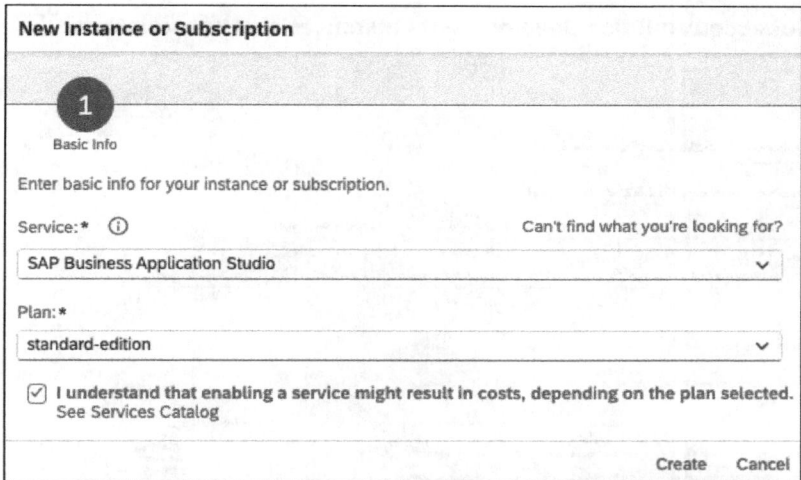

Figure 7.3 Creating New SAP Business Application Studio Instance

A window like the one shown in Figure 7.4 opens, confirming the start of the subscription creation process. Click the **View Subscription** button and you can verify that the creation has been completed.

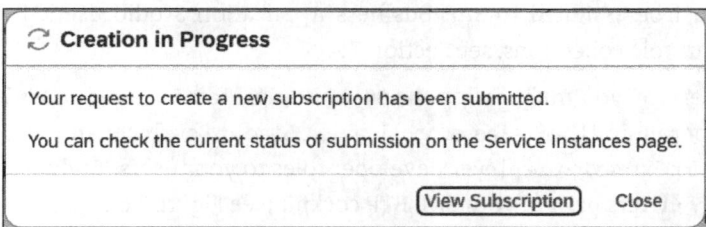

Figure 7.4 Create Subscription

This brings you back to the overview of the applications and instances of your subaccount (see Figure 7.5). Clicking **SAP Business Application Studio** will take you to the application, where you can start creating the subscription.

299

7   Activating and Setting Up SAP Business Application Studio

URI for Browser Favorites and Sharing with Users

The link to the application, as shown in Figure 7.5, is a persistent link. This means that it can also be used outside the SAP BTP cockpit to log onto SAP Business Application Studio. The link has the form *https://<org name>.eu20cf.applicationstudio.cloud.sap/*, where the value of *<org name>* is automatically assigned to your subaccount and can be changed as described in SAP Note 3115060. We recommend that you save this link so that you can provide it to your SAP Business Application Studio users.

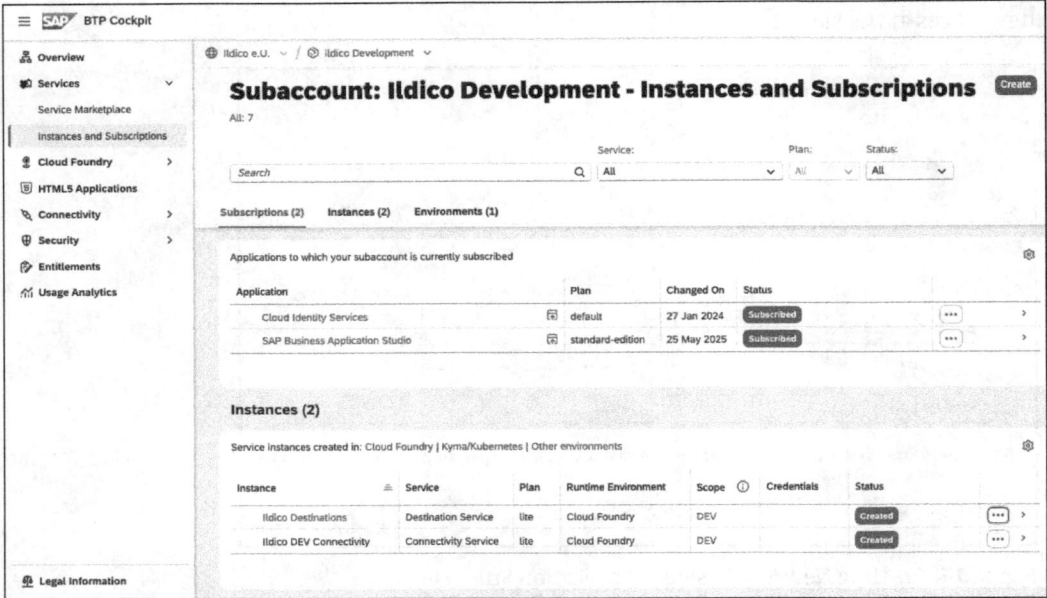

Figure 7.5 Instances and Subscriptions in Subaccount

However, before you can start setting up SAP Business Application Studio, there are still some steps to be taken. The subscription automatically adds new role collections to the subaccount, which must be assigned to SAP Business Application Studio users. For more information about role collections, see Section 7.2.

To be able to use the service, you must assign the `Business_Application_Studio_Administrator` administrator role and the `Business_Application_Studio_Developer` and `Business_Application_Studio_Extension_Deployer` developer roles to your users. To do this, navigate to the **Security** • **Users** path in your SAP BTP cockpit (see Figure 7.6).

Click the three-dot button to access the **Assign Role Collection** point, where you have to assign the **Business_Application_Studio_Administrator** role collection to yourself to be able to set up SAP Business Application Studio (see Figure 7.7). You can also assign other roles, but these are not essential for the IDE setup.

300

7.1   Setting Up SAP Business Application Studio

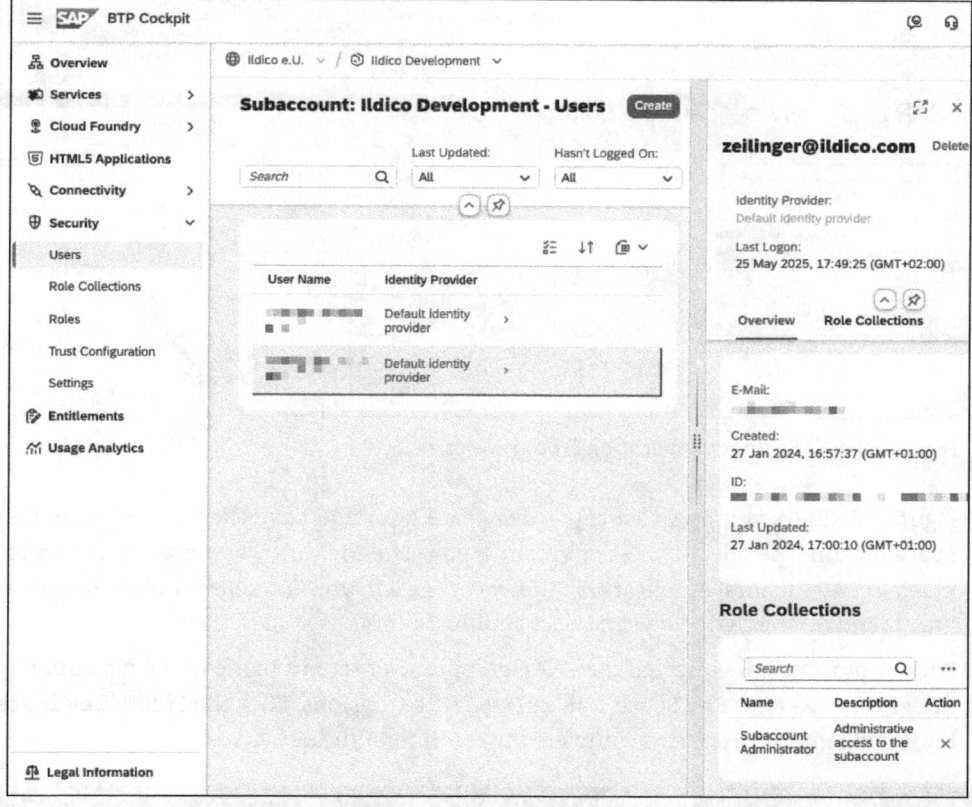

Figure 7.6 Users Within Subaccount in SAP BTP Cockpit

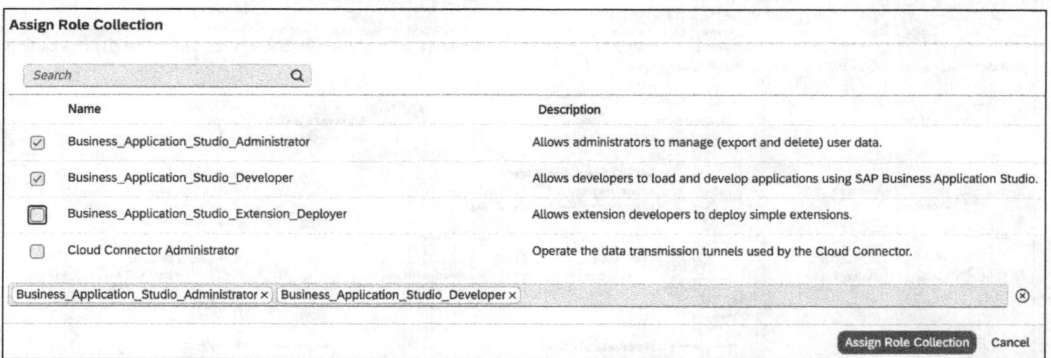

Figure 7.7 Assigning Role Collections

Now you can start SAP Business Application Studio with the persistent link (*https:// <org name>.eu20cf.applicationstudio.cloud.sap/*), as previously discussed. First you will be asked to create a dev space (see Figure 7.8). Such a dev space can be shared by several developers, such as those working on the same project.

7 Activating and Setting Up SAP Business Application Studio

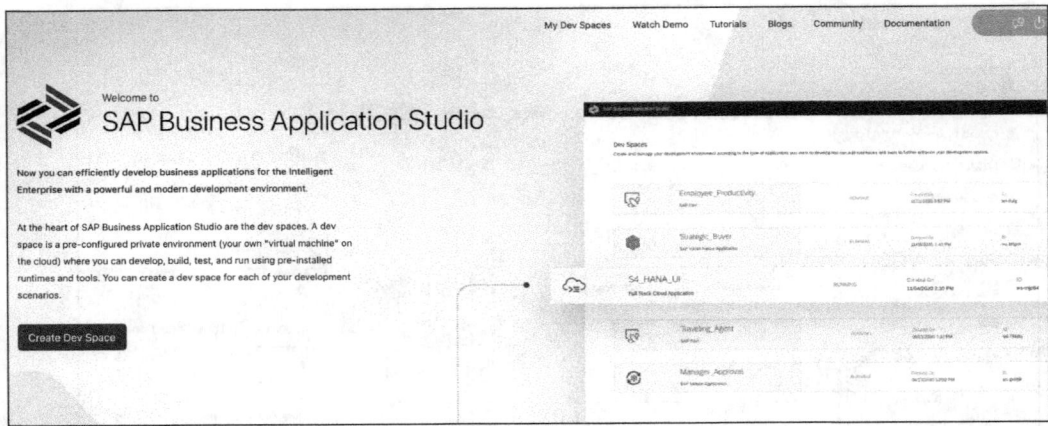

Figure 7.8 SAP Business Application Studio Welcome Screen

Figure 7.9 shows you how to create a dev space after you have clicked the **Create Dev Space** button. The selection shows you how powerful the various tools are that are provided in SAP Business Application Studio. On the left, you can select the development group, and on the right, you can select additional tools.

For our purposes, we selected the **SAP Fiori** option, entered a name in the field directly under **Create a New Dev Space**, and selected no extensions. Click the **Create Dev Space** button when you're done to complete the creation of the dev space.

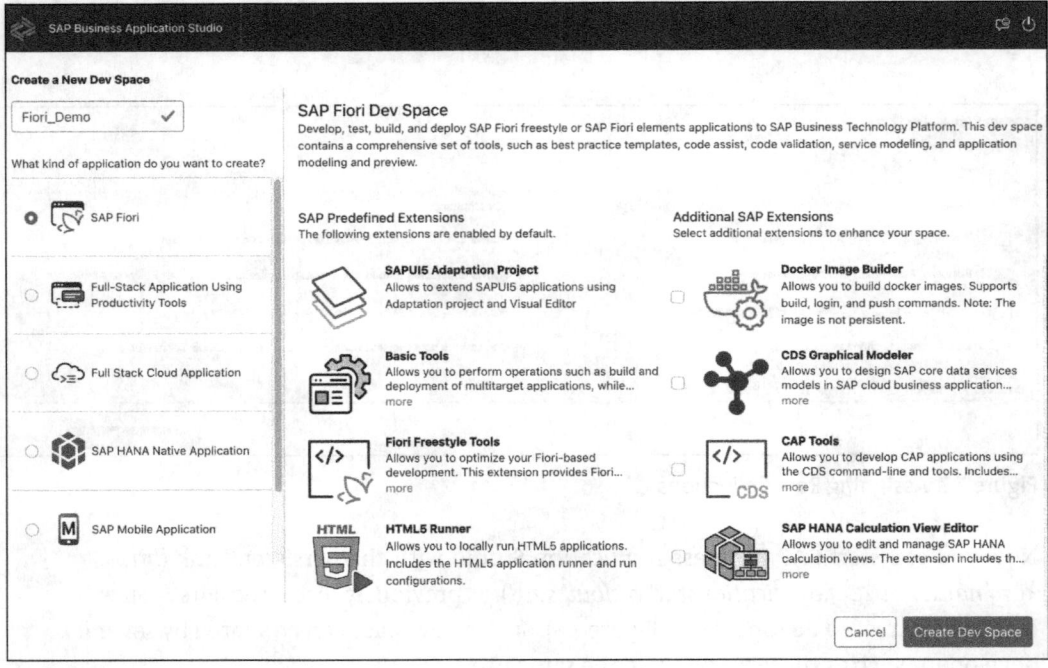

Figure 7.9 Dev Space Creation

302

SAP BTP then displays an overview of the dev spaces and the text **STARTING** for a bit while the setup is being performed. When you see the text **RUNNING**, you can click the name of the dev space to start SAP Business Application Studio with the previously selected dev space (see Figure 7.10).

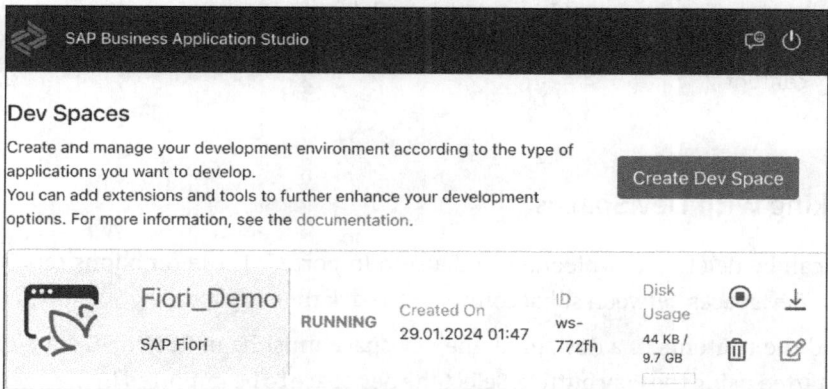

Figure 7.10 Dev Space in RUNNING Status

The spaces terminate themselves if they are not used for a certain period, which is very advantageous for administration. Resources are saved, and the usual problem of never knowing exactly who needs a space and where is solved—even if only for later. If you have a bottleneck or want to restart a space, you can click the **Stop** button (see Figure 7.10). After the dev space has been stopped, clicking **Edit** (the pencil button) takes you back to the selection shown in Figure 7.9, where you can change the dev space type again if necessary.

7.2 Granting Authorizations

In this section, we explain which permissions you should grant to which groups of people. SAP Business Application Studio has the following role collections:

- `Business_Application_Studio_Developer`
  This role collection provides full developer authorizations.

- `Business_Application_Studio_Extension_Deployer`
  This role collection provides developer access to SAP Business Application Studio extensions.

- `Business_Application_Studio_Administrator`
  This role collection allows you to restart, delete, and download spaces.

We recommend that you authorize as few people as possible to be administrators. As convenient as the ability to restart dev spaces may be for developers, the problems associated with it are equally complex: We recommend not restarting dev spaces while they

7 Activating and Setting Up SAP Business Application Studio

are being developed. Downloading spaces is also problematic, as they may contain personal data.

> **Personal Data**
> Make your development department aware that the data in the dev space can be viewed by other developers. Test files, such as images, should contain neither personal nor a proprietary content.

7.3 Working with Dev Spaces

Dev spaces can be deleted, downloaded, and also reimported. These functions can be used to copy dev spaces between subaccounts or to back them up locally.

To download the contents of a dev space, the dev space must be in **RUNNING** state or have been started using the **Play** button. Select the dev space to be imported in the overview and click the arrow ⬇ button to download the contents (see Figure 7.11).

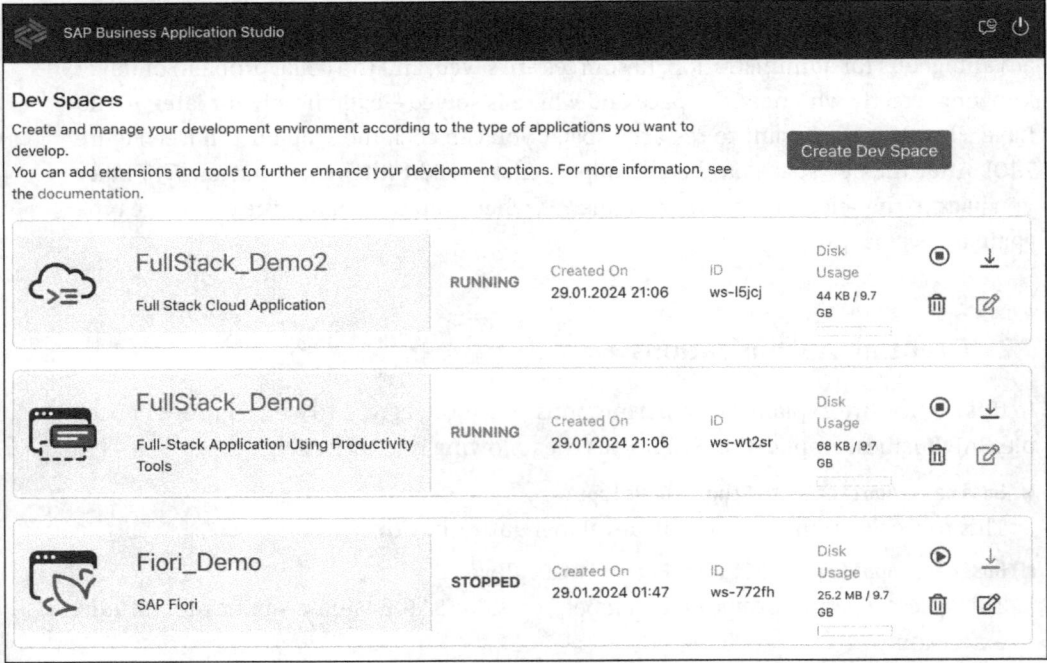

Figure 7.11 Selecting Dev Spaces as Administrator

If you now click the arrow button, you will see instructions for how to proceed with the downloaded data to be able to use it in another project (see Figure 7.12). This means that

304

to use the content in a different context, you must first create the dev space and then import the downloaded archive.

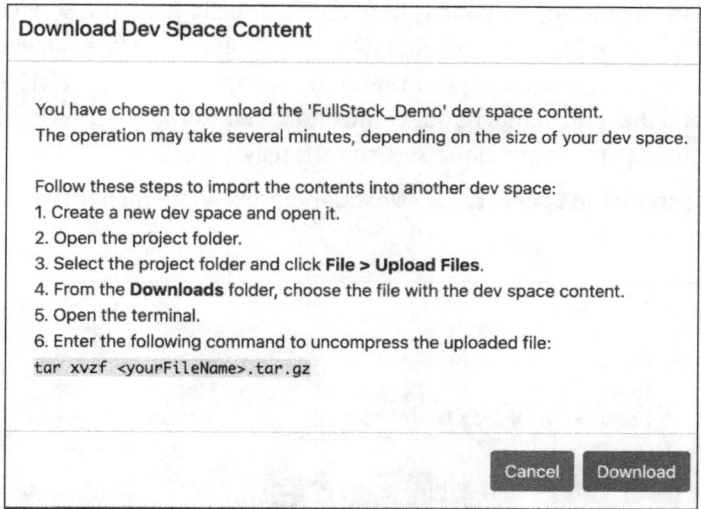

Figure 7.12 Downloading Dev Space Content

> **Command Line**
>
> The administration of dev spaces can also be used from the command line; that is, it can also be scripted. For more information, see SAP Help Portal at *https://help.sap.com/ docs/bas/sap-business-application-studio/restart-dev-space*. The available operations include restarting, exporting, and stopping dev spaces.

7.4 Using External Systems

To connect to a local system from SAP Business Application Studio, you must create a destination. This destination not only is required to access local systems such as ABAP systems, Git on-premise, or npm on-premise, but also is needed in certain cases to perform the exploration of OData services. It is also used to select an OData service for creating and displaying applications.

The SAP Business Application Studio dev spaces already have an integrated web proxy that allows you to access local systems. However, it is important to protect your access data for accessing external systems—for example, by using a keystore or an artifact manager.

For the connection to a local system via this web proxy, you must also configure a destination. This configuration is done from your Cloud Foundry subaccount. All HTTP

7 Activating and Setting Up SAP Business Application Studio

requests, including hosts and ports, made through the proxy will go through this pre-configured destination.

You can create a destination pointing to your system either directly from the Service Center or conveniently from the SAP BTP cockpit. It is advisable always to keep an eye on the security of your access to external systems and to take appropriate protective measures. We recommend that you manage your connections centrally as well-secured connections are an essential part of your cloud security strategy.

To create a connection, choose the **Connectivity • Destinations (New)** menu path in the SAP BTP cockpit (see Figure 7.13).

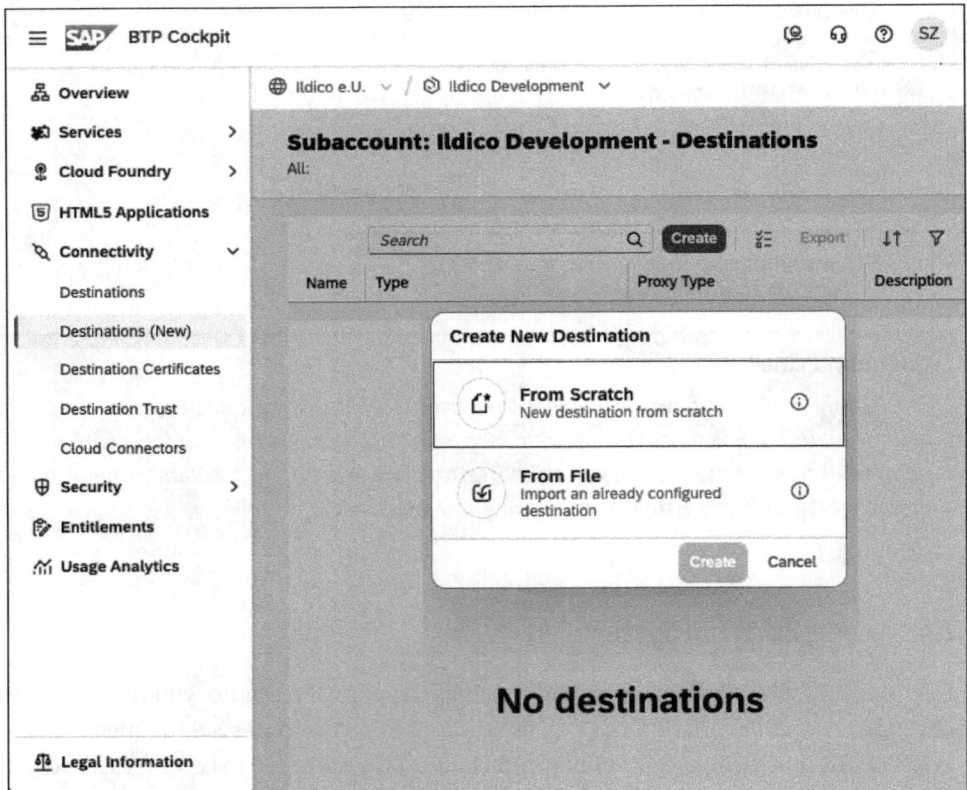

Figure 7.13 Overview of Destinations in SAP BTP Cockpit

Click **Create Destination**. In the next dialogue, select **From Scratch** (see Figure 7.13), then click **Create** to navigate to the **Create Destination** screen. Figure 7.14 shows an example of a connection setup.

7.4 Using External Systems

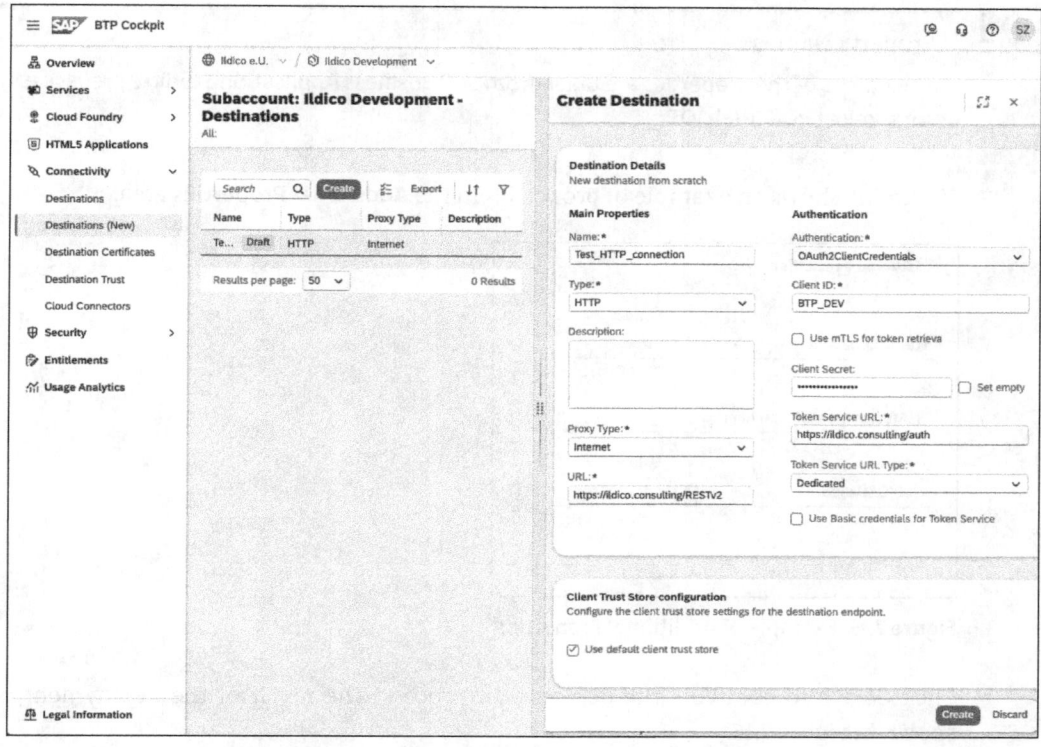

Figure 7.14 Example of Creating Connection in SAP BTP

Scrolling further down the screen shown in Figure 7.14, you will reach the **Additional Properties** section. To create additional properties, click **Add Property**. To be able to use the connection in SAP Business Application Studio, you need four additional properties (see Table 7.1).

Property	Value
`WebIDEEnabled`	true
`HTML5.Dynamic-Destination`	true
`WebIDEUsage`	- `odata_abap` (used to explore ABAP service catalogs) - `dev_abap` (used to roll out the ABAP repository and develop enhancement projects in SAPUI5) - `odata_c4c` (used to access SAP Cloud for Customer catalogs) - `odata_gen` (for an OData service URI after login) - `apihub_sandbox` (used to explore the SAP API hub sandbox)
`WebIDEAdditionalData`	`full_url` (only for `odata_gen` if an absolute URI is to be used)

Table 7.1 Properties and Their Values for Connecting to Local System from SAP Business Application Studio

7 Activating and Setting Up SAP Business Application Studio

> [»] **Property Names**
> The names of the properties are taken from SAP Business Application Studio's predecessor product: SAP Web IDE.

Figure 7.15 shows an example of properties in the **Additional Properties** area.

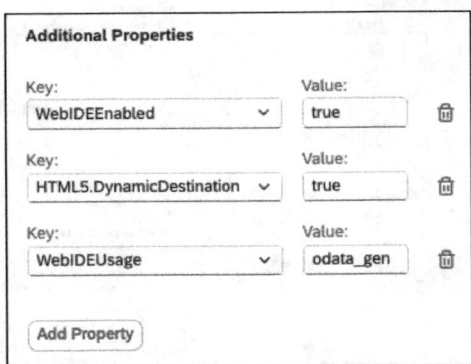

Figure 7.15 Example of Additional Properties

Click **Create** to complete the deployment process. The result of the deployment is shown in Figure 7.16.

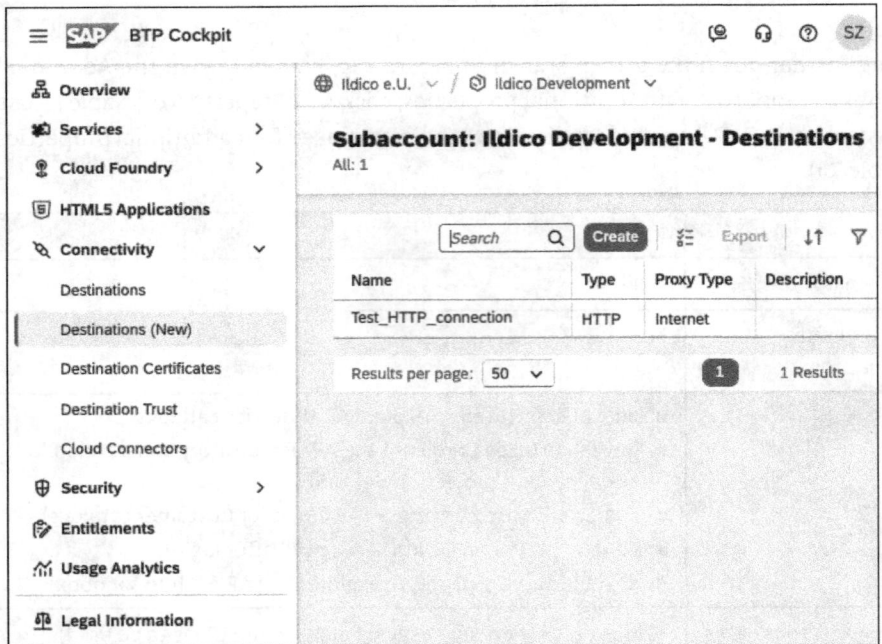

Figure 7.16 Example Destination for Use in SAP Business Application Studio

7.4 Using External Systems

To verify that the connections have been created correctly (and that the parameters have been set so that the developers can see them) and that the connection is accessible from SAP Business Application Studio, proceed as follows:

1. Start SAP Business Application Studio with the URI you noted earlier (Section 7.1).
2. Select any dev space (it may need to be started).
3. On the SAP Business Application Studio start screen (see Figure 7.17), click the plug button on the left to go to the Service Center.

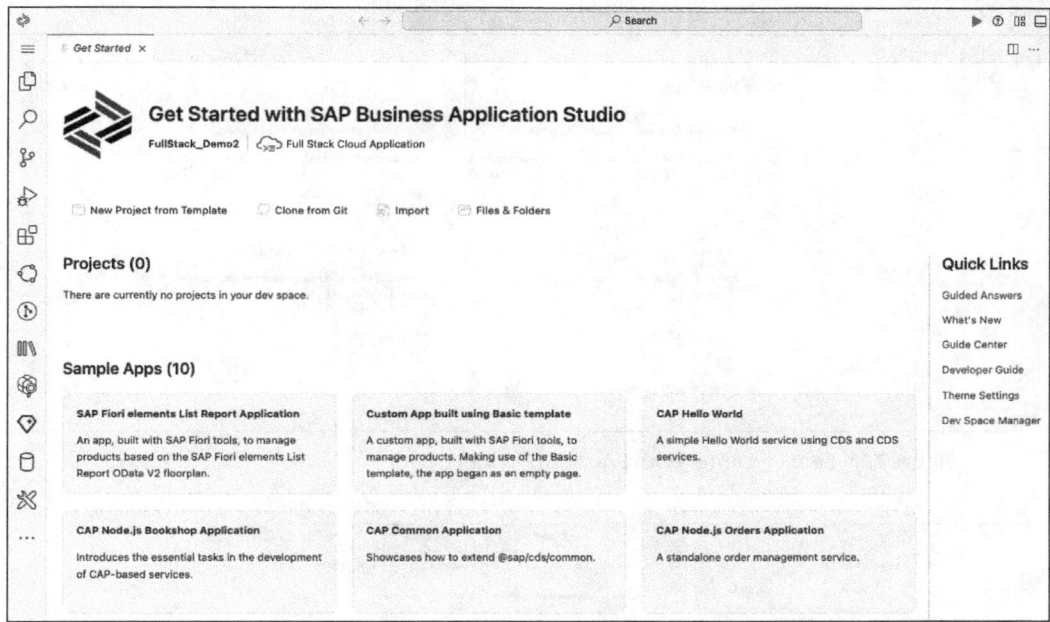

Figure 7.17 Welcome Screen in SAP Business Application Studio

4. In the Service Center, open the **SAP SYSTEM** node and find your connection (see Figure 7.18).
5. If you click the connection, the connection details are displayed in the right-hand area (see Figure 7.19). Depending on the connection, a test can be performed there.

The responsibility of the administrator usually ends here; now the development department takes over. If the connection is not visible, check the previously mentioned parameters for completeness. If the connection test is not successful, it is advisable to check the network or the intermediate cloud connector.

7   Activating and Setting Up SAP Business Application Studio

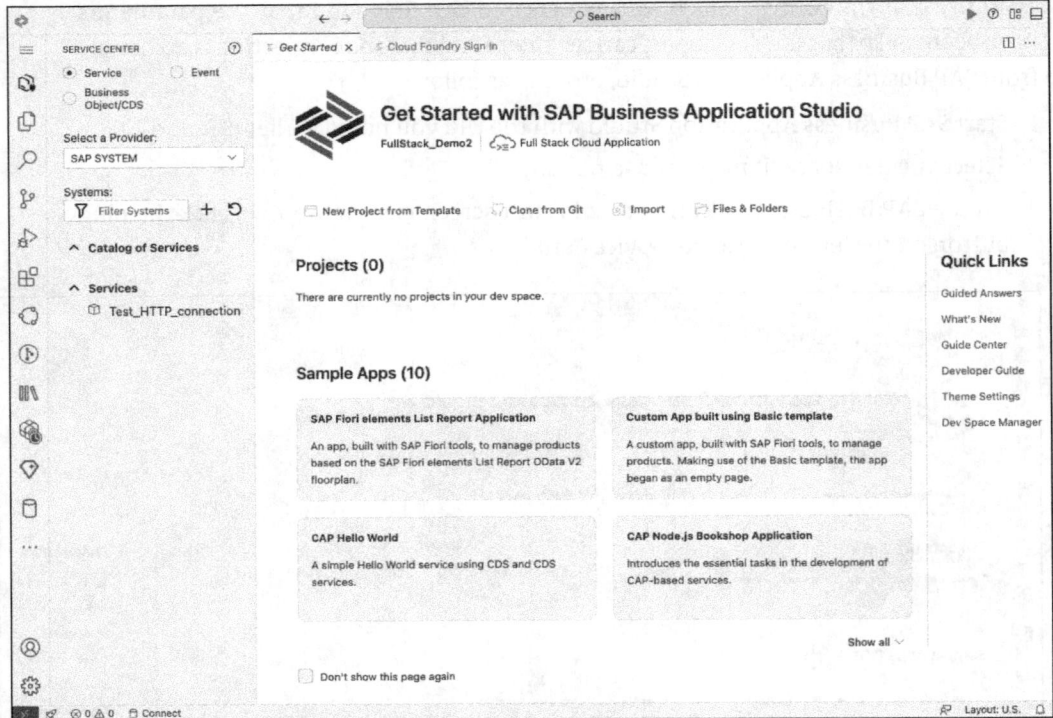

Figure 7.18 Service Center with SAP SYSTEM Tab Open

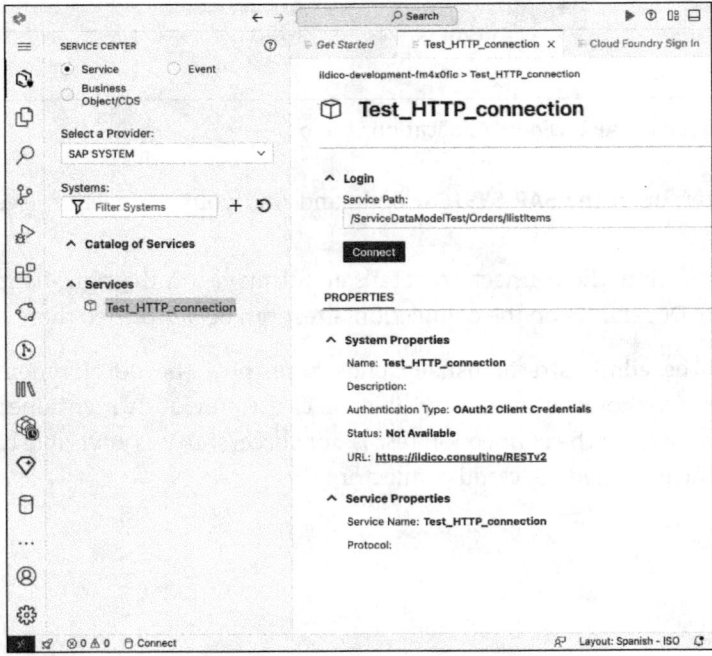

Figure 7.19 Connection Details and Test Option

7.5 Versioning with Git Repositories

In the rapidly evolving world of software development, efficient collaboration between development and system administration is of critical importance. Git, as a distributed version control system, plays a central role in this. This section is aimed at system administrators who want to use Git to configure and maintain a smooth development environment on SAP BTP, integrated with SAP Business Application Studio.

Git allows the development department not only to manage the source code, but also to seamlessly coordinate changes to the code. For administration, it is of great importance to configure and maintain the Git infrastructure correctly in order to create an optimal environment for collaboration. We recommend that you host Git yourself on premise and then integrate it with SAP BTP using the cloud connector. Alternatively, you can use online Git repositories—though they are of course more challenging from a security point of view.

As an administrator, you are responsible for setting up remote repositories and branches, managing access rights, and configuring workflow policies. Clear structures and processes help the development team to work together efficiently and without collisions.

The merging and conflict resolution is done either by the development management or by the administration.

The security of Git repositories is about the rights of individual developers. Sensitive parts of the repository should always be well protected and backed up regularly.

> **SSL/TLS**
>
> In SAP Business Application Studio, the connection to the Git server must be established using SSL/TLS.

The cloud connector is used to connect to the on-premise system. The first step is to create a mapping for the Git server in the cloud connector. Open the connection to the subaccount in the cloud connector and select **Cloud to On-Premises** (see Figure 7.20). Click the plus button on the **Access Control** tab.

> **SSL Certificate and Git**
>
> Note that if the internal host name differs from the virtual host name, you will have a problem: The SSL certificate provided by the backend will be issued for a different server name than the one you have chosen as the virtual server name.
>
> In our example, both servers are in the same domain, and the backend server we are using has a wildcard certificate installed that identifies the entire domain as trustworthy.

7 Activating and Setting Up SAP Business Application Studio

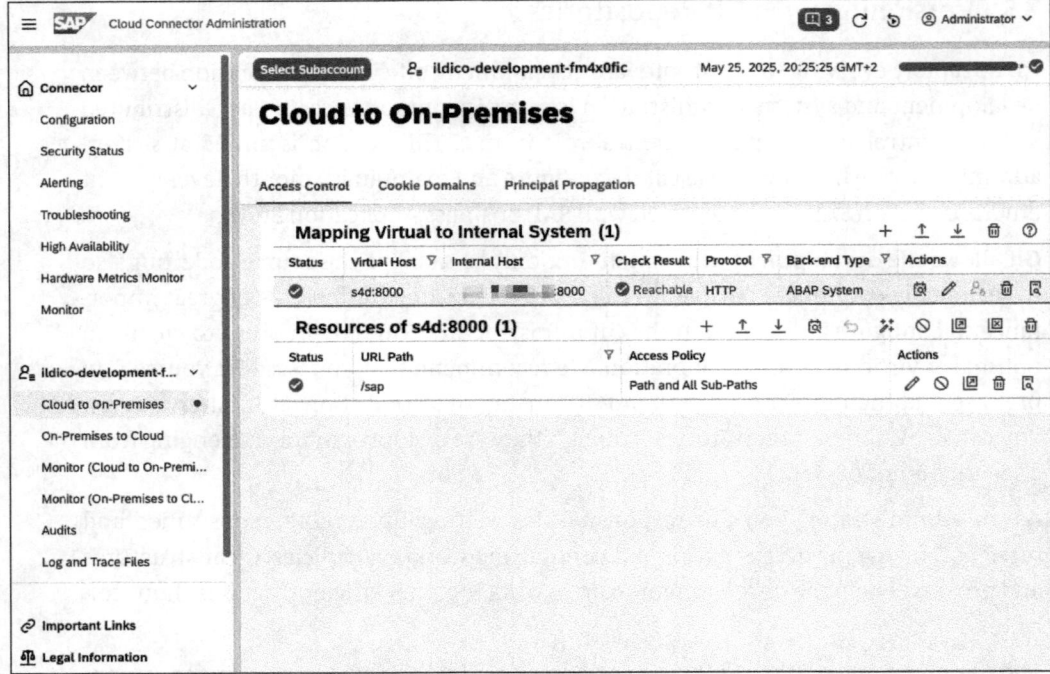

Figure 7.20 Adding Git Server to Cloud Connector

Select the **Non-SAP System** option for **Backend Type** (see Figure 7.21). Then click **Next**.

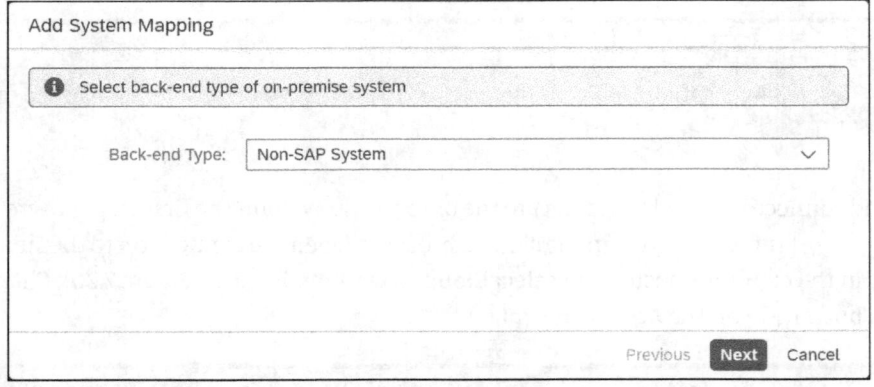

Figure 7.21 Select Backend Type

In the **Protocol** field, select **HTTPS** (see Figure 7.22). When you are done, click **Next**.

7.5 Versioning with Git Repositories

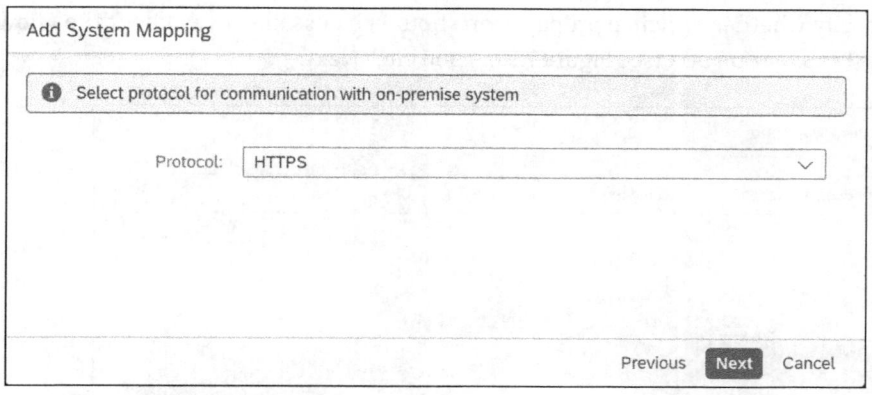

Figure 7.22 Select Protocol

Enter the **Internal Host** and **Internal Port** (see Figure 7.23). Then click **Next**.

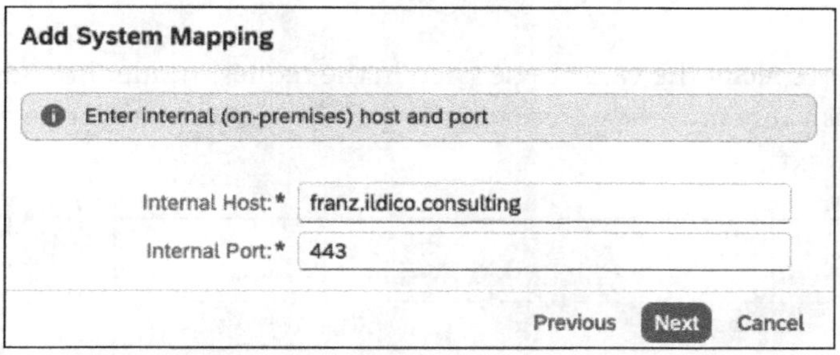

Figure 7.23 Enter Internal Host

Enter the **Virtual Host** and **Virtual Port** (see Figure 7.24). Then click **Next**.

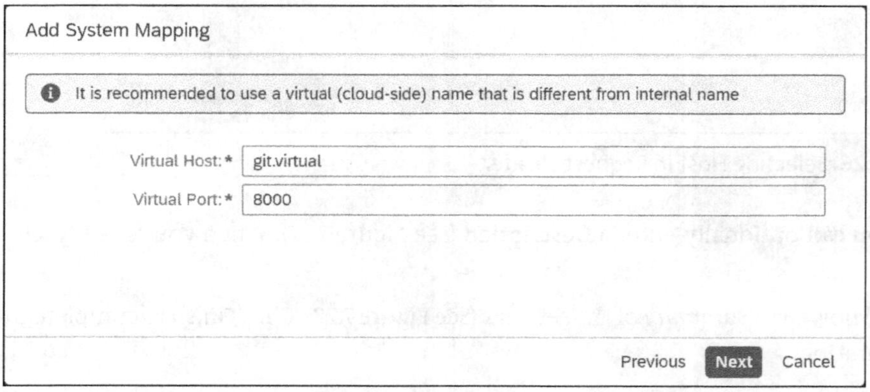

Figure 7.24 Enter Virtual Host

7 Activating and Setting Up SAP Business Application Studio

Next, specify whether principal propagation should be possible. If yes, check the **Allow Principal Propagation** box (see Figure 7.25). Then click **Next**.

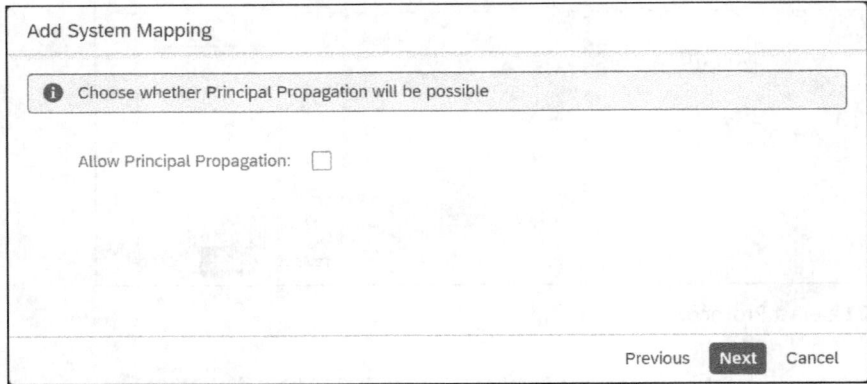

Figure 7.25 Configuring Principal Propagation

In the next step, you must specify the value to be filled in the request header host, as shown in Figure 7.26. This value must be entered in the **Host in Request Header** field. When you're done, click **Next**.

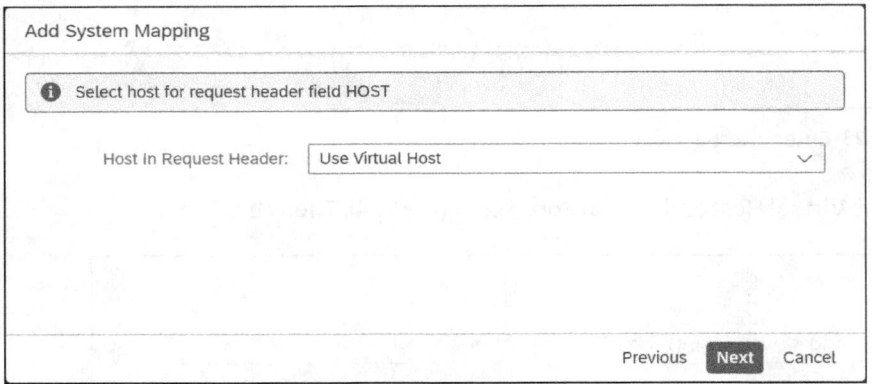

Figure 7.26 Selecting Host in Request Header

Now you can optionally enter a **Description** (see Figure 7.27). When you're ready, click **Next**.

You will now see a **Summary** of the settings (see Figure 7.28). Click **Finish** to complete the configuration.

After completing the configuration, you should see the screen shown in Figure 7.29. Now you must assign the resources. To do this, first click the plus button ➕ in the **Resources** section of *git.<yourserverURL>* (where you replace *<yourserverURL>* with your Git server URL).

7.5 Versioning with Git Repositories

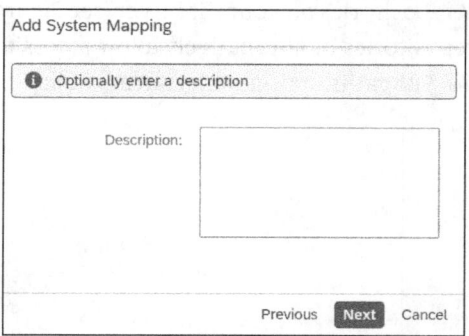

Figure 7.27 Add Description

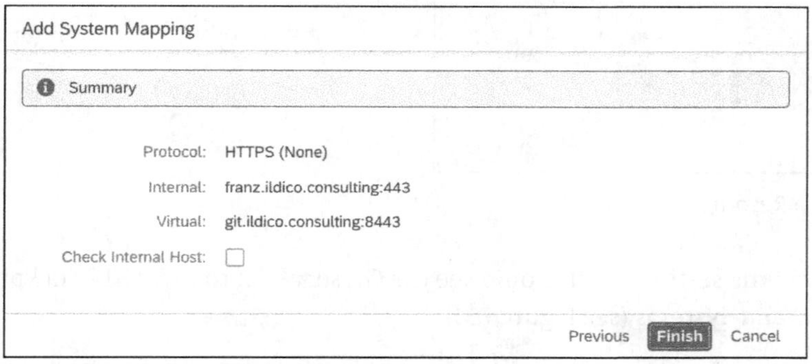

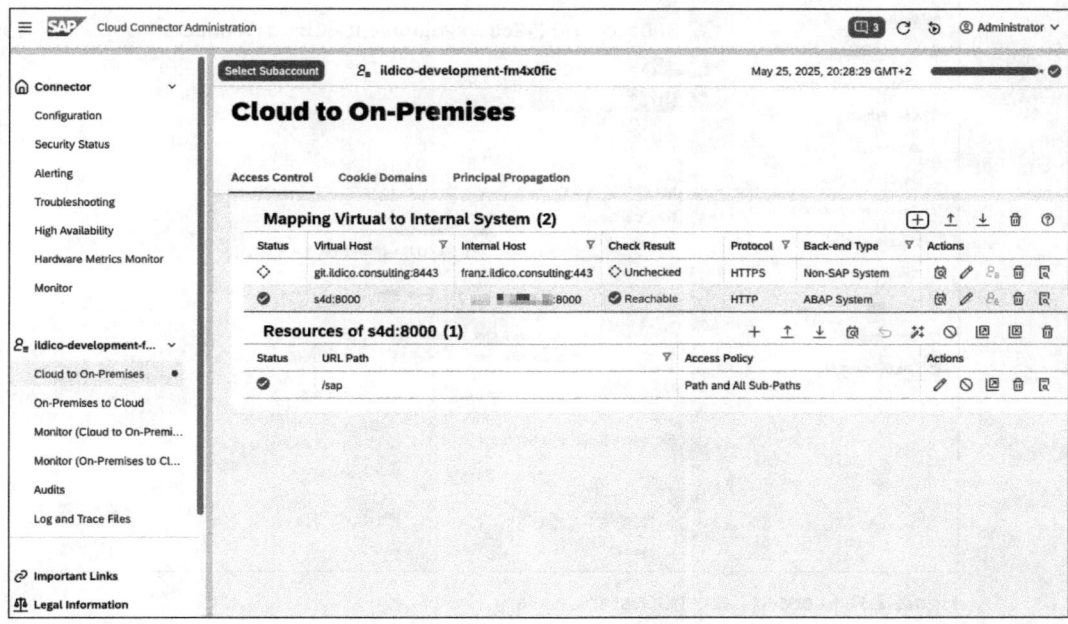

Figure 7.28 Configuration Summary

Figure 7.29 Access Control Overview

7   Activating and Setting Up SAP Business Application Studio

In the **URL Path** field, enter the path to the Git repositories on your Git server (see Figure 7.30). You can either allow access to all Git repositories or alternatively allow access to individual repositories. Select the **Path and All Subpaths** option under **Access Policy**.

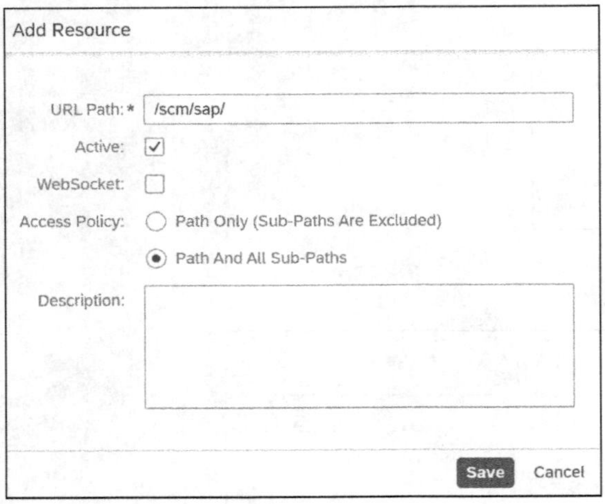

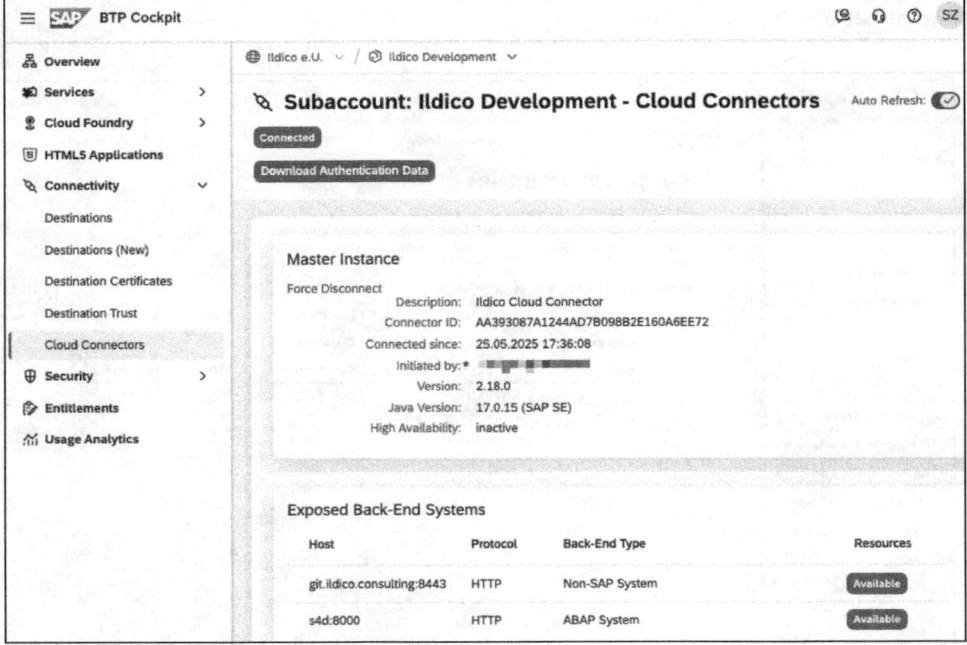

Figure 7.30 Adding a Resource

After you have saved the settings, you should see the Git server in the SAP BTP cockpit under **Exposed Backend Systems** (see Figure 7.31).

Figure 7.31 Exposed Backend Systems

7.5 Versioning with Git Repositories

Navigate to **Connectivity • Destinations (New)** in the side menu (see Figure 7.32). Click **Create** to create a new destination.

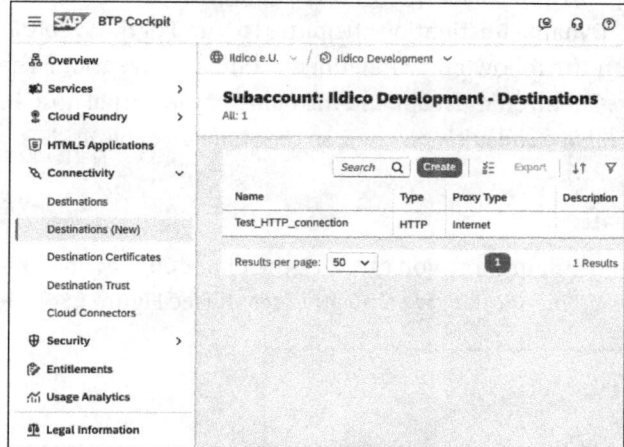

Figure 7.32 Destinations in SAP BTP Cockpit

You can now maintain the destination properties as usual (see Figure 7.33).

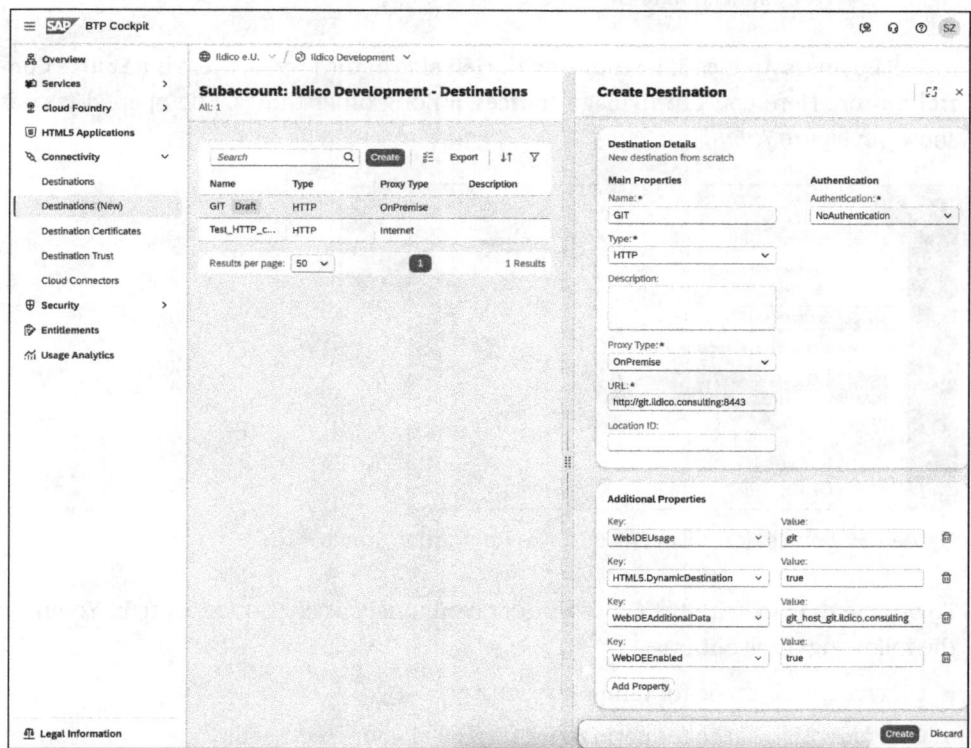

Figure 7.33 Add New Destination

For the **URL** property, you must use the virtual host and the virtual port. Define four additional properties under **Additional Properties**. You can select the names of the additional properties from the dropdown list. Select **git** for the **WebIDEUsage** property. Set the **WebIDEEnabled** and **HTML5.DynamicDestination** attributes to **true**. For the **WebIDE-AdditionalData** attribute, you must follow an SAP-defined naming convention. The value must start with *git_host_*. Then you must append the name of the virtual host. In the example, the virtual host *git.ildico.consulting* is used, so the value must be *git_host_git.ildico.consulting*.

When you're finished, click **Create**.

After you have saved the target configuration, you can click the **Check Connection** button to perform a connection test. This should give a positive result (see Figure 7.34).

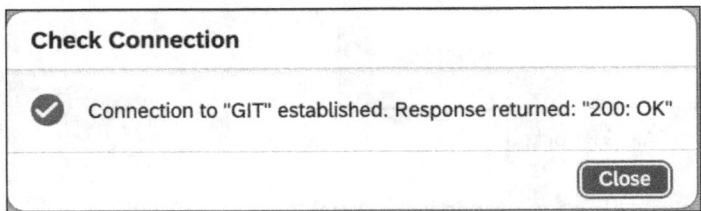

Figure 7.34 Test Connection to Git Server

In SAP Business Application Studio, on the left side of the screen, there is a **Source Control** button. Here you can manage sources, among other things. The opened view is shown in Figure 7.35.

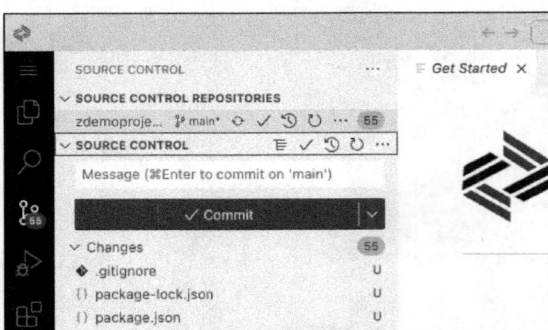

Figure 7.35 Source Control in SAP Business Application Studio

To be able to work with the Git repository, you must specify Git credentials. You have the following three options:

- Git credentials cache for temporary storage
- Git credentials cache for permanent storage of your credentials
- Personal access token, if you have an access token from your Git repository

7.5 Versioning with Git Repositories

To test the function, enter the code in Listing 7.1 in the command line in SAP Business Application Studio. To access the command line, click the **Terminal** tab (see Figure 7.36).

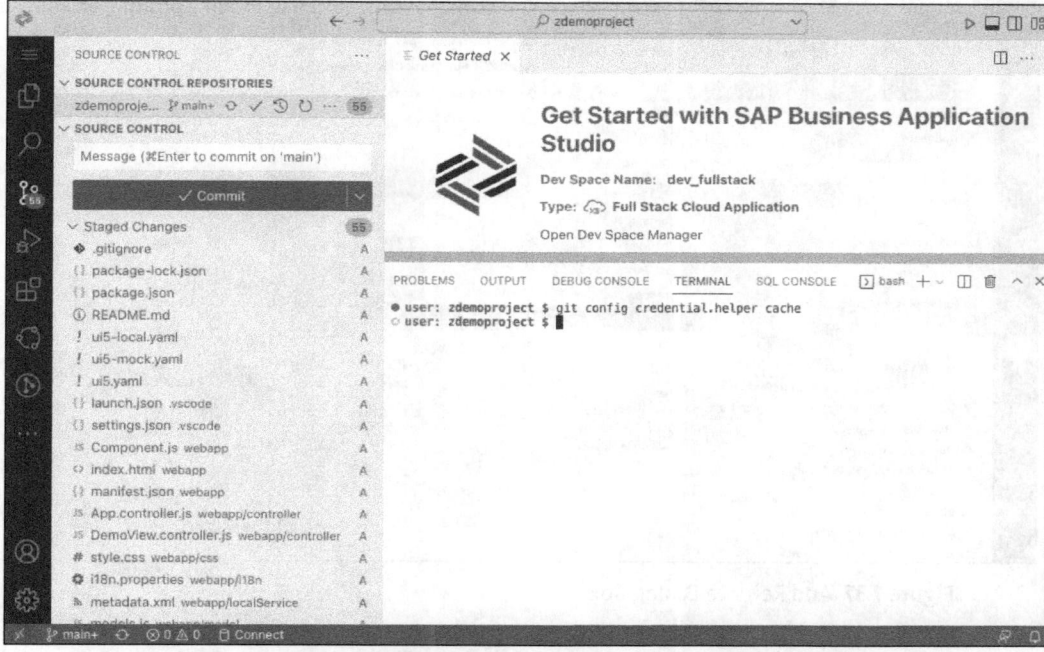

Figure 7.36 Accessing Git Credentials Command Line

```
$ git config credential.helper 'cache --timeout=3600
$ git push https://git.ildico.consulting:8443/<reponame>.git
Username: <git username>
Password: <git password>
```

Listing 7.1 Entering Your Git Credentials

Once you have completed this step, you will be able to work with your Git repository credentials for one hour, after which you will need to reenter them.

> **Learn More About the Git Cache**
> To learn more about the Git cache, visit *https://git-scm.com/docs/git-credential-cache*.

Now let's add the sources of a sample development to the repository. Under **SOURCE CONTROL**, you can see a three-point button [...] that opens the menu. Navigate to the path **Remote • Add Remote…** (see Figure 7.37).

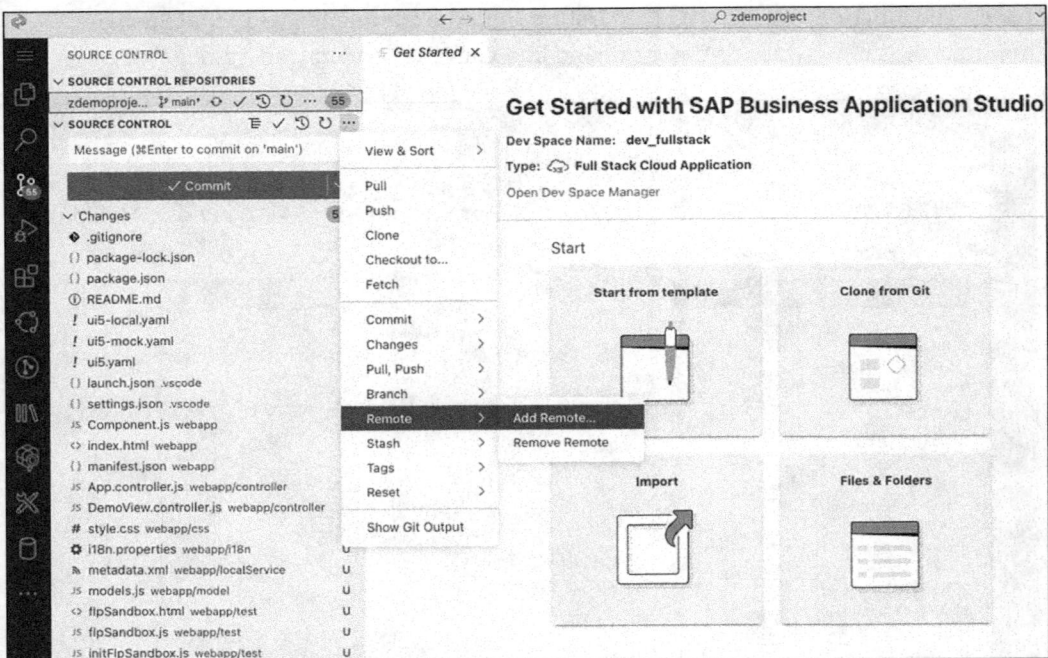

Figure 7.37 Add Remote Dialog Box

Enter the Git server in the SAP Business Application Studio search field (see Figure 7.38).

Figure 7.38 Add Remote Git Repository

In the next step, you can assign a name to the Git connection. For our example, we have entered "ConsultingGit" (see Figure 7.39).

Once you have assigned a name, you can use the repository throughout SAP Business Application Studio. Many of the operations are built into SAP Business Application Studio itself, while others must be performed from the terminal.

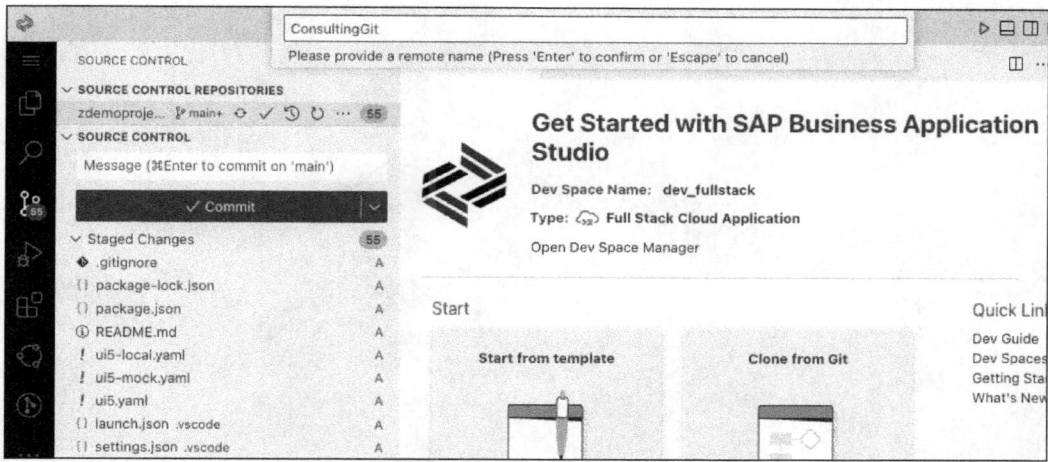

Figure 7.39 Assigning Git Connection Name

> **More Information About Git in SAP Business Application Studio**
>
> For more information about working with Git and SAP Business Application Studio, see *https://help.sap.com/docs/bas/sap-business-application-studio/connecting-to-corporate-git-repository*.

7.6 Summary

In this chapter, we explored how SAP Business Application Studio serves as the central tool for cloud-based development on SAP BTP. The chapter guided you through activating the service, assigning roles, and setting up isolated dev spaces.

You learned how to configure permissions through the predefined role collections and how to manage dev spaces as needed. We also covered how to securely connect to external systems (like ABAP or Git) by creating destinations in the SAP BTP cockpit. Finally, you saw how Git-enabled version control can be used directly from SAP Business Application Studio.

Chapter 8
Activating and Setting Up SAP Integration Suite

The key to success in hybrid environments is the integration of cloud and on-premise systems. SAP offers SAP Integration Suite for this purpose.

In today's fast-paced and digitally connected world, the integration of systems and applications has become a critical success factor for companies of all sizes. The ability to seamlessly navigate between internal and external data flows has a direct impact on a company's efficiency, agility, and innovative strength. Luckily, SAP Integration Suite is here to help! It's a platform that acts as a central hub for digital transformation.

SAP Integration Suite is a comprehensive integration platform as a service (iPaaS) offering. It's a game-changer that goes far beyond the limitations of traditional on-premise systems. It enables organizations to efficiently link their heterogeneous system landscapes—consisting of a variety of SAP and non-SAP applications—and automate business processes. This chapter is your gateway to the world of modern integration technologies, which play a crucial role in the digital transformation era. We'll also highlight the central position of SAP Integration Suite in this landscape.

SAP Integration Suite is not only an evolutionary advancement of its on-premise predecessor, SAP Process Orchestration, but also a revolutionary platform that impresses with cloud flexibility and an extensive range of ready-made content. The broad market acceptance of the platform is a clear sign that companies in all industries have recognized the need to integrate their systems into an increasingly complex digital world.

In Section 8.1, we'll dive into the exciting features and background of this remarkable platform. Section 8.2 will reveal how to set up a subaccount and assign the necessary entitlements. Section 8.3 will guide you through the process of creating a subscription. Then you'll discover how to activate capabilities within SAP Integration Suite in Section 8.4. After that, you'll learn how to create the SAP Process Integration runtime in Section 8.5. Finally, you'll learn how to create service keys in Section 8.6.

8.1 Functions and History of SAP Integration Suite

The SAP Integration Suite has a long history, starting in 2013 with SAP HANA Cloud Integration, which replaced SAP Process Integration and SAP Process Orchestration in

SAP HANA Cloud Platform. SAP HANA Cloud Integration was based on the open-source product Apache Camel, and SAP added SAP-specific components to meet enterprise customer requirements. In 2017, SAP dropped the HANA suffix from the name SAP HANA Cloud Platform, which was henceforth called *SAP Cloud Platform*. SAP HANA Cloud Integration was also renamed *SAP Cloud Platform Integration*, a mere rebranding with no change in functionality. SAP Integration Suite represents not merely an enhancement but a rebranding effort that consolidates multiple integration tools and solutions under a unified platform. This strategic move simplifies the user experience while addressing the growing complexities of modern integration landscapes.

SAP Cloud Platform Integration covered typical integration requirements for the following scenarios:

- Application-to-application (A2A)
- Business-to-business (B2B)
- Business-to-government (B2G)

The connections with systems are made using common protocols and technologies, such as HTTPS, FTP, SFTP, SOAP, OData, REST, JDBC, and IMAP. These protocols are mapped via adapters. In addition to classic technology adapters, SAP also delivers adapters that have been specially developed for SAP cloud products and applications, such as the SAP SuccessFactors adapter and the SAP Ariba adapter. In the B2G environment, SAP delivers the ERiC/ELSTER adapter. If your requirements cannot be met by the existing adapters, you can use the Adapter Development Kit (ADK) to develop and provide your own.

In addition to traditional integration, many customers want to be able to provide APIs. SAP has developed API Management for this purpose.

In addition, many companies need to integrate various cloud solutions and SaaS offerings that are not from SAP, such as Microsoft Office 365, Salesforce, ServiceNow, and Atlassian Jira. To address this, SAP partnered with Cloud Elements to develop the Open Connectors product. Later, for electronic data interchange (EDI) scenarios, the Integration Advisor solution was introduced to help companies accelerate the implementation and realization of EDI interfaces. Each of these products had its own pricing model with different metrics. As you can imagine, it was very difficult for customers to keep track of all the components and different pricing. In addition, each of these solutions was delivered separately, which increased the administrative burden.

SAP listened to customer feedback and merged these products into SAP Integration Suite. Since then, all components can be used with the SAP Integration Suite license. In addition, these components have been combined into a single application and integration has been improved. Around the same time, SAP introduced the Cloud Foundry environment in parallel with the Neo environment. SAP Integration Suite is available only in the Cloud Foundry environment.

8.1   Functions and History of SAP Integration Suite

SAP Integration Suite now includes the following components:
- Cloud Integration
- API Management including Graph
- Event Mesh
- Trading Partner Management
- Integration Advisor
- Open Connectors
- Integration Assessment
- Migration Assessment
- Edge Integration Cell

SAP Integration Suite is also offered in a *free tier* version, which allows you to try the service free of charge for a limited period.

SAP Integration Suite is impressive due to the large number of standard integrations provided by SAP. These depend on the product used and can be found in SAP Business Accelerator Hub (*https://api.sap.com/*). Figure 8.1 shows the integrations for SAP S/4HANA.

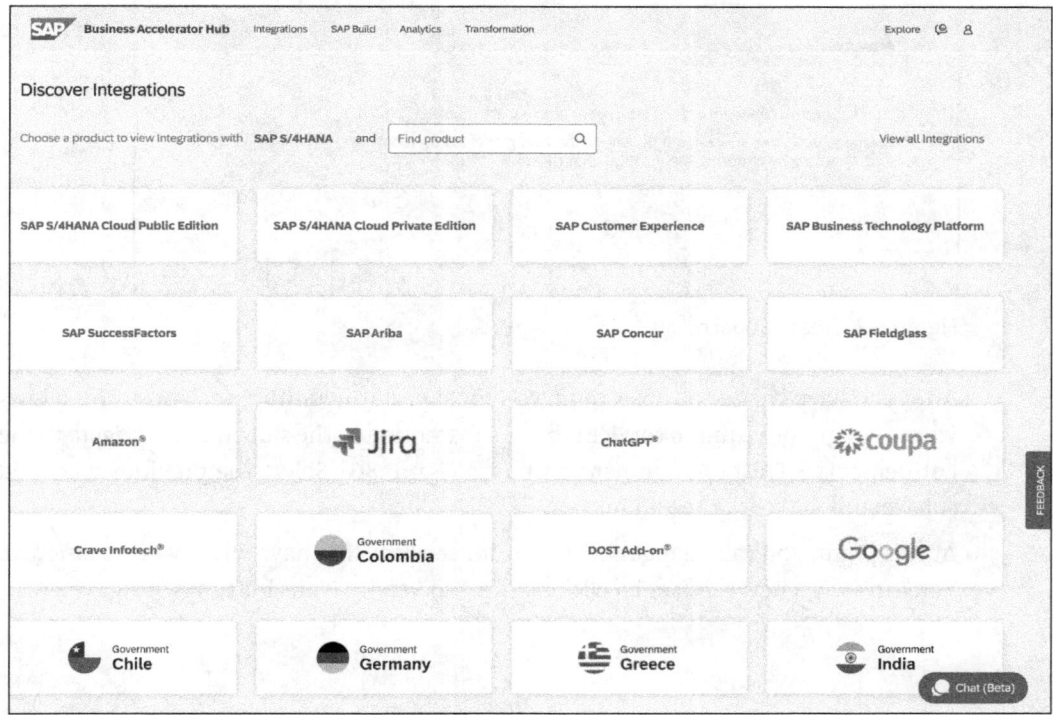

Figure 8.1 Standard Integrations for SAP S/4HANA

8 Activating and Setting Up SAP Integration Suite

8.2 Creating a Subaccount and Assigning Entitlements

Although SAP provides several boosters for various services on SAP BTP, there is no booster for the installation and configuration of SAP Integration Suite. Therefore, it is necessary to perform some steps manually at the global account and subaccount level.

The first step is to create a subaccount. To do this, you must be logged into the SAP BTP cockpit at the global account level. We discussed how to create a subaccount in Chapter 2. Figure 8.2 shows the settings for the subaccount used in the following example. As always, you should first check SAP Discovery Center to see for which hyperscalers and data centers SAP Integration Suite is available.

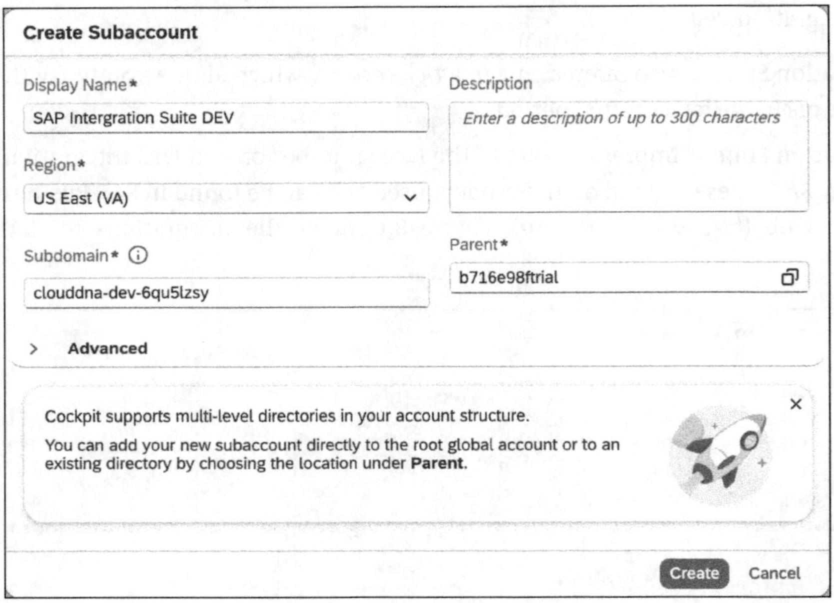

Figure 8.2 Create Subaccount

After you have created a subaccount, you must perform entity association. This allows you to assign the required services to the subaccount. In the side menu, navigate to the **Entitlements • Entity Assignment** path (see Figure 8.3). Select the previously created subaccount and click the **Edit** button.

At this point, you can change the quotas for services that have already been assigned. You can assign new services by clicking the **Add Service Plans** button (see Figure 8.4).

8.2 Creating a Subaccount and Assigning Entitlements

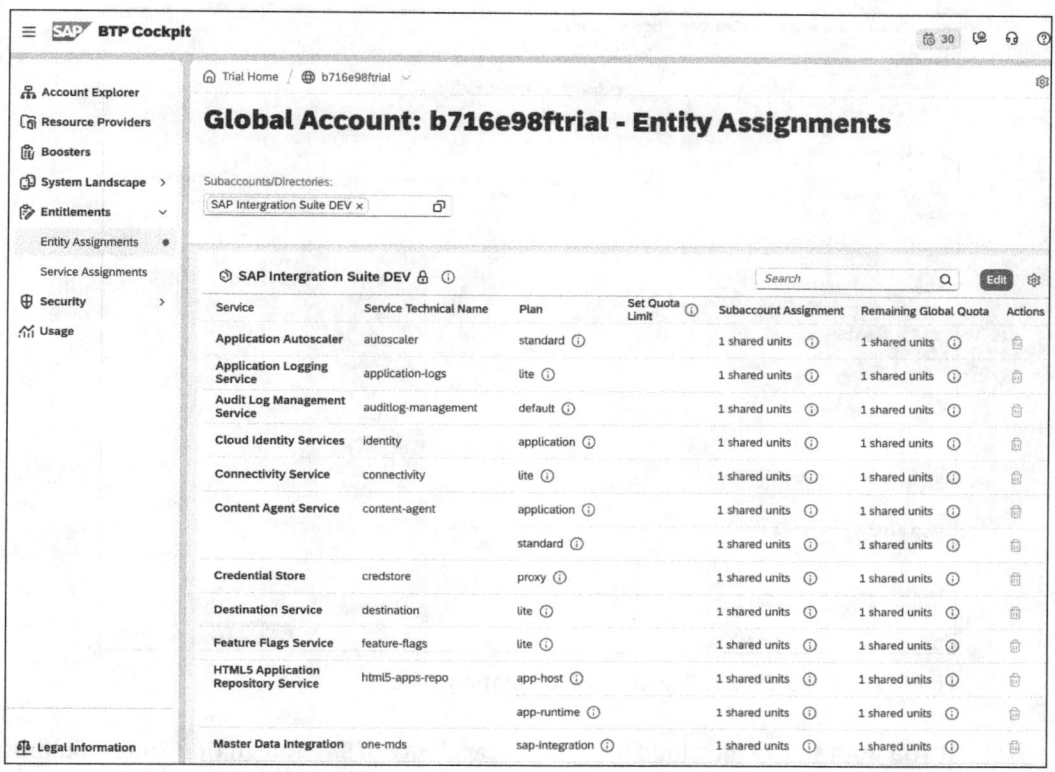

Figure 8.3 Configure Entitlements

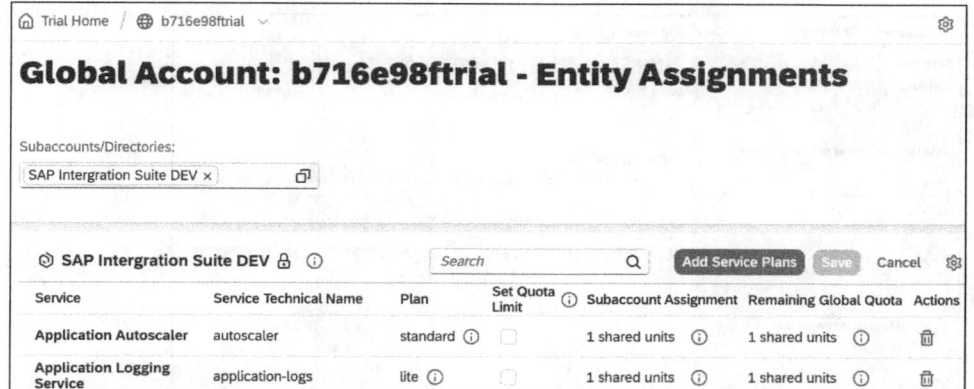

Figure 8.4 Add Service Plans

To use SAP Integration Suite, the **Integration Suite** service must be assigned. Activate the **trial (Application)** indicator (the free service plan) to use SAP Integration Suite free of charge for 90 days. In this example, we use a trial account. You must select the **trial (Application)** plan for this case (see Figure 8.5). You can find the other available service plans in SAP Discovery Center.

8   Activating and Setting Up SAP Integration Suite

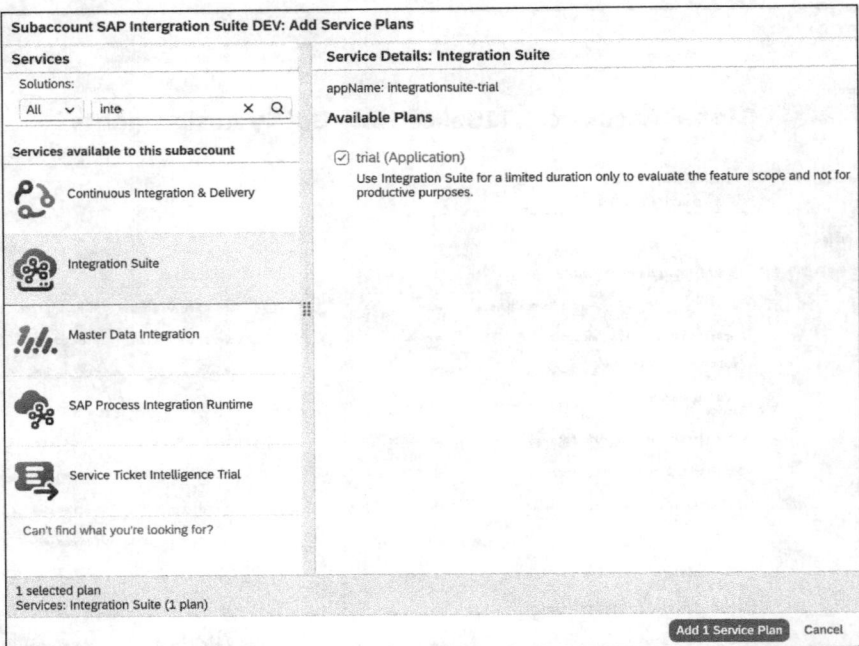

Figure 8.5 Select Service Plan for SAP Integration Suite

If you want to use the Cloud Integration capability of SAP Integration Suite, you must also add the **SAP Process Integration Runtime** service. This service is available under the **api** and **integration-flow** service plans (see Figure 8.6).

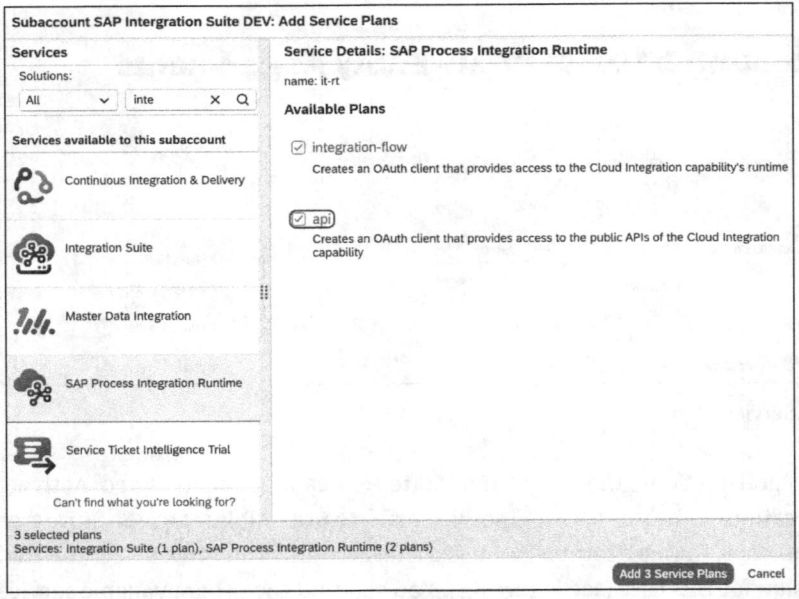

Figure 8.6 Selecting Service Plan for SAP Process Integration Runtime Service

The API service plan provides access to the Cloud Integration public APIs. The integration-flow service plan is required to generate the OAuth client credentials needed to authenticate the sender systems. The SAP Process Integration runtime service plans are included in the SAP Integration Suite license, so there is no additional license cost. After assigning the service plans, close the dialog by clicking **Add 3 Service Plans**. OData v2 APIs are provided to access Cloud Integration. These include access to integration content, security content, message processing logs, log files, message stores, and the partner directory.

> **API Documentation**
>
> If you plan to access Cloud Integration using APIs, you can find an overview of the available APIs in SAP Business Accelerator Hub at *https://api.sap.com/package/CloudIntegrationAPI/odata* (see Figure 8.7).

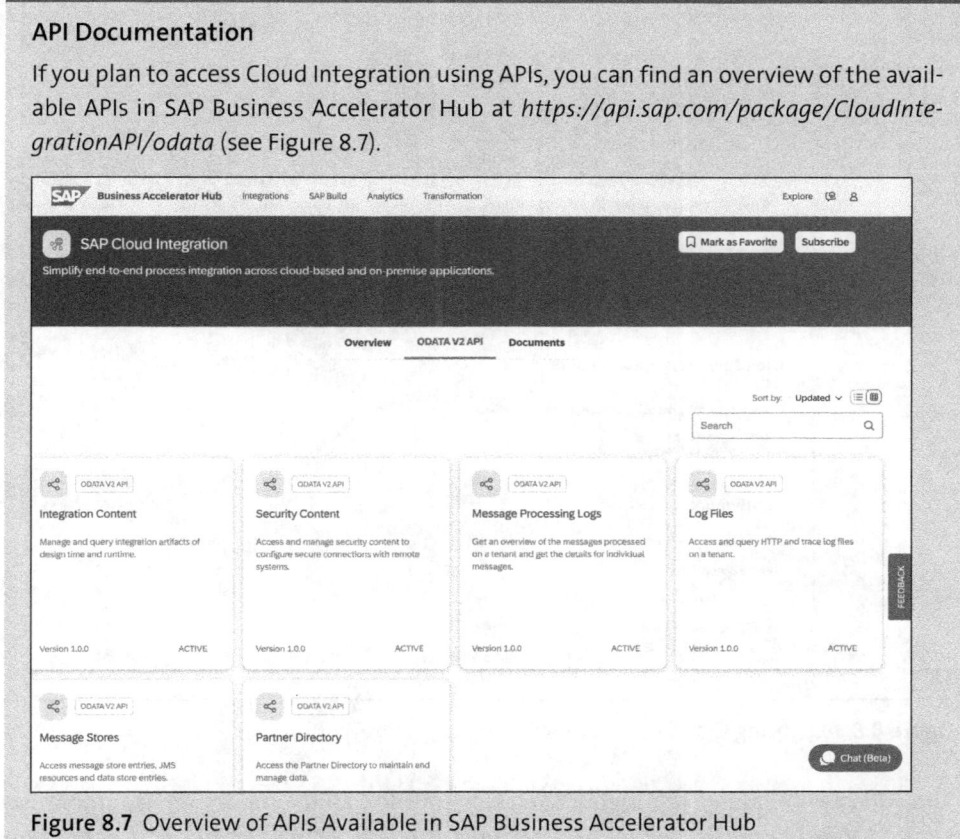

Figure 8.7 Overview of APIs Available in SAP Business Accelerator Hub

After assigning service plans to the subaccount, save the assignment by clicking **Save**. Note that no license costs are incurred at this point; they only arise after the service has been subscribed to or instantiated in the subaccount.

8.3 Creating a Subscription

After the entitlements have been assigned to the subaccount, you can start setting up SAP Integration Suite. To do so, open the SAP BTP cockpit of the subaccount. The SAP

8   Activating and Setting Up SAP Integration Suite

Integration Suite subscription does not require a Cloud Foundry environment, whereas the SAP Process Integration runtime does. Therefore, first activate the Cloud Foundry environment. To do so, navigate to the **Overview** section in the side menu and click the **Enable Cloud Foundry** button (see Figure 8.8).

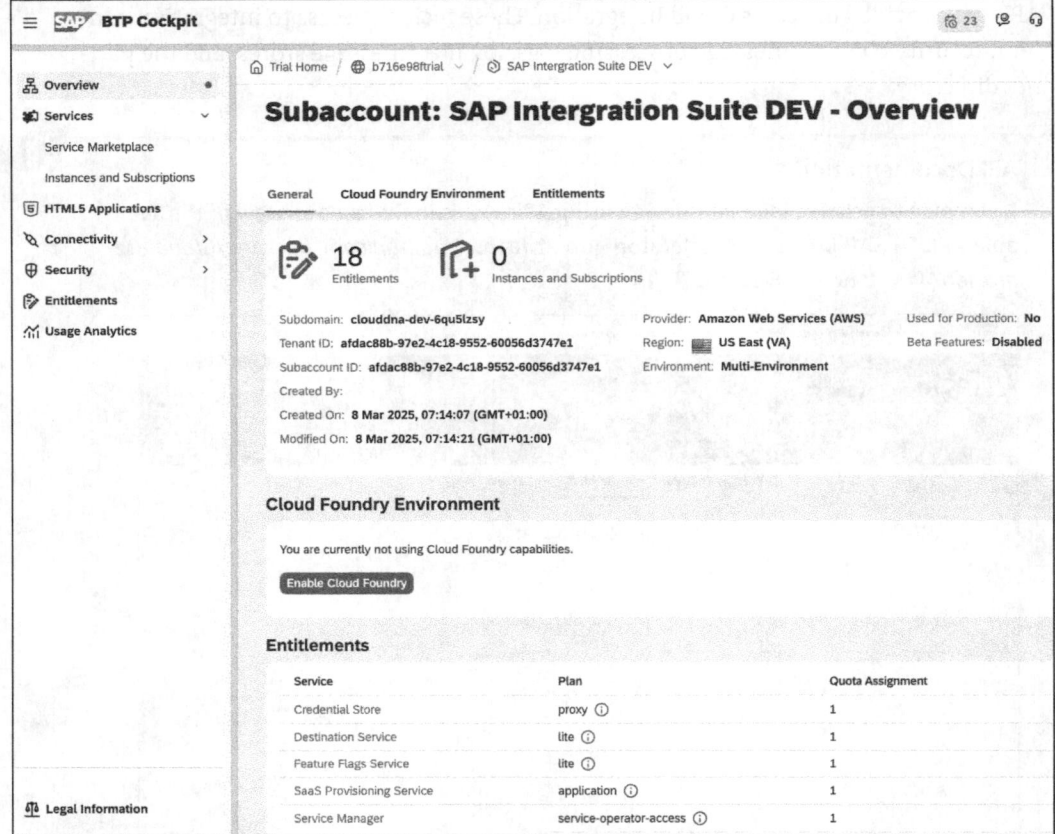

Figure 8.8 Activating Cloud Foundry Environment

You will now see the preconfigured settings for the Cloud Foundry environment (see Figure 8.9). You can customize these settings as needed. For example, you might want to customize **Instance Name** and **Org Name** to match your own naming conventions.

To get started, go to the **Services • Instances and Subscriptions** side menu. There you'll see the active Cloud Foundry environment (see Figure 8.10). You can also start the SAP Integration Suite subscription here. To do so, click the **Create** button. If you prefer, you can also go to the **Services • Service Marketplace** path in the side menu and start the subscription there.

8.3 Creating a Subscription

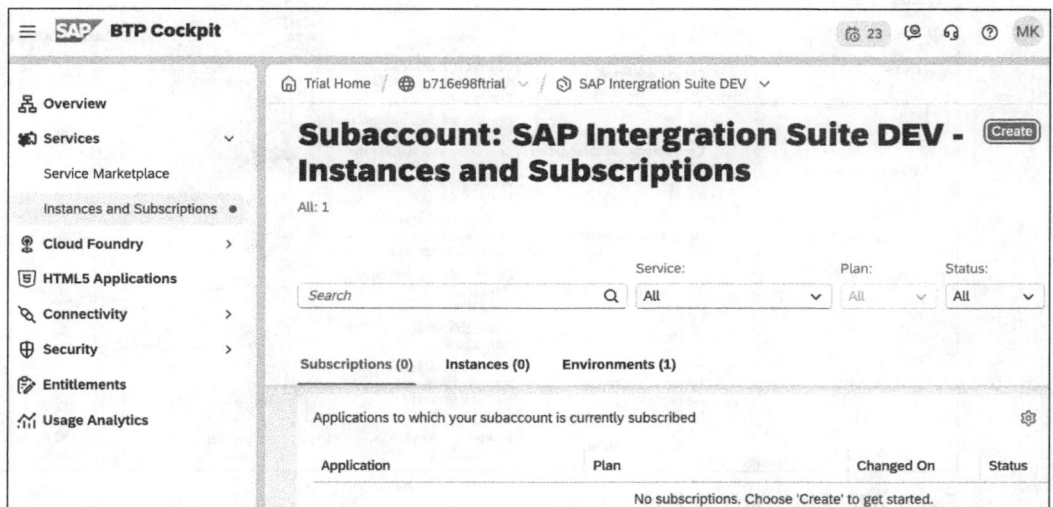

Figure 8.9 Configure Cloud Foundry Environment

Figure 8.10 Create Subscription

Choose the **Integration Suite** option in the **Service** field. In the **Plan** field, choose either **trial**, if you are in the trial account, or **free**, if you are using the free tier (see Figure 8.11). Then click **Create**.

331

8   Activating and Setting Up SAP Integration Suite

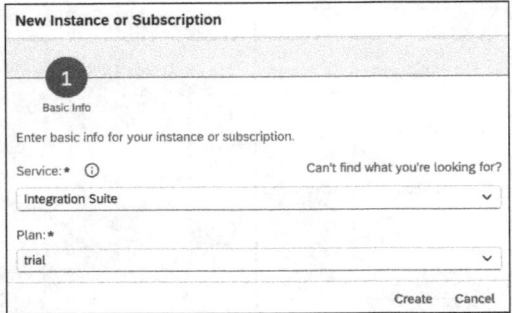

Figure 8.11 Select Service Plan

The subscription should be created in a few seconds. To access SAP Integration Suite, you must assign the required role collections to the desired users. To do this, use the side menu to navigate to **Security • Role Collections** (see Figure 8.12). Then, click the **Integration Provisioner** role collection.

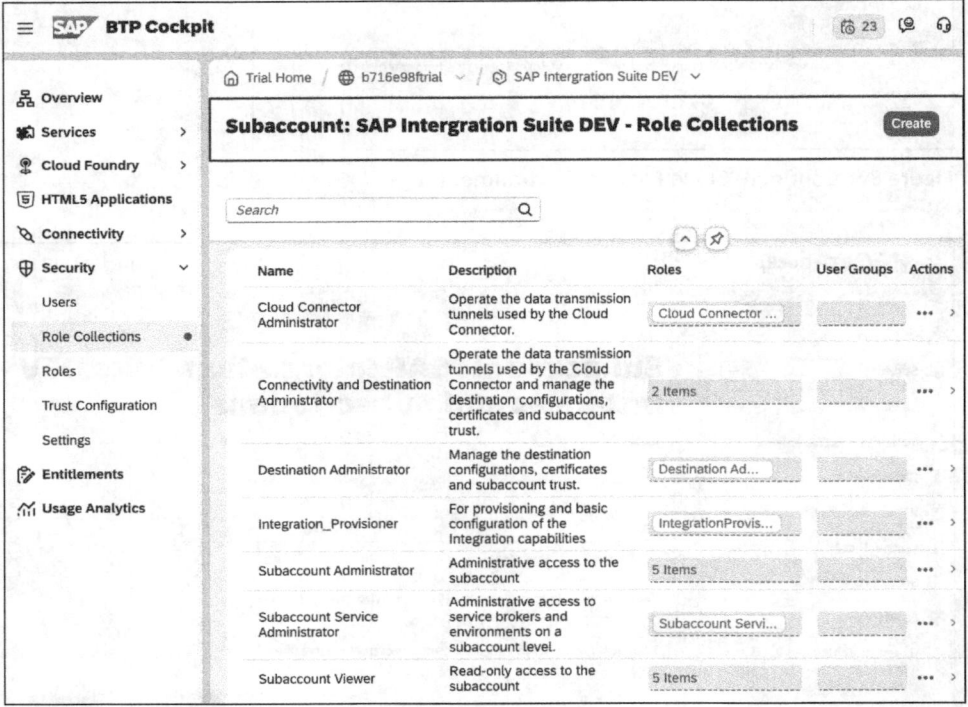

Figure 8.12 Assign Role Collections

You are now in the role collection details section (see Figure 8.13). As you can see here, the role collection includes the IntegrationProvisioningAdmin role, but no **Users** or **User Groups** are assigned. Click the **Edit** button to assign users to the role collection. We generally recommend that role collections be mapped to user groups of the underlying

8.3 Creating a Subscription

identity providers via a mapping. However, we deliberately omitted this step in this practical example because we want to focus on the installation and configuration of SAP Integration Suite.

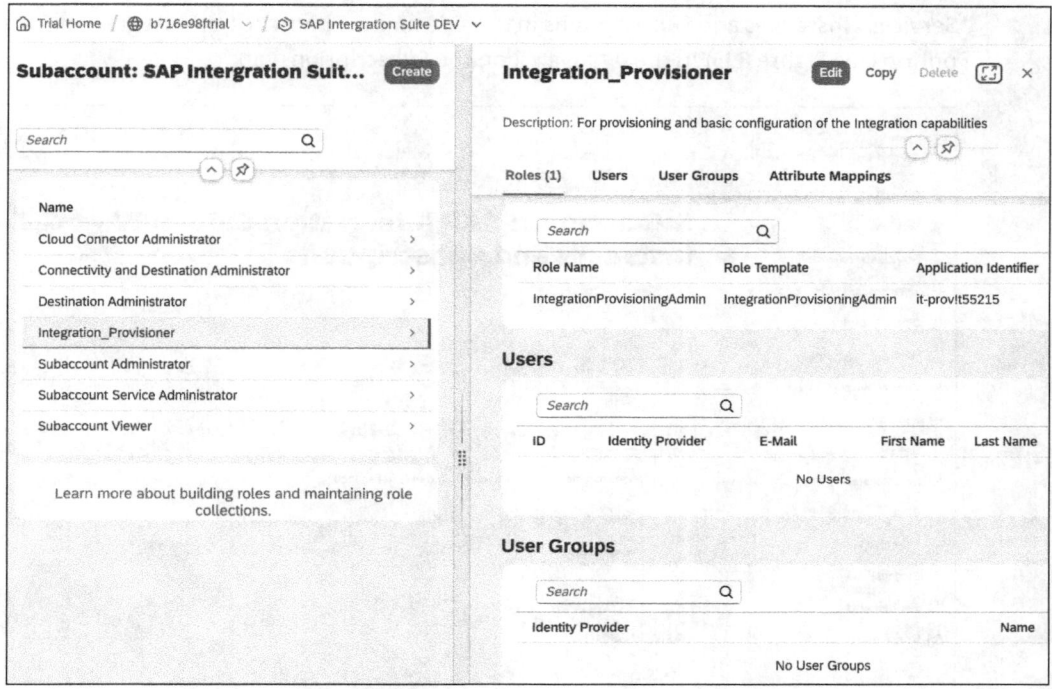

Figure 8.13 Edit Role Collection

You can now enter the email address of the desired user in the **ID** field in the **Users** area (see Figure 8.14). Then click the **Save** button.

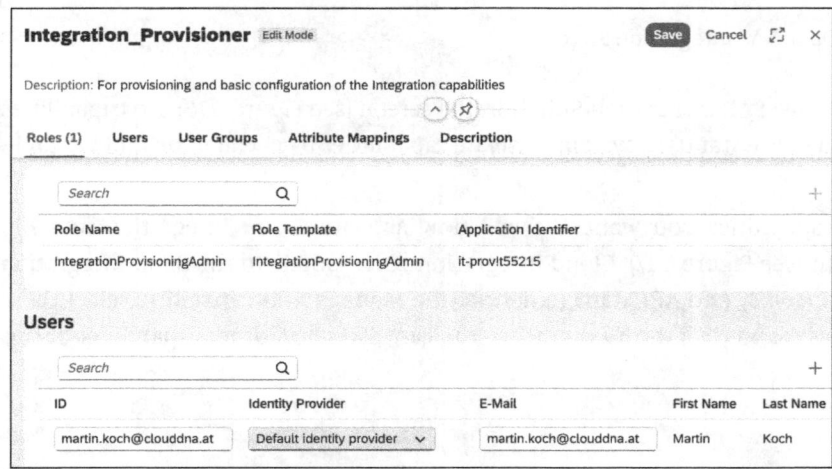

Figure 8.14 Add Users and Save Assignment

333

8.4 Activating Capabilities

You have now created all the prerequisites for accessing SAP Integration Suite. Next, you must activate the desired capabilities in SAP Integration Suite. Follow menu path **Services • Instances and Subscriptions** in the side menu. Then, click the **Integration Suite** option (see Figure 8.15) in the detail area on the **Subscriptions** tab.

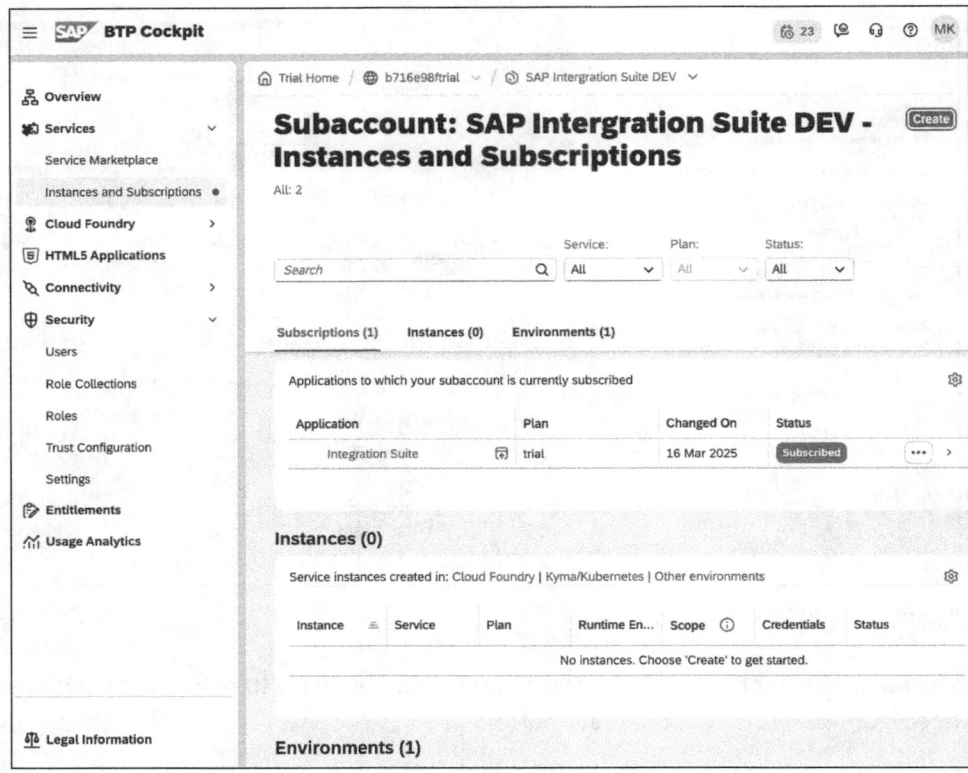

Figure 8.15 Open SAP Integration Suite

You will now see SAP Integration Suite's initial screen (see Figure 8.16). No capabilities are activated in the standard system. Activate capabilities by clicking the **Add Capabilities** button.

Select the capabilities you want. We will now activate Cloud Integration and API Management (see Figure 8.17). Cloud Integration corresponds to the **Build Integration Scenarios** capability and API Management to the **Manage APIs** capability. Select these two capabilities and click the **Next** button. You can also select other capabilities at this point.

8.4 Activating Capabilities

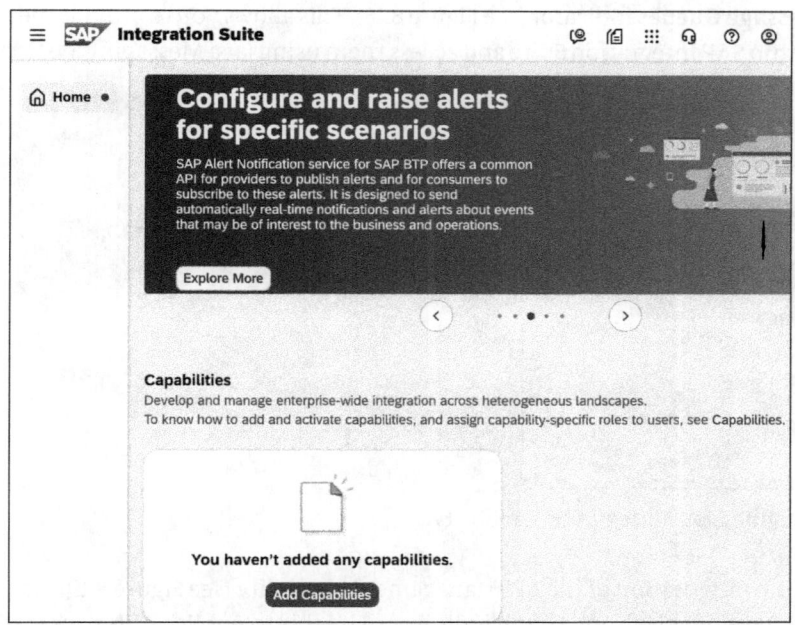

Figure 8.16 Add Capabilities to SAP Integration Suite

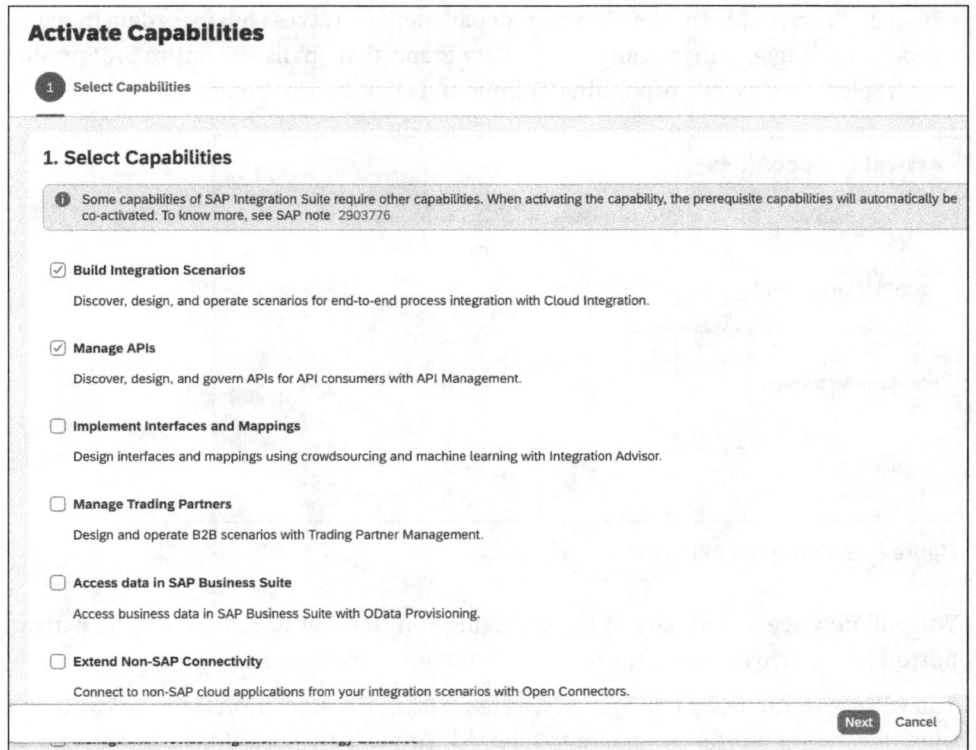

Figure 8.17 Select Capabilities

Activate the **Message Queues** indicator (see Figure 8.18). This allows you to provide message queues within SAP Integration Suite and access them using Java Messaging System (JMS). Then click the **Next** button.

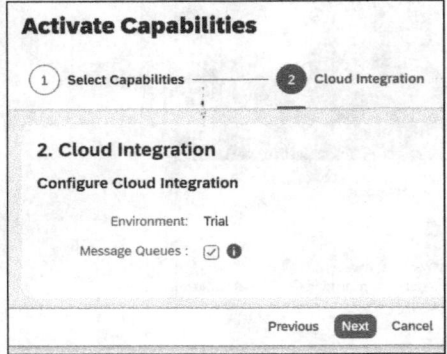

Figure 8.18 Configure Cloud Integration Capability

Proceed with the configuration of the API Management capability (see Figure 8.19). Activate the **Enable Developer Hub** and **Graph** indicators. Use this to publish APIs packaged in products and make them available to the development department. Graph is a new and unified API for SAP that uses modern open standards such as OData V4 and GraphQL. With Graph, the development department can access business data managed by SAP in a single, semantically linked data graph that spans the entire SAP product range. Select the two corresponding options and click the **Next** button.

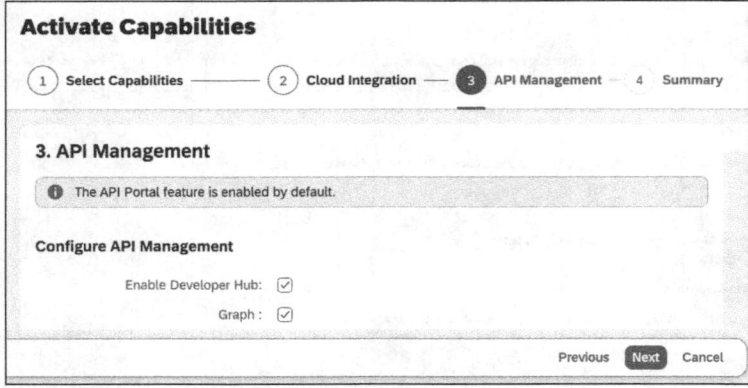

Figure 8.19 Configure API Management

You will now see a **Summary** of the configuration (see Figure 8.20). Click the **Activate** button to confirm and start the process of providing the capabilities.

You will see the activation progress (see Figure 8.21). The activation takes up to 60 minutes, depending on the components selected. You will also be informed of any errors that occur.

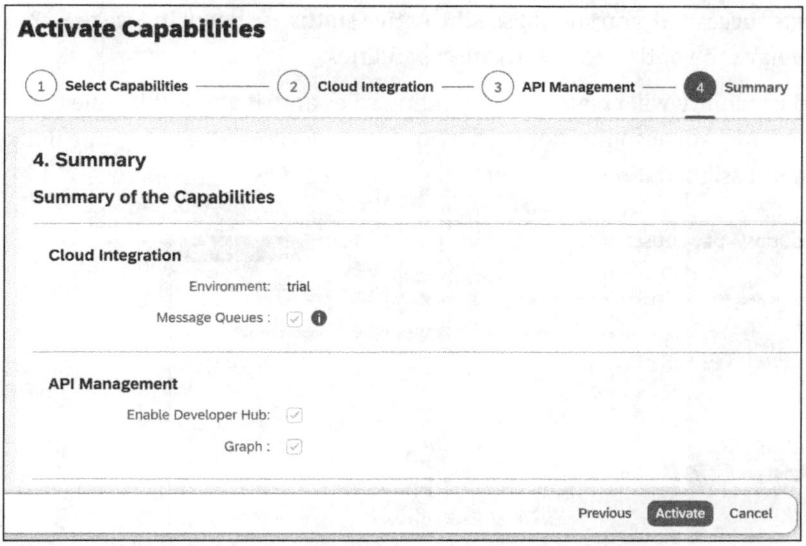

8.4 Activating Capabilities

Figure 8.20 Configuration Summary

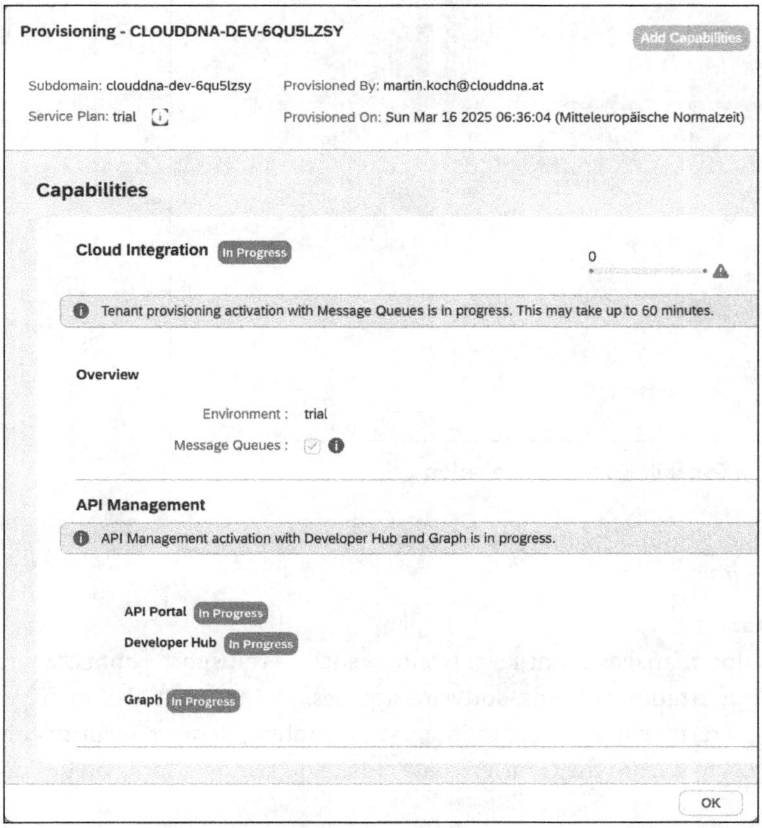

Figure 8.21 Installation Progress

If activation was successful, you should see the **Active** status as shown in Figure 8.22. At this point, you have the option to deactivate capabilities.

Each activated capability will create corresponding roles and, if applicable, role collections in the SAP BTP subaccount. Role collections are collections of roles, but unlike roles, they can be assigned directly to users.

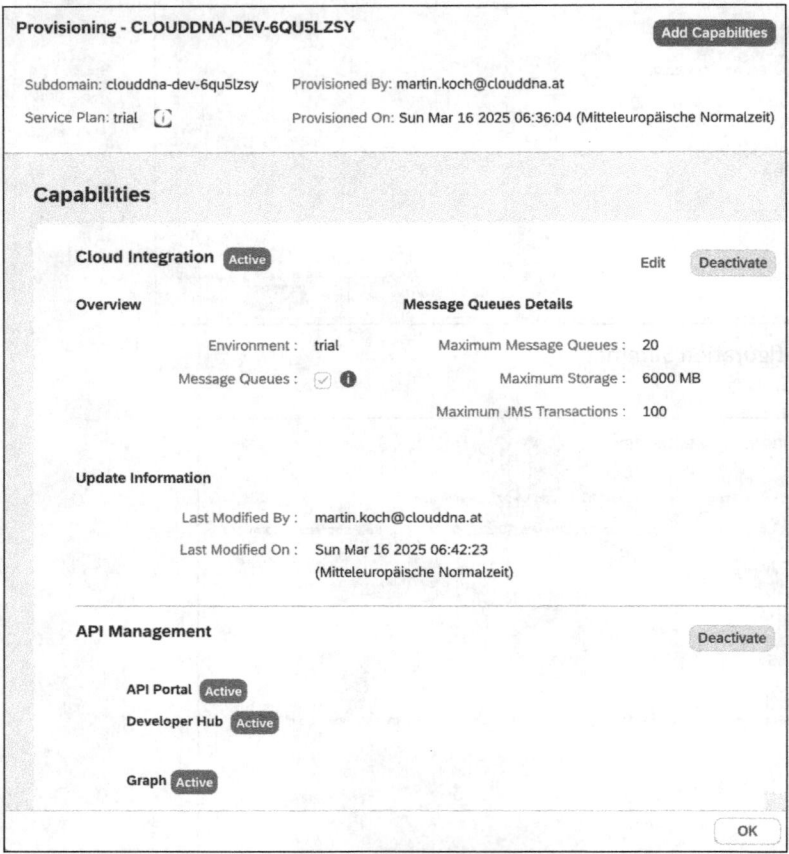

Figure 8.22 Status of Capabilities After Installation

When the Cloud Integration capability is activated, the following role collections are created (see Figure 8.23):

- PI_Administrator
  This role collection manages client-level settings, such as transport, connection to SAP Process Orchestration systems, software updates, and more. It also manages access policies to restrict user access to integration content, deploys security content, deletes messages from the transient data store, and removes locks on design-time artifacts.

- `PI_Business_Expert`
  You can also copy standard packages, monitor integration flows, edit the trace configuration, and change the protocol levels and the archiving configuration. You can display the entries in the data store, check the usage of the integration resources, and edit B2B partner profiles and contacts.
- `PI_Read_Only`
  This allows you to monitor integration flows, view packages and package artifacts in the design workspace, and display entries in the datastore, access policies, B2B partner profiles, and agreements, as well as locks on design-time artifacts.
- `PI_Integration_Developer`
  With this role collection, you can perform the tasks of `PI_Read_Only` and `PI_Business_Expert`. You can create, edit, import, export, and delete packages with their artifacts and you can deploy artifacts.

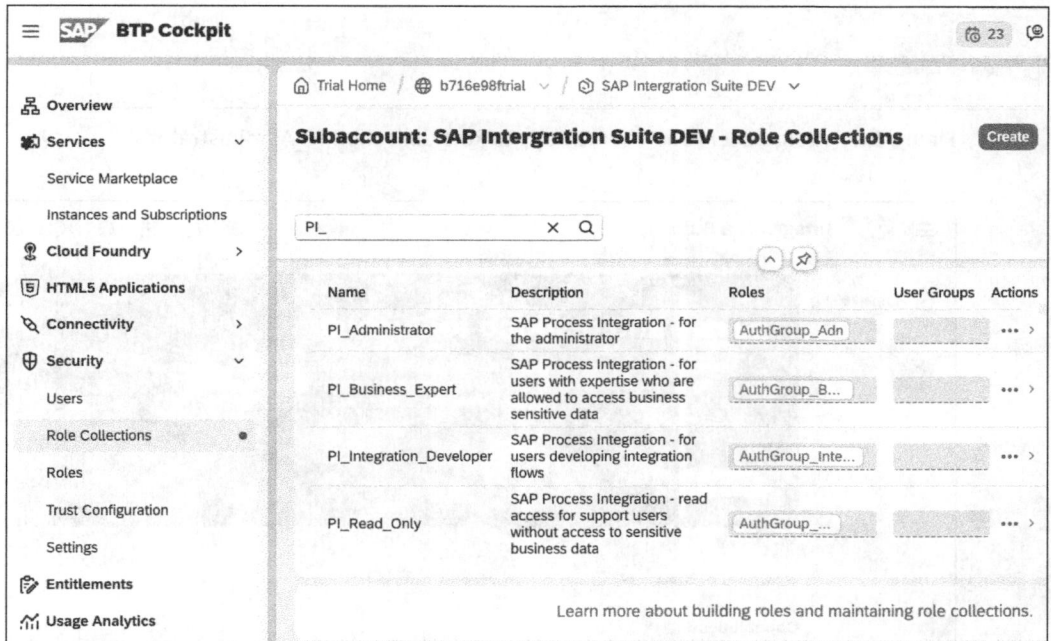

Figure 8.23 Check Role Collections

Navigate to the role collection details to assign **Users** or **User Groups** (see Figure 8.24).

After assigning the role collection to your user, you must reopen SAP Integration Suite and authenticate yourself. This will ensure the assignment is resolved correctly at runtime, and you will then see the menu entries displayed in Figure 8.25 in the side menu.

8   Activating and Setting Up SAP Integration Suite

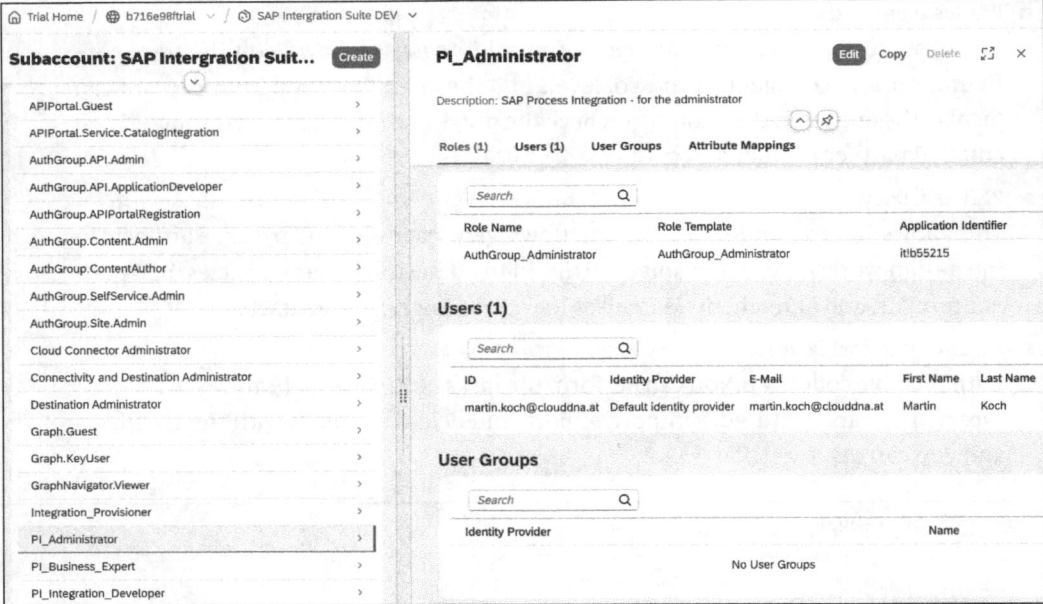

Figure 8.24 Assign Users and User Groups to Role Collection PI_Administrator

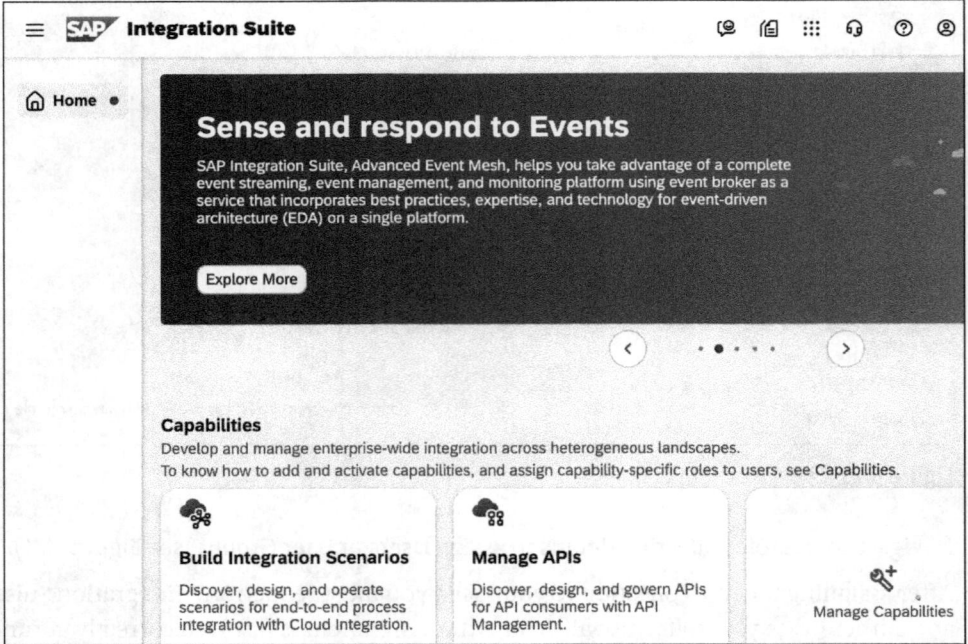

Figure 8.25 Open SAP Integration Suite

8.5 Instantiating the SAP Process Integration Runtime

Send messages to Cloud Integration for processing while the interfaces are running by creating an SAP Process Integration runtime service instance. In the subaccount's SAP BTP cockpit, go to the **Services • Service Marketplace** path in the side menu (see Figure 8.26). Use the search field or scroll to find the **SAP Process Integration Runtime** option. Click the ellipsis button in the tile, then click **Create**.

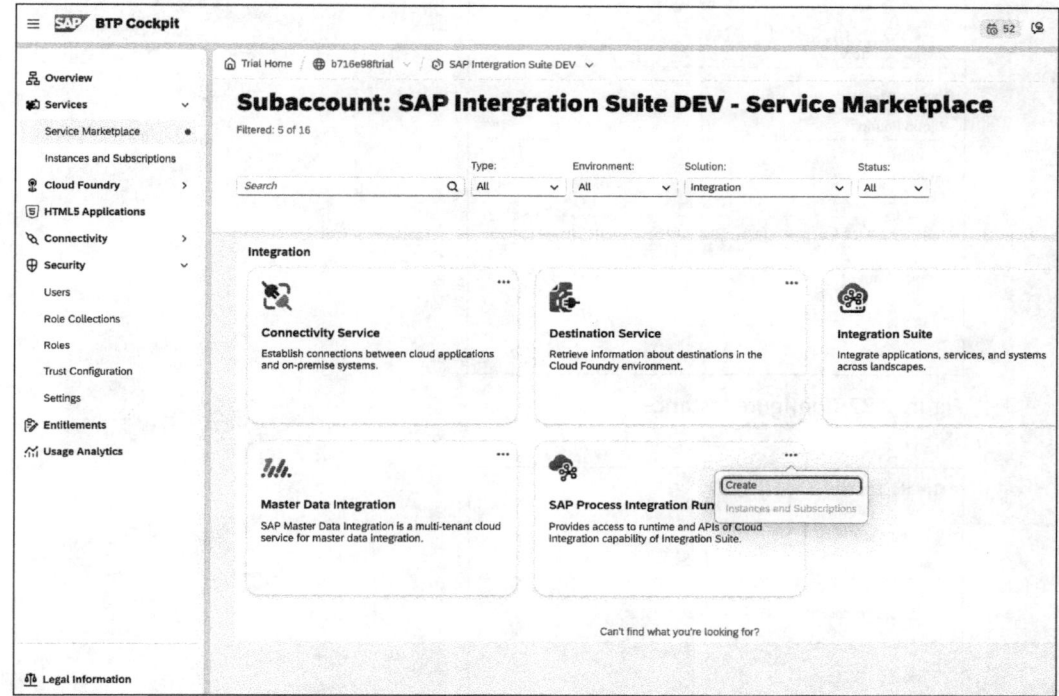

Figure 8.26 Create SAP Process Integration Runtime Service Instance

Configure the SAP Process Integration runtime service instance. The service has already been selected correctly in Figure 8.27: Select **integration-flow** in the **Plan** field and select **Cloud Foundry** in the **Runtime Environment** field. Then select a **Space**. A space was not deliberately created in advance here, so you must go through the entire process. Click the **Create a Space** link in the infobox below the **Space** field.

Enter a space name in the **Create Space** field (see Figure 8.28). You are not required to adhere to any naming conventions from SAP. You also can select the space roles assigned to the user who creates the space. Click the **Create** button.

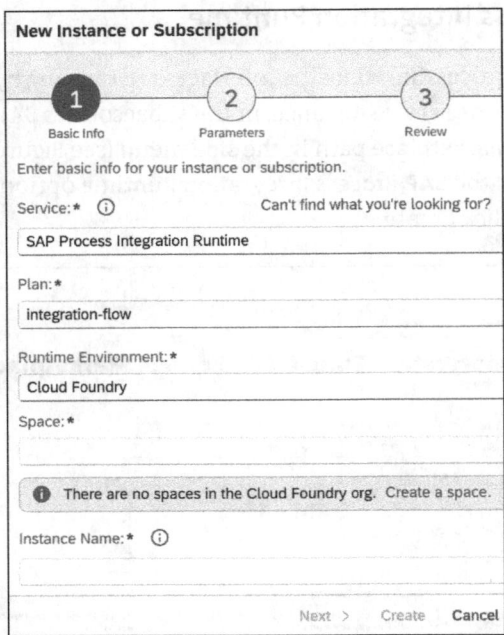

Figure 8.27 Configure Instance

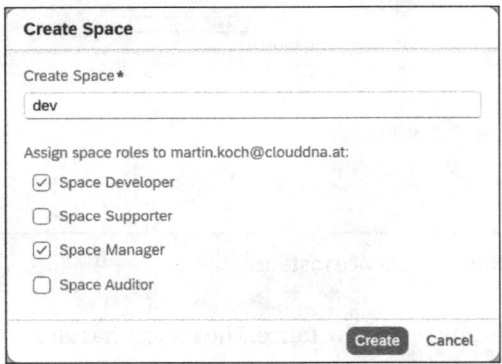

Figure 8.28 Creating Cloud Foundry Space

Next, select the space that has just been created in the dialog for creating the SAP Process Integration service instance (see Figure 8.29). Enter an instance name in the **Instance Name** field; choose a meaningful name. Then click **Next**.

You will see the parameters of the service instance in the next step. No adjustments are necessary at this point. As shown in Figure 8.30, the **ESBMessaging.send** role and the **Client Credentials** grant type have been assigned to the service instance. You can assign the role to the sender later in iFlows. Now click **Next**.

8.5 Instantiating the SAP Process Integration Runtime

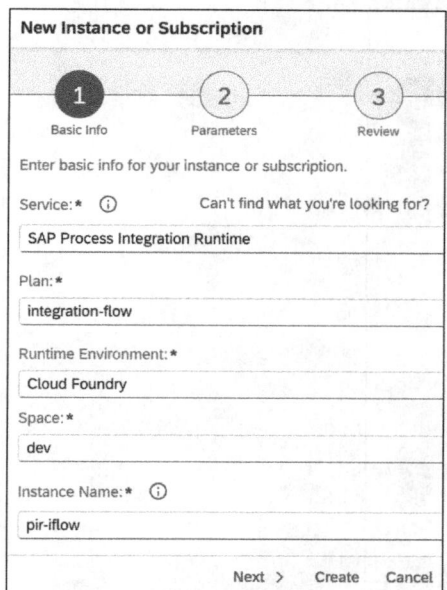

Figure 8.29 Configure Instance

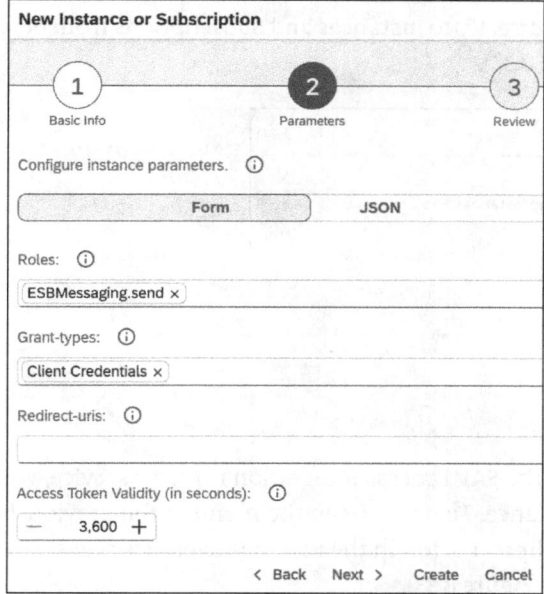

Figure 8.30 Check Parameters

You will now see a final summary of your settings (see Figure 8.31). Confirm these by clicking the **Create** button.

8   Activating and Setting Up SAP Integration Suite

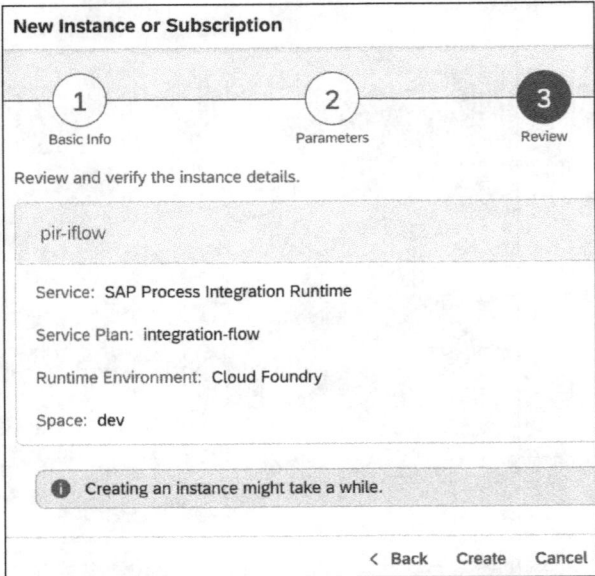

Figure 8.31 Check Settings

The service instance will be created at this point. This step can take up to a minute, as experience has shown. You can jump directly to **Instances and Subscriptions** from here via the corresponding link (see Figure 8.32).

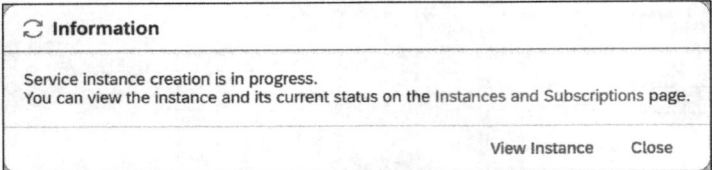

Figure 8.32 Check Installation Progress

8.6   Create Service Key

After creating the service instance of the SAP Process Integration runtime service, you must create a service key for this instance. To do so, open the menu of the previously created instance by clicking on the ellipsis button in the instance overview and selecting the **Create Service Key** option (see Figure 8.33).

You must assign a unique **Service Key Name**. Click the **Create** button to initiate the creation of the service key (see Figure 8.34).

8.6 Create Service Key

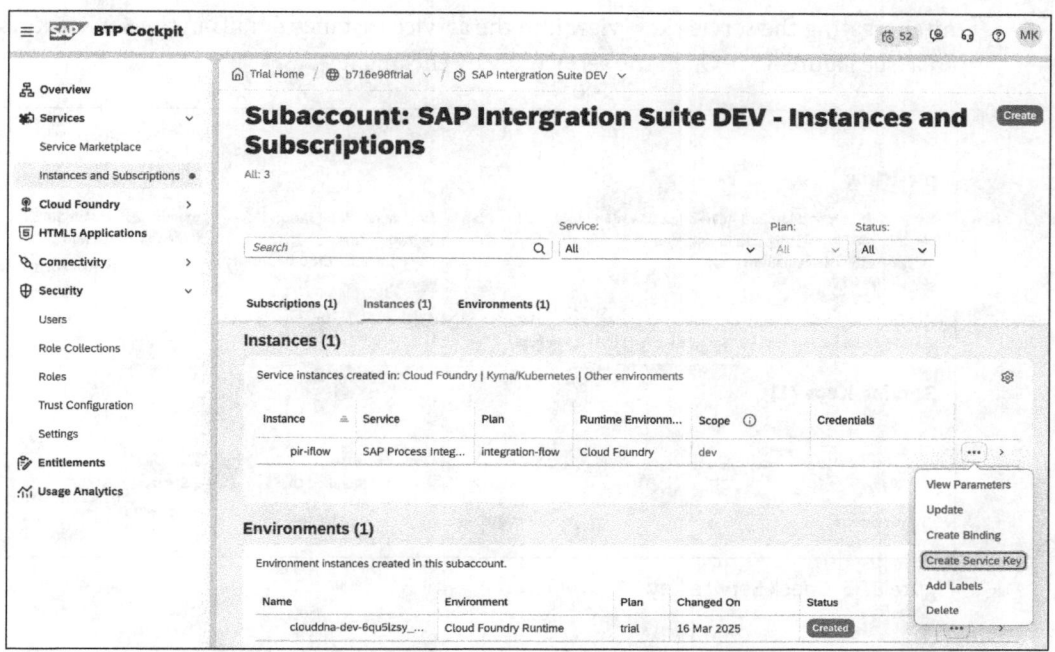

Figure 8.33 Create Service Key

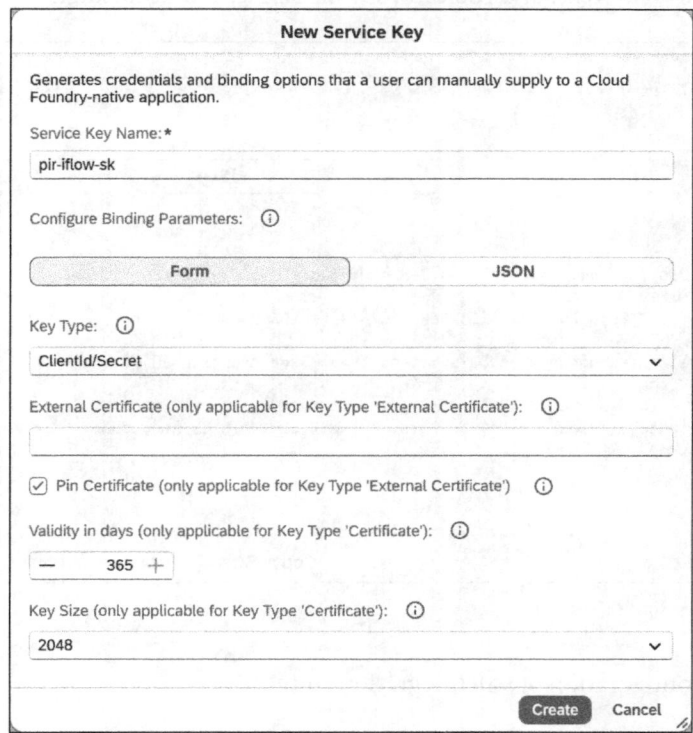

Figure 8.34 Configure Service Key

After creating the service key, view it in the service instance details in the **Service Keys** area (see Figure 8.35). Open the service key by clicking it.

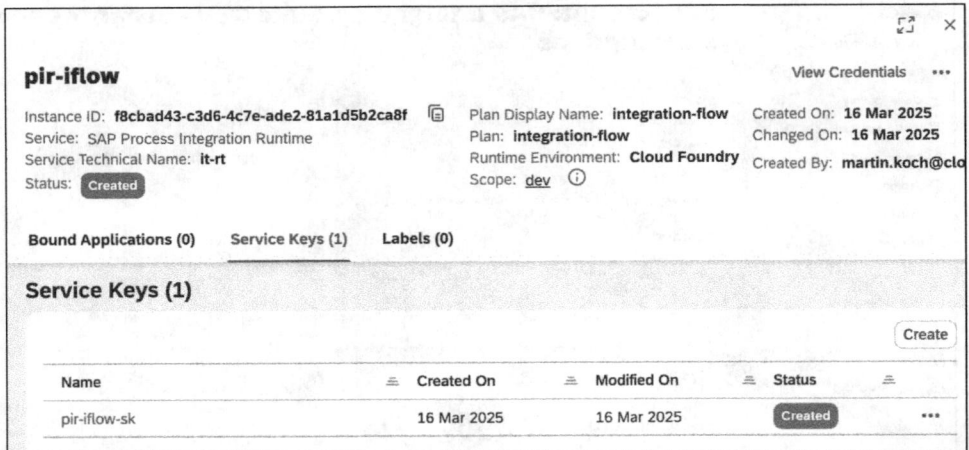

Figure 8.35 Check Service Key

Figure 8.36 clearly shows that the service key is in JSON format. It contains all the details that a sender system needs to authenticate itself using OAuth. These include the `clientid`, `clientsecret`, `url`, and `tokenurl`. You can view the service key again later.

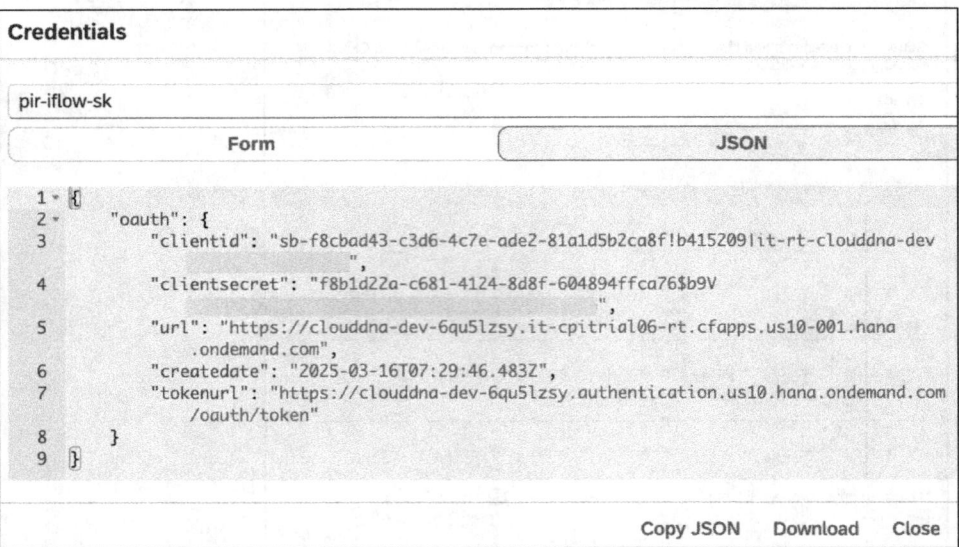

Figure 8.36 Check Service Key

This finalizes the basic configuration of SAP Integration Suite.

8.7 Summary

This chapter is your key to unlocking a world of possibilities with SAP Integration Suite! It's your step-by-step guide to a smooth and seamless setup for cloud-based integration scenarios. You are now ready to dive into the exciting world of cloud-based integration, where the possibilities are endless. This chapter started by giving you a comprehensive overview of SAP Integration Suite's functions and history (Section 8.1). You learned about its role in modern enterprise integration and how it's evolved from previous SAP integration solutions.

Then, we jumped into the technical setup, starting with creating a subaccount and assigning entitlements (Section 8.2). This step is crucial for provisioning SAP Integration Suite within SAP BTP. Once the subaccount was set up, the next step was creating a subscription (Section 8.3) to unlock the suite's amazing functionalities.

With the subscription active, you then activated the required capabilities (Section 8.4), such as Cloud Integration, API Management, Open Connectors, and Event Mesh, depending on your specific integration needs. To enable integration flows and message processing, you had to instantiate the SAP Process Integration runtime service (Section 8.5). To finalize the setup, you created a service key (Section 8.6), which provides authentication and programmatic access to the SAP Integration Suite services.

Chapter 9
Activating and Setting Up SAP Cloud Transport Management for SAP Integration Suite

SAP Cloud Transport Management facilitates the management of software deliverables between accounts in disparate environments (e.g., Cloud Foundry, ABAP, and Neo) by transporting these deliverables across varying runtimes. This includes both application artifacts and their respective application-specific content.

SAP Cloud Transport Management ensures transparency in terms of the audit trail of changes, meaning that you can track which changes were made in your production environment, by whom, and when. The service also enables a separation of interests: A developer of an application or SAP cloud content artifacts can initiate the transport of changes from the development environment, while importing into the test and production environment is carried out by a central operations team.

These features underscore the pivotal role of SAP Cloud Transport Management within the broader context of SAP Integration Suite. Consider a complex system landscape with numerous interfaces or iFlows between disparate systems. The standard transport route of SAP Integration Suite, involving file export from the development system and subsequent import into the test and productive system, carries the risk of a potential source of error. Experience has shown that incorrect imports can occur quickly—for example, by importing an older file by mistake or by not taking important dependencies into account.

Using SAP Cloud Transport Management for cloud integration artifacts solves this problem by automating and centralizing the entire transport process. This approach mitigates human error and ensures consistent, traceable distribution of artifacts across all environments.

In addition, SAP Cloud Transport Management offers a clear and flexible approach to mapping complex transport routes and processes. This significantly simplifies the administration of large system landscapes and ensures faster, more efficient, and more secure deployments.

As the setup of SAP Cloud Transport Management is not entirely trivial and there is currently no booster available, this chapter provides detailed step-by-step instructions

9   Activating and Setting Up SAP Cloud Transport Management for SAP Integration Suite

first on how to install the service and then on how to configure it optimally. We also address common issues and best practices to facilitate a seamless integration of the service into your operations.

To begin, in Section 9.1, we explain how to activate the service. Then, in Section 9.2, we show you how to provide the service in test and productive instances. In Section 9.3, we will focus on setting up a system landscape within SAP Cloud Transport Management. This is followed by an explanation of how to add the SAP Content Agent service to the respective subaccount in Section 9.4. Finally, in chapter Section 9.5, we will show you how to configure SAP Cloud Transport Management within SAP Integration Suite.

9.1   Activating SAP Cloud Transport Management

We recommend that you install the Cloud Transport Management Service in a separate subaccount. Although this is not strictly necessary, our experience has shown that it streamlines operations. From a technical standpoint, utilizing a subaccount does not incur any license costs beyond those associated with the installed services. The first step is to create a subaccount, as shown in Figure 9.1. Be sure to assign an expressive **Display Name** for it. SAP Cloud Transport Management is exclusively available in multicloud environments. Therefore, it's necessary to select a hyperscaler and an associated data center.

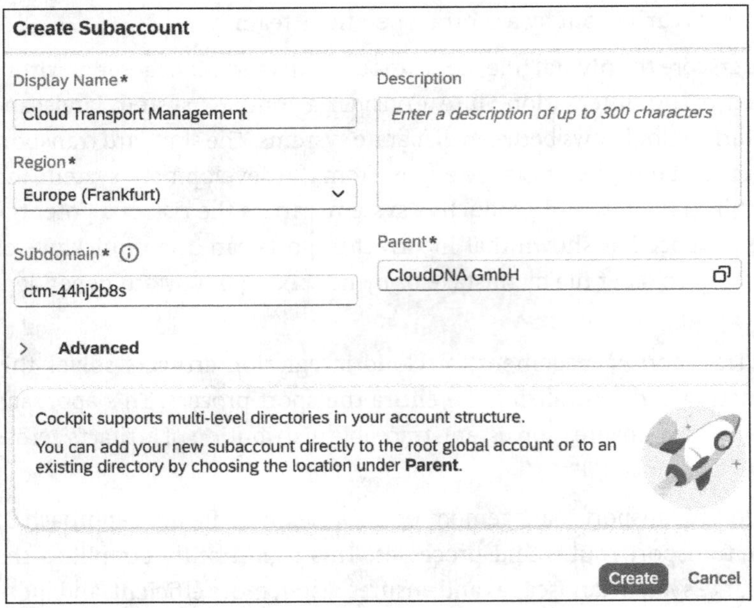

Figure 9.1 Create Subaccount

9.1 Activating SAP Cloud Transport Management

In addition, it is necessary to establish a separate account for the SAP Content Agent service. SAP Content Agent is a service based on Cloud Foundry that is included in your overall SAP BTP contract. SAP Content Agent can be integrated with SAP Cloud Transport Management. Content with its dependencies and related content can be exported between subaccounts. The user interface will display the content details required for transport activities and the activities performed.

For a three-tier system landscape of SAP Integration Suite, it is recommended to have five subaccounts, as illustrated in Figure 9.2.

Name	Type	Environment	Provider	Region	Changed On
∨ ⊕ CloudDNA GmbH	Global Account				4 Dec 2024, 01:11:57 (...
∨ ☐ SAP Integration Suite	Directory				2 Apr 2025, 19:43:30 (...
Cloud Transport Management	Subaccount	Multi-Environment	Amazon Web Services (AWS)	Europe (Frankfurt)	2 Apr 2025, 19:43:39 (...
Content Agent	Subaccount	Multi-Environment	Amazon Web Services (AWS)	Europe (Frankfurt)	2 Apr 2025, 19:43:52 (...
SAP Integration Suite DEV	Subaccount	Multi-Environment	Amazon Web Services (AWS)	Europe (Frankfurt)	2 Apr 2025, 19:44:05 (...
SAP Integration Suite PROD	Subaccount	Multi-Environment	Amazon Web Services (AWS)	Europe (Frankfurt)	2 Apr 2025, 19:44:10 (...
SAP Integration Suite TEST	Subaccount	Multi-Environment	Amazon Web Services (AWS)	Europe (Frankfurt)	2 Apr 2025, 19:44:15 (...

Figure 9.2 Subaccounts

In the next step, assign the corresponding entitlements to the SAP Cloud Transport Management subaccount. To do so, first navigate to the **Entitlements • Entity Assignments** section within the SAP BTP cockpit for the global account. Then, click the **Edit** button, followed by clicking the **Add Service Plans** option (see Figure 9.3).

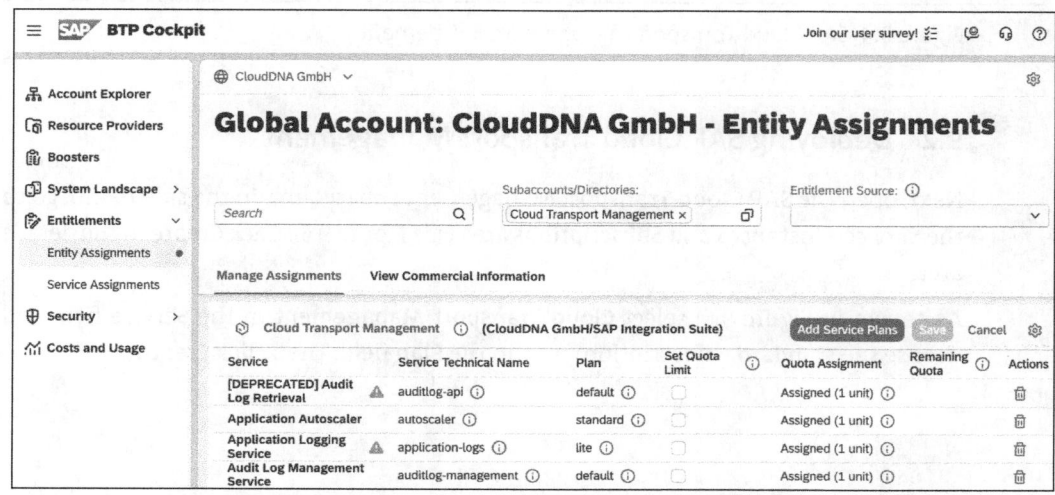

Figure 9.3 Add Entitlements

351

9 Activating and Setting Up SAP Cloud Transport Management for SAP Integration Suite

Select the **Cloud Transport Management** entitlement, as shown in Figure 9.4, and then select the **standard** and **standard (Application)** service plans. Finally, save the assignment of the service plans to the subaccount.

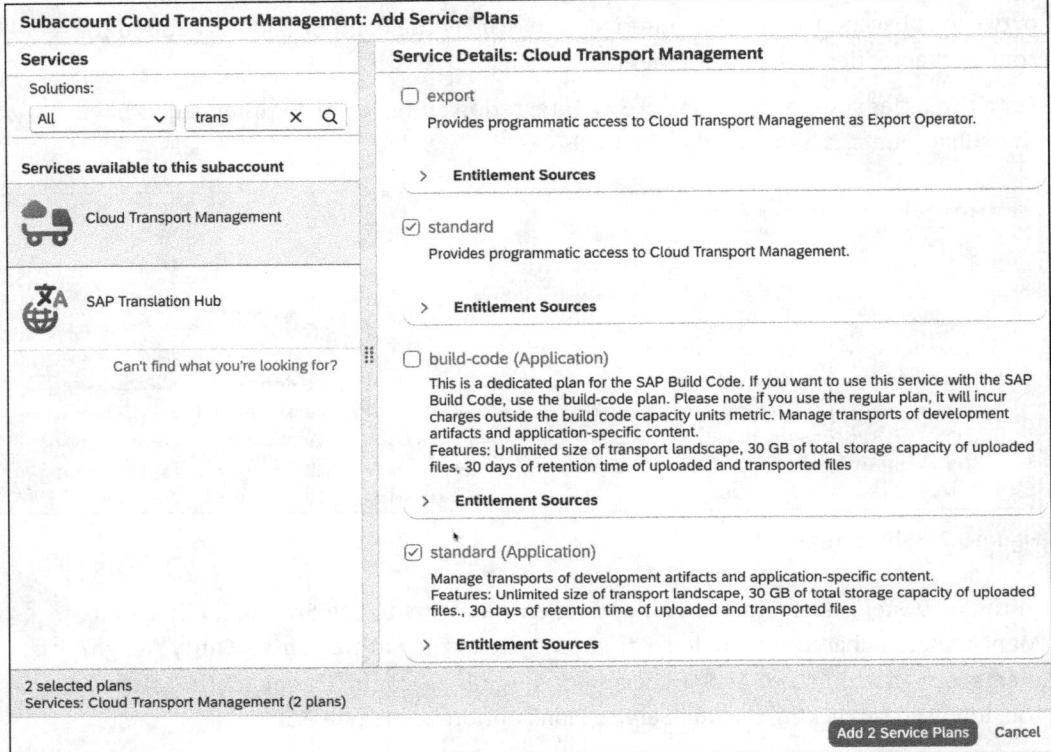

Figure 9.4 SAP Cloud Transport Management Entitlement

9.2 Deploying SAP Cloud Transport Management

Next, open the SAP Cloud Transport Management subaccount. In the side menu, go to the **Service • Instances and Subscriptions** area (see Figure 9.5). Click **Create** in the details area.

As shown in Figure 9.6, select **Cloud Transport Management** in the **Service** field and choose the **standard** (subscription) plan in the **Plan** field. Then click **Create**.

9.2 Deploying SAP Cloud Transport Management

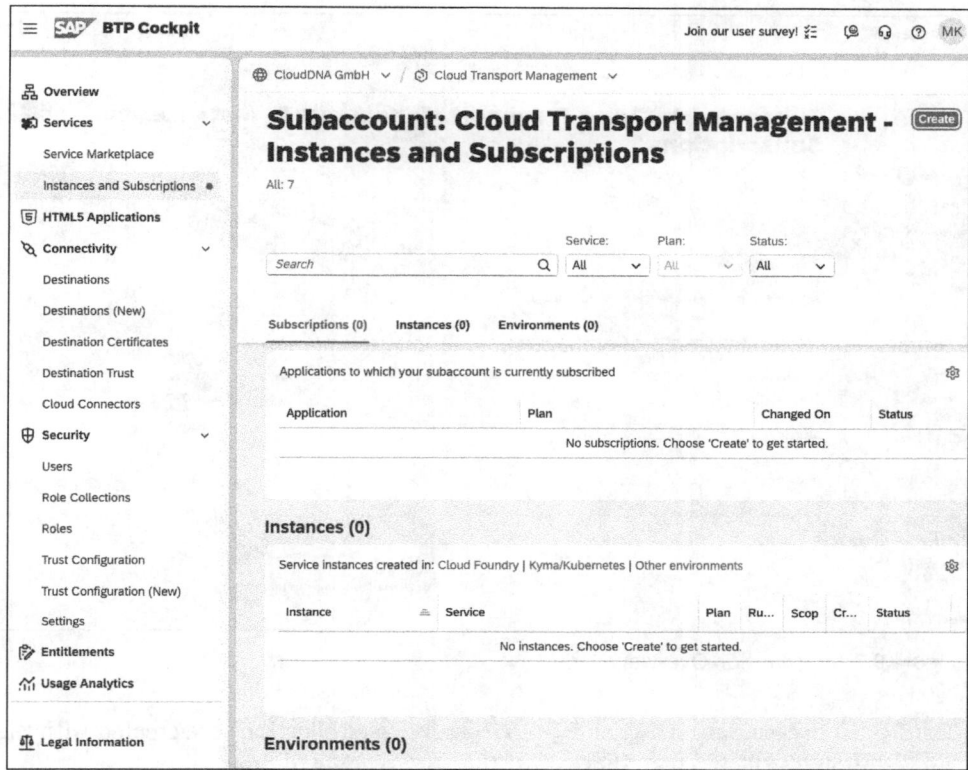

Figure 9.5 Subaccount Instances and Subscriptions

Figure 9.6 Create New Subscription

Our experience shows that creating the subscription takes up to a minute. Once the subscription is successfully created, you'll see the subscription named **Cloud Transport Management** and the status set to **Subscribed**, as shown in Figure 9.7.

353

9   Activating and Setting Up SAP Cloud Transport Management for SAP Integration Suite

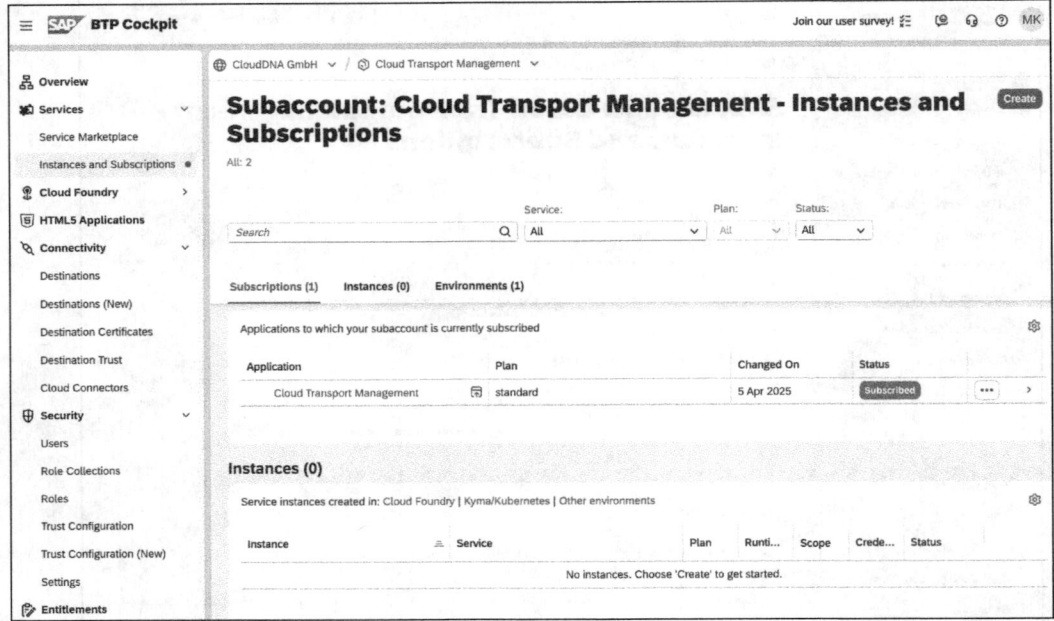

Figure 9.7 Subscription Overview

The `TMS_LandscapeOperator_RC` and `TMS_Viewer_RC` role collections are created with the subscription (see Figure 9.8). These must then be assigned to users.

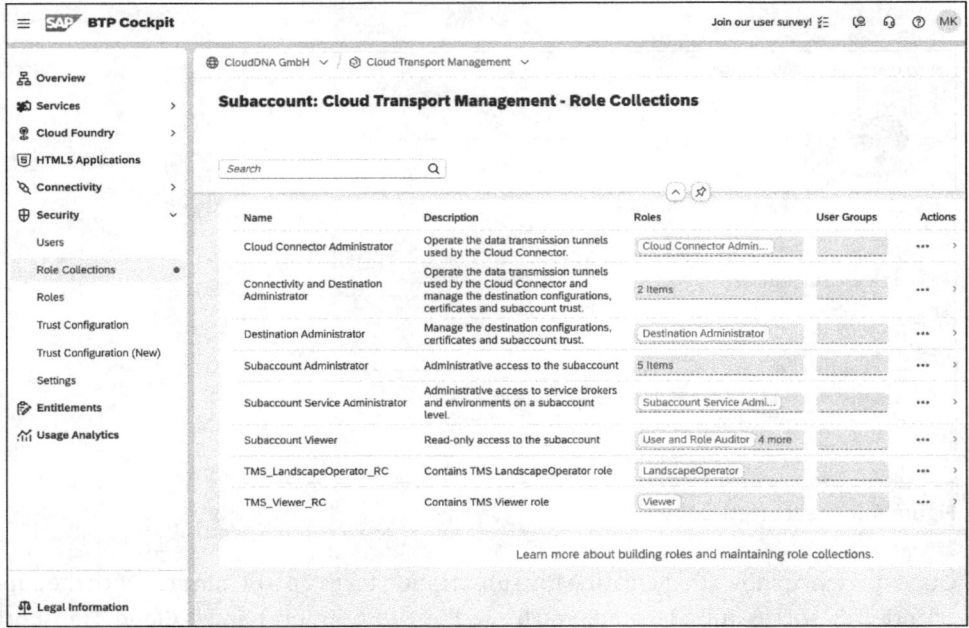

Figure 9.8 SAP Cloud Transport Management Role Collections

9.2 Deploying SAP Cloud Transport Management

Open the **TMS_LandscapeOperator_RC** role collection and switch to edit mode (see Figure 9.9). Then assign the desired users to the role collection and click **Save**.

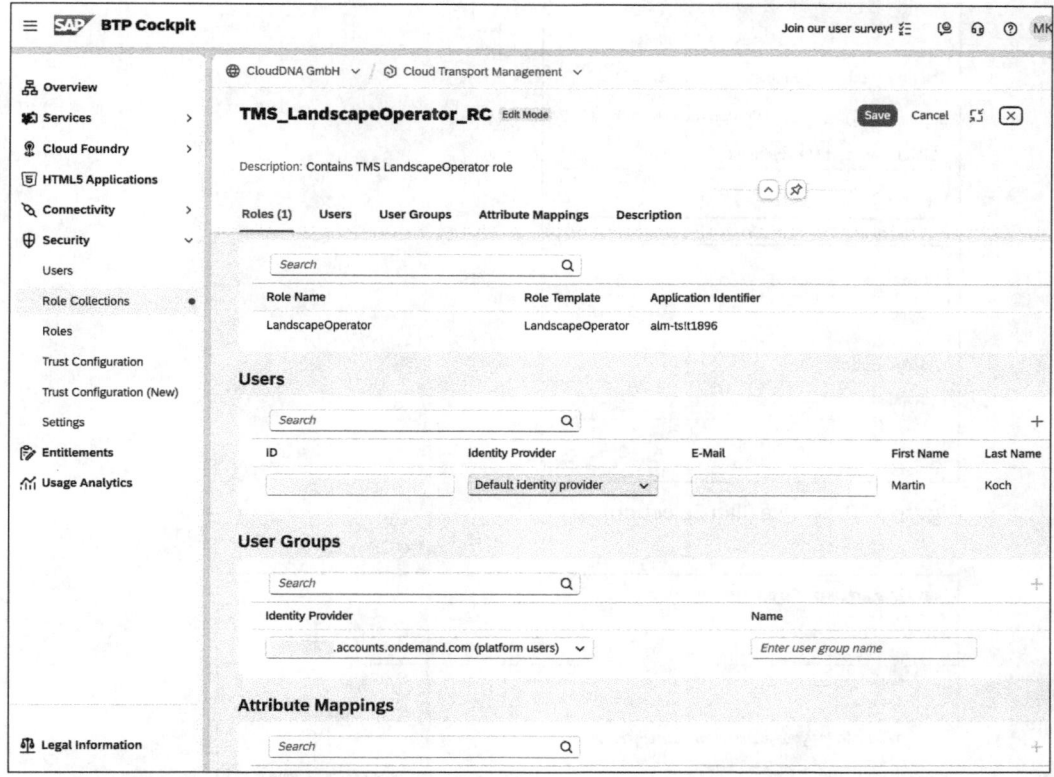

Figure 9.9 User Assignment

Next, create a service instance. Navigate to the **Service • Instances and Subscriptions** area in the side menu (see Figure 9.5). Click **Create** in the details area. As shown in Figure 9.10, select the **Cloud Transport Management** entry in the **Service** field and the **standard (Instances)** plan in the **Plan** field.

Next, select **Cloud Foundry** in the **Runtime Environment** field. Then, select a **Space**. If no space exists, you can create a new space directly at this point. After creating the space, select it as shown in Figure 9.11. Enter a meaningful name in the **Instance Name** field. Finally, click **Next**.

9   Activating and Setting Up SAP Cloud Transport Management for SAP Integration Suite

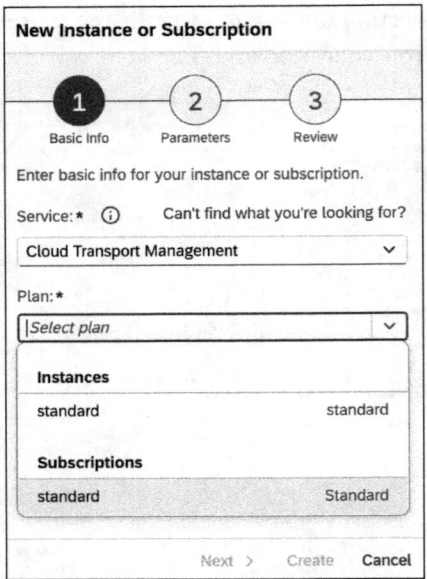

Figure 9.10 Service Plan Selection

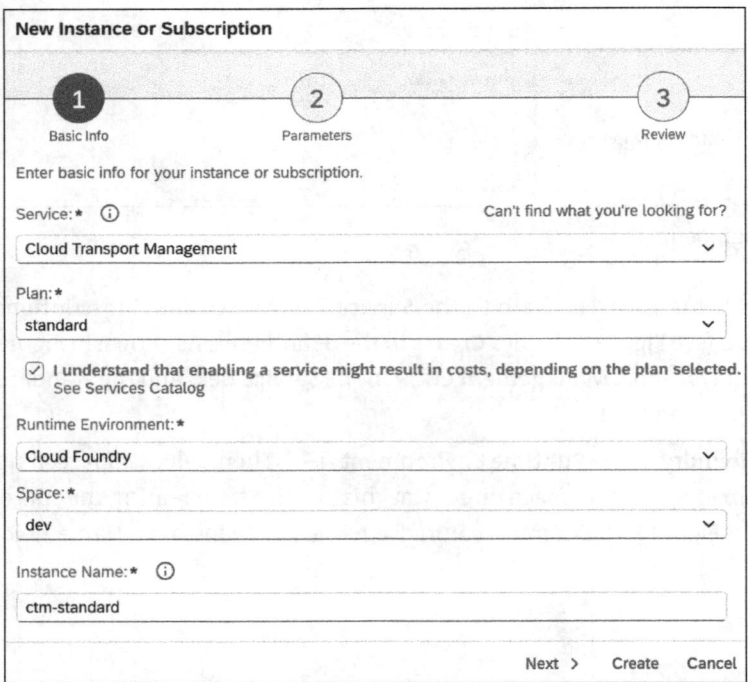

Figure 9.11 Create Service Instance and Maintain Details

9.2 Deploying SAP Cloud Transport Management

You will now see the step for maintaining the service instance parameters. No changes are necessary at this point (see Figure 9.12). Click **Next**.

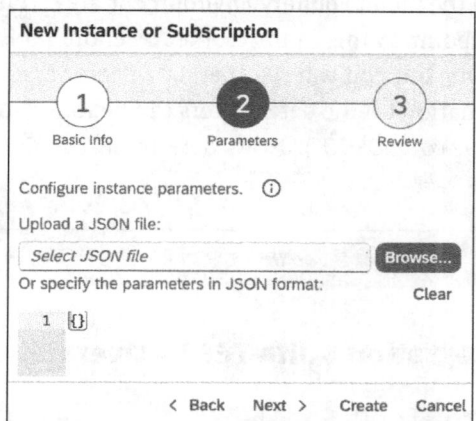

Figure 9.12 Maintain Service Instance Parameters

You will now see a summary of the settings made so far, as shown in Figure 9.13. Click **Create** to create the service instance.

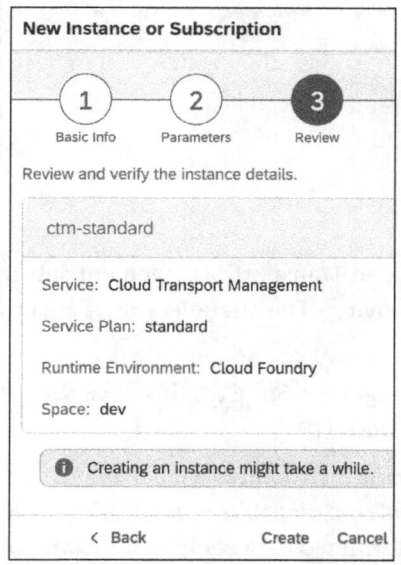

Figure 9.13 Service Instance Summary

After activation, you need to set up destinations for the deployment in the test and productive instances of SAP Integration Suite, in the subaccount subscribed to SAP

Cloud Transport Management. Open the SAP BTP cockpit of the test instance of SAP Integration Suite and navigate to the **Overview** section in the side menu (see Figure 9.14). You will see the **API Endpoint** listed in the **Cloud Foundry Environment** area. You can derive the data center from the API endpoint. In this example, the API endpoint is *https://api.cf.eu10-004.hana.ondemand.com*, and you can see that data center *eu10-004* is part of the URL. More detailed information on the data centers can be found in the official documentation (see *http://s-prs.co/v608007*). Now, determine the **Org Name** and the **Space**.

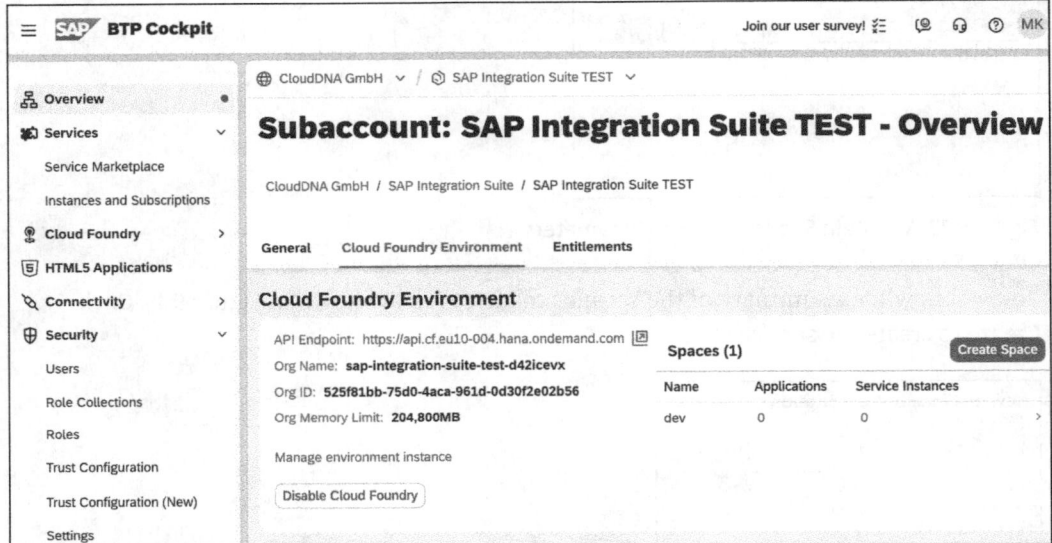

Figure 9.14 Determine API Endpoint of TEST Instance

Jump back into the SAP BTP cockpit for the SAP Cloud Transport Management subaccounts. Navigate in the side menu to the **Connectivity · Destinations (New)** area as shown in Figure 9.15. Next, click **Create**.

Create a new destination that points to the SAP Integration Suite test instance. Assign a meaningful name as shown in Figure 9.16. Select the **HTTP** type.

Enter the URL of the deploy service in the **URL** field. It is structured as follows: *https://deploy-service.cfapps.<data center>.hana.ondemand.com/slprot/<org name>/<space>/slp*. Replace <data center> with the previously determined data center—for example, eu10-004—and replace <org name> with the previously determined **Org Name** and <space> with the previously determined **Space**. In the **Authentication** field, select the **Basic Authentication** option and enter a technical user that is assigned the SpaceDeveloper role in the target subaccount in the space.

9.2 Deploying SAP Cloud Transport Management

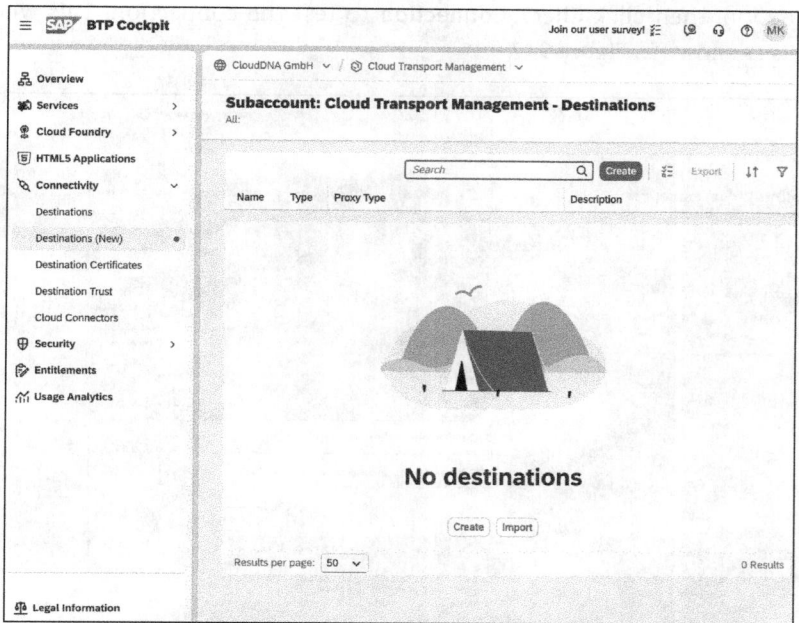

Figure 9.15 Open Destination Overview

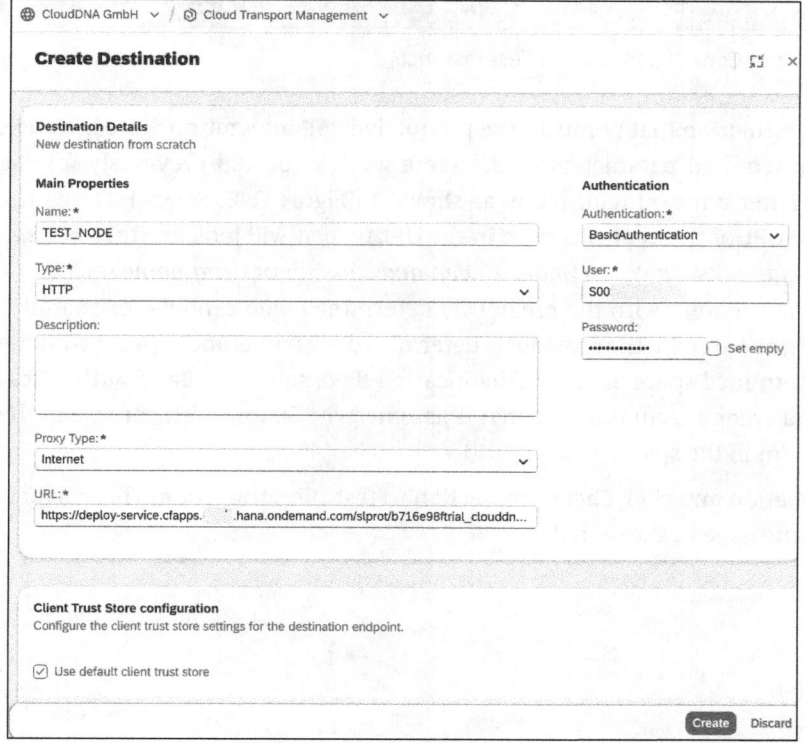

Figure 9.16 Create Destination to Test Node

9   Activating and Setting Up SAP Cloud Transport Management for SAP Integration Suite

Save the destination, then click **Check Connection** to test the connection. This will return the status as shown in Figure 9.17.

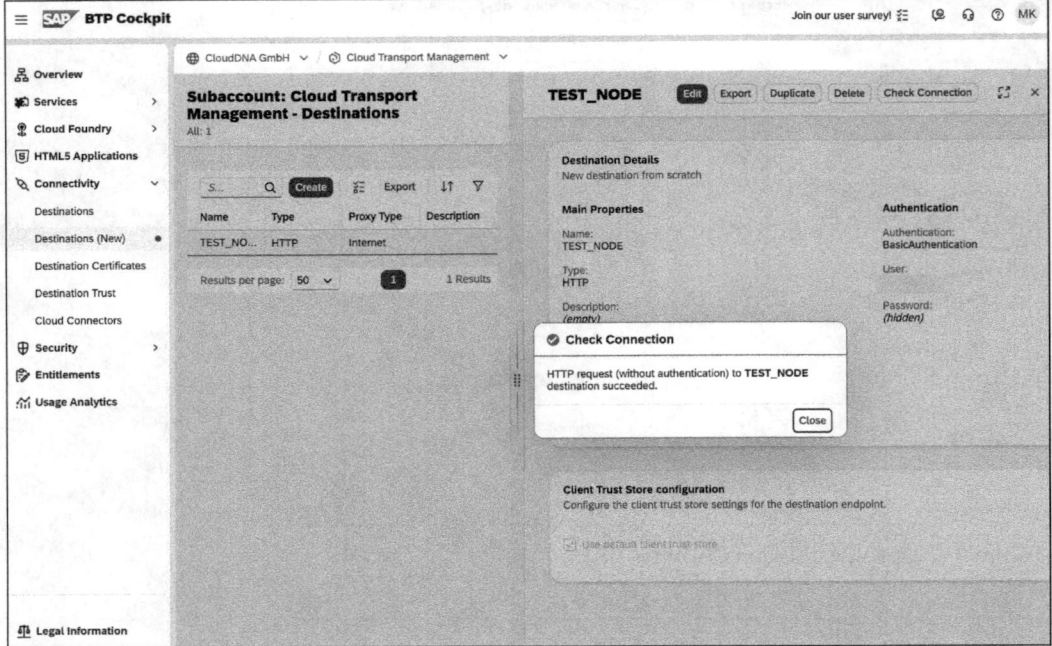

Figure 9.17 Result of Connection Test for Test Instance

Create a new destination that points to the productive SAP Integration Suite instance. Determine the required parameters in the same way as you did previously for the test instance. Enter a meaningful name as shown in Figure 9.18. Select **HTTP** as the **Type**. Enter the **URL** of the deploy service in the **URL** field. It will look like this: *https://deploy-service.cfapps.<data center>.hana.ondemand.com/slprot/<org name>/<space>/slp*. Replace <data center> with the previously determined data center—for example, eu10—and <org name> with the previously determined org name, and <space> with the previously determined space. In the **Authentication** field, select the **Basic Authentication** option and enter a technical user that is assigned the SpaceDeveloper role in the target subaccount in the space.

Save the destination and click **Check Connection** to test the connection. This will provide a success message as shown in Figure 9.19.

9.3 Creating a System Landscape in SAP Cloud Transport Management

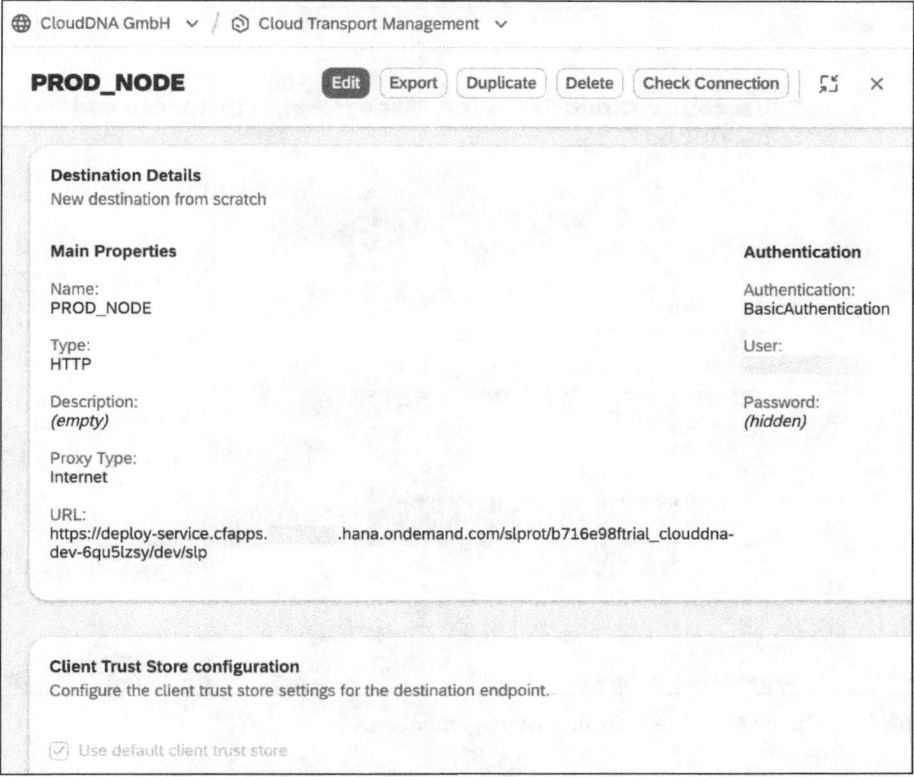

Figure 9.18 Create Destination for Production Instance

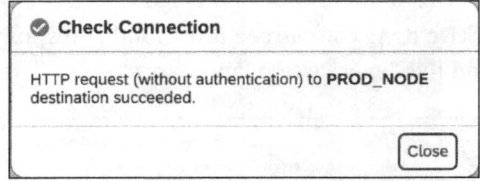

Figure 9.19 Connection Check for Production Node

9.3 Creating a System Landscape in SAP Cloud Transport Management

Next, you must create the system landscape in SAP Cloud Transport Management. To do so, navigate as shown in Figure 9.20 in the SAP BTP cockpit of the SAP Cloud Transport Management subaccount to the **Services • Instances and Subscriptions** area. You will find the SAP Cloud Transport Management subscription in the details area. Click the **Cloud Transport Management** link to open SAP Cloud Transport Management.

9   Activating and Setting Up SAP Cloud Transport Management for SAP Integration Suite

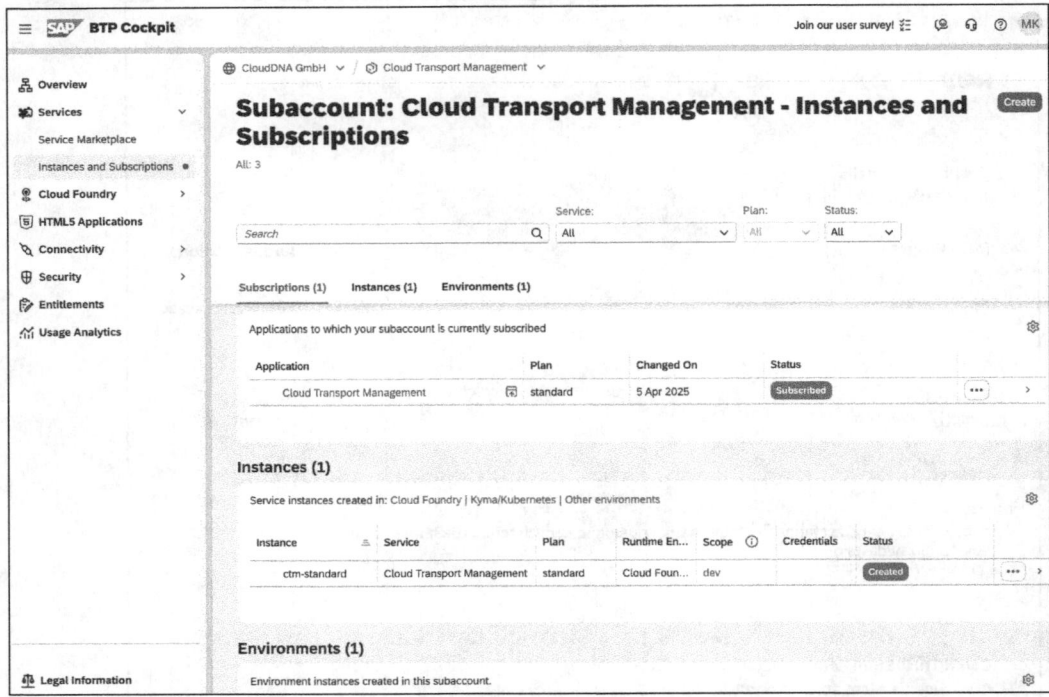

Figure 9.20 Open SAP Cloud Transport Management

You can perform this setup manually or use the Transport Landscape Wizard. We will show you how to use the Transport Landscape Wizard in this example as it is the easier option. To begin, navigate to the **Landscape Wizard** area as shown in Figure 9.21. Select the **Three-Node Landscape** template and click **Next**. As you can see, SAP Cloud Transport Management supports two-, three-, four-, and five-level system landscapes.

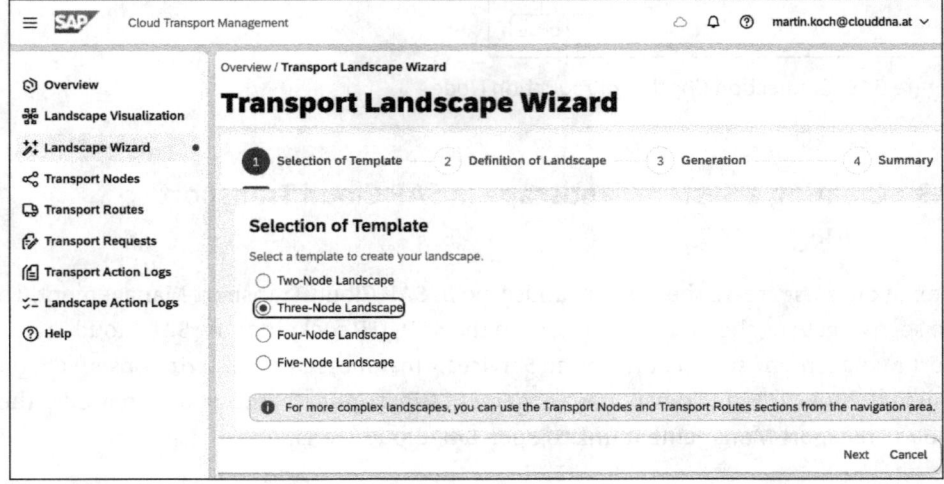

Figure 9.21 Transportation Landscape Wizard

9.3 Creating a System Landscape in SAP Cloud Transport Management

Maintain the nodes of the system landscape. Give each node a meaningful name, as shown in Figure 9.22 (e.g., use DEV, TEST, and PROD as shown in the example). Enter a suitable description in the **Description** field. Select the **Allow Upload to Node** option for all three nodes. Finally, select the **Auto** option for the **Forward Mode** parameter for all three nodes. For the TEST and PROD nodes, select the **Multi-Target Application** option for the **Content-Type** parameter. Finally, select the previously created destinations for the TEST node and the PROD node for the **Destination** parameter. The result should look like Figure 9.22.

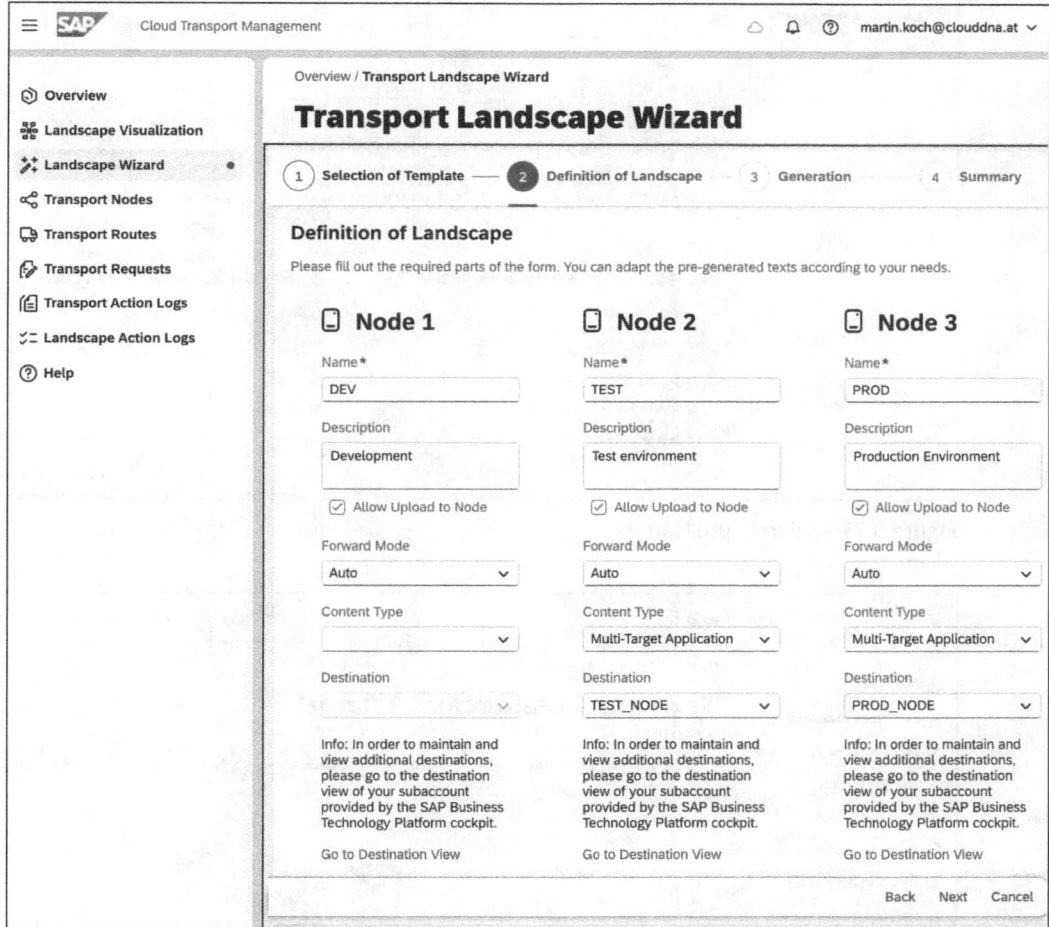

Figure 9.22 Definition of System Landscape

Scroll down and enter a descriptive name for Route 1 from the DEV to the TEST node and for Route 2 from the TEST to the PROD node, as shown in Figure 9.23. Click **Next**.

You should now see the result shown in Figure 9.24 in the **Generation** step. Click **Summary**.

9 Activating and Setting Up SAP Cloud Transport Management for SAP Integration Suite

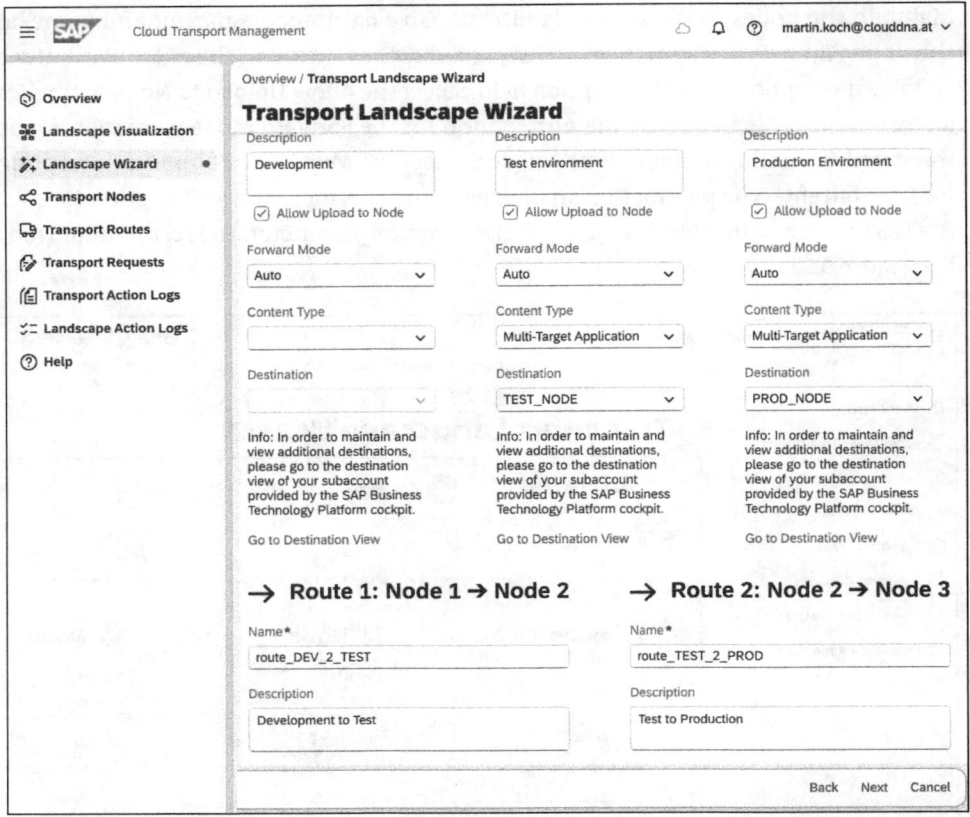

Figure 9.23 Assign Route Names

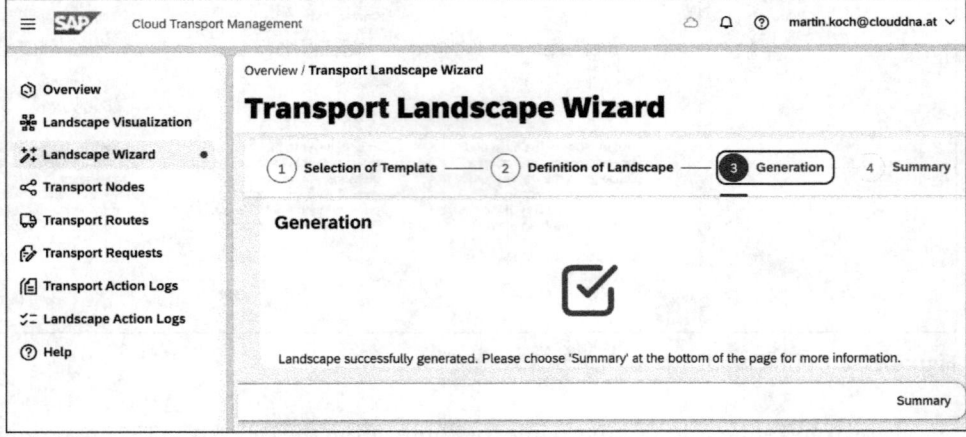

Figure 9.24 Wizard Generation Step

You are now in the final step of the wizard, as shown in Figure 9.25. You will see a summary of the configuration you have created so far. Check this summary, then click **Finish**.

9.4 Adding the SAP Content Agent Service to a Subaccount

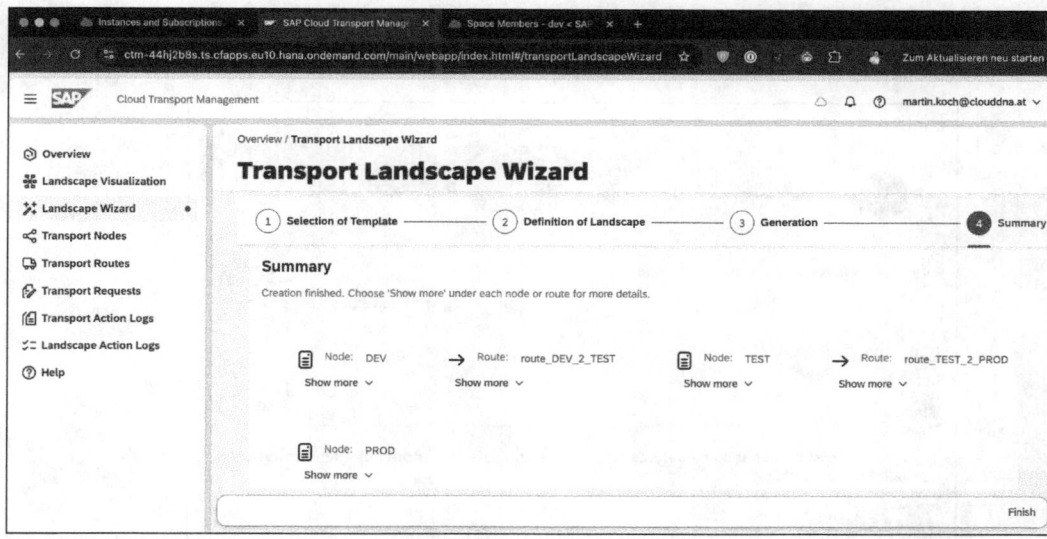

Figure 9.25 Wizard Summary Step

9.4 Adding the SAP Content Agent Service to a Subaccount

You have now completed the configuration in SAP Cloud Transport Management. Next, open the SAP BTP subaccount in which the SAP Content Agent service is to be added. Navigate to the **Overview** area as shown in Figure 9.26. Click **Enable Cloud Foundry**. You need to use the Cloud Foundry environment to add the service instances.

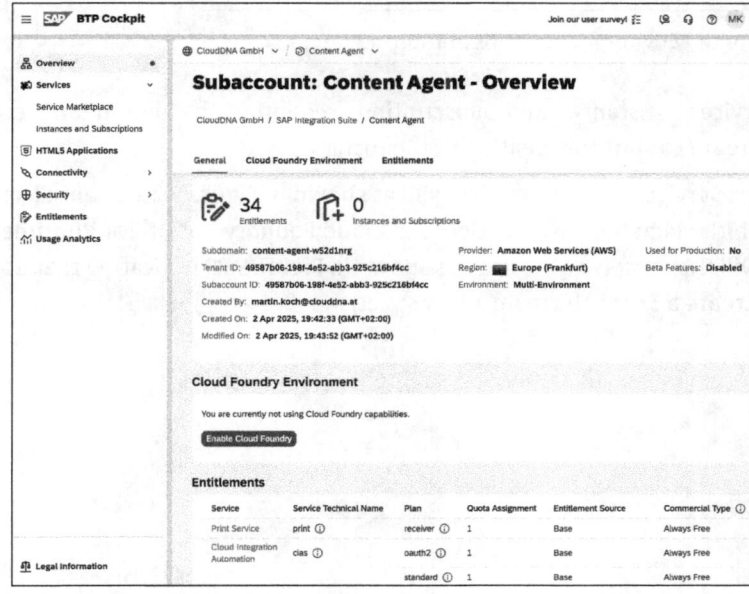

Figure 9.26 Content Agent Subaccount Overview

An **Instance Name** and an **Org. Name** are suggested. Change them if necessary. Then click **Create** (see Figure 9.27).

Figure 9.27 Cloud Foundry Environment Configuration

Navigate to the **Services • Instances and Subscriptions** section in the side menu (see Figure 9.28). Click **Create** to start the creation of the instance.

Select **Content Agent Service** from the **Service** field as shown in Figure 9.29. Then select the **standard** plan in the **Plan** field. Next, select the **Cloud Foundry** option for **Runtime Environment**. You will then receive a message as shown in Figure 9.29 indicating that no space exists. Click **Create a Space** to create a new space.

9.4 Adding the SAP Content Agent Service to a Subaccount

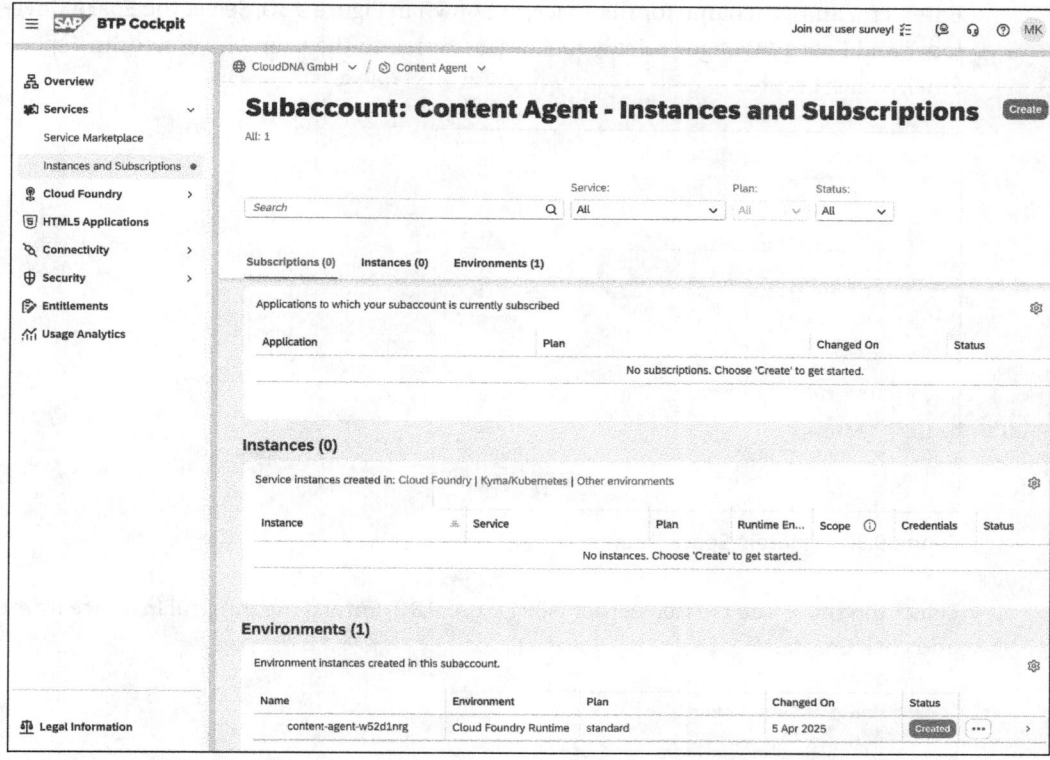

Figure 9.28 Services and Instances Overview

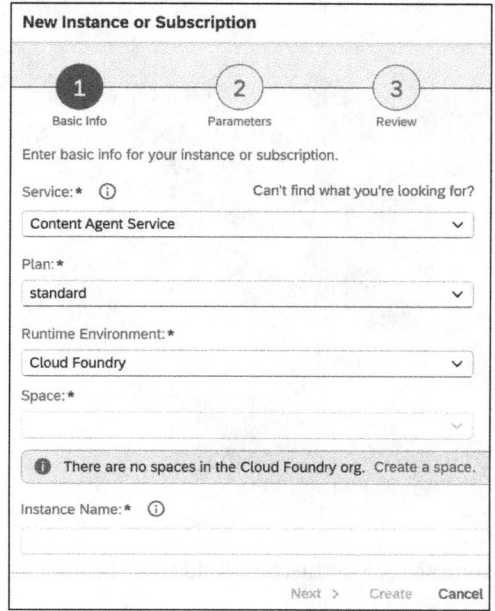

Figure 9.29 Configure SAP Content Agent Service Instance

9 Activating and Setting Up SAP Cloud Transport Management for SAP Integration Suite

Enter a meaningful name for the space, as shown in Figure 9.30. Select the **Space Developer** and **Space Manager** roles, which are assigned to the user who creates the space. Finally, click **Create**.

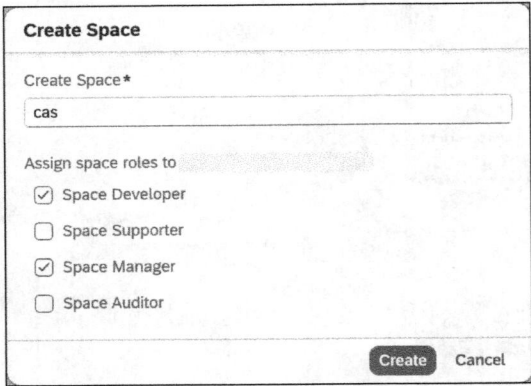

Figure 9.30 Maintain Space Details

Select the space you created earlier (see Figure 9.31). Enter a meaningful **Instance Name** and click **Create**.

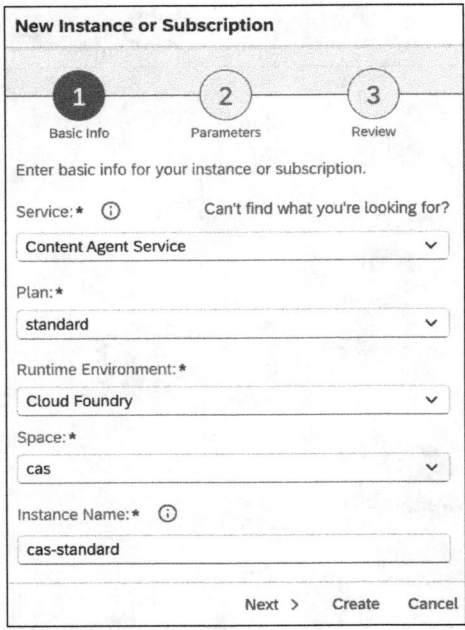

Figure 9.31 Maintain Service Details

In the next step of the wizard, select the **Assemble** role in the **roles** field (see Figure 9.32). Then click **Next**.

368

9.4 Adding the SAP Content Agent Service to a Subaccount

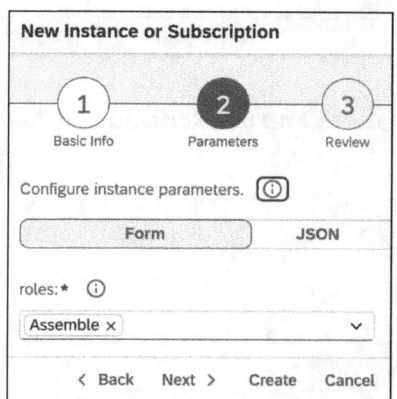

Figure 9.32 Maintain Service Instance Parameters

You will now see the configuration summary, as shown in Figure 9.33. Check this summary, then click **Create**.

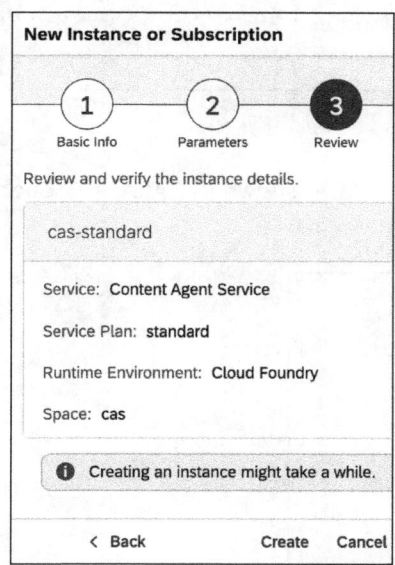

Figure 9.33 Summary of Service Instance Configuration

Creating the service is a roughly one-minute process. After the service instance has been created, you must create a service key as shown in Figure 9.34. Click **Create Service Key** in the popover menu of the service instance you just created.

9   Activating and Setting Up SAP Cloud Transport Management for SAP Integration Suite

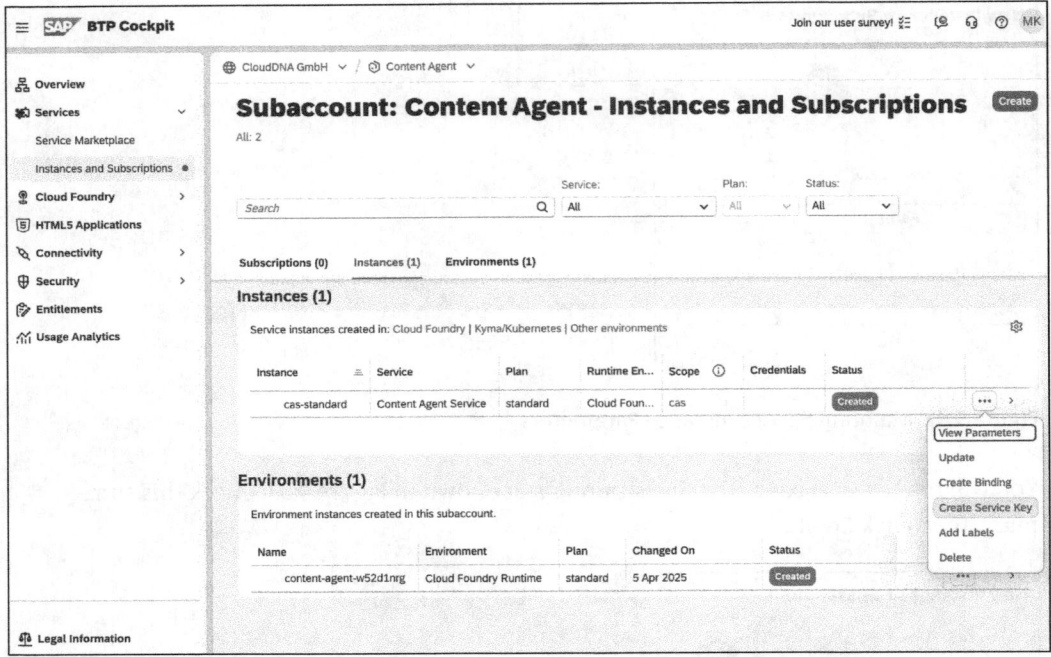

Figure 9.34 Create Service Key

Enter a meaningful name in the **Service Key Name** field, as shown in Figure 9.35. Click **Create**.

Figure 9.35 Configure Service Key

It takes a few seconds to create the service key. After that, you can open it. The service key should resemble the one shown in Figure 9.36. This key contains a client secret and a client ID. You will need the details from the service key in the next step.

370

9.4 Adding the SAP Content Agent Service to a Subaccount

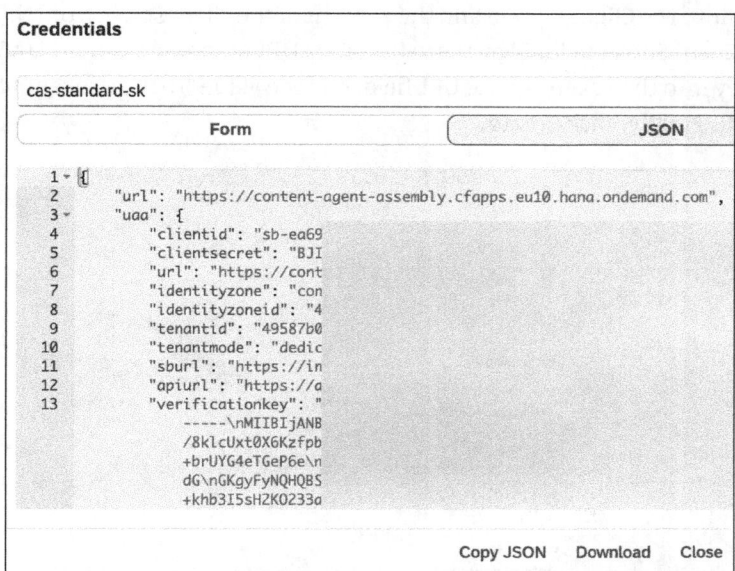

Figure 9.36 Show Service Key

Create a destination in the SAP Integration Suite development instance subaccount that points to the SAP Content Agent service. To do so, open the subaccount and navigate to the **Connectivity • Destinations (New)** area (see Figure 9.37). Click **Create** to create a new destination.

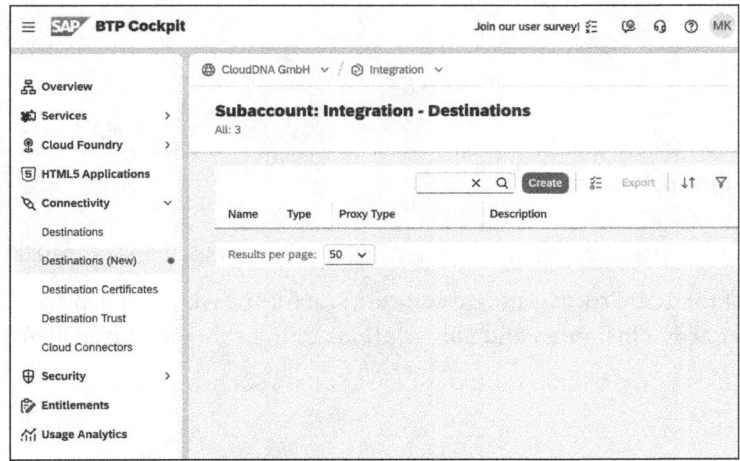

Figure 9.37 Create Destination

Enter "ContentAssemblyService" in the **Name** field. Remember, this value is case-sensitive, and the name cannot be chosen freely. In the **URL** field, copy the URL from the previously created service key. Select the **Internet** option for **Proxy Type** and the **Oauth2ClientCredentials** option for **Authentication** (see Figure 9.38). Copy the client ID from the service key into the **Client ID** field and the content of the client secret from the service key into the **Client Secret** field. Copy the value of the URL attribute from the **UAA** area of the service key into the **Token Service URL** field. Add the value "/oauth/token" to the token service URL. Finally, click **Create**.

Figure 9.38 Maintain Destination Details

Now perform a connection test. The result should look like the one shown in Figure 9.39.

Create an instance of the SAP Process Integration runtime for the API service plan. To do so, navigate to **Services • Instances and Subscriptions** in the side menu (see Figure 9.40). Click **Create**.

9.4 Adding the SAP Content Agent Service to a Subaccount

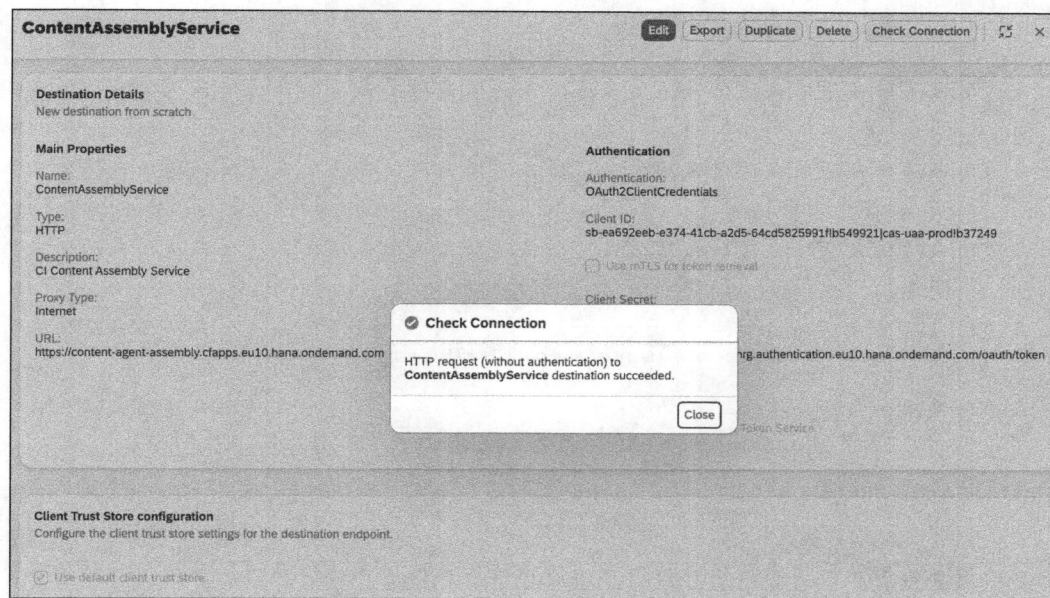

Figure 9.39 Result of Connection Test

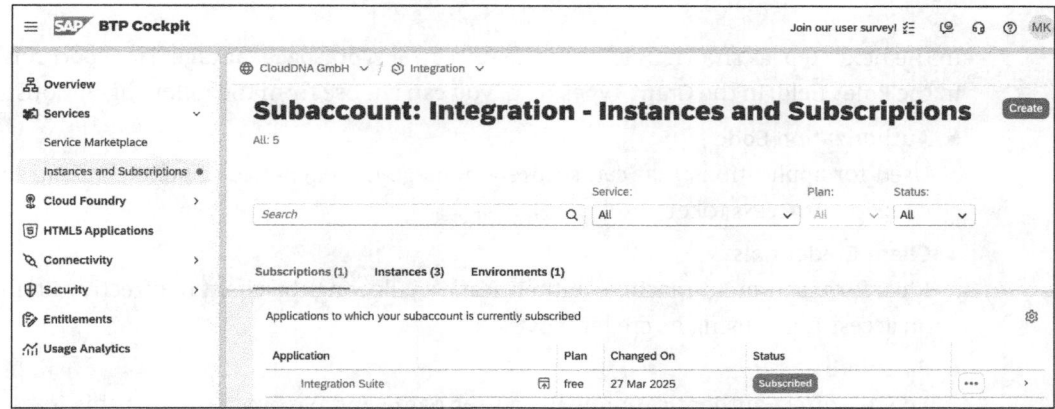

Figure 9.40 Create SAP Process Integration Runtime Service Instance

In the **Service** field, select **SAP Process Integration Runtime** (see Figure 9.41). Next, select **api** under **Plan** and **Cloud Foundry** for **Runtime Environment**. Select a **Space** and enter a descriptive name in the **Instance Name** field. Then click **Next**.

9   Activating and Setting Up SAP Cloud Transport Management for SAP Integration Suite

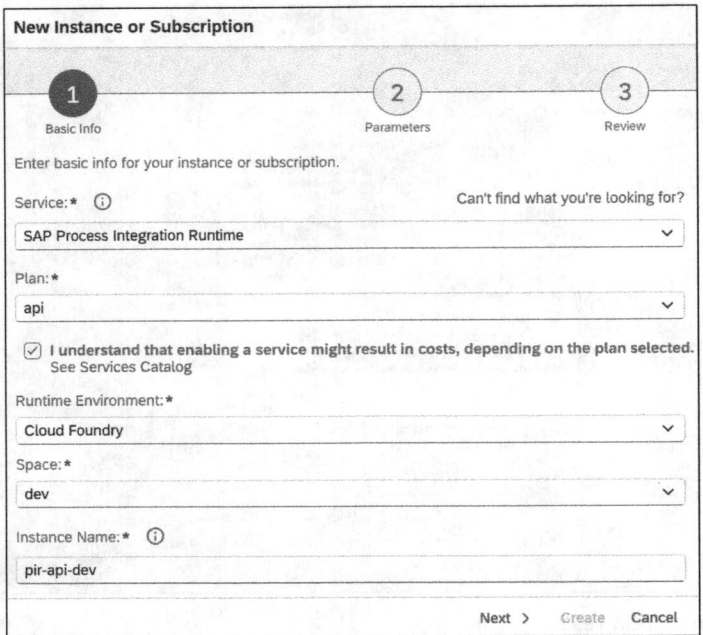

Figure 9.41 SAP Process Integration Runtime: Create API Plan: Basic Info

In the next step, as shown in Figure 9.42, select the **WorkspacePackagesTransport** role in the **Roles** field. In the **Grant Types** field, you can choose from the following options:

- **Authorization Code**
  Used for applications that can securely manage the exchange of an authorization code for an access token

- **Client Credentials**
  Ideal for machine-to-machine authentication, allowing the client to directly obtain an access token using its credentials

- **Password**
  Enables direct authentication using a user name and password, though this is less commonly recommended due to security concerns

- **Refresh Token**
  Allows the client to request a new access token without the need for reauthentication, ensuring seamless user experiences

- **SAML2 Bearer**
  Utilizes SAML assertions for obtaining an access token; commonly used in federated identity scenarios

- **JWT Bearer**
  Relies on JSON Web Tokens for access token acquisition; often used for secure, token-based authentication systems

Selecting the appropriate grant type depends on your specific authentication needs and the integration scenario. For example, the OAuth2ClientCredentials grant type mentioned earlier is particularly suited for secure system-to-system communication, ensuring that destinations leverage robust security mechanisms.

Now click **Next**.

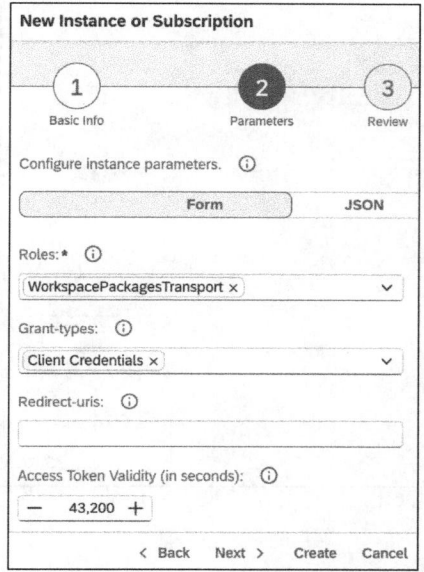

Figure 9.42 SAP Process Integration Runtime: Create API Plan: Parameters

You will now see the configuration summary as shown in Figure 9.43. Click **Create** to create the service instance.

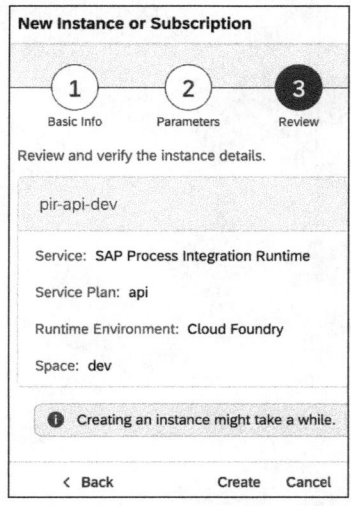

Figure 9.43 Summary of Service Instance Configuration

9 Activating and Setting Up SAP Cloud Transport Management for SAP Integration Suite

To create a service key for this service instance, click **Create Service Key** under the ... button on the line of the service instance you just created (see Figure 9.44).

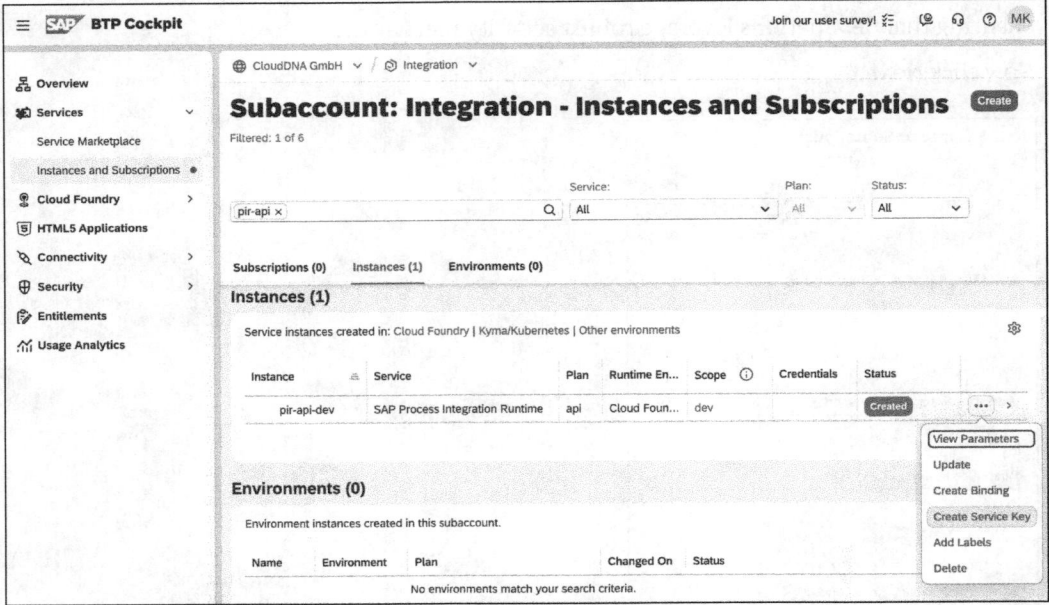

Figure 9.44 Create Service Key

Enter a descriptive name in the **Service Key Name** field and click **Create** (see Figure 9.45). You will need the details from the service key in the next step.

Figure 9.45 Maintain Service Key Details

9.4 Adding the SAP Content Agent Service to a Subaccount

Open the subaccount in which the SAP Content Agent service was added. Create a new destination; you've walked through this process several times before, so it should be familiar. Enter "CloudIntegration" in the **Name** field, and remember that this name is case-sensitive (see Figure 9.46). Copy the value of the URL from the service key into the **URL** field. Append the "/api/1.0/transportmodule/Transport" path to the URL. Select **Internet** for **Proxy Type** and **OAuth2ClientCredentials** for **Authentication**. For the **Client ID**, **Client Secret**, and **Token Service URL** fields, use the corresponding values from the service key. Note that the token service URL must include the */oauth/token* path. Finally, click **Save**.

Figure 9.46 Create Cloud Integration Destination

Run a connection test. This will provide the results shown in Figure 9.47.

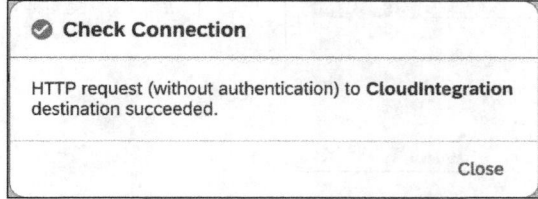

Figure 9.47 Connection Check Result

9   Activating and Setting Up SAP Cloud Transport Management for SAP Integration Suite

Create a service key for the service instance in the SAP Cloud Transport Management subaccount. Click **Create Service Key** in the corresponding service instance, as shown in Figure 9.48.

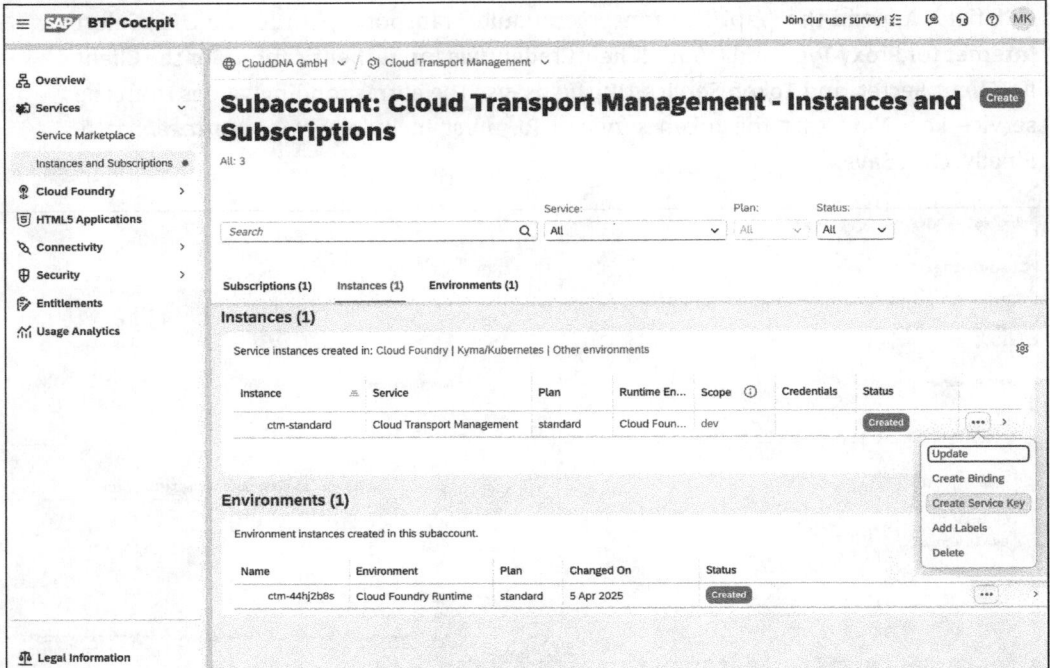

Figure 9.48 Create Service Key

Enter a meaningful name for the service key, as shown in Figure 9.49, then click **Create**.

Figure 9.49 Maintain Service Key Name

378

You will need the details of the service key later. Now, reopen the subaccount in which the SAP Content Agent service was added. You must create a destination there that points to SAP Cloud Transport Management. To do this, navigate to **Connectivity • Destinations (New)** and click **Create** (see Figure 9.50).

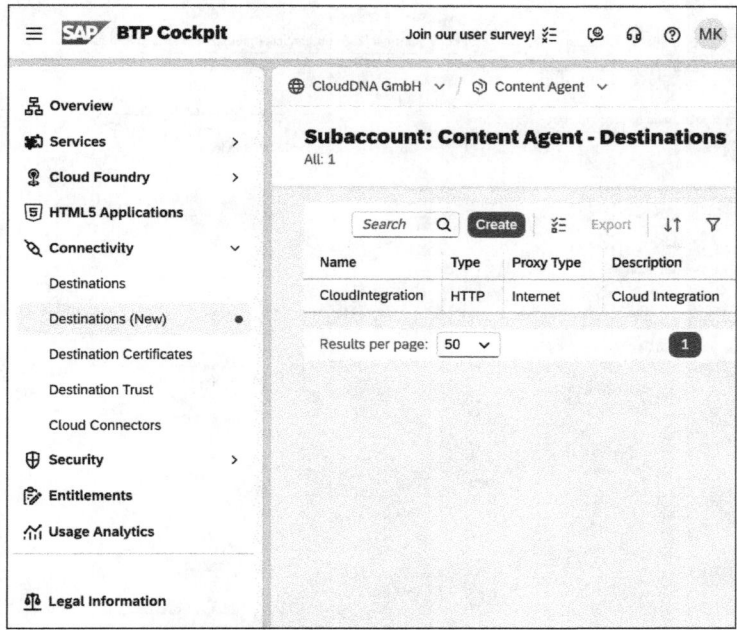

Figure 9.50 Create Destination

Enter "Transport Management Service" in the **Description** field (see Figure 9.51). Note that this value is case-sensitive. Next, copy the URI of the previously created service key and paste it into the **URL** field. Now select **Internet** for **Proxy Type** and the **OAuth2Client-Credentials** option for **Authentication**. Use the corresponding values from the service key for the **Client ID**, **Client Secret**, and **Token Service URL** fields. Remember, the token service URL must include the */oauth/token* path. In the **Additional Properties** area, create a property named **sourceSystemId**. The value must match the name of the node of the SAP Integration Suite development instance in SAP Cloud Transport Management, which you chose when you created the system landscape in SAP Cloud Transport Management. Finally, click **Save**.

Run a connection test. This will display a success message as shown in Figure 9.52.

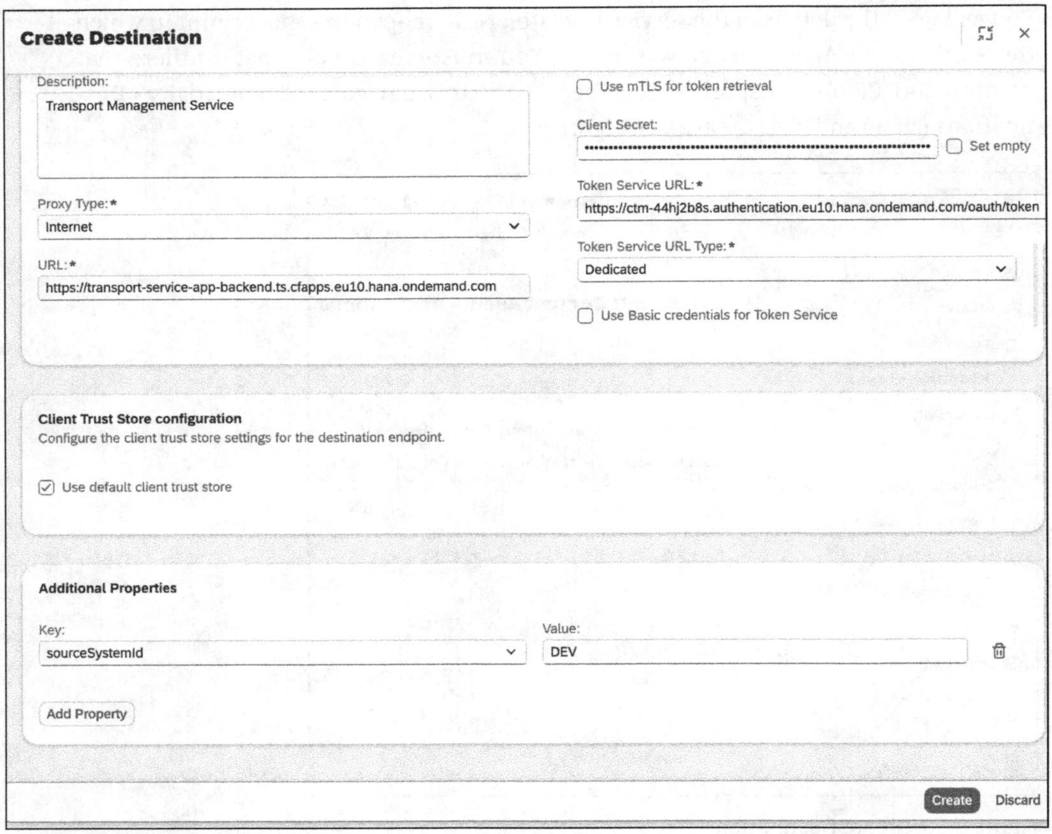

Figure 9.51 Transportation Management Service: Create Destination

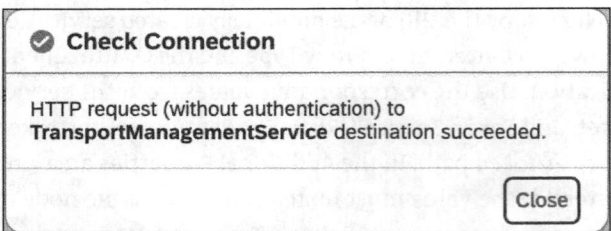

Figure 9.52 Connection Check Result

9.5 Configuring SAP Cloud Transport Management in SAP Integration Suite

You can now configure SAP Cloud Transport Management in SAP Integration Suite. This must be done in the development system. To do so, open the subaccount in which the

9.5 Configuring SAP Cloud Transport Management in SAP Integration Suite

development instance of SAP Integration Suite is provided. Navigate in the side menu to the **Services • Instances and Subscriptions** area, as shown in Figure 9.53. Click the **Integration Suite** link to open SAP Integration Suite.

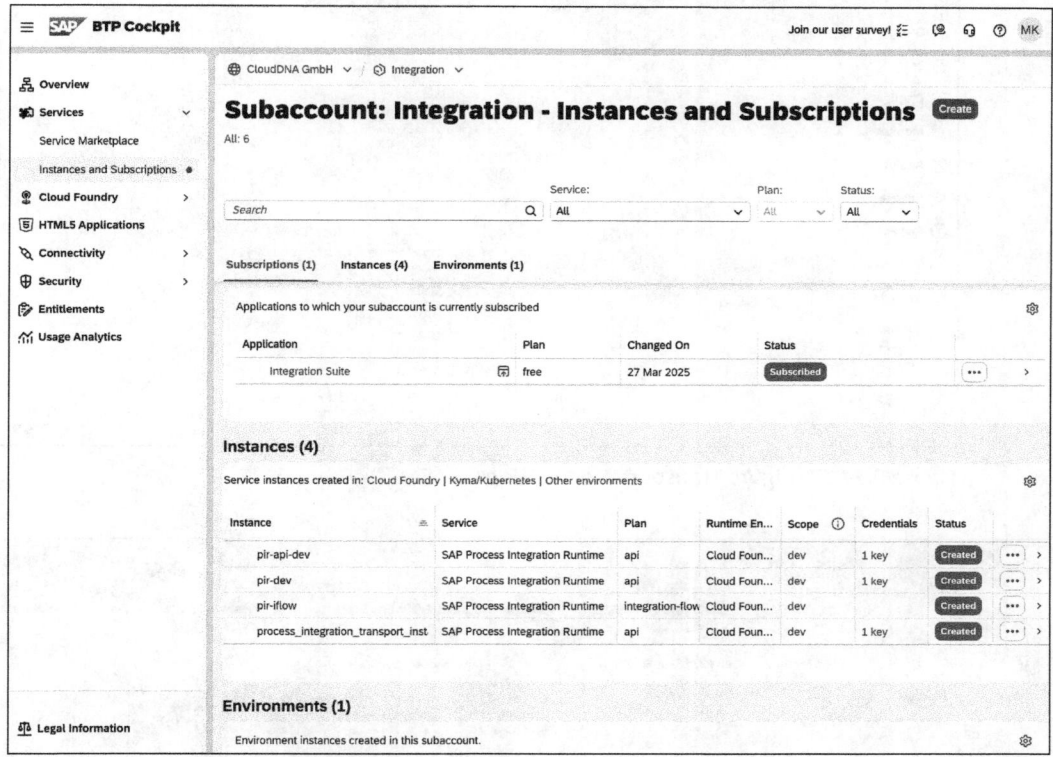

Figure 9.53 Open SAP Integration Suite

In SAP Integration Suite, go to the **Settings • Integrations** area as shown in Figure 9.54. Open the **Transport** tab page and click **Edit** in the bottom-right corner. Select the **Cloud Transport Management** option in the **Transport Mode** field. Finally, click **Check Configuration**.

You will see a **SUCCESS** status in the response, as shown in Figure 9.55. This confirms that the configuration is correct and all destinations are operational.

9 Activating and Setting Up SAP Cloud Transport Management for SAP Integration Suite

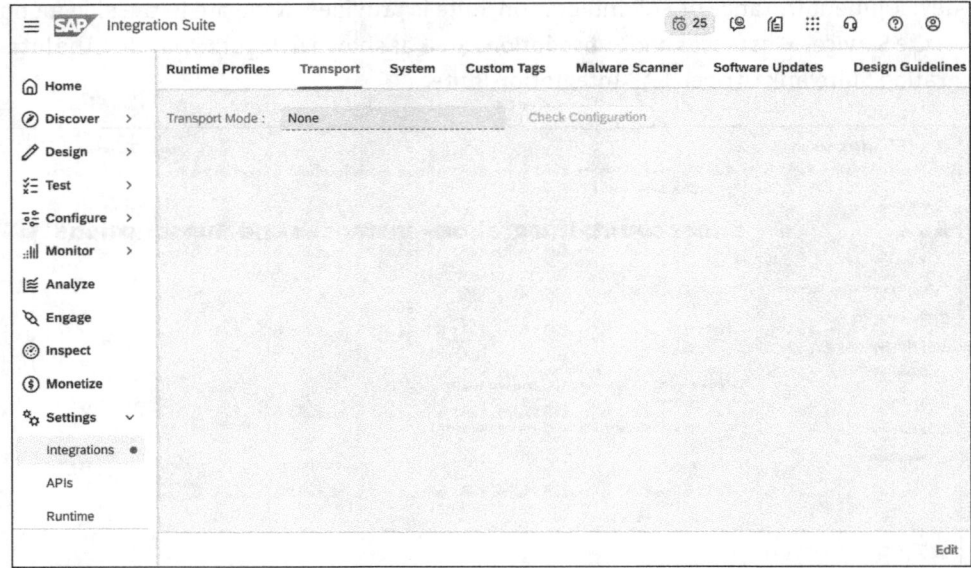

Figure 9.54 Configure Transportation Settings

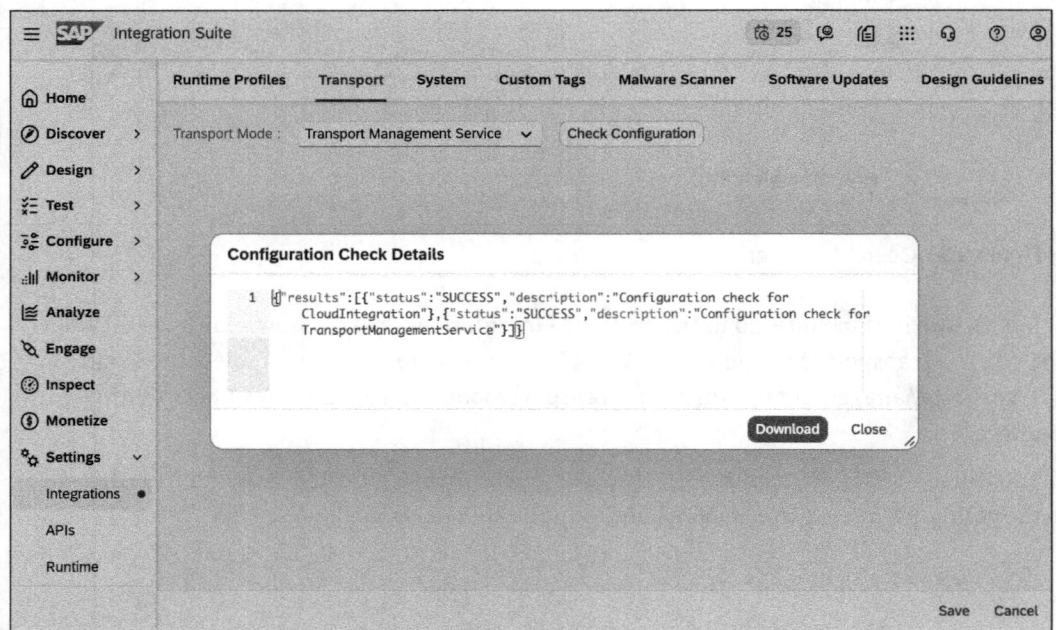

Figure 9.55 Result of Connection Test

Users must have the `WorkspacePackagesTransport` role to perform a transport from SAP Integration Suite. This role cannot be assigned to users directly. Instead, it must be packaged in a role collection. First, click **WorkspacePackagesTransport** to open the role, as

9.5 Configuring SAP Cloud Transport Management in SAP Integration Suite

shown in Figure 9.56. Ensure that there is no assignment to a role collection in the **Role Collections** area.

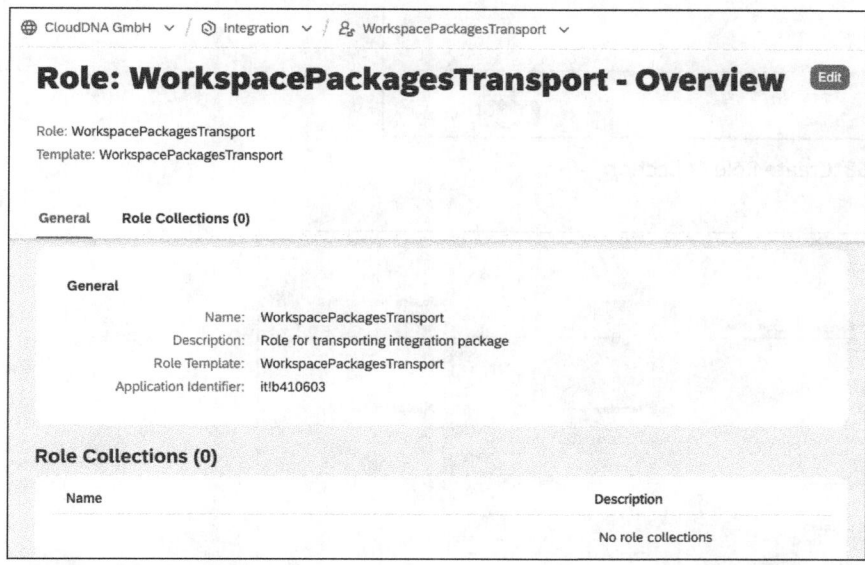

Figure 9.56 Check Role

Now open the **Role Collection** overview (see Figure 9.57) and click **Create**.

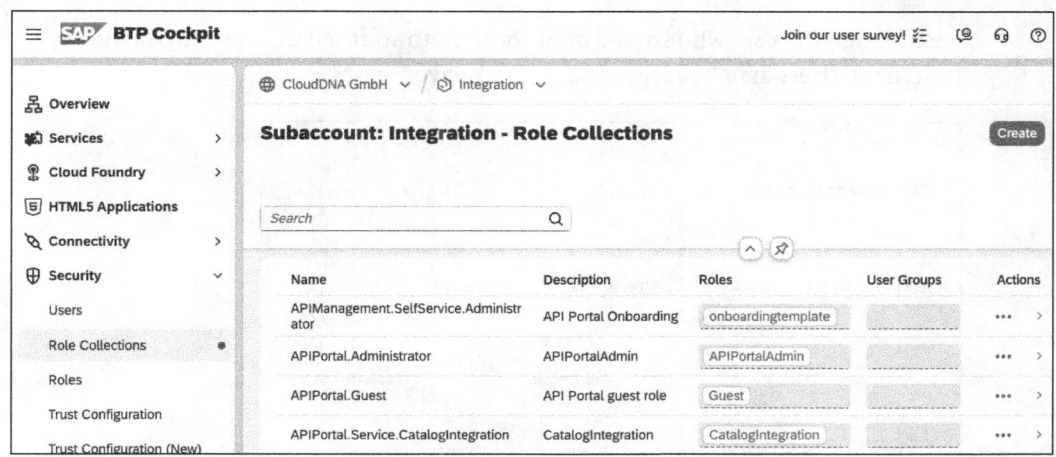

Figure 9.57 Role Collection Overview

Enter a name in the **Name** field—for example, "CI_Transport"— as shown in Figure 9.58, then click **Create**.

Assign the WorkspacePackagesTransport role to the role collection as shown in Figure 9.59. Then click **Add**.

9 Activating and Setting Up SAP Cloud Transport Management for SAP Integration Suite

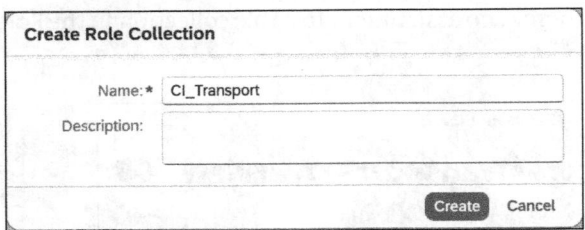

Figure 9.58 Create Role Collection

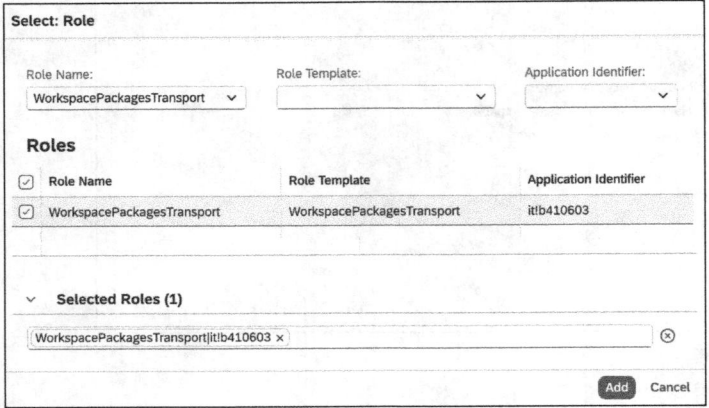

Figure 9.59 Assign Role

Next, assign the user who should be authorized to start the transport to the role collection in the **Users** area (see Figure 9.60). Click **Save**.

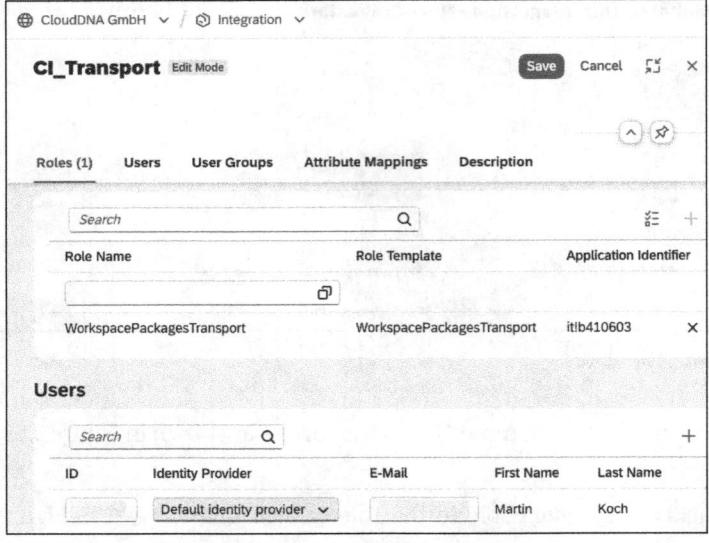

Figure 9.60 Role Collection User Assignment

9.5 Configuring SAP Cloud Transport Management in SAP Integration Suite

Start using SAP Integration Suite. Open an integration package as shown in Figure 9.61, and click **Transport**.

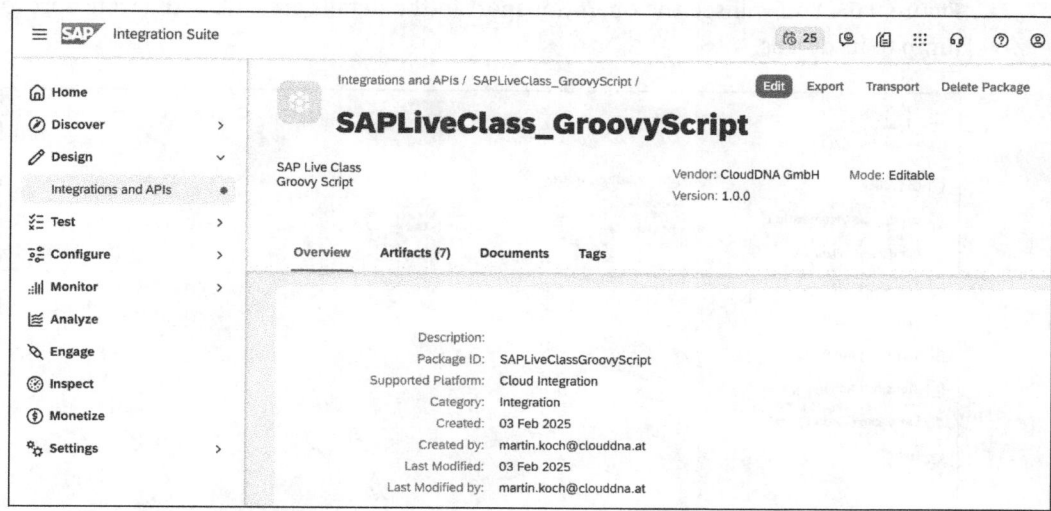

Figure 9.61 Start Transportation

Enter a comment in the **Comments** field as shown in Figure 9.62. This will be displayed in SAP Cloud Transport Management. Then click **Transport**. Use the **Propagate Logged-in User as Transport Owner** checkbox to propagate the user identity to SAP Cloud Transport Management.

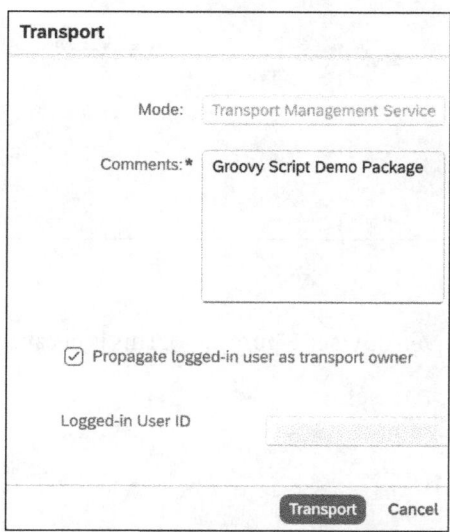

Figure 9.62 Maintain Transportation Name

The transport is now visible in SAP Cloud Transport Management. Open SAP Cloud Transport Management. Navigate in the side menu to the **Overview** area as shown in Figure 9.63. You will see the open transport in the details area. Click the transport to jump to its details.

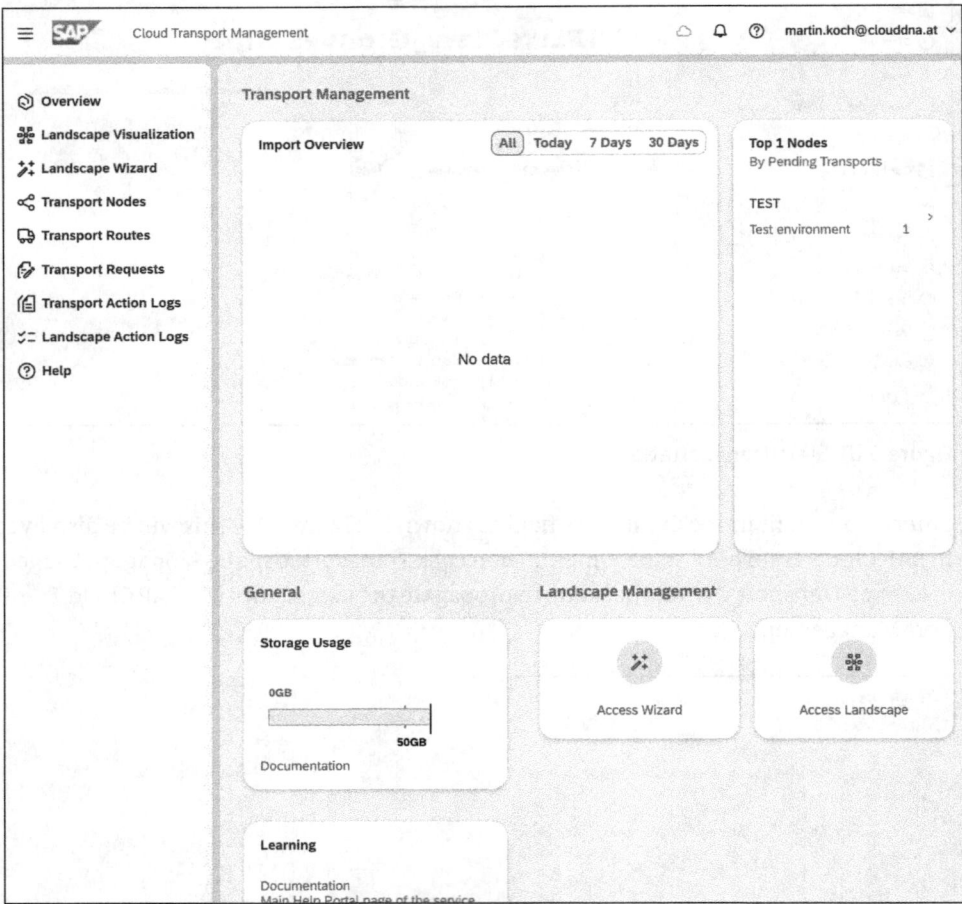

Figure 9.63 Transportation Overview

You will notice that the **Import All** button is grayed out (see Figure 9.64). This is because the user does not have the appropriate role.

9.5 Configuring SAP Cloud Transport Management in SAP Integration Suite

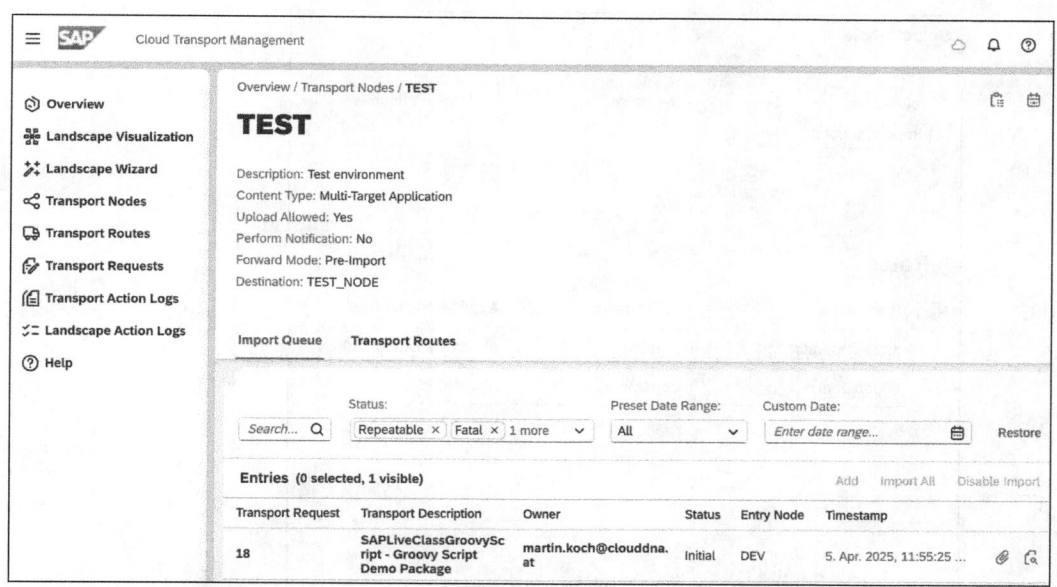

Figure 9.64 Display Import Queue

Create a role collection to authorize the import. Creating a role collection has already been shown several times in this chapter, so we won't provide step-by-step instructions again here. Enter a meaningful **Name** for the role collection as shown in Figure 9.65. Then click **Add**.

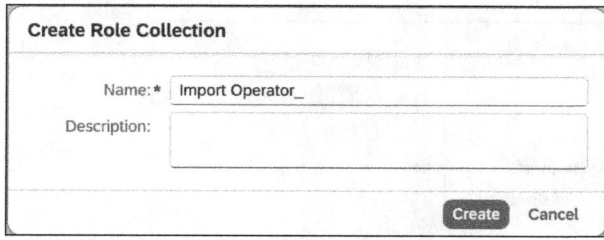

Figure 9.65 Create Role

Assign the `ImportOperator` role to the role collection as shown in Figure 9.66. Then click **Save**.

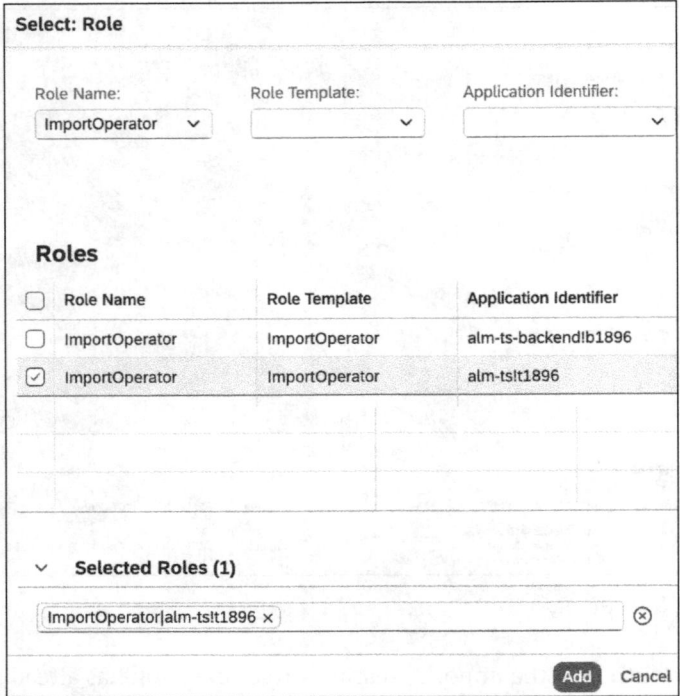

Figure 9.66 Assign Role

Assign the desired users to the role collection (see Figure 9.67) and save it.

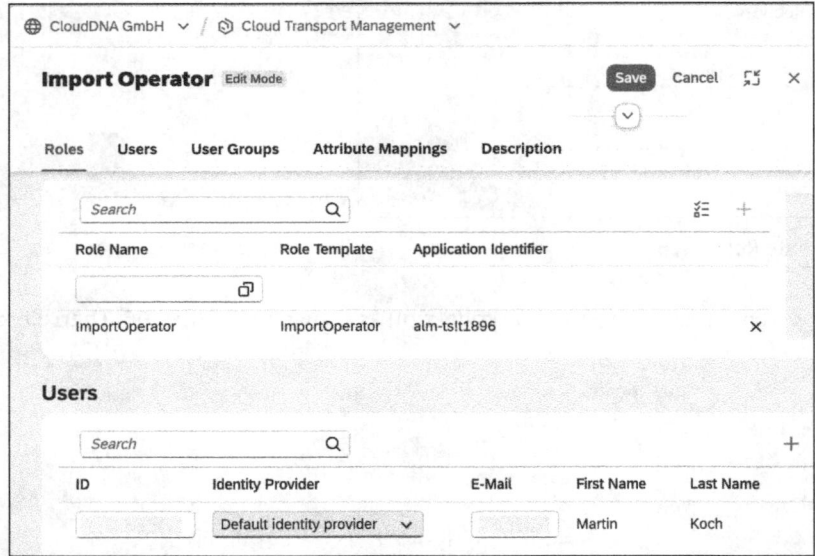

Figure 9.67 Assign Import Operator Role Collection

9.6 Summary

When you reenter SAP Cloud Transport Management, the **Import All** button will be active (see Figure 9.68). Click the button to start the import.

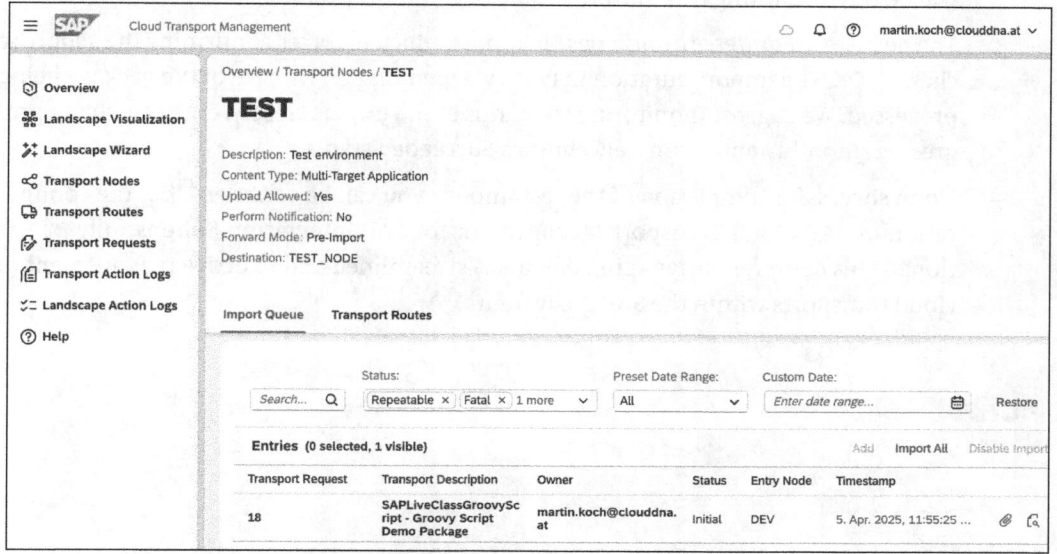

Figure 9.68 Display Import Queue

Authorize the import, as shown in Figure 9.69. Click **OK** to proceed.

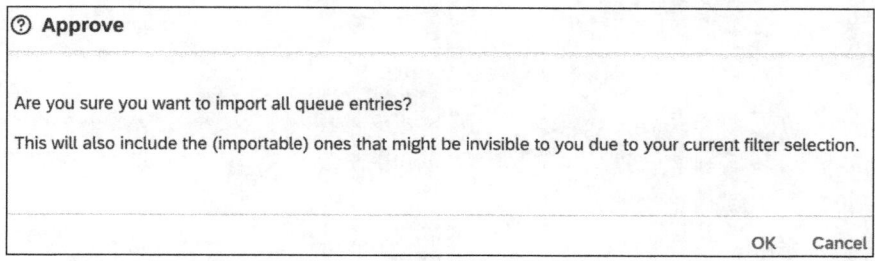

Figure 9.69 Authorize Import

The import will take some time depending on the size of the package. Check the status of the import, which should show the **Succeeded** status.

You have now completed the configuration of SAP Cloud Transport Management for SAP Integration Suite and have successfully performed a test import.

9.6 Summary

This chapter provided a detailed guide to configuring SAP Cloud Transport Management for SAP Integration Suite. The process begins with assigning the appropriate roles to users, specifically via the Import Operator role collection. Once this step is completed, you can reenter SAP Cloud Transport Management, where the **Import All** button will be active. Clicking this button initiates the import process.

The next step requires authorizing the import, which involves confirming the action by clicking **OK**. The import duration may vary depending on the size of the package being processed. We suggest monitoring the status of the import closely, ensuring that it progresses smoothly and ultimately shows a **Succeeded** status.

Upon successful completion of the test import, you can be confident that the configuration of SAP Cloud Transport Management for SAP Integration Suite is fully operational. This comprehensive setup ensures a streamlined and effective management of cloud transports within the SAP ecosystem.

Chapter 10
Activating and Setting Up SAP Build

SAP Build integrates no-code and low-code tools under the names SAP Build Apps, SAP Build Process Automation, and SAP Build Work Zone. These tools empower you to map your requirements on SAP BTP with ease.

In today's fast-paced business world, your employees must drive innovation and deliver solutions quickly. With low-code tools from SAP Build, anyone can participate in the development and automation process. SAP Build offers a suite of powerful tools, including SAP Build Apps, SAP Build Process Automation, and SAP Build Work Zone. These tools enable you to create, improve, and optimize business applications, automate processes, and design business pages.

SAP Build Apps provides a visual development environment that allows users to create applications and solutions by dragging and dropping prebuilt components. This low-code approach eliminates the need for manual coding, reducing development time and effort significantly. Section 10.1 explains how to set up SAP Build Apps. This offering empowers users to develop visually on SAP BTP and create enterprise-ready applications tailored to their specific requirements. SAP Build's capabilities extend beyond visual development, offering seamless integration with a wide range of SAP and non-SAP systems. The platform provides prebuilt connectors and business content that enable users to accelerate development by leveraging existing integrations. The integration-centric approach is supported by SAP Build Process Automation. In Section 10.2, we explain how to install and configure SAP Build Process Automation. Section 10.3 provides clear instructions for installing and configuring SAP Build Work Zone, advanced edition. This offering enables users to work together efficiently as a team.

Building on the possibilities offered by SAP Build, Section 10.4 explores a key feature that unlocks even more potential for users: SAP Build Code. This feature introduces advanced customization capabilities for developers and business experts alike.

10.1 SAP Build Apps

Are you seeking a solution that will enable you to quickly and efficiently develop business applications? SAP Build Apps is a low-code platform that enables users of all skill levels to create custom applications without extensive programming knowledge. With

SAP Build Apps, you can develop user interfaces using simple drag-and-drop methods. With a visual interface that allows for component arrangement and the design of user interfaces, you can create custom, enterprise-grade applications.

A notable feature of SAP Build Apps is its ability to enable the visual creation of data models and business logic without requiring any coding. This feature allows users to create cloud services and backend functionalities tailored to their business needs. In addition, it offers seamless integration, enabling secure connections with both SAP and non-SAP solutions. Prebuilt components, connectors, and integrations allow you to integrate disparate systems, utilize existing resources, and expedite development. This allows you to integrate custom applications with other enterprise systems, ensuring smooth data flow and a consistent user experience. SAP Build Apps is a tool that allows users to develop applications more easily and quickly. It enables users to focus on their expertise rather than on complex technical details. It eliminates the conventional barriers associated with application development, allowing professionals with diverse roles and skill levels to participate in the application development process. SAP Build Apps is designed to scale, whether you are developing a small application or a large enterprise solution.

SAP Discovery Center is an invaluable resource for gaining an initial understanding of SAP Build Apps. In addition to detailed service and pricing information, SAP Discovery Center provides insight into the geographical distribution of the various data centers used for service delivery (see Figure 10.1). The cornerstones of the roadmap are also documented there.

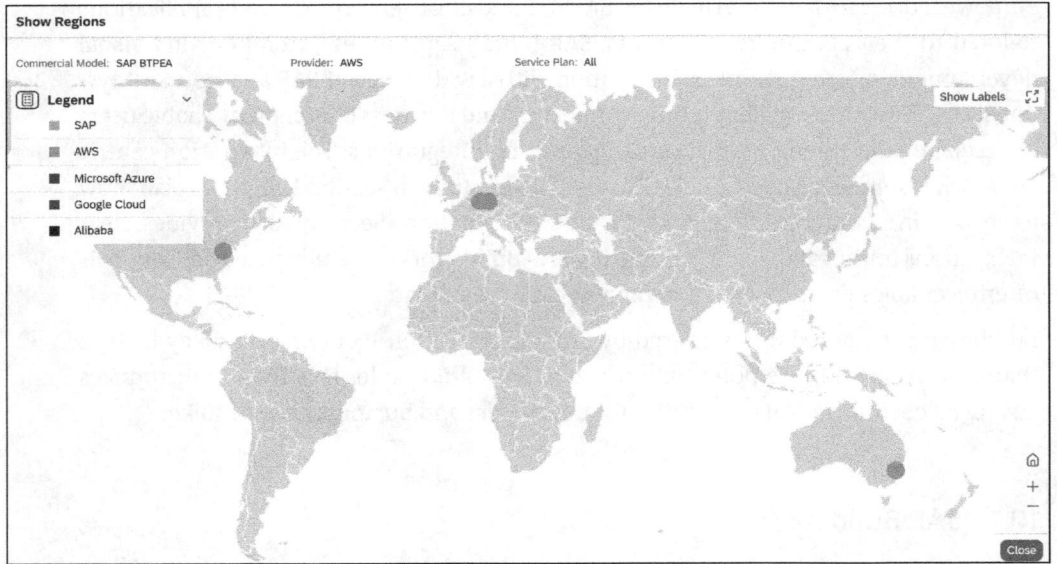

Figure 10.1 Display of Distribution of Data Centers in SAP Discovery Center

10.1 SAP Build Apps

SAP offers two plans for SAP Build Apps: a standard plan and a free plan. The standard plan is ready for production use and includes the full range of SAP Build Apps features—with the added security of enterprise-level support. The free plan has the following limitations:

- The number of builds is limited to two successful builds per app and platform.
- The development runtime is the only available cloud runtime; it cannot be used for production purposes.
- It is important to note that community support is the only available option. This support is not subject to the service-level agreement (SLA).

Let's now look at the process of installing and configuring SAP Build Apps.

10.1.1 Installation

SAP BTP's boosters at the global account level streamline the installation and configuration of services in a subaccount. These boosters act as automatic assistants, performing standardized setups and configurations. They minimize manual effort and reduce sources of error during setup by automatically performing the steps required to activate a service. These boosters save developer and system administrator teams time, allowing them to focus on more specific customizations and optimizations after completing the basic service setup.

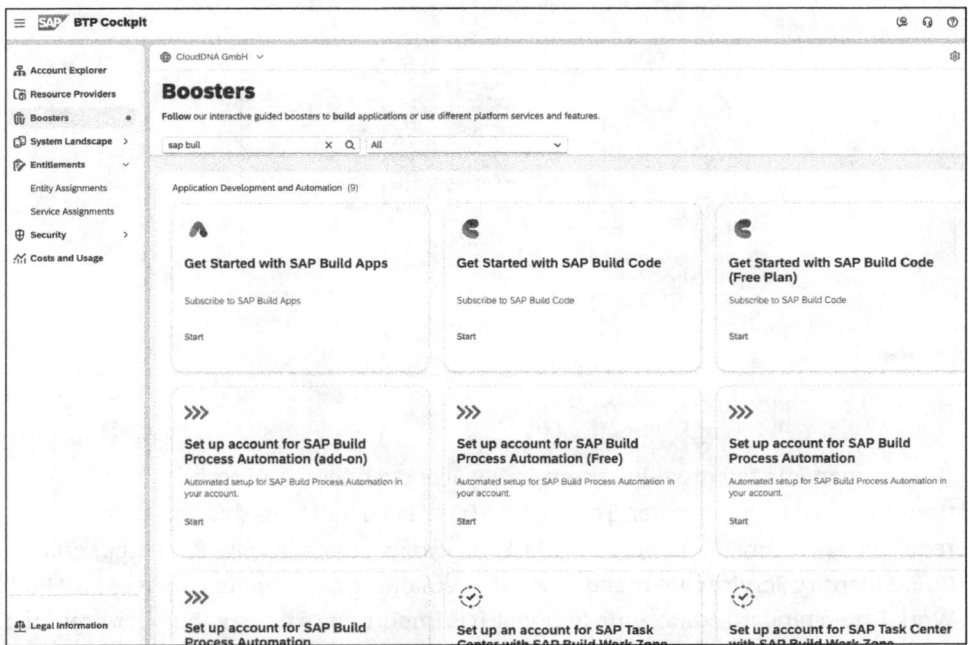

Figure 10.2 SAP Build Apps Booster

10 Activating and Setting Up SAP Build

Within the SAP BTP global account cockpit, the boosters are accessible via the side menu. Select the **Boosters** option to find the available automation tools (see Figure 10.2). Use the search function to filter specifically for "SAP Build." You will see two boosters for SAP Build Apps. One booster is for detailed account setup (**Get Started with SAP Build Apps—Detailed Account Setup**). It provides comprehensive account configuration. The other booster is for quick account setup (**Get Started with SAP Build Apps—Quick Account Setup**). It provides a fast and simplified setup process. These boosters differ in scope and level of detail, but both are designed to efficiently set up and configure SAP Build Apps in your subaccount. We'll look specifically at the booster for detailed account setup here. To begin, click the corresponding tile to open the booster.

The **Overview** tab contains an architecture overview (see Figure 10.3). This includes all components installed by the booster, including optional components. It integrates with other cloud and on-premise systems.

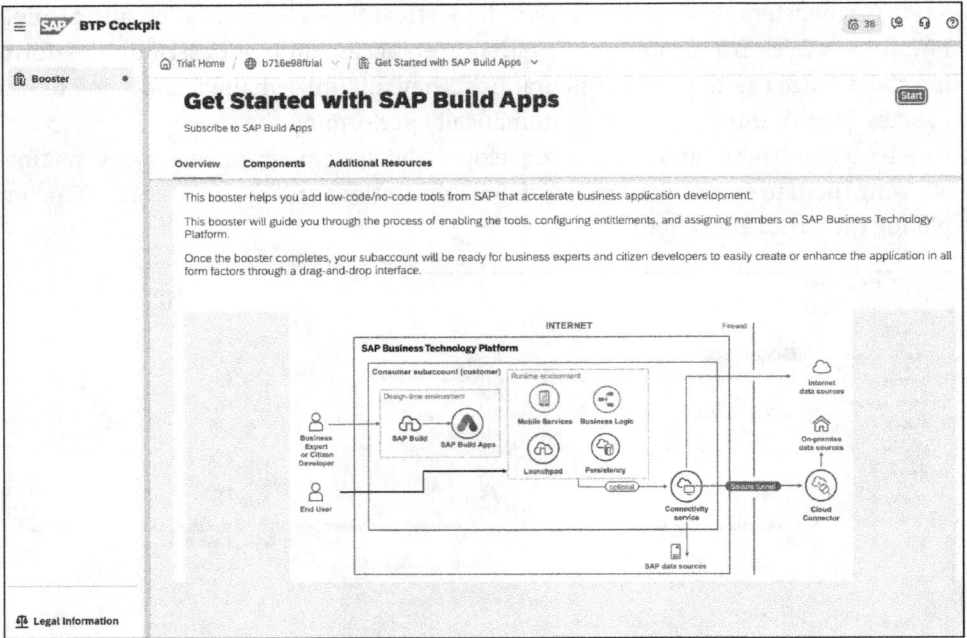

Figure 10.3 Architecture Overview

The **Components** tab provides a comprehensive overview of all services and subscriptions installed by the booster. The **MANDATORY** label indicates that this component is required (see Figure 10.4). For SAP Build Apps, it's clear that only SAP Build Apps and SAP Cloud Identity Services are mandatory. The remaining components, such as SAP Build Work Zone, standard edition, are optional. It is important to note that the services incur costs as soon as a subaccount subscribes to them. Click the **Start** button to initiate the booster.

10.1 SAP Build Apps

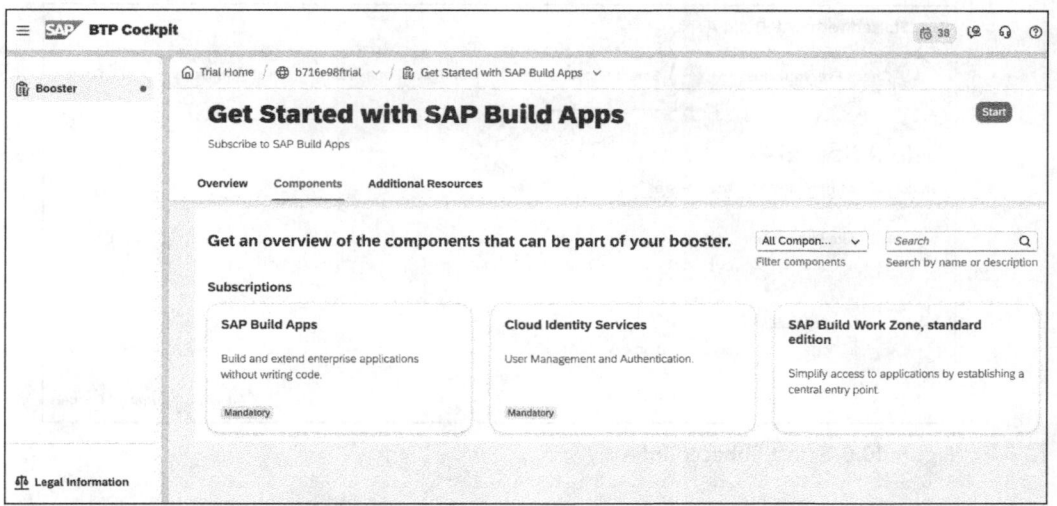

Figure 10.4 Booster Components

The first step of the booster, **Check Prerequisites**, is to check the prerequisites, as shown in Figure 10.5. The booster checks three things: whether you have the appropriate permissions to run it, whether a user-defined identity provider is available, and whether the necessary permissions exist. If all prerequisites have been successfully checked, proceed to the next step of the configuration by clicking **Next**.

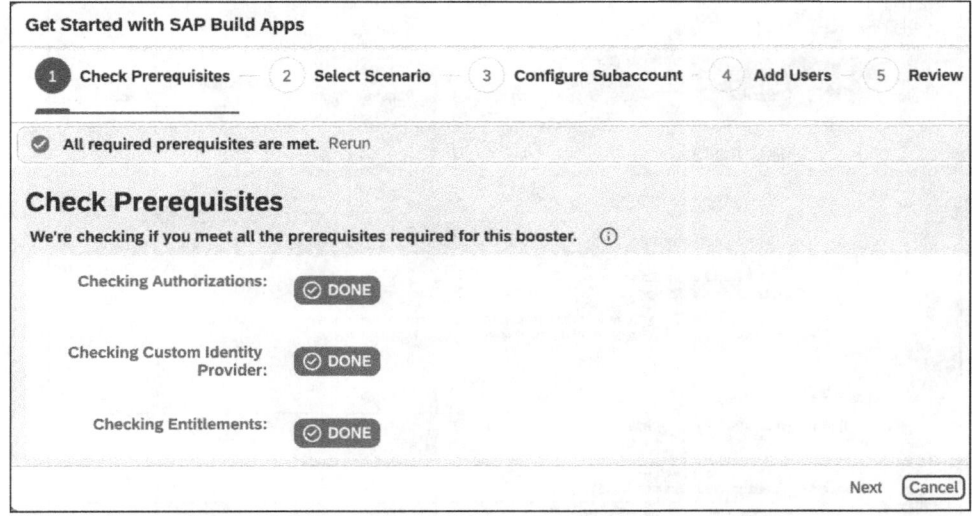

Figure 10.5 Check Prerequisites

In the second step, **Select Scenario**, you must choose whether to use an existing subaccount or whether the booster should create a new subaccount for this use case (see Figure 10.6). Select the appropriate action and click **Next** to continue.

10   Activating and Setting Up SAP Build

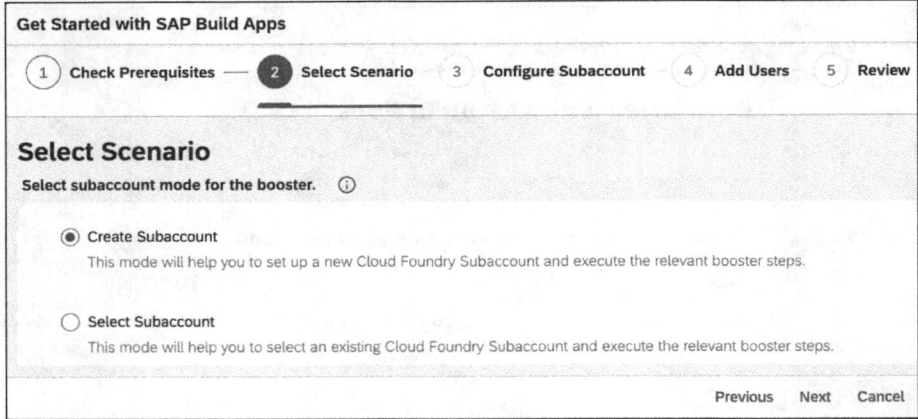

Figure 10.6 Select Subaccount

In the third step, **Configure Subaccount**, you can customize the permissions (see Figure 10.7).

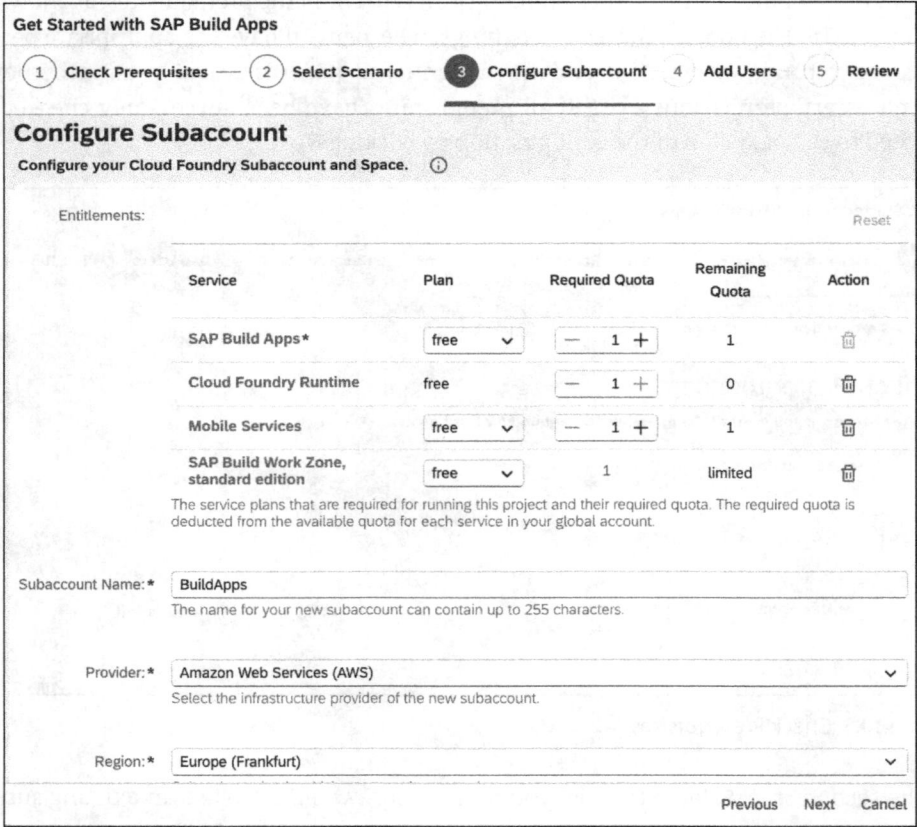

Figure 10.7 Configure Entitlements

10.1 SAP Build Apps

At this point, all components—services and subscriptions, both mandatory and optional—are selected. Delete optional components by clicking the trash can button next to each one. You can then change the name of the subaccount. By default, this consists of the global account name combined with a generated name. Use a descriptive name here. We strongly advise against using spaces in the name. Next, select the provider (AWS, Azure, or Google) and the associated data center or region. SAP Build Apps is not available in all data centers of all providers. Proceed to the next step of the configuration by clicking **Next**.

In the fourth step, **Add Users**, you must select a platform identity provider (**Custom Identity Provider for Platform Users**) and an application identity provider (**Custom Identity Provider for Applications**; see Figure 10.8). The *application identity provider* is used to authenticate developers who want to use SAP Build Apps. It is also responsible for authenticating end users when you deploy the apps you have created in this subaccount and make them available via SAP Mobile Services or SAP Build Work Zone, standard edition. The *platform identity provider* must authenticate users who manage subaccounts and create targets there. Enter the email addresses of the users assigned the Subaccount Administrator and BuildApps_Administrator roles in the **Administrators** field. The platform identity provider authenticates these users. In the **Developers** field, you must maintain the email addresses of the users who are used as developers in SAP Build Apps. Add new users of both types to the subaccount later.

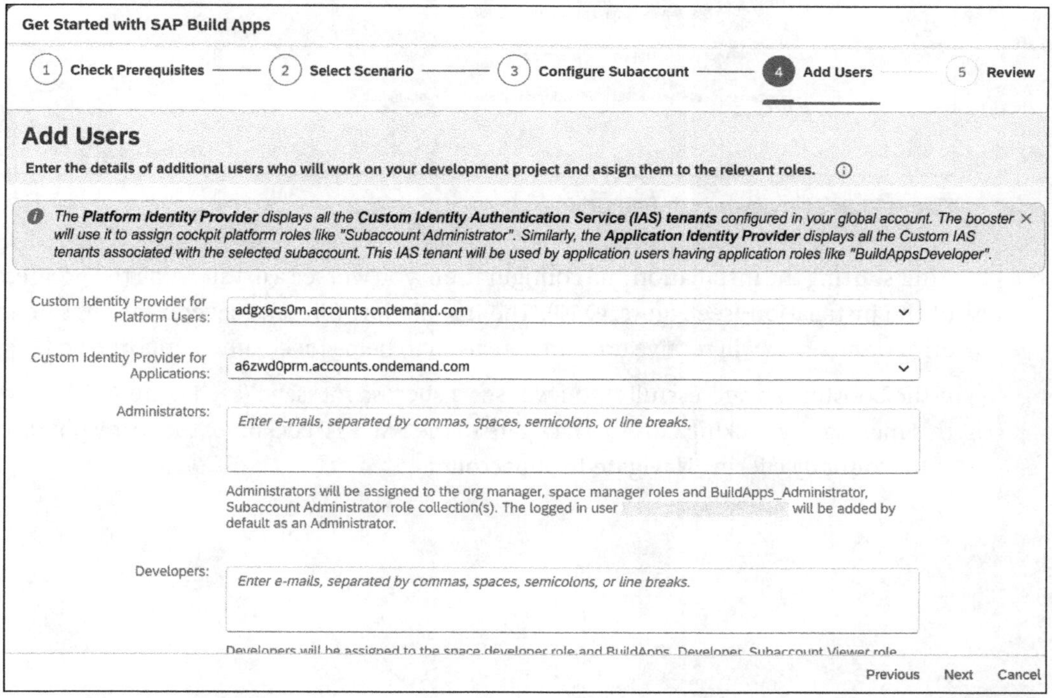

Figure 10.8 Configure Users

10 Activating and Setting Up SAP Build

In the **Review** step, you will see a summary of the configuration you just created (see Figure 10.9). Click **Finish** to start installing and configuring the services.

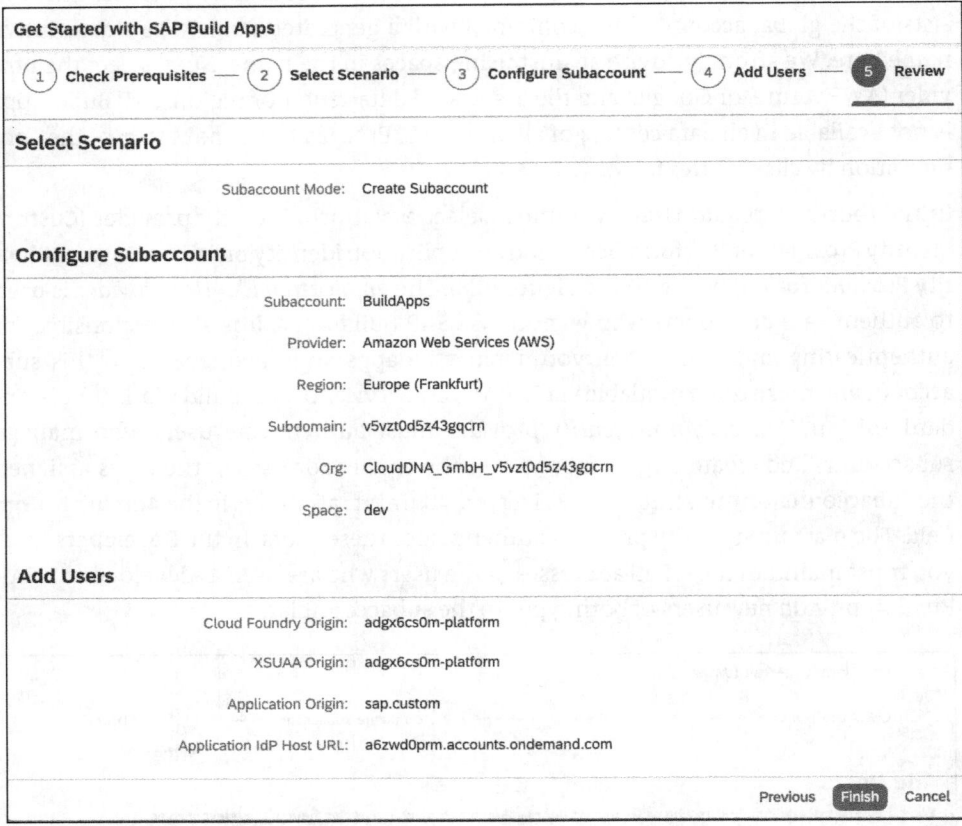

Figure 10.9 Overview of Configurations

After starting the installation and configuration, you will see a list showing the progress of the installation (see Figure 10.10). The installation will take several minutes. If an error occurs, you will receive error information to help you create a support ticket.

If the booster ran successfully, you will see a success message (see Figure 10.11). Close this message by clicking **Close**, or navigate to the SAP BTP cockpit of the corresponding subaccount by clicking **Navigate to Subaccount**.

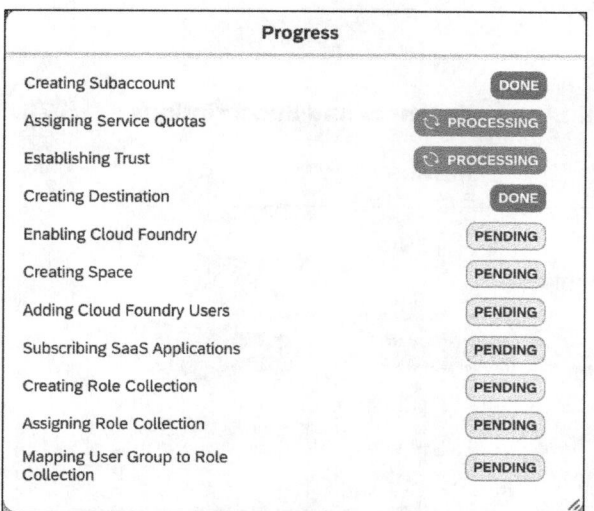

Figure 10.10 Installation Progress

> ✓ **Success**
>
> **Booster executed successfully**
>
> **Your subaccount is ready for SAP Build Apps Development.**
> Navigate to Subaccount
>
> **Follow the guide below to learn more about subaccounts in the cockpit**
> Subaccounts in SAP BTP cockpit
> **Learn how to manage entitlements and quotas in SAP cockpit**
> Managing Entitlements and Quotas Using the Cockpit
>
> Close

Figure 10.11 Success Message

10.1.2 Configuration

The booster has now performed a series of background activities. This includes subscribing to and setting up the subscriptions and services. The SAP BTP cockpit provides a clear overview of all created instances and subscriptions. To see this, navigate to **Services • Instances and Subscriptions** in the side menu (see Figure 10.12). You will find two subscriptions for the booster you just ran: one for **SAP Build Apps** and one for **SAP Build Work Zone, standard edition**.

10   Activating and Setting Up SAP Build

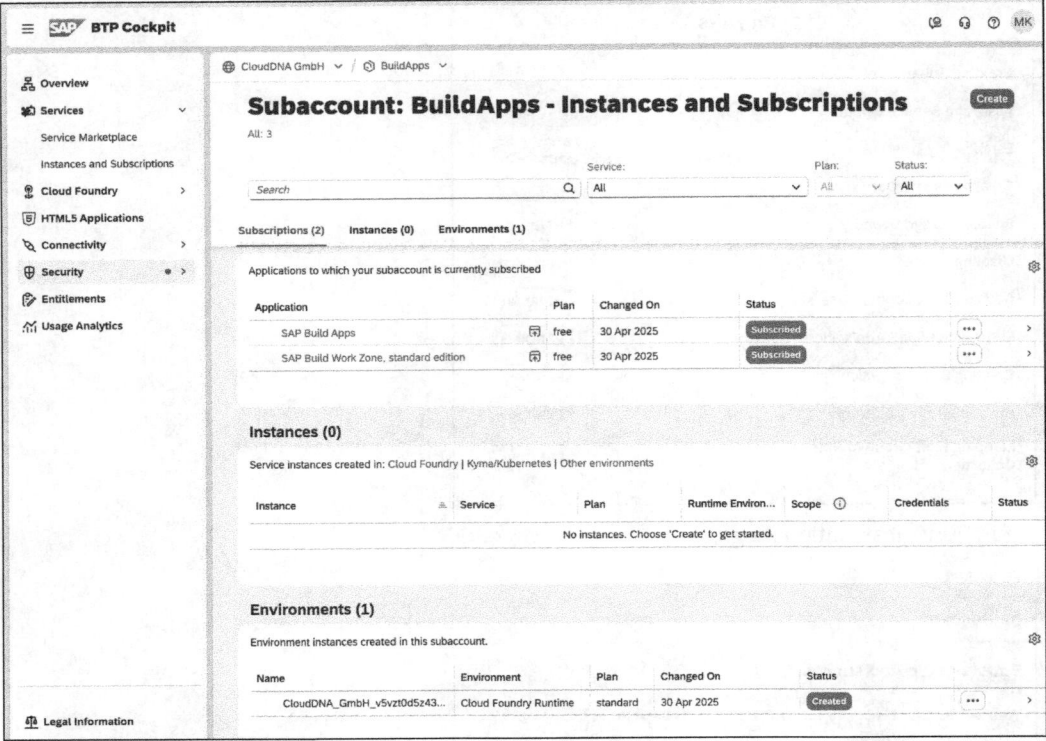

Figure 10.12 Overview of Instances and Subscriptions

You will then be redirected to Identity Authentication to log in. Once you have successfully logged in, the SAP Build Apps lobby will open.

Roles are created on SAP BTP with each subscription. However, roles cannot be assigned directly to users. Instead, the concept of role collections is used. A *role collection* is a collection of different, technically related roles. Navigate to **Security • Role Collections** to see all role collections available in the subaccount (see Figure 10.13). The following role collections are delivered with the SAP Build Apps subscription:

- BuildApps_Administrator
- BuildApps_Developer

Figure 10.13 also shows the following role collections that were created for SAP Build Work Zone, standard edition:

- Launchpad_Admin
- Launchpad_Admin_Read_Only
- Launchpad_Advanced_Theming
- Launchpad_External_User

400

If the available role collections do not meet your requirements, you can create your own role collections by clicking the **Create** button.

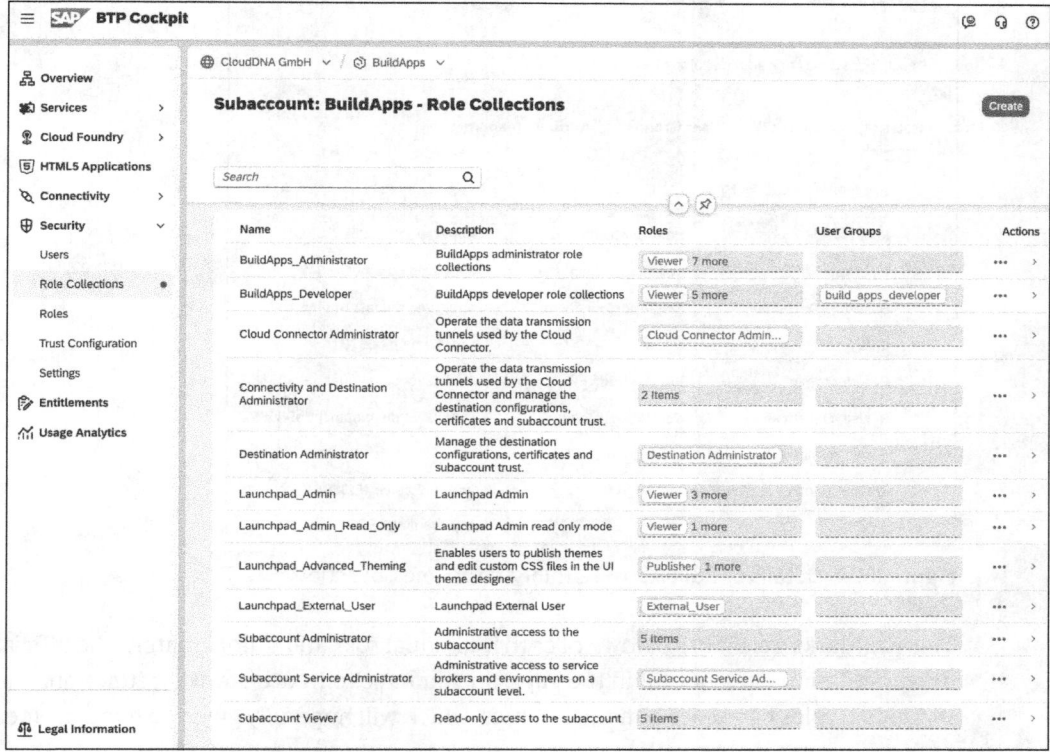

Figure 10.13 Overview of Role Collections

Now let's take a closer look at the two role collections delivered with SAP Build Apps. You can click a role collection in the overview to see its details. Role collections are assigned to users either directly or via user groups, which in turn are mapped to groups in the underlying identity provider. However, you also have the option of assigning role collections using attribute mappings. The role collection is derived based on certain attributes that are sent by the identity provider after successful registration. These can include, for example, the department or country in which the user is located.

Figure 10.14 shows the `BuildApps_Administrator` role collection. It consists of the following roles:

- `BuildAppsAdmin`
- `BuildAppsDeveloper`
- `Editor`
- `RegistryAdmin`
- `RegistryDeveloper`
- `Super_Admin`
- `Theme_Admin`
- `Viewer`

10 Activating and Setting Up SAP Build

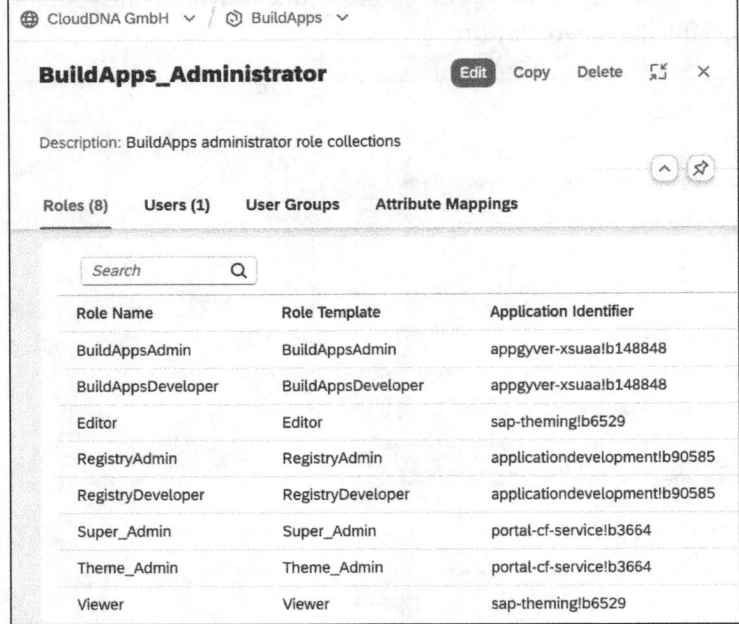

Figure 10.14 Details of BuildApps_Administrator Role Collection

This page lacks a clear breakdown of each individual role, and unfortunately, the official documentation does not fill in the gaps. So you have to figure out what functions the individual roles have based on their names, which will hopefully give you enough clues to piece things together.

Figure 10.15 shows the `BuildApps_Developer` role collection. It contains the following roles:

- `BuildAppsDeveloper`
- `Editor`
- `RegistryDeveloper`
- `Super_Admin`
- `Theme_Admin`
- `Viewer`

You may be wondering why the `Super_Admin` role is included in the `BuildApps_Developer` role collection. Another key point to consider is the connectivity of the role collection with the `build_apps_developer` user group. This connection allows you to assign this user group in Identity Authentication, offering significant convenience. It eliminates the need to assign individual role collections to each user in the SAP BTP cockpit at the subaccount level.

The booster has also created the `SAP-Build-Apps-Runtime` destination in the SAP BTP subaccount. This destination is a prerequisite for the visual cloud functions. Navigate to **Connectivity · Destinations (New)** in the side menu to view the details of this destination (see Figure 10.16).

10.1 SAP Build Apps

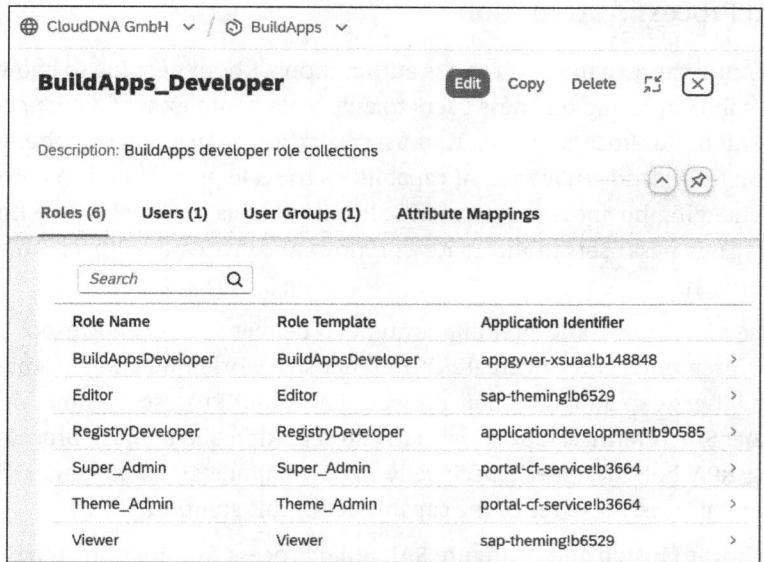

Figure 10.15 Details of BuildApps_Developer Role Collection

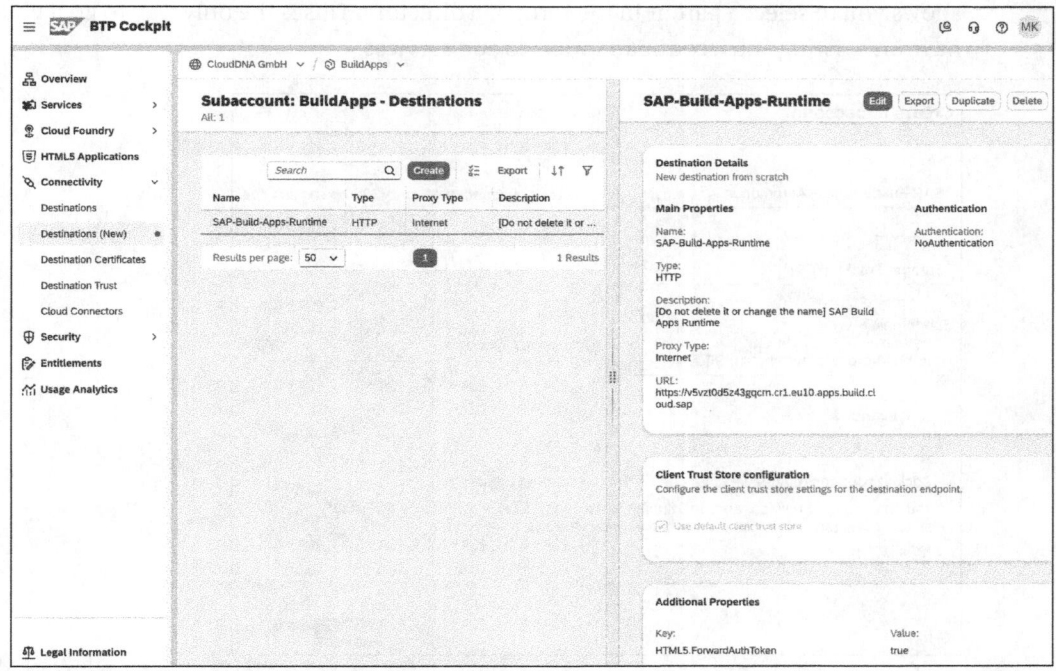

Figure 10.16 Details of SAP Build Apps Runtime Destination

10.2 SAP Build Process Automation

SAP Build Process Automation allows you to use automation without needing to know how to code. This solution allows business users to automate complex workflow processes and tasks. SAP Build Process Automation uses workflow management, robotic process automation (RPA), and embedded AI capabilities to scale process automation in order to meet changing business requirements. Intuitive tools require little to no coding, empowering business users to automate workflows and processes with a simple drag-and-drop approach.

Developers can use visual tools and prebuilt content to deliver results and respond quickly to new requirements. You can create comprehensive workflows and automations that business users can adopt in their projects. SAP Build Process Automation integrates with other SAP offerings. It provides native integration and prebuilt process content, including RPA bots designed specifically for SAP applications. AI-powered intelligent document processing extends the capabilities of this solution.

We will show you how to install and configure SAP Build Process Automation step by step. First, you need to create a subaccount (see Figure 10.17). The booster can also create a subaccount, but we recommend creating the subaccount manually in advance as it allows you to select a parent in the form of a directory. This is the only way to go if you have an existing subaccount and want to add services.

Figure 10.17 Create Subaccount

SAP offers different boosters for SAP Build Process Automation, one for the free quota and different ones for productive use (see Figure 10.18). Click the desired booster to jump to the booster overview.

10.2 SAP Build Process Automation

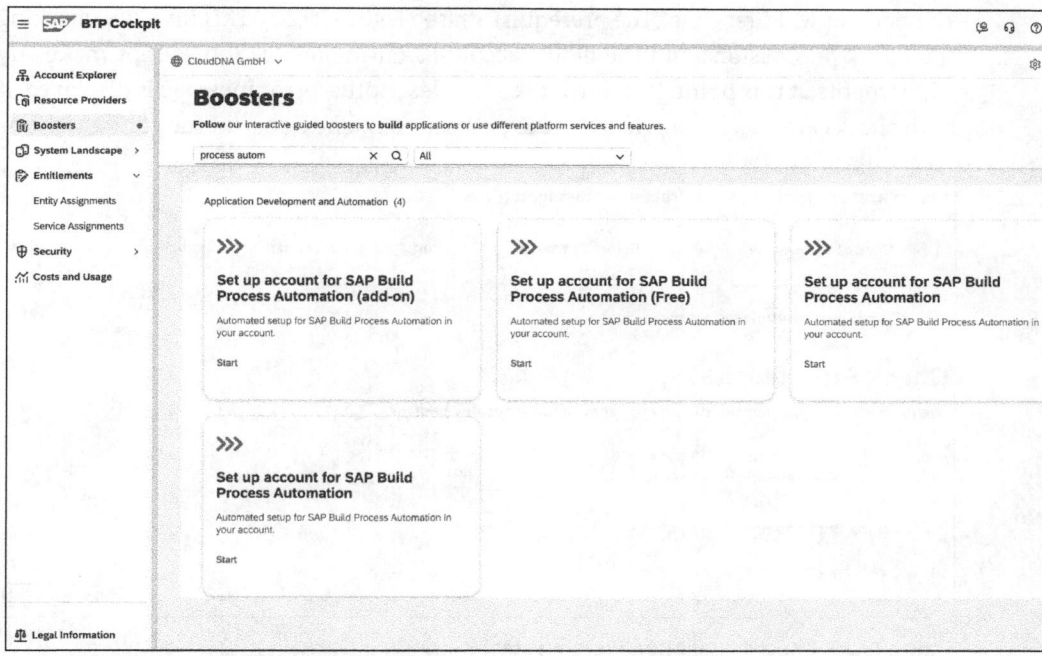

Figure 10.18 SAP Build Process Automation Boosters

We will use the booster for the free quota for the following demonstration. Open the **Components** tab in the booster to see the components you need (see Figure 10.19). As you can see in the figure, SAP Build Process Automation requires a service and a subscription. When you're ready, click the **Start** button to start the booster.

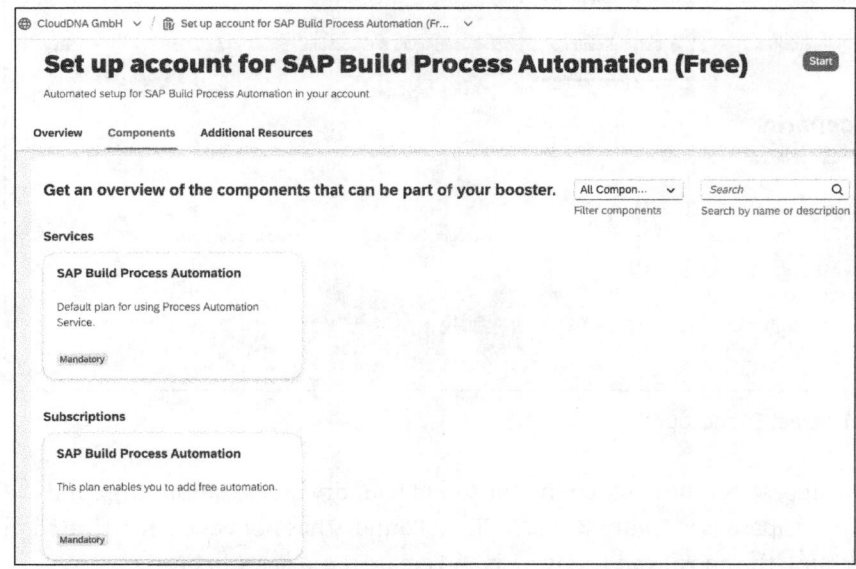

Figure 10.19 SAP Build Process Automation Booster Components

10 Activating and Setting Up SAP Build

The booster will first check the prerequisites (see Figure 10.20). This involves checking the user's permissions and the global account's entitlements. You cannot make any adjustments at this point. If an error occurs, a descriptive error message is displayed. If both checks are successful, click **Next** to proceed to the next step of the configuration.

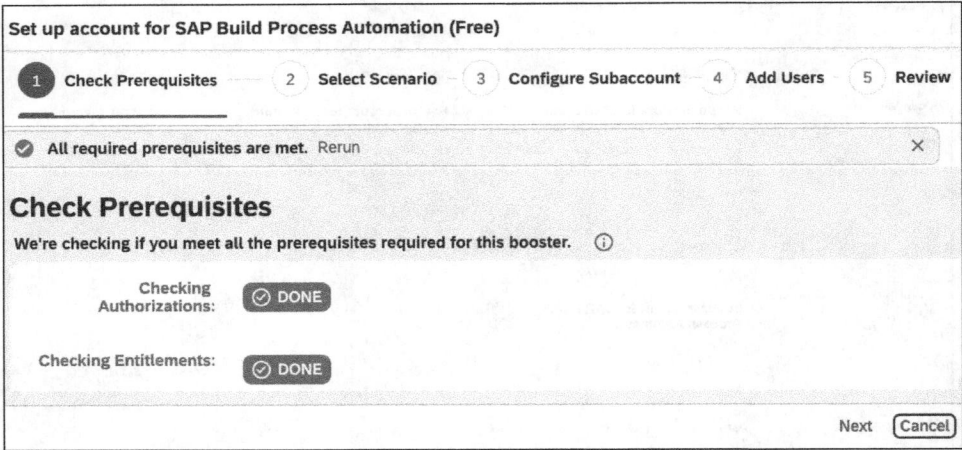

Figure 10.20 Check Installation Prerequisites

In the second step, you must decide whether to use an existing subaccount or create a new subaccount for the deployment of SAP Build Process Automation (see Figure 10.21). In this example, we are using the subaccount that was created previously, so choose the **Select Subaccount** option. Click **Next**.

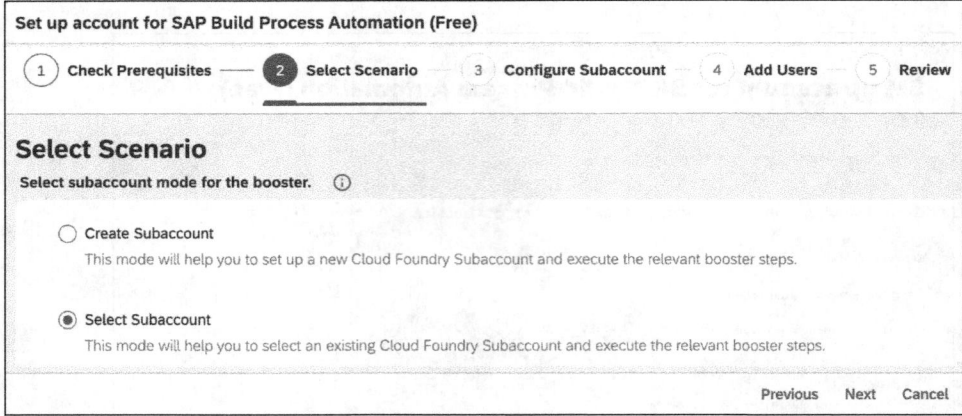

Figure 10.21 Select Subaccount

In the third step, select the subaccount, the Cloud Foundry organization (**Org**), and the Cloud Foundry **Space** (see Figure 10.22). If Cloud Foundry has not yet been activated in this subaccount, the booster will activate it and create the space. Click **Next**.

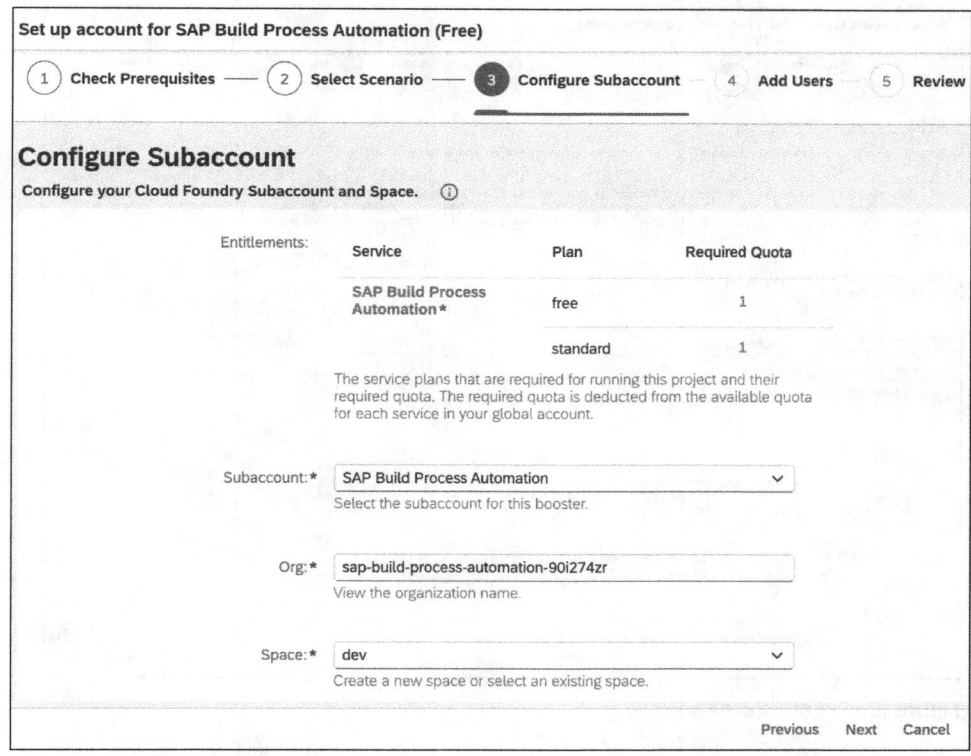

Figure 10.22 Configure Subaccount

In the fourth step, you must now perform the initial assignment of users (see Figure 10.23). Select which identity provider should be used for the platform and application users. You can also maintain the users who are to be initially assigned administrator permissions in the **Administrators** field. These users are assigned the Org Manager and Space Manager roles for Cloud Foundry and the Subaccount Administrator role collection at the subaccount level. In the **Developers** field, you can maintain the users who are to be initially authorized as developers. These users are assigned the following role collections:

- ProcessAutomationDeveloper
- ProcessAutomationAdmin
- ProcessAutomationParticipant
- Subaccount Viewer

Click **Next**. In the last step, you will see a summary of the configuration you have just made (see Figure 10.24). Click **Finish** to start the setup process via the booster.

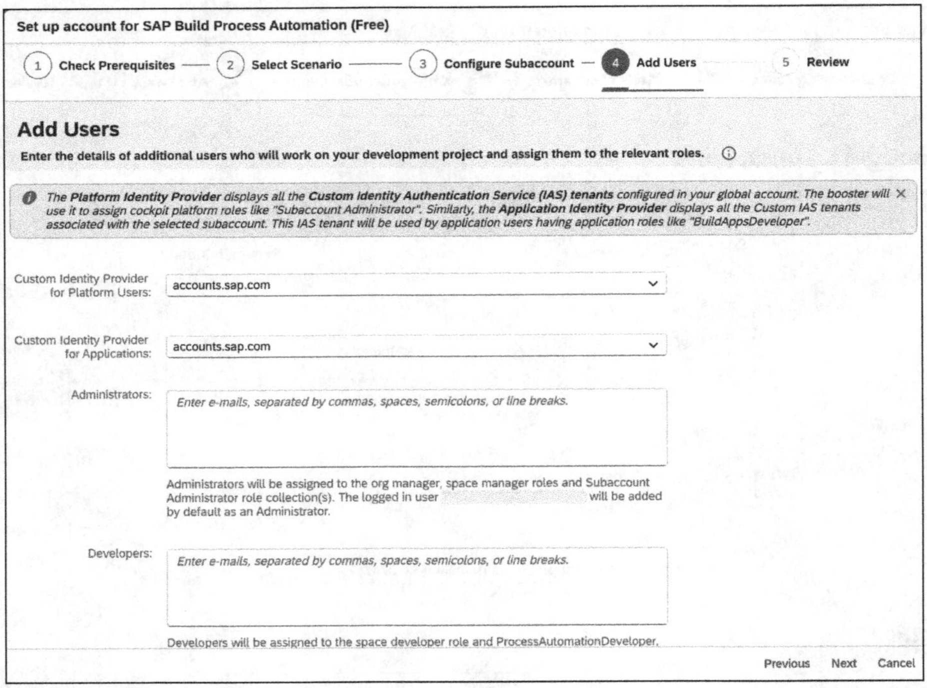

10 Activating and Setting Up SAP Build

Figure 10.23 Configure Users

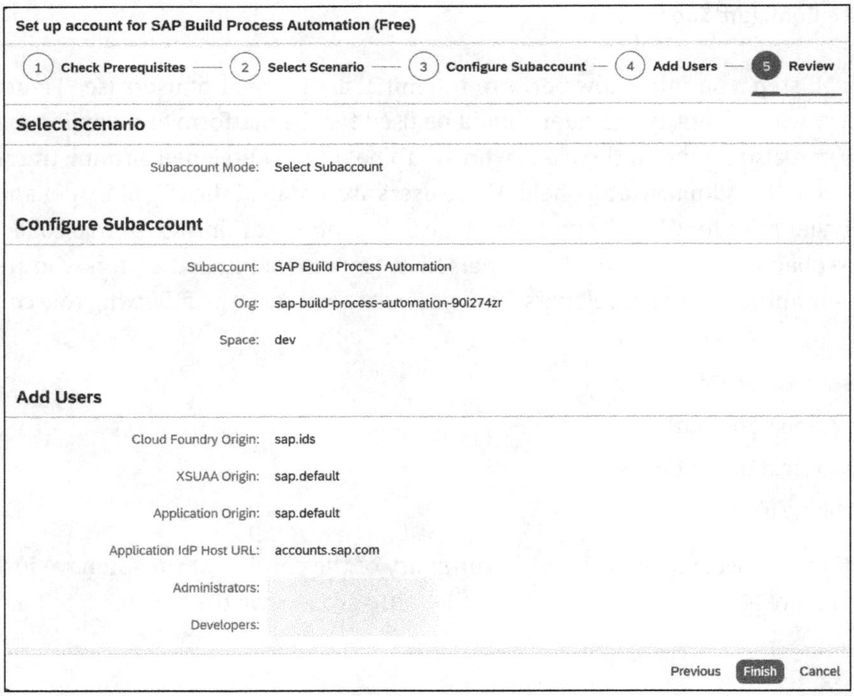

Figure 10.24 Summary of Configuration

10.2 SAP Build Process Automation

As with the installation of the booster for SAP Build Apps, you will then see the progress of the installation (see Figure 10.25).

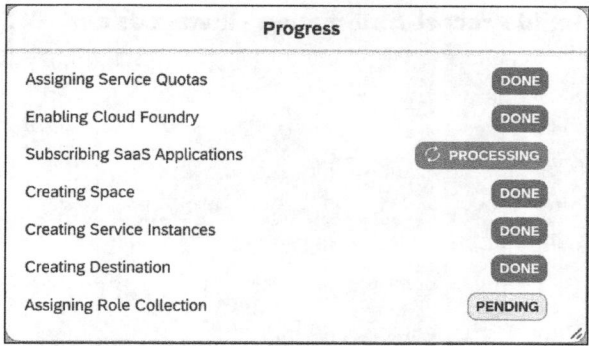

Figure 10.25 Installation Progress

Once installation and configuration have been completed successfully, you will see a success message (see Figure 10.26). Navigate to the SAP BTP cockpit of the subaccount by clicking **Navigate to Subaccount**. Open the instance and service overview.

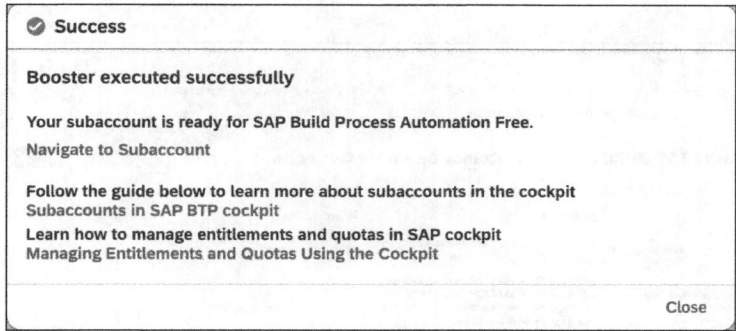

Figure 10.26 Booster Success Message

Navigate to **Services • Instances and Subscriptions** in the side menu (see Figure 10.27). Find the **SAP Build Process Automation** application in the **Subscriptions** area. Click the name to open the app. The sap_process_automation service instance is installed in the dev space. You can find it in the **Instances** area.

Once the subscription is successful, the corresponding roles are provided in the subaccount (see Figure 10.28). To do this, navigate to **Security • Role Collections** in the side menu. You will see the following roles:

- ProcessAutomationAdmin
- ProcessAutomationDelegate
- ProcessAutomationDeveloper
- ProcessAutomationParticipant

409

10 Activating and Setting Up SAP Build

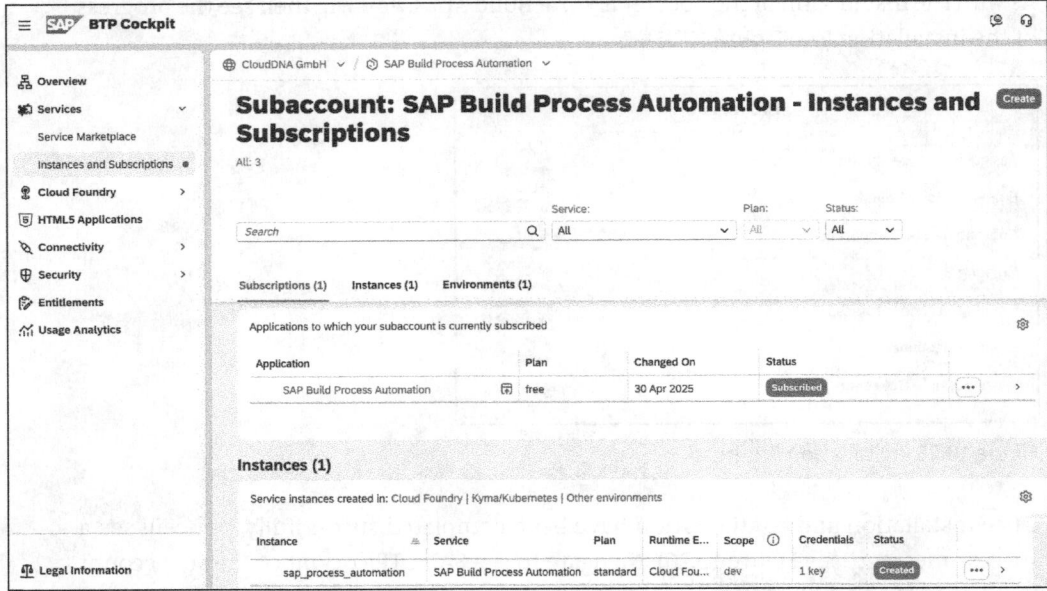

Figure 10.27 SAP Build Process Automation Instance and Subscription Overview

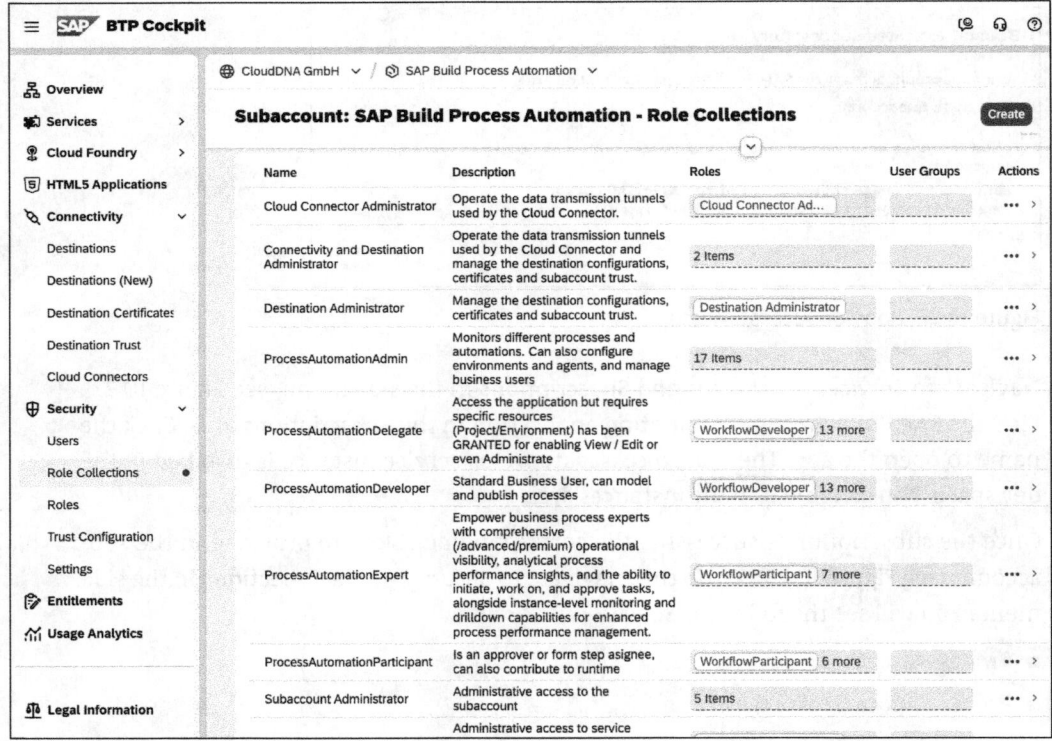

Figure 10.28 Role Collection Overview

The SAP Build Process Automation booster execution automatically creates both the sap_process_automation_service_user_access and the sap_process_automation_service destinations (see Figure 10.29).

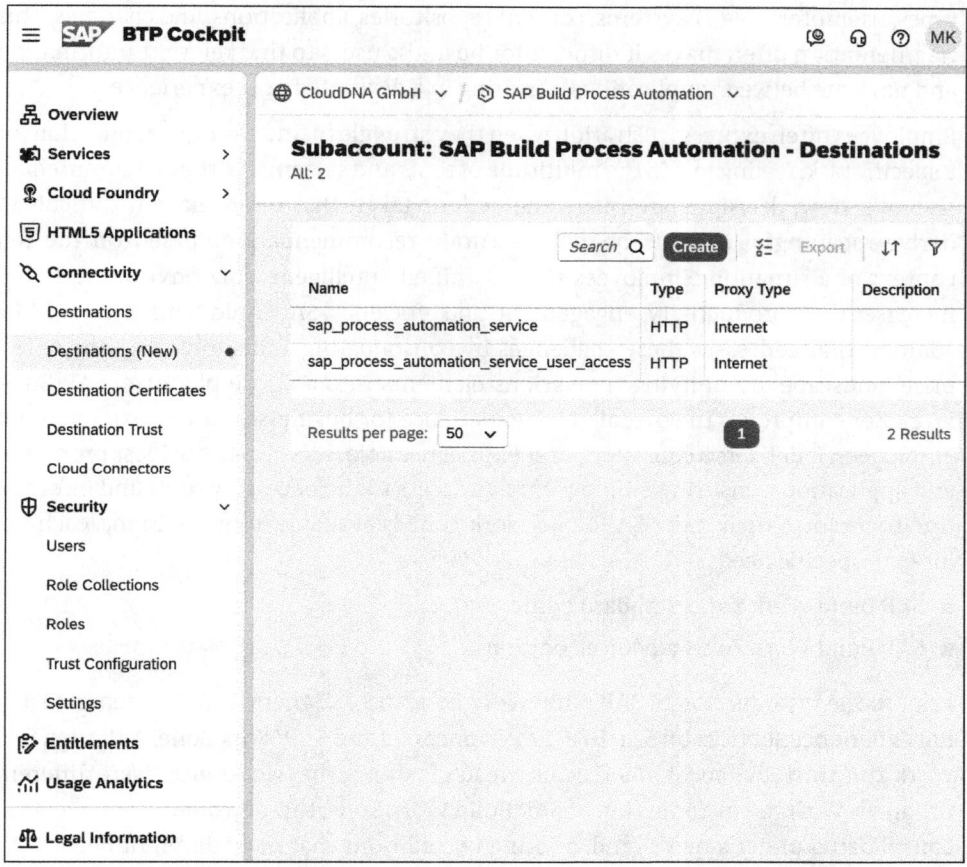

Figure 10.29 SAP Build Process Automation Destinations

The sap_process_automation_service destination is a necessity for technical scenarios—specifically, scenarios in which there are no logged-in user details available. These scenarios include ready-to-use live process content packages.

The sap_process_automation_service_user_access destination is essential for connecting client applications with the primary propagation to SAP Build Process Automation. This applies to HTML5 apps served through managed app routers, such as SAP Build Work Zone, and applications built with SAP Build Apps.

You can then start the SAP Build Process Automation application. This takes you to the SAP Build Process Automation lobby, which serves as the central entry point.

10.3 SAP Build Work Zone

Today's complex business landscapes present organizations with the challenge of managing heterogeneous and fragmented ecosystems encompassing various content types, user interfaces, IT systems, content repositories, applications, and channels. This fragmentation often makes it difficult for business users to find relevant information and navigate between applications, resulting in a disjointed user experience.

Employees often express frustration when they struggle to find the right application for a specific task, feeling lost in the multitude of tools and systems. Without a comprehensive overview, decisions are made and actions taken that often make it difficult to derive meaningful insights or make accurate recommendations based on the full context of a situation. Employees want a unified, intelligent work environment that increases their productivity, engagement, and efficiency. SAP Build Work Zone is SAP's solution that addresses these challenges by consolidating and simplifying the enterprise landscape. By unifying the various elements into a single platform, SAP Build Work Zone improves the overall work experience for businesses, IT departments, and employees. It delivers a consistent user experience across channels, business processes, and applications, ensuring employees have access to the necessary tools and information to perform their tasks. SAP Build Work Zone is available in two editions, each tailored to specific needs:

- SAP Build Work Zone, standard edition
- SAP Build Work Zone, advanced edition

Prior to the introduction of SAP Build Work Zone in 2022, there were two separate digital experience services on SAP BTP: SAP Launchpad and SAP Work Zone. Although SAP Work Zone included most of SAP Launchpad's features, the two services were different products. With the introduction of SAP Build Work Zone, these two services have been consolidated under a new brand, offering two editions that meet different needs. SAP Launchpad is now SAP Build Work Zone, standard edition, and SAP Work Zone is now SAP Build Work Zone, advanced edition.

Ahead, we'll walk through the step-by-step process of installing and configuring SAP Build Work Zone, advanced edition.

10.3.1 Initial Steps

Because the process for SAP Build Work Zone is the same as installing the boosters for SAP Build Apps and SAP Build Process Automation, we will not provide detailed descriptions with screenshots for most of the steps. As before, you will start by creating a subaccount (see Figure 10.30).

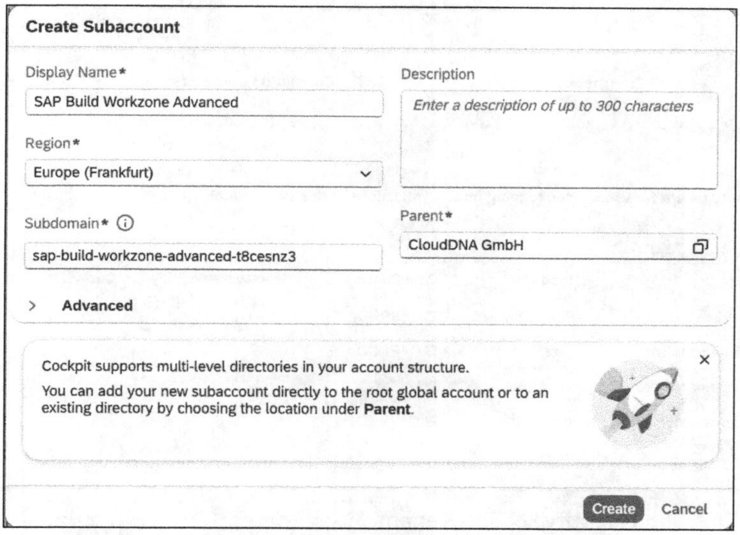

10.3 SAP Build Work Zone

Figure 10.30 Create Subaccount for SAP Build Work Zone

The next step is to establish a trust relationship with SAP Cloud Identity Services. Open the SAP BTP cockpit for the subaccount and navigate to the **Security • Trust Configuration** area in the side menu. Click **Establish Trust**, as shown in Figure 10.31.

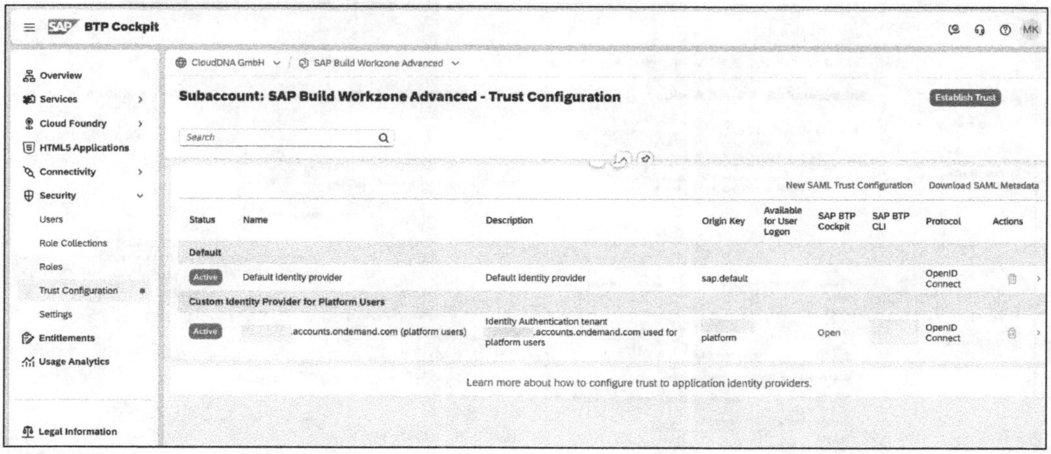

Figure 10.31 Establish Trust

In the **Configure Tenant** dialog, select the desired instance of SAP Cloud Identity Services, as shown in Figure 10.32.

10 Activating and Setting Up SAP Build

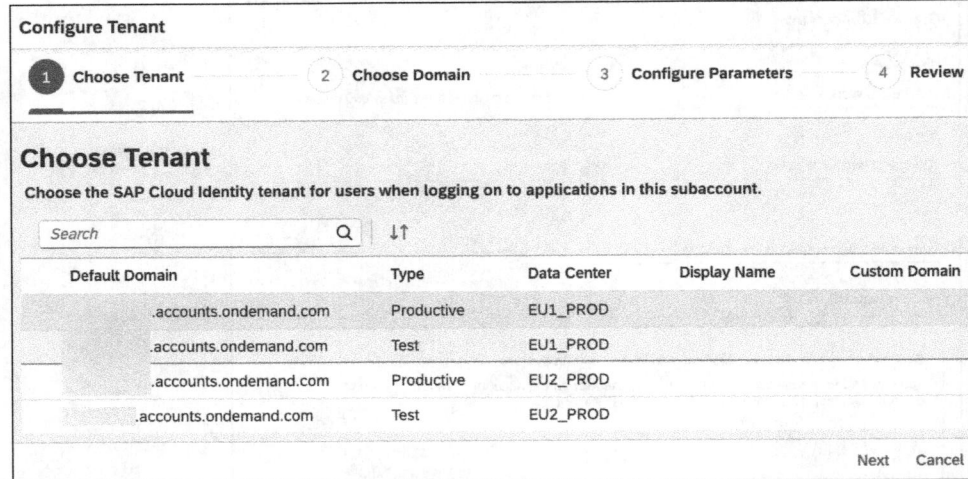

Figure 10.32 Choose SAP Cloud Identity Services Tenant

The next step is to configure SAP Cloud Identity Services. To do this, navigate to the **Security • Trust Configuration** area in the side menu, as shown in Figure 10.33. Select the identity provider you created earlier under **Custom Identity Provider for Applications**. Click the **Administration Console** link in the **Details**.

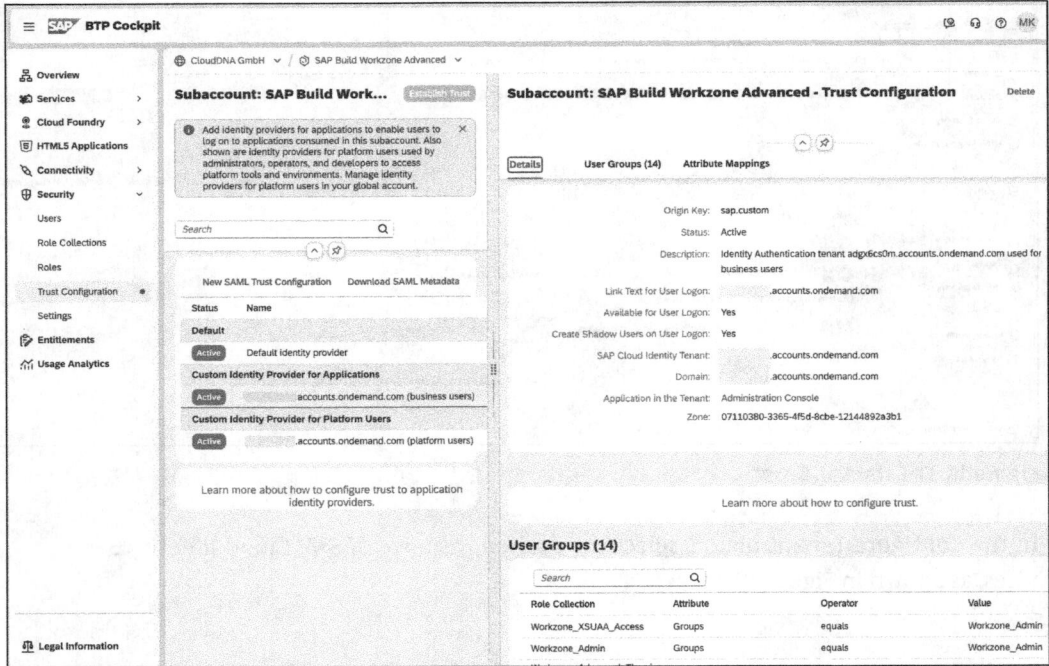

Figure 10.33 Open SAP Cloud Identity Services Admin Console

10.3 SAP Build Work Zone

You will now be taken directly to the previously registered application, as shown in Figure 10.34. In the **Single Sign-On** area, click the **Subject Name Identifier** entry. In the **Primary Attribute** area, select **Identity Directory** for **Source** and **Global User ID** for **Value**. Then click **Save**.

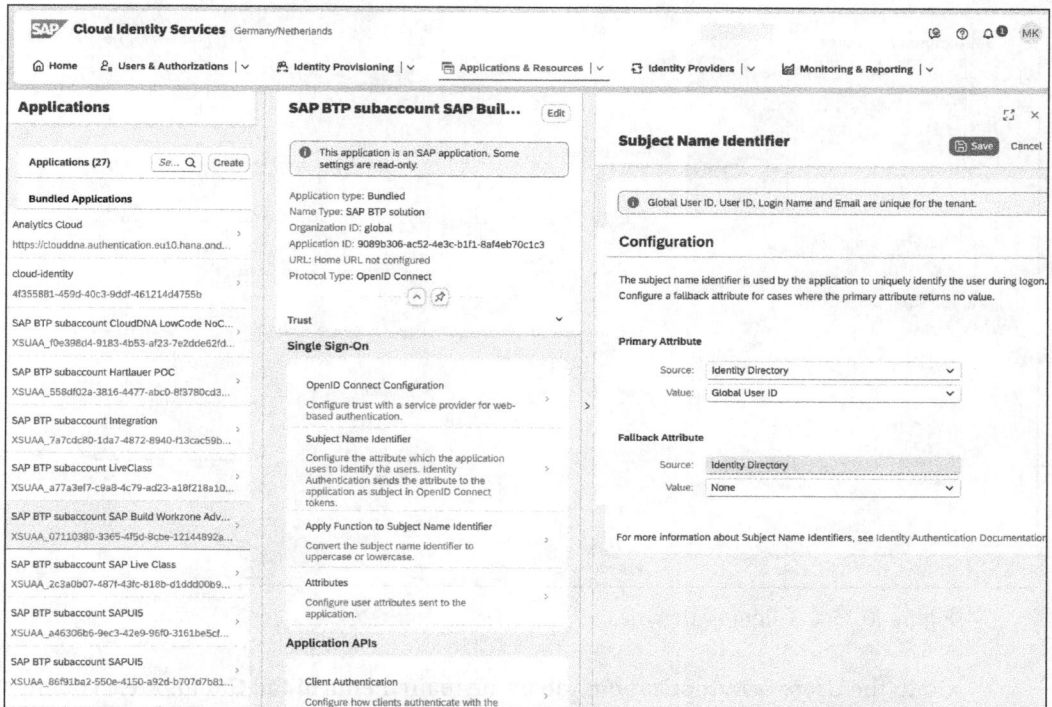

Figure 10.34 Configure Subject Name Identifier

Next, access the **Attributes** area by following this path: **Trust · Single Sign-On** (see Figure 10.35). There are six attributes available by default. These must be manually expanded for the interaction between SAP Cloud Identity Services and SAP Build Work Zone to function correctly. Click **Add** in the upper-right corner to insert a new attribute in the table. Insert the attributes as listed in Table 10.1 and click **Save**.

Name	Source	Value
first_name	Identity Directory	First Name
last_name	Identity Directory	Last Name
mail	Identity Directory	Email
Groups	Expression	Workzone_User_Type_${type}

Table 10.1 Attributes for Single Sign-on Response to Application

10   Activating and Setting Up SAP Build

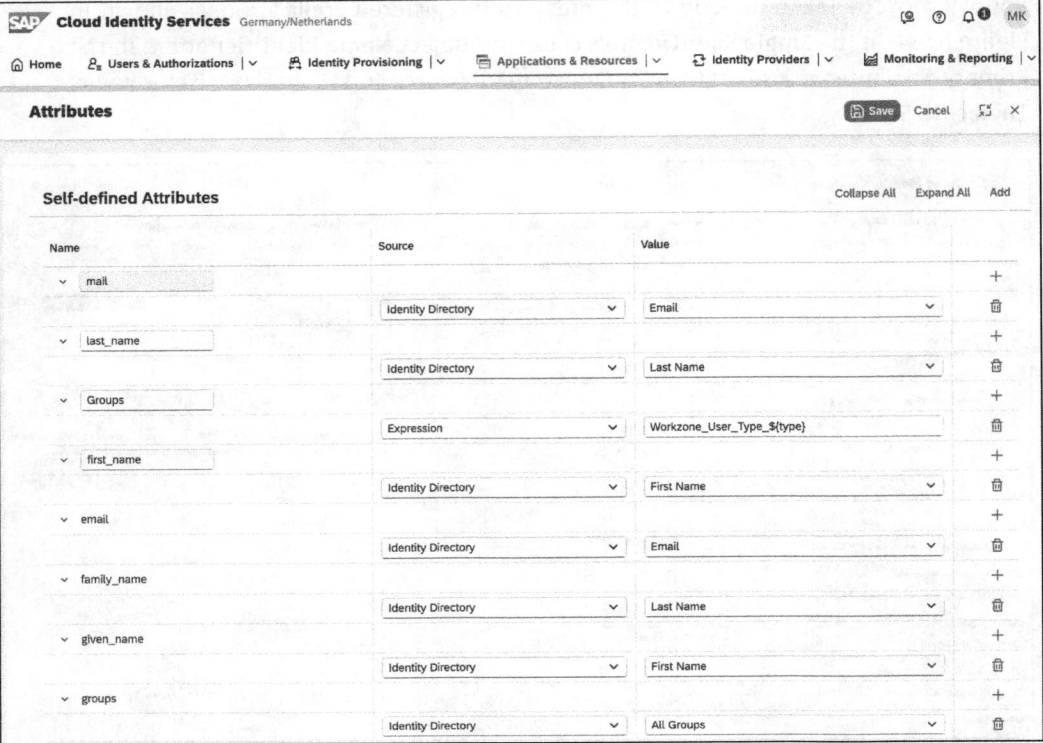

Figure 10.35 Configure Attributes

Go to the **Users & Authorizations** tab in the main menu. In the **Groups** area, you must manually create new groups. These groups will be added to the role collections in the subaccount. Click the **+ Create** button to create a new group (see Figure 10.36). Create the following groups in this way:

- `Workzone_Admin`
- `Workzone_Area_Admin`
- `Workzone_End_User`
- `Workzone_Page_Content_Admin`
- `Workzone_Support_Admin`
- `Workzone_User_Type_public`

Next, activate the **Cloud Foundry Environment** and create a space within it. Then, as shown in Figure 10.37, navigate to the **Overview** area in the side menu and check that everything has been created as desired.

10.3 SAP Build Work Zone

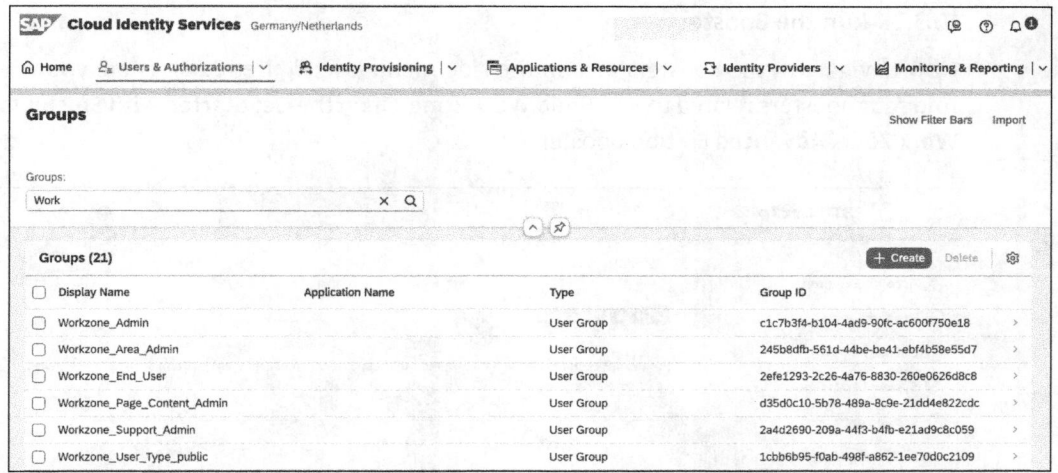

Figure 10.36 Create Groups

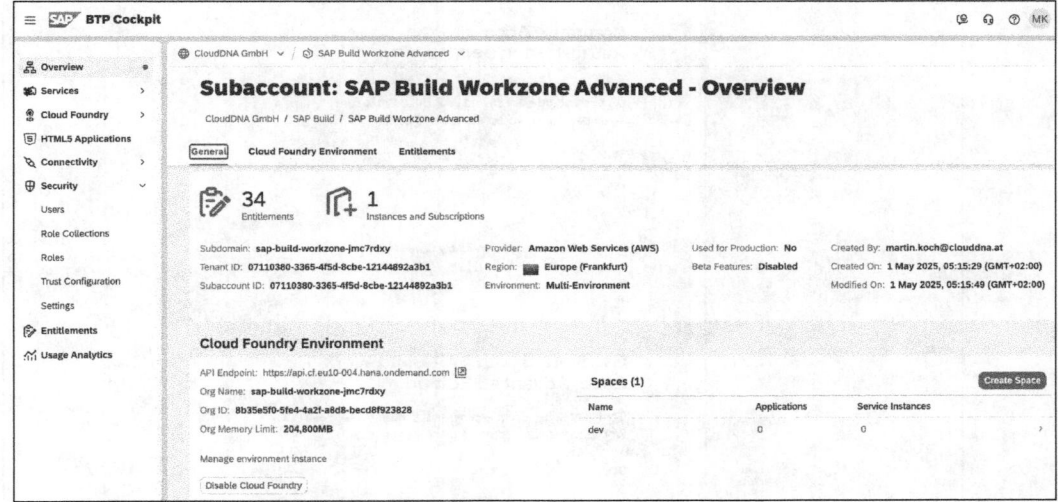

Figure 10.37 Enable Cloud Foundry and Create Space

You have now configured SSO in SAP Cloud Identity Services. First, you adjusted the subject name identifier, and then you defined which attributes are sent to SAP Build Work Zone after successful login. Finally, you created the groups required for SAP Build Work Zone.

10 Activating and Setting Up SAP Build

10.3.2 Run the Booster

Now navigate to the **Boosters** area in the side menu (see Figure 10.38). There you will find four boosters related to SAP Build Work Zone. Open the **Get Started with SAP Build Work Zone, Advanced Edition** booster.

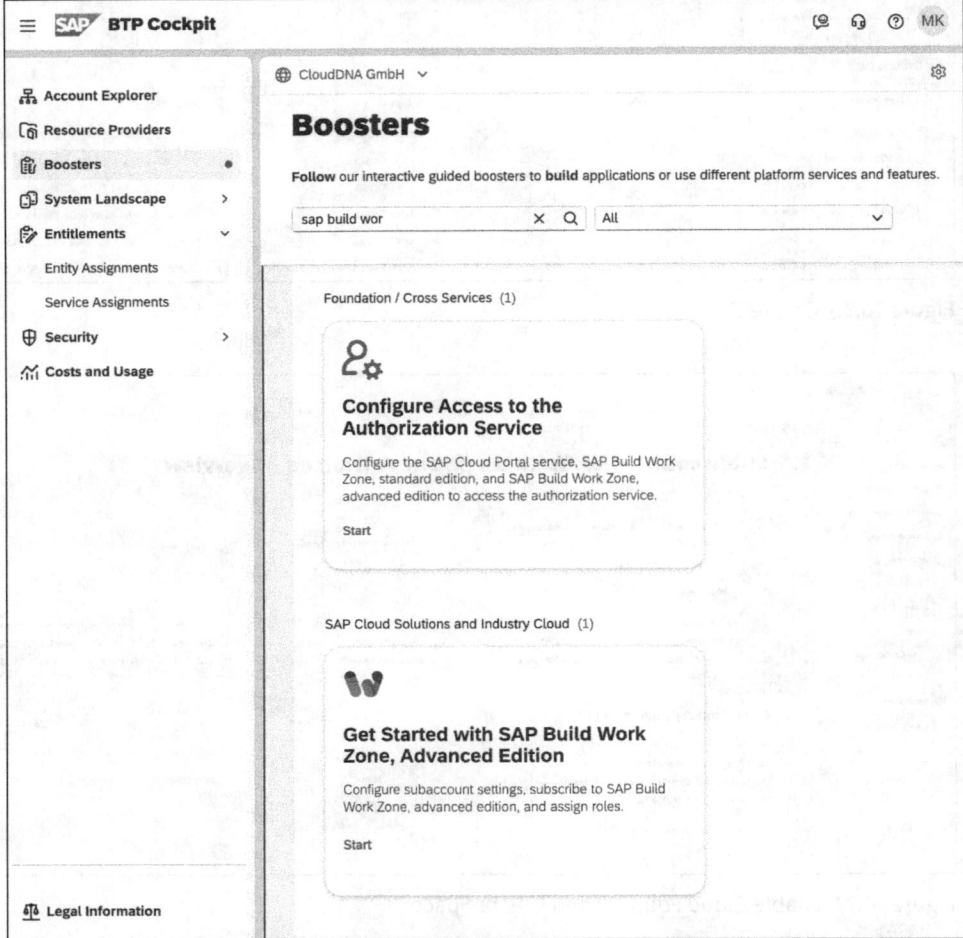

Figure 10.38 SAP Build Work Zone, Advanced Edition Booster

Open the **Components** tab of the booster to see an overview of the required services and subscriptions (see Figure 10.39). Then, click **Start** to begin using the booster.

First, click the **Continue** button to confirm that you want to run the SAP Build Work Zone booster and not the SAP SuccessFactors Work Zone booster (see Figure 10.40).

10.3 SAP Build Work Zone

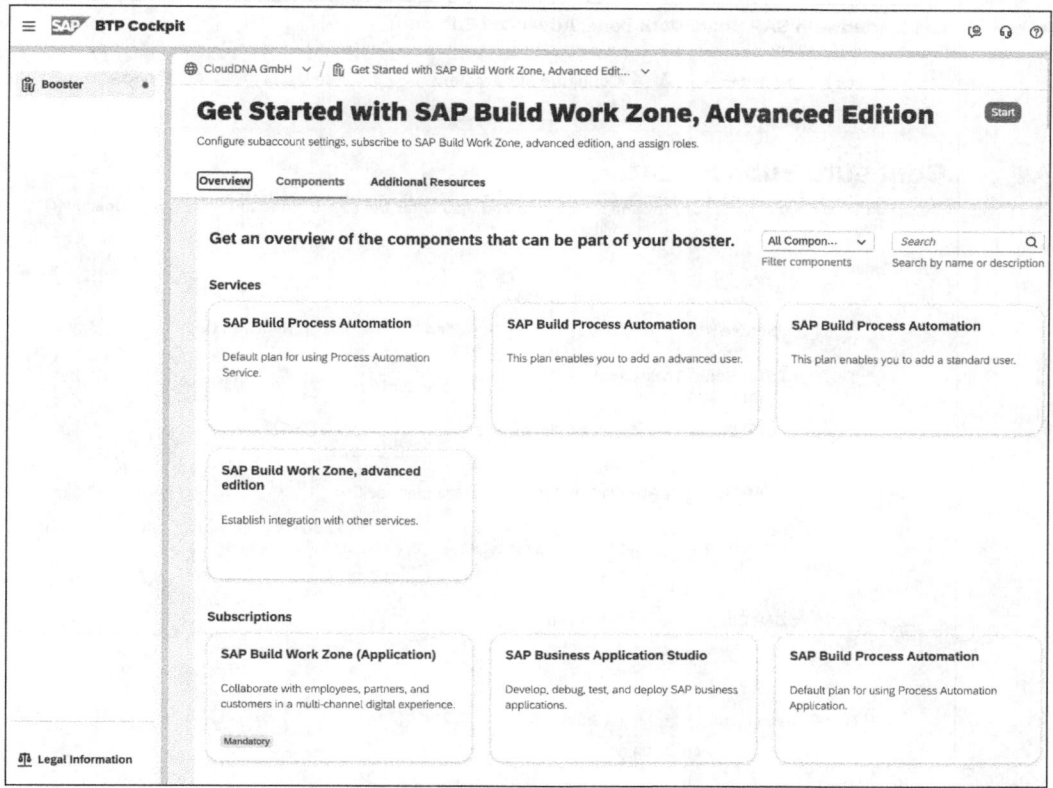

Figure 10.39 Component Overview in SAP Build Work Zone

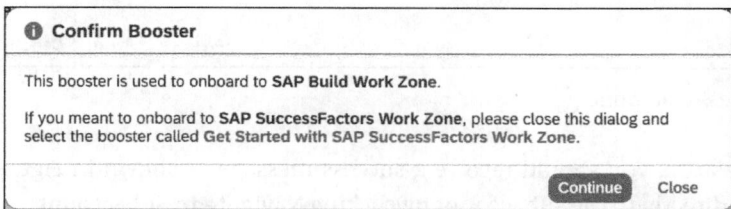

Figure 10.40 Confirm Selection of Correct Booster

At this point, we will only show the **Configure Subaccount** section of the booster. The other steps should already be familiar to you from the boosters covered earlier. Select the **Entitlements** shown in Figure 10.41. In the **Subaccount** section, select the subaccount you created earlier. The **Org** field is automatically populated, as only one Cloud Foundry organization is allowed or can be created per subaccount. In the **Space** area, select the previously created space, if it's not already preselected.

10 Activating and Setting Up SAP Build

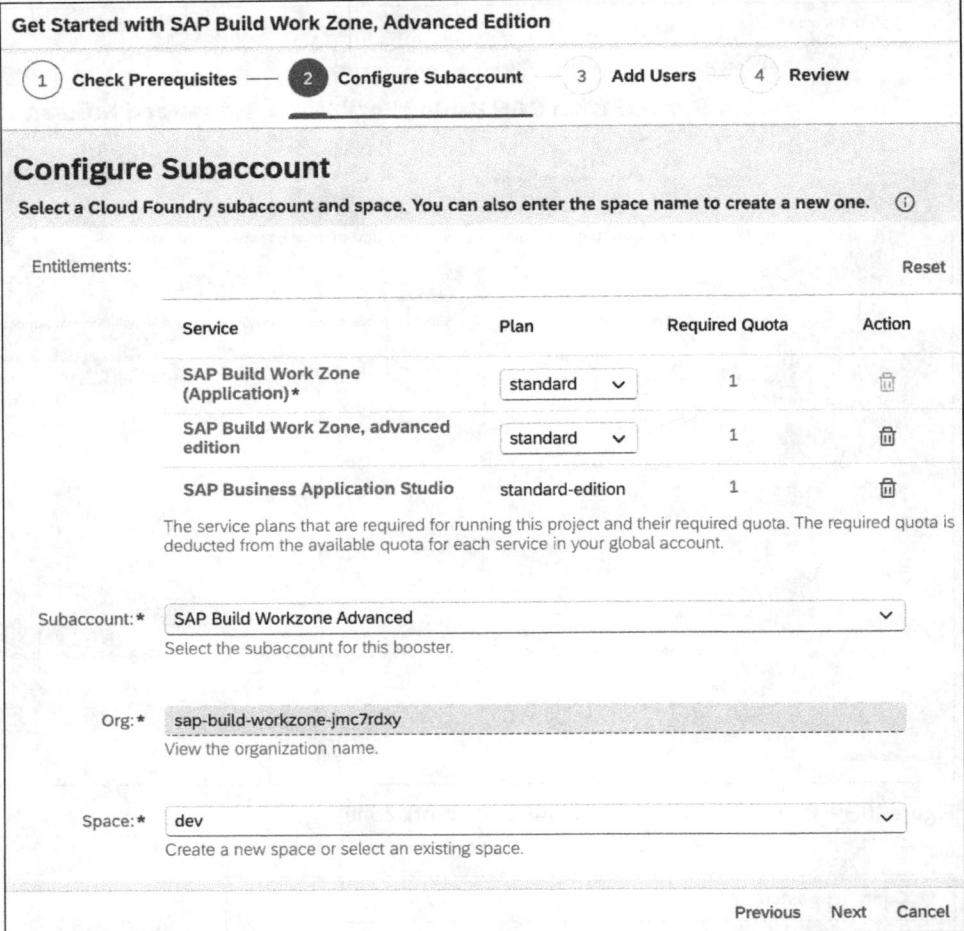

Figure 10.41 Configure Subaccount

After the booster has run, you should receive a success message as shown in Figure 10.42. You can jump directly to the subaccount by clicking **Navigate to Subaccount**.

Figure 10.42 Success Message

In the side menu of the SAP BTP cockpit, navigate to the **Security · Role Collections** area. There you will see that different roll collections have been created for both the workflow and SAP Build Work Zone (see Figure 10.43).

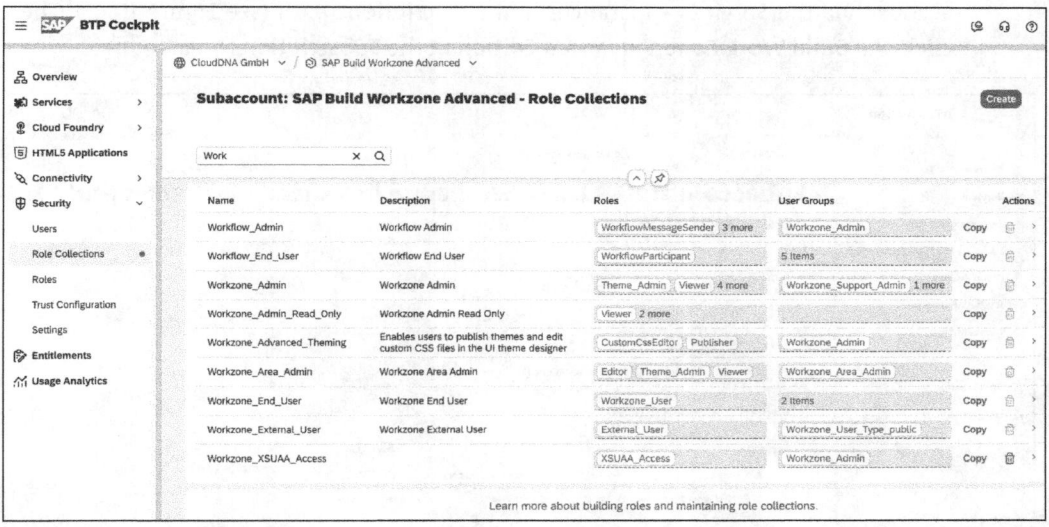

Figure 10.43 Check Role Collections

Open the **Workzone_Admin** role collection. Navigate to the **User Groups** area. You should see the mappings for the **Workzone_Admin** and **Workzone_Support_Admin** user groups, as shown in Figure 10.44. This link was created by the booster, provided that you previously created the corresponding groups in SAP Cloud Identity Services.

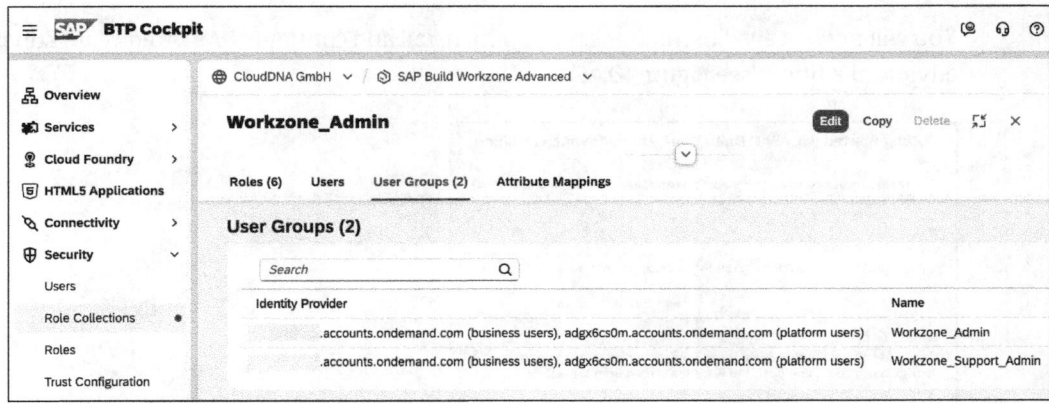

Figure 10.44 Verify User Group Mappings

10.3.3 Configuring SAP Build Work Zone, Advanced Edition

In the next step, you'll perform the necessary basic configuration within SAP Build Work Zone, advanced edition. To start, navigate to the SAP BTP cockpit of the subaccount via the **Services • Instances and Subscriptions** path (see Figure 10.45). There, click **SAP Build Work Zone, Advanced Edition** in the **Subscriptions** area.

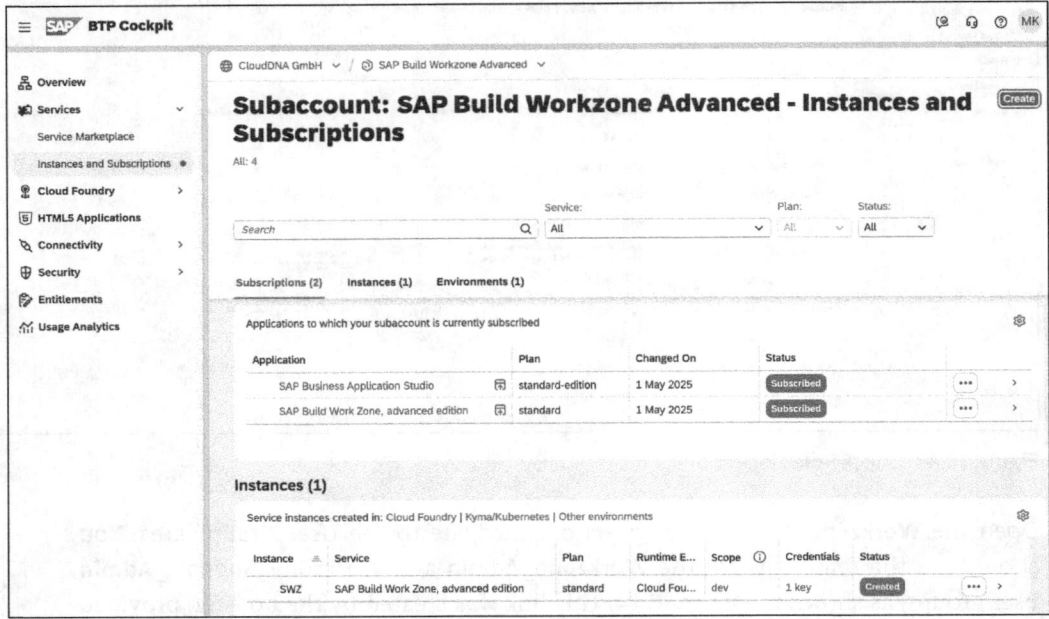

Figure 10.45 SAP Build Work Zone in Overview of Instances and Subscriptions

You will now receive instructions on how to install and configure SAP Build Work Zone, advanced edition (see Figure 10.46).

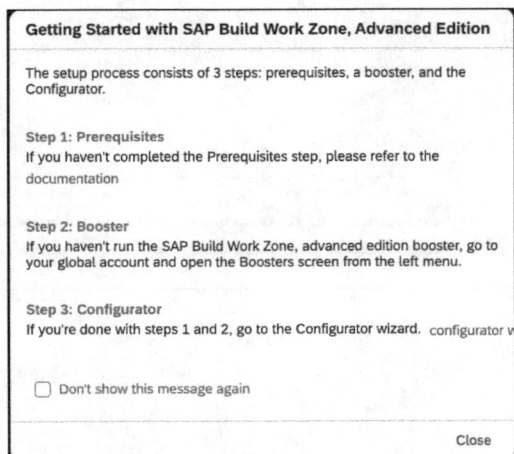

Figure 10.46 Configuration Notes for SAP Build Work Zone

10.3 SAP Build Work Zone

From there, you can jump to the documentation by clicking the **documentation** link, which is very helpful: It contains the mappings for the Identity Provisioning service that you will need later. You can close this dialog by clicking **Close**.

Now you can start the configurator (see Figure 10.47). Select the **I want to create a new service instance.** radio button, then click the **Next** button.

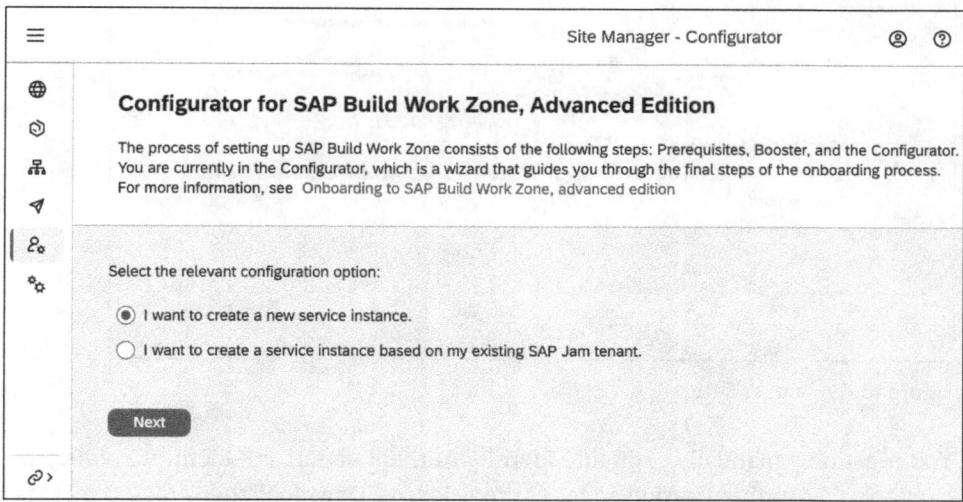

Figure 10.47 Configurator

You can skip the first step, which involves creating a destination for SAP SuccessFactors to integrate with. Therefore, click the **Skip Step** button (see Figure 10.48).

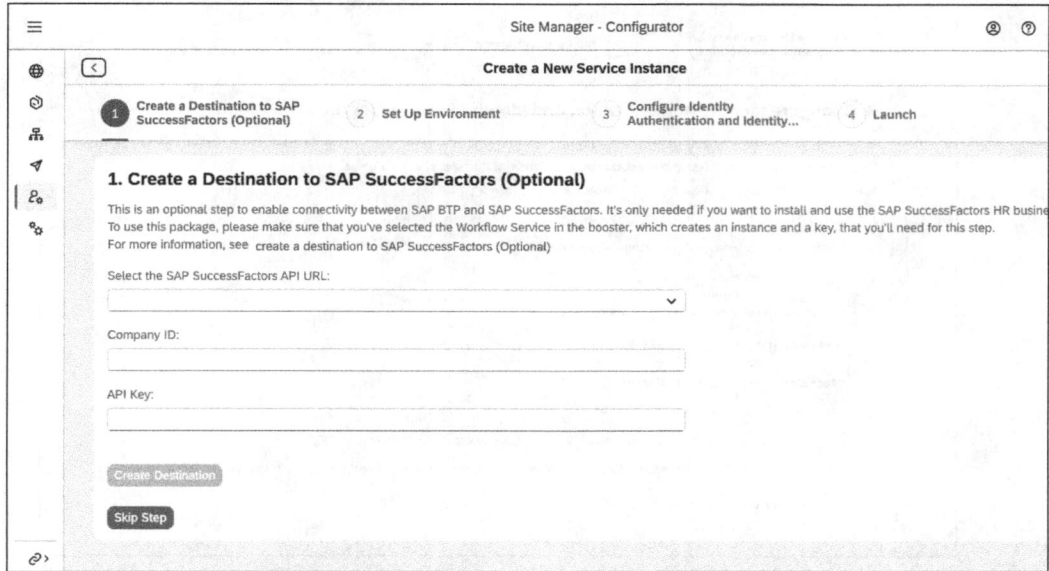

Figure 10.48 Skip SAP SuccessFactors Step

10 Activating and Setting Up SAP Build

In the second step, select **Set Up Environment** in the configurator for SAP Build Work Zone, advanced edition, and choose **Default** in the **Select Domain Type** area (see Figure 10.49). (If you are using a custom domain, then you must select the **Custom** option instead.) Now click the **Trigger Setup** button.

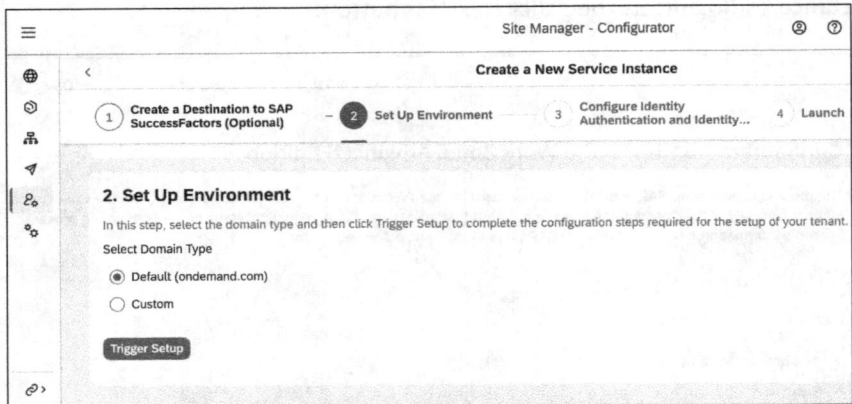

Figure 10.49 Trigger Setup

You must now manually configure Identity Authentication and Identity Provisioning to enable user authentication and user provisioning. Download the SAML 2.0 metadata of the service provider from the configurator by clicking the **Download Metadata** link (see Figure 10.50).

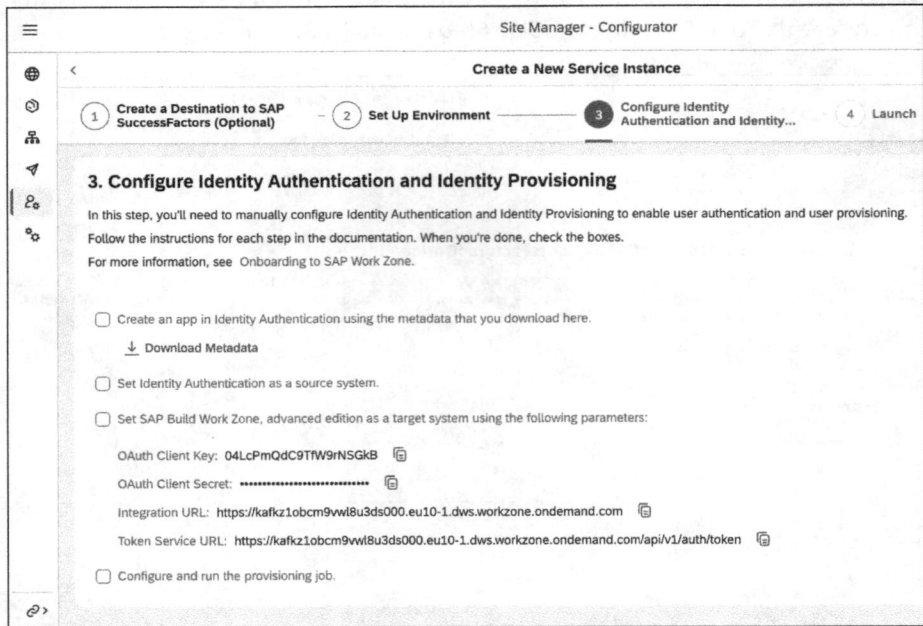

Figure 10.50 Configure Identity Authentication and Identity Provisioning

10.3 SAP Build Work Zone

In SAP Cloud Identity Services, go to **Applications & Resources** • **Applications** and click **Create** to create a new application (see Figure 10.51).

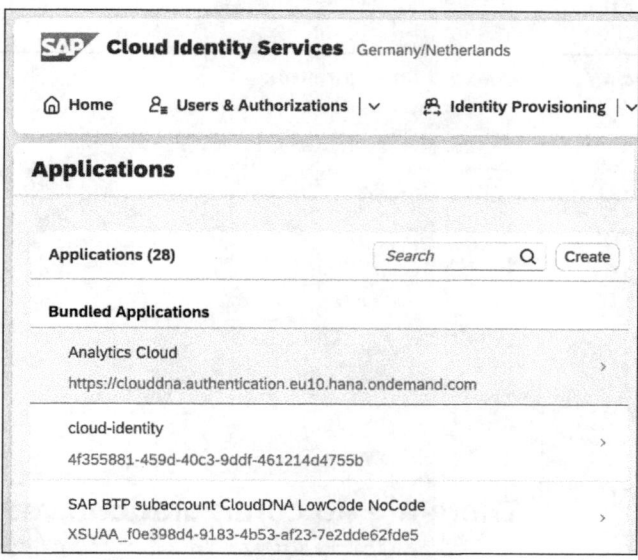

Figure 10.51 Create New Application

Enter a meaningful name in **Display Name**, such as "SAP Build Work Zone Advanced." Select **SAP BTP solution** for **Type**, and select **SAML 2.0** for **Protocol Type**. Then click the **+ Create** button (see Figure 10.52).

Figure 10.52 Provide Application Details

10   Activating and Setting Up SAP Build

Now open the SAML 2.0 configuration for the application you created (see Figure 10.53). To do this, click the **SAML 2.0 Configuration** entry in the **Single Sign-On** area. Then click the **Define from Metadata** button.

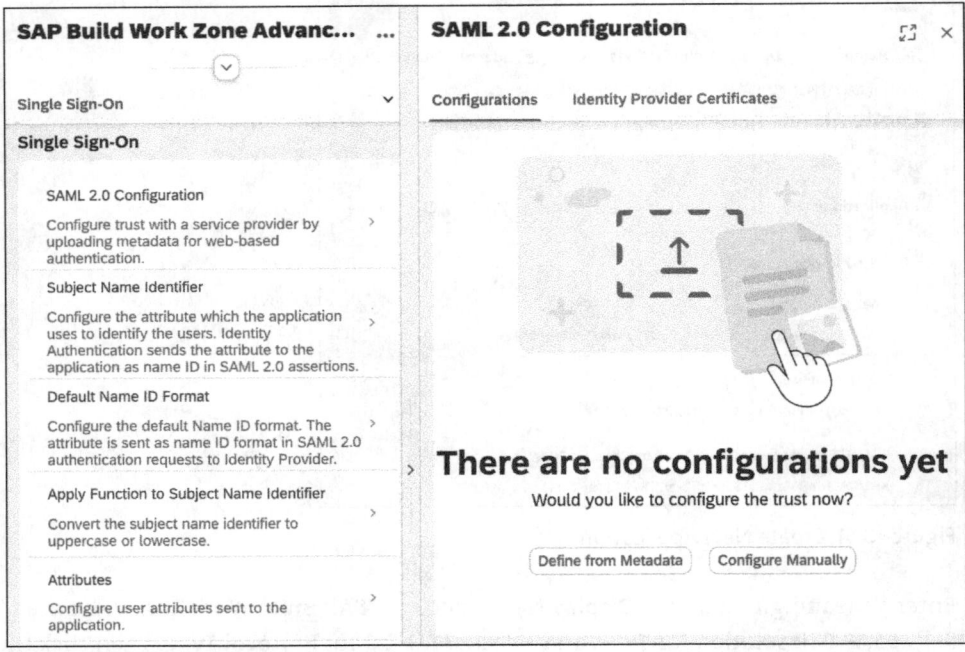

Figure 10.53 Define New Configuration

Insert the metadata of the service provider by clicking the **Browse...** button, and save your changes by clicking the **Save** button (see Figure 10.54).

Figure 10.54 Choose Metadata File

10.3 SAP Build Work Zone

You must now open the **Subject Name Identifier** editor from SAP Build Work Zone, advanced edition. Change the **Primary Attribute Source** from **User ID** to **Global User ID**, then click the **Save** button (see Figure 10.55).

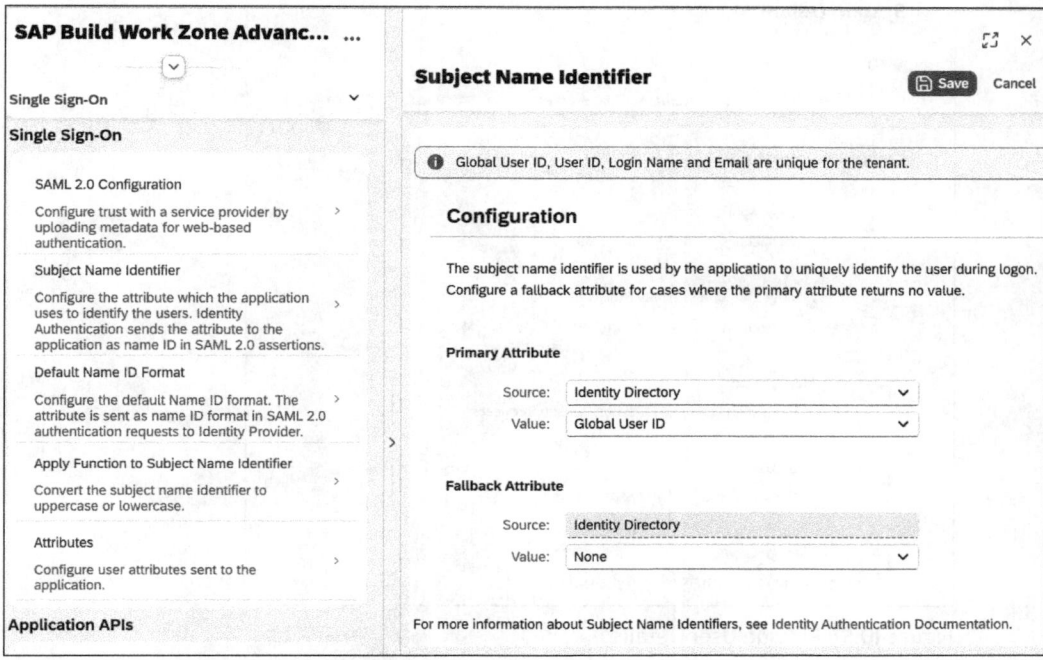

Figure 10.55 Customize Subject Name Identifier

In the administration console for SAP Cloud Identity Services, navigate to the **Administrators** tile and create a technical user by clicking the **Add** button and selecting **System** from the popover (see Figure 10.56).

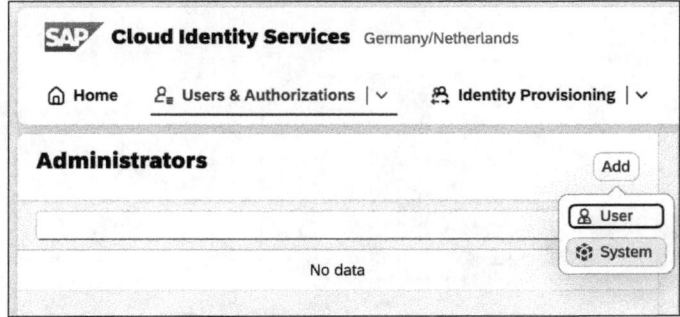

Figure 10.56 Create System User

Assign a descriptive **Name** and select the permissions shown in Figure 10.57. Then click **Save**.

10 Activating and Setting Up SAP Build

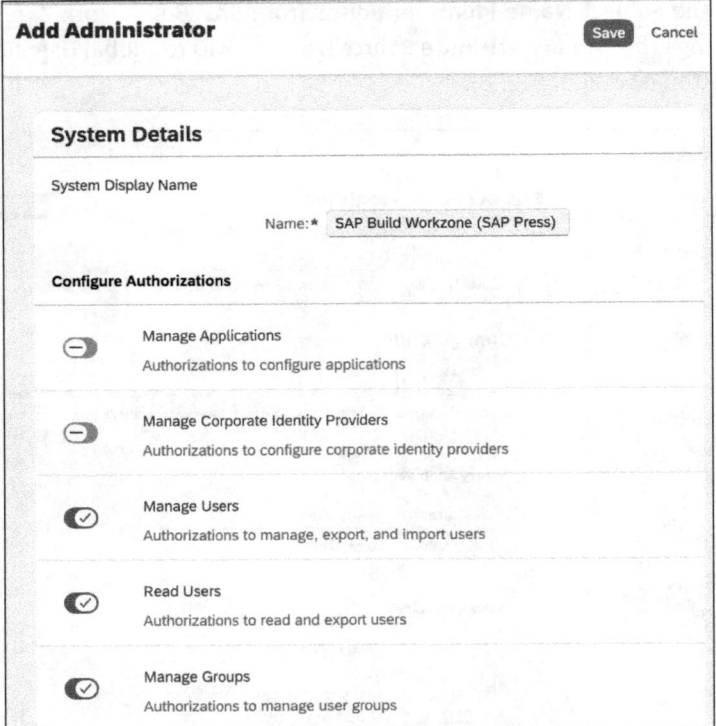

Figure 10.57 Provide User Details

The authentication between the Identity Authentication service and the Identity Provisioning service is done via basic authentication with a password and a generated **Client ID** (see Figure 10.58). Click **+ Add** to create a client secret that will be used as the password.

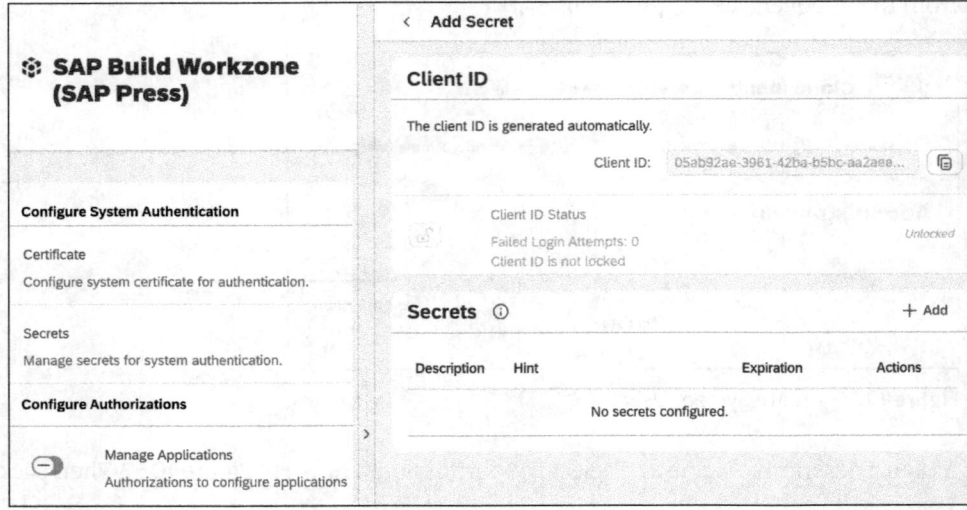

Figure 10.58 Credentials

Assign a **Description** as shown in Figure 10.59, and select **Never** for the **Expire in** field. Finally, click the **Save** button.

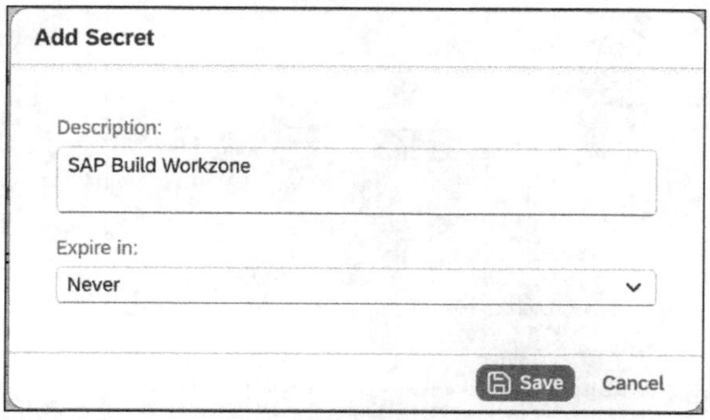

Figure 10.59 Create Client Secret

You must now set up the Identity Authentication service as a source system. To do this, navigate to the **Identity Provisioning** • **Source System** area and then click **Add** (see Figure 10.60). Select **Identity Authentication** as the **Type** and assign a meaningful **System Name**.

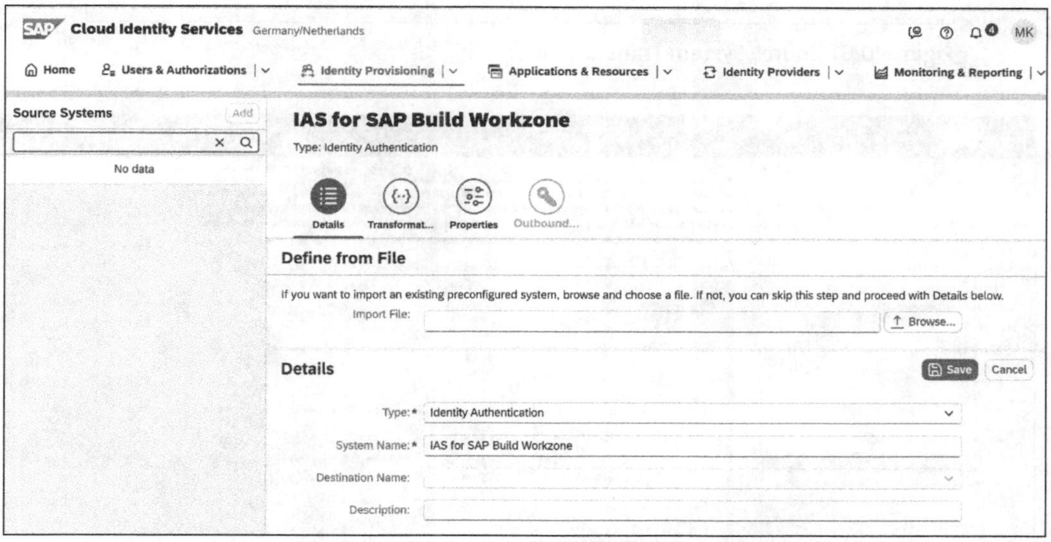

Figure 10.60 Create Source System

You must now create a transformation. Transformations are used to map user attributes from the source system's data model to the target system's data model and vice versa. Replace the default transformation code (displayed under the **Transformations** tab after saving its initial configuration) with the transformation that matches SAP Build Work Zone, advanced edition. To do so, open the **Transformation** tab and click the **Edit** button (see Figure 10.61).

10 Activating and Setting Up SAP Build

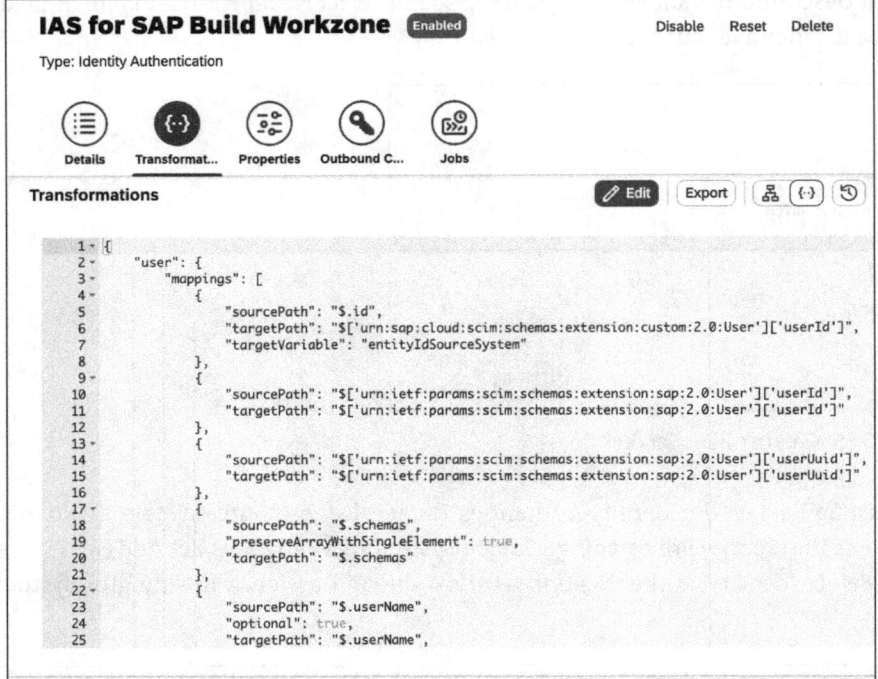

Figure 10.61 Source System Transformation

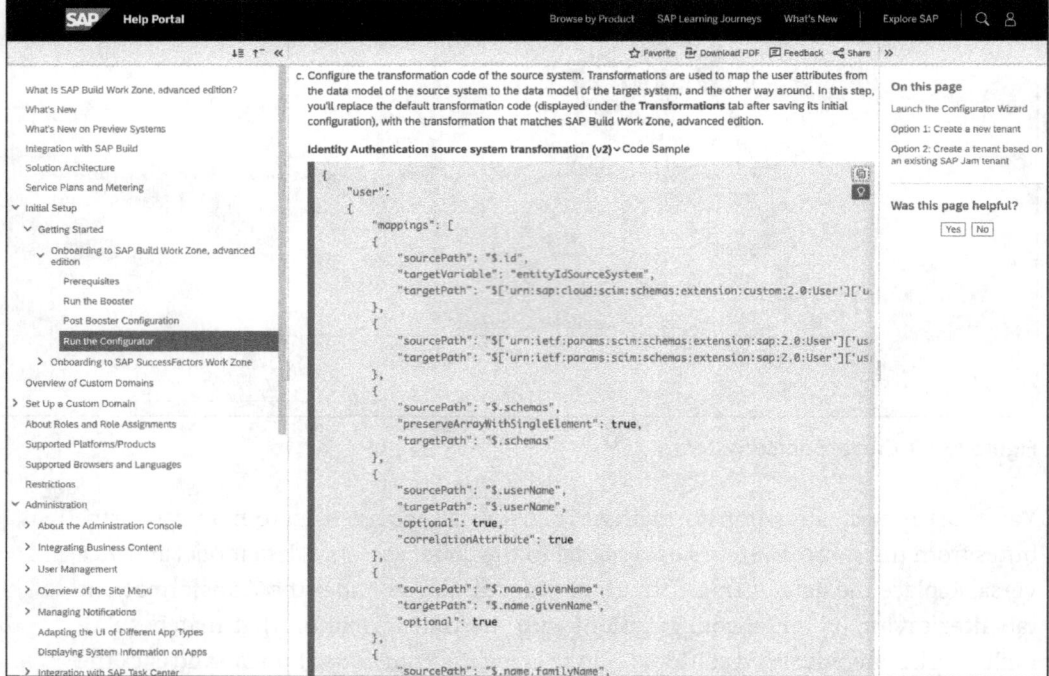

Figure 10.62 Copy Source Transformation

10.3 SAP Build Work Zone

You can find the corresponding transformation in the official SAP Help. As shown in Figure 10.62, open the **Run the Configurator** section in the SAP Help Portal and navigate to the code for the corresponding transformation. You can copy this code to the clipboard using the **Copy** button.

Paste the transformation code from the clipboard into the appropriate field (see Figure 10.63), then click **Save**. If you are in the visual view, you can switch to the code view by clicking the corresponding icon.

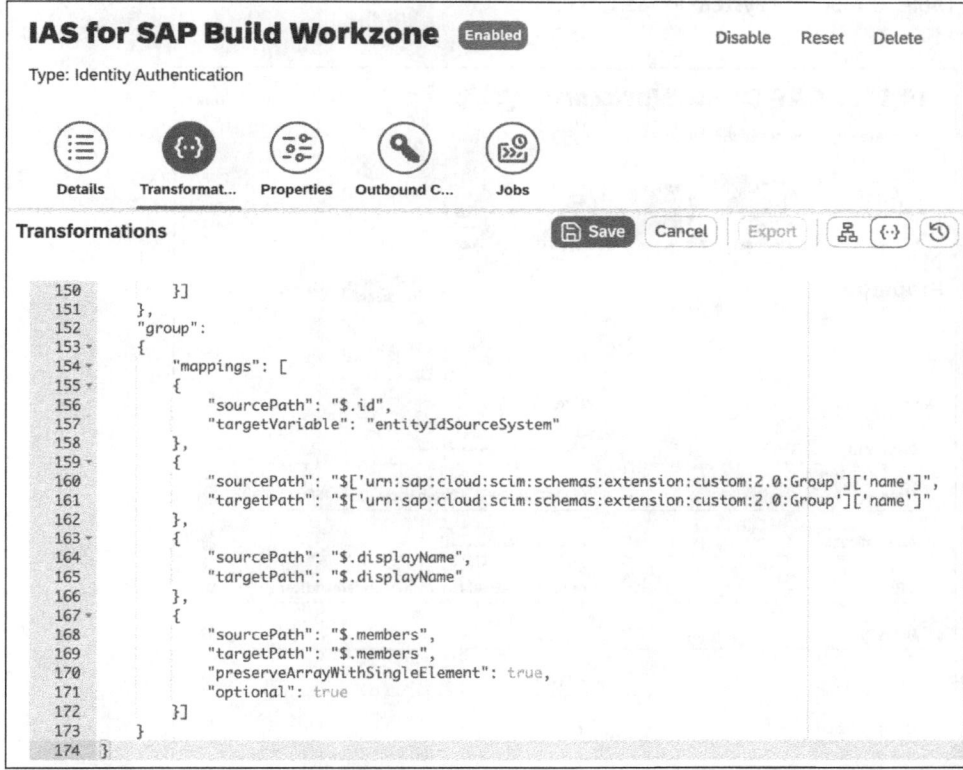

Figure 10.63 Edit Transformation

Click the **Properties** tab (see Figure 10.64). Confirm that the properties shown in the figure are present. If not, add them manually. You will need the properties shown in Table 10.2 in place. Finally, click the **Save** button.

Property Name	Description and Value
Type	http
URL	Specify the URL of the Identity Authentication tenant of your company. For example: https://mytenant.accounts.ondemand.com

Table 10.2 Source System Properties

10 Activating and Setting Up SAP Build

Property Name	Description and Value
ProxyType	Internet
Authentication	BasicAuthentication
User	ClientID
Password	Client Secret

Table 10.2 Source System Properties (Cont.)

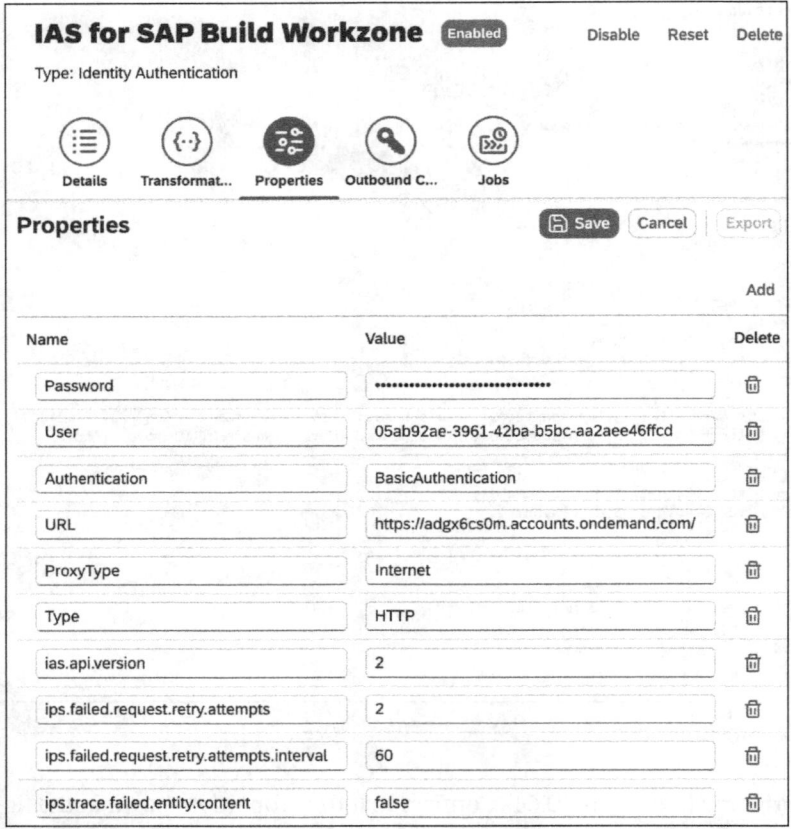

Figure 10.64 Add Properties

Now create a target system. To do this, navigate to **Identity Provisioning • Target Systems**. Click **Add**. Select **SAP Build Work Zone, advanced edition** for **Type**. Enter a meaningful name in the **System Name** field. Finally, click **Save** (see Figure 10.65).

10.3 SAP Build Work Zone

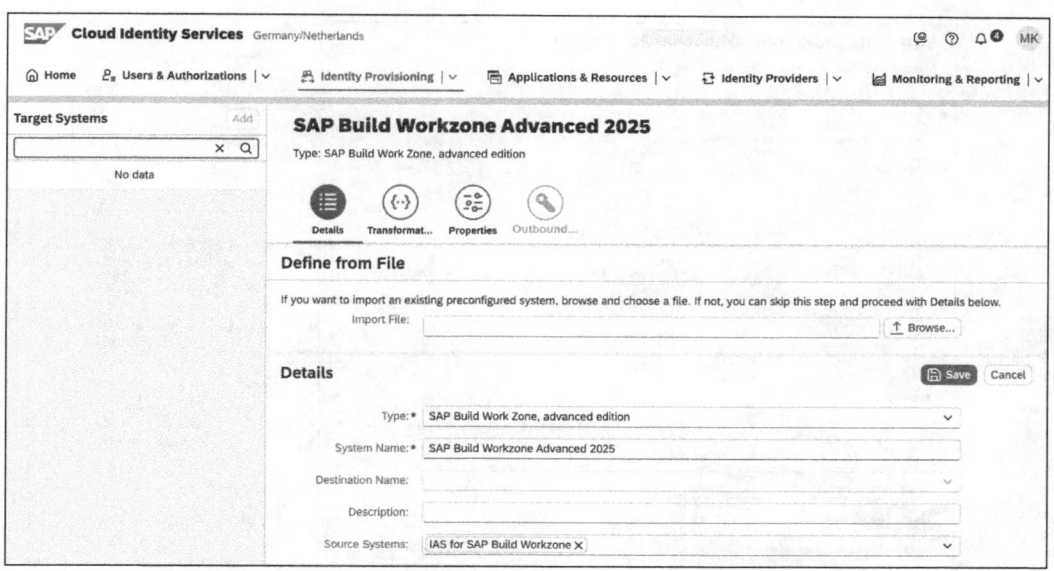

Figure 10.65 Create Target System

You must maintain the properties here. Open the **Properties** tab (see Figure 10.66) and maintain the properties shown in Table 10.3 to complete this task.

Identity Provisioning Property Name	Value
Type	HTTP
URL	Copy this value from the Integration URL field.
ProxyType	Internet
Authentication	BasicAuthentication
User	Copy this value from the **OAuth Client Key** wizard field.
Password	Copy this value from the **OAuth Client Secret** field in the wizard.
OAuth2TokenServiceURL	Copy this value from the **Token Service URL** wizard field.
ips.failed.request.retry.attempts	3
ips.failed.request.retry.attempts.interval	60
ips.delete.existedbefore.entities	true
ips.trace.failed.entity.content	true

Table 10.3 Target System Properties

10 Activating and Setting Up SAP Build

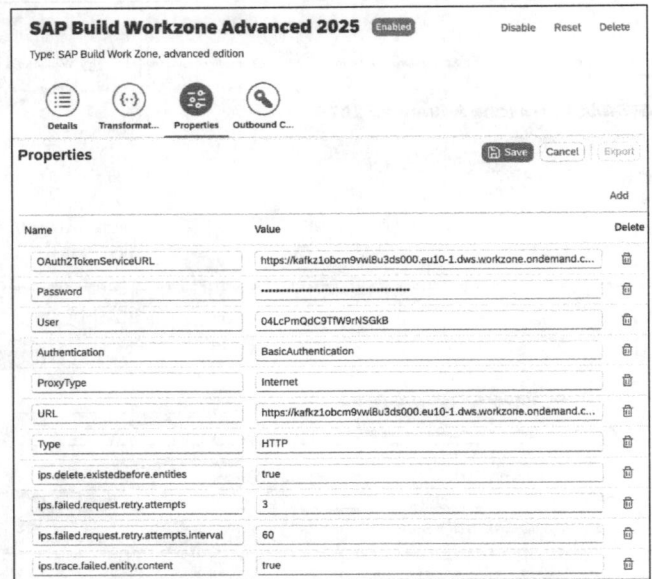

Figure 10.66 Target System Properties

Here too you must insert a mapping. Again, copy the mapping from the official product documentation (see Figure 10.67).

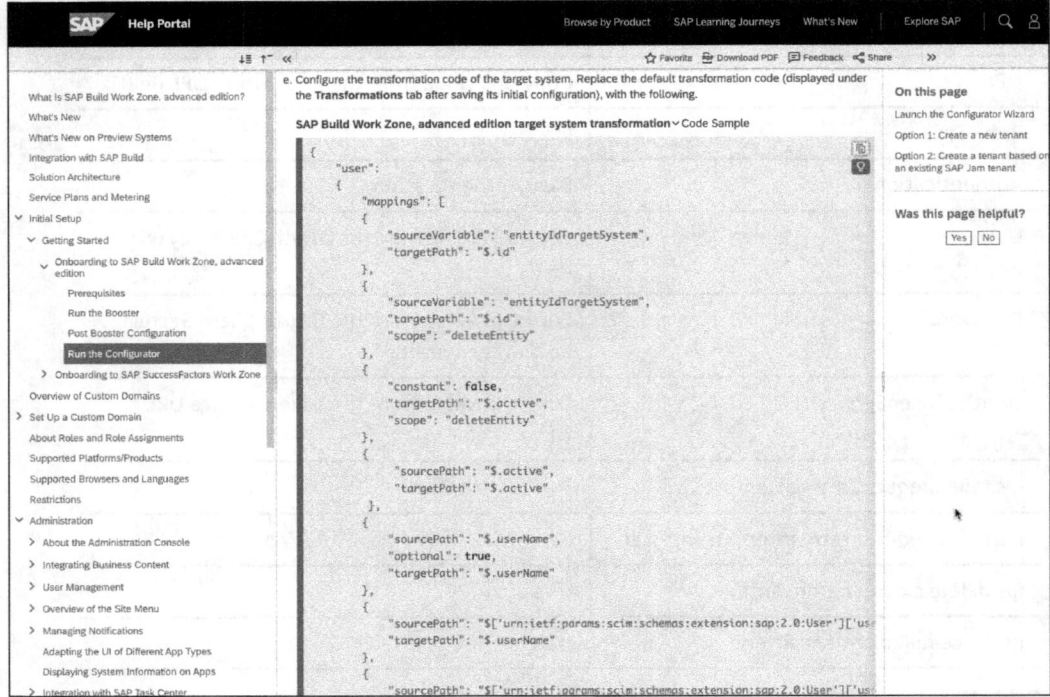

Figure 10.67 Target System Mapping

434

10.3 SAP Build Work Zone

Insert the mapping into the code editor of the **Transformations** tab and click **Save** (see Figure 10.68).

```
SAP Build Workzone Advanced 2025  [Enabled]        Disable  Reset  Delete
Type: SAP Build Work Zone, advanced edition

Details  Transformat...  Properties  Outbound C...

Transformations                              Save  Cancel  Export

219    "mappings": [
220      {
221        "sourceVariable": "entityIdTargetSystem",
222        "targetPath": "$.id"
223      },
224      {
225        "constant": "urn:ietf:params:scim:schemas:core:2.0:Group",
226        "targetPath": "$.schemas[0]"
227      },
228      {
229        "sourcePath": "$['urn:sap:cloud:scim:schemas:extension:custom:2.0:Group']['name']",
230        "targetPath": "$.displayName"
231      },
232      {
233        "sourcePath": "$.members[*].value",
234        "preserveArrayWithSingleElement": true,
235        "optional": true,
236        "targetPath": "$.members[?(@.value)]",
237        "functions": [
238          {
239            "type": "resolveEntityIds"
240          }
241        ]
242      }
243    }
```

Figure 10.68 Mapping

Now that all the necessary settings have been made, start the first provisioning. This is always done from the source system. To do this, navigate to the source system you created earlier, open the **Jobs** tab, and click the **Run Now** button under **Read Job** (see Figure 10.69). Schedule a job that performs provisioning at regular intervals to ensure productive operation.

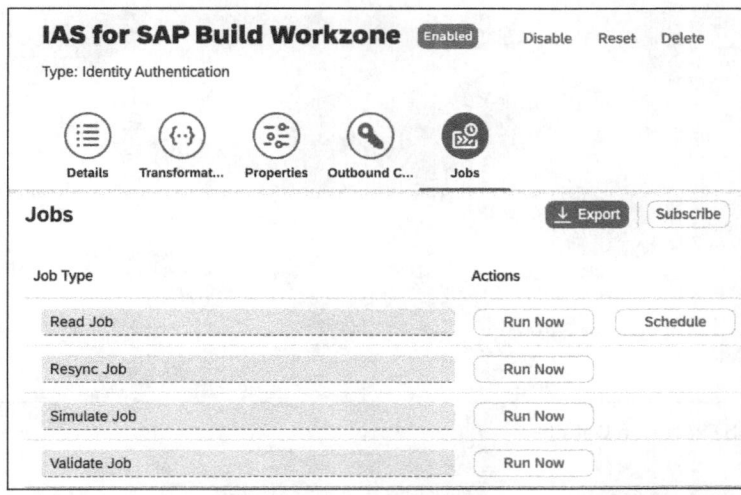

Figure 10.69 Run Read Job in Source System

435

Next, open the **Provisioning Logs**. To do this, navigate to **Identity Provisioning • Provisioning Logs** and open the **Job Logs** tab (see Figure 10.70). As the figure clearly shows, the job has been completed with the status **Finished Successfully**. Click the corresponding entry in the table to jump to the details.

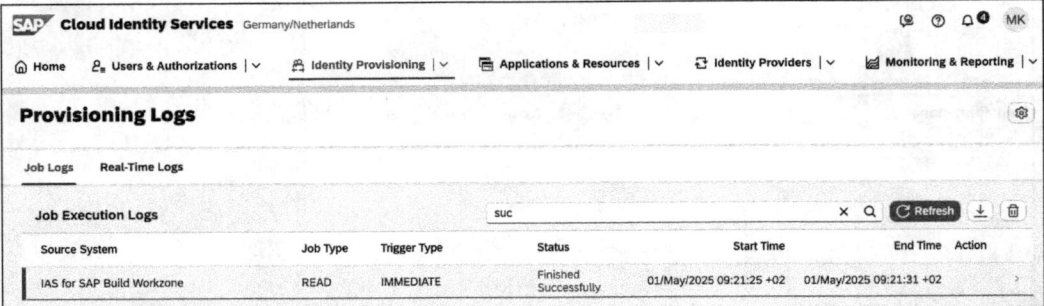

Figure 10.70 Check Provisioning Log

In the **Job Execution Details**, you will find all relevant information about the provisioning run (see Figure 10.71). This report clearly shows how many users and groups were read from the source system and adapted in the target systems. This is also where you would find error messages if the provisioning run encountered an error. This can happen if a transformation was incorrect.

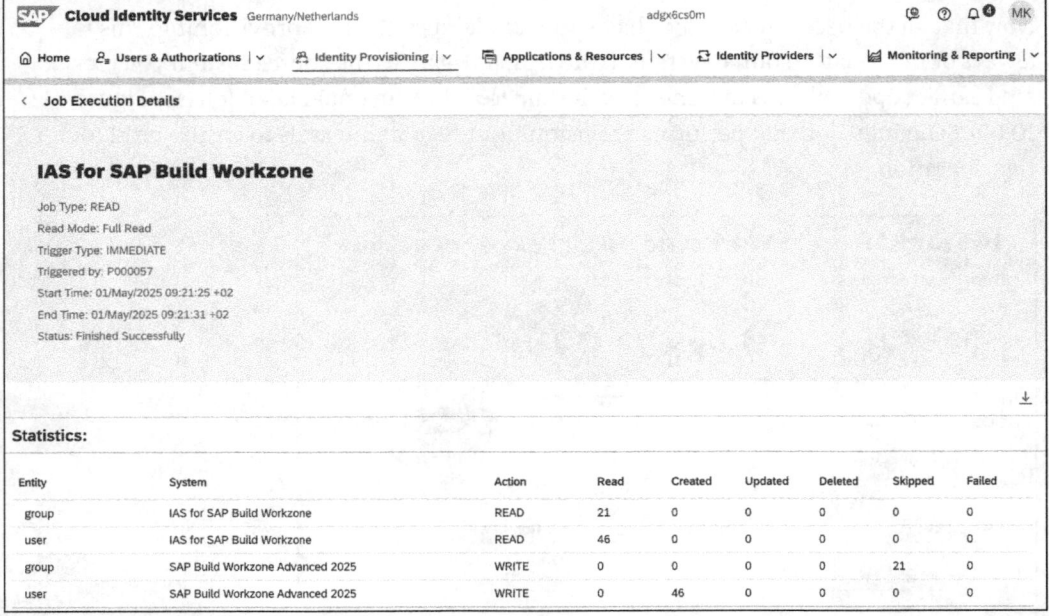

Figure 10.71 Check Job Execution Details

10.3 SAP Build Work Zone

Now that you have configured SAP Cloud Identity Services, continue with the configuration in SAP Build Work Zone, advanced edition. Select the appropriate checkboxes for all tasks, then click **Step 4** (see Figure 10.72).

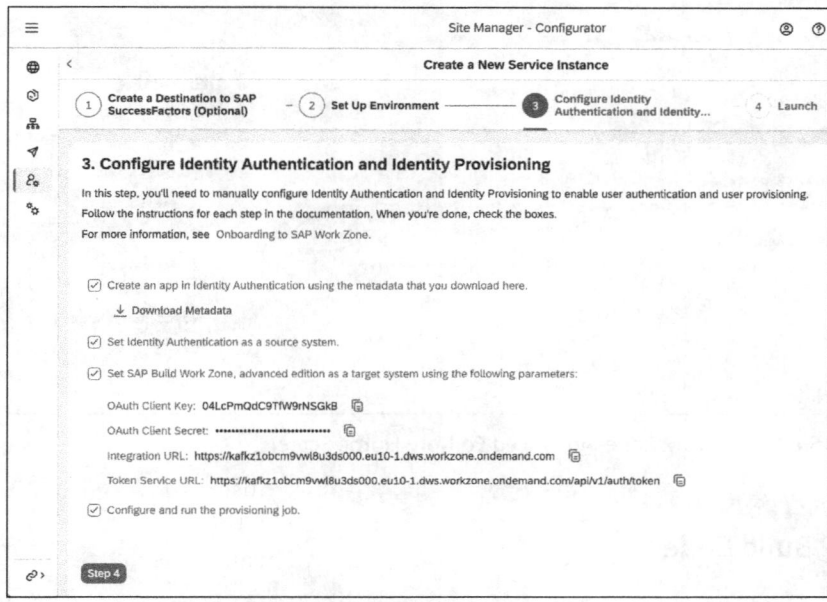

Figure 10.72 Continue Configurator

You should now see that the onboarding has been successfully completed (see Figure 10.73). Click the **Open SAP Build Work Zone, advanced edition** link to access the application for end users.

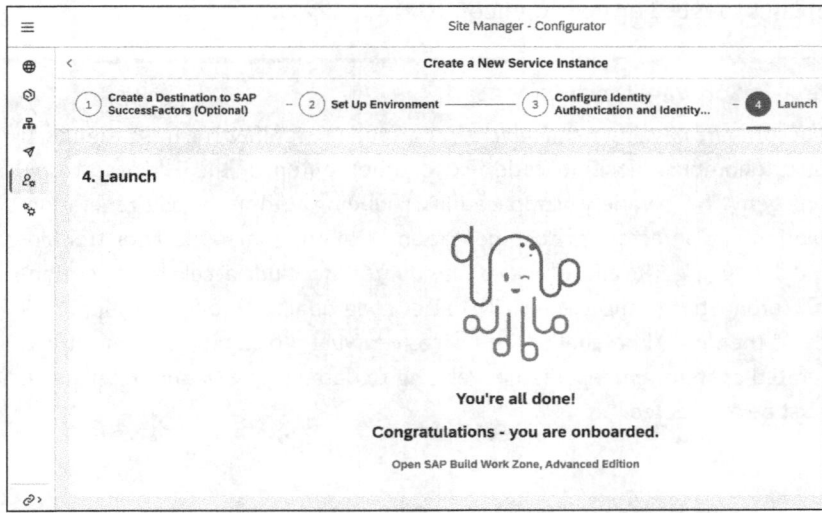

Figure 10.73 Launch SAP Build Work Zone

After switching to the end user view, you will see the image shown in Figure 10.74 after successful authentication.

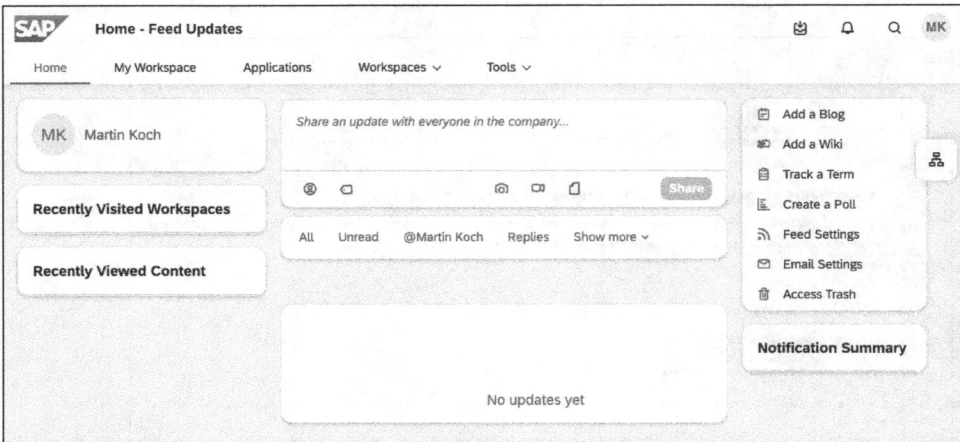

Figure 10.74 SAP Build Work Zone, Advanced Edition: Home Screen

10.4 SAP Build Code

SAP Build Code is a cloud-based development environment for JavaScript and Java. It provides an easy solution for coding, testing, integrations, and lifecycle management. SAP Build Code allows developers to build applications, extend SAP systems, and collaborate with other developers and business experts. Joule, embedded within SAP Build Code, integrates AI-powered code generation, enabling efficient creation of application logic, data models, and test scripts. SAP Build Code provides guided experiences and prebuilt templates to speed up development.

> **Generative AI in Software Development**
>
> In the field of software development, *generative AI* (gen AI) signifies the utilization of AI models that autonomously generate code, text, or other content. In the field of software development, gen AI has a variety of applications, including automatic code generation, code completion and refactoring, documentation creation, and support for troubleshooting and debugging. The advantages of this approach include accelerated development, higher productivity, and potentially better code quality through AI-supported suggestions. At the same time, challenges such as verifying the quality and correctness of the generated content and legal issues relating to data protection and intellectual property must be considered.

10.4 SAP Build Code

SAP Build Code can be installed using a booster. To do this, navigate as usual in the SAP BTP cockpit to the global account level in the side menu, go to the **Boosters** area, and search for "SAP Build Code" (see Figure 10.75).

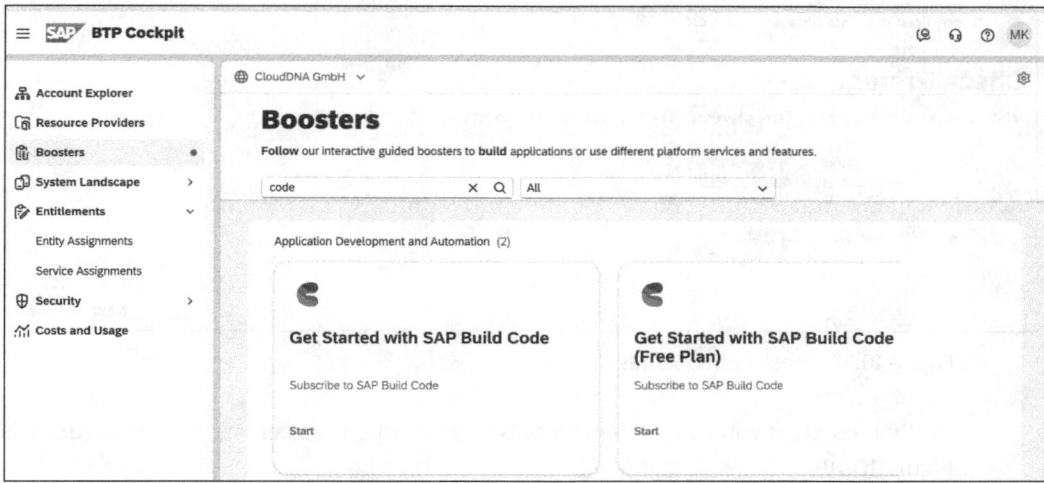

Figure 10.75 Booster for SAP Build Code

Click the desired booster to access the details. Open the **Components** tab. You will see that both an SAP Build Code subscription and a subscription for SAP Business Application Studio are required. Then click **Start** (see Figure 10.76).

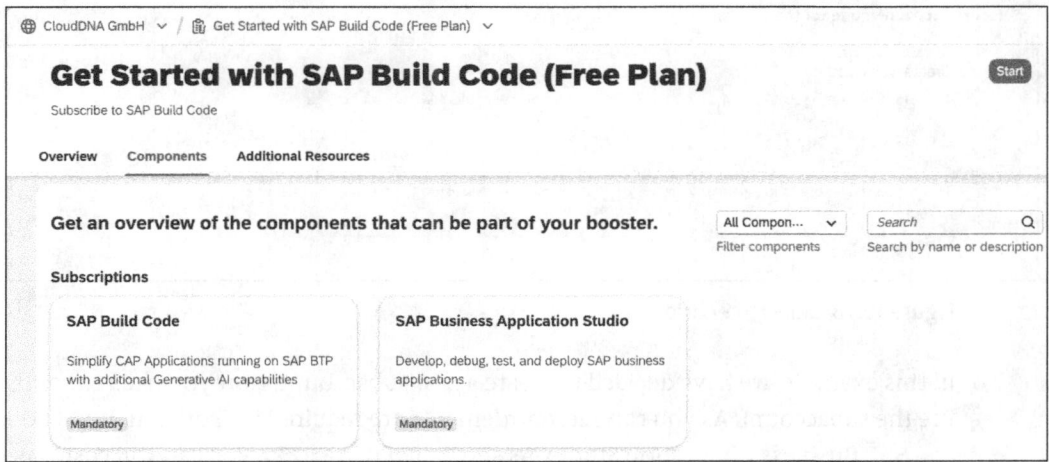

Figure 10.76 Booster Components

In the first step, as shown in Figure 10.77, the system checks whether your global account has the required entitlements and whether your user has the necessary permissions.

10   Activating and Setting Up SAP Build

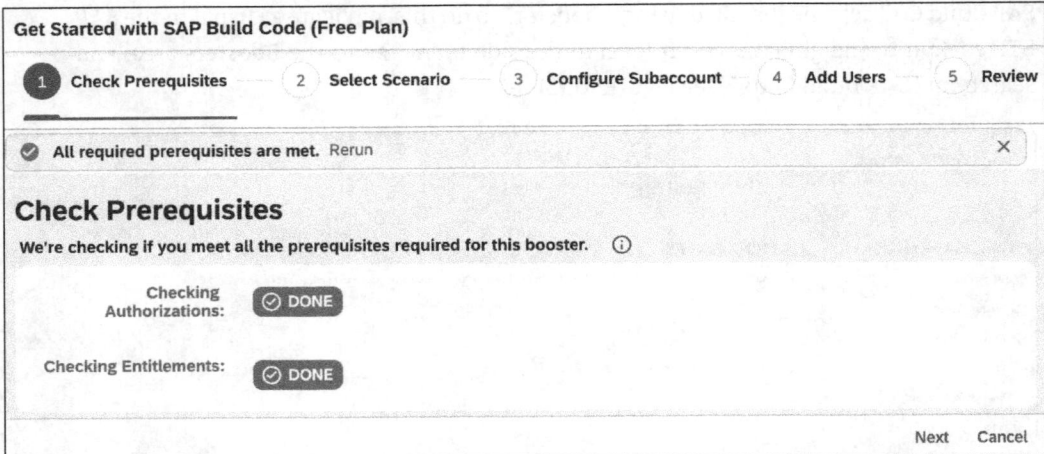

Figure 10.77 Check Prerequisites

In the next step, you must select an existing subaccount or create a new account (see Figure 10.78).

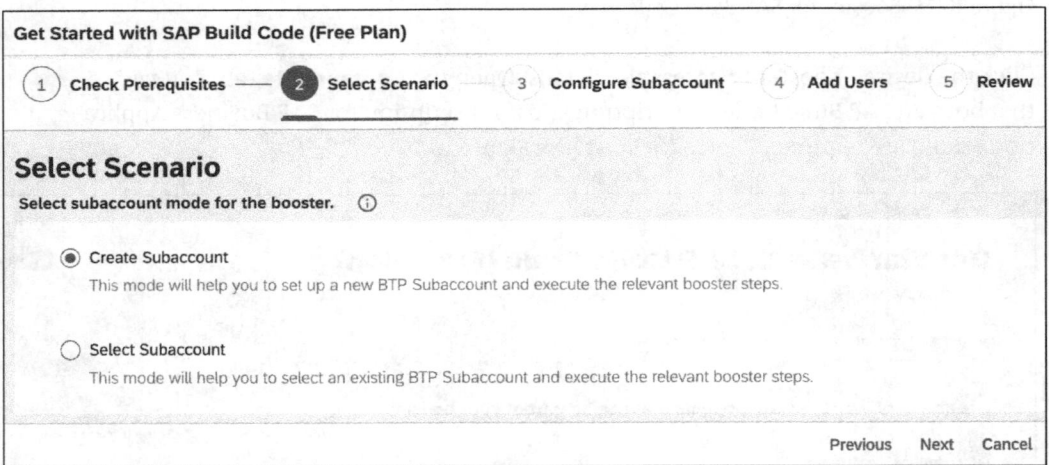

Figure 10.78 Select Scenario

In this example, we have decided to create a new subaccount. Now you need to configure the subaccount. As you can see, entitlements are required for both SAP Build Code and SAP Business Application Studio. As shown in Figure 10.79, you can still customize the **Subaccount Name** and select a data center (in the **Provider** field).

In the next step, you must define which identity provider should be used for platform users and which for application users. You will also see a note indicating that the user executing the booster will automatically be added as an administrator and developer (see Figure 10.80).

10.4 SAP Build Code

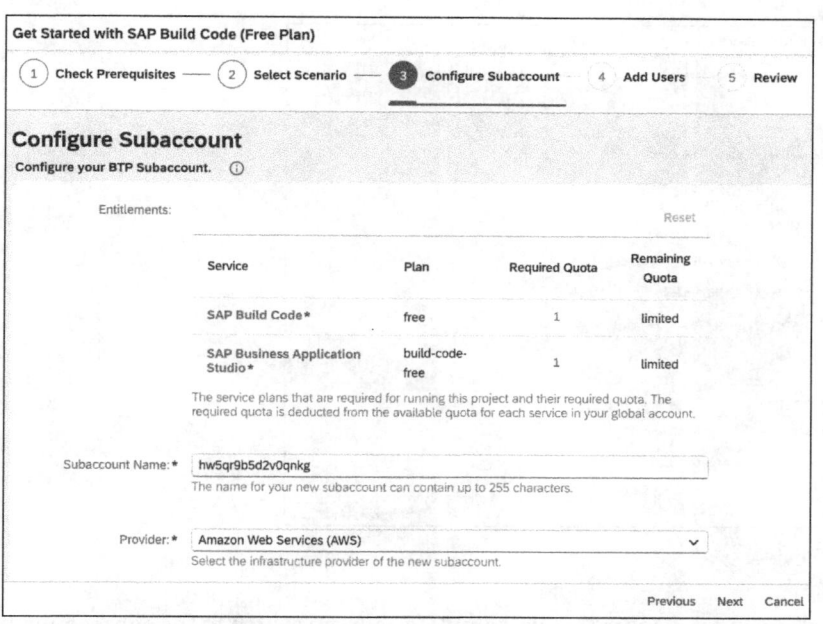

Figure 10.79 Configure Subaccount

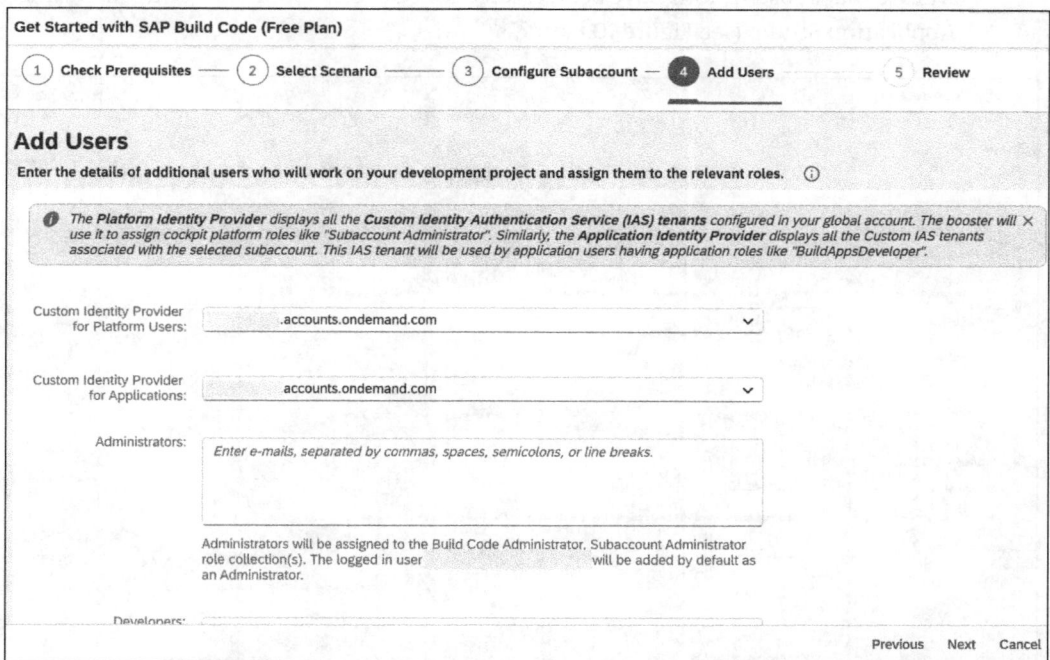

Figure 10.80 Authentication and Users

Finally, you will see a summary of the settings you have made. You can confirm these by clicking **Finish** (see Figure 10.81).

10 Activating and Setting Up SAP Build

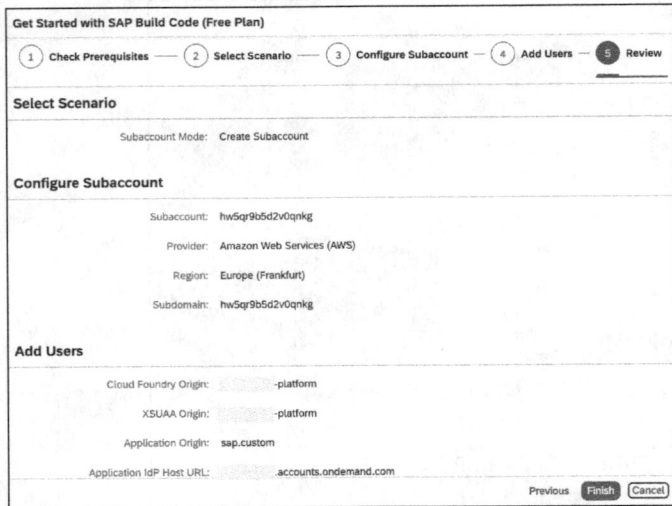

Figure 10.81 Review

Once installation and configuration are complete, you can switch to the subaccount. In the side menu, navigate to the **Services • Instances and Subscriptions** area. There you will see that subscriptions have been created for both SAP Build Code and SAP Business Application Studio (see Figure 10.82).

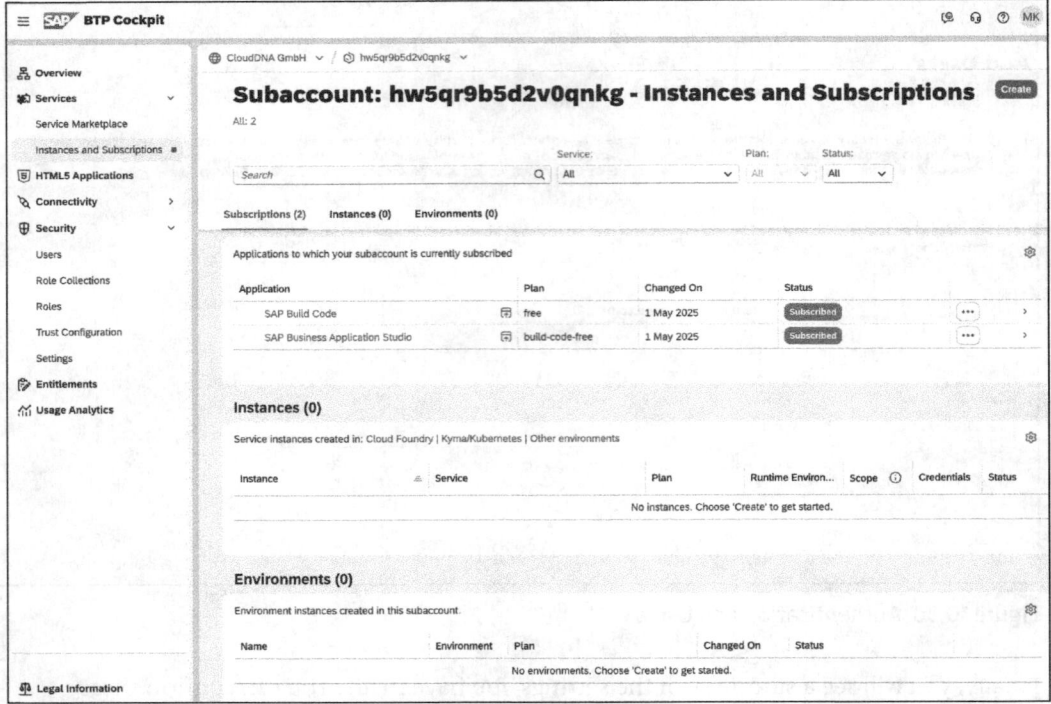

Figure 10.82 Instances and Subscriptions

10.4 SAP Build Code

Now navigate to the **Security • Role Collections** area in the side menu. There you will see, as shown in Figure 10.83, that series of role collections have been created for both SAP Build Code and SAP Business Application Studio.

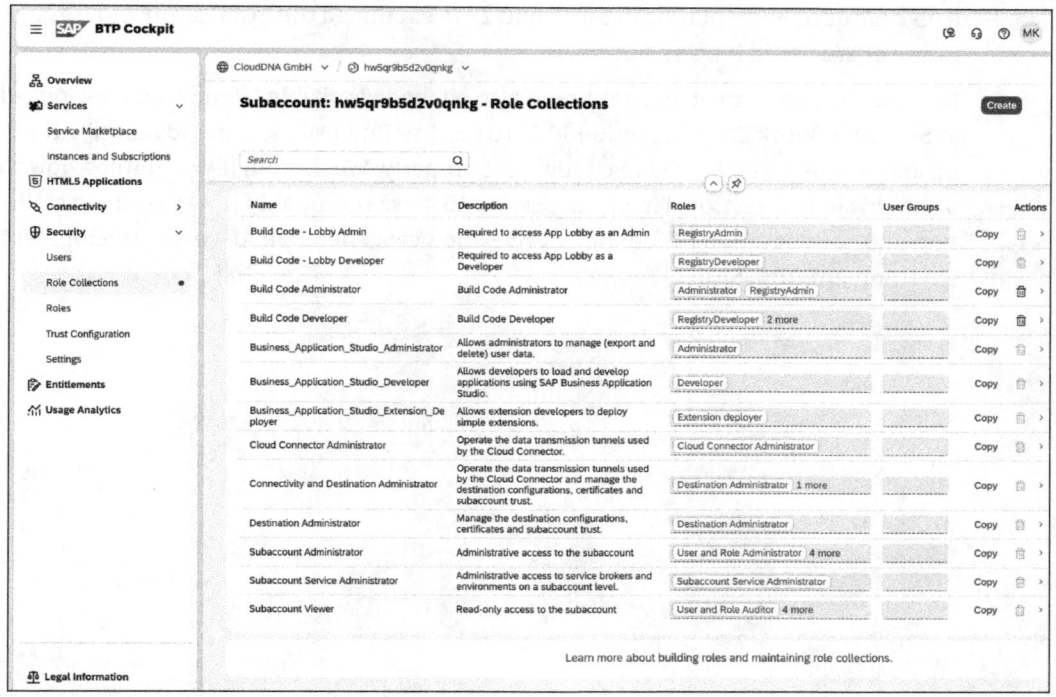

Figure 10.83 Role Collections

By clicking **SAP Build Code**, you can jump to the SAP Build lobby (see Figure 10.84).

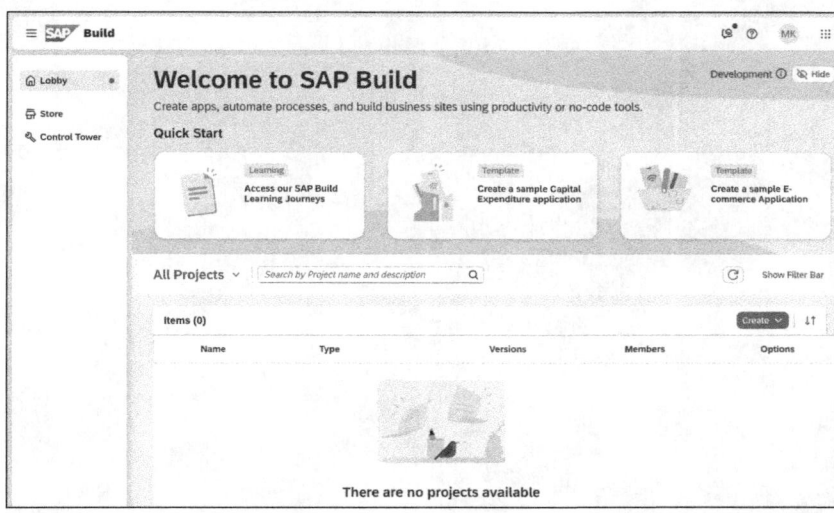

Figure 10.84 SAP Build Code Lobby

10.5 Summary

In Section 10.1, you learned how to install and configure SAP Build Apps. SAP Build Apps is a tool for creating applications without any programming knowledge—what we call a *no-code* development tool. In Section 10.2, we examined the installation and configuration of SAP Build Process Automation.

Because the content you create should also be made available to end users, we looked at SAP Build Work Zone in Section 10.3. To get SAP Build Work Zone, advanced edition up and running, you'll need to configure it properly. We thoroughly examined how to do so this in this section. Finally, in Section 10.4, we thoroughly reviewed the installation and configuration of SAP Build Code, the new generative AI–based development environment from SAP.

The Authors

Martin Koch is the managing director of CloudDNA GmbH, an SAP partner based in Austria with 20-plus employees. His company specializes in SAP BTP, SAP Integration Suite, full-stack SAP development (ABAP RESTful application programming model, SAP Cloud Application Programming Model, SAPUI5, SAP Fiori, SAP Fiori elements), and clean core strategies. Martin and his team are authors of several SAP training courses on SAPUI5, SAP Fiori, Cloud Integration, and SAP BTP security. As an architect, consultant, and developer, he advises international SAP customers of all sizes. Originally trained as a commercial pilot and air traffic controller, he joined SAP Austria in 2007 as a trainee, focusing first on SAP NetWeaver and integration. Over time, he expanded his expertise to mobile applications, SAP HANA, and modern SAP cloud architectures. In recognition of his community contributions, Martin was named an SAP Champion in 2023.

Siegfried Zeilinger is self-employed as the managing director of a small consulting company. His consulting expertise includes SAP architecture; development strategies for ABAP, Java, and cloud; and SAP Identity Management. Since 2016, he has been a certified information systems auditor (CISA). Siegfried's most recent experience was in the pharmaceutical industry and the public sector. Before starting his own business in 2011, he worked for SAP Austria as an SAP NetWeaver and SAP Enterprise Portal consultant, leading large international projects. Today, he regularly offers SAP training courses on the topics of authorizations, SAP Cloud, and SAP NetWeaver. From 2003 to 2019, he supervised diploma theses at the TU Vienna and the FH Wiener Neustadt and gave several lectures on SAP.

Index

A

Access control 206
Account model 44
   directories and subaccounts 47
   directories per functional area 48
   directories per subsidiary 49
   directory per geographical area 48
Adapter
   Development Kit 324
   FTP 324
   HTTPS 324
   IMAP 324
   JDBC 324
   OData 324
   REST 324
   SFTP 324
   SOAP 324
Administration use 81
Alibaba Cloud 21
Amazon Web Services (AWS) 21
API Management 324, 325, 336
Application identity provider 65, 118, 397
Application programming
   interfaces (APIs) 43
Artificial intelligence (AI) 20
Asymmetric encryption 59
Authentication 62, 96, 157, 204
Authorizations 57, 71, 115, 157, 204
Azure 21

B

Boosters 182, 326, 405
Break glass account 166
Brute force attacks 205

C

Center of excellence (CoE) 41
Certificates 60
Cloud 17
Cloud connector 253
   CA approach 271
   cipher suites 266
   cloud configuration 267
   configuring the UI 264

Cloud connector (Cont.)
   directory structure 260
   failover 284
   initial steps 261
   installation 255
   installer versions 256
   JVM 276
   local user store 268
   on-premise configuration 270
   port 257
   portable version 256
   prerequisites 254
   reporting configuration 274
   RFC protocol 273
   shadow host 282
   shadow instance 284
   subaccount 263
   user store file 262
Cloud development teams 41
Cloud Foundry 173
   environment 324, 416
   Foundation 21
   organization 28
Cloud Integration 325
   APIs 329
   APIs for OData v2 329
   role collections 338
Cloud Platform Enterprise
   Agreement (CPEA) 23
Cloud service status 53
Conditional authentication 150
Corporate identity provider 67, 125

D

Destinations 287, 289
Dev spaces 298, 304
DevOps 41
Directories 175
   splitting 176

E

Edge Integration Cell 325
Entitlements 26, 36, 192, 329
EU access 28
Event Mesh 325

447

E

Events 246
Extended Services for User Account and
  Authentication (XSUAA) 212

F

Feature Flags Service application 131
Free tier 325

G

Generative AI 438
Git 311, 316, 319
Global account 26, 156, 158
Google Cloud 21
Governance model 41
Grant types 115, 374
Graph 325
Group mapping 238
Groups 416
Guided Answers 54

H

High availability (HA) 277, 281
Horizontal scaling 277
HTTPS proxy 267

I

Identity Authentication 67, 68, 70, 72, 111,
  145, 158, 165, 173, 230, 424, 429
  B2B 75
  B2C 74
  B2E 76
  menu 80
  notification emails 92
  tenant 210
  tenant login 77
  tenant settings 89
  user management 82
Identity provider 64, 69, 132, 163, 208, 225
  initiated SSO 112
  metadata 125
Identity Provisioning 101, 424
  source system 102
  target system 106
iFlows 342
Infrastructure as a service (IaaS) 21
Integration Advisor 324, 325

Integration Assessment 325
Integration patterns
  application-to-application (A2A) 324
  business-to-business (B2B) 324
Integration platform as a service (iPaaS) 323

J

Java Development Kit (JDK) 257
Java Messaging System (JMS) 336
Java Virtual Machine (JVM) 254
JSON Web Tokens (JWTs) 136

K

Kerberos-authenticated users 273

L

License models 22
Lightweight Directory Access
  Protocol (LDAP) 70

M

Master instance 277
Message queues 336
Microsoft Azure Active Directory --> Microsoft
  Entra ID 118
Microsoft Entra ID 118, 124, 226
  subaccount 233
Migration Assessment 325
Multicloud environment 113
Multifactor authentication (MFA) 205

N

Neo environment 113, 202, 324

O

OAuth 2.0 114
Onboarding document 42
On-premise 17, 18
Open Connectors 324, 325
OpenID Connect (OIDC) 111, 114, 118, 131
  claim 136
openSAP 35
Organization 241
Organization Manager role 247

Index

P

Passcode 147
Passwords 87, 94, 263
Pay as you go 23
Platform as a service (PaaS) 72
Platform engineering team 41
Platform identity provider 65, 118, 209, 397
Principal propagation 314
Provisioning 108
Proxy system 103
P-user ID 64, 162

Q

Quotas 26, 36, 242
    assignment 243

R

RADIUS 99
Reference architecture 52
Resource provider 190
Risk-based authentication 146
Robotic process automation (RPA) 404
Role 166, 215
    templates 216
Role collections 160, 166, 219, 338, 383, 387, 421
    create 168
    mapping 223
    reporting 226
Routes 245

S

SAML 2.0 .... 111, 112, 118, 212, 426
SAP Analytics Cloud 20
SAP Audit Log Viewer service 249
SAP BTP 393
SAP BTP ABAP environment 22
SAP BTP cockpit 157
SAP BTP command line interface (CLI) 43
SAP BTP Guidance Framework 40
SAP BTP, Cloud Foundry environment 21, 294
SAP BTP, Kyma runtime 22
SAP BTP, Neo environment 21
SAP BTPEA 23
SAP Build 391

SAP Build Apps 391, 444
    plans 393
SAP Build Code 438, 439, 444
    booster 439
    role collections 443
SAP Build Process Automation 391, 404, 444
    boosters 404
SAP Build Work Zone 391, 412, 444
    booster 418
    initial steps 412
SAP Build Work Zone, advanced edition 412, 422
    configure 422
    properties 433
    provisioning 436
    subject name identifier 427
    target system mapping 434
    transformations 429
SAP Build Work Zone, standard edition 412
SAP Business Accelerator Hub 325
SAP Business Application Studio 20, 192, 232, 297, 439
    authorizations 303
    connections 309
    destinations 306
    dev space 302
    external systems 305
    plan 299
    role collections 300
    roles 300
    source control 318
SAP Cloud ALM 274
SAP Cloud Identity Services 72, 158, 169, 173, 227, 413, 425
SAP Cloud Transport Management 349
    activate 350
    deployment 352
    destinations 357
    entitlements 351
    nodes 363
    role collections 354
    SAP Integration Suite 380
    service instance 355
    system landscape 361
SAP Connectivity service 254, 258, 286, 290
SAP Content Agent 351, 371, 377
    add to subaccount 365
SAP Datasphere 20
SAP Destination service 59, 287
SAP Discovery Center 18, 29, 204, 326, 392
    missions 29
    pricing 31

449

Index

SAP Discovery Center (Cont.)
  project board 35
  reference architecture 29, 33
  SAP business AI features 29
  service 31
SAP Extension Suite 20
SAP Fiori launchpad 76
SAP for Me 53, 161
SAP HANA 19
SAP ID 63, 66, 161, 166, 207, 209
SAP Integration Suite 20, 323, 358
  capabilities 334
  entitlements 326
  role collections 332
  subscriptions 329
  transport 382
SAP Passport 63
SAP Platform Identity Provider service
  for SAP BTP 95
SAP Process Integration runtime 329
  service 341, 372
SAP Service Marketplace 172
SAP Support Portal 76
SAP Universal ID 35, 63, 161
Scalability 277
Secure communication 58
Security 57
Service key 344, 346, 370, 376
Service plan 36
Service provider–initiated SSO 112
Services 29, 248
Session timeout 91
Setup automator 43
Shadow instance 277
Shared responsibility model 25
SICM protocol 81
Single roles 166
Single sign-on (SSO) 111, 415, 417
Software as a service (SaaS) 17
Spaces 28, 242, 245
SSL/TLS 311
Subaccount 157, 158, 170
  administration 199
  authentication 227

Subaccount (Cont.)
  configure 396
  create 199
  directories 44
  subdomain 202
Subscriptions 247
S-user ID 64, 162
Symmetric encryption 58
System landscape 188

T

Third-party identity providers 212
Time-based one-time password
  (TOTP) 99, 147
Tokens 190
Trading Partner Management 325
Transport Landscape Wizard 362
Trust configuration 208
Trust store 61
Two-factor authentication 144

U

Usage analytics 38
Usage monitoring 193
Use cases 19
User account 83
User administration 57, 206
User groups 88
User management 157, 179

V

Versioning 311
Vertical scaling 277

W

Workflow management 404

X

X.509 client certificate 270

- Develop low-code and no-code applications with SAP Build Apps
- Create centralized business sites with SAP Build Work Zone
- Automate workflow processes with SAP Build Process Automation

Glavanovits, Haider, Koch, Krancz

SAP Build

No-Code Development, Centralized Access, and Process Automation

The new SAP Build is here—dive into its tools for low-code and no-code development! Looking for a new development environment to create full stack applications? Learn how to implement SAP Build Apps! Need better tools to design and build a central access point—like SAP Fiori launchpad—for business applications? Get SAP Build Work Zone up and running! Want to create, maintain, and automate business processes? Look no further than SAP Build Process Automation! With practical guidance on the whole SAP Build suite, you'll be developing in no time.

801 pages, pub. 05/2024
E-Book: $84.99 | **Print:** $89.95 | **Bundle:** $99.99

www.sap-press.com/5772

- Integrate your enterprise landscape: on-premise and cloud, SAP and non-SAP systems
- Design integration scenarios with prepackaged content, APIs, and SaaS connectors
- Configure B2B connections with the Integration Advisor

Aron, Gakhar, Vij

SAP Integration Suite

SAP's integration technologies are now combined—but what is SAP Integration Suite, and how do you use it to manage an integrated enterprise landscape? In this book, get the answers to these questions and more as you take a tour of the new suite. Then get step-by-step instructions for using key capabilities such as prepackaged integrations, open APIs, integration scenarios, the Integration Advisor, and more. Master the complete integration suite!

343 pages, pub. 07/2021
E-Book: $74.99 | **Print:** $79.95 | **Bundle:** $89.99

www.sap-press.com/5326

- Install and configure the cloud connector for SAP
- Set up connections for common use cases, including SAP Business Application Studio, SAP Web IDE, and more
- Run cloud connector securely, monitor errors, configure principal propagation and more

Martin Koch, Siegfried Zeilinger

Cloud Connector for SAP

Establish quick and secure communication between your cloud and on-premise systems with SAP Connectivity service's cloud connector! Set up and configure the cloud connector, from performing sizing to implementing connectivity APIs. Link on-premise SAP products to SAP BTP and its services, including SAP Business Application Studio, SAP Integration Suite's Cloud Integration, and more. With information on creating secure connections, administering the cloud connector, and monitoring, this guide has everything you need!

352 pages, pub. 04/2023
E-Book: $84.99 | **Print:** $89.95 | **Bundle:** $99.99

www.sap-press.com/5683

- Configure security for the Neo and Cloud Foundry environments
- Set up secure connections with the cloud connector
- Protect key cloud services like SAP Business Application Studio and SAP Integration Suite

Martin Koch, Siegfried Zeilinger

Security and Authorizations for SAP Business Technology Platform

Learn what it takes to protect SAP Business Technology Platform! Walk through the cloud security mechanisms of SAP BTP (formerly SAP Cloud Platform). See how to set up users and permissions for your unique circumstances and configure secure connection to cloud and on-premise systems. Work with SAP BTP's administration tools, including the command line interface and APIs. With information on safeguarding key cloud services, this guide will leave you confident in your cloud system's security!

355 pages, pub. 11/2022
E-Book: $84.99 | **Print:** $89.95 | **Bundle:** $99.99

www.sap-press.com/5627

- Learn about SAP's latest technology platform
- Explore products, services, and tools for application development, automation, integration, analytics, and AI
- Walk through customer use cases to see how SAP BTP can bring value to your business

Banda, Chandra, Gooi

SAP Business Technology Platform

Discover SAP's unified technology platform with this introductory guide! Get started with the building blocks of SAP Business Technology Platform: architecture design, runtime environments, and the development approach. Take a tour of the integrated tools and services for application development, business logic, automation, integration, security, and more. With detailed implementation examples for practical use cases, this is your guidebook to the complete SAP BTP ecosystem!

729 pages, 2nd edition, pub. 08/2024
E-Book: $84.99 | **Print:** $89.95 | **Bundle:** $99.99

www.sap-press.com/5919

Acharya, Bajaj, Dhar, Ghosh, Lahiri

Application Development with SAP Business Technology Platform

Develop cloud applications customized for your business needs! Master the basics of SAP Business Technology Platform (SAP BTP) and its development environments; then get step-by-step instructions for developing and operating your own applications. Build your backend with Java, Node.js, or ABAP, and set up your frontend using SAPUI5 and SAP Fiori. With detailed code examples throughout, this book is your complete guide to building cloud applications on SAP BTP!

- Build and deploy cloud applications on SAP BTP using Java, Node.js, and ABAP
- Work with SAP Business Application Studio, SAP Cloud Application Programming Model, cloud services, and more
- Manage, monitor, and secure your applications

574 pages, pub. 12/2022
E-Book: $84.99 | **Print:** $89.95 | **Bundle:** $99.99

www.sap-press.com/5504

Interested in reading more?

Please visit our website for all new book
and e-book releases from SAP PRESS.

www.sap-press.com